**AA**

# GUESTHOUSES FARMHOUSES & INNS IN BRITAIN

*Editor:* Joan Fensome

*Designer:* Ashley Tilleard

*Cover design by:* Jadzia Koltonowska

Gazetteer compiled by the AA Publications Research Unit

Maps by AA Cartographic Services Department

---

**OUR COVER PICTURE**
**Mrs Marion Cornish, who, with her husband Eric, runs Leworthy Farm, winner of the AA Farmhouse of the Year Competition 1980.**
Photo: Home & Freezer Digest

# Contents

Produced by the Publications Division of the Automobile Association, Fanum House, Basing View, Basingstoke, Hampshire RG21 2EA

Phototypeset by Tradespools Ltd, Frome, Somerset

Printed in Great Britain by Collins, Glasgow

Town plans in this book (other than those for London) are based on the Ordnance Survey map with the sanction of the Controller, HMSO.

# Contents

4

# GUESTS IN THE HOUSE

**Remember when holiday accommodation fell into one of two categories – hotel or boarding house? And all boarding houses seemed to smell of cabbage, boarders queued for the one lavatory, baths were unobtainable and you washed at a marble-topped stand with a jug of hot water brought up by the skivvy?**

***What a long way we have come since then!***

Improvement probably started in the 1930s with a change of name. We thought it an affectation at the time, but once 'boarders' became 'guests' accommodation and food began to improve.

The AA has done its bit, too, by introducing standards which have given owners an incentive to make their homes into places where it is really a pleasure to stay. Certain it is that the establishments listed in this guide bear no resemblance to those boarding houses for which some people seem to have a nostalgia. But perhaps those people have forgotten the lumpy flock mattresses, the flies dancing round the gas light, wet cabbage, sour plums and custard, and dreary décor. No, we do not weep for the demise of the boarding house!

To be listed in this book, establishments have to attain standards which the AA considers essential for a comfortable stay, but in travelling around we are constantly surprised by the number which offer accommodation and facilities which far exceed the minimum requirements. Bathrooms or shower rooms en suite, well-furnished bedrooms, comfortable lounges, cordon-bleu cookery, and the provision of entertainment and sports facilities, are no longer found only in luxury hotels. All these things involve capital investment, much thought, and hard work; and we congratulate those owners who are not only willing to plough back profits in order to improve their product, but also expend a great deal of effort to make their house the sort of place people will wish to return to and to recommend to their friends.

Readers sometimes query the inclusion of hotels in this book and wonder why they appear here rather than in *AA Hotels & Restaurants in Britain*. The explanation is that, to be classified by the AA as a hotel, an establishment has to meet certain criteria which we feel are traditionally required but which not every one will need. For instance AA hotels provide all meals to residents, but a lot of establishments which call themselves 'hotels' do not serve lunches, and some only offer bed and breakfast. To hold three stars or more, hotels have also to serve meals to certain non-residents, which guesthouses rarely do. The AA 'guesthouse' category is therefore different from, but not necessarily inferior to, the 'hotel' category and, in fact, the best guesthouses are sometimes superior in many ways. It should be mentioned, though, that these top class guesthouses (and some farmhouses) are usually as expensive as the more modest hotels.

Inns (as distinct from Public Houses) are different again, in that they are licensed premises which serve meals to casual customers and are obliged, by law, to afford overnight accommodation for *bona fide* travellers. They may be quite small and in some respects do not meet AA requirements for hotel classification, but they are not necessarily inferior to, or cheaper than, one-star or two-star hotels.

Some of the very best of our guesthouses were finalists in the 'Guesthouse of the Year' competition featured in our colour section (see page 15). They set a very high standard and offer a degree of luxury for which many people are willing to pay a little extra. We hope many other owners will strive to emulate them, but at the same time we do realise that some people look for basic accommodation at a low price. There is a place for both in this book. Gazetteer entries give the range of prices, as supplied to us by owners. These are liable to alteration, but do give an indication of the likely cost and can be used to compare the charges of the various establishments. Whether you plump for *de luxe* and ignore the price, or seek out the cheapest place available, you should be sure, if you choose from this book, of clean and comfortable accommodation.

6

# How to use the gazetteer

**Arrangement of gazetteer**
The first part of the gazetteer lists Guesthouses and
Inns; the second part lists Farmhouses. Each section
is arranged in alphabetical order by placename. The
establishments are generally more modest in the
way of facilities than the AA hotels classified by stars
(listed in *AA Members' Handbook* and the AA guide
*Hotels and Restaurants in Britain*).

At the back of the book is a 16-page atlas showing
the location of establishments.

**To find a guesthouse, farmhouse or inn**
Look at the area you wish to visit in the atlas. *Towns
with guesthouses or inns* are marked with a solid
dot ●.
*Towns with guesthouse/s and/or inn/s plus
farmhouse/s* are marked with a dot in an open
circle ◉.
*Towns with farmhouses only* are marked with an
open circle ○.
Farmhouses are listed under the nearest identifiable
town or village and may in fact be a few miles away.

**Reading a map reference**
In the gazetteer section of this guide, the main
placename is given a two-figure map reference to
key with the location atlas. In the Farmhouse section
six-figure references have also been given which can
be used in conjunction with a larger scale Ordnance
Survey map to pinpoint the exact position.

Example: Two-Figure Reference
*Map 3 ST76:* This is the map reference for Bath in the
county of Avon. Turn to Map 3 in the atlas, refer to
the group of squares, ST. Find sub-division 7 from
*left* to *right* and sub-division 6 from *bottom* to *top.*
While every effort has been made to ensure the
correct gazetteering of establishments, in some
cases the information received by us has been
insufficient. In these instances the establishments
have been marked at the nearest town.

**Town Plans**
A number of town plans have been included in the
text to show the positions of establishments in some
of the larger towns or cities. Included on these maps
are the following: one-way streets, car parks, post
offices, information centres, cathedrals, and castles.
As the gazetteer information is continually being
updated, some of the establishments shown on the

town plans may have been deleted from the text; conversely some more recent gazetteer entries do not appear on the relevant town plans. The mileages at road exits are calculated from the border of the plan. A list of town plan symbols appears on page 14.

## Gazetteer notes
A key to abbreviations and symbols in gazetteer entries appears on the inside covers.

## Accommodation for under £6
Not all guesthouses or inns shown in this publication provide bed and breakfast for under £6 per person per night. Those which expect to do so during 1982 carry the appropriate symbol (⋈).

## Annexes
The number of bedrooms in an annexe is shown in the gazetteer entry, eg (A6). It should be noted that annexes (often used only during the season) may lack some of the facilities available in the main building. It is advisable to check the nature of the accommodation and the charges should be checked before reservations are confirmed.

## Bathrooms
The gazetteer entry indicates the number of rooms with private bath or shower and wcs where applicable.

## Central Heating
The heating symbol (▥) in an establishment's entry does not mean that this facility is available all year round. Some places only operate their central heating in the winter months, and then at their own discretion.

## Children
Guesthouses and farmhouses usually accommodate children of all ages unless a minimum age is given (eg nc8 – no children under eight), but it does not necessarily follow that they are able to provide special facilities. If you have very young children find out, before you reserve accommodation, what special amenities (such as cots and high chairs) are available and whether reductions are made for children. In the gazetteer, establishments which do have special facilities for children are indicated by the symbol Ch. All the following amenities will be found at these establishments: baby-sitting service or baby intercom system, playroom or playground,

laundry facilities, drying and ironing facilities, cots and high-chairs, and special meals.

### Complaints
If you have any complaints you should inform the proprietor immediately so that the trouble can be dealt with promptly. If a personal approach fails, members should inform the AA regional office nearest to the establishment concerned.

### Deposits
Some establishments, particularly in large towns and holiday centres, require a deposit – especially from chance callers staying for only one night. If you are paying a deposit at the time of advance booking it is advisable to effect insurance cover against possible cancellation, eg *AA Travelsure.*

### Disabled Persons
If the wheelchair symbol &. is shown in an establishment's entry it means that the disabled can be accommodated. This information has been supplied to the AA by the proprietor but it is advisable to check before making reservations. Details more relevant to disabled persons may be obtained from *The AA Guide for the Disabled* priced £1 from AA offices (free to members). Members with any form of disability should notify proprietors so that appropriate arrangements can be made to minimise difficulties, particularly in the event of an emergency.

### Dogs
Establishments which do not accept dogs are indicated by the symbol ✗ but other establishments may impose restrictions on the size of dog allowed. The conditions under which pets are accepted should be confirmed with the management when making reservations. Generally dogs are not allowed in the dining room.

### Family bedrooms
The gazetteer indicates whether family bedrooms are available by the abbreviation fb together with the relevant number of rooms, eg (2fb).

### Farms
Within each gazetteer entry is the six-figure reference to be used in conjunction with Ordnance Survey maps. This number follows the establishment name and is in *italics.*

The acreage of each establishment is shown in the body of each entry (eg 55 acres) followed by the type of farming that predominates in the relevant farm (eg dairy, arable etc).

Although the AA lists working farms, some may have become 'non-working' before publication if, for instance, the farmer has sub-let or sold land. Potential guests should ascertain the true nature of the farm's activity before booking to ensure their requirements are met.

## Fire Precautions

So far as can be ascertained at the time of going to press, every unit of accommodation listed in this publication, provided it is subject to the requirements of the Act, has applied for and not been refused a fire certificate. The Fire Precautions Act 1971 does not apply to the Channel Islands or the Isle of Man, both of which exercise their own rules with regard to fire precautions for accommodation units.

## Gazetteer Entry

Establishment names shown in *italics* indicate that particulars have not been confirmed by the management in time for this 1982 edition.

## Licences

An indication is given in each entry where a guesthouse is licensed. Most places in the guesthouse category do not hold a full licence but all inns do. Licensed premises are not obliged to remain open throughout the permitted hours and may do so only when they expect reasonable trade. Note that at establishments which have registered clubs, club membership does not come into effect – nor can a drink be bought – until 48 hours after joining. For further information refer to leaflet HH20 'The Law about Licensing Hours and Children/Young Persons on Licensed Premises' available from AA offices.

## London

It is common knowledge that in London prices tend to be higher than in the provinces. For hotels, we have tried to select establishments where the accommodation is inexpensive and where bed and breakfast is normally provided. We have also included a few which provide a full meal service and whose charges are consequently higher.

## Meals

In some parts of the country, high tea is generally

11

served in guesthouses although dinner is often also available on request. The latest time that the evening meal can be **ordered** is indicated in the text. On Sundays, many establishments serve their main meal at midday and will charge accordingly. However it is possible that a cold supper will be available in the evening.

## Opening dates
Unless otherwise stated, establishments are open all year. Where dates are shown these are inclusive: eg *Apr–Oct* indicates that the establishment is open from the beginning of April to the end of October.

## Prices
Prices are liable to fluctuation and it is advisable to check when you book. Also, make sure you know exactly what facilities are being offered when you are verifying charges, because there are variations in what an establishment may provide within inclusive terms. Weekly terms, for instance, vary from full board to bed and breakfast only. This is shown in the text by the symbol **Ł** (no lunches) and **M** (no main meals). Some establishments provide packed lunches, snacks or salads at extra cost – inns providing snacks are identified in entries by the abbreviation sn. All prices quoted normally include VAT and service, where applicable.

## *1981 Prices
When proprietors have been unable to furnish us with their proposed 1982 prices, those for 1981 are quoted, prefixed by an asterisk (*).

## Requests for Information
If you are writing to an establishment requesting information it is important to enclose a stamped, addressed envelope. Please quote this publication in any enquiry.

## Reservations
*Please book as early as you possibly can* or you may be disappointed. If you are delayed or have to change your plans, let the proprietor know at once. You may be held legally responsible if the room you booked cannot be re-let. Some establishments, especially those in short-season holiday centres, do not accept bookings for bed and breakfast only. Additionally, some guesthouses – particularly in seaside resorts – do not take bookings from midweek to midweek, and a number will not accept period bookings other than at full board rate, *ie* not

at nightly bed and breakfast rate plus individual meals.

It is regretted that the AA cannot at the present time undertake to make any reservations.

The hotel industry's Voluntary Code of Booking Practice was introduced in June 1977. Its prime object is to ensure that the customer is clear about the precise services and facilities he or she is buying, and what price he will have to pay, before he commits himself to a contractually binding agreement. The guest should be handed a card at the time of registration, with a full tariff including the total obligatory charge, and details may also be displayed prominently at the reception office.

The Tourism (Sleeping Accommodation Price Display) Order 1977 was introduced in February 1978. It compels hotels, motels, guesthouses, inns and self-catering accommodation with four or more letting bedrooms to display in entrance halls the maximum and minimum prices charged for each category of room. This order complements the Voluntary Code of Booking Practice.

Every effort is being made by the AA to encourage the use of the Voluntary Code in appropriate establishments.

---

### Restricted Service
Some establishments operate a restricted service during the less busy months. This is indicated by the prefix rs. For example, rs Nov–Mar indicates that a restricted service is operated from November to March. This may be a reduction in meals served and/or accommodation available.

---

### Telephone Numbers
Unless otherwise stated the telephone exchange name given in the gazetteer is that of the town under which the establishment is listed. Where the exchange for a particular establishment is not that of the town under which it appears, the name of the exchange is given after the telephone symbol ☎ and before the number.

In some areas telephone numbers are likely to be changed by the telephone authorities during the currency of this publication. In case of difficulty check with the operator.

---

### Television
If the gazetteer entry shows 'CTV' or 'TV', either colour or monochrome television is available in a lounge.

## VAT and Service Charge

In the United Kingdom and the Isle of Man, Value Added Tax is payable on both basic prices and any service. The symbol S% in the gazetteer indicates that the inclusive prices shown reflect any separate accounting for service made by the establishment. VAT does not apply in the Channel Islands. With this exception, prices quoted in the gazetteer are inclusive of VAT.

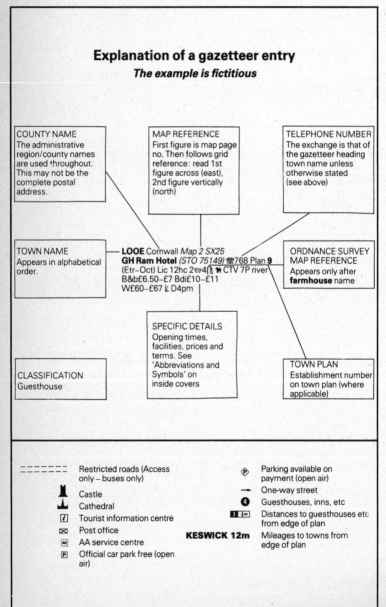

## Explanation of a gazetteer entry
*The example is fictitious*

**COUNTY NAME**
The administrative region/county names are used throughout. This may not be the complete postal address.

**MAP REFERENCE**
First figure is map page no. Then follows grid reference: read 1st figure across (east), 2nd figure vertically (north)

**TELEPHONE NUMBER**
The exchange is that of the gazetteer heading town name unless otherwise stated (see above)

**TOWN NAME**
Appears in alphabetical order.

**LOOE** Cornwall *Map 2 SX25*
**GH Ram Hotel** *(STO 75149)* ☎768 Plan **9**
(Etr–Oct) Lic 12hc 2⇔4⋔ ⚹ CTV 7P river
B&b£6.50–£7 Bdi£10–£11
W£60–£67 ⚓ D4pm

**ORDNANCE SURVEY MAP REFERENCE**
Appears only after **farmhouse** name

**SPECIFIC DETAILS**
Opening times, facilities, prices and terms. See 'Abbreviations and Symbols' on inside covers

**CLASSIFICATION**
Guesthouse

**TOWN PLAN**
Establishment number on town plan (where applicable)

---

| | |
|---|---|
| ‐‐‐‐‐‐‐ Restricted roads (Access only – buses only) | ⓟ Parking available on payment (open air) |
| 🏰 Castle | → One-way street |
| ⛪ Cathedral | ❹ Guesthouses, inns, etc |
| 𝑖 Tourist information centre | ⬛ ¾m Distances to guesthouses etc from edge of plan |
| ✉ Post office | **KESWICK 12m** Mileages to towns from edge of plan |
| AA AA service centre | |
| Ⓟ Official car park free (open air) | |

14

# How we chose the Guesthouse of the Year

In choosing the 1981 Guesthouse of the Year we followed the procedure which has worked well over the past three years. Each AA region was asked to nominate establishments, basing their choice on reports from inspectors after their routine visits, followed by special visits to all 'possibles'. Brian Langer, Head of Administration in the AA Head Office Hotel & Information Department, drove your editor all round Great Britain to stay (incognito) in these regional nominations. We visited guesthouses in locations as far apart as Kent, Cornwall, Anglesey, Yorkshire and the Trossachs.

Brian and I assessed the guesthouses independently of one another, awarding marks for the building and its environment; hospitality; recreational facilities; cleanliness; bathrooms etc; public rooms including furnishings and heating; bedrooms including the comfort of the bed and adequacy of other furnishings, availability of heating, and facilities such as tea-making and radio; and meals including the amount of choice, the service, and the quality and quantity of the food.

Naturally we had some slight differences of opinion regarding what one should expect of a good guesthouse, but over all our markings were very similar and we had absolutely no doubt about the national winner. Not that we were the final arbiters, for we had to go back to a committee which chose the regional and national winners, basing their decision on our written and verbal reports.

It may be noticed that no mark was given for 'value for money' but we did bear this in mind, and expected better facilities, more choice of food, etc, from the higher-priced places. In particular, we had to accept that the provision of a private shower or bathroom and WC would increase the room price considerably. Proprietors differed in their opinions regarding the desirability of installing private facilities, some being convinced that most people who stay in guesthouses prefer modest accommodation at a modest price, and others stating that many visitors ask for a room with private bathroom and do not mind paying extra for this. We had also to bear in mind that guesthouses in tourist spots were likely to be more expensive, especially if their season was short. We found that most places charged extra when a double room was occupied as a single – which happened in our case. Although this comes hard on single people one can see the proprietors' point of view because they may have to turn away a couple when a double room is occupied by one person. Two points should be made, though: it should be made quite clear at the time of booking that an extra charge will be made; and if there are spare rooms and it is obvious that no-one has been turned away guests will appreciate it if the additional charge is waived, or at least reduced.

All the guesthouses we visited had washbasins with hot and cold water in each room and an adequate number of bathrooms and WCs, all well-equipped and clean. Within the colour feature mention is made of toilet facilities only where integral shower rooms and WCs are available.

Except for our Scottish winner, which was run as a hotel rather than as a guesthouse, there was no choice of main course at dinner. In all but one of our winners, vegetables were served in separate dishes and this seems to us a refinement which is not difficult to put into practice. Most (but not all) gave a choice of starter and pudding, and all were licensed. Breakfast usually consisted of fruit juice or cereal; bacon and egg with variable additions such as sausage, tomato, mushrooms, fried bread; toast and marmalade; tea or coffee. An alternative to the fried dish was usually offered and was always available if one asked.

The people who run guesthouses seem to fall into three categories;
a) Those who have large houses and decide to take guests to help with expenses or just because they enjoy meeting people; in these cases the husband often follows another profession.
b) Those who are able to put quite a lot of capital into starting a guesthouse.
c) Those who decide to give up some other employment and move to a nice place where they hope to make a living taking guests. Some of these people have only a little capital and have to work very hard, doing building and decorating work themselves and developing their business bit by bit.

We met all three types on our travels and admired those who had created very pleasant guesthouses starting more or less from scratch. But we had to look at establishments from the point of view of potential guests and were faced with a choice between, perhaps, a well-run little guesthouse cleverly adapted and extended to take as many guests as possible, and a fine Georgian house with spacious rooms and lovely gardens. Not that the building was the most important aspect, but it was one of the things which could swing the final decision.

In practice the one thing which makes the difference between a happy stay and a mere temporary shelter is the attitude of the people running the place – not just the proprietors but any employees who come into contact with visitors as well. To treat strangers as guests, making them feel welcome and aware of a concern for their comfort, cannot always be easy. We often arrived rather late, having booked for only one night, so it would not have surprised us if we had been treated in an impersonal manner, but in almost every instance we were greeted with a smile and a friendly word, and our hosts seemed really keen that we should be comfortable and enjoy our stay. In fact we felt as though we were guests in the house, which is just as it should be.

*You can read all about the AA Guesthouse of the Year and about the five regional winners in the colour pages which follow.*

# GUESTHOUSE
## OF THE YEAR

**Rydal Lodge, Rydal, Ambleside, Cumbria**
**(Ernest, Joan and David Warren and Lily Shaw)**

Comfort — good food — beautiful surroundings . . . What more could one ask for? Rydal Lodge does offer quite a bit more: marvellous hospitality, historical and literary connections, accessibility by public transport as well as ample car-parking space, and very good value for money.

*David Warren and Lily Shaw (left)*
*with Ernest and Joan Warren*

Ernest and Joan Warren are both master bakers and used to own restaurants in Blackburn and Ashton-under-Lyne. Their businesses were successful but they felt they had too little control at 'point of sale' as they were both very much involved with the cooking. So three years ago they made up their minds to look for a guesthouse which would be small enough to manage without staff yet large enough for them to offer a high standard of comfort. They were joined in this venture by their son David, who had been farming, and by Joan's widowed sister, Lily Shaw. Ernest and Joan are still particularly concerned with the kitchen and the good food which emanates from it; Lily looks after the business side and supervises the housekeeping, as well as helping to serve meals; and David's main function is to greet guests and make sure they enjoy their stay, though he does help in many other ways — even to making the beds.

A coaching inn constructed of stone without mortar — just like the drystone walls which divide the fields — was built in the mid 17th century, and towards the end of the 18th century an elegant house was built onto the old inn. These two dissimilar buildings — the golden-brown drystone inn and the white-painted Georgian residence — make up Rydal Lodge.

Lawns and flower beds slope down to the fast-flowing River Rothay, and a private riverside path leads to a footbridge and, within a few minutes' stroll, to beautiful Rydal Water where Wordsworth's host of daffodils danced and fluttered in the breeze. All around, tree-clad fells reach to skies which are almost always beautiful, whether flying ribbons of torn cloud in a clean blue heaven or shadowing the hills with towering cumulus. Even when

*The garden from my bedroom window*

*The river Rothay runs swiftly past the guesthouse on its way from Rydal Water*

*At dusk we strolled by Rydal Water and I took this photograph of Brian, silhouetted against the silvery lake.*

rain comes in from the Atlantic and the tops are wreathed in mist the countryside has a calm serenity, the woods are sweetly-scented, and the lake mirrors the green hills in its quiet depths.

No wonder Wordsworth (who for many years lived just up the hill at Rydal Mount) and the other Lakeland poets loved this area. In the evening, when you sit in the lounge at Rydal Lodge, you may imagine them in that room, exchanging views with Dr Matthew Arnold. That famous headmaster of Rugby School and his family stayed at Rydal Lodge while their own house, Fox Howe, was being built, and he is known to have entertained Wordsworth and Coleridge there. The artist William Hull also lived in the house for a time.

The Warrens have furnished this first-floor sitting room, which has several long windows looking onto the garden and river, with very comfortable chairs and sofas. Decorations here, and throughout the house, are light and cheerful. The eight bedrooms are all well furnished, with very comfortable beds (in which electric blankets provide warmth when needed), wall heaters for use on cooler evenings, and good pieces of old furniture, as well as such items as chairs and a luggage rack which are all too often missing.

I was given a room in the old part of the house and found it comfortably warm on a dull day because the very thick drystone walls provide good insulation against cold or heat. The floor sloped to the extent that the bed had to be chocked up at one end to make it level, which was rather fun. Brian had a room in the Georgian house, quite different from mine, with a high ceiling and a big window looking onto the garden, but equally characterful.

Few are the people who do not like good food, and enjoyable meals are an essential part of a successful holiday. Not only did we enjoy the food at Rydal Lodge, but it was quite obvious that the other guests did too. One lady went so far as to refuse a first course so that she would have room for two of the delicious sweets, and another asked for the recipe for apple and mint sauce, a speciality which Joan serves with lamb. We were offered, as starter, the choice of cream of celery soup, melon with grapefruit, or fruit juice. The main course was leg of lamb with (served in separate dishes for one to help oneself) roast potatoes, petits pois, and onions in a creamy sauce. The sweets that evening — and all the guests awaited them eagerly — were lemon Pavlova, strawberries and cream, or ice-cream with a choice of home-made sauces. Most people chose the Pavlova, and then David offered everyone strawberries and cream as an extra. How I wished I had room! Biscuits and a selection of English cheeses were then brought round, just in case anyone needed more.

Coffee is served in the lounge but luckily other guests informed us that it was available all evening so we went off to explore before it became too dark. I took some photographs of Rydal Water and its surroundings and we rambled along the bank, enjoying the freshness of the evening air.

When we returned we found, as we had been told, that coffee was still to be had. The pot stands on a hotplate, with cream and sugar available, and guests can help themselves at any time during the evening. In addition there was a dish of sweets — chocolate ginger, fudge, and peppermint creams — for guests to sample. We had not been back long when Lily came to see whether the coffee pot needed refilling, and later David came in to take orders for alcoholic drinks if anyone wanted them.

For an additional charge of 25p guests could have tea or coffee brought to them in the morning. This was served in a pot with milk or cream and sugar and with a selection of biscuits, all nicely presented on a tray brought in by Lily with a smiling 'good-morning'. Breakfast (which can be taken early if anyone has to leave betimes), was most enjoyable, the usual bacon and eggs being supplemented by Cumberland sausage.

Although Rydal is set amongst hills and lakes, it is not cut off. David will meet anyone coming by train (Windermere is the nearest station), buses go through the village at reasonable intervals, and the 'mountain goat' mini-bus, which takes holidaymakers to the more remote parts of the fells, will pick people up at the house. There is a sports centre at Kendal, swimming and roller-skating at Ambleside (the nearest town), golf and a sailing school at Windermere, and, in the near vicinity, facilities for wind-surfing, pony trekking, nature trails and 'discovery walks'. This is a very good area for bird-watching, too, and is very attractive to all nature-lovers. There was a painter staying at Rydal Lodge when we were there and it would certainly be a good base for any artist or photographer. A folder of literature about places of interest nearby is placed in each bedroom.

Most people are content to stay in during the evening, and cards, board games and books are available, as well as TV in a separate room. There is quite often a show at one of the local halls, staged by an amateur theatrical society, which some guests enjoy for a change; and there are cinemas and night spots not many miles away. When the guests seem likely to enjoy it,

David organises games, and both David and Lily are ready to help and advise about places to visit and things to do.

If 'guesthouse' means what it says — a house where guests are entertained and cared for — then Rydal Lodge meets the bill. From the moment you arrive and David shows you around, takes you to your room, and offers you a drink (tea, coffee, or something stronger), you feel welcome. Ernest Joan, Lily and David all seem so happy living and working in this lovely place, and their happiness is contagious.

**There could be no worthier 'Guesthouse of the Year' than Rydal Lodge.**

*Rydal Water, only a few minutes' stroll from the house, is one of the most beautiful of the English Lakes.*

# WINNER, WALES
## Plas Llanfaes, Beaumaris, Isle of Anglesey
### (Mary and Arwel Hughes)

*Plas Llanfaes, once a rectory, is built of local Penmon stone*

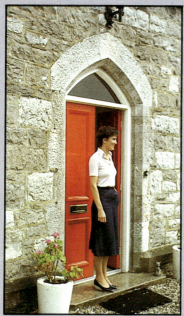

*Mary Hughes at the guesthouse door*

It took us a long time to reach Plas Llanfaes, partly because we took the tourist route through Shropshire and round the North Wales coast. We telephoned to warn Mary Hughes that we would be a bit late for dinner but she told us not to worry. She and her husband, Arwel, could not have been kinder to two weary travellers, extending a hospitality which was to last throughout our stay.

We were glad of the good dinner, cooked by Mary and her mother Mrs Mary Hannon, who come from Yorkshire. Mrs Hannon is a professional cook and displays the flair for which Yorkshirewomen are famous. Quite a lot of the vegetables and fruit come from the garden, and meat is often from local farms, so one can always be sure of appetising fresh food. We were served by Arwel Hughes, very correctly and with friendly concern for our well-being, with fruit cocktail; a traditional main course of roast beef, crisp and light Yorkshire pudding, with roast potatoes, carrots, peas and gravy served in separate dishes; and a delicious sweet called Cherry Jubilee which consisted of ice cream with a hot sauce made of cherries and brandy.

Plas Llanfaes used to be a rectory and Arwel and Mary bought it from the Church Commissioners. It is typical of the comfortable rural rectories of the 19th century, solidly built of local stone and with its own paddock and wooded grounds extending to 7 acres.

Beaumaris, with its moated castle and small harbour, is an attractive little town and a good centre for touring both Ynys Mon (as the Isle of Anglesey is called in Welsh) and the mainland of Wales which is easily reached by Telford's fine bridge or over the new road bridge which spans the Menai Straits.

Anglesey is an island of gentle countryside and attractive coves and beaches. Besides its natural advantages it has three sports centres and facilities for fishing, sailing, golf and pony trekking. Within sight of Plas Llanfaes are the mountains of Snowdonia, and there are many places of interest, including National Trust properties, steam railways and craft centres, within easy reach. Penmon Priory and Dovecote, with views of the lighthouse and Puffin Island, are within walking distance of the house. There is also an outdoors activity centre at nearby Llangoed and Arwel can arrange for guests to be picked up at the guesthouse if they wish to spend a day there.

The house is tastefully furnished and very comfortable, with log fires burning on cooler evenings. There is colour TV in one lounge and tourist literature is to hand. Bedrooms are very well equipped with plenty of storage space, comfortable beds and central heating. Orders for newspapers and early morning tea or coffee are taken the previous evening. Plas Llanfaes would easily lend itself to extension, but Arwel and Mary have taken a conscious decision to keep it small enough for them to run with little or no assistance other than from Mrs Hannon, who is a tower of strength in the kitchen. Arwel follows his own profession but takes a very active part in running the guesthouse and making sure that guests are well looked after.

We left Anglesey with the feeling that we had been refreshed and revived by a night in an extremely pleasant and well-run home.

# WINNER, SCOTLAND
## Lubnaig Hotel, Callander, Perthshire
**(Morna and Ian Dalziel)**

1 & 2 Lubnaig Hotel
3 Morna and Ian Dalziel
4 The annexe contains two
comfortable rooms
5 Loch Lubnaig at dusk
6 Entrance to the dining room

The little town of Callander is familiar to most people who are old enough to remember 'Dr Finlay's Casebook' on television, for its alias is Tannochbrae. The Lubnaig Hotel is in a quiet cul-de-sac off the main shopping street and is just the sort of house where one of the doctor's more affluent patients might have lived, a many-gabled stone-built house in a large lawned garden backed by wooded hills.

Everything is special about the Lubnaig, from the tartan carpet on the hall floor to the private shower and WC provided for each bedroom. Decorations are certainly individualistic, many of the ideas coming from the fertile brain of Morna Dalziel, with husband Ian providing much of the practical ability needed to put them into practice. Ian once worked in his family's garage business in Edinburgh as a coachpainter — a skill which comes in handy when redecorating time comes round — and Morna is the daughter of a chef who started a chain of restaurants in Fife. Morna certainly seems to have inherited her father's culinary talent, and she and her husband owned a restaurant before taking their first guesthouse nine years ago.

They have owned the Lubnaig Hotel for five years and have done much to extend and improve it during that time. It now has a fine lounge overlooking the garden, with comfortable seating, colour television and a selection of books, magazines and games. The dining room has been decorated in the style of a baronial hall, with rapiers displayed against the beamed ceiling and horned heads around the walls. Popular with most guests is the attractive cocktail bar, with banquette seating arranged in groups.

All the bedrooms have private well-equipped showers and lavatories and are of a good size, with bright modern décor, central heating and facilities for making tea and coffee. A holiday information folder is provided for each room.

An unusually wide choice of food is offered, guests being asked to order their evening meal earlier in the day. Starters include such items as egg mayonnaise and delicate patés as well as the usual soups and fruit juices. Morna uses wines and cream to good effect — one inspector says that a *gigot* of lamb in a cream and herb sauce was quite delicious. Brian and I had the more straightforward gammon with apricots, which was very enjoyable. Vegetables, served separately, were hot and fresh and the whole was attractively presented. A sweet from the trolley followed, with a selection of everybody's favourites from gateaux and profiteroles to fresh fruit salad with cream.

Callander is an ideal centre for touring and is a good base for many outdoor pursuits, be it fishing or shooting (in season), pony trekking, birdwatching, or just plain walking. Ian Dalziel, who is on the committee of the Scottish Wildlife Trust and is also a licensed falconer, is a mine of information about birds in the area.

After dinner Brian took me for a tour of the magnificent lochs and mountains which form the area known as the Trossachs. It was well after ten o'clock when we got back, after a round trip of 65 miles, but the northern light was only just fading — another plus to Scotland in summer.

Prices match facilities offered, so the Lubnaig Hotel is rather more expensive than the other establishments we visited, but this is an ideal place for anyone who wants an element of luxury and does not mind paying extra to obtain it.

# WINNER, SOUTH-EAST ENGLAND
## Snailham House, Icklesham, East Sussex
**(Denis and Irene Coxell)**

*Creeper-clad Snailham House is quietly situated amidst farmlands*

*Denis and Irene Coxell*

If we gave a separate award for good value, Snailham House would be well in the running. It is quite the cheapest place we visited but accommodation and environment are well up to standard and meals are ample.

Denis Coxell was an engineer in the London Docks and when he and Irene decided to look for a guesthouse he insisted that it should be small enough for them to run on their own as he had had enough of coping with staff. Although Snailham House comes in this category (though they do have some help in the holiday season), it is a fine residence, part creeper-clad, part tile-hung in typical Sussex fashion, within a large landscaped garden and surrounded by gently undulating, well-wooded countryside. It was, in fact, originally a farmhouse, having started as a modest building in the mid 19th century and been extended and improved over the years. The present farmer decided to move to an older house nearby and so the mainly-Victorian house came onto the market.

Entering the house one is immediately impressed by its spaciousness, as one walks into a large square hall with a lovely flower arrangement on the central table, loads of tourist information (with booklets and cards for sale) on one side, and walls decorated with interesting maps and pictures. In fact flowers and maps are a feature throughout the public rooms, and the decorations — alcoves in deep pastel green and quiet, unobtrusive wallpapers — seem designed as a background for flowers and pictures.

There are two fine lounges, one with television, the other a 'quiet' room, and a pleasant dining room. Bedrooms are furnished with comfortable beds and serviceable wardrobes, etc., and I was glad to see that there were an adequate number of chairs. Tea and coffee-making facilities are placed in each room.

When we arrived we were at once shown round and offered tea, which was served in the lounge five minutes later. Both Denis and Irene showed us every consideration during our short stay.

Our meal consisted of chicken soup; lamb chops, with broccoli, braised celery and new potatoes served in separate vegetable dishes; and gateau. Irene says she was used to cooking for a family of six and just prepares the same sort of meals for her guests, increasing the quantities as necessary. She makes no pretension to being a *cordon bleu* cook but the food is enjoyable and nicely presented.

Snailham House is actually at Broad Street (which consists of nothing much other than the house and farm) near Icklesham, a tiny village near the town of Winchelsea, which is itself near Rye, a most interesting old town which is one of the Cinque Ports and was once on the coast. This is a very good centre for visiting the many interesting places in East Sussex and Kent. Sports facilities abound in the area and it is, of course, quite near the sea too. For evening entertainment, theatres, cinemas, discos, etc., can be found at Hastings or Eastbourne, but most guests are happy to stay in either to watch television or to make use of the skittle board, cards, games and books which are provided.

Irene says they usually have some children staying there during the school holiday, but she is careful not to have too many in the house at one time. This is certainly a fine place for a family holiday or for adults who enjoy the peace of the countryside.

# WINNER, WEST OF ENGLAND
## Coombe Farm Guest House, Widegates, Cornwall
### (Alexander and Sally Low)

*Sally, Mandy, Charlie and Alex Low with Lorraine Tamblin and Prince the dog (Coombe Farm Guest House in the background)*

*Mallard Ducks feather their way to bed*

*Mandy on Pepper and Charlie on Buttons*

*Photos on this page by Alex Low*

Running a guesthouse is a new venture for Alex and Sally Low and this is only their second season, but already they have given Coombe Farm Guest House a character quite of its own. Alex is primarily a photographer and was the original picture editor of the Telegraph Magazine. He had been a journalist for a good many years when he decided that he would like a change. His wife, Sally, had at one time run a restaurant so taking on a guesthouse was a reasonable proposition and one which appealed to them both.

They viewed quite a number of 'for sale' properties and were almost despairing of finding the right place when they heard that Coombe Farm was on the market. They had often spent holidays at Looe (which is about four miles away) and remembered the house, which they had frequently passed. In fact Alex says he had coveted it for years and they hardly needed to view it before they made up their minds to buy. The property was originally part of a large estate and the house was built in 1928 for a nephew of the landowner. It was constructed to the design of an Indian Hill Station bungalow, but with rooms added in the deep roof.

The public rooms are decorated in fresh, light colours, with good furniture and drapes, lots of flowers and plants and, on cooler days, log fires for comfort and cheerfulness. Bedrooms are clean and comfortable and each has a pleasant outlook.

This really was a farmhouse when it was first built, but the house, with 10½ acres of garden, paddock and woodland, was sold away from the farm. Although Alex does not attempt to farm his land, he takes a great delight in the wildlife and keeps a number of animals for the pleasure of his family and guests. Goats crop the grass which stretches between the entrance drive and a pond inhabited by mallards and moorhens, and there are ponies in the paddock. A bit of wild woodland is a contribution towards wildlife conservation as well as providing logs for those splendid fires.

As in a family house, the evening mealtime varies a little, a gong warning guests when it is ready — some time between 7 and 7.30 p.m. This arrangement has virtues in that there is no waiting around once the gong sounds, and the food is all served fresh and hot. No choice is offered — though Sally would find an alternative for any dish that a guest really disliked — and this again means both that all the food is fresh-cooked and that the Lows can offer very good value for money.

We each had a good bowl of steaming home-made soup, chicken with a variety of vegetables, and apricot sponge with cornish cream. Cheese with biscuits were offered and there was good coffee to follow. Certainly no-one need go hungry while Sally looks after the catering. Mealtime service was by a quiet and efficient girl, Lorraine Tamblin, described by Alex as 'very much part of the establishment'.

One of our inspectors said (with unaccustomed enthusiasm) that if ever she owns a guesthouse she would want it to be like Coombe Farm and I know just what she means. There is a happy-go-lucky feeling about the place, as though everyone is doing just what suits them best and taking a pleasure in doing it.

# WINNER, MIDLANDS
## Shottle Hall Farm Guest House
## Shottle, Derbyshire
## (Phyllis and Philip Matthews)

*Shottle Hall Farm Guest House*

*Phyllis and Philip Matthews*

*Massed rhododendrons in the extensive and well-kept garden*

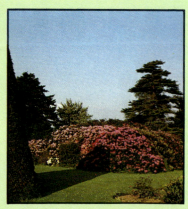

Shottle Hall is owned by the Chatsworth Estate and is situated amongst the gentle hills of southern Derbyshire. The large house had been divided into two separate entities early this century and in 1960 Philip and Phyllis Matthews became tenants of the 'farmhouse' side and ran the farm. It was the *Farmers' Weekly* Hospitality Club that first encouraged them to take guests, but only on a small scale.

Then the 'desirable residence' half fell empty and they were asked whether they would like to take it on. At first they said 'No' because the whole building contains 36 rooms, many of them spacious and high-ceilinged. But after some thought and discussion with the Chatsworth agent they changed their minds on condition that they were allowed to use the main house for business purposes. They planned a major operation, installing firedoors, rewiring, putting in central heating and extra bathrooms, and redecorating, the whole job being carried out between April and July 1977. They now have two separate businesses, the farm and the guesthouse. For this reason we list Shottle Hall as a guesthouse although it is set amidst farmlands.

Except that visitors are not expected to go into the farm area (Philip says this is for safety reasons and because he feels it would be unfair to his farm employees), staying at Shottle Hall is very much like visiting a farmhouse; except that the house is rather superb and was obviously built for an early Victorian gentleman farmer. The first tenant known to have occupied it was the Master of Blantyre who brought his sheep with him. The story goes that when the head of the flock reached the farm, sheep were still leaving the trucks in Belper sidings. He was only at Shottle a little while before moving to New Zealand, where no doubt he found more room for the sheep. The farm is now given over to dairy cows and cereal growing. Shottle Hall is a delightful house with most beautiful landscaped gardens and soothing views. The spacious public rooms are decorated in quiet colours and contain comfortable seating; a room which gets lots of morning sun is used for breakfast and there is another dining room where the evening meal is served. The bedrooms are large and attractively decorated.

Our evening meal consisted of egg mayonnaise, roast beef with Yorkshire pudding and plenty of fresh vegetables served in separate dishes, Black Forest gateau, and biscuits with a selection of English cheeses as well as coffee or tea. All good farmhouse food, and no need to go hungry. Phyllis says she usually starts the week with straightforward roasts, etc. If the guests seem the gastronomically adventurous type she introduces some less usual dishes, but she always makes a point of offering English cheeses and plenty of cream.

She likes to get to know her visitors and always comes into the dining room towards the end of the meal to have a chat, which helps to break down barriers between guests too. Although Philip has the farm to run he takes a great deal of interest in the guesthouse and he and Phyllis know all there is to know about their area and will help plan the week's activities for anyone who asks. In addition to Chatsworth, which is one of the most stately of Britain's Stately Homes, many places of interest in the area are open to the public. There are swimming pools at Belper (which has a sports centre) and Ashbourne, and opportunities exist locally for walking, riding and golf.

I really enjoyed staying at Shottle Hall and it will linger in my mind even though I was there for only one night. Whether for a complete holiday or for a break on the journey between North and South, it has a lot to recommend it.

# The Best of the Rest

Woodlea Guest House, at Symonds Yat West, is perched on the steep wooded banks of the River Wye. Sue and 'Goff' Parr have put in a tremendous amount of work to create a comfortable and welcoming guesthouse. Latest addition is a swimming pool.

The Cona Guest House at Shottenden is in an ideal position for people going to or coming from Dover or Folkestone. English-born Joy Jones and her American husband reckon that 60% of their guests are Dutch.

Bank Villa stands at the edge of Masham, a little town on the banks of the River Ure in North Yorkshire. It is run by Anton van der Horst and Phillip Gill, who does most of the cooking. The food here was some of the best we came across. Parking space is very limited but there is a public car park by the bowling green just across the road, from whence my picture of Masham was taken.

# Gazetteer

## GUEST HOUSE AND INN SECTION

**For details of AA-listed Farmhouses see separate section page 233**

The gazetteer gives locations and details of AA-listed guest houses and Inns in England, Wales and Scotland, Channel Islands and Isle of Man.

Details for islands are shown under individual placenames; the gazetteer text also gives appropriate cross-references. A useful first point of reference is to consult the location maps which show where guesthouses or Inns are situated.

N.B. *There is no map for Isles of Scilly.*

**ABERDARE** Mid Glam *Map 3 S000*
**GH Cae-Coed Private Hotel** Craig St, off Monk St ☎871190 Lic 7hc (3fb) nc3 CTV 10P ▥ S% B&b£8 Bdi£10.50 W£73.50 ⅃ D4pm

**ABERDEEN** Grampian *Aberdeens Map 15 NJ90* **(See Plan)**
**GH Broomfield Private Hotel** 15 Balmoral Pl ☎28758 Plan:**1** 8hc (1fb) CTV 16P ▥ S% B&bfr£8.50 Bdifr£12 D6pm

**GH *Carden Hotel*** 44 Carden Pl ☎26813 Plan:**2** 7hc nc5 CTV 6P ▥

**GH Crown Private Hotel** 10 Springbank Ter ☎26842 Plan:**3** 8hc (2fb) ⊁ nc4 CTV S% B&b£8 Bdi£11.50 W£50 M D5pm

**GH Dunromin** 75 Constitution St ☎56995 Plan:**4** 5hc (1fb) CTV ▥ S% B&b£6–£7

**GH Klibreck** 410 Great Western Rd ☎36115 Plan:**5** Closed Xmas & New Year 7hc (2fb) ⊁ CTV 3P ▥ S% ✳ B&bfr£7 Bdifr£10.50 Wfr£45.50 M D3pm

**GH Mannofield Hotel** 447 Great Western Rd ☎35888 Plan:**6** Lic 10rm 7hc (2fb) nc5 CTV 14P ▥ ✳ B&bfr£13.80 Bdifr£19.55 Wfr£136.85 ⅃ D6pm

**GH Tower Hotel** 36 Fonthill Rd ☎24050 Plan:**7** Lic 7hc (3fb) CTV 8P ▥ S% ✳ B&b£9 Bdi£13.25 W£83.50 ⅃ D6.45pm

**GH *Urray House*** 429 Great Western Rd ☎35204 Plan:**8** 6hc (3fb) nc5 CTV 5P 1♨ ▥ S% ⅃ D3pm

**GH *Western*** 193 Great Western Rd ☎56919 Plan:**9** 6hc (2fb) ⊁ CTV 8P ▥ S% B&bfr£7

| | | |
|---|---|---|
| **1** Broomfield Private Hotel | **4** Dunromin | **7** Tower Hotel |
| **2** Carden Hotel | **5** Klibreck | **8** Urray House |
| **3** Crown Private Hotel | **6** Mannofield Hotel | **9** Western |

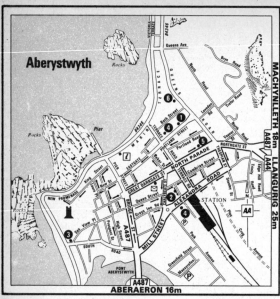

1 Four Seasons Hotel
2 Glan-Aber Hotel
3 Glyn-Garth
4 Railway Hotel
5 Shangrila
6 Swn-y-Don
7 Windsor Private Hotel

**ABERDOVEY** Gwynedd *Map 6 SN69*
⊠⊣**GH Cartref** ☎273 6hc (1fb) CTV 6P
B&bfr£5.50

**GH Maybank Private Hotel** ☎500
Feb–Nov Lic 7hc 1⇔ 1🛁 (3fb) CTV 🔳 sea
S% B&b£8–£1.5 Bdi£12–£19.50 W£53–£95
M D9.30pm

**ABERFELDY** Tayside *Perths Map 14 NN84*
**GH Balnearn Private Hotel** Crieff Rd
☎20431 13hc (2fb) CTV 13P 2🏤 ఈ
B&b£10.35 Bdi£14.55 W£80.50 ৳ D7pm

**GH Guinach House** Urlar Rd ☎20251
Mar–Oct Lic 8hc (2fb) CTV 8P S%
B&b£8.50–£10 Bdi£12.50–£15 W£80–£95
D7pm

**GH Nessbank Private Hotel** Crieff Rd
☎20214 Mar–Oct rsNov–Feb Lic 7hc CTV
7P B&bfr£10.50 Bdifr£15.50 Wfrf£95 ৳ D6pm

**ABERGAVENNY** Gwent *Map 3 SO21*
**GH Park** 36 Hereford Rd ☎3715 Lic 6hc
(1fb) CTV 8P 🔳 S% B&b£6.50 Bdi£10
W£43.50 ৳ D5pm

**INN** *Great George Hotel* Cross St ☎4230
Lic 4hc CTV 11🏤 🔳 D9.30pm

**ABERGELE** Clwyd *Map 6 SH97*
⊠⊣ **GH Coed Mor** Groes Lwyd ☎822261
6hc (2fb) TV 3P 🔳 S% B&bfr£5 Bdi fr£6.50
Wfr£45.50 ৳ D5pm

**INN Bull Hotel** Chapel St ☎822115 6hc 🛳
⊁CTV 12P S% B&b£7 Bdi£12 W£84 sn
L£2.50–£5&alc D8pm£4–£5 &alc

**ABERPORTH** Dyfed *Map 2 SN25*
**GH Fynonwen County** ☎810312 Lic 12hc
1⇔ (2fb) 40P 🔳 B&bfr£8.50 Bdifr£12 Wfrf£84 ৳

**ABERSOCH** Gwynedd *Map 6 SH32*
**GH Llysfor** ☎2248 Etr–Oct Lic 8hc 1⇔ 1🛁
(2fb) CTV 12P river sea S% B&b£8 Bdi£12.50
Wfrf£87 ৳ Dnoon

**ABERYSTWYTH** Dyfed *Map 6 SN58* **(See Plan)**

**GH** *Four Seasons Hotel* 50–54 Portland St
☎612120 Plan:**1** Closed Xmas Lic 17hc
6⇔🛁 (3fb) ⊁ nc5 CTV 12P 🔳 S%
D7.30pm

**GH Glan-Aber Hotel** Union St ☎617610
Plan:**2** Lic 14hc (1fb) CTV S% B&b£7.50
Bdi£11 Wfr£55 ৳ D7pm

**GH Glyn-Garth** South Rd ☎615050 Plan:**3**
Closed 2wks Xmas rsOct–Etr Lic 12hc 2🛁
(2fb) ⊁ nc7 CTV 🔳 sea S% B&b£7–£9 Bdi£11–
£13.50 W£68–£82 ৳ D4pm

⊠⊣ **GH Shangrila** 36 Portland St ⎮
☎617659 Plan:**5** 6hc (1fb) CTV 🔳 S%
B&b£5.50 Bdi£8 Wfrf£56 ৳ D4pm

**GH Swn-Y-Don** 40–42 North Pde ☎615059
Plan:**6** Lic 26hc (3fb) CTV 7P 🔳 ✱ B&bfr£8.05
Bdifr£11.50 Wfrf£74.75 ৳

⊠⊣ **GH Windsor Private Hotel** 41 Queens
Rd ☎612134 Plan:**7** 10hc (2fb) ⊁ CTV 6P 🔳
S% B&b£5.50–£7.50 Bdi£9–£11.50 W£60–£74
৳ D5pm

**INN Railway Hotel** Alexandra Rd ☎611258
Plan:**4** 4hc 🛳 ⊁ S% B&b£6.50 Bar lunch
£1.25alc

**ACASTER MALBIS** N Yorks *Map 8 SE54*
**INN Ship** ☎York 703888 Closed Xmas day
5hc 27P 🔳 S% B&b£7.50–£10 sn L£3.95
D9pm £5.50–£7.50 &alc

**ACLE** Norfolk *Map 9 TG41*
**GH** *Fishley Manor Hotel & Country Club*
South Walsham Rd ☎ Great Yarmouth
750377 Lic 12hc nc6 CTV 40P D9.30pm

**AINSTABLE** Cumbria *Map 12 NY54*
**INN Heather Glen Country Hotel** ☎Croglin
219 Closed 1–19 Mar 3hc 1⇔ ⊁ nc8 25P 🔳
S% B&b£9–£14 Bdi£16.50–£22 Bar lunch
£1.15–£2.50 D9.15pm £8 alc

**ALDEBURGH** Suffolk *Map 5 TM45*
**GH** *Granville Hotel* 243–247 High St
☎2708 Closed Xmas wk Lic 9hc 2⇔ (2fb) ⊁
CTV 1🏤 🔳 D8.30pm

**ALDERSHOT** Hants *Map 4 SU85*
**GH Glencoe Hotel** 4 Eggars Hill ☎20801
11hc 1🛏 (1fb) ✶nc7 CTV 12P 🅿 S% B&b£9–
£15 Bdi£15 W£80–£100 Ł D1pm

**ALMONDSBURY** Avon *Map 3 ST58*
**GH** *Hill Farm* 6 Gloucester Rd ☎613206
11rm 10hc ✶ Ch CTV 10P D6.30pm

**ALNMOUTH** Northumb *Map 12 NU21*
**GH Marine House Private Hotel** 1 Marine
Dr ☎349 Lic 8hc 2🛏 (4fb) Ch CTV 8P 🅿 sea
S% B&b£10–£11.50 Bdi£14–£17.80 W£103–
£118 D4pm

**ALNWICK** Northumb *Map 12 NU11*
**GH Aln House** South Rd ☎602265 Closed
Xmas & New Year 7hc (3fb) ✶nc5 CTV 7P 🅿

B&b£7–£8 Bdi£11–£12.50 W£73.50–£84 Ł
D5.30pm

**GH Bondgate House Hotel** Bondgate
Without ☎602025 Lic 8hc 1🛏 (3fb) CTV 7P
🅿 S% B&b£6–£8 Bdi£10–£13 D4pm

**GH Eradell** 1 Beaconsfield Ter, Upper
Howick St ☎602619 8hc (5fb) ✶nc5 TV 🅿
S% B&b£7–7.50 Bdi£11–£11.50 W£75–£80 Ł
D4pm

**GH Georgian** 3–5 Hotspur St ☎603165
Closed Dec–9 Jan 7rm 6hc (1fb) ✶ TV in all
bedrooms 6P 🅿 S% ✻B&b£5.75–£6.75
Bdi£9.25–£10.25 W£37–£42 ⋈ D7pm

**GH Hope Rise** The Dunterns ☎602930 7hc
(2fb) ✶nc5 CTV 12P 🅿 S% B&b£6.50–£7.50
Bdi£10–£11 W£70–£75 Ł D4pm

**ALTRINCHAM** Gt Manchester *Map 7 SJ78*
**GH Bollin Hotel** 58 Manchester Rd ☎061-928 2390 Closed 1 wk Xmas & New Year 10hc (3fb) CTV 12P B&b£10

**AMBLESIDE** Cumbria *Map 7 NY30*
**GH *Compston House*** ☎2305 Lic 10hc (2fb) ★ CTV Dnoon

**GH Gables** Church Walk, Compston Rd ☎3272 mid Mar–Nov Lic 15hc 1⊜ (5fb) nc3 CTV 8P ▥ B&b£8.05 Bdi£11.90 W£80.50 Ⱡ D6pm

**GH Gale Crescent** Lower Gale ☎2284 Mar–Nov 7hc (2fb) ★ CTV 6P S% B&b£7

**GH Hillsdale Private Hotel** Church St ☎3174 8hc (3fb) ★ CTV ▥ S% B&b£6.75 Bdi£10.50 W£68.60 Ⱡ D5.30pm

**GH Horseshoe** Rothay Rd ☎2000 Feb–Dec 12hc 5⋔ (6fb) CTV 11P ▥ S% B&bfr£7.95 Wfr£55.65 M

**GH Norwood House** Church St ☎3349 8hc (5fb) CTV ▥ S% ✱B&b£7–£8 Bdi£9–£10 W£65–£70 Ⱡ D2pm

**GH Oaklands Country House Hotel** Millans Park ☎2525 Feb–Nov Lic 7hc 1⊜ (4fb) ★ CTV 8P ▥ S% B&b£7–£10 Bdi£12.50–£16 W£80–£105 Ⱡ D4pm

**GH Riverside Hotel** Gilbert Scar ☎2395 Lic 11hc 3⊜ 1⋔ (2fb) ★ nc10 CTV 12P ▥ river Bdi£15.50–£21 W£108.50–£145 Ⱡ D7.30pm

**GH Rothay Garth Hotel** Rothay Rd ☎2217 Lic 14hc 2⊜ 3⋔ (2fb) CTV 12P ▥ S% B&b£13.22–£14.50 Bdi£16.67–£18.30 W£106.95–£117.60 Ⱡ D6pm

**GH Rydal Lodge Hotel** (2m NW A590)
☎3208 Apr–Oct Lic 8hc (1fb) CTV 12P river
B&b£8.80 Bdi£14.80 W£97 ⅃ D2pm

**GH Smallwood Hotel** Compston Rd ☎2330
Apr–Oct rsNov–Mar (wknds only) 13hc 1⇌
1🛏 (5fb) nc1 CTV 10P ⊞ S% B&bfr£8 Bdifr£12
Wfr£82 ⅃ D6pm

**AMROTH** Dyfed Map 2 SN10
**GH Sunnyridge** ☎Saundersfoot 812335
Jun–Aug 8hc (5fb) nc3 CTV 8P sea S%
B&b£6 W£42 ⋈

**ANCHOR** Salop Map 7 SO18
**INN Anchor** ☎Kerry 250 8hc 2⇌ CTV 250P
⊞ B&b£9–£12 sn L£3.50–£4.50 D9.30pm
£4.50 alc

**ANNAN** Dumfries & Galloway
*Dumfriesshire Map 11 NY16*
**GH Ravenswood** St Johns Rd ☎2158 Mar–
Jan Lic 9hc (2fb) ✵ CTV S% B&b£7.50–£8
Bdi£11–£11.60 W£77–£80.50 ⅃ D5pm

**APPLEBY** Cumbria *Map 12 NY62*
**GH Bongate House** ☎51245 Lic 7hc 1⇌ 1🛏
(3fb) ⊡ CTV 4P 2⚘ ⊞ S% B&b£7 Bdi£10
W£60 ⅃ D6.30pm

⊨ **GH Howgill House** ☎51574 Etr–Oct
6hc (3fb) ✵ CTV 6P S% B&bfr£5.50

**ARBROATH** Tayside *Angus Map 12 NO64*
⊨ **GH Kingsley** 29–31 Market Gate
☎73933 14hc (4fb) ✵ CTV 10P ⊞ S%
B&b£5.70–£6.85 Bdi£8–£9.20 W£49–£56 ⅃
D6pm

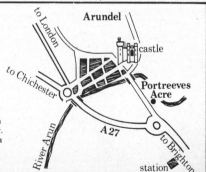

**ARDROSSAN** Strathclyde *Ayrs Map 10 NS24*
**GH Ellwood House** 6 Arran Pl ☎61130 7hc (1fb) CTV sea S% B&b£6

**ARNSIDE** Cumbria *Map 7 SD47*
**GH Grosvenor Private Hotel** The Promenade ☎761666 Mar–Oct & Xmas Lic 13hc (6fb) CTV 10P river S% B&b£7.50–£8.50 Bdi£12–£13 W£80–£87 ⅃ D5pm
**See advert on page 40**

**ARRAN, ISLE OF** Strathclyde *Bute Map 10*
See **Blackwaterfoot, Corrie, Lamlash, Lochranza, Sannox, Whiting Bay**

**ARRETON** Isle of Wight *Map 4 SZ58*
**GH Stickworth Hall** ☎233 May–Sep Lic 25hc 12ft (6fb) ✻nc5 CTV 45P ▥
✱B&b£9.65–£11.30 Bdi£16.15–£17.80 W£89–£98.90 ⅃ D7pm

**ARUNDEL** W Sussex *Map 4 TQ00*
⋈**GH Arden** 4 Queen's Lane ☎882544 8hc (2fb) ✻CTV 6P ▥ S% B&b£5–£6 Bdi£8.50–£9.50 W£56–£66.50 ⅃ Dnoon
**GH Bridge House** 18 Queen St ☎882142 Closed Xmas wk 11hc 2ft (5fb) 匚ħ CTV 4P 2🏠 ▥ river S% B&b£6–£11 W£40–£70 Ⲙ
**GH Portreeves Acre** The Causeway ☎883277 Apr–Oct 5⇆ CTV 6P ▥ river S% B&b£7.50

**ASCOT** Berks *Map 4 SU96*
**GH Highclere House** Kings Rd Sunninghill ☎25220 Lic 6hc (1fb) 匚ħ CTV 8P 2🏠 ▥ S% B&b£9.50 Bdi£14 D9.30pm

**ASCOTT-UNDER-WYCHWOOD** Oxon *Map 4 SP31*
**INN Wychwood Arms Hotel** ☎Shipton-under-Wychwood 830271 5⇆ 🏠 nc14 CTV in all bedrooms 30P ▥ B&b£12.50–£18 Bdi£20 sn L£6alc D9.30pm£9alc

**ASHBURTON** Devon *Map 3 SX76*
**GH Clitheroe House** St Lawrence Ln ☎52916 Closed Xmas Lic 9hc 4ft (3fb) ✻ nc5 CTV 7P ▥ S% B&b£8–£10 Bdi£11.50–£14 W£75–£85 ⅃ D10.30pm
**GH Gages Mill** Buckfastleigh Rd ☎52391 Lic 7hc 2ft (1fb) ✻ nc5 CTV 7P S%
✱B&b£6.50–£7 Bdi£10.50–£11 W£66–£69 ⅃

**ASHBY-DE-LA-ZOUCH** Leics *Map 8 SK31*
**GH *Fernleigh*** 37 Tamworth Rd ☎4755 6hc CTV 8P ▥ D6.30pm

**ASHFORD** Kent *Map 5 TR04*
**GH Croft Hotel** Canterbury Rd, Kennington ☎22140 Closed Xmas Lic 16hc 1⇆ 3ft (A6hc 2⇆ 4ft) (5fb) ✻CTV 22P ▥
✱B&b£9.20–£11.50 Bdi£13.20–£15.50 W£90–£105 ⅃ D8pm
**GH Downsview** Williesborough Rd, Kennington ☎21953 Lic 17hc 3ft (1fb) CTV 20P ▥ S% ✱B&b£11.40 W£68.40 ⅃ D9pm

**ASHWELL** Herts *Map 4 TL23*
**INN Three Tuns Hotel** 6 High St ☎2387 6hc 🏠 nc3 CTV 30P ▥ S% B&b£11.50–£15sn L95p–£3.95 D10pm£3.95

**AUSTWICK** N Yorks *Map 7 SD76*
**GH Traddock** ☎Clapham (N Yorks) 224 Etr–Oct Lic 11hc 1⇆ 7ft (4fb) nc5 CTV 14P ▥ B&b£9.20 Bdi£14.95 W£101.20 ⅃ D4.30pm

**AVIEMORE** Highland *Inverness-shire Map 14 NH81*
**GH Aviemore Chalets Motel** Aviemore Centre ☎810618 Lic 76🛏 (72fb) CTV 300P ▥ S% B&Bf8.40–£9.50 Bdif12.65–£14 Wf109–£120 D10pm

**GH Corrour House** Inverdruie ☎810220 Dec–Oct Lic 10rm 9hc (5fb) CTV 12P ▥ S% B&bf11.50 Bdif18.40 Wf128.80 ⅃ D6.30pm

**GH Craiglea** Grampian Rd ☎810210 11hc 1🛏 (4fb) ⃒Ch⃒ CTV 10P S% B&bf7–£8 Wf45.50–£52.50 M

**GH Ravenscraig** ☎810278 5rm 4hc (2fb) CTV 10P ▥ S% B&bf7.50–£8.50 Bdif11–£12.50 Wf72–£80 ⅃

**AYR** Strathclyde *Ayrs Map 10 NS32*
**GH Clifton Hotel** 19 Miller Rd ☎264521 Lic 11hc 4🛏 (1fb) ⊁nc5 CTV 16P B&bf6.50–£7 Bdif10.50–£12 Wf70–£75 D5.30pm

⊨◄ **GH Inverlea** 42 Carrick Rd ☎266756 7hc (1fb) CTV 4P S% B&bf5–£7 Bdif7–£9 (W only Oct–Apr) D5pm

**GH Kingsley Hotel** 10 Alloway Pl ☎262853 6hc (4fb) ⊁CTV P ▥ sea S% B&bf8 Bdif12 Wf54–£77.05 ⅃ D8pm

**GH Lochinver Hotel** 32 Park Circus ☎265086 Closed Xmas & New Year Lic 8hc (1fb) ⊁CTV 3P ▥ S% ✱B&bf5.75 Bdif9.20 Wf64.40 ⅃ Dam (W only Jul & Aug)

**GH Windsor Hotel** 6 Alloway Pl ☎264689 10hc (5fb) CTV ▥ B&bf9.50–£10.50 Bdif13–£14 Wf85–£90 ⅃ D4.30pm

**AYTON, GREAT** N Yorks *Map 8 NZ51*
**INN Royal Oak Hotel** High Green ☎722361 5hc 1⇌ CTV 10P ▥ S% ✱B&bf9.50–£10.50 sn Lf4alc D9pmf8.50alc

**BACTON** Norfolk *Map 9 TG33*
**GH Keswick Hotel** Walcott Rd ☎Walcott 650468 Lic 6hc 2⇌ 1🛏 ⊁nc12 CTV 40P ▥ D10pm

**BACUP** Lancs *Map 7 SD82*
**GH** *Burwood* Todmorden Rd ☎3466 Lic 6rm 5hc (1fb) ⊁CTV 8P ▥ S% D7pm

**BAKEWELL** Derbys *Map 8 SK26*
**GH Merlin House** Ashford Ln, Monsal Head ☎Great Longstone 475 mid Mar–mid Jan Lic 8hc 1⇌ 2🛏 (1fb) nc5 CTV 8P ▥ S% B&bf9–£14 Bdif15–£20 Wf100–£120 ⅃ D6.30pm

**BALA** Gwynedd *Map 6 SH93*
**GH Frondderw** ☎520301 Closed Xmas Lic 8hc 2⇌ (3fb) ⊁⃒Ch⃒ CTV 10P lake S% B&bf7.50 Bdif12.50 Wf82 ⅃ D6pm

**GH** *Plas Teg* Tegid St ☎520268 Closed Xmas Lic 8hc (4fb) CTV 10P lake D7pm

**BALDOCK** Herts *Map 4 TL23*
**GH Butterfield House** Hitchin St ☎892701 Lic 11⇌ (1fb) ⊁TV 12P ▥ S% B&bf11.50–£17.25 Bdif15–£21.75 D8pm

**BALLACHULISH** Highland *Argyll Map 14 NN05*
⊨◄ **GH Lyn-Leven** White St ☎392 8hc ⊁ CTV 9P ▥ lake S% B&bf4.50–£5.90 Bdif8–£9.40 D8pm

**BALLANTRAE** Strathclyde *Ayrs Map 10 NX08*
**INN Ardstinchar** Main St ☎383 4🛏 6P ▥ river S% B&bf7 Bdif10 Bar lunch £1.50–£2.50 D9.30pm

**BALLATER** Grampian *Aberdeens* Map 15 NO39
**GH Moorside** Braemar Rd ☎492 Apr–Oct Lic 8hc 1⇨ 3🛏 (2fb) nc5 CTV 10P ⊞ S% B&bfr£8 Bdifr£12 Wfr£78 ⟁ D7pm

**GH Morvada** ☎501 Apr–Oct Lic 7rm 6hc 2🛏 (2fb) CTV 6P ⊞ S% ✳B&bfr£6.50 Bdifr£10 D6.30pm

**GH Netherley** 2 Netherley Pl ☎792 Feb–Oct 10rm 9hc (1fb) nc2 CTV S% ✳B&b£6 Bdi£10 W60 ⟁ D7pm

**BALLOCH** Strathclyde *Dunbartons* Map 10 NS48
**INN Lomond Park Hotel** Balloch Rd ☎Alexandria 52494 7hc 1⇨ 2🛏 🚿 ✟ CTV 50P ⊞ S% ✳B&b£10–£14 Wf£70–£98 ⋈

**BALMAHA** Central *Stirlings* Map 10 NS49
⊢⊣ **GH Arrochoile** ☎231 Apr–Oct 6hc (2fb) ✟ CTV 12P ⊞ S% B&b£5 W£35 ⋈

**BAMPTON** Devon Map 3 SS92
**GH Bridge House Hotel** Luke St ☎298 (due to change to 31298) Closed Xmas Lic 6hc 2⇨ 1🛏 (2fb) CTV ⊞ B&bfr£8.05 Bdifr£11.05 Wfr£82.22 ⟁ D9.30pm

**BAMPTON** Oxon Map 4 SP30
**GH Bampton House** Bushey Row ☎Bampton Castle 850135 Closed Xmas wk Lic 6rm 5hc 1⇨ 3🛏(lfb) Ⓒ CTV 12P ⊞ S% B&b£9–£11 Bdi£15.50–£17.50 W£97.25–£110.25 ⟁ D5pm

**BANBURY** Oxon Map 4 SP44
**GH Lismore Private Hotel** 61 Oxford Rd ☎62105 Closed 24 Dec–3 Jan Lic 10hc 1⇨ (4fb) ✟CTV 6P 2🅿 ⊞ S% B&b£9–£11

**GH Tredis** 15 Broughton Rd ☎4632 6hc (1fb) CTV ⊞ S% B&b£6.50–£7.50 Bdi£9.50–£10.50 Dmid-day

**BANFF** Grampian *Banffs* Map 15 NJ66
**GH Carmelite House Private Hotel** Low St ☎2152 Closed Xmas & New Year Lic 8hc (3fb) ✟ CTV 6P S% B&b£6.50–£7.50 Bdi£9–£10.50 W£60–£65 ⟁ D5pm

⊢⊣ **GH Ellerslie** 45 Low St ☎5888 6hc (1fb) ✟ CTV S% B&b£5.50 Bdi£7.75 W£50 ⟁ D3pm

**BANGOR** Gwynedd Map 6 SH57
**GH Dilfan** Garth Rd ☎53030 8hc CTV 6P ⊞ D6pm

**GH Telford Hotel** Holyhead Rd ☎52543 Lic 9hc 3⇨🛏 (1fb) ✟ CTV P ⊞ sea D9pm

**BANTHAM** Devon Map 3 SX64
**INN Sloop** ☎Thurlestone 489 6hc 1⇨ 🚿 30P ⊞ sea B&b£7.50–£10.50 Bdi£12.50–£15.50 sn L£2–£5.50&alc D10pm£4–£6&alc

**BARMOUTH** Gwynedd Map 6 SH61
**GH Lawrenny Lodge** ☎280466 Etr–Oct Lic 10hc CTV 15P sea
**See advert on page 42**

**GH Morwendon** Llanaber (1m N A496) ☎280566 Apr–Oct Lic 7hc (3fb) ✟nc5 CTV 10P sea S% B&b£6.50–£6.75 Bdi£10–£10.75 W£68–£72 ⟁ D5.30pm

**BARNSTAPLE** Devon Map 2 SS53
**GH Cresta** Sticklepath Hill ☎74022 Closed Xmas 5hc (A 2rm 1hc 1⇨) (3fb) ✟nc5 CTV 8P ⊞ S% B&b£7.50–£9 Bdi£11–£12.50 W£74.50–£84 ⟁ Dmid-day

**GH Northcliff** 8 Rhododendron Av (off A39)
☎2524 Lic 8hc (1fb) ⼤ CTV 12P ⬛ S%
✱B&b£7.25 Bdi£11.50 W£72.50–£75 Ł

**GH Yeo Dale Hotel** Pilton Bridge ☎2954
Closed Xmas 10hc (4fb) CTV 4P S% B&b£7
Bdi£9.75 W£63 Ł Dmid-day

**BARRY** S Glam *Map 3 ST16*
**GH Maytree** 9 The Parade ☎734075 Lic 5hc
(2fb) CTV sea S% B&b£6–£8

**GH Sheridan** 11 The Parade ☎738488 5hc
(5fb) ⼤ CTV P ⬛ sea S% B&b£6–£9

**BARTON-ON-SEA** Hants *Map 4 SZ29*
**GH *Binley Hotel*** Beach Av ☎New Milton
610460 Mar–Oct rsNov–Mar Lic 9hc CTV 9P
⬛ D7pm

**GH Cliff House Hotel** Marine Drive West
☎New Milton 619333 mid Feb–Nov Lic
11hc (1fb) CTV 20P ⬛ S% B&b£10.50–£11
Bdi£15.50 W£92.50–£95 Ł D8pm

**GH *Dome Hotel*** Barton Court Av ☎New
Milton 616164 Lic 10hc 3⇔🛏 (4fb) CTV 18P
1🅿 ⬛ sea D7.30pm

**GH Gainsborough Hotel** 39 Marine Drive
East ☎New Milton 610541 Lic 9hc 1⇔ (1fb)
⼤ nc8 CTV 15P 5🅿 ⬛ sea S% B&b£9–£9.75
Bdi£13.50–£14 W£94.50–£98 Ł
D6.30pm

**GH Old Coastguard Hotel** 53 Marine Drive
East ☎New Milton 612987 Lic 8hc nc12 CTV
10P ⬛ sea S% B&b£8.63–£9.78 Bdi£11.50–
£13.80 W£74.75–£92 Ł D7pm

**BASINGSTOKE** Hants see **Sherfield-on-
Loddon**

**BASSENTHWAITE** Cumbria *Map 11 NY23*
**GH Bassenfell Manor Hotel**
☎Bassenthwaite Lake 366 Mar–Nov Lic
19hc 6🛏 (4fb) ⼤ nc2 CTV 20P ⬛ lake S%
B&b£10–£10.50 Bdi£15.50–£16.50 W£97.65–
£104 Ł D8.30pm

**BATH** Avon *Map 3 ST76* **(See Plan)**
**GH Apsley Garden House Hotel**
Newbridge Hill ☎21368 Plan:**1** Lic 11hc 1⇔
(2fb) CTV 10P ⬛ S% B&b£10.50–£11.50
Bdi£16–£17 W£100–£120 Ł D7.30pm

**GH Arden Hotel** 73 Great Pulteney St
☎66601 Plan:**2** Lic 12hc 3🛏 (4fb) nc7
CTV 2🅿 ⬛ B&b£9.50–£10.50 Bdi£14–£15
W£60–£67 Ⓜ D6.30pm

**GH Ashley Villa Hotel** 26 Newbridge Rd
☎21683 Plan:**3** 15hc 2⇔ 5🛏 (1fb) CTV 10P
⬛ & ✱B&b£16–£18 Bdi£21–£23 D9.30pm

**GH Avon Hotel** Bathwick St ☎22226 Plan:**4**
18hc 1⇔ 10🛏 (12fb) CTV 21P 2🅿 ⬛ S%
B&b£7–£12.50
**See advert on page 44**

**GH Carfax Hotel** Great Pulteney St ☎62089
Plan:**5** rs25 & 26 Dec (B&b only) Tem 38hc
4⇔ 3🛏 (4fb) ⼤ CTV 12P 4🅿 ⬛ lift & S%
B&b£9–£11.60 Bdi£13–£15.45 W£80–£105 Ł
D7.15pm

**GH Coningsby** 20 Park Ln ☎21119 Plan:**6**
Lic 3hc (2fb) CTV 3P ⬛ S% B&b£13–£15
Wfr£10 Ⓜ

◄►**GH Dorset Villa** 14 Newbridge Rd
☎25975 Plan:**7** Mar–Nov 6hc ⼤ nc10 CTV
6P ⬛ S% B&b£5.75–£6

**GH *Eastfield House*** 57 Upper Oldfield Pk
☎314990 Plan:**8** Feb–20 Dec Lic 10hc 1⇔🛏
(3fb) ⼤ CTV 8P D6pm

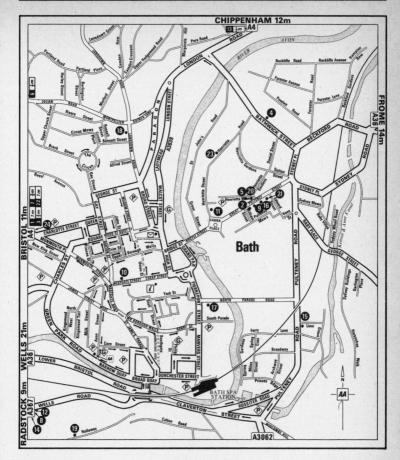

CHIPPENHAM 12m

Bath

1 Apsley Garden
 House Hotel
2 Arden Hotel
3 Ashley Villa Hotel
4 Avon Hotel
5 Carfax Hotel
6 Coningsby
7 Dorset Villa
8 Eastfield House
9 Edgar Hotel

10 Edwardian Hotel
 (Inn)
11 Georgian
12 Glenbeigh Hotel
13 Grove Lodge
14 Kingsley House
 Private Hotel
15 Lynwood
16 Millers Hotel
17 North Parade Hotel

18 Oxford Private
 Hotel
19 Paradise House
 Hotel
20 Richmond Hotel
21 St Monica's Hotel
22 Tacoma
23 Villa Magdala
 Private Hotel
24 Waltons

**GH Edgar Hotel** 64 Great Pulteney St
☎20619 Plan:**9** Lic 11hc 4⋔ (3fb) ✱CTV ⅢⅢ
S% B&b£9–£11.50 Bdi£13.50–£15.50
**See advert on page 44**

**GH Georgian** 34 Henrietta St ☎24103
Plan:**11** Lic 9hc (3fb) CTV 2☎ ⅢⅢ lift S%
✱B&b£8.50

**GH Glenbeigh Hotel** 1 Upper Oldfield Pk
☎26336 Plan:**12** Feb–Dec Lic 8hc (3fb)
CTV 8P 3☎ ⅢⅢ S% B&b£7–£9 W£50–£55
Ⓜ

**GH Grove Lodge** 11 Lambridge, London Rd
☎310860 Plan:**13** Lic 8hc (2fb) TV available
in some bedrooms S% B&b£8.50

**GH Kingsley House Private Hotel** 53 Upper
Oldfield Pk ☎25749 Plan:**14** Feb–Dec Lic
6hc 4⋔ ✱⋔ nc 6P ⅢⅢ

**GH Lynwood** 6 Pulteney Gdns ☎26410
Plan:**15** Closed Xmas 15hc (4fb) nc2 CTV ⅢⅢ

S% B&b£7.50–£10

**GH Millers Hotel** 69 Great Pulteney St
☎65798 Plan:**16** Closed Xmas Lic 11hc 2➾
(3fb) CTV 3P ⅢⅢ S% B&b£10–£11 Bdi£14.60–
£15.60 W£98–£105 Ⅳ D5pm

**GH North Parade Hotel** North Parade
☎60007 Plan:**17** Lic 17hc (3fb) CTV ⅢⅢ river
S% B&bfr£9.50

**GH Oxford Private Hotel** 5 Oxford Row,
Lansdown Rd ☎314039 Plan:**18** 9hc 2⋔ ✱
CTV ⅢⅢ S% B&b£6.90–£7.50

**GH Paradise House Hotel** Holloway
☎317723 Plan:**19** Closed Xmas wk 5hc (1fb)
✱TV available in some bedrooms 3P 3☎ ⅢⅢ
S% B&b£9–£12 W£54–£75 Ⓜ

**GH Richmond Hotel** 11 Gt Pulteney St
☎25560 Plan:**20** Lic 32rm 18hc 12➾ (4fb)
CTV ⅢⅢ S% B&b£7.50–£14 Bdi £11.50–£18
W£75–£85 Ⅳ (W only Oct–Feb) D5pm

43

**GH** *St Monica's Hotel* Gt Pulteney St
☎62092 Plan:**21** Lic 23hc Ch CTV 2♨ ⊮
D7.50pm

**GH** *Tacoma* 159 Newbridge Hill ☎310197
Plan:**22** Jan–20 Dec 8hc (3fb) ⅄ CTV 5P ⊮

**GH Villa Magdala Private Hotel** Henrietta
Rd ☎25836 Plan:**23** 9hc 6⇌ 3⋔ (2fb) ⅄ CTV
available in some bedrooms 12P 3♨ S%
B&b£14–£15

**GH** *Waltons* 17 Crescent Gdns ☎26528
Plan:**24** 20hc (3fb) CTV ⊮ D8.30pm

**INN** *Edwardian Hotel* 38 Westgate St
☎61642 Plan:**10** Closed Xmas Day Lic 26hc
15⇌⋔ ⊮ D11.15pm

**BEAULY** Highland *Inverness-shire Map 14
NH54*

**GH Chrialdon** Station Rd ☎2336 Jun–Oct
rsApr & May Lic 11hc (4fb) CTV 14P S%
B&b£6–£6.50 Bdi£9.75–£10.25 D7.45pm

**GH** *Grulnard* ☎2417 Apr–Oct 6hc (2fb) TV
6P

**BEAUMARIS** Gwynedd *Map 6 SH67*
**GH Plas Llanfaes Country House** ☎810480
Closed Xmas wk Lic 6hc (1fb) ⅄ CTV 12P ⊮
S% B&b£8.50–£10 Bdi£13–£15.50 W£79–£98 ⊮
D6pm

**GH Sea View** West End ☎810384 6hc ⅄
nc10 TV 5P sea S% ✻B&b£5.50 Bdi£9.50
W£66.50 ⊮ D4pm

**INN White Lion Hotel** Castle Sq ☎810589
9hc ⅄ CTV ⊮ sea S% ✻B&b£8.05 Bdi£12.65
Bar lunch 40p–£2.25 Dnoon£4.60&alc

**BEAUMONT** Jersey, Channel Islands *Map 16*
**GH *Seawold Private Hotel*** St Aubin's Rd ☎Jersey 20807 22hc 22⇔🛉 ⚊ CTV 5P ⧈ sea (W only May–Sep) D6.45pm

**BECKERMET** Cumbria *Map 11 NY00*
**INN Royal Oak Hotel** ☎84551 8⇔🛉 ⚊ CTV in all bedrooms 20P 20☜ ⧈ S% B&b£14–£16 Bdi£18–£20 Bar meals £1–£6.50

**BEDDGELERT** Gwynedd *Map 6 SH54*
**GH Sygyn Fawr** ☎258 Lic 7hc 4🛉 (1fb) CTV 20P ⧈ S% B&b£10–£12 Bdi £16–£18 W£107–£114 ⚊ D7.30pm

**BEDFORD** Beds *Map 4 TL04*
**GH Kimbolton Hotel** 78 Clapham Rd ☎54854 rsXmas day Lic 16hc (1fb) CTV 20P ⧈ B&bfr£11.50 Bdifr£16 W£fr£136.50 D7pm

**BEER** Devon *Map 3 SY28*
**GH Bay View** Fore St ☎Seaton (Devon) 20489 Etr–Oct 6hc (2fb) nc5 CTV sea B&b£6.50–£8.50 W£42–£45 M

**BEESTON** Notts *Map 8 SK53*
**GH Brackley House Hotel** 31 Elm Av ☎Nottingham 251787 Lic 14hc 3⇔ 1🛉 CTV 14P ⧈ S% ✱B&bfr£10.42 D9pm

**BELFORD** Northumb *Map 12 NU13*
**INN Black Swan** Market Sq ☎266 9hc 1⇌ TV 30P 2☜ ⧈ B&b£9.20 Bdi£15.20 sn L£4.20alc D8.30pm£6alc

**BELSTONE** Devon *Map 2 SX69*
**INN Tors** ☎Sticklepath 689 3hc CTV P 2☜ ⧈ ✱B&b£8 Bdi£11 W72 ⚊ sn L£3.50 S% D8.30pm£3&alc

**BENSON** Oxon *Map 4 SU69*
**INN White Hart Hotel** ☎Wallingford 35244 10hc nc5 TV 60P B&b£12.50 sn L£2.50 D8.30pm£2.50&alc

**BERRIEW** Powys *Map 7 SJ10*
**INN *Talbot Hotel*** ☎260 Lic 8hc 1⇔🛉 CTV 40P D9.30pm (Dining room in annexe across lane)

**BERRYNARBOR** Devon *Map 2 SS54*
**GH *Seacliffe Country Hotel*** ☎Combe Martin 3273 10hc (3fb) ⚊ CTV 12P ⧈ sea D9pm

**BETWS GARMON** Gwynedd *Map 6 SH55*
**I⚊I GH Bryn-Gloch Farm** ☎Waunfawr 216 Lic 3hc (A 2hc) (1fb) TV 8P S% B&b£5.50 Bdi£9.50 W£66.50 ⚊ D7.30pm

**BETWS-Y-COED** Gwynedd *Map 6 SH75*
**GH Bod Hyfryd** Holyhead Rd ☎220 6hc TV 6P river S% B&bfr£6.50 Bdifr£8.50 Wfr£59.50 ⚊ D6pm

**GH Glenwood** ☎508 Closed Xmas 6hc (3fb) nc4 CTV 12P ⧈ river S% ✱B&b£7.50–£9 Bdi£11–£12.50 D7.30pm

**GH *Gwynant*** ☎372 Etr–Oct 5rm 4hc (1fb) TV 5P

**GH Hafan** ☎233 Closed Xmas Lic 7hc 3🛉 (2fb) nc2 CTV 10P 1☜ ⧈ S% B&b£7–£9 Bdi£12–£14

**GH Henllys (Old Court) Private Hotel** ☎534 Feb–Dec Lic 10hc 2⇔ 4🛉 nc6 CTV 14P river B&bfr£7.50 Bdifr£12.75 Wfr£79 ⚊ D7pm

**GH Mount Garmon Hotel** ☎335 Jan–Oct Lic 5hc 3🛉 ⚊ nc5 CTV 5P ⧈ S% B&bfr£7.50 Bdifr£13.50 Wfr£90 ⚊ D5pm

**BEXHILL-ON-SEA** E Sussex *Map 5 TQ76*
**GH *Alexandra Hotel*** 2 Middlesex Rd ☎210202 Feb–Nov rsDec & Jan Lic 9hc (2fb) nc3 CTV 1P ⧈ D4pm

**GH Dunselma Private Hotel** 25 Marina ☎212988 Etr–5 Oct 11hc 2⇔ (2fb) nc5 sea S% B&b£9.20–£11.50 Bdi£13.80–£16.10 W£71.30–£87.40 ⚊ D7.30pm

**GH Radclive Private Hotel** 36 Woodville Rd ☎212007 Lic 8hc (3fb) CTV P ⧈ S% B&b£7–£8 Bdi£10–£11 W£66–£70 ⚊ D8.30pm

**GH Victoria House** 1 Middlesex Rd ☎210382 Mar–mid Oct Lic 11hc (3fb) CTV 6P S% B&b£8.74–£10.12 Bdi£8.50–£12 W£57.50–£62.79 ⚊ D6.30pm

**BICKINGTON** *(Nr Newton Abbot)* Devon *Map 3 SX77*
**GH Privet Cottage** ☎319 Etr–Oct 9hc CTV 8P S% B&b£6.50 Bdi£11.50 W£80 ⚊ D6.30pm

**BICKLEIGH** *(Nr Tiverton)* Devon *Map 3 SS90*
**GH Bickleigh Cottage** ☎Tiverton 230 May–Sep rsApr & Oct 11rm 9hc 2⇔ (2fb) ⚊ TV 10P river ✱B&b£7–£9 Bdi£11.75–£13.75 D5pm

**BIDEFORD** Devon *Map 2 SS42*
**GH Edelweiss** 2 Buttgarden St ☎2676 Apr–Oct rsNov–Mar Lic 11hc (5fb) CTV river S% ✱B&b£6–£6.80 Bdi£9.50–£10.30 W£52.75–£62.50 ⚊ D9.30pm

**GH Mount Private Hotel** Northdown Rd ☎3748 Mar–Nov Lic 6hc 2🛉 (2fb) TV 1☜ ⧈ S% B&b£7–£7.50 Bdi£10.50–£11 W£65–£75 D9.30pm

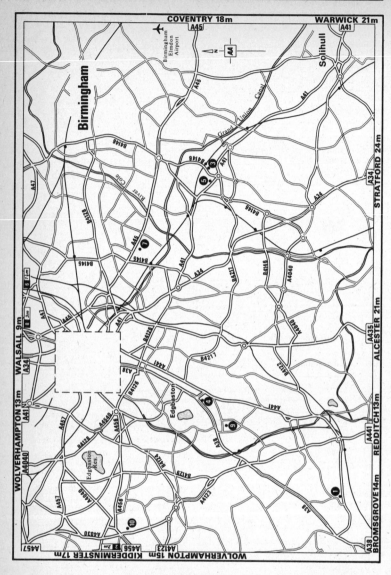

1 Alexander
2 Highfield House
  (see under
  Rowley Regis)
3 Bridge House
  Hotel
4 Bristol Court
  Hotel
5 Kerry House
  Hotel
6 Lyndhurst Hotel
7 Park View
8 Standbridge
  Hotel (see
  under Sutton
  Coldfield)
9 Wentsbury Hotel
10 Wentworth Hotel

**GH** *Sonnenheim Private Hotel* Heywood
Rd, Northam ☎4989 Lic 9hc 1⇔ 1🛏 (4fb) CTV
10P ▥▥ D6.30pm

**GH** *Tresillian Hotel* ☎6664 Lic 10hc 1⇔ 1🛏
(2fb) ⒸⒽ CTV 10P ▥▥ S% B&b£7–£8.50
Bdi£11–£12.90 W£63–£73 ⎷ D8pm

**BIGBURY-ON-SEA** Devon *Map 3 SX64*
**GH** *Easton House Private Hotel* ☎296
Mar–Nov & Xmas Lic 15hc 9⇔ (9fb) ⒸⒽ CTV
20P ▥▥ D8.30pm

**BILBROOK** Somerset *Map 3 ST04*
⊨⊣ **GH** **Bilbrook Lodge Hotel**
☎Washford 561 6hc ✱nc6 CTV 12P ▥▥
S% B&b£5.50–£6.50 Bdi£8.50–£9
D6.30pm

**BINGLEY** W Yorks *Map 7 SE13*
**GH** **Hall Bank Private Hotel** Beck Ln
☎Bradford 565296 Closed Xmas 8hc 3⇔
(1fb) ✱nc2 CTV 20P ▥▥ S% B&b£8.16–£10.69
Bdi£12.19–£15.72 W£78.20–£87.86 ⎷

**BIRMINGHAM** W Midlands *Map 7 SP08*
**(See Plan)**
**GH Alexander** 44 Banbury Rd ☎021-475
4341 Plan:**1** Lic 12hc (2fb) CTV 12P ▥ S%
B&bfr£9.20 Bdifr£16 Wfr£84 ⅃ D6pm

**GH Bridge House Hotel** 49 Sherbourne Rd,
Acocks Gn ☎021-706 5900 Plan:**3** Lic 10hc
(1fb) CTV 15P ▥ S% B&b£6.90 Bdi£9.50
W£67.50 D9.30pm

**GH Bristol Court Hotel** 250 Bristol Rd
☎021-472 0413 Plan:**4** Lic 30hc 4⇌ 6♒ (2fb)
Ⓒⱨ CTV 30P 3♨ ▥ S% B&b£12–£14
Bdi£15.50–£17.50 Wfr£140 D9pm

**GH Kerry House Hotel** 946 Warwick Rd,
Acocks Gn ☎021-707 0316 Plan:**5** Lic 23hc
CTV 21P ▥ S% B&b£12.65–£14.95

Bdi£17.65–£19.95 Wfr£90 ⅃ D7.30pm
**GH Lyndhurst Hotel** 135 Kingsbury Rd,
Erdington ☎021-373 5695 Plan:**6** Closed
Xmas 20hc 1♒ (3fb) ⚟ CTV 15P ▥ S%
B&b£10.35 Bdi£14.95 W£94.14 ⅃ D6.30pm

**GH Park View** 42 Tennyson Rd, Small Heath
☎021-772 5000 Plan:**7** Lic 6hc (4fb) CTV ▥
S% ✳ B&bfr£7 Bdifr£8.50

**GH Wentsbury Hotel** 21 Serpentine Rd,
Selly Park ☎021-472 1258 Plan:**9** Closed
Xmas 8hc (1fb) CTV 10P ▥ S% B&bfr£8
Bdifr£12.50 D6.30pm

**GH Wentworth House Hotel** 103
Wentworth Rd, Harborne ☎021-427 2839
Plan:**10** Closed Xmas 18hc (A 3hc) CTV 14P
3♨ ▥ S% B&b£8–£14 Bdi£12–£16 D8.30pm

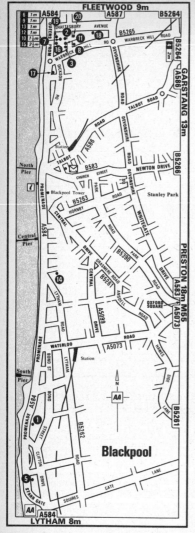

1 Arandora Star Private Hotel
2 Arosa Hotel
3 Beaucliffe Private Hotel
4 Breck Hotel (*see under Poulton-le-Fylde*)
5 Channings
6 Cliftonville Hotel
7 Croydon Private Hotel
8 Denely Private Hotel
9 Edenfield Private Hotel
10 Garville Hotel
11 Lynstead Private Hotel
12 Manxonia Hotel
13 Mavern Private Hotel
14 Motel Mimosa
15 New Heathcote Hotel
16 North Mount Private Hotel
17 Sunnycliff
18 Sunray Private Hotel
19 Surrey House Hotel
20 Ventnor Private Hotel

---

**BIRNAM** Tayside *Perths Map 11 NO04*
**GH Waterbury House** Murthly Ter
☎Dunkeld 324 6hc (1fb) CTV P ▥ S%
B&b£5.50–£6 Bdi£9.50–£11 W£39–£66 ⅃ D6pm

**BISHOP'S CLEEVE** Glos *Map 3 SO92*
**GH Old Manor House** 43 Station Rd ☎4127
6hc (3fb) CTV 8P S% B&b£6.50–£7.50
Bdi fr£12 Dnoon

**BISHOPSTON** W Glam *Map 2 SN58*
**GH Winston Hotel** 11 Church Ln,
Bishopston Valley ☎2074 Lic 13hc 3🛁 (2fb)
CTV 18P ▥ S% ✳B&b£8.50 Bdi£13.50
**See advert on page 47**

**BISHOP WILTON** Humberside *Map 8 SE75*
**INN Fleece** ☎251 4hc ⇔ ⊁ CTV 20P ▥
B&b£7.50 Bdi£14 Bar lunch 45p–£3.50
D9.30pm£6.25–£8&alc

**BLACKAWTON** Devon *Map 3 SX85*
**INN Normandy Arms** Chapel St ☎316 5hc
2⇔ 11P S% B&b£7.25–£8 Bar lunch 45p–
£4&alc D10.30pm£5–£7&alc

**BLACKPOOL** Lancs *Map 27 SD33* **(See Plan)**
**GH Arandora Star Private Hotel** 559 New
South Prom ☎41528 Plan:**1** Jan–Oct Lic
18hc (3fb) CTV 12P 4🅿 sea S% B&bfr£6.35
Bdifr£9.50 D5pm

**GH Arosa Hotel** 18–20 Empress Dr
☎52555 Plan:**2** Etr–Nov & Xmas Lic 21hc
4🛁 (6fb) ⊁ CTV 7P ▥ S% B&b£8–£9 D4pm
**See advert on page 50**

**GH Beaucliffe Private Hotel** 22 Holmfield
Rd, North Shore ☎51663 Plan:**3** Mar–Dec
12hc (2fb) ⊁ nc3 CTV 10P ▥ S% B&b£7.76
Bdi£8.91 W£59.57 ⅃

**GH Channings** 557 New South Prom ☎41380 Plan:**5** Lic 20hc (6fb) CTV 16P ▥ sea S% ✳ B&bf5.50–£6.50 Bdif7–£8 D4pm

╟┥ **GH Cliftonville Hotel** 14 Empress Dr ☎51052 Plan:**6** Apr–Nov & 4 days Xmas Lic 21hc 11♒ (7fb) CTV 6P ▥ B&bf5.75–£12 Bdif8.50–£15 Wf57–£85 ⫝̸ D5.45pm

**GH Croydon Private Hotel** 12 Empress Dr ☎52497 Plan:**7** Etr–Oct Lic 11hc 2♒ (3fb) ✶ CTV 8P S% B&bf6.90–£8.33 Bdif8.10–£9.48 Wf56.70–£66.36 ⫝̸ D5.30pm

**GH Denely Private Hotel** 15 King Edward Av ☎52757 Plan:**8** 8hc (2fb) ✶ CTV 5P ▥ D4.30pm

**GH Edenfield Private Hotel** 42 King Edward Av ☎51538 Plan:**9** Apr–Oct Lic 10hc (2fb) ✶ nc10 CTV 2P S% B&bf7–£8

Bdif8.50–£10.50 Wf58–£72 ⫝̸ D3pm

**GH Garville** 3 Beaufort Av, Bispham (2m N) ☎51004 Plan:**10** Jan–Nov Lic 7hc 2➪ (2fb) CTV 4P ▥ lift S% B&bfrf7 Bdifrf8.25 Wfrf57.75 ⫝̸ D5.30pm

**GH Lynstead Private Hotel** 40 King Edward Av ☎51050 Plan:**11** Lic 11hc (5fb) ✶ CTV S% B&bf7.76–£8.63 Bdif8.81–£9.78 Wf62.37–£68.46 ⫝̸ D3pm

**GH Manxonia Hotel** 248 Queens Prom, Bispham (1m N A584) ☎51118 Plan:**12** Xmas, Etr & Spring Bank Hol–Oct Lic 18hc (5fb) CTV 9P ▥ sea Dnoon

**GH Mavern Private Hotel** 238 Queens Prom, Bispham (1m N A584) ☎51409 Plan:**13** 22hc 1➪ (2fb) ✶ 12P 1☎ ▥ S% ✳ B&bf8.05–£9.20 Bdif9.20–£10.35 D5pm

**GH Motel Mimosa** 24a Lonsdale Rd ☎41906 Plan:**14** Closed Xmas 15☺ ✦nc11 CTV 12P 1☎ ⑩ S% B&b£10–£11 W£68.43–£76.48 Ⓜ

**GH New Heathcote Hotel** 270 Queens Prom ☎52083 Plan:**15** Lic 9hc CTV 6P ⑩ B&bfr£6 Bdifr£7.50

⋈**GH North Mount Private Hotel** 22 King Edward Av ☎55937 Plan:**16** May–Oct Lic 8hc (2fb) ✦CTV ⑩ S% B&b£5.50–£5.75 Bdif£7.75–£8 W£54.25–£56 Ⓛ D5pm

**GH Sunnycliff** 98 Queens Prom ☎51155 Plan:**17** Etr–Nov & Xmas 12hc (4fb) CTV 12P sea S% B&b£6.90–£8 Bdif£9–£10.50 W£63–£73.50 Ⓛ D5pm

**GH Sunray Private Hotel** 42 Knowle Av, Queens Prom ☎51937 Plan:**18** Jan–Nov 6hc (1fb) CTV 6P ⑩ S% B&b£7.10–£8.50

Bdi£11.25–£12.80 W£78.75–£89.60 Ⓛ D4.30pm

⋈**GH Surrey House Hotel** 9 Northumberland Av ☎51743 Plan:**19** Mid Mar–early Nov 12hc 1☺ 4fi (2fb) CTV 6P 1☎ ⑩ S% B&b£5.75–£7.25 Bdif£7.50–£10.75 W£50–£73.50 Ⓛ D5pm

**GH Ventnor Private Hotel** 57 Holmfield Rd ☎51314 Plan:**20** Closed 2wks Xmas/New Year 8hc (2fb) ✦CTV ⑩ S% B&b£7–£8.75 Bdif£8.50–£10.50 W£55–£65 Ⓛ D3pm

**BLACKWATERFOOT** Isle of Arran Strathclyde *Bute Map 10 NR92* **INN Greannan Hotel** ☎Shiskine 200 Apr–Oct 12hc CTV 40P ⑩ S% B&b£7.30–£7.50 Bdif£11–£11.30 W£77–£79.10 Ⓛ Bar lunch £1–£2 D£5.50

**BLACKWOOD** Gwent *Map 3 ST19*
**INN Plas** Gordon Rd ☎224674 6hc CTV 50P
▥ S% B&bfr£12.65 Bdifr£17 sn L£2.50alc
D9.30£5alc

**BLAENAU FFESTINIOG** Gwynedd *Map 6
SH74*
✕ **GH Don Restaurant & Guest House**
147 High St ☎403 Lic 6hc (3fb) ⚹ CTV 2P 2⚘
▥ B&b£5.50–£6 Bdif£8.50–£9 D9pm

**BLAIRGOWRIE** Tayside *Perths Map 11
NO14*
**GH Kintrae House Hotel** Balmoral Rd
☎2106 Lic 9hc (3fb) CTV 16P ▥ S%
B&b£8.50 Bdif£13 Wfrf£91 ⅃ D9pm

**BLEADNEY** Somerset *Map 3 ST44*
**GH Threeway Country House Hotel &
Restaurant** ☎Wells 78870 Closed Xmas Lic
10hc 1⇔ 1🛁 (2fb) ⚹ CTV 40P ▥ S%
✳B&b£7.50–£10.50 D9pm

**BLETCHINGLEY** Surrey *Map 4 TQ35*
**INN Whyte Harte** ☎Godstone 843231 9hc
4⇔ ⚗ ⚹ CTV 60P ▥ B&b£14 sn Lfr£6&alc
D10pmfr£9

**BLUE ANCHOR** Somerset *Map 3 ST04*
**GH Camelot** ☎Dunster 348 Feb–Nov 7hc
(1fb) ⚹nc12 CTV 6P ▥ sea S% B&b£7–£8
Bdif£10.25–£11.25 W£65–£70 D5pm

**BLYTH** Northumb *Map 12 NZ38*
**INN *Kitty Brewster*** 549 Cowpen Rd ☎2732
Lic 7hc ⚹ CTV 20P ▥ D9.30pm

**BOAT OF GARTEN** Highland *Inverness-
shire Map 14 NH91*

**GH Moorfield House Hotel** Deshar Rd
☎646 Jan–Oct Lic 5hc (2fb) ⚹nc5 TV 12P ▥
✳B&b£7.50–£8 Bdi£10.50–£12 W£70–£80 ⅃
D5.30pm

**BODEDERN** Gwynedd *Map 6 SS38*
**INN Crown Hotel** ☎Valley 740734 5hc
100P ▥ S% B&b£6.50

**BODIAM** E Sussex *Map 5 TQ72*
**GH Justins Hotel** ☎Staplecross 372 Closed
Nov Lic 10hc 2⇔ 6🛁 (3fb) CTV 20P ▥ S%
B&b£12.88 Bdi£19.20 W£127.40 ⅃ D8pm

**BODMIN** Cornwall *Map 2 SX06*
**GH Washaway Your Troubles** Washaway
☎4951 Lic 5hc (A 3rm 2hc) (1fb) ⚹nc5 CTV
10P ▥ S% B&b£7.50–£9 Bdif£13–£14.50
W£78–£85 ⅃

**BOGNOR REGIS** W Sussex *Map 4 SZ99*
✕ **GH Homestead Private Hotel** 90
Aldwick Rd ☎823443 Lic 6hc (A 2🛁) (6fb)
CTV 10P S% B&bfr£5.50 Bdifr£7.50
Wfrf£49 ⅃

**GH Landsdowne Hotel** 55–57 West St
☎865552 rsXmas Lic 10hc (5fb) CTV 3P ▥
sea ✳B&b£7–£10 Bdi£11.50–£14.50
W£76–£98 ⅃ D6pm

**BOLLINGTON** Cheshire *Map 7 SJ97*
**INN Turners Arms Hotel** 1 Ingersley Rd
☎73864 5rm 4hc TV 5P ▥ S% B&b£10 sn
L£1.80&alc D10pm£4alc

**BONAR BRIDGE** Highland *Sutherland Map
14 NH69*
**GH Glengate** ☎Ardgay 318 Mar–Oct 3hc
CTV 4P sea S% B&b£6

1 Alcombe Private Hotel
2 Anfield Hotel
3 Arundale
4 Braemar Private Hotel
4A Hotel Bristol
5 Britannia Hotel
6 Bursledon Hotel
7 Carisbroke Hotel
8 Carysfoot Lodge Private Hotel
9 Hotel Cavendish
10 Charles Taylor Hotel
11 Chilterns Hotel
12 Cintra
13 Cliffside Hotel
14 Clock House Hotel
15 Crescent Grange Hotel
16 Dean Court Hotel
17 Derwent House
18 East Cliff Cottage Private Hotel
19 Eglan Court Hotel
20 Fallowfield Hotel
21 Farlow Private Hotel
22 Freshfields Touring Hotel
23 Gervis Court Hotel
24 Hamilton Hall Private Hotel
25 Hawaiian
26 Heather Mount Hotel
27 Highlin Private Hotel
28 Hollyhurst Hotel
29 Kensington Hotel
30 King's Barton Hotel
31 Linwood House Hotel
32 Loddington Grange Hotel
33 Mae-Mar Private Hotel
34 Mon Bijou
35 Monreith
36 Mount Stuart Hotel
37 Penmone Hotel
38 Pine Beach
40 St John's Lodge Hotel
41 St Ronans
42 Sandelheath
43 Sea Shells
44 Seastrole Private Hotel
45 Sea View Court Hotel
46 Hotel Sorrento
47 Southlea Hotel
48 Tower House Hotel
49 Tudor Grange Hotel
50 Wellington Hotel
51 Wenmaur House
52 West Bay Hotel
53 Whitley Court Hotel
54 Windsor Court Hotel
55 Wood Lodge Hotel

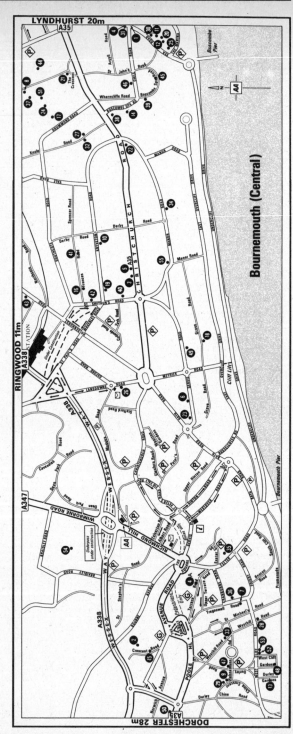

**BONTDDU** Gwynedd *Map 6 SH61*
**INN** *Halfway House Hotel* ☎635 Etr–Dec
Lic 4hc (A 1⇨) 🄌 ⊁ CTV 12P 3🅰 ⬆ D9pm

**BONTNEWYDD** Gwynedd *Map 6 SH46*
**GH** *Dwynfa* ☎Llanwnda 830414 Mar–Oct
12hc ⊁ nc10 CTV 15P river

**BOOT** Cumbria *Map 7 NY10*
**GH** *Brook House* ☎Eskdale 288 Lic 6hc
(2fb) CTV 8P D6pm

**BOSCASTLE** Cornwall *Map 2 SX09*
**GH St Christophers Country House** High
St ☎412 Mar–Oct Lic 6hc 1🄌 (2fb) CTV 6P
🄌 sea S% B&b£8–£8.50 Bdi£12.50–£13
W£84.50–£88.50 ⬇ D7.30pm

**GH Tolcarne Private Hotel** ☎252 Lic 12hc
1⇨ (3fb) 🄬 CTV 30P 🄌 B&b£8.50–£9.50
Bdi£12.50–£13 W£80–£86 ⬇ D8pm

**BOSWINGER** Cornwall *Map 2 SW94*
**GH Van Ruan House** ☎Mevagissey 842425
Etr–Oct Lic 7hc (1fb) ⊁ nc7 CTV 🄌 sea S%
✱B&bfr£7.50 Bdifr£11.50 Wfr£75 ⬇ D4pm
(W only Jul & Aug)

**BOURNEMOUTH AND BOSCOMBE**
Dorset *Map 4 SZ09*
*Telephone Exchange 'Bournemouth'*
**(See Central and District Plans)**
For additional guesthouses see **Poole** and
**Christchurch**
**GH Alcombe Private Hotel** 37 Sea Rd,
Boscombe ☎36206 Central plan:**1**Closed
Xmas 12hc (4fb) CTV 6P S% B&b£6–£8.75
Bdi£8.50–£12 W£56.40–£86 ⬇ D4.30pm

**GH Alum Bay Hotel** 19 Burnaby Rd, Alum
Chine ☎761034 District plan:**56** Mar–Oct

Lic 13hc (4fb) CTV 10P 🄌 S% B&b£6.50–
£7.50 Bdi£8–£11 D6.30pm

**GH Alumcliff Hotel** 121 Alumhurst Rd,
Westbourne ☎764777 District plan:**57** mid
Mar–Oct Lic 17hc 2⇨ 9🄌 (4fb) ⊁ nc7 CTV
14P 🄌 sea S% B&b£10 Bdi£14.80 W£85–£105
⬇ D6pm (W only Jul & Aug)

**GH** *Alum Court Hotel* 10 Studland Rd
☎761069 District plan:**58** Lic 12hc 1⇨ CTV
9P 1🅰 🄌 sea D10pm

**GH Alum Grange Hotel** 1 Burnaby Rd,
Alum Chine ☎761195 District plan:**59** Feb–
Oct & Xmas Lic 14hc 2⇨ 4🄌 (5fb) nc3 CTV
9P 🄌 S% B&b£10.25–£12 Bdi£13.90–£16.50
W£88.55–£108.79 ⬇ D6pm

**GH Anfield Private Hotel** 12 Bradburne Rd
☎20749 Central plan:**2** Mar–Oct & Xmas Lic
16hc (3fb) ⊁ nc5 CTV 12P S% B&b£8–£9.15
Bdi£10.25–£12.65 W£63.25–£86.25 ⬇
D4pm

**GH Arundale Hotel** 38 Christchurch Rd
☎28088 Central plan:**3** Lic 43hc 1⇨ (17fb)
CTV 20P 🄌 S% ✱B&bfr£10 Bdi fr£14.35
(W only during Summer)

⊬ **GH Balmer Lodge Hotel** 23 Irving Rd,
Southbourne ☎424879 District plan:**61** 8hc
(6fb) CTV 7P S% B&bfr£5.50 Bdi fr£8 Wfr£53 ⬇
D5pm

**GH Bay Tree Hotel** 17 Burnaby Rd, Alum
Chine ☎763807 District plan:**62** Lic 12hc
(2fb) nc3 CTV 6P sea S% B&b£6–£9 Bdi£8–
£11.50 W£56–£75 ⬇ D6pm (W only Jul & early
Aug)

**GH Blinkbonnie Heights Hotel** 26 Clifton
Rd, Southbourne ☎426512 District plan:**64**
12hc 1⇨ (3fb) 🄬 CTV 12P 🄌 ⅚ S% B&b£7–
£9 Bdi£9–£11 W£54–£66 ⬇ D6pm

**GH Bracken Lodge Private Hotel**
5 Bracken Rd, Southbourne ☎428777
District plan:**66** Etr–9 Oct Lic 12hc (2fb) ✸
nc2 CTV 14P 🅿 B&b£6.90–£11.50 Bdi£13.80–
£15 W£55.50–£80 ⅃ D6.15pm

**GH Braemar Private Hotel** 30 Glen Rd,
Boscombe ☎36054 District plan:**4** Etr–Oct
& Xmas Lic 11hc 1⇔ (4fb) ✸ CTV 8P 🅿 S%
B&b£6.90–£7.50 Bdi£8–£11 W£63–£72 ⅃ (W
only Jul & Aug)

**GH Hotel Bristol** Terrace Rd ☎27007
Central plan:**4A** Etr–mid Oct & Xmas Lic
27hc 4⇔ (6fb) nc5 CTV 23P 🅿 lift S%
✳B&b£8.05–£10.35 Bdi£9.20–£14.95
W£63.25–£95.45 ⅃

**GH Britannia Hotel** 40 Christchurch Rd
☎26700 Central plan:**5** Closed Xmas
28hc ✸ nc3 CTV 30P 🅿 D6pm

**GH Brun-Lea Hotel** 94 Southbourne Rd
☎425956 District plan:**68** Lic 16hc 4🔥 (3fb)
✸ nc7 CTV 11P S% B&b£6.90–£10.35
Bdi£11.50–£14.95 W£57.50–£86.25 ⅃ D7pm

**GH Bursledon Hotel** Gervis Rd ☎24622
Central plan:**6** 23hc 1⇔ 7🔥 (4fb) nc3 CTV
14P 5⌆ 🅿 S% ✳B&b£9.20–£11.50
Bdi£12.65–£17.25 W£73.60–£105.80 D6.30pm

**GH Carisbrooke Hotel** 42 Tregonwell Rd
☎20432 Central plan:**7** Apr–Oct Lic 25hc
(3fb) nc4 CTV 19P S% B&b£10–£15.50
Bdi£13–£18.50 W£68–£99 D4.30pm

**⋈ GH Carysfort Lodge Private Hotel** 19
Carysfort Rd, Boscombe ☎36751 Central
plan:**8** Lic 11hc (4fb) ✸ CTV 10P S% B&b£5–
£7 Bdi£7–£10 W£45–£69 ⅃ Dnoon

**GH Hotel Cavendish** 20 Chine Cres, West
Cliff ☎20489 Central plan:**9** Etr–Nov 19hc

(5fb) ✸ CTV 14P S% B&b£6.90–£9.20
Bdi£8.62–£11.50 W£55.20–£85.10
⅃ D5pm

**GH Charles Taylor Hotel** 40/44 Frances Rd,
Knyveton Gdns ☎22695 Central plan:**10**
Mar–Nov Lic 28hc 11⇔ (9fb) ✸ nc3 CTV 12P
🅿 sea ✳B&b£6.50–£10 Bdi£9.75–£13.80
W£63.82–£91.80 ⅃ D6.30pm

**GH Chilterns Hotel** 44 Westby Rd ☎36539
Central plan:**11** Apr–Oct Lic 19hc (8fb) CTV
17P 2⌆ S% B&b£6.50–£10.25 Bdi£9.75–
£13.75 W£63.25–£86.25 ⅃ D5pm

**GH Chine Cote Private Hotel** 25 Studland
Rd, Alum Chine ☎764108 District plan:**69**
Etr–Oct 9hc (7fb)✸ CTV 4P D6pm

**GH Chineside Private Hotel** 15 Studland
Rd, Alum Chine ☎761206 District plan:**70**
Apr–Oct 13hc 3🔥 (4fb) ✸ nc4 CTV 13P 🅿 S%
B&b£6.90–£8 Bdi£10.50–£13.25 W£69–£86 ⅃
D5.30pm (W only 17 Jul–14 Aug)

**⋈ GH Cintra Hotel** 10–12 Florence Rd,
Boscombe ☎36103 Central plan:**12** Apr–
Oct Lic 39hc 3⇔ 5🔥 (10fb) 🅲🅷 CTV 12P
B&b£5.70–£9.20 Bdi£6.90–£11 W£55–£80.50
Dnoon

**GH Cliffside Hotel** 7 Durley Gdns, West Cliff
☎27833 Central plan:**13** Lic 21hc (9fb) ✸ nc3
CTV D9.30am

**GH Clock House Hotel** 13 Boscombe Spa
Rd ☎36988 Central plan:**14** Lic 19hc (3fb)
CTV 12P sea S% B&bfr£6.50 Bdifr£8 Wfr£45 ⅃
D6pm (W only Jun–Aug)

**GH Collingdale Lodge** 145 Richmond Park
Rd ☎514540 District plan:**71** Lic 20hc 3🔥
(4fb) ✸ nc8 CTV 18P B&bfr£10.12 Bdi£13.92–
£16.45 W£61.99–£95.51 ⅃ D4pm

**GH Crescent Grange Hotel** 6–8 Crescent Grange Rd, The Triangle ☎26959 Central plan:**15** Closed Nov rsDec–Feb Lic 23hc 1⇨ (4fb) ✻ nc3 CTV 20P ▥ S% B&b£8.05–£10.35 Bdi£11.50–£13.80 W£69–£98.90 D5.30pm

⊩⊣ **GH Crossroads Hotel** 88 Belle Vue Rd, Southbourne ☎426307 District plan:**72** 10hc (4fb) ✻ nc5 CTV 10P S% B&b£5.17–£8.05 Bdi£8.05–£12.08 W£40–£66 ⱪ D4.30pm

**Dean Court Hotel** 4 Frances Rd ☎28165 Central plan:**16** Closed Nov Lic 11hc (4fb) nc3 CTV 5P ▥ S% B&b£6–£9 Bdi£8.50–£11.50 W£48–£68 ⱪ Dnoon

**GH Derwent House** 36 Hamilton Rd, Boscombe ☎39102 Central plan:**17** Lic 11rm 10hc (4fb) ✻ CTV 12P ▥ S% B&b£6.35–£7.45 Bdi£10.95–£12.05 W£57–£70 ⱪ

**GH *Dorchester Hotel*** 64 Lansdowne Rd

North ☎21271 District plan:**74** Lic 15⇨ (11fb) ⸰Ch⸰ CTV 15P ▥ & D5.30pm
**See advert on page 57**

**GH Dorset Westbury Hotel** 62 Lansdowne Rd ☎21811 District plan:**75** Lic 21hc 3⇨ (3fb) nc6 CTV 20P ▥ S% B&b£7.87–£11.96 Bdi£11.90–£15.98 W£76.93–£104.36 ⱪ D6.30pm

**GH Earlham Lodge** 91 Alumhurst Rd, Alum Chine ☎761943 District plan:**76** Feb–Dec Lic 14hc 6ⅰ (4fb) ✻ CTV 9P ▥ B&b £8.05–£10.35 Bdi£10.93–£13.80 W£74.75–£92 ⱪ D6pm

**GH East Cliff Cottage Private Hotel** 57 Grove Rd ☎22788 Central plan:**18** Apr–Oct 10hc 4⇨ (1fb) nc5 CTV 9P S% B&b£8.62–£12.37 Bdi£13.20–£16.77 W£80.75–£100.62 ⱪ D3.30pm

56 Alum Bay Hotel
57 Alumcliff Hotel
58 Alum Court Hotel
59 Alum Grange
60 Avalon Private Hotel (*see under Poole*)
61 Balmer Lodge
62 Bay Tree Hotel
63 Belvedere Hotel (*see under Christchurch*)
64 Blinkbonnie Heights
65 Blue Shutters (*see under Poole*)
66 Bracken Lodge
67 Broomway Hotel (*see under Christchurch*)
68 Brun-Lea
69 Chine Cote
70 Chineside Private Hotel
71 Collingdale Lodge
72 Crossroads
73 Dene Hotel (*see under Poole*)
74 Dorchester Hotel
75 Dorset Westbury
76 Earlham Lodge
77 Ferndale (*see under Christchurch*)
78 Gordons
79 Grassmere
80 Heathcote Hotel
81 Holmcroft Hotel
82 Holme Lacy Hotel
83 Hurley Lodge
84 Kingsley Hotel
85 Laurels (*see under Christchurch*)
86 Lewina (*see under Poole*)
87 Lynrene Private Hotel
88 Mariner's
89 Moorings
90 Mount Lodge
91 Myrtlehouse
92 Naseby-Nye
93 Newfield
94 Northover
95 Oak Hall
96 Ormonde House (*see under Poole*)
97 Park House (*see under Christchurch*)
98 Perran Court
99 Pines (*see under Christchurch*)
100 Redcroft Private Hotel (*see under Poole*)

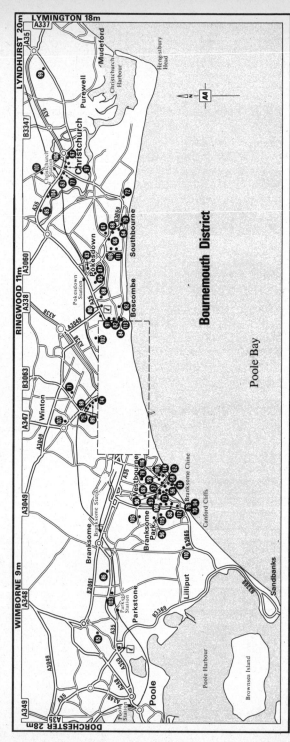

**101–116** see top of next page

**101** St Albans Hotel (*see under Christchurch*)
**102** St Wilfred's
**103** Sandbourne (*see under Poole*)
**104** Sea Witch Hotel (*see under Christchurch*)
**105** Sheldon Lodge (*see under Poole*)
**106** Shortwood House (*see under Christchurch*)
**107** Silver Trees Hotel
**108** Hotel Sorrento
**109** Stratford Hotel
**110** Teesdale Hotel (*see under Poole*)
**111** Tree Tops Hotel
**112** Twin Cedars Hotel (*see under Poole*)
**113** Valberg
**114** West Dene
**115** Westminster Cottage Hotel (*see under Poole*)
**116** Woodford Court


**GH Eglan Court Hotel** 7 Knyveton Rd ☎20093 Central plan: **19** Etr–Oct Lic 14hc 2⋔ (2fb) ✱nc5 CTV 10P ▥ S% B&b£6–£7 Bdi£8.50–£9 W£52–£65 ⱡ D5.30pm

**GH Fallowfield Hotel** 25 Florence Rd, Boscombe ☎37094 Central plan: **20** Jan–Oct & Xmas Lic 15hc (8fb) CTV 12P S% B&b£8–£10.75 Bdi£10.50–£13.25 W£65.25–£79.35 ⱡ D6pm (W only Jul & Aug)

**GH Farlow Private Hotel** 13 Walpole Rd, Boscombe ☎35865 Central plan: **21** Closed 1wk Spring & 2wks Oct 12hc (2fb) ✱nc4 CTV 14P S% B&b£6.33–£7.48 Bdi£9.78–£10.93 W£57.50–£69 ⱡ D4pm (W only Jul & Aug)

**GH Freshfields Hotel** 55 Christchurch Rd ☎34023 Central plan: **22** Lic 12hc (4fb) ✱nc5 CTV 9P ▥ S% B&b£6.90–£9.20 Bdi£10.35–£12.65 W£68.43–£84.53 ⱡ D1pm

**GH Gervis Court Hotel** 38 Gervis Rd ☎26871 Central plan: **23** Etr–Oct Lic 18hc (2fb) Ⓒⓗ CTV 20P 1⌂ S% B&b£8.50–£10.20 Bdi£12.57–£13.72 W£73.02–£90.31 ⱡ D7pm

**GH Gordons Hotel** 84 West Cliff Rd ☎765844 District plan: **78** Mar–Oct rsJan–Mar Lic 17hc 4⋔ (3fb) CTV 16P ▥ B&b£8.63–£9.78 Bdi£13.23–£14.38 W£80.50–£92 ⱡ

**GH Grassmere** 5 Pine Av, Southbourne ☎428660 District plan: **79** Etr–Oct 10hc (3fb) ✱nc3 CTV 8P S% B&b£6.50–£7.50 Bdi£8.50–£9.50 W£55–£65 ⱡ D5pm

⊢⊣ **GH Hamilton Hall Private Hotel** 1 Carysfort Rd, Boscombe ☎35758 Central plan: **24** Lic 10hc 1⇌ 2⋔ (3fb) nc5 CTV 9P ▥ S% B&b£5.75–£8.05 Bdi£9.75–£11.50 W£68.25–£80.50 ⱡ Dnoon

**GH Hawaiian Hotel** 4 Glen Rd, Boscombe ☎33234 Central plan: **25** Apr–Oct 12hc 5⇌ 1⋔ (3fb) ✱nc4 CTV 9P ▥ S% B&b£7.48–£9.20 Bdi£9.20–£11.20 W£64.40–£78.20 ⱡ

**GH Heathcote Hotel** 2 Heathcote Rd, Boscombe ☎36185 District plan: **80** Lic 16hc 2⇌ 2⋔ (7fb) ✱CTV 16P S% B&b£6–£10 Bdi£9.50–£13.50 W£57.50–£82.80 D6.15pm

**GH Heather Mount Hotel** 70 Lansdowne Rd ☎24557 Central plan: **26** Lic 20hc 4⇌ 2⋔ (5fb) ✱nc7 CTV 16P S% B&b£6.90–£9.20 Bdi£10.35–£12.65 W63.80–£80.50 ⱡ D3pm

**GH Highlin Private Hotel** 14 Knole Rd ☎33758 Central plan: **27** Closed Nov Lic 12hc (9fb) ✱nc9 CTV 7P S% B&b£7–£7.50 Bdi£10.50–£11 W£60–£75 ⱡ

**GH Hollyhurst Hotel** West Hill Rd, West Cliff ☎27137 Central plan:**28** Mar–Nov & Xmas Lic 24hc 5⇆ 🛏 (10fb) CTV 21P sea D6.15pm

**GH Holmcroft Hotel** 5 Earle Rd, Alum Chine ☎761289 District plan:**81** Apr–Oct Lic 22hc 5🛏 (7fb) nc3 CTV 17P S% B&b£7–£10 Bdi£10.50–£13.50 W£64–£80 ⌽ D6.30pm

**GH Holme Lacy Hotel** Florence Rd ☎36933 District plan:**82** Etr–Oct 30hc 5⇆ (8fb) CTV 16P S% B&b£7.50–£8.50 Bdi£9.95–£11.25 W£63–£75 ⌽ D6pm

⊨⊣ **GH Hurley Lodge** 20 Castlemain Av, Southbourne ☎427046 District plan:**83** Etr–Oct 6hc (3fb) ✸ nc6 CTV 5P ⊪ S% B&b£6–£7 Bdi£8.50–£9.50 W£48–£58 ⌽ D4pm (W only mid Jul–Aug)

**GH Kensington Hotel** 18 Chine Cres, Westcliff ☎27434 Central plan:**29** Apr–Nov Lic 27hc 9🛏 (8fb) ⒸⒽ CTV 23P ⊪ S% B&b£8–£9.75 Bdi£11.25–£14.65 W£50–£87.40 ⌽ D7.30pm

**GH Kings Barton Hotel** 22 Hawkwood Rd, Boscombe ☎37794 Central plan:**30** Lic 15hc 1⇆ 1🛏 (5fb) ✸ CTV 16P ⊪ S% B&b£9–£11 Bdi£11–£12.50 W£60–£69 ⌽ D4pm

**GH Kingsley Hotel** 20 Glen Rd, Boscombe ☎38683 District plan:**84** Lic 12hc (4fb) ✸ CTV 6P S% B&b£7.65–£8.85 Bdi£9.25–£11.10 W£64.70–£74.12 ⌽ D4.30pm

**GH Linwood House Hotel** 11 Wilfred Rd ☎37818 Central plan:**31** Mar–Oct Lic 10hc (5fb) nc5 CTV 6P ⊪ S% B&b£6.50–£9 Bdi£8–£10.50 W£52–£75 D5pm

**GH Loddington Grange Hotel** 13 Knowle Rd ☎36117 Central plan:**32** 10hc (5fb) ✸ CTV 6P S% B&bf6.90–£9.20 Bdif10.50–£13.50 Wf63.25–£80.50 ⌶ D6pm

⊢⊣ **GH Lynrene Private Hotel** 31 Parkwood Rd, Boscombe ☎424743 District plan:**87** Lic 14hc (4fb) ✸ CTV 12P S% B&bf5.75–£9.25 Bdif7.25–£13 Wf46–£86.60 ⌶

**GH *Mae-Mar Private Hotel*** 91–93 Westhill Rd, West Cliff ☎23167 Central plan:**33** Lic 28hc (7fb) CTV ▥ lift D10am

**GH Mariner's Hotel** 22 Clifton Rd, Southbourne ☎420851 District plan:**88** Feb–Oct 15hc (2fb) Ch CTV 20P ▥ sea S% B&bf6.50–£7.50 Bdif8.50–£9.50 Wf57–£64.50 ⌶ D6.30pm

**GH Mon Bijou Hotel** 47 Manor Rd, East Cliff ☎21389 Central plan:**34** 11hc 2🛏 CTV 8P ▥ S% ✳B&bf8.50–£9.50 Bdif9–£12 Wf55–£70 D6pm

**GH Monreith Hotel** Exeter Park Rd ☎20344 Central plan:**35** Mar–Nov rsXmas Lic 28hc (3fb) ✸nc4 CTV 23P sea S% ✳B&bf8.05–£10.35 Bdif11.50–£13.80 Wf75.90–£92 D6pm

**GH Moorings Hotel** 66 Lansdowne Road North ☎22705 District plan:**89** Lic 18hc (2fb) nc5 CTV 18P ▥ S% ✳B&bf7–£8 Bdif10–£12.50 Wf60.50–£75 ⌶ D7pm

**GH Mount Lodge Hotel** 19 Beaulieu Rd, Westbourne ☎761173 District plan:**90** Closed Nov Lic 11hc 1🛏 (2fb) Ch CTV 6P ▥ S% B&bf8.05–£8.63 Bdif12.65–£14.38 Wf82.80–£86.25 D7pm

**GH Mount Stuart Hotel** 31 Tregonwell Rd ☎24639 Central plan:**36** Mar–Nov Lic 17hc

1🛏 5🛏 (2fb) ✸ CTV 14P ▥ S% B&bf8.50–£11 Bdif11.50–£14 Wf75–£97 ⌶

**GH Myrtlehouse Hotel** 41 Hawkwood Rd, Boscombe ☎36579 District plan:**91** 10hc (5fb) Ch CTV 7P ▥ S% B&bf6.32–£8.63 Bdif8.05–£12.07 Wf52.33–£80.50 ⌶ D5pm

**GH *Naseby-Nye Hotel*** Byron Rd, Boscombe ☎34079 District plan:**92** Lic 13hc 3🛏 nc4 CTV 10P ▥ sea D6.30pm

**GH Newfield Private Hotel** 29 Burnaby Rd, Alum Chine ☎762724 District plan:**93** Lic 12hc 3🛏 (2fb) ✸ CTV 6P S% ✳B&bf6.50–£8 Bdif9.50–£12 Wf65–£77 ⌶ D6pm

**GH Northover Private Hotel** 10 Earle Rd, Alum Chine ☎767349 District plan:**94** Apr–Oct 11hc 2🛏 (3fb) nc3 CTV 10P S% B&bf7.20–£10 Bdif10–£13 Wf68–£90 ⌶ D5pm

**GH Oak Hall Private Hotel** 9 Wilfred Rd, Boscombe ☎35062 District plan:**95** Mar–Oct Lic 12hc (2fb) nc5 CTV 8P ▥ S% B&bf6.75–£7.38 Bdif9.20–£10.90 Wf63.75–£80.50 ⌶ D7pm

**GH Penmone Hotel** 17 Carysfort Rd, Boscombe ☎35903 Central plan:**37** Lic 9hc CTV 10P ▥ D6pm

**GH Perran Court Hotel** 58 Lansdowne Rd ☎27881 District plan:**98** Apr–Oct rsJan–Mar Lic 14hc 3🛏 (5fb) nc7 CTV 14P ▥ S% B&bf8.05–£10.50 Bdif11.50–£13 Wf65–£85 ⌶ D6.30pm (W only Jul & Aug)

**GH Pine Beach Hotel** 31 Boscombe Spa Rd ☎35902 Central plan:**38** Etr–Oct Lic 21hc (3fb) ✸nc7 CTV 17P sea D6pm B&bf9–£11 Bdif12.50–£16.50 Wf82–£92 ⌶ D6.30

**GH St Johns Lodge Hotel** 10 St Swithuns Rd ☎20677 Central plan:**40** Closed Xmas

Lic 18hc (3fb) CTV 14P S% B&b£6.90–£9.77 Bdi£9.20–£13.80 W£64.40–£89.70 ⅃ D6pm

**GH St Ronans Hotel** 64–66 Frances Rd ☎23535 Central plan:**41** Etr–Nov & Xmas rsJan–Apr Lic 13hc (7fb) CTV 8P ⊞ S% ✱ B&b£6.32–£9.20 Bdi£8.20–£11.50 W£51.75–£78.70 Dnoon (W only Jul & Aug)

**GH St Wilfreds Private Hotel** 15 Walpole Rd, Boscombe ☎36189 District plan:**102** 8hc (4fb) ✟ CTV 2P 1🐾 S% B&b£6–£6.50 Bdi£7.50–£8 W£50–£56 ⅃ D6pm

**GH** *Sandelheath Hotel* 1 Knyveton Rd, East Cliff ☎25428 Central plan:**42** Lic 15hc (4fb) ✟ nc4 CTV 12P ⊞ D7pm

**GH Sea Shells** 201–205 Holdenhurst Rd ☎292542 Central plan:**43** Closed Xmas 12hc (A 8hc) (11fb) CTV 30P 1🐾 S% B&b£7–£9.20 W£44.25–£60.75 Ⓜ

⋈ **GH Seastrole Private Hotel** 12 Campbell Rd, Boscombe ☎36996 Central plan:**44** Lic 9hc (5fb) CTV 8P S% B&b£5.75–£10.35 Bdi£7.50–£11.50 W£52–£69 ⅃ D1pm

**GH Sea View Court Hotel** 14 Boscombe Spa Rd ☎37197 Central plan:**45** Mar–Nov Lic 15hc 1➾ 1🔥 (4fb) nc3 CTV 20P ⊞ sea S% B&b£8.05–£10.35 Bdi£11.50–£1? W£57.50–£80.50 ⅃ D12.30pm

**GH Silver Trees Hotel** 57 Wimborne Rd ☎26040 District plan:**107** 10hc 2🔥 (1fb) ✟ nc5 CTV 12P S% ✱ B&b£7–£11.25 Bdi£11–£15.25 W£68–£94 ⅃ D6pm

**GH Hotel Sorrento** 16 Owls Rd, **Boscombe** ☎34019 Central plan:**46** Mar–Oct 19hc 8🔥 (4fb) nc3 CTV 20P 1🐾 B&b£6.90–£8.63 Bdi£10.63–£13.05 W£49–£79.50 ⅃ D6pm

**GH Hotel Sorrento** 8 Studland Rd, **Alum Chine**, Westbourne ☎762116 District plan:**108** Lic 19hc 4➾ 3🔥 (4fb) nc5 CTV 12P ⊞ sea S% B&bfr£9.25 Bdifr£13.25 W£89–£109 ⅃ D5.30pm

**GH Southlea Hotel** Durley Rd, West Cliff ☎26075 Central plan:**47** May–Oct Tem 20hc (6fb) nc3 CTV 15P ✱ B&b£7.50–£9.20 Bdi£9–£12.30 W£63.25–£86.25 ⅃ D6pm

**GH Stratford Hotel** 20 Grand Av, Southbourne ☎424726 District plan:**109** Lic 14hc (6fb) CTV 10P ⊞ S% ✱ B&b£7–£8 Bdi£9–£10 W£60–£65 ⅃ D5pm

**GH Tower House Hotel** West Cliff Gdns ☎20742 Central plan:**48** Lic 34hc 11➾ 1🔥 (17fb) nc5 CTV 20P sea S% B&b£8.50–£11.50 Bdi£10.50–£16 W£65–£105 ⅃ D7pm

**GH Tree Tops Hotel** 16 Grand Av, Southbourne ☎426933 District plan:**111** Etr–Oct Lic 14hc (4fb) CTV 12P S% B&bfr£6.90 Bdifr£9.20 W£64.40–£82.80 ⅃ D5pm (W only mid Jul–Aug)

**GH Tudor Grange Hotel** 31 Gervis Rd ☎291472 Central plan:**49** Mar–15 Nov Lic 12hc 1➾ (3fb) CTV 8P ⊞ B&b£7.50–£13.50 Bdi£11–£17 W£70–£110 ⅃ D7pm

⋈ **GH Valberg Hotel** 1A Wollstonecraft Rd, Boscombe ☎34644 District plan:**113** Closed Xmas day 10hc 7🔥 (3fb) ✟ nc5 CTV 8P ⊞ S% B&b£5–£8 W£32–£49 Ⓜ (W only mid Jun–mid Sep)

**GH Wellington Hotel** 10 Poole Rd ☎768407 Central plan:**50** Lic 28hc 1➾ 3🔥 (8fb) CTV 35P lift B&b£8.05–£9.75 Bdi£12.50–£15 W£69.60–£92 ⅃ D9.30pm

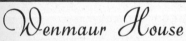

**GH Wenmaur House Hotel** 14 Carysfort Rd, Boscombe ☎35081 Central plan:**51** Lic 12hc (4fb) ✝ CTV 10P ⅢⅢ S% B&b£6.90–£8.05 Bdi£10.35–£11.50 W£57.50–£72.45 ↳ (W only Jul & Aug)

**GH West Bay Hotel** West Cliff Gdns ☎22261 Central plan:**52** Mid May–early Oct 13hc (4fb) CTV 6P B&b£7.48–£9.78 Bdi£10.35–£12.65 W£57.50–£80.50 ↳ D6pm (W only mid Jun–mid Sep)

**GH West Dene Private Hotel** 117 Alumhurst Rd, Westbourne ☎764843 District plan:**114** Etr–Oct Lic 17hc 5⇆ 2🛁 (4fb) ✝ CTV 20P sea B&b£10–£11.50 Bdi£13–£14.50 W£81–£88 ↳ D5.45pm

**GH Whitley Court Hotel** West Cliff Gdns ☎21302 Central plan:**53** Dec–Oct Lic 15hc (6fb) nc3 CTV 10P sea S% B&b£6–£9 Bdi£9–£12 W£50–£80 ↳

**GH Windsor Court Hotel** 34 Bodorgan Rd ☎24637 Central plan:**54** Lic 37hc 16⇆ 🛁 (10fb) [Ch] CTV 22P ⅢⅢ D7.30pm

**GH Woodford Court Hotel** 19–21 Studland Rd, Alum Chine ☎764907 District plan:**116** Etr–Nov 23hc 2⇆ 9🛁 (7fb) nc2 CTV 14P ⅢⅢ sea S% B&b£7.50–£10 Bdi£10–£12.50 W£60–£84 D6.15pm

**GH Wood Lodge Hotel** 10 Manor Rd, East Cliff ☎20891 Central plan:**55** Apr–Oct Lic 16hc 2⇆ 6🛁 (3fb) CTV 12P ⅢⅢ S% B&b£10.25–£15.25 Bdi£13.75–£18.75 W£82.50–£112.50 ↳ D7pm

**BOURTON-ON-THE-WATER** Glos *Map 4 SP12*

**INN Mousetrap Inn** ☎20579 3hc ⇘ nc14 TV in all bedrooms 16P ⅢⅢ S% B&b£8.75–£9.50 Bar lunch £1.20alc D9pm£5alc

**BOWLAND BRIDGE** Cumbria *Map 7 SD48* **INN Hare & Hounds** ☎Crosthwaite 333 4hc (A 4⇆) ⇘ TV available in some bedrooms 80P S% B&b£10.50–£12.50 Bar lunch£2–£2.50 D9pm£6.50&alc

**BOWNESS-ON-WINDERMERE** Cumbria *Map 7 SD49* **Guesthouses are listed under Windermere**

**BRADFORD** W Yorks *Map 7 SE13* **GH Belvedere Hotel** 19 North Park Rd, Manningham ☎492559 Closed 2wks Xmas Lic 13hc (1fb) ✝ nc5 CTV 10P ⅢⅢ S% ✱B&b£11.50 Bdi£14.95 D7pm

**GH Maple Hill** 3 Park Dr, Heaton ☎44061 10hc (2fb) CTV 10P 4🐕 ⅢⅢ S% B&b£6.90

**GH Midway** 218 Keighley Rd, Frizinghall ☎42667 6hc (1fb) CTV S% ✱B&b£6.95

**BRAEMAR** Grampian *Aberdeens Map 15 NO19*

**GH Braemar Lodge** ☎617 May–Sep rsMay Lic 12hc (3fb) TV 12P ⅢⅢ S% B&b£7.50–£8.50 Bdi£13–£14.50 D6.30pm

**GH Callater Lodge** ☎275 26 Dec–mid Oct Lic 9hc (1fb) 42P ⅢⅢ S% B&b£9.54 Bdi£16 D8pm

**BRAUNTON** Devon *Map 2 SS43* **GH Brookdale Hotel** 62 South St ☎812075 Lic 9hc (3fb) ✝ [Ch] CTV 10P 1🐕 ⅢⅢ S% B&b£6–£6.50 Bdi£8.50–£9 W£56–£60 ↳ D4.30pm

**BREAGE** Cornwall *Map 2 SW62* **GH Hillsdale Hotel** Polladras ☎Germoe 3334 Lic 9hc (7fb) [Ch] CTV 9P ⅢⅢ S% B&b£8.05–£9.20 Bdi£11.05–£12.20 W£59.80–£71.30 ↳ D4pm

**BREDE** E Sussex *Map 5 TQ81* **GH Roselands Private Hotel** ☎882338 16 Jan–14 Dec 16hc (2fb) CTV 12P ⅢⅢ ✱B&b£7.75–£8.75 Bdi£11.65–£12.65 D6pm

**BRENT KNOLL** Somerset *Map 3 ST35* **GH Woodlands** Hill Lane ☎760232 rsXmas Lic 10hc 6🛁 (3fb) ✝ [Ch] CTV 20P ⅢⅢ S% B&b£11–£13.50 Bdi£13–£15 W£75–£95 ↳ D6.15pm

**BRIDFORD** Devon *Map 3 SX88* **GH Bridford** ☎Christow 52563 Mar–Nov rsDec–Feb (closed Xmas) 6hc (1fb) ✝ CTV 6P ⅢⅢ D4.30pm

**BRIDGNORTH** Salop *Map 7 SO79* **GH Severn Arms Hotel** Underhill St ☎4616 Lic 10hc CTV

**INN Ball Hotel** East Castle St ☎2478 5hc ⇘ ✝ TV available in some bedrooms 10P 1🐕 ⅢⅢ S% B&b£8.50–£9.50 Bar lunch80p–£3

**BRIDLINGTON** Humberside *Map 8 TA16* **GH Shirley Private Hotel** 47/48 South Marine Dr ☎72539 Etr–Oct Lic 38hc 1⇆ 8🛁 (12fb) CTV 5P lift sea ✱B&b£9.20 Bdi£13.22 W£69–£91.42 D7pm

**GH Southdowne Hotel** South Marine Dr ☎73270 Etr–mid Oct Lic 10hc (3fb) CTV 10P ⅢⅢ S% B&b£8 Bdi£10 W£70–£72 ↳ D6pm

**BRIDPORT** Dorset *Map 3 SY49* **GH Britmead House** 154 West Bay Rd ☎22941 Lic 9hc 3⇆ (3fb) nc3 CTV TV in some bedrooms 15P ⅢⅢ river S% B&b£9–£10 Bdi£13–£14 W£82–£88 ↳ D4.30pm **See advert on page 62**

# Britmead House Hotel

Small family run private hotel with a big reputation for friendliness, cleanliness and excellent home cooking. Very pleasant location, level walks to beach, harbour and shops. Television in all bedrooms, some private bathrooms. Licensed. AA and Members West Country Tourist board. BTA Approved Winter and Spring breaks. Open all year.

Mid-week bookings taken at all times.

Ample Parking

Brochure on request:
**154, West Bay Road,
Bridport, Dorset. DT6 4EG
Tel: Bridport (0308) 22941**

# Roundham House Hotel

**West Bay Road, Bridport, Dorset.
Tel: Bridport 22753 (STD 0308)**

Special commendation recommended by British Tourist Authority.

A fine old, mellowed stone house in lovely surroundings with every comfort and convenience. Standing in its own grounds of three quarters of an acre, overlooking Eype Down, cliffs and sea.

Full choice of interesting and varied menus daily with fresh homegrown vegetables.

Hot, cold and shaving points in all rooms, colour television, library and bar. Restaurant and residential licence.

Guests warmly welcomed with personal attention.

Inclusive terms: dinner, bed & breakfast — £14.50 daily and £97.00 weekly inclusive of Value Added Tax.

Telephone or write for brochure, tariff and sample menus.

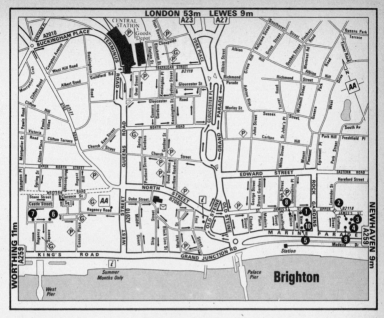

**1** Ascott House
**2** Downlands
Private Hotel
**3** Langham
**4** Marina House
Hotel

**5** Melford Hall
Hotel
**6** Prince Regent
Hotel
**7** Regency Hotel
**8** Trouville

**9** Twenty One
Hotel
**10** Twenty Three

---

**GH Roundham House Hotel** West Bay Rd
☎22753 8 Jan–Nov Lic 8hc (3fb) CTV 6P ⅢⅢ
sea S% B&bf9–£9.50 Bdif14–£14.50 Wf94–
£97 ⅃ D6.30pm

**INN King Charles Tavern** 114 St Andrews
Rd ☎22911 4hc ⚓ 6P 2☎ S% B&bf6–£7 Bdi
£8–£10 Wf40–£47 Ⅲ Bar lunch30p–£3
D9pmf2–£6

**BRIGHTON** E Sussex Map **4** TQ30 **See also
Hove (See Plan)**
**GH Ascott House** 21 New Steine, Marine
Pde ☎688085 Plan:**1** 11hc (5fb) ⚓ nc12 CTV
sea S% B&bf7–£8.50 Wf47–£56 Ⅲ

**GH Downlands Private Hotel** 19 Charlotte
St ☎601203 Plan:**2** Closed Xmas wk 10hc
(3fb) CTV ⅢⅢ S% B&bf6.50–£7 Bdif10–£11
Wf42–£70 ⅃ D10.30am

**GH Langham** 16 Charlotte St ☎682843
Plan:**3** Jan–Nov 8hc ⚓ nc7 TV ✻B&bf6.50
Bdif9.50 Wf60

**GH Marina House Hotel** 8 Charlotte St
☎605349 Plan:**4** Lic 10hc 1fⅢ (3fb) CTV ⅢⅢ
sea S% B&bf8.50–£9 Bdif12.50–£13 Wf85–
£89 D10am

**GH Melford Hall Hotel** 41 Marine Pde
☎681435 Plan:**5** Closed Xmas & New Year
Lic 12hc (5fb) CTV 6P ⅢⅢ sea B&bf10–£14

**GH Prince Regent Hotel** 29 Regency Sq
☎29962 Plan:**6** Lic 18fⅢ ⚓ nc2 CTV in some
bedrooms ⅢⅢ S% B&bf18

**GH Regency Hotel** 28 Regency Sq
☎202690 Plan:**7** Lic 13hc 1⇆ 5fⅢ ⚓ nc8 CTV
ⅢⅢ S% B&bf12–£19 Bdif16.50–£23.50
D4.30pm

**GH Rowland House** 21 St George's Ter,
Kemp Town ☎603639 Not on plan Lic 10hc
(2fb) nc5 CTV 1P ⅢⅢ B&bf8–£8.50 Bdif11.50–
£12 Wf80.50–£84 ⅃ D5pm

**GH Trouville** 11 New Steine, Marine Pde
☎697384 Plan:**8** Lic 9hc (3fb) ⚓ nc4 CTV S%
B&bf8–£12 Bdif12–£16 Wf59–£105 ⅃

**GH The Twenty-One Hotel**21 Charlotte St,
Marine Pde ☎35407 Plan:**9** Lic 6hc (2fb) ⚓
CTV CTV in all bedrooms ⅢⅢ sea S% B&bf10–
£12 Bdif17.95–£19.95 Wf70–£84 Ⅲ D5pm

⊢⋈⊣ **GH Twenty-Three** 23 New Steine
☎684212 Plan:**10** 9hc (5fb) CTV S%
B&bf5.50–£6.50 Bdif8.50 Wf38.50 Ⅲ Dam

**BRISTOL** Avon Map **3** ST57 **(See Plan)**
**GH Alandale Hotel** Tyndall's Park Rd,
Clifton ☎35407 Plan:**1** Closed Xmas Lic
13hc 3⇆ (1fb) TV in all bedrooms 10P ⅢⅢ S%
B&bf7.50–£12.35

**GH Birkdale Hotel** 11 Ashgrove Rd,
Redland ☎33635 Plan:**2** Closed Xmas Lic
18hc 4fⅢ (2fb) TV in all bedrooms 12P ⅢⅢ
B&bf10.92–£16.67 Bdif16.10–£21.85
D7.30pm

**GH Cambridge Hotel** 15 Iddesleigh Rd
☎36020 Not on plan Closed Xmas & New
Years day Lic 11hc (3fb) CTV ⅢⅢ S% B&bf8.62
Bdif12.65 D5pm

**GH Cavendish House Hotel** 18 Cavendish
Rd, Henleaze ☎621017 Plan:**3** 6hc (3fb) CTV
5P ⅢⅢ ✻B&bf6.90 Wf48.30 Ⅲ

**GH Chesterfield Hotel** 3 Westbourne Pl,
Clifton ☎34606 Plan:**4** Closed Xmas 13hc
nc5 CTV ⅢⅢ S% ✻B&bf7.93

63

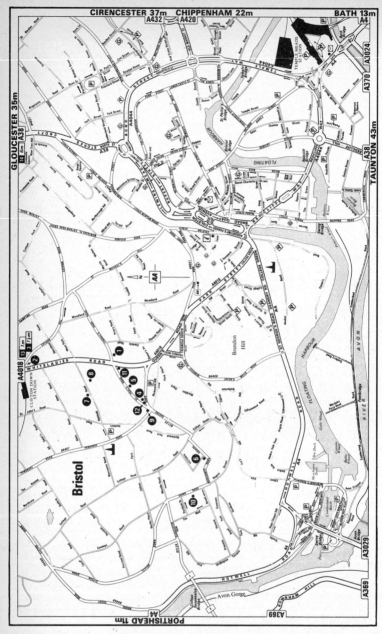

1 Alandale
2 Birkdale
3 Cavendish House Hotel
4 Chesterfield Hotel
5 Hotel Clifton
6 Glenroy Hotel
7 Oakdene Hotel
8 Oakfield Hotel
9 Pembroke Hotel
10 Rodney Hotel
11 Seeley's Hotel
12 Washington Hotel
13 Westbury Park Hotel
14 Willow (see under Patchway)

**GH Hotel Clifton** St Pauls Rd, Clifton
☎36882 Plan:**5** Lic 64hc 3⇔ 29🛏 (5fb) CTV
14P 🅿 lift S% ✳B&£7.82–£10.92 D10pm

**GH Glenroy Hotel** 30 Victoria Sq, Clifton
☎39058 Plan:**6** Closed Xmas Lic 32hc 4⇔ 🛏
(10fb) CTV in all bedrooms 16P 🅿
✳B&bfr£7.76 Wfr£54.32 Ⓜ

**GH Oakdene Hotel** 45 Oakfield Rd ☎35900
Plan:**7** Closed Xmas 8hc (3fb) ✶ nc4 TV in all
bedrooms S% ✳B&bfr£9.66

**GH Oakfield Hotel** 52–54 Oakfield Rd
☎35556 Plan:**8** 23 Dec–28 Dec 27hc (4fb)
CTV 10P 2🚗 🅿 S% B&bf9–£9.50 Bdif£12.50–
£13 D7pm

**GH** *Pembroke Hotel* 13 Arlington Villas
☎35550 Plan:**9** Closed Xmas 15hc (2fb) CTV
🅿

**GH Rodney Hotel** 4 Rodney Pl, Clifton
Down Rd ☎35422 Plan:**10** Closed Xmas &
New Year 30hc (5fb) ⊁CTV 🅿 B&bf£11.50

**GH Seeleys Hotel** 19–27 St Pauls Rd,
Clifton ☎38544 Plan:**11** Closed Xmas Lic
40hc 8⇔ 24🛏 (A 20hc 14🛏) (20fb) ⊁ Ⅽⅹ CTV
in all bedrooms 10P 18🚗 🅿 S% B&bf£7.32–
£8.25 Bdif£11.57–£12.50 D10.30pm

**GH Washington Hotel** 11–15 St Pauls Rd,
Clifton ☎33980 Plan:**12** 32hc (3fb) CTV 13P
🅿 S% ✳B&bf£7.94

**GH Westbury Park Hotel** 37 Westbury Rd,
Westbury-on-Trym ☎620465 Plan:**13** Lic 9hc
(1fb) CTV in all bedrooms 6P 🅿 S% B&bf9–
£11 Bdif£14–£16 Wf£98 ⅃ D8pm

**BRIXHAM** Devon *Map 3 SX95* **(See Plan)**
**GH Beverley Court Private Hotel** Upton
Manor Rd ☎3149 Plan:**1** May–Sep Lic 11hc
(5fb) ⊁CTV 15P 🅿 S% B&bf£8.05–£10.35
Bdif£11.50–£13.80 Wf£69–£82.80 ⅃ D6.30pm

**GH Brioc Private Hotel** 11 Prospect Rd
☎3540 Plan:**2** Lic 10hc (2fb) ⊁CTV 🅿 sea
S% B&bfr£6.50 Bdif£8.60–£9.70 Wf£60–£68 ⅃
D7pm

**GH Cottage Hotel** Mount Pleasant Rd
☎2123 Plan:**3** May–Oct Lic 10hc (2fb) nc3
CTV 6P sea S% B&bf£7–£8 Bdif£9–£10 Wf£55–
£70 ⅃ D6pm

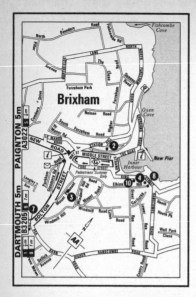

**Brixham**

PAIGNTON 5m A3022 NEW ROAD

DARTMOUTH 5m B3205

| | |
|---|---|
| 1 Beverley Court Private Hotel | 6 Orchard House |
| 2 Brioc Private Hotel | 7 Parkway House Private Hotel |
| 3 Cottage Hotel | 8 Pola |
| 4 Harbour View Hotel | 9 Raddicombe Lodge |
| 5 Holwell | 10 Sampford House |

**GH Harbour View Hotel** King St ☎3052 Plan:**4** Closed Xmas 10hc 1🛗 (3fb) TV sea S% B&b£7.50 W£52.50 🅜

⊁⊣ **GH Holwell** 119 New Rd ☎3496 Plan:**5** 7hc (4fb) CTV 10P S% B&b£5.50–£6.50 Bdi£8–£9 W£48–£54 ⅃ Dam

**GH** *Orchard House* St Marys Rd ☎3590 Plan:**6** Closed Jan & Feb Lic 5hc (2fb) ⊁ CTV 12P Dnoon

**GH Parkway House Private Hotel** 2 Greenswood Rd ☎2730 Plan:**7** Closed Xmas 7hc (4fb) CTV 6P 1🐾 S% ✷B&b£7 Bdi£9 W£62 ⅃ D5pm

**GH Pola** 63–65 Berry Head Rd ☎2019 Plan:**8** 16 Jan–19 Dec 12hc (6fb) CTV sea S% B&b£6–£6.50 W£42–£45.50 🅜

**GH Raddicombe Lodge** 105 Kingswear Rd

☎2125 Plan:**9** 10hc (3fb) ⊁ nc1 CTV 10P ▥ sea S% B&b£7.90–£8.75 Bdi£11.80–£13.10 W£82.60–£91.70 ⅃ D5.30pm (W only last wk Jul & 1st wk Aug)

**GH Sampford House** 57–59 King St ☎7761 Plan:**10** 6hc ⊁ CTV ✷B&bfr£6.50 Bdifr£9 Wfr£42 ⅃ D6pm (W only Jul & Aug)

**BRIXTON** Devon *Map 2 SX55*
**GH Rosemount** ☎Plymouth 880770 Closed 23 Dec–4 Jan Lic 6hc (2fb) ⊁ CTV 15P ▥ S% ✷B&b£6 Bdi£10.25 W£66.75 ⅃ Dnoon

**BROADFORD** Isle of Skye, Highland *Inverness-shire Map 13 NG62*
**GH** *Hilton* ☎322 Apr–Oct 10rm 9hc TV 10P ▥

**BROAD HAVEN** (Nr Haverfordwest) Dyfed *Map 2 SM81*
**GH Broad Haven Hotel** ☎366 Jan–Sep rsXmas Lic 38hc 26⇌ 4🛗 (12fb) 🄲🄷 CTV 100P sea B&b£7–£9 Bdi£11.50–£14 W£67.50–£98 ⅃ D7pm

**BROADHEMPSTON** Devon *Map 3 SX86*
**GH Downe Manor** ☎Ipplepen 812239 Apr–Sep 9rm 7hc (1fb) ⊁ CTV 6P 2🐾 S% ✷B&b£5 Bdi£7.25 W£50 ⅃ D6.30pm

**BROAD MARSTON** Heref & Worcs *Map 4 SP14*
**GH** *Broad Marston Manor* ☎Stratford-upon-Avon 720252 Mar–Nov 7hc 1⇌ 🛗 (1fb) ⊁ nc12 CTV 30P ▥

**BROADSTAIRS** Kent *Map 5 TR36*
**GH Bay Tree Hotel** 12 Eastern Esp ☎62502 Mar–Oct rsNov–Feb Lic 9hc (3fb) nc3 CTV 9P ▥ sea S% B&b£6.50–£8.50 Bdi£9.50–£11.50 W£60–£75 ⅃ D2pm

**GH Corner Ways** 49/51 West Cliff Rd ☎Thanet 61612 Apr–Sep Lic 12hc (7fb) CTV 15P ▥ S% ✷B&b£8.63–£9.66 Bdi£9.78–£10.93 W£57.50–£65.55 ⅃ D6.30pm

**GH Denmead Hotel** 13 Granville Rd ☎Thanet 62580 Lic 8hc (5fb) TV in all bedrooms 10P ▥ B&b£8.05–£9.65 Bdi£12.50–£13.80 W£68.80–£80.50 ⅃

**GH Dutch House Hotel** 30 North Foreland Rd ☎Thanet 62824 Lic 10hc (4fb) ⊁ CTV 6P ▥ sea S% B&b£10.50–£11.50 Bdi£14.50–£16 W£75–£80 ⅃ D6.30pm

**GH East Horndon Private Hotel** 4 Eastern Esp ☎Thanet 68306 9hc (4fb) 🄲🄷 CTV TV available in some bedrooms 2🐾 ▥ sea B&b£11.50–£12.65 Bdi£16–£17.25 W£100–£110 ⅃ D9.30pm

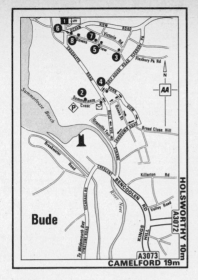

1 Cliff
2 Edgcumbe
3 Kisauni
4 Links View
5 Pencarrol
6 Sandiways
7 Shoreline
8 Surf Haven

**GH Keston Court Private Hotel** 14 Ramsgate Rd ☎Thanet 62401 Lic 9hc (3fb) ⚊ nc1 CTV 6P ⅢⅢ S% B&bf8–£8.50 Bdif11–£11.50 Wf63–£69 ⅃ D8pm

**GH *Kingsmead Hotel*** Eastern Esp ☎Thanet 61694 Lic 14hc (4fb) CTV 12P ⅢⅢ sea D6pm

**GH *Seapoint Private Hotel*** 76 West Cliff Rd ☎Thanet 62269 May–Oct rsMar–May Lic 10hc (4fb) CTV 10P 1☎ ⅢⅢ sea D6pm

**BROADWAY** Heref & Worcs *Map 4 SP03*
**GH Olive Branch** 78–80 High St ☎853440 Closed Xmas 8hc (2fb) ⚊ TV 8P S% B&bf8

**BROCKENHURST** Hants *Map 4 SU30*
**GH Fern Lodge Hotel** Sway Rd ☎Lymington 22092 Lic 8hc 2⋔ (3fb) CTV 12P S% B&bf9–£10 Bdif13.50–£15 Wf91.35–£101.50 ⅃ D8pm

**BROMLEY** Gt London *London plan 4 D6 (page 135)*
**GH Bromley Continental Hotel** 56 Plaistow Ln ☎01-464 2415 Lic 14hc (3fb) ⚊ CTV 14P ⅢⅢ B&bf9.75 Bdif14.50 Dnoon

**GH Bromley Villa St Philomena Hotel** 1–3 Lansdowne Rd ☎01-460 6311 Lic 20hc 4⇌ (5fb) ⚊ CTV 6P ⅢⅢ S% B&bf8.62 Wfrf70 Ⓜ

**BRUTON** Somerset *Map 3 ST63*
**GH Fryerning** Frome Rd, Burrowfield ☎2343 8 Jan–25 Feb & 13 Mar–16 Dec Lic 4hc 3⇌ 1⋔ ⚊ nc8 8P ⅢⅢ B&bf11–£12 Bdif15–£17.50 Wf105–£116 ⅃ D7pm

**BUCKFASTLEIGH** Devon *Map 3 SX76*
**GH Black Rock** Buckfast Rd, Dart Bridge (at Buckfast 1m N) ☎2343 Lic 12hc 1⋔ (4fb) Ⓒⓗ CTV 20P ⅢⅢ river B&bf7.50–£8 Bdif11–£11.50 Wf69–£76 ⅃ D5pm

**GH *Furzeleigh Mill*** ☎2245 Closed Xmas & New Year Lic 16hc TV 20P

**BUDE** Cornwall *Map 2 SS20* **(See Plan)**
**GH *Cliff*** Maer Down, Crooklets ☎3110 Plan:**1** Mar–Oct 12⇌ ⋔ (6fb) CTV 14P sea D8pm

**GH Edgcumbe Hotel** 19 Summerleaze Cres ☎2314 Plan:**2** Feb–Nov & Xmas 15hc 2⋔ (5fb) CTV 11P ✱B&bf6.50–£8.50 Bdif9.50–£11.50 Wf60–£80 ⅃ D6.30pm

**GH Kisauni** 4 Downs View ☎2653 Plan:**3** Apr–Sep 6hc (3fb) CTV 5P S% ✱B&bf5–£6 Bdif7.50–£8.50 Wf47–£50 ⅃ D5pm

**GH Links View** 13 Morwenna Ter ☎2561 Plan:**4** Closed Xmas Lic 7hc (2fb) CTV ⅢⅢ sea S% ✱B&bf5.50–£6 Bdif8–£9 Wf52–£58 ⅃ D5.30pm

⊶ **GH Pencarrol** 21 Downs View ☎2478 Plan:**5** Apr–Oct 7hc (2fb) 1☎ S% B&bf4.50–£6.50 Bdif6–£6.50 Wf42–£56 ⅃ D5pm

**GH Sandiways** 35 Downs View ☎2073 Plan:**6** Mar–Oct Lic 11hc (5fb) ⚊ nc3 CTV 6P S% B&bf6–£6.50 Bdif8.50–£9 D6pm

⊶ **GH Shoreline** 23 Downs View ☎3134 Plan:**7** Mar–Oct Lic 9hc (5fb) ⚊ CTV 5P ⅢⅢ S% B&bf5–£6 Bdif7.50–£9 Wf48–£61 ⅃ D6.30pm (W only late Jul & Aug)

**GH Surf Haven** 31 Downs View ☎2998 Plan:**8** Mar–Oct Lic 10hc (5fb) Ⓒⓗ CTV 7P B&bf6–£7.50 Bdif9–£10.50 Wf56–£64 ⅃ D5.30pm

**BUDLEIGH SALTERTON** Devon *Map 3 SY08*
**GH Park House Hotel** 7 Park Ln, Little Knowle ☎3303 Lic 10hc (6fb) ⚊ Ⓒⓗ CTV 15P S% ✱B&bf9–£11 Bdif13–£15 Wf78–£90 ⅃ D6pm

**GH *Tidwell House Country Hotel*** ☎2444 Closed Xmas 9hc Ⓒⓗ CTV 10P 2☎ D5pm

**GH Willowmead** 12 Little Knowle ☎3115 6hc CTV 7P ⅢⅢ S% B&bf9–£9.50 Bdif12–£13 Wfrf70 D7pm

**BUILTH WELLS** Powys *Map 3 SO05*
**INN Lion Hotel** ☎553670 18hc 5⇌ CTV 14P ⅢⅢ river B&bf8.75–£12 Bdif13.75–£17 Wf95–£120 sn Lf4.50–£6&alc D9pm £4.50–£6.50&alc

**BURFORD** Oxon *Map 4 SP21*
**GH Corner House Hotel** High St ☎3151 Mar–10 Nov Lic 10hc 1⇌ (2fb) CTV ⅢⅢ B&bfr10 Bdi frf14 D7.45pm

**BURLEY** Hants *Map 4 SU20*
**GH Tree House** New Forest ☎3448 Mar–Nov Lic 8hc (3fb) ⚊ nc5 CTV in all bedrooms S% B&bf11 Wf70 Ⓜ

**BURLEY IN WHARFEDALE** W Yorks *Map 7 SE14*
**INN Burley Gates Freehouse** ☎864102 (A 6⇌) ⚊ 100P ⅢⅢ S% ✱B&bf15 Bdif19 Wf105 Bar lunch £1.25–£4.25 D10pmf1.25–£4.25

**BURNSALL** N Yorks *Map 7 SE06*
**GH Manor House** ☎231 Feb–Oct Lic 8hc (2fb) CTV 8P river S% ✱B&bf6.50–£7 Bdif10.75–£11.25 Wf75 ⅃ Dnoon

**BURNTISLAND** Fife *Map 11 NT28*
⊶ **GH Forthaven** 4 South View, Lammerlaws ☎872600 4hc (2fb) TV 4P river S% B&bf5 Wf30 Ⓜ

**BURROW BRIDGE** Somerset *Map 3 ST33*
**GH Old Bakery** ☎234 Lic 6hc 1⇌ CTV 12P 1☎ S% B&bfrf6 Bdi frf11 Wfrf60 ⅃ D10.30pm

**BURTON UPON TRENT** Staffs *Map 8 SK22*
**GH Delter Hotel** 5 Derby Rd ☎35115 Lic
6hc 1🛋 (5fb) ✻ TV in all bedrooms 10P 🏴 S%
B&b£9.50 Bdi£13 W£91 ⅃ D9pm

**BURWASH** E Sussex *Map 5 TQ62*
**INN Admiral Vernon** Etchingham Rd
☎882230 5hc nc10 CTV 30P 1🛋 🏴 S%
B&b£9–£10 Bdi£12–£14 W£55–£60 sn
L£1.75–£3.95&alc D9pm£3.50–£4.50&alc

**INN Bell** High St ☎882304 Closed Xmas 5hc
TV 14P 🏴 ✻ B&b£6.75–£8.25 W£42.50–£53
M sn L£3alc D9pm£5alc

**BURY ST EDMUNDS** Suffolk *Map 5 TL86*
**GH Swan** 11 Northgate St ☎2678 Closed
Xmas 6hc (1fb) ✻ CTV S% B&b£8.50

**BUTE, ISLE OF** Strathclyde *Bute Map 10*
See Rothesay

**BUTTERTON** Staffs *Map 7 SK05*
**INN Black Lion** ☎Onecote 232 3🖙 🛁 ✻ TV
14P 🏴 S% B&b£10–£10.50 Bdi£12.75 sn
L£1–£2.75 D£3–£5

**BUXTON** Derbys *Map 7 SK07*
**⼦⼉GH Fairhaven** 1 Dale Ter ☎4481 Jan–
Nov 6hc (3fb) CTV 🏴 S% B&b£5.50–£6 Bdi
£8–£9 W£53–£60 ⅃ D4pm

**GH Griff** 2 Compton Rd ☎3628 rs14 Dec–
14 Jan 6hc (1fb) CTV 4P 🏴 B&b£6.50–£7
W£42–£45 M

**GH *Hawthorn Farm*** Fairfield Rd ☎3230
Closed Xmas rsOct–Etr 6hc (A 8hc) TV 14P
2🛋 (W only May–Sep) Dnoon

**GH Kingscroft** 10 Green Ln ☎2757 Lic 7hc
(2fb) CTV 9P 2🛋 🏴 S% B&b£7 Bdi£9 W£55 ⅃
D6pm

**GH Old Manse** 6 Clifton Rd, Silverlands
☎5638 Feb–Nov Lic 8hc (3fb) CTV 4P 🏴 S%
B&b£6–£7 Bdi£10–£11 W£63–£70 ⅃ D4pm

**GH Roseleigh Private Hotel** 19 Broadwalk
☎4904 Closed Xmas rsNov–Mar Lic 13hc
(2fb) ✻nc7 CTV 12P lake S% B&bfr£7.45
Bdifr£12 Wfr£80 ⅃ D5.30pm

**GH Templeton** Compton Rd ☎5275 6hc
(1fb) ✻ CTV 6P 🏴 S% ✳B&b£6 Bdi£8 D3pm

**GH Thorn Heyes Private Hotel** 137 London
Rd ☎3539 Apr–Dec Lic 7hc 3🛋 (2fb) nc2
CTV 7P 🏴 S% B&b£10.25–£10.40 Bdi£16.25–
£16.40 W£99.50 ⅃ D7pm

**GH Westminster Hotel** 21 Broadwalk
☎3929 Lic 14hc (1fb) CTV 10P S% B&b£8.25
Bdi£12 Wfr£81 ⅃ D5pm

**CAERNARFON** Gwynedd *Map 6 SH46*
**GH *Bryn-Menai*** Llanbellig Rd ☎2120 Etr–
mid Dec 7hc 🅲🅷 CTV P sea D6.30pm

**⼦⼉GH Caer Menai** 15 Church St ☎2612
6hc (2fb) CTV S% B&b£5.50–£6 W£38.50–
£42 M

**GH Menai View Hotel** North Rd ☎4602
Mar–Oct 6hc (1fb) ✻ TV 🏴 sea B&b£8.05
W£56.35 M D8pm

**INN Black Boy** Northgate St ☎3604 Closed
Xmas 16hc 6🛋 CTV 9P S% B&b£7.50–£9.75
Bdi£13–£15.25 sn L£3–£3.50 D9pm£5.50

**CALLANDER** Central *Perths Map 11 NN60*
**GH Abbotsford Lodge** Stirling Rd ☎30066
Lic 18hc (7fb) CTV 20P 🏴 S% B&b£7.20
Bdi£12.40 W£79.90 ⅃ D7pm

**⼦⼉GH Annfield** 18 North Church St
☎30204 Apr–Oct 8hc (1fb) CTV 9P 🏴 S%
B&b£5.50–£6

---

# 𝔅𝔩𝔞𝔠𝔨 𝔅𝔬𝔶 𝔦𝔫𝔫

**Northgate Street, Caernarfon, Gwynedd.**
**Telephone Reception: 3604**

(Free House). Situated within Caernarfon Castle walls is almost as old as the castle itself.
Oak beams and inglenooks make a delightful setting for a restful holiday. Hot and cold
water in all bedrooms. Plus six with private showers and bathrooms. Private car park at
rear of hotel. Wine, dine and enjoy your stay in the olde worlde atmosphere of this lovely
14th century inn.

**Reservation and SAE for tariff, telephone 3604, attention Mr & Mrs Williams.**

---

# 𝔎𝔦𝔫𝔫𝔢𝔩𝔩 𝔥𝔬𝔲𝔰𝔢

## 24 Main Street, Callander, Perthshire

Kinnel is an attractive Victorian Town House which
backs onto the scenic beauty of the River Teith. It
is convenient for the shops, bus service and other
amenities. The house has a reputation for good food
and comfortable accommodation. Facilities include
a private car park, wash hand basins in all rooms, a
colour TV in the lounge and electric blankets on all
beds. Callander is set in the beautiful Trossachs
area and is the ideal centre for those interested in
sport, scenic beauty and history. Write, or
telephone Callander (0877) 30181, for brochure.

**GH** *Ashlea House Hotel* Bracklinn Rd
☎30325 Mar–Nov 20hc 2⇌ ⋔ (3fb) ⋔ CTV
17P ▥ D7.15pm

⊢⊣ **GH Edina** 111 Main St ☎30004 9hc
(2fb) CTV 7P S% B&b£5.47–£6.21 Bdi£8.92–
£10.17 Wfr£64.50 ⌊ D7.30pm

**GH Highland House Hotel** South Church St
☎30269 Mar–Oct Lic 10hc 4⋔ (1fb) ⋔ CTV
▥ river B&b£7.50–£10 Bdi£14–£16.50 W£94–
£110 ⌊ D7.30pm

**GH Kinnell** 24 Main St ☎30181 Mar–Nov
9hc (2fb) CTV 8P river S% B&b£6.25–£7
Bdi£10.50–£11.50 W£80 ⌊ D7.30pm

**GH** *Lubnaig* Leny Feus ☎30376 Mar–14
Oct Lic 10hc 10⇌ ⋔ (A 2⋔) ⋔ nc7 CTV 14P
▥ (W only mid May–mid Sep) D8pm

⊢⊣ **GH Rock Villa** 1 Bracklinn Rd ☎30331
Etr–mid Oct 7hc (1fb) ⋔ 7P S% B&b£5.50–
£6

**GH Tighnaldon Private Hotel** 156 Main St
☎30703 Etr–Oct, Xmas & New Year Lic 6hc
(1fb) ▥ TV river ✳B&b£5–£5.50 Bdi£9–£10
W£60–£65 ⌊ D6pm

**CALNE** Wilts *Map 3 ST97*
**GH Chilvester Lodge** ☎812950 Mar–Dec
4rm 2⇌ 1⋔ nc10 CTV 3P 1☎ ▥ S% B&b£14–
£17.50 Bdi£19.75–£26 W£138–£157.50 ⌊
D5pm

**INN White Hart Hotel** 2 London Rd
☎812413 10hc 1⇌ ⋔ TV 10P ▥ S%
B&b£8.05 sn L£3–£5

**CALSTOCK** Cornwall *Map 2 SX46*
**INN Boot** Fore St ☎Tavistock 832331 3hc
1⋔ ⋔ CTV 7P ▥ ✳ B&b£7.50–£8.50 Bar lunch
fr50p D9pm£8alc

**CAMBORNE** Cornwall *Map 2 SW64*
**GH Pendarves Lodge** ☎712691 Closed Oct
Lic 8hc (2fb) ⋔ CTV 12P S% B&b£7.50
Bdi£11.50 W£80 ⌊

**GH Regal Hotel** Church Ln ☎713131 Lic
13hc 2⇌ (1fb) ⋔ CTV 13P ▥ ✳ B&b£8 Bdi£12
W£80 ⌊ D9.45pm

**GH St Clair Hotel** Basset Rd ☎713289 Lic
12hc (2fb) ⋔ CTV 40P ▥ S% B&b£12.75
Bdi£14.95 W£100 ⌊ D8.30pm

**CAMPBELTOWN** Strathclyde *Argyll Map 10
NR72*
**GH** *Westbank* Dell Rd ☎2452 Feb–Nov 7hc
CTV

**CAMBRIDGE** Cambs *Map 5 TL45*
**GH All Seasons** 219 Chesterton Rd

☎353386 10hc (3fb) ▣ TV in all bedrooms
4P ▥ & S% B&b£6–£6.50 Bdi£8.50–£9.50
W£56–£60 ⌊ D2pm

**GH Belle Vue** 33 Chesterton Rd ☎51859
8hc (2fb) 6P river S% B&b£6.50–£7.50

**GH Guest House Hotel** 139 Huntingdon Rd
☎352833 Closed Xmas wk 13hc (4fb) ▣
CTV 10P ▥ S% B&b£11 Bdi£13.50
D7.15pm

**GH Helen's Hotel** 167–169 Hills Rd
☎46465 10 Jan–10 Dec Lic 19hc 1⇌ 10⋔
(A 5hc) (3fb) CTV 20P ▥ S% B&b£10–£16
Bdi£15–£21 D7.30pm

**GH Lensfield Hotel** 53 Lensfield Rd
☎355017 Closed 2wks Xmas 30hc 10⋔
(4fb) ⋔ CTV 10P 3☎ ▥ S% B&b£8.50–£17

**GH Suffolk House** 69 Milton Rd ☎352016
7hc 1⇌ (2fb) ⋔ CTV TV in all bedrooms 7P ▥

**CAMELFORD** Cornwall *Map 2 SX18 During
the currency of this guide Camelford
telephone numbers are likely to change*
**GH Sunnyside Hotel** 7 Victoria Rd ☎2250
Closed Nov Lic 9hc (5fb) CTV 16P ▥ S%
B&b£8.50–£9.50 Bdi£14–£15 W£68–£84 ⌊
D6pm

**GH Warmington House** 32 Market Pl
☎3380 Lic 7hc (3fb) ▣ CTV 3P 2☎ ▥ S%
B&b£7.50–£8.50 Bdi£12–£14 W£78–£90 ⌊
D9.30pm

**CANONBIE** Dumfries & Galloway
*Dumfriesshire Map 11 NY37*
**INN** *Riverside* ☎295 (Closed last 2wks Jan)
Lic 7hc ⋔ CTV 25P ⇨ D8.30pm

**CANTERBURY** Kent *Map 5 TR15* **(See Plan)**
**GH Abba Hotel** Station Rd West ☎64771
Plan:**1** Lic 14hc (1fb) ⋔ CTV 6P ▥ S%
✳B&b£8–£10 Bdi£8.50–£14 D10pm

**GH** *Canterbury Hotel* 71 New Dover Rd
☎68750 Plan:**2** rsSun (no evening meal) Lic
8⇌ ⋔ (6fb) CTV 20P ▥ D9.30pm

**GH Carlton** 40 Nunneryfields ☎65900
Plan:**3** Lic 11hc (3fb) TV 3P ▥ S% B&b£6–
£8.50 Bdi£9–£13 W£70–£84 ⌊ D5pm

**GH Ebury Hotel** New Dover Rd ☎68433
Plan:**4** 15 Jan–Dec Lic 15hc 13⇌ 2⋔ (4fb)
▣ CTV in all bedrooms 24P 2☎ ▥ B&b£11–
£16 Bdi£15–£18.50 W£84–£120 ⌊
D8.30pm

**GH Ersham Lodge** 12 New Dover Rd
☎63174 Plan:**5** 15 Jan–Xmas Lic 15hc
1⇌ (A 10hc 1⇌ 4⋔) (7fb) TV in all
bedrooms 17P 2☎ ▥ S% B&b£8.50–£12
Bdi£12.50–£16 D5pm

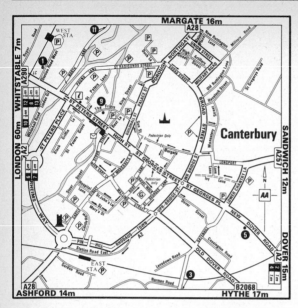

1 Abba Hotel
2 Canterbury Hotel
3 Carlton
4 Ebury Hotel
5 Ersham Lodge
6 Harbledown Court
7 Highfield Hotel
8 Magnolia House
9 Pilgrims
10 Pointers
11 St Stephens
12 Victoria Hotel
13 Wesley Manse

**GH *Harbledown Court*** 17 Summer Hill, Harbledown ☎60659 Plan:**6** 7hc 1⇨ ⋒ CTV 8P ▥

**GH Highfield Hotel** Summer Hill, Harbledown ☎62772 Plan:**7** Closed Xmas Lic 11hc 1⋒ (3fb) nc3 CTV 12P ▥ B&b£8.50–£11

**⋈ GH Magnolia House** 36 St Dunstans Ter ☎65121 Plan:**8** Closed Xmas & New Year 6hc (3fb) ✸ 3P ▥ S% B&bf£5.50–£6.50

**GH Pilgrims Guest House** 18 The Friars ☎64531 Plan:**9** 14hc 2⋒ (2fb) CTV 4P 4☎ ▥ S% B&bf£6–£9

# *The ideal hotel for visiting south east Kent*

★ Charming Victorian hotel

★ 6 miles Canterbury, 9 miles coast

★ 2½ acres including lawns, flower beds and vegetable garden

★ Childrens' play area including sandpit & swing

★ Happy atmosphere and good service

★ Horse riding, fishing, golf & tennis nearby

★ A wealth of historical places to visit just a short car ride away

★ **Farm Holiday Guide diploma winner for accommodation & food 1979 & 1980**

# The Woodpeckers Country Hotel Ltd.

**Womenswold, Nr Canterbury, Kent
Barham 319 (STD 022782)**

★ Heated swimming pool, water slide & diving board

★ Television lounge and quiet lounge

★ 16 comfortable rooms all with H/C water & tea & coffee-making facilities

★ **Four-poster, Georgian, brass bedstead, bridal bedrooms all en' suite**

★ Warm air central heating

★ Highly recommended for traditional country home baking as reported in 'The Daily Express' 'The Guardian', the 'Dover Express' and 'The Telegraph'

★ Packed lunches

★ Licensed

'A Taste of England'

*Personal attention from resident proprietors*

**GH Pointers** 1 London Rd ☎56846 Plan:**10**
Lic 15hc 2⇔ 1⋔ (2fb) CTV in all bedrooms
10P ⠀ ✱B&b£11.50–£15.55 Bdi£17.50–£23
W£110–£130 ⋈ D9.30pm

**GH Red House Hotel** London Rd,
Harbledown (1m W A2) ☎63578 Not on plan
Closed Xmas day Lic 10hc 5⇔ 2⋔ (4fb) CTV
17P ⠀ S% B&b£9.80–£16.10 Bdi£16–£22.70
W£87–£132 ⥾ D8pm

**GH St Stephens** 100 St Stephen's Rd
☎62167 Plan:**11** Lic 9hc (1fb) ✹ TV 8P ⠀ S%
✱B&b£7.48–£8.05 D5pm

**GH Victoria Hotel** 59 London Rd ☎59333
Plan:**12** Lic 27rm 10hc 16⇔ 1⋔ (5fb) CTV
30P ⠀ ✱B&b£8–£9.90 D8.30pm

⊢⊣ **GH Wesley Manse** 71 Whitstable Rd
☎55164 Plan:**13** Lic 8hc (2fb) ⒸⒽ CTV 5P ⠀
S% B&b£5.50–£7.50 Bdi£8.50–£10.50
D5pm

**CAPEL ISAAC** Dyfed *Map 2 SN52*
**GH *Maesteilo Mansion Country House
Hotel*** ☎Dryslwyn 510 Lic 8rm 7hc 6⇔ ⋔ ✹
nc14 CTV 20P 4⩍ ⠀ D7pm

**CARDIFF** S Glam *Map 3 ST17*
**GH *Ambassador*** 4 Oakfield St ☎33288
Closed Xmas Lic 16hc ✹ CTV ⠀ D3pm

**GH Balkan Hotel** 144 Newport Rd
☎491790 13hc 1⇔ 1⋔ (3fb) CTV 15P ⠀ S%
✱B&b£6.90–£8.05 Bdi£11.50–£12.65
W£57.50–£63.25 ⥾ D6pm

**GH Clayton Hotel** 65 Stacey Rd, Roath
☎492345 Closed Xmas & New Year Lic 9hc
(1fb) ✹ CTV 6P ⠀ S% ✱B&bfr£9.20
Bdifr£13.34 Dnoon

**GH Domus** 201 Newport Rd ☎495785 Lic
10hc 2⋔ (2fb) ✹ CTV 10P ⠀ ✱B&b£6.25
Bdi£10 Dnoon

**GH Dorville Hotel** 3 Ryder St ☎30951 13hc
(3fb) ✶ CTV ⬛ S% ✱B&bf8–£8.50 Wf56 M

**GH Ferrier's** (Alva Hotel) 132 Cathedral Rd
☎23413 Closed 2wks Xmas Lic 27hc 1⇆
(3fb) ✶ CTV 12P ⬛ B&bf13.50 Bdif19.50
D1pm

**GH Princes** 10 Princes St, Roath ☎491732
7hc (2fb) ✶ CTV 3P ⬛ S% B&bf7–£8
Bdif10.50–£11.50 Dnoon

**GH St Winnow's Hotel** Tygwyn Rd,
Penylan ☎45577 9hc 1⇆ 🛁 (A 2hc) CTV 11P
⬛ Dnoon

**GH Tane's Hotel** 148 Newport Rd ☎491755
9hc (1fb) ✶ CTV 10P ⬛ S% B&bf6.90–£8.05
Bdif11.50–£12.65 Wf57.50–£63.25 ⅃ D6pm

**CAREY** Heref & Worcs *Map 3 SO53*
**INN Cottage of Content** ☎242 3hc CTV
30P ⬛ B&bf10 sn Lf6alc D9.30pmf7.50alc

**CARLISLE** Cumbria *Map 11 NY35*
**GH Angus Hotel** 14 Scotland Rd ☎23546
Closed Xmas & New Year Lic 8hc (3fb) CTV
⬛ D5pm

**GH Cumbria Park Hotel** 32 Scotland Rd
☎22887 Closed Xmas Lic 19hc 1⇆ 8🛁 (1fb)
✶ CTV 26P ⬛ S% ✱B&bf11 Bdif16 Wf77 M
D6.45pm

**⊬⊣ GH East View** 110 Warwick Rd
☎22112 9hc 1⇆ 1🛁 (4fb) ✶ TV ⬛ S%
B&bf5.50–£7

**GH Kenilworth Hotel** 24 Lazonby Ter
☎26179 6hc (2fb) CTV 5P ⬛ S% ✱B&bf5–£6

**CARNFORTH** Lancs *Map 7 SD47*
**GH Holmere Hall** 76 Milnthorpe Rd, Yealand
Conyers (2m N off A6) ☎5353 Lic 6hc (1fb) ✶

TV available in some bedrooms 12P ⬛ S%
✱B&bf8.25 Wf54.25 M D9pm

**CARNOUSTIE** Tayside *Angus Map 12 NO53*
**GH Dalhousie Hotel** 47 High St ☎52907
Feb–Dec Lic 7rm 5hc (2fb) CTV 6P sea S%
B&bf7 Bdif11 Wf77 ⅃ D8.30pm

**CARRADALE** Strathclyde *Argyll Map 10
NR83*
**GH Ashbank Hotel** ☎650 Etr–Oct Lic 5hc
(2fb) ✶ CTV 7P sea ✱Bdif12 Wfrf72 ⅃
D8.30pm

**GH Drumfearne** ☎232 Apr–Sep 6rm 5hc
(3fb) ✶ TV P D6pm

**GH Duncrannag** ☎224 Apr–Sep Tem 11hc
8P

**GH Dunvalanree** Portrigh ☎226 Etr–Sep
12hc (3fb) ✶ nc2 TV 9P ⬛ sea S% ✱B&bf5–
£6 Bdif7–£7.50 Wf49 ⅃ D3pm

**CARRBRIDGE** Highland *Inverness-shire
Map 14 NH92*
**GH Ard-na-Coille** Station Rd ☎239 4hc (1fb)
TV 7P ⬛ river S% ✱B&bfrf6 Bdifrf10.50
Wfrf70 ⅃ D2pm

**GH Dalrachney Lodge Private Hotel** ☎252
Closed Nov & Dec (except Xmas) 9hc (3fb)
nc5 CTV 10P ⬛ river B&bfrf8 Bdifrf12 D7pm

**GH Old Manse Private Hotel** Duthil (2m E
A938) ☎278 Closed Nov 9hc (2fb) CTV 9P ⬛
B&Bf7.50 Bdif11.50 Wf70 ⅃ D1pm

**CASTLE DONINGTON** Leics *Map 8 SK42*
**GH Delven Hotel** 12 Delven Ln ☎810153
Lic 7hc ✶ nc16 CTV 4P 4⇱ ⬛ S% B&bf16–
£18 Bdif21–£23 Wf126 ⅃ D9.30pm

**CASTLE DOUGLAS** Dumfries & Galloway *Kirkcudbrights Map 11 NX76*
**GH Rose Cottage** Gelston ☎2513 5rm 4hc ★nc3 CTV 14P ▥ S% B&b£6.50–£7 Bdi£8.50–£9.50 W£45.50–£66.50 Ⱡ D5pm

**CATÊL** Guernsey, Channel Islands *Map 16*
**GH *Lilyvale Private Hotel*** Hougue Du Pommier, Route De Carteret ☎Guernsey 56868 May–Oct Lic 13hc 5🛁 🚿 (10fb) ★nc2 CTV 12P D6.30pm

**CATON** Lancs *Map 7 SD56*
**INN Ship Hotel** Lancaster Rd ☎770265 3hc ⊗ ★nc TV 20P 3🚗 ▥ S% B&b£8.50–£9 Bar lunch £2alc D9pm

**CAWOOD** N Yorks *Map 8 SE53*
**GH *Compton Court Hotel*** ☎315 Closed Xmas & New Year Lic 7hc 1🛁 🚿 (A 3hc 1🛁 🚿) (2fb) CTV 12P ▥ D7pm

**CHAGFORD** Devon *Map 3 SX78*
**GH Bly House** Nattadon Hill ☎2404 Jan–Nov 8hc 5🛁 nc12 CTV 10P ▥ S% *B&b£6.50–£9 Bdi£11–£13.50 W£69–£85 Ⱡ D7pm

**GH Glendarah** ☎3270 Closed Nov Lic 8hc (1fb) CTV 9P ▥ S% B&b£8.35–£9.20 Bdi£13.80–£15 W£94–£118 Ⱡ D7.30pm

**CHALE** Isle of Wight *Map 4 SZ47*
**INN Clarendon Hotel & Wight Mouse** ☎Niton 730431 12hc 3🛁 1🚿 CTV 150P ▥ sea B&b£9 Bdi£16.10–£18.40 W£90–£100 Ⱡ L£2–£4&alc sn D10pm£3–£6&alc

**CHALFONT ST PETER** Bucks *Map 4 TQ09*
**INN Greyhound** High St ☎Gerrards Cross 83404 11hc ⊗ ★30P ▥ S% B&b£12.50 Bar lunch40p–£1.20 D10pm£3.45–£6.95

**CHANNEL ISLANDS** *Map 16*
**Information is shown under individual placenames. Refer first to Guernsey or Jersey for details**

**CHAPELHALL** Strathclyde *Lanarks Map 11 NS76*
**GH Laurel House Hotel** 101 Main St ☎Airdrie 63230 Lic 6rm 5hc (1fb) ★CTV 6P ▥ *B&b£8.50 Bdi£11

**CHARD** Somerset *Map 3 ST30*
**GH Watermead** 83 High St ☎2834 Lic 9hc (2fb) [ch] CTV 9P ▥ S% B&b£6 Bdi£9.50 W£62 Ⱡ D6pm

**CHARLTON** W Sussex *Map 4 SU81*
**GH Woodstock House Hotel** ☎Singleton 666 Feb–Nov Lic 12hc 2🛁 2🚿 ★nc9 CTV 10P ▥ B&b£11.50–£15 Bdi£15.50–£21 W£100–£123 Ⱡ D7.30pm

**CHARLWOOD** Surrey *Map 4 TQ74*
**For accommodation details see under Gatwick Airport**

**CHARMOUTH** Dorset *Map 3 SY39*
**GH *Cottage*** High St ☎60407 Closed Xmas 5hc (A 1hc) (4fb) CTV 30P D7.30pm

**GH Newlands House** Stonebarrow Ln ☎60212 Apr–Oct Lic 9rm 7🛁 2🚿 (2fb) ★nc5 CTV TV in all bedrooms 12P ▥ S% B&b£8–£9 Bdi£11.75–£12.75 W£70.25–£79.25 Ⱡ D5pm

**GH White House** 2 Hillside ☎60411 Mar–Oct Lic 9hc 1🛁 (4fb) ★nc4 CTV 15P ▥ *B&b£8–£9.50 Bdi£11.75–£13.25 W£74–£83 Ⱡ D7pm

**CHEDDAR** Somerset *Map 3 ST45*
**GH Gordons Hotel** Cliff St ☎742497 Closed Dec rsOct–Mar Lic 14hc (3fb) [ch] CTV 10P S% B&b£7 Bdi£11 D8pm

**CHELMSFORD** Essex *Map 5 TL70*
**GH Beechcroft Private Hotel** 211 New London Rd ☎352462 Closed Xmas 26hc (2fb) CTV 15P ▥ B&b£11.40

**GH Boswell House Hotel** 118–120 Springfield Rd ☎87587 Closed Xmas–New Year Lic 13hc 9🛁 4🚿 (2fb) CTV 25P ▥ *B&bfr£19.26 Bdifr£24.32 D7pm

**GH Newholme Hotel** 440 Baddow Rd, Gt Baddow ☎76691 Lic 10hc 1🛁 (2fb) CTV 8P ▥ S% B&b£11.50 Bdi£16.50 Wfr£80.50 M D8.30pm

**GH Tanunda Hotel** 219 New London Rd ☎354295 Lic 21hc 2🛁 5🚿 ★nc5 CTV 21P ▥ S% *B&b£10.25 Bdi£15.15 D8pm

**CHELTENHAM** Glos *Map 3 SO92*
**GH Askham Court Hotel** Pittville Circus Rd ☎25547 Lic 17hc 2🛁 CTV TV in 2 bedrooms P ▥ S% B&b£10.35–£11.50 Bdi£16.10 Wfr£107 Ⱡ D6.30pm

**GH Beaumont House** 56 Shurdington Rd ☎45986 Closed Xmas Lic 8hc (2fb) [ch] CTV 12P 1🚗 ▥ S% B&b£10–£12 Bdi£13–£16 W£79 Ⱡ D9.30pm

**GH Bowler Hat Hotel** 130 London Rd ☎23614 Lic 6hc (4fb) ★CTV 6P ▥ S% B&b£8

**GH Brennan** 21 St Lukes Rd ☎25904 5hc (1fb) CTV S% B&b£6

**GH Cotswold Grange Hotel** Pittville Circus Rd ☎515119 Lic 20hc 7⇨ (2fb) CTV 20P ⬛ S% B&bf10.92–£16 Bdif16–£22 D7pm

**GH Hollington House Hotel** 115 Hales Rd ☎519718 Closed Xmas Lic 6hc ⊀ CTV 7P ⬛ B&bf9 Bdif14.50 D6pm

**GH Ivy Dene** 145 Hewlett Rd ☎21726 10hc (3fb) CTV 8P ⬛

**GH North Hall Hotel** Pittville Circus Rd ☎20589 Lic 22hc (3fb) CTV 20P ⬛ B&bf8.62 Bdif11.79 D6.45pm

**GH Wellington Hotel** Wellington Sq ☎21627 Lic 10hc (2fb) CTV 8P ⬛ S% B&bf8.75 Bdif13.75 Wf82 ⅃ D5pm

**GH Willoughby** 1 Suffolk Sq ☎22798 Closed Xmas 11hc (2fb) CTV 10P S% B&bf8.90 Bdif12.07 Wf80.50 ⅃

**CHESTER** Cheshire *Map 7 SJ46*
**GH *Abbotsford Hotel*** 17–19 Victoria Rd ☎26118 Lic 16hc ⊀ TV ⬛

**GH Brookside Private Hotel** 12 Brook Ln ☎381943 Closed Xmas Lic 21hc 4⇨ 3🛏 (6fb) CTV 14P ⬛ S% B&bf8.62–£9.77 D8.30pm

**GH *Buckingham Private Hotel*** 38 Hough Green ☎673374 8hc (3fb) CTV 8P ⬛ D7pm

**GH Cavendish Hotel** 44 Hough Green ☎675100 Lic 11hc 1⇨ (4fb) CTV in all bedrooms 15P ⬛ S% B&bf9.50–£12.50 Bdif14.50–£17.50 Wf95–£112.50 ⅃ D8pm

**GH Chester Court Hotel** 48 Hoole Rd ☎20779 Closed Xmas wk Lic 8hc 1⇨ 2🛏 (3fb) CTV in all bedrooms 15P ⬛ B&bf8.75–£10.25 Bdif13–£15 D7pm

**GH Eversley Private Hotel** 9 Eversley Pk
☎373744 Lic 8hc (4fb) ✝nc3 CTV 12P ▥ S%
B&b£6.25 Bdif£10 W£70 ⌊ D10am

**GH Gables** 5 Vicarage Rd, Hoole ☎23969
7hc (4fb) CTV 7P S% B&b£6–£6.50

**GH Green Bough Hotel** 60 Hoole Rd
☎26241 Closed 2wks Xmas Lic 11hc 2⇔ 4⋔
(2fb) CTV 11P ▥ B&b£8–£10.50 Bdif£12–£15
W£85–£100 ⌊ D6.30pm

**GH Hamilton** 5–7 Hamilton St ☎45387 Lic
10hc (4fb) CTV 2P 4⋒ ▥ S% B&b£7–£8
Bdif£10–£11 D4pm

**GH Malvern** 21 Victoria Rd ☎380865
Closed Xmas & New Year rsJan–Mar & Oct–
Dec 7hc (1fb) ✝nc2 CTV ▥ S% B&b£6–£7
W£40–£45 Ⓜ

**GH Redland Private Hotel** 64 Hough Green
☎671024 Closed Dec 10hc (5fb) ✝CTV 10P
3⋒ S% B&b£7–£9 W£40–£60 Ⓜ

**GH Riverside Private Hotel** 22 City Walls,
off Lower Bridge St ☎26580 16hc 8⇔ (3fb)
CTV 25P ▥ river S% ✱B&b£7.50–£11 Bdif£9–
£12.50 D10pm

**GH Weston Hotel** 82 Hoole Rd ☎26735
Closed Xmas Lic 9hc (A 14⇔ ⋔) ✝nc5 CTV
▥ D9pm

**CHICKLADE** Wilts Map 3 ST93
**GH Old Rectory** ☎Hindon 226 Closed 4–18
May, 3–18 Oct, Xmas 8hc (2fb) CTV 8P 1⋒
S% ✱B&b£7–£8 Bdif£10.40–£11.70
W£57.50–£67.50 ⌊ D2pm

**CHIDEOCK** Dorset Map 3 SY49
**GH Thatch Cottage** ☎473 Feb–mid Dec Lic

3hc ✝nc10 CTV 4P 2⋒ ▥ S% ✱B&b£6–£6.50
Bdif£10–£10.50 W£40–£43 Ⓜ D7.30pm

**CHILLINGTON** Dorset Map 3 SX74
**GH Fairfield** ☎Kingsbridge 580388 Lic 12hc
1⋒ (9fb) Ⓒⓗ CTV 20P ▥ ⓖ B&b£8.05–£9.35
Bdif£12.08–£13.22 W£80.50–£88.55 ⌊ D7pm

**CHIPPING SODBURY** Avon Map 3 ST78
**GH Moda Hotel** 1 High St ☎312135 Closed
Xmas Lic 7hc (1fb) ✝nc5 TV ▥ S%
✱B&b£8.50–£9

**CHITTLEHAMHOLT** Devon Map 3 SS62
**GH Beares Farm** ☎523 Closed Xmas &
New Year Lic 6hc 12P ▥ D9pm

**CHRISTCHURCH** Dorset Map 4 SZ19
For locations and additional guesthouses see
**Bournemouth**

**GH Belvedere Hotel** 59 Barrack Rd
☎485978 Bournemouth district plan:**63** Lic
12hc (3fb) CTV ▥ S% B&b£6–£6.50
Bdif£8.50–£9.50 Wfr£70 ⌊ Dam

**GH Broomway Hotel** 46 Barrack Rd
☎483405 Bournemouth district plan:**67**
Closed Xmas Lic 10hc (3fb) nc2 CTV 12P S%
B&b£8.63–£10.35 Bdif£13.80–£16.10 W£63.25–
£80.50 ⌊

**GH Ferndale** 41 Stour Rd ☎482616
Bournemouth district plan:**77** 6hc (1fb) ✝
CTV 6P ▥ S% ✱B&b£5–£7 Bdif£8–£10
W£52.50–£66.50 ⌊

**GH Laurels** 195 Barrack Rd ☎485530
Bournemouth district plan:**85** Lic 14hc (2fb)
CTV 14P ▥ S% ✱B&b£5.50–£7.50 Bdif£9–£11
D6pm

**GH Park House Hotel** 48 Barrack Rd ☎482124 Bournemouth district plan:**97** Lic 10hc 1⇌ 1🏠 (4fb) Ⓒʰ CTV 12P 1☎ 🛏 S% B&b£9–£10 Bdi£12–£13.50 D6.30pm (W only Jun–Sep)

**GH Pines** 39 Mudeford Rd ☎475121 Bournemouth district plan:**99** Lic 13hc 2🏠 (3fb) Ⓒʰ CTV 12P 🛏 S% B&b£8.05–£9.20 Bdi£11.50–£12.65 W£70.84–£78.50 ⚓ D6pm

**GH St Albans Hotel** 8 Avenue Rd ☎471096 Bournemouth district plan:**101** Etr–Oct rsOct–Etr Lic 9hc (4fb) CTV 12P 🛏 lift S% B&b£6.50–£7.50 Bdi£10–£11 W£68–£75 ⚓ D4pm

**GH Sea Witch Hotel** 153–5 Barrack Rd ☎482846 Bournemouth district plan:**104** Lic 9hc (2fb) 🛠 CTV 20P 🛏 D5pm

**GH Shortwood House Hotel** 1 Magdalen Ln ☎485223 Bournemouth district plan:**106** 8rm 7hc 1🏠 (3fb) 🛠 CTV 8P 🛏 S% B&b£6–£7.50 Bdi£9–£11 W£58–£65 ⚓ D5pm

**INN Somerford Hotel** Somerford ☎482610 Not on plan 8hc 1🏠 CTV 100P 🛏 B&b£11.50–£12.50 sn L£3.50&alc D9.30pm£5.25&alc

**CHURCH STRETTON** Salop Map 7 SO49
**GH Mynd House Private Hotel** Ludlow Rd, Little Stretton (2m S B4370) ☎722212 Feb–Dec Lic 13hc 1🏠 (2fb) CTV 16P 🛏 S% B&b£6.25–£10.45 Bdi£10.65–£14.95 W£67.55–£97.65 ⚓ D5pm

**CILIAU AERON** Dyfed Map 2 SN55
**GH Ty Lôn** ☎Aeron 470726 5hc (2fb) CTV 6P 🛏 S% B&b£6.50 W£42 Ⓜ

---

DINNER, BED AND BREAKFAST
LICENSED BAR

# 𝕭elvedere 𝕳otel

TELEPHONE: CHRISTCHURCH 48-5978

**59 BARRACK ROAD, CHRISTCHURCH DORSET**

Proprietors:
**Mr and Mrs R. J. Jefferis**

---

# 𝕸ynd 𝕳ouse 𝕻rivate 𝕳otel

**CHURCH STRETTON
SHROPSHIRE SY6 6RB
Tel. CHURCH STRETTON 722212**

This family run hotel offers:
★ A warm and genuine welcome coupled with friendly courteous service
★ Varied menus, excellent table
★ Sensibly-priced tariff
★ Residents lounge with CTV
★ Games room with Table Tennis
★ Lounge Bar
★ All rooms H&C plus shaver points (4 with showers)
★ Fully Centrally Heated
★ Fire Certificate
★ Free Car Parking
★ Morning Tea, Evening Refreshments and Packed Lunches available

**Please send SAE for brochure and tariff**

---

# 𝖂hite 𝖍art 𝕴nn

Cinderford 23139

Proprietors: Sue and James Newman
Situated close to centre of Forest of Dean, with views of the Forest from the front rooms. All rooms have H&C. TV if required. B&B accommodation from £8. Bistro and Restaurant available. Traditional Sunday lunches. Cold buffet daily throughout the summer.

**CINDERFORD** Glos *Map 3 SO61*
**GH Overdean** 31 St White's Rd ☎22136
6hc (1fb) CTV 5P 2㋱ ⫿⫿⫿ S% B&bf£6.50

**INN *White Hart Hotel*** St Whites Rd,
Ruspidge (B4227) ☎23139 Lic 6hc 60P
D9.45pm
**See advert on page 77**

**CIRENCESTER** Glos *Map 4 SP00*
**GH Raydon** 3 The Avenue ☎3485 Closed 24
Dec–2 Jan Lic 10hc (2fb) CTV 6P S%
B&bfr£9 Bdi fr£13 D7pm

**GH Rivercourt** Beeches Rd ☎3998 Closed
Xmas & New Year 6hc (2fb) ⊁ TV 10P 9㋱ ⫿⫿⫿
S% ✻ B&b£7–£7.50

**GH La Ronde** 52–54 Ashcroft Rd ☎4611 Lic
10hc (4fb) ⊁CTV ⫿⫿⫿ B&b£8.50–£9 Bdi£13.75–
£14.75 D8pm

**GH Wimborne** Victoria Rd ☎3890 Feb–Nov
6hc ⊁ nc5 CTV 6P B&b£8–£9 Bdi£13–£14
Dnoon

**CLACTON-ON-SEA** Essex *Map 5 TM11*
**GH Argyll Private Hotel** 8 Colne Rd
☎23227 Apr–Dec Lic 25hc 1㋙ (4fb) ⊁ nc6
CTV 6P B&b£9–£10 Bdi£12–£14 Wf£90–£95
D6pm

**GH Sandrock Hotel** 1 Penfold Rd ☎28215
(liable to change) Closed Jan Lic 6hc ⊁CTV
6P ⫿⫿⫿ sea S% B&bf£10

**GH York House** 19 York Rd, Holland-on-Sea
(2m NE B1032) ☎814333 Feb–Oct rsXmas
Lic 7hc 1㋙ (4fb) CTV 4P 2㋱ ⫿⫿⫿ S% B&b£9.50–
£11 Bdi £13.50–£16 Wf£85–£110 Dnoon

**CLARE** Suffolk *Map 5 TL74*

**GH Old Bear & Crown Hotel** 20 Market Hill
☎440 Lic 5hc (1fb) CTV 6P 2㋱ S% B&bf£12–
£14 Bdi£18–£21 D8.30pm

**CLEARWELL** Glos *Map 3 SO50*
**INN Wyndham Arms** ☎Dean 33666 Closed
Mon & Xmas 3hc ⇔ TV in all bedrooms 30P
1㋱ ⫿⫿⫿ B&b£8 sn L£3.15&alc D10pm£10alc

**CLEHONGER** Heref & Worcs *Map 3 SO43*
**GH Thistledein** Church Rd ☎Belmont 338
rsXmas Lic 8hc (5fb) ⊁ TV 7P ⫿⫿⫿
B&b£6.50–£7 Bdi£11–£12 D6.30pm

**CLIFTON** *(Nr Penrith)* Cumbria *Map 12 NY52*
**GH *Whitrigg House*** ☎Penrith 64851 Lic
5hc 1⇔ ㋙ (2fb) ⊁nc5 CTV 6P 3㋱ ⫿⫿⫿ D7pm

**CLITHEROE** Lancs *Map 7 SD74*
**GH Fairway House** 48 King St ☎22025 Lic
10hc 4㋙ (5fb) CTV 9P ⫿⫿⫿ S% B&b£8–£13.75
Bdi£12–£18 Wf£101.50–£143 D8pm

**CLUN** Salop *Map 7 SO38*
**INN Sun** ☎559 4hc ⊁ nc14 CTV 10P ⫿⫿⫿ S%
B&b£8–£11 Bdi£13–£16 Wf£82–£100 ⫽ Bar
lunch60p–£3.50 D9.30pm£5&alc

**COCKERMOUTH** Cumbria *Map 11 NY13*
**GH Hundith Hill Hotel** Lorton Valley (2m SE
B5292) ☎822092 Mar–Nov Lic 14rm 7⇔
(4fb) CTV 30P ⫿⫿⫿ B&b£9.50–£11.50 Bdi£15–£17
Wf£98–£112 ⫽ D7pm

**COLCHESTER** Essex *Map 5 TM02*
**GH *Cloisters Hotel*** 94 Maldon Rd ☎73756
Feb–Nov Lic 9hc 1⇔ ㋙ (2fb) ⊁ nc5 CTV
10P ⫿⫿⫿

---

---

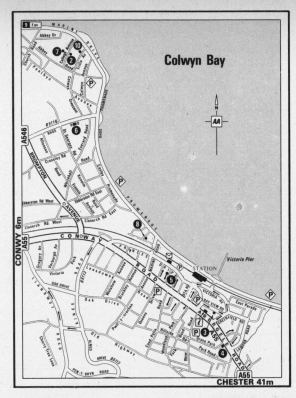

Colwyn Bay

2 Cabin Hill Private Hotel
3 Green Lawns
4 Grosvenor Hotel
5 Idaho Hotel
6 Northwood Hotel
7 St Luke's
8 Southlea
9 Sunny Downs Private Hotel
10 West Mains Private Hotel

**COLDINGHAM** Borders *Berwicks Map 12 NT96*
**INN Anchor** ☎338 Lic 4rm 3hc ⍟ CTV P 〽 ⇛ D8pm£4

**COLEFORD** Devon *Map 3 SS70*
**INN New** ☎Copplestone 242 4hc 2⇔ ⇛ CTV 60P S% B&b£6.90 Bar lunch50p−£3

**COLLYWESTON** Northants *Map 4 TF00*
**INN Cavalier** Main St ☎Duddington 288 6hc nc2 60P 〽 B&b£10.35−£17.25 sn L£9alc D9.30pm£9alc

**COLWYN BAY** Clwyd *Map 6 SH87* **(See Plan)**
**GH Cabin Hill Private Hotel** College Av, Rhos-on-Sea ☎44568 Plan:**2** Mar−Oct Lic 10hc 3🛁 (4fb) ⍟ CTV 6P 〽 S% B&bfr£7.50 Bdi fr£9 Wfr£63 ⅃ D6pm

**GH Green Lawns** 14 Bay View Rd ☎2207 Plan:**3** Closed Nov Lic 16hc (A 2hc) nc4 CTV 10P D6pm

**GH Grosvenor Hotel** 106−108 Abergele Rd ☎31586 Plan:**4** Lic 16hc 2⇔ 🛁 (8fb) ⍟ CTV 12P D5.30pm
**See advert on page 80**

**GH Idaho Hotel** 19 Wynnstay Rd ☎30730 Plan:**5** Lic 7hc (4fb) ⍟ nc2 CTV 6P S% B&b£6.25 Bdi£9.50 W£52 ⅃

**GH Northwood Hotel** Rhos Rd, Rhos-on-Sea ☎49931 Plan:**6** May−Oct Lic 14hc 4🛁 (4fb) nc2 CTV 14P 〽 S% B&bf£7.50−£13.50 Bdi£11.50−£14.50 Wfr£50 D6.30pm

**GH St Luke's** 20 College Av, Rhos-on-Sea ☎48035 Plan:**7** Closed Xmas & New Year Lic 18hc (4fb) ✻ CTV 10P ▥ lift S% B&b£9 Bdi£13 Wfr£90 D7pm

**GH Southlea** 4 Upper Prom ☎2004 Plan:**8** Lic 9hc (4fb) ⓒh S% ✻ B&b£8.05–£9.20 Bdi£10.92–£12.08 Wf£62.10–£69 ᴸ D6pm

**GH Sunny Downs Private Hotel** 66 Abbey Rd, Rhos-on-Sea ☎44256 Plan:**9** Lic 17hc (7fb) ✻ CTV 10P ▥ B&b£8.05–£8.25 Bdi£10.15–£10.35 Wf£56.35–£57.75 ᴸ D5.30pm

**GH West Mains Private Hotel** Trillo Av, Rhos-on-Sea ☎44664 Plan:**10** May–Sep Lic 10hc CTV 15P sea D6.30pm

**COLYFORD** Devon *Map 3 SY29*
**GH Elmwood Hotel** Swanhill Rd ☎Colyton

52750 Lic 9hc (A 3hc) ✻ CTV 12P 1🏠 ▥ D7pm

**GH St Edmunds** ☎Colyton 52431 Apr–Sep 7rm 6hc (1fb) CTV 8P ▥ S% B&b£6.75 Wf£45.50 ᴹ

**COLYTON** Devon *Map 3 SY29*
**GH Old Bakehouse** ☎52518 Feb–Dec Lic 7hc TV 10P ▥ S% B&b£14–£17 Bdi£25–£30 D9pm

**COMBE MARTIN** Devon *Map 2 SS54*
**GH Coulsworthy House Hotel** ☎2463 Lic 13hc 5🏠 (5fb) ⓒh CTV 20P ▥ B&b£10–£11 Bdi£15.50–£16.50 Wf£97–£101 ᴸ D7.30pm

**GH Firs** Woodlands ☎3404 Lic 9hc (6fb) ✻ ⓒh CTV 10P ▥ sea S% ✻ B&b£6.32–£7 Bdi£10.35–£10.50 Wf£45–£52 ᴸ D5pm

**GH** *Miramar Hotel* Victoria St ☎3558 Lic
11hc (5fb) Ch CTV 9P 2☂ ⬛ D5.30pm

**GH Newberry Lodge Hotel** Newberry Rd
☎3316 Lic 15hc 2♪ (4fb) Ch CTV 12P sea
B&bf8.65–£9.25 Bdi£12.65–£13.25 Wf81.65–
£86.25 ⅃ D7pm

**COMPTON** Berks *Map 4 SU57*
**INN Swan Hotel** ☎269 4hc TV 40P S%
B&bf9.50–£10.50 Bdi£14–£18 sn L£3.95alc
D9pm£4.90alc

**COMRIE** Tayside *Perths Map 11 NN72*
⤬ **GH Mossgiel** ☎567 Closed Nov,
rsDec–Etr 6hc nc2 CTV 6P ⬛ S% B&bf5
Bdi£8.50 Wf59.50 ⅃ D5pm

**CONISTON** Cumbria *Map 7 SD39*
**GH Low Bank Ground Country House
Hotel** ☎525 Feb–Xmas Lic 4⇋ (2fb) Ch 10P
⬛ lake S% B&bf13.50–£14.75 Bdi£22–£25
Wf154–£175 ⅃ D6pm

**INN Crown** ☎243 6hc CTV 40P 3☂ ⬛ S%
B&bf8.50 Bdi£14–£16 Wf98–£112 ⅃ sn
L£2.30–£5 D8pm£5–£6.50

**CONNOR DOWNS** Cornwall *Map 2 SW53*
**GH Pine Trees** ☎Hayle 753249 Apr–Oct Lic
10rm 9hc (6fb) ✸ CTV 10P S% ✱B&bf6–£7
Bdif9.75–£11.50 Wf57.50–£74.75 ⅃ D3pm

**CONSTANTINE** Cornwall *Map 2 SW72*
⤬**GH High Cross** ☎40373 Mar–Oct 5hc
(2fb) ✱ CTV 6P S% B&bf5–£6 Bdif6.50–£8

**INN Trengilly Wartha** Nancenoy ☎40332
5hc ⬛ nc14 20P ⬛ S% B&bf8 Wf56 M sn
L£2.75–£4.50 D9.30pm£5.75–£10

**CONWY** Gwynedd *Map 6 SH77*
**GH Cyfnant Private Hotel** Henryd Rd
☎2442 Feb–Dec Lic 6hc (2fb) ✱ CTV 6P
B&bf7–£8.25 Bdi£10.75–£12.25 Wf71.75–
£82.25 ⅃ D6pm

**GH Leys Gwilym** 3 Mountain Rd, off
Cadnant Pk ☎2351 Lic 6hc (2fb) ⬛
river sea S% B&bf6–£7 Bdif9–£10 Wf55–£60 ⅃
D8pm

**GH Sunnybanks** Llanrwst Rd, Woodlands
☎3845 Etr–Sep 7hc (2fb) TV 6P ⬛ S%
B&bf5.50 Bdifr£8.50 Wf48 ⅃ D7pm

**CORRIE** Isle of Arran, Strathclyde *Bute Map
10 NS04*
**GH Blackrock House** ☎282 Mar–Oct 9hc
(4fb) CTV 8P ⬛ sea S% B&bf6.50–£7.50
Bdif9–£9.50 Wf63–£66.50 ⅃ D6pm

**CORWEN** Clwyd *Map 21 SJ04*
**GH *Central Hotel*** ☎2462 Closed 24–26
Dec 10hc (6fb) CTV 20P 1☂ ⬛ D9.30pm

**COSHESTON** Dyfed *Map 2 SN00*
**INN Hill House** ☎Pembroke 4352 8hc 4♪
CTV available in 4 bedrooms 20P ⬛
✱B&bfr£10 Wfr£70 ⅃ Bar lunch£1.90–£4.30
D9pm£5.75

**COVENTRY** W Midlands *Map 4 SP37*
**GH Croft Hotel** 23 Stoke Green (off Binley
Rd) ☎457846 Lic 13hc (1fb) CTV 14P ⬛ S%
B&bfr£11.50 Bdifr£16.25 D7.15pm

**GH *Fairlight*** 14 Regent St ☎24215 12hc
(2fb) CTV 8P ⬛

**GH Mount** 7–9 Coundon Rd ☎25998 10rm
9hc (2fb) CTV ⬛ S% B&bf6.50 Wf45.50 M

**GH Northanger House** 35 Westminster Rd ☎26780 Closed Xmas 7hc (2fb) ★ CTV 1🚗 ▥ S% B&bfr£7

**GH Ravenswood** 31 Westminster Rd ☎20656 7hc 1⇔ (2fb) CTV 6P ▥ S% B&bfr£6

**COWDENBEATH** Fife *Map 11 NT19*
**GH Struan Bank Private Hotel** 74 Perth Rd ☎511057 Lic 7hc (1fb) CTV 8P ▥ S% ✱B&b£7 Bdi£10 D7pm

**CRAFTHOLE** Cornwall *Map 2 SX35*
**INN Finnygook** ☎St Germans (Cornwall) 338 (due to change to 30338) rsXmas 5⇔ 🚗 ★ nc14 CTV 50P S% B&b£10 sn L60p–£4 D9.30pm£7alc

**CRAIL** Fife *Map 12 NO60*
**GH Caiplie House** 51–53 High St ☎564 7hc (2fb) CTV 12P B&b£6.50–£7.50 Bdi£10–£11 W£63–£70 ⱡ D8.30pm

**CRANBROOK** Kent *Map 5 TQ73*
**INN *George Hotel*** Stone St ☎713348 Lic 13hc CTV 30P 2🚗

**CRANTOCK** Cornwall *Map 2 SW76*
**GH Crantock Cottage Private Hotel** West Pentire Rd ☎830232 May–Sep Lic 10hc (2fb) nc7 CTV 20P sea S% B&b£7.50–£8 Bdi£9–£10.80 W£63.25–£69 ⱡ D5pm

**CRAWLEY** W Sussex *Map 4 TQ23* **For accommodation details see under Gatwick Airport**

**CREETOWN** Dumfries & Galloway *Kircudbrights Map 6 NX45*
**GH *Mayburn*** ☎317 Etr–Sep 5hc (2fb) Ch TV 5P D7.30pm

**INN Creetown Arms Hotel** St Johns St ☎282 6hc CTV 20P S% B&bfr£7.50 Bdifr£10.50 Wfr£75 ⱡ sn L£2–£5.50 D9pmfr£5.50&alc

**CRESSAGE** Salop *Map 7 SJ50*
**INN Cound Lodge** ☎322 7hc ★ 40P ▥ river S% B&b£7–£9 Bar lunch £1.50alc D9.30pm£6alc

**CRIANLARICH** Central *Perths Map 10 NN32*
⊢⊣ **GH Glenardean** ☎236 Lic 6hc (3fb) CTV 5P ▥ river S% B&b£5.50–£6 Bdi£8.25–£9 W£51–£54 ⱡ D7pm

**GH Mountgreenan** ☎286 Closed Xmas Day 5hc (1fb) CTV P ▥ S% ✱B&bfr£5 D6.30pm

**CRICCIETH** Gwynedd *Map 6 SH53*
**GH Min-y-Gaer Private Hotel** Portmadoc Rd ☎2151 Lic 10hc (4fb) CTV 12P sea S% ✱B&b£7.50–£9.50 Bdi£10.50–£12.50 W£70–£84 D8pm

**GH Moorings** Marine Ter ☎2802 Mar–Oct 7hc (3fb) CTV ▥ sea S% B&b£6–£7.50 Bdi£10–£12 W£68–£82 ⱡ D6pm

**GH *Môr Heli Private Hotel*** Marine Ter ☎2794 Etr–Sep rsOct Lic 16hc (6fb) CTV 24P sea D6.30pm

**GH *Neptune Private Hotel*** Marine Ter ☎2794 Etr–Sep rsOct Lic 14hc (6fb) CTV 24P sea D6.30pm


**Finnygook Inn**

**Crafthole, Cornwall.**

Small friendly 16th century inn yet catering to modern needs, the restaurant is open to non-residents who will also find good meals served in the bar.

The inn overlooks Whitesand Bay Golf Course and the sea beyond.

All rooms have H&C and coloured TV.

**Write for brochure or telephone: St Germans 338.**



**Neptune & Môr Heli Hotels**

**Min-y-Môr, Criccieth, Gwynedd LL52 0EF**
**Telephone: 2794/2878 – STD 076671**

Two, well-established, family-run hotels situated on sea-front, noted for good food and friendly atmosphere. Comfortably furnished throughout with an attractive licensed bar for guests and diners.
For brochure and terms contact resident proprietors:- WJ J & E Williams.
*Fire certificate granted*
*Licensed*
*Car park*

**CRICKHOWELL** Powys *Map 3 SO21*
**GH Dragon Country House Hotel** High St
☎810362 Lic 11rm 10hc 1⇨ (2fb) Ⓒʰ CTV
15P ▥ S% ✱B&bfr£7.25 Bdifr£12.50
Wfr£82.50 ⅃ D8.30pm

**INN Beaufort Arms Hotel** ☎810402 4⋔ TV
▥ S% ✱B&b£9 Bdi£16

**CRIEFF** Tayside *Perths Map 11 NN82*
**GH Comely Bank** 32 Burrell St ☎3409 Feb–
Nov 6hc (2fb) CTV S% B&b£6 Bdi£8.50 W£52
⅃ D6pm

**GH Heatherville** 31 Burrell St ☎2825 5hc
(3fb) ✸CTV 5P S% ✱B&b£5.50–£6 Bdi£8.50–
£9 D5pm

**GH Lockes Acre Hotel** Comrie Rd ☎2526
Apr–Oct Lic 6hc (2fb) CTV 5P ▥ S% B&b£7
Bdi£12 D6.30pm

**CROMER** Norfolk *Map 9 TG24*
**GH Brightside** 19 Macdonald Rd ☎513408
Apr–Oct Lic 6hc (3fb) ✸nc5 CTV 4P ▥ S%
B&b£7–£8 Bdi£8.50–£9.50 W£54–£65
⅃ Dnoon

**GH Chellow Dene** 23 Macdonald Rd
☎513251 Closed Xmas Lic 7hc (2fb) nc3
CTV 6P ▥ S% B&b£6–£6.50 Bdi£8.50–£9
W£54–£59 ⅃ D6pm

**GH** *Coolhurst* 25 Macdonald Rd ☎512073
7hc (4fb) CTV 2P D5.30pm

**GH Westgate Lodge Private Hotel** 10
Macdonald Rd ☎512840 Lic 12hc (6fb) ✸
nc3 CTV 14P ▥ S% B&bf£7.75–£8 Bdi£10.35–
£11.50 W£66.50–£73.50 ⅃ D6.30pm

**CROSS GATES** Powys *Map 3 SO06*
**GH** *Guidfa* ☎ Penybont 241 mid May–Sep
Lic 5hc 2⇨ ⋔ (1fb) TV 6P ▥

**CROSSWAY GREEN** Heref & Worcs *Map 7
SO86*
**INN Mitre Oak** ☎Hartlebury 352 7hc CTV
50P 1☎ ▥ S% B&b£9.25 sn L£2.95–£3.95&alc
D9.30pm

**CROWDECOTE** Derbys *Map 7 SK16*
**INN Pack Horse** ☎Longnor 210 2hc CTV
25P ▥ ✱B&b£7–£8.50 Bdi£11.50–£13
W£75 sn Lfr£4.50&alc D10.30pm£4.50

**CROYDE** Devon *Map 2 SS43*
**GH Moorsands House Hotel** Moor Ln
☎890781 Apr–Oct Lic 8hc (2fb) ✸nc5 CTV
8P ▥ S% B&bfr£7.50 Bdifr£11 Wfr£77 ⅃
D6.30pm

**GH Seabirds Hotel** Baggy Point ☎890224
Etr–Sep Lic 9hc (1fb) CTV 20P ▥ sea
✱B&b£8–£10 Bdi£13–£15 W£86–£99 ⅃
D9pm

**CROYDON** Gt London *London plan 4 E4*
*(page 135)*
**GH Central Hotel** 3–5 South Park Hill Rd
☎01-688 5644 Closed Xmas wk Lic 27hc
6⇨ 8⋔ CTV available in some bedrooms 10P
▥ S% B&bfr£15 D7.30pm

**GH Friends** 50 Friends Rd ☎01-688 6215
10hc (4fb) ✸CTV 5P S% ✱B&b£8.50–£9.50
W£52.50–£59.50 Ⓜ

**GH Markington Hotel** 9 Haling Park Rd,
South Croydon ☎01-688 6530 Lic 16hc 1⇨
6⋔ (3fb) ✸CTV 7P ▥ ✱B&b£12 Bdi£15 W£90
⅃ D7pm

**GH Oakwood Hotel** 69 Outram Rd ☎01-
654 2835 Lic 16hc 9⇨ ⋔ (3fb) CTV 15P 3☎ ▥
S% ✱B&b£12.50–£16.50 Bdi£16.50–£20.50
D7pm

**CULLEN** Grampian *Banffs Map 15
NJ56*
⊶⊣ **GH Wakes** Seafield Pl ☎40251 Apr–
Oct Lic 23rm 22hc (3fb) CTV 20P B&b£5.50–
£6.50 Bdi£8–£9 W£45–£50 ⅃ D5pm

**CURY CROSS LANES** Cornwall *Map 2
SW62*
**GH Pendragon Private Hotel** ☎Mullion
240631 6hc (1fb) ✸nc5 CTV 12P S%
✱B&b£6–£6.50 Bdi£8.25–£9.25 W£57.75–
£64.75 ⅃

**DARLINGTON** Co Durham *Map 8 NZ21*
**GH Raydale Hotel** Stanhope Road South
☎58993 Lic 11hc (2fb) ✸CTV 12P ▥ S%
B&bfr£13.80 Bdifr£18.97 D3pm

**DARTINGTON** Devon *Map 3 SX76*
**INN Cott** ☎Totnes 863777 6hc ⇌ CTV 35P
B&b£13.25 sn L£1.50–£3 D10pm£2–£4

**DARTMOUTH** Devon *Map 3 SX84*
**GH Downderry** 6 Church Rd ☎2788 6hc
(1fb) ✸nc4 CTV 5P S% ✱B&b£6.50–£7.50
Bdi£10.75–£11.75 W£67–£74 ⅃ D10am

**GH Orleans** 24 South Town ☎2967 5hc ✸
TV ▥ river sea S% B&b£8–£9.50 Wfr£55 Ⓜ

**DAWLISH** Devon *Map 3 SX97*
**GH** *Barton Grange Private Hotel* 5 Barton
Villas ☎863365 rsNov–Apr 9hc (1fb) nc5
CTV 7P ▥ D4.30pm

**GH** *Brockington* 139 Exeter Rd ☎863588
9hc nc10 CTV 8P ▥ ⅃

**GH Broxmore Private Hotel** 20 Plantation
Ter ☎863602 Feb–Dec Lic 8hc (3fb) ✸nc8
CTV ▥ S% ✱B&b£5.50–£6.50 Bdi£8.50–£9.50
W£55–£65 ⅃ D5.30pm

**GH *Lamorna Private Hotel*** 2 Barton Ter ☎862242 Lic 10hc (5fb) ★ CTV D7pm

**GH Lynbridge Private Hotel** Barton Villas ☎862352 Apr–Sep rsMar 8hc (2fb) ★ CTV 7P ▥ S% B&b£6.50–£7 Bdi£8.50–£9 W£59–£62 Ⱡ D6pm

**GH Marldon House Hotel** 6 Barton Villas ☎862721 7hc (3fb) nc2 CTV 6P ▥ S% *B&b£5.50–£5.90 Bdi£8.40–£9 W£56–£59.50 Ⱡ D4.30pm

**GH Mimosa** 11 Barton Ter ☎863283 Mar–Oct 9hc (4fb) ★ nc5 CTV 2P S% B&b£5.50–£6.50 Bdi£7.50–£8.50 W£45–£51 Ⱡ D1pm

⊢⊣ **GH Portland House** 14 Marine Pde ☎864040 Etr–Oct 7hc (3fb) ★ CTV 6P sea S% B&b£4.50–£6 Bdi£7.50–£9 W£50–£60 Ⱡ D10am

**GH Radfords** Dawlish Water ☎863322 Mar–Nov Lic 19⊜ (A 2rm 1hc 1⊜) Ch CTV 50P ▥ B&b£10.35–£12.65 Bdi£17.25–£21.85 Wfr£108 Ⱡ D6pm (W terms only Jul & Aug)

**DEAL** Kent *Map 5 TR35*
**GH Pension Castle Lea** 2 Gladstone Rd ☎2718 Mar–Nov 4rm 3⊜ 1⋒ ★ nc2 CTV ▥ S% B&b£8 Bdi£12 W£84 Ⱡ D7pm

**DENBIGH** Clwyd *Map 6 SJ06*
**GH Cayo** 74 Vale St ☎2686 Lic 7hc (3fb) CTV 2P ▥ S% B&b£7.50 Bdi£10.50 W£70 Ⱡ D5.30pm

**DENT** Cumbria *Map 7 SO78*
**INN George & Dragon** ☎256 9hc ⌂ CTV 14P ▥ B&b£9.50 W£60 M Bar lunch£1.30alc D9.30pm£5alc

**DENTON** Gt Manchester *Map 7 SJ99*
**GH *Elsinore*** 121 Town Ln ☎061-320 7606 Lic 12⊜ ⋒ CTV 18P ▥ D8pm

**DERBY** Derbys *Map 8 SK33*
**GH Ascot Hotel** 724 Osmaston Rd ☎41916 Lic 18hc (2fb) CTV 12P ▥ S% B&bfr£9.50 Bdifr£13 D6.30pm

**GH Georgian House Hotel** 34 Ashbourne Rd ☎49806 Lic 17hc 1⊜ (3fb) ★ CTV 15P ▥ S% *B&bfr£9.49 Bdifr£13.29

**DERSINGHAM** Norfolk *Map 9 TF63*
**GH Westdene House Hotel** 60 Hunstanton Rd ☎40395 Closed Xmas Lic 5hc (1fb) ★ CTV 15P ▥

**DEVIZES** Wilts *Map 4 SU06*
**INN *Castle Hotel*** New Park St ☎2046 Lic 13hc CTV 8⌂ ▥ D9pm

**DEVORAN** Cornwall *Map 2 SW73*
**GH Driffold Hotel** 8 Devoran Ln ☎863314 Lic 8rm 3hc 2⋒ ★ CTV 12P ▥ B&b£6.50–£9.50 Bdi£10.50–£14

**DINAS MAWDDWY** Gwynedd *Map 6 SH81*
**INN Buckley Arms Hotel** ☎261 14hc 1⊜ 1⋒ CTV 50P ▥ S% B&b£8.50–£9.50 Bdi£14.50–£15.50 Wfr£98 Ⱡ Bar lunch£1–£2.50 D9pm£6–£6.50

**DINORWIC** Gwynedd *Map 6 SH50*
**GH Hafodty** ☎Llanberis 548 (liable to change to Llanberis 870548 during 1981) Apr–Sep Lic 6rm 5hc (2fb) nc8 6P ▥ S% B&b£8.25 Bdi£12 W£74 Ⱡ D6pm

**DIRLETON** Lothian *E Lothian Map 12 NT58*
**INN Castle** ☎221 rsNov–Apr 5hc (A 4hc)
CTV 12P ▦ B&b£10.50 Bdi£16 W£95 ⫽ Bar
lunch fr£1.50 D8.30pmfr£5.50

**DODDISCOMBSLEIGH** Devon *Map 3 SX88*
**INN Nobody** ☎Christow 52394 Closed
Xmas rsSun & Mon 4hc 1⋔ ⇌ ✸nc14 TV in
all bedrooms 50P B&b£10–£15 Bar lunch£3alc
D9.30pm£7alc

**DOLWYDDELAN** Gwynedd *Map 6 SH75*
**INN Gwydyr** ☎209 Lic 2hc ✸nc14 12P sn
D9.30pm

**DONINGTON** Lincs *Map 8 TF23*
**INN Red Cow** ☎298 Lic 7hc TV 30P sn

**DORCHESTER** Dorset *Map 3 SY69*
**INN White Hart Hotel** High East St ☎3545
Closed Xmas Lic 6hc TV 12P 6⇌ ▦ D9.30pm

**DORMINGTON** Heref & Worcs *Map 3 SO54*
**GH Dormington Court Hotel** ☎Hereford
850370 Lic 6hc (1fb) CTV 15P ▦ B&b£7–£7.50
Bdi£11.25–£11.75 W£75–£80 ⫽ D5pm

**DOUGLAS** Isle of Man *Map 6 SC37*
**GH Ainsdale** 2 Empire Ter, Central Prom
☎6695 May–Sep 19hc (11fb) CTV sea S%
B&b£6–£6.50 Bdi£6.75–£7.50 D7pm

**GH Rosslyn Private Hotel** 3 Empire Ter,
Central Prom ☎6056 Lic 18hc (6fb) ✸CTV
sea S% B&b£6.50–£7.50 W£7.75–£8.50

**GH Rutland Hotel** Queens Prom ☎21218
Apr–Oct Lic 120hc 10⇌ 7⋔ (23fb) ✸CTV
sea S% B&b£6.90–£9.50 Bdi£8.75–£12
W£84.50–£98.60 D6.30pm

**DOVER** Kent *Map 5 TR34*
**GH Allwyn Cottage** 337 Folkestone Rd
☎201126 Closed Xmas 6hc (2fb) ✸CTV 10P
1⇌ ▦ S% B&b£6.50–£7

**GH Beulah House** 94 Crabble Hill, London
Rd ☎Kearsney 4615 7hc 1⋔ (3fb) ✸ Ⓒⓗ 8P
2⇌ ▦ river S% B&b£7–£8 W£49–£56 ▯

**GH Dover Stop** 45 London Rd, River (2m
NW A256) ☎Kearsney 2751 Lic 7rm (A 5rm)
(7fb) ✸CTV 14P ▦ river S% B&b£8–£10.50

**GH Number One** 1 Castle St ☎202007 5hc
1⇌ 3⋔ (3fb) CTV in all bedrooms 1P 2⇌ ▦
S% B&b£7–£8

**GH Peverell House Private Hotel** 25 Park
Av ☎202573 Feb–Nov Lic 7hc (4fb) ✸CTV
6P ▦ S% B&b£8–£9 Bdi£12.50–£13.50
W£84.50–£91.50 ⫽ Dnoon

**GH St Brelade's** 82 Buckland Av ☎206126
Mar–Oct rsNov–Feb Lic 8hc (4fb) ✸TV 6P
1⇌ ▦ S% B&b£7.50–£8.50

**DOWNTON** Wilts *Map 4 SU12*
**GH Warren** High St ☎20263 6hc 1⇌ ⋔ (1fb)
nc6 CTV 7P ▦

**DRUMNADROCHIT** Highland *Inverness-shire Map 14 NH53*
**INN Lewiston Arms Hotel** Lewiston ☎225
4hc (A 4hc) ⇌ CTV 40P S% B&b£7.50
Bdi£12.50–£15 W£52 ▯ Bar lunch£2alc
D8.30pm£5.50alc

**DULOE** Cornwall *Map 2 SX25*
**GH Duloe Manor Hotel** ☎Looe 2795 Etr–
mid Oct Lic 11hc 9⇌ (3fb) CTV 20P ▦ S%
B&b£15.50–£18.40 Bdi£23.50–£27.50
W£162.50–£190.20 ⫽ D8pm

**DUMFRIES** Dumfries & Galloway
*Dumfriesshire Map 11 NX97*
⊁⊣ **GH Fullwood Private Hotel** 30 Lovers
Walk ☎2262 5hc (2fb) TV S% B&b£5.50
W£37.50 ▯

**GH Newall House** 22 Newall Ter ☎2676 Lic
7rm 6hc (3fb) CTV 7P ▦ S% ✳B&b£7 Bdi£10
W£65 ⫽ D5pm

**DUNBAR** Lothian *E Lothian Map 12 NT67*
**GH Cruachan** East Links Rd ☎63595 6hc
(1fb) CTV ▦ sea S% B&bfr£7 Bdifr£10 Wfrf£67
⫽

⊁⊣ **GH Marine** 7 Marine Rd ☎63315 11hc
(3fb) ✸CTV ▦ S% B&b£4.45–£6.50 Bdi£7–
£8.50 W£44–£54 ⫽ D6pm

**GH St Laurence** North Rd ☎62527 Etr–Oct
6hc ✸sea S% ✳B&bfr£6.50 Bdi fr£10 Wfrf£60
⫽ D5pm

**GH Springfield House** Edinburgh Rd
☎62502 Apr–Oct 6hc (2fb) CTV 9P ▦

**DUNBLANE** Tayside *Perthshire Map 11 NN70*
**GH Altair Neuk Hotel** Doune Rd ☎822562
Lic 8hc 2⋔ (2fb) CTV 10P ▦ S% B&bfr£10
Bdifr£16 D8.45pm

**DUNOON** Strathclyde *Argyll Map 10 NS17*
**GH Cedars Private Hotel** Alexandra Pde
☎2425 Feb–Dec Lic 14hc 2⇌ (2fb) CTV ▦
sea S% ✳B&b£7.47–£8.91 Bdi£11.50–£12.93
W£72.45–£82.80 ⫽ D5.30pm

**DUNSFORD** Devon *Map 3 SX88*
**INN Royal Oak** ☎Christow 52256 3hc ✸

# THE ALTAIR NEUK HOTEL

Doune Road, Dunblane, Perthshire.
Telephone: (STD Code 0786) 822562 — Visitors 822187
Proprietors: Frank & Elizabeth Johnson

The Altair Neuk Hotel is an attractive, stone-built, small country hotel, situated in the
Cathedral City of Dunblane, just six miles from Stirling. In an ideal situation for
touring the Trossachs, Loch Lomond, Central Highlands. Edinburgh and Perth. The
hotel offers comfort and a friendly atmosphere. Personally run by the proprietors, the
accommodation includes, double, twin, family and single rooms, all with central
heating and H&C, some private facilities. The hotel has a licence, TV lounge, dining
room and plenty of private parking. Large flat garden with umbrella tables for
afternoon tea or a quiet drink. Table d'hôte menu plus steak grill. Mini Breaks.

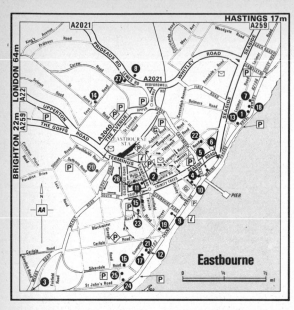

**HASTINGS 17m A259**

**Eastbourne**

1 Aberfoyle Hotel
2 Alfriston Hotel
3 Beachy Rise
4 Cavendish
5 Le Chalet
6 Chesleigh Hotel
7 Courtlands Hotel
8 Downland Private Hotel
9 Eastbourne Health Hotel
10 Edelweiss
11 Edmar
12 Elmscroft Private Hotel
13 Far End
14 Flamingo Private Hotel
15 Hanburies Hotel
16 Little Crookham
17 Lynwood Hotel
18 Marina
19 Mowbray
20 Orchard House
21 Saffrons
22 St Clare
23 Somerville Private Hotel
24 South Cliff House
25 Southcroft
26 Traquair Private Hotel
27 Wynstay Private Hotel

15P 2🏠 ▥ S% B&b£8.62 sn L£1.65–£3.90 D9.30pm£1.65–£3.90

**DUNVEGAN** Isle of Skye, Highland
*Inverness-shire Map 13 NG24*
⋈ **GH Argyll House** Kensalrog, Roskhill (3m S A863) ☎230 Etr–Oct 6rm 5hc (1fb) TV 6P ▥ lake S% B&b£5.25 Bdi£8 D7pm

**GH Roskhill** Roskhill (3m S A863) ☎317 Mar–Dec 5hc (2fb) TV 6P ▥ S% B&b£6.50– £6.90 Bdi£10.25–£10.75 D6.15pm

**DUXFORD** Cambs *Map 5 TL44*
**GH Highfield House** 55 St Peter's Street ☎Cambridge 833160 Lic 8hc 3⇌ ⋔ (1fb) Ⓒⱨ CTV 12P 2🏠 ▥ D7pm

**EASTBOURNE** E Sussex *Map 5 TV69* **(See Plan)**
⋈ **GH Aberfoyle Hotel** 83 Royal Pde ☎22161 Plan:**1** Lic 6hc (2fb) ⋔ nc5 2P ▥ sea S% B&b£5.50–£10 Bdi£7.50–£12 Wf£55–£67 ⌁ D6pm (W only Jul & Aug)

**GH Alfriston Hotel** Lushington Rd ☎25640 Plan:**2** Closed Xmas & 1st 3 wks Nov rs last wk Nov–Mar Lic 10hc ⋔ nc5 CTV 1🏠 D10am

**GH Beachy Rise** Beachy Head Rd ☎639171 Plan:**3** Mar–Oct 6hc (1fb) nc5 CTV ▥ S% B&b£7.50–£8.50 Bdi£9.50–£10.50 Wf£63– £70 ⌁ D4pm

**GH Cavendish** 1 Cavendish Pl ☎24284 Plan:**4** Closed Nov & Dec 11hc (3fb) nc3 TV sea ⌁ D4pm

**GH Le Chalet** 7 Marine Pde ☎20029 Plan:**5** 10hc (2fb) CTV sea B&b£7.50–£9.20

**GH Chesleigh Hotel** 4 Marine Pde ☎20722 Plan:**6** Etr–Oct 6hc 2⇌ 1⋔ ⋔ nc7 CTV sea S% B&b£7.50–£8

**GH Courtlands Hotel** 68 Royal Pde ☎21068 Plan:**7** Lic 7hc (A 7hc) (5fb) ⋔ CTV 1P 2🏠 sea S% B&bfr£12.08 Bdifr£14.38 Wfrf£94.30 ⌁ D6pm

**GH Downland Private Hotel** 37 Lewes Rd ☎32689 Plan:**8** Lic 16hc 7⇌ 5⋔ (4fb) Ⓒⱨ

CTV 16P ▥ S% B&bf11–£13 Bdif16–£19
Wf90–£118 ⌇ D7.15pm

**GH Eastbourne Health Hotel** 17 Burlington
Pl ☎23604 Plan:**9** 8hc (2fb) ✕ nc10 CTV 2P
▥ S% ✳ B&bf8 Bdif11 Wf77–£87 ⌇ D10am

**GH Edelweiss** 10 Elms Av ☎32071 Plan:**10**
May–Sep Lic 8hc (1fb) ✕ nc6 CTV ▥ B&bfrf9
Wfrf49 ℳ

**GH Edmar** 30 Hyde Gdns ☎33024 Plan:**11**
Etr–mid Oct 9hc 1⇔ 1🛆 (1fb) ✕ nc5 CTV S%
B&bf6.25–£9.50 Bdif10–£14 Wf55–£97 ⌇
D6pm

**GH Elmscroft Private Hotel** 53 Jevington
Gdns ☎21263 Plan:**12** 12hc (3fb) ✕ CTV

**GH Far End** 139 Royal Pde ☎25666 Plan:**13**
Jan–Oct 10hc (3fb) ✕ nc3 CTV 8P 2🚗 ▥ sea
S% B&bf7–£8.50 Bdif8.50–£10 Wf59–£75
D6pm (W only mid May–mid Sep)

**GH Flamingo Private Hotel** 20 Enys Rd
☎21654 Plan:**14** Lic 12hc 8⇔ 🛆 (1fb) ✕ nc8
CTV ▥ ✳ B&bf8–£13 Bdif12–£17 Wf74–£105 ⌇
D6.30pm

**GH Hanburies Hotel** 4 Hardwick Rd
☎30698 Plan:**15** Lic 14hc 10⇔ (2fb) nc5
CTV ▥ S% B&bf10–£12.50 Bdif11.50–
£14.50 Wf93–£107 D3pm

**GH Little Crookham** 16 Southcliffe Av
☎34160 Plan:**16** rsOct–Apr (B&b only) 8hc
(1fb) nc5 CTV ▥ D6pm

**GH Lynwood Hotel** Jevington Gdns
☎23982 Plan:**17** Lic 78hc 15⇔ 🛆 (6fb) nc2
CTV 4P 4🚗 lift D7.45pm

**GH Hotel Marina** 86–87 Royal Pde ☎20297
Plan:**18** Etr–Oct Lic 18hc 1⇔ (2fb) nc2 CTV
sea S% B&bf8–£8.50 Bdif9.50–£10.50 Wf65–
£80 ⌇ D6pm

**GH Mowbray Hotel** Lascelles Ter ☎20012
Plan: **19** Apr–Oct 16hc 4🛏 (1fb) nc7 CTV lift
B&bf£9.60–£10.55 Wf£57.39–£67.72 Ⓜ

**GH Orchard House** 10 Old Orchard Rd
☎23682 Plan: **20** Feb–Nov 7hc 3🖛 1🛏 ✸ nc3
CTV 3P 1🅰 B&bf£8.50–£9.50 Bdif£10.50–£12.50
Wf£64–£71 ⌇ D4pm

**GH Saffrons Hotel** 30–32 Jevington Gdns
☎25539 Plan: **21** Apr–Oct Lic 25hc 5🖛 5🛏
(4fb) CTV S% B&bf£10.50–£12.50 Bdif£15.50–
£17.25 Wf£99.50–£113 ⌇ D6.15pm

**GH St Clare** 70 Pevensey Rd ☎29483
Plan: **22** Closed Nov 8hc (4fb) ✸ nc4 CTV 🚻
S% B&bf£6–£7.50 Bdif£8.50–£10.50 Wf£52.50–
£63 ⌇ D4pm (W only Jun–Aug)

**GH Somerville Private Hotel** 6 Blackwater
Rd ☎29342 Plan: **23** Lic 11hc (2fb) ✸ CTV
S% B&bf£11.11–£11.82 Bdif£11.11–£11.82
Wf£66.66–£72.21 D3pm

**GH South Cliff House** 19 South Cliff Av
☎21019 Plan: **24** rsXmas (B&b only) Lic 6hc
CTV 🚻 D6pm

**GH Southcroft** 15 South Cliff Av ☎29071
Plan: **25** Lic 7hc (3fb) nc3 CTV 🚻 S%
B&bf£7.50–£8 Bdif£9.50–£10 Wf£64–£68 ⌇
D4.10pm (W only mid Jun–Sep)

**GH Traquair Private Hotel** 25 Hyde Gdns
☎25198 Plan: **26** Lic 11rm 6hc 5🛏 (3fb) CTV
✷ B&bf£8–£15 Bdif£13–£20 Wf£80–£120 ⌇
D6.15pm

**GH Wynstay Private Hotel** 13 Lewes Rd
☎21550 Plan: **27** 7hc (3fb) ✸ CTV 7P 🚻 S%
B&bfr£7 Bdif£10 Wf£50–£68 ⌇ D3pm

**EAST COWTON** N Yorks *Map 8 NZ30*
**INN Beeswing** ☎North Cowton 349 3🖛
20P 🚻 S% B&bf£12.50–£14 Bdif£17.50–£19 sn
Lf£3alc D10pmf£6alc

**EAST GRINSTEAD** W Sussex *Map 5 TQ33*
**GH Cranfield Hotel** Maypole Rd ☎21251
Lic 19rm 15hc TV 12P ✸ B&bf£9.20

**EASTLEIGH** Devon *Map 2 SS42*
**GH Pine's Farmhouse Hotel** (2½m NE of
Bideford off A39) ☎Instow 860561 Etr–Sep
Lic 7hc (2fb) ✸ nc3 CTV 12P 🚻 S% ✸ B&bf£8
Bdif£11 Wf£68 ⌇ D5pm (W only Aug & Spring
Bank Hol wk)

**EAST WITTERING** W Sussex *Map 4 SZ79*
**GH Wittering Lodge Hotel** Shore Rd
☎West Wittering 3207 Etr–Oct Lic 10hc
(2fb) CTV 22P 1🅰 🚻 sea S% B&bf£11–£13
Bdif£16.50–£18.50 Wf£105–£120 ⌇ D8.30pm

**EBBERSTON** N Yorks *Map 8 SE88*
**GH Foxholm Hotel** (on B1258)
☎Scarborough 85550 Mar–Nov Lic 10hc 1🖛
2🛏 (2fb) CTV 12P 2🅰 🚻 B&bf£9.50–£12
Bdif£14.50–£17 Wf£92–£107 ⌇ D7.30pm

**EDINBURGH** Lothian *Midlothian Map 11
NY27* **(See Plan)**
**GH Adam Hotel** 19 Lansdowne Cres ☎031-
337 1148 Plan: **1** Lic 9hc (1fb) CTV ⌇ D6pm

**GH Ben Doran Hotel** 11 Mayfield Gdns
☎031-667 8488 Plan: **2** Closed 23–30 Dec
9hc (5fb) CTV 7P S% B&bf£6–£7.50 Wf£35–£48
Ⓜ (W only Nov–Jun)

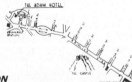

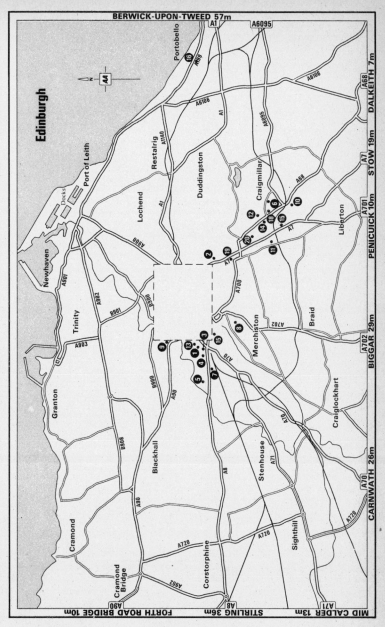

| | | |
|---|---|---|
| **1** Adam Hotel | **7** Eden | **14** Hillview |
| **2** Ben Doran Hotel | **8** Elmington House | **15** Kildonan Lodge |
| **3** Boisdale Hotel | Private Hotel | **16** Park Lodge |
| **4** Clans Hotel | **9** Galloway | **17** Quinton Lodge |
| **5** Cumberland | **10** Glendale | **18** Sharon |
| Hotel | **11** Glenisla Hotel | **19** Southdown |
| **6** Dorstan Private | **12** Golf View Hotel | **20** Thrums Private |
| Hotel | **13** Grosvenor | Hotel |

**GH Boisdale Hotel** 9 Coates Gdns ☎031-337 4392 Plan:**3** 11hc 3⇨ 8⋔ (4fb) CTV ⅢⅢ S% B&b£5.50–£10 Bdi£8–£12.50 D7.30pm

**GH Clans Hotel** 4 Magdala Cres ☎031-337 6301 Plan:**4** 8hc (3fb) ⊁ CTV ⅢⅢ S% B&b£7–£9.50

**GH Cumberland Hotel** 1 West Coates ☎031-337 1198 Plan:**5** 8hc (4fb) ⊁ CTV 9P ⅢⅢ S% B&b£9–£11 W£56–£70 Ⓜ

**GH Dorstan Private Hotel** 7 Priestfield Rd ☎031-667 6721 Plan:**6** Closed Xmas & New Year 14hc 3⇨ 1⋔ CTV 10P ⅢⅢ S% B&b£8.22–£9 Bdi£14.54–£15.32 W£100 ⊬ Dam

**GH Eden** 12 Osbourne Ter ☎031-337 4185 Plan:**7** 6hc (2fb) ⊁ 8P ⅢⅢ S% B&b£8–£9

**GH Elmington House Private Hotel** 45 Leamington Ter ☎031-229 1164 Plan:**8** Lic 7hc 3⋔ (2fb) CTV TV available in some bedrooms ⅢⅢ S% B&b£6.50 Bdi£9 D6pm

**GH** *Galloway* 22 Dean Park Cres ☎031-332 3672 Plan:**9** 8hc 1⇨ ⋔ (2fb) CTV ⅢⅢ D5pm

**GH Glendale** 5 Lady Rd ☎031-667 6588 Plan:**10** 7hc (2fb) ⊁ nc3 CTV 8P ⅢⅢ S% B&b£7.50–£9

**GH Glenisla Hotel** 12 Lygon Rd ☎031-667 4098 Plan:**11** 9hc (1fb) CTV 5P ⅢⅢ S% B&bfr£8.50 Bdifr£12 D2.30pm

**GH Golf View Hotel** 2 Marchall Rd (off Dalkeith Rd) ☎031-667 4812 Plan:**12** Apr–Oct Lic 11hc 4⇨ 2⋔ (3fb) CTV 12P ⅢⅢ S% B&b£8.05–£11.50

# Glendale House Hotel

Mrs K Philip, Proprietrix

5 Lady Road, **Edinburgh**

EH16 5PA

Tel: 031-667 6588

Glendale House where comfort and cleanliness are our first priority. A warm welcome is extended to everyone by friendly hostess. Enjoy your breakfast in the wood-panelled dining room. Adjacent to bus route, 10 minutes' from town centre, buses direct every few minutes. Leave your car in the large private car park. Full central heating. TV in most bedrooms.

# DORSTAN PRIVATE HOTEL

7 Priestfield Road, Edinburgh
EH16 5HJ Tel: 031-667 6721

Private car park. Off Dalkeith Road. Near Commonwealth Pool.
Modernised to a high standard.
Fitted wardrobes, H & C, razor points in all bedrooms.
2 bathrooms, TV lounge. Full central heating.
Reduced terms for children. Babysitting.
Evening meals available.

Fire precautions carried out.

Member of the Scottish Tourist Board, and Edinburgh Guest House & Private Hotel Association. Under the personal supervision of the Proprietors: Mr. & Mrs. W. S. Bradford. Send SAE for brochure.

EDINBURGH

# Golf View Hotel

Residents' licence. Adjacent to the Royal Commonwealth Swimming Pool and Tennis Courts. A short putt from the first tee of the Prestonfield Golf Course. Large private car park. All rooms hot and cold, shaver points. Full central heating. Private bathrooms and shower rooms. Under the personal supervision of Mr and Mrs D'Ambrosio.

**2 Marchhall Road, Edinburgh EH16 5HR. (off Dalkeith Road) Tel: 031 667 4812**

**GH Greenside Hotel** 9 Royal Ter ☎031-557 0022 Not on plan Feb–Nov 12hc 1🛏 1🛤 (3fb) CTV ⬛ river B&b£10.35–£12.65

**GH *Grosvenor*** 1 Grosvenor Gdns, Haymarket ☎031-337 4143 Plan:**13** 7hc 2🛏🛤 (3fb) TV ⬛

**GH Halcyon Hotel** 8 Royal Ter ☎031-556 1033 Not on plan *Where meal terms are included in the prices, these meals are taken at Peppermills Restaurant, 4A Royal Terrace.* Feb–Nov 16hc (6fb) ✶ CTV river S% B&b£6.90–£9.20 Bdi£10.90–£13.70 W£71.47–£89.46 ⅃ D7.30pm

**GH Hillview** 92 Dalkeith Rd ☎031-667 1523 Plan:**14** 8hc 1🛏 nc3 CTV 4P ⬛ S% B&b£6.50–£7.25 Bdi£10.45–£11.50 W£72.50–£79 ⅃ D4.30pm

**GH Kildonan Lodge Hotel** 27 Craigmillar Pk ☎031-667 2793 Plan:**15** Lic 8hc (5fb) nc5 CTV 15P ⬛ B&b£9.20 D9.30pm

**GH Kirkridge** 8 Kilmaurs Ter ☎031-667 6704 Not on plan *Students taken during university terms* 7hc (1fb) TV in all bedrooms ⬛ S% B&b£6–£7.50 W£36–£45 Ⓜ

**GH Park Lodge** 13–15 Abercorn Ter, Portobello ☎031-669 9325 Plan:**16** 14rm 11hc 6🛏 (4fb) ✶ Ⓒⓗ CTV 8P ⬛ sea S% B&b£7.50–£9 Bdi£10.50–£12 W£70–£80 ⅃ D10am

**GH *Quinton Lodge*** 24 Polwarth Ter ☎031-229 4100 Plan:**17** Closed Xmas & New Year 6hc (2fb) ✶ CTV 8P ⬛ D6.30pm

**GH Salisbury Hotel** 45 Salisbury Rd ☎031-667 1264 Not on plan 15hc 2🛤 (4fb) CTV 12P ⬛ S% B&b£6.50–£10 Wfr£40 Ⓜ

**GH Sharon** 1 Kilmaurs Ter ☎031-667 2002 Plan:**18** 9hc (3fb) ✶ CTV 5P ⬛ S% B&b£6.50–£9.50

**GH Southdown** 20 Craigmillar Pk ☎031-667 2410 Plan:**19** 8hc (4fb) ✶ CTV 8P ⬛ B&b£5–£6.50 Bdi£8.50–£9.50 D6pm

**GH Thrums Private Hotel** 14 Minto St, Newington ☎031-667 5545 Plan:**20** Lic 6hc 1🛤 (2fb) CTV S% B&b£7–£8

**EGGLESTON** Co Durham *Map 12 NY29*
**INN Moorcock** Hilltop ☎Teesdale 50395 rsNov–May 6hc ⇌ 50P ⬛ river S% B&b£7–£8 Bdi£11–£13 Bar lunch£1.60–£2.20 D9.45pm£5.50alc
See advert on page 92

**ELIE** Fife *Map 12 NO40*
**GH Elms** Park Pl ☎330404 Lic 6rm (2fb) ✶ CTV 8P ⬛ B&b£7 Bdi£11 W£73 ⅃ D6pm

**ELLESMERE** Salop *Map 7 SJ33*
**GH Grange** Grange Rd ☎2735 Lic 12hc 6🛏 1🛤 (2fb) TV available in some bedrooms 20P B&b£9.50–£11 Bdi£14–£15.50 W£90–£100 ⅃ D8.30pm
See advert on page 92

**EMPINGHAM** Leics *Map 4 SK90*
**INN White Horse** ☎221 4rm 3hc TV available in some bedrooms 50P 6⚭ S% B&bfr£10.50 sn Lf3–£6 D9.30pm£4–£8

**EMSWORTH** Hants *Map 4 SU70*
**GH Jingles** 77 Horndean Rd ☎3755 9hc (1fb) CTV 10P ⬛ S% ✳B&b£8–£9 Bdi£10.25–£12 D5pm

**GH Merry Hall Hotel** 73 Horndean Rd ☎2424 Closed Xmas Lic 10hc 7🛏 3🛤 (4fb) ✶ TV in all bedrooms 14P ⬛ S% ✳B&b£9.90–£14.30 Bdi£15.20–£19.80 D7.30pm

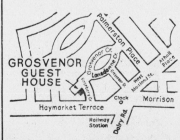

**EVESHAM** Heref & Worcs *Map 4 SP04*
**GH Waterside Family Hotel** 56–59
Waterside ☎2420 Lic 10hc 5🛏 (A 3hc 1🛏)
(6fb) CTV 18P 🎑 B&bfr£8.62 Bdifr£11.97
Wfr£80 ⅃ D7.30pm

**EXETER** Devon *Map 3 SX99* **(See Plan)**
**GH Brayside** 21 New North Rd ☎56875
Plan:**1** 8hc (3fb) ✻nc3 TV in all bedrooms
S% ✳B&b£7–£9

**GH Hotel Gledhills** 32 Alphington Rd
☎71439 Plan:**2** Closed Xmas 12hc (5fb) ✻
CTV 9P 3🍴 🎑 S% B&b£8.05–£13.80
Bdi£11.50–£20.70 W£63.25 ⅃ D5pm

**GH Park View Hotel** 8 Howell Rd ☎71772
Plan:**4** Closed Xmas wk 10hc 2🛏 2🛏 (A 4hc)
(2fb) 🆑 CTV 6P 🎑 B9b£8.63–£10.35
Bdi£12.95–£15.05 W£57.50–£65.50 Ⓜ
(W only Oct–Jun)

**GH Radnor Hotel** 79 St David's Hill ☎72004
Plan:**5** Closed Xmas 9hc (2fb) CTV 7P 🎑
B&bfr£7 Bdifr£11 D2.30pm

**GH Regents Park Hotel** Polsloe Rd ☎59749
Plan:**6** Closed 2wks Xmas 11hc (2fb) CTV
16P S% B&b£8 Bdi£12.50 W£87.50
⅃ D5pm

**GH Sylvania House Hotel** 64 Pennsylvania
Rd ☎75583 Plan:**7** Closed Xmas & New
Year 8hc 1🖙 5🛏 (2fb) CTV 4P 🎑 S% B&b£7–
£8.25

**GH Telstar Hotel** 77 St David's Hill ☎72466
Plan:**8** Closed Xmas 7hc (2fb) ✻ CTV 5P 🎑
S% B&b£6.90–£7.47 Bdi£9.78–£10.35
W£68.46–£72.45 ⅃ D3pm

**GH Trees Mini Hotel** 2 Queen's Cres, York
Rd ☎59531 Plan:**9** rs18 Dec–1 Jan 12hc
(1fb) ✻nc2 CTV 2P 3🍴 🎑 S% B&b£7–£7.50

---

---

---

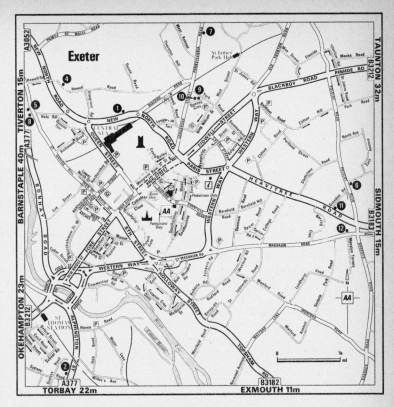

| | | | | | |
|---|---|---|---|---|---|
| 1 | Brayside | 6 | Regents Park Hotel | 9 | Trees Mini Hotel |
| 2 | Hotel Gledhills | 7 | Sylvania House Hotel | 10 | Trenance House Hotel |
| 4 | Park View Hotel | 8 | Telstar House | 11 | Westholme Hotel |
| 5 | Radnor Hotel | | | 12 | Willowdene Hotel |

Bdi£11–£12 W£70–£78 ⅃ D6.30pm
**See advert on page 94**

**GH Trenance House Hotel** 1 Queen's Cres,
York Rd ☎73277 Plan:**10** 10hc 1⇘ (4fb) CTV
9P ▥ S% B&bfr£7 Bdifr£11 D1pm

**GH Westholme Hotel** 85 Heavitree Rd
☎71878 Plan:**11** Closed Xmas & New Year
7hc (1fb) CTV 8P S% ✳ B&b£7

**GH Willowdene Hotel** 161 Magdalen Rd
☎71925 Plan:**12** 8hc (1fb) ⊁ CTV S%
B&b£7.50 W£49 ᛗ

**EXFORD** Somerset *Map 3 SS83*
**GH** *Exmoor House* ☎304 Mar–Oct 5hc (A
12hc) TV 18P ▥ D6pm

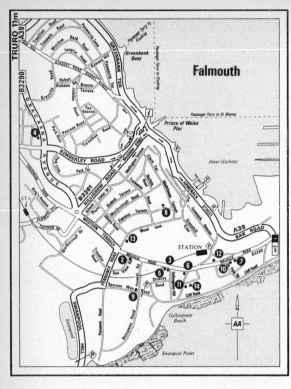

1 Bedruthan
2 Collingbourne
  Hotel
3 Cotswold House
  Private Hotel
4 Hotel Dracaena
5 Evendale Private
  Hotel
6 Gyllyngvase
  House
7 Homelea
8 Langton Leigh
9 Maskee House
10 Milton House
11 Rosemary Hotel
12 Tregenna
13 Trevone Hotel
14 Wickham

**EXMOUTH** Devon *Map 3 SY08*
**GH Anchoria** 176 Exeter Rd ☎72368
Closed Xmas rsOct/Etr 8hc 2⇌ (2fb) ✶ CTV
8P S% ✳ B&b£7 Bdi£11 D4.30pm

**GH Carlton Lodge Free House** Carlton Hill
☎3314 Lic 7hc (2fb) CTV 9P ⦙⦙⦙ S%
✳ B&b£10–£11.50 Bdi£13.50–£15 Dam

**GH Clinton House** 41 Morton Rd ☎71969
Apr–Oct 8hc (2fb) nc5 CTV B&b£6 Bdi£8
W£56 Ⱡ D5.30pm

**GH Dawson's** 8 Morton Rd ☎72321 Etr–
Oct 6hc (2fb) ✶ CTV 2P S% ✳ £5.75–£6.32
Bdi£8.62–£9.20 W£57.50–£63.25 Ⱡ D6.30pm

**GH Dolphin House** 4 Morton Rd ☎3832 Lic
28hc 5⇌ ⦙⦙ (14fb) CTV 6P ⦙⦙⦙ D7.30pm

**GH Morton Villa** 37 Morton Rd ☎73164
Etr–Sep Lic 7hc (3fb) ✶ CTV ⦙⦙⦙

**GH Summerleaze Private Hotel** 79
Salterton Rd ☎79349 Apr–Oct Lic 7hc 1⇌
2⦙⦙ (1fb) ✶ nc10 CTV 12P ⦙⦙⦙ S% B&b£8–£8.50
Bdi£12–£13 W£76.50–£80.50 Ⱡ D8pm

**FAIRBOURNE** Gwynedd *Map 6 SH61*
**GH Liety Heulog** 2–4 Alyn Rd ☎250228
Mar–Oct Lic 12hc (5fb) CTV 12P ⦙⦙⦙ S%
B&bfr£6.90 Wfr£50 Ⱡ D8pm

**FAKENHAM** Norfolk *Map 9 TF92*
**INN Lime's Hotel** Bridge St ☎2726 5hc ✶
CTV 25P ⦙⦙⦙ ✳ B&b£10.50 sn L£5alc
D9pm£6alc

**FALMOUTH** Cornwall *Map 2 SW83* **(See
Plan)**
**GH Bedruthan** 49 Castle Dr ☎311028

**Plan:1** Closed Xmas Lic 6hc (2fb) ⚹ CTV 4P ⨇ sea S% B&b£7–£8 Bdi£10–£11 D2pm

**GH Collingbourne Hotel** Melvill Rd ☎311259 Plan:**2** Apr–Oct Lic 16hc 8ⁿ ⚹ CTV 16P ⨇ sea S% ✱B&b£6.05–£9.50 Bdif£7.75–£11.50 W£52.90–£79.35 ⫽ D8pm

**GH Cotswold House Private Hotel** 49 Melvill Rd ☎312077 Plan:**3** Closed Xmas wk Lic 11hc 2⇔ ⚹ nc13 CTV 12P B&b£7.95–£8.95 Bdi£11.70–£12.50 W£70–£85 ⫽ D5.45pm

**GH Hotel Dracaena** Dracaena Av ☎314470 Plan:**4** Lic 9hc 2⇔ (A 9hc) (6fb) CTV 20P S% B&b£6.90–£8.05 Bdi£8.05–£10.35 D6.30pm

**GH Evendale Private Hotel** 51 Melvill Rd ☎314164 Plan:**5** May–Oct 10hc 3⇔ (4fb) CTV 10P ✱B&b£7.50–£9 Bdi£10.75–£13 W£71.30–£85

**GH Gyllyngvase House Hotel** Gyllyngvase Rd ☎312956 Plan:**6** Mar–Oct Lic 16hc 1⇔ 6ⁿ (2fb) ⚹ CTV 15P B&b£8.63–£9.77 Bdi£12–£13.23 W£86.25–£97.75 ⫽ D7.15pm

**GH Homelea** 31 Melvill Rd ☎313489 Plan:**7** May–Sep 7hc ⚹ nc14 TV 4P B&b£7–£7.50 Bdi£9.50–£10.50 W£65–£69 ⫽ D5pm

**GH Langton Leigh** 11 Florence Pl ☎313684 Plan:**8** Mar–Oct 8hc (4fb) CTV 6P 1⚘ ⨇ sea S% B&b£6.25–£7.50 Bdi£8.50–£10 W£55–£65 ⫽

**GH Maskee House** Spernen Wyn Rd ☎311783 Plan:**9** Apr–Oct 7hc (2fb) ⚹ CTV 6P 2⚘ ⨇ sea S% ✱B&b£6–£8 W£40–£52 M

**GH Milton House** 33 Melvill Rd ☎314390 Plan:**10** rsOct–Apr (booking only) 7hc ⚹ nc5 CTV 6P sea

**GH Rosemary Hotel** 22 Gyllyngvase Ter ☎314669 Plan:**11** End Mar–Oct Lic 11hc (6fb) CTV 4P sea S% ✱B&b£8.05–£10 Bdi£9.20–£12 W£59.80–£81.65 ⫽ D6.30pm

**GH Tregenna** 28 Melvill Rd ☎313881 Plan:**12** Lic 6hc (2fb) CTV 4P sea S% B&b£6 Bdi£8–£9.50 W£53–£63.50 ⫽

**GH Trevone Hotel** 33 Wood Ln ☎313123 Plan:**13** Apr–Oct Lic 16hc 1⇔ 3ⁿ (4fb) CTV 12P sea S% B&b£8.50–£11 Bdi£12.50–£17 W£78–£95 ⫽ D6.30pm
**See advert on page 96**

**GH Wickham** 21 Gyllyngvase Ter ☎311140 Plan:**14** Mar–Oct 10hc (2fb) ⚹ nc3 CTV 3P sea S% B&b£6.50–£7.50 Bdi£9–£10.50 W£60–£70 ⫽ D5pm

**FAREHAM** Hants *Map 4 SU50*
**GH Carrick House** 11–13 East St ☎234678 Lic 9hc (4fb) CTV S% ✱B&b£7.50–£8.50 D8pm

**GH Maylings Manor Hotel** 11A Highlands Rd ☎286451 Lic 28hc 20⇔ ⁿ (4fb) ⨇ D9.30pm

**FARNHAM** Surrey *Map 4 SU84*
**GH Eldon Hotel** 43 Frensham Rd, Lower Bourne ☎Frensham 2745 Lic 14hc 7⇔ 2ⁿ 60P ⨇ S% ✱B&b£12.50–£16 Bdi£16.50–£26 D9.45pm

**FAZELEY** Staffs *Map 4 SK20*
**GH Buxton House Hotel** 65 Coleshill St ☎Tamworth 4392 Lic 12rm 11hc 4⇔ ⁿ (3fb) CTV 15P ⨇ D5pm

**FEATHERSTONE PARK** Northumb *Map 12 NY66*

---

**INN** *Wallace Arms Hotel* ☎Haltwhistle
20375 Lic 3hc nc5 CTV 36P ⓜ ⇔ D9pm

**FENITON** Devon *Map 3 ST19*
**GH Colestocks House** Colestocks (1m N
unclass rd) ☎Honiton 850633 Mar–Sep Lic
6hc 2⇝ 2⋔ (2fb) ✹ nc12 CTV 6P S%
✱B&b£8–£12 Bdi£10.50–£13.50 W£66.50–
£87.50 ⓁD7.30pm

**FERNDOWN** Dorset *Map 4 SU00*
**GH Broadlands Hotel** West Moors Rd
☎877884 Lic 12hc 1⇝ (2fb) CTV 15P S%
B&b£9.75–£10.50 Bdi£13.75–£15 W£91.50–
£99.50 ⓁD6.30pm

**FFESTINIOG** Gwynedd *Map 6 SH64*
**GH Newborough House Hotel** Church Sq
☎2682 Lic 6hc (4fb) nc4 CTV 4P S%
B&bfr£8.25 Bdi fr£12.65 Wfr£80.50 Ⓛ

**FIDDLEFORD** Dorset *Map 3 ST81*
**INN** *Fiddleford* ☎Sturminster Newton
72489 Closed Xmas day 4hc nc14 30P ⓜ
D10pm

**FILEY** N Yorks *Map 8 TA18*
**GH Beach Hotel** The Beach ☎Scarborough
513178 Apr–Oct Lic 22hc (12fb) CTV sea S%
B&b£8.05 Bdi£8.91–£11.21 W£67.37–
£78.47 ⓁD6pm

**GH Downcliffe Hotel** The Beach
☎Scarborough 513310 Apr–Oct Lic 17hc 4⋔
(9fb) CTV 9P 1⚓ sea ✱B&b£7.50 Bdi£8.25–
£8.95 W£57.75–£62.65 ⓁD6pm

**GH Southdown Hotel** The Beach
☎Scarborough 513392 Etr–Sep Lic 25hc 1⇝
1⋔ (12fb) CTV 4P sea S% B&b£9.20

Bdi£10.92 W£68.82–£96.60 ⓁD6pm (W only
18 Jul–29 Aug)

**FLAX BOURTON** Avon *Map 3 ST56*
**INN Jubilee** Farleigh Rd ☎2741 4hc nc14
45P S% ✱B&b£8.05 Bar lunch fr£1&alc
D10pm£5alc

**FLEETWOOD** Lancs *Map 7 SD34*
**GH** *Southbrook Private Hotel* 41 The
Esplanade ☎3944 Lic 10hc (2fb) CTV 4P
D9pm

**FLUSHING** Cornwall *Map 2 SW83*
**GH Nankersey Hotel** St Peters Rd ☎Penryn
74471 Lic 7hc (3fb) ✹ nc3 CTV river sea S%
✱B&b£8.05–£9.20 Bdi£12.65–£13.80
W£76.48–£84.52 Ⓛ

**FOLKESTONE** Kent *Map 5 TR23* **(See Plan)**
**GH Argos Private Hotel** 6 Marine Ter
☎54309 Plan:**1** Lic 9hc (2fb) nc3 CTV ⓜ S%
B&b£8–£8.62 Bdi£10.35–£12.07 W£74.75–
£86.25 ⓁD9pm

**GH Arundel Hotel** 3 Clifton Rd ☎52442
Plan:**2** 16 Feb–Oct Lic 13hc (4fb) ✹ CTV ⓜ
S% B&b£6.90–£9.20 Bdi£9.20–£11.50
W£52.90–£64.40 ⓁD3pm

⋈**GH Beaumont Private Hotel** 5 Marine
Ter ☎52740 Plan:**3** Lic 8hc (2fb) CTV ⓜ
B&b£5.75–£6.90 Bdi£8.75–£10.35 Dam

**GH Belmonte Private Hotel** 30 Castle Hill
Av ☎54470 Plan:**4** Apr–Oct 10hc (A 4hc)
(2fb) ✹ nc3 CTV 8P S% B&b£8–£8.75 Bdi£10–
£11 W£53–£60 D6pm

**GH Claremont Private Hotel** 20–22
Claremont Rd ☎54897 Plan:**5** Lic 14hc (4fb)

**Trevone Hotel**

**33 Woodlane, Falmouth,
Cornwall.
Tel: Falmouth (0326) 313123**

Very comfortable LICENSED Georgian style
hotel conveniently situated between town,
beaches and harbour. 17 bedrooms; some
family rooms — children sharing rooms at
reduced rates — and "en suite" rooms. Sea
views. Large garden with sun terrace. Mid-week
bookings — home cooking — car park. Relaxed
friendly atmosphere.
*Brochure with pleasure from Cornish proprietors:
Mr & Mrs A Holmes.*

**Colestocks House**

**Colestocks, Feniton, Honiton, Devon, EX14 0JR.
Telephone: (0404) 850633**

Thatched Georgian house, painted pink
and set in 2 acres of beautiful
landscaped gardens. A delightful place
to stay. Hotel facilities of 2 lounges,
colour TV, licensed, separate tables,
and choice of menu. Most bedrooms
have private bath/shower and toilet.
Colestocks is between Feniton and
Payhembury, in a quiet country setting.
*Brochure from R W and G A Denton.*

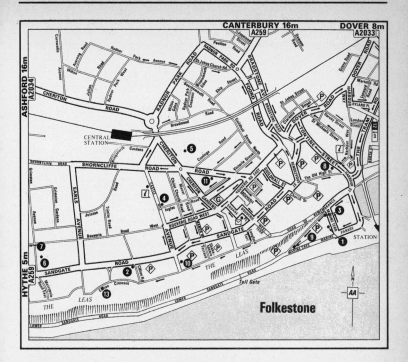

**Folkestone**

1 Argos Private
  Hotel
2 Arundel Hotel
3 Beaumont
  Private Hotel
4 Belmonte Private
  Hotel

5 Claremont
  Private Hotel
6 Horseshoe
  Private Hotel
8 Micheal's
9 Pier Hotel

11 Shannon Private
   Hotel
12 Wearbay
13 Westward Ho!
   Private Hotel

✳ nc8 CTV 7P 卿 S% B&bfr£10.35 Bdifr£15.23
W£56.92–£75.90 ㋏

**GH Horseshoe Private Hotel** 29
Westbourne Gdns ☎52184 Plan:**6** Etr–Oct
10hc (2fb) ✳ nc6 CTV 15P 卿 S% B&b£7.50–
£8 Bdi£9–£9.50 W£54–£60 ㋏ Dnoon

**GH Michael's** 35 Tontine St ☎55961 Plan:**8**
Mar–Dec Lic 12hc (2fb) ✳ CTV 卿 D10.30pm

**GH Pier Hotel** 1 Marine Cres ☎54444
Plan:**9** Lic 28hc (7fb) CTV sea D6pm

**GH Shannon Private Hotel** 59–61 Cheriton
Rd ☎52138 Plan:**11** Apr–Sep Lic 24hc 2⇔ 🏠
CTV 11P D7.15pm

**GH Wearbay Hotel** 25 Wearbay Cres
☎52586 Plan:**12** Lic 12hc 1⇔ (1fb) CTV 1☎
sea S% B&b£7–£12.10 Bdi£12–£17.95
W£77–£118.65 ㋏ D11pm

**GH Westward Ho! Private Hotel** 13 Clifton
Cres ☎52663 Plan:**13** Lic 11hc (6fb) CTV 卿
lift sea S% B&b£9.20–£10.35 Bdi£12.65–
£13.80 W£57.50–£80.50 ㋏ D5pm

**FONTMELL MAGNA** Dorset Map 3 ST81
**GH Estyard House Hotel** ☎811460 Closed
Nov & Xmas 6hc nc10 8P 卿 S% B&b£7.75
Bdi£11.50 W£74 D3pm

**FORDINGBRIDGE** Hants Map 4 SU11
**GH Oakfield Lodge** 1 Park Rd ☎52789 Feb–
Oct 10hc (2fb) ✳ CTV 10P B&b£7–£7.50

**FORRES** Grampian Moray Map 14 NJ05

⊬ **GH Regency** 66 High St ☎72558 Lic
7hc CTV S% B&b£5–£6 D6pm

**FORT WILLIAM** Highland Inverness-shire
Map 14 NN17
**GH Benview** Beford Rd ☎2966 Mar–Nov
15hc (2fb) CTV 20P B&b£6.90–£9.20
Bdi£11.50–£13.80 D7pm

**GH Guisachan** Alma Rd ☎3797 15hc (4fb)
CTV 14P 卿 lake S% B&b£6–£7.50 Bdi£9–
£11.50 W£63–£80.50 ㋏ D5.30pm

**GH Hillview** Achintore Rd ☎4349 Apr–Sep
9hc (2fb) CTV 9P 卿 lake S% ✳ B&b£5.50
Bdi£9.50

**GH Innseagan** Achintore Rd ☎2452 Apr–
Oct Lic 26hc 12⇔ (2fb) CTV 30P 卿 lake S%
B&b£6–£8.50 Bdi£10.50–£13 D7pm

⊬ **GH Loch View** Heathercroft, off Argyll
Ter ☎3149 Etr–Oct 7hc 1⇔ (3fb) CTV 8P 卿
lake S% B&b£5.50–£6

**GH Rhu Mhor** Alma Rd ☎2213 Mar–Oct
7hc (2fb) ✳ CTV 7P lake S% B&b£6–£6.50
Bdi£9–£9.50 D5pm

**GH Stronchreggan View** Achintore Rd
☎4644 Apr–Oct 7hc (5fb) ✳ CTV 7P 卿 lake
S% Bdifr£10 Wfr£70 ㋏ D6.30pm

**FOVANT** Wilts Map 4 SU02
**INN Cross Keys Hotel** ☎284 Closed 2wks
autumn 4hc ✳ nc CTV 20P 卿 ✳ B&b£7.15
Bar lunch55p–£2.95 D9pm£7–£9

97

**FOWEY** Cornwall *Map 2 SX15*
**GH Ashley House Hotel** 14 Esplanade
☎2310 Mar–Nov Lic 8hc (3fb) CTV sea S%
B&b£7.50–£8.50 Bdi£11.50–£12.50 W£70–£80
↳ D5pm

**GH Carnethic House** Lambs Barn ☎3336
Mar–Oct Lic 7hc 2⋔ (2fb) ⊁ nc10 CTV in all
bedrooms 20P ⦏ S% B&b£9.46–£11.77
Bdi£14.37–£16.68 W£95.56–£110.92 ↳ D6pm

**GH Polmear** 62 Esplanade ☎3464 6hc (1fb)
⊁ nc8 TV sea S% B&b£6–£8 Bdi£10–£12
W£56–£70 ↳ D5pm

**FOWNHOPE** Heref & Worcs *Map 3 SO53*
**GH Bowens Farm** ☎430 rsXmas Lic 6hc
(1fb) nc10 CTV 6P 4🏖 ⦏ B&b£8.50–£9 Bdi£13–
£14 W£85–£89 ↳ D9pm

**FOYERS** Highland *Inverness-shire Map 14
NH42*
**GH Foyers Bay House** Lower Foyers
☎Gorthleck 631 6hc (2fb) CTV P 4🏖 ⦏ lake
S% ✳B&b£6.25 Bdi£11.25 W£70 ↳ D8.30pm

**FRADDON** Cornwall *Map 2 SW95*
**GH Denmar** ☎St Austell 860359 Lic 6hc
(2fb) ⊁ Cⁿ CTV 8P ⦏ S% B&bfr£6 Bdi£7–£8
W£52–£59 ↳ D6.30pm (W only late Jul & Aug)

**GH St Margaret's Private Hotel** ☎St
Austell 860375 Lic 13hc CTV 20P ⦏ S%
B&bfr£8.05 Bdifr£10.35 Wfr£69 ↳

**FRESHWATER** Isle of Wight *Map 4 SZ38*
**GH Blenheim House** Gate Ln ☎752858
May–Oct Lic 9hc 5⋔ (5fb) ⊁ nc5 CTV 8P 4🏖

# The Bowens Farmhouse

*Country Guest House*

Fownhope, Hereford
Telephone: (043277) 430
Have you discovered our hospitable hideaway nestling
under the Herefordshire hills?
Intimate, comfortable 18th century farmhouse, recently
completely refurbished, providing high standard
accommodation. 5 double/twin rooms with showers
H & C, tea/coffee making facilities, central heating. 1
single room. Oak beamed dining room. Log fire. Sitting
room. Colour TV. All rooms tastefully decorated. Highly
recommended for traditional cooking, own/local fresh
produce. Peaceful village setting in large attractive
grounds with putting & croquet. Superb views.
Excellent centre for walking/touring Wye Valley, Welsh
Marches, Malverns etc. Bicycles for hire. Bargain
breaks October — May. Licensed. No children under
10. On B4224 Ross — Hereford. B & B from £8.50 per
person, dinner optional.

# ...Bed & breakfast

## Foyers Bay House
### Lower Foyers, Inverness
### Tel: Gorthleck 631

Stay for a night or two at Foyers Bay House
where we have 6 bedrooms to let, each with
wash-hand basin. Residents' dining room and
lounge with television. Evening meal available.
The house stands in its own grounds along a
quiet, private drive. Loch Ness is a short walk
away as are the famous Falls of Foyers.

**Lambs Barn, Fowey, Cornwall.**
**Telephone: (072 683) 3336**
*For those who appreciate peace, comfort and
old-fashioned standards.*
This delightful Regency house, peacefully
situated in tranquil countryside, ten minutes
from the sea at Fowey. Newly refurbished,
Carnethic provides gracious accommodation
and good food under the personal
supervision of your hosts Timothy and
Kathryn Tozer. All bedrooms are centrally
heated and have colour TV. Most have a
shower en suite. A licensed bar, and heated
outdoor swimming pool are available for
guests' enjoyment. Ample parking for cars
and boats. Brochure on request.

**Carnethic House**

⭢ sea S% B&bf£7.80–£8.40 Bdi£12–£12.60
W£78–£81.60 ⭠ D7pm
**GH Saunders Hotel** Coastguard Ln
☎752322 Lic 13hc (7fb) [ch] CTV 10P sea S%
B&bf£8–£9 Bdi£11–£13 W£77–£80 ⭠ D5pm

**FRINTON-ON-SEA** Essex *Map 5 TM21*
**GH Forde** 18 Queens Rd ☎4758 6hc (1fb) ⭢
nc5 TV 1P ⭢ S% B&bf£7 Bdi£10.50 W£60 ⭠
D6.30pm

**GH Montpellier** 2 Harold Gr ☎4462 Feb–
Oct 8hc (3fb) CTV 7P S% B&bf£9 Bdi£15
W£90 ⭠ D7pm

**GH Uplands** 41 Hadleigh Rd ☎4889 Closed
Xmas rsOct–Feb (wknds only) Lic 6hc (2fb)
CTV 8P ⭢ S% B&bf£8–£8.50 Bdi£10–£10.50
W£63.50–£65.50 ⭠ D5pm

**GAERWEN** Gwynedd *Map 6 SH47*
**INN *Holland Arms*** ☎651 Lic 6hc CTV 40P
⭢ D9pm

**GAIRLOCH** Highland *Ross & Crom Map 14
NG87*
**GH Horisdale House** Strathgairloch ☎2151
Apr–Sep rsMar & Oct 9hc (3fb) ⭢ nc7 CTV
20P ⭢ lake S% B&bf£7–£8 Bdi£11–£12 W£73–
£80 ⭠ D5pm

**GARFORTH** W Yorks *Map 8 SE43*
**GH Coach House Hotel** 58 Lidgett Ln
☎Leeds 862303 5 Jan–21 Dec 6hc (A 3hc)
(1fb) CTV 10P 2⭢ ⭢ S% B&bf£9

**GARGRAVE** N Yorks *Map 7 SD95*
**GH Kirke Syke** 19 High St ☎356 Lic 5hc (A

# *Saunders Hotel*

### Coastguard Lane, Freshwater Bay, PO40 9QX.
### Telephone: Freshwater 752322

*Relax in a quiet Area of
Outstanding Natural Beauty*
Saunders Hotel is superbly situated amid National
Trust country, 150 yards from the sea and near to
the Golf Course. The Hotel has a comfortable TV
Lounge, Bar Lounge, Games Room and a spacious
Sun Lounge overlooking a lawned garden. All
bedrooms have washbasins. The Resident
Proprietors have a reputation for making their
Guests feel welcome and for providing excellent
food. Bookings accepted on any day for any length
of stay.

# HORISDALE HOUSE
### Strath, Gairloch, Wester Ross. Tel: Gairloch 0445-2151

Amenities offered at Horisdale House:
Centrally heated throughout. Hot & Cold in all
bedrooms. Shaving light & point over basin
mirrors. Continental quilts. Fully carpeted.
Ample wardrobes. Spacious lounge and dining
room. Car park for twenty cars. Home baking.
Breakfast and evening meal. Afternoon teas
available. Modern very comfortable Guest
House with panoramic views of the loch and
Torridon peaks. Use our house as a centre for
exploring Wester Ross: Inverewe Gardens 6
miles, Loch Maree 9 miles, Beinn Eighe Nature
Reserve 19 miles, or enjoy Gairloch's sandy
beaches, nine hole golf course, sea angling and
hill walking. Please write for our brochure.

# 𝕿rumble's Hotel & Restaurant

### Stanhill, Charlwood, Surrey
### Telephone: Crawley (0293) 862212

A family-run country house offering
accommodation and well cooked food. The
Restaurant is highly noted for its excellent
food. 5 bedrooms, 2 with traditional four-
poster beds—all with private bathrooms, tea
& coffee making facilities, colour TV and
radio. Full central heating. Open for lunch
and dinner.

*BTA Commendation award.*          *Gatwick 4 miles*

4hc 3⇔ 2⋒) CTV 10P ▥ S% B&bf7.50 Bdif12 Wf84 ⫶ Dnoon

**GARTMORE** Central *Perths Map 11 NS59*
**GH Baad Springs Farm** ☎Aberfoyle 207 Apr–Oct Lic 3rm 1⇔ 2⋒ (1fb) CTV 6P S% ✶B&bf8 Bdif13 Wf50 D5pm

**GATWICK AIRPORT, LONDON** W Sussex *Map 4 TQ24*
**GH Barfield Farm** Stanhill, Charlwood ☎Norwood Hill 862545 Closed Xmas & New Year 5hc (3fb) ⊁ nc4 CTV 8P 4⋒ ▥ S% B&bf8–f10

**GH Barnwood Hotel** Balcombe Rd, Crawley ☎Crawley 882709 Closed Xmas Lic 28hc 1⇔ 26⋒ (14fb) ⊁ (except guide dogs) CTV 35P ▥ ⅙ S% B&bf17.25 D8.45pm

**GH Frames Skylodge Motel** London Rd,

County Oak, Crawley (2m S of airport on A23) ☎Crawley 514341 Lic 21hc 21⇔ ⋒ ⊁ CTV 45P ▥

**GH Gainsborough Lodge** 39 Massetts Rd, Horley (2m NE of airport adjacent A23) ☎Horley 3982 9hc 3⋒ (1fb) ⊁ TV 10P ▥ B&bf19–f24

**GH Trumbles Hotel & Restaurant** Stanhill, Charlwood ☎Crawley 862212 Closed Xmas & New Year Lic 5hc 2⇔ 3⋒ ⊁ nc9 CTV in all bedrooms 20P ▥ B&bf15 D8.45pm
**See advert on page 99**

**GIGGLESWICK** N Yorks *Map 7 SD86*
**GH Woodlands** The Mains ☎Settle 2576 Closed Xmas & New Year Lic 10hc (2fb) ⊁ nc3 CTV 10P ▥ S% B&bf10.35 Bdif16 Wf105 ⫶ Dnoon

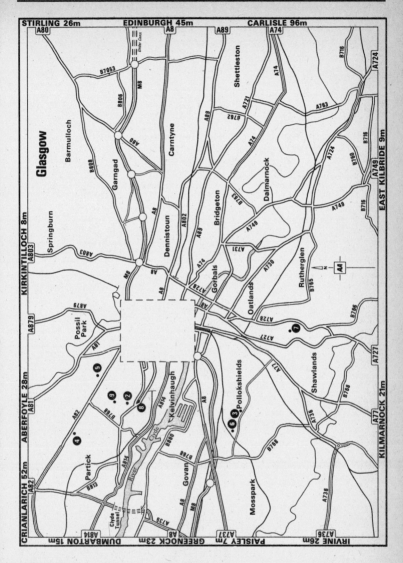

| | | | | |
|---|---|---|---|---|
| **2** | Chez Nous | **5** | Kelvin Private | |
| **3** | Dalmeny Hotel | | Hotel | |
| **4** | Devonshire Hotel | **6** | Linwood House | |

| | | |
|---|---|---|
| **7** | Marie Stuart Hotel | |
| **8** | Smith's Hotel | |
| **9** | Wilkie's | |

**GLASGOW** Strathclyde *Lanarks* Map 11 *NS56* **(See Plan)**

**GH** *Burnbank Hotel* 67–85 West Prince's St ☎041-332 4400 Not on plan 36hc 5⇨ ⋔ (4fb) CTV ⊪ D7pm

**GH Chez Nous** 33 Hillhead St, Hillhead ☎041-334 2977 Plan:**2** Lic 15rm 14hc (2fb) CTV 9P ⊪ S% B&bf6.90–£7.50 Bdif11.65–£12.25 D4.30pm

**GH Dalmeny Hotel** 62 St Andrews Dr, Nithsdale Cross ☎041-427 1106 Plan:**3** Lic 10hc 2⇨ 2⋔ (1fb) ⊁ CTV 20P ⊪ S% B&bf12.42–£20.13

**GH Devonshire Hotel** 5 Devonshire Gdns, Gt Western Rd, Kelvinside ☎041-334 1308 Plan:**4** Tem 22hc 2⇨ 2⋔ (5fb) CTV 8P ✳ B&bfrf8.05 Bdi frf12 D8pm

**GH Kelvin Private Hotel** 15 Buckingham Ter, Hillhead ☎041-339 7143 Plan:**5** 14hc (2fb) Ch CTV 5P ⊪ S% B&bf10–£12.50 Wf65–£82.50 ℳ

**GH Linwood House** 356 Albert Dr, Pollokshields ☎041-427 1642 Plan:**6** 16hc (2fb) ⊁ CTV 7P ⊪ S% B&bf7.50–£8.50

**GH Marie Stuart Hotel** 46–48 Queen Mary Av, Cathcart ☎041-423 6363 Plan:**7** Closed 1 Jan Lic 34hc 8⇨ 1⋔ (4fb) CTV 20P ⊪ S% ✳ B&bf12.50 Bdif16.50 D7.30pm

**GH Smith's Hotel** 963 Sauchiehall St ☎041-339 7674 Plan:**8** 26hc (7fb) ✻ CTV ⪢ S% B&bf8.05–£10.35

**GH Wilkie's** 14–16 Hillhead St, Hillhead ☎041-339 6898 Plan:**9** Closed Xmas & New Year 13hc (12fb) CTV 5P B&bf6.50–£7.50

**GLASGOW AIRPORT** Strathclyde *Renfrews Map 11 NS46*
**GH Ardgowan** 92 Renfrew Rd, Paisley ☎041-889 4763 11 Jan–19 Dec 6hc (3fb) TV available in some bedrooms 6P ⪢ S% B&bf8.50–£10.50

**GH Broadstones Private Hotel** 17 High Calside, Paisley ☎041-889 4055 8hc (2fb) CTV 12P ⪢ S% B&bf9–£10

**GLASTONBURY** Somerset *Map 3 ST53*
**GH Hawthorn House Hotel** 8–10 Northload St ☎31255 Lic 12hc (2fb) ✻ CTV 2☎ ⪢ B&bf7.47–£8.05 Wf50.60–£54.59 Ⓜ D8pm

**GLENCOE** Highland *Argyll Map 14 NN15*
**GH Dunire** ☎Ballachulish 318 6hc (4fb) TV 10P ⪢ S% ✳B&bf5.50–£6 Bdif8–£8.50 D6.30pm

ⵀ **GH Scorrybreac** ☎Ballachulish 354 Jan–Oct 5hc (2fb) ✻ nc5 CTV 8P ⪢ lake S% B&bfr£5.50 Bdifr£8.50 D6.30pm

**GLENRIDDING** Cumbria *Map 11 NY31*
**GH Bridge House** ☎236 Mar–Oct 6hc (3fb) 7P ⪢ lake S% B&bfr£6.50

**GLOSSOP** Derbys *Map 7 SK09*
**GH Crowton's** 14 High St East ☎63409 Closed Xmas Lic 6hc ✻ nc5 TV in all bedrooms 20P ⪢ ✳B&bf10 D9pm

**GH Hurst Lee** Derbyshire Level, Sheffield Rd ☎3354 Closed Xmas & New Year Lic 6hc (1fb) CTV 6P ⪢

**GLOUCESTER** Glos *Map 3 SO81*
**GH Alma** 49 Kingsholm Rd ☎20940 8hc (2fb) ✻ nc10 TV 5P 1☎ ⪢ S% B&bf6.50–£8

**GH Claremont** 135 Stroud Rd ☎29540 6hc (3fb) TV in all bedrooms 6P ⪢ S% B&bf5.50–£7.50 Wfrf35 Ⓜ

**GH Hucclecote Garden Hotel & Restaurant** 164 Hucclecote Rd ☎67374 Lic 12hc 2🛏 1🚿 (1fb) ✻ CTV 20P ⪢ S% B&bf10 Bdif14.50 Wf82.50 ⅃ D10.30pm

**GH Monteith** 127 Stroud Rd ☎25369 8hc (3fb) CTV 8P ⪢ S% ✳B&bf6.50–£7

**GH New Bridge Hotel** West End Ter ☎34792 Lic 10hc (3fb) CTV 8P S% B&bf7.50–£8.50 Bdif10.50–£12 Wf45–£50 Ⓜ D9pm

**GH Stanley House Hotel** 87 London Rd ☎20140 Lic 5hc 2🛏 (A 11hc 5🛏) (2fb) Ⓒʰ CTV 35P 1☎ ⪢ S% B&bf8.22–£8.85 Bdif11.22–£11.85 Wf53.13 ⅃ D7pm

**GOLSPIE** Highland *Sutherland Map 14 NH89*
ⵀ **GH Glenshee** Station Rd ☎3254 6hc (2fb) Ⓒʰ CTV 12P ⪢ S% B&bf5–£5.50

**GOMSHALL** Surrey *Map 4 TQ04*
**INN Black Horse** ☎Shere 2242 6hc 🚿 ✻ nc12 CTV 60P B&bf14.95 Bdif23 sn Lf4–£5.50 D9.30pm£7–£9.50

**GOONHAVERN** Cornwall *Map 2 SW75*
**GH Reen Cross Farm** ☎Perranporth 3362

Closed Xmas Lic 9hc (3fb) CTV 15P 1🐾 S%
B&b£6–£6.50 Bdi£9–£10 W£65–£68 ⊬

**GOREY** Jersey, Channel Islands *Map 16*
**GH Lavender Villa Hotel** Grouville ☎Jersey
54937 Apr–Oct Lic 17hc 11⇌ (2fb) ⚲nc6
CTV 18P ⅏ S% B&b£13–£16 D6.30pm

**GORRAN HAVEN** Cornwall *Map 2 SX04*
**GH Perhaver** ☎Mevagissey 2471 Etr–mid
Oct Lic 5hc ⚲ nc CTV 5P sea S% Bdi£12–
£12.50 W£72.50–£75 ⊬ D5pm

**GOSPORT** Hants *Map 4 SZ69*
**GH Bridgemary Manor Hotel** Brewers Ln
☎Fareham 232946 Lic 16hc CTV 15P
D5.30pm

**GOUROCK** Strathclyde *Renfrews Map 10
NS27*
**GH Claremont** 34 Victoria Rd ☎31687 6hc
(2fb) CTV ⅏ river S% B&b£7 W£49 Ⓜ

**GOVILON** Gwent *Map 3 SO21*
**GH Llanwenarth House** ☎Gilwern 830289
Lic 4rm 3⇌ 1🛁 (1fb) ⒸⒽ CTV 10P ⅏ B&b£13–
£15 Bdi£20–£25 W£120 ⊬ D7.30pm

**GRAMPOUND ROAD** Cornwall *Map 2
SW95*
**INN Midway** ☎St Austell 882343 Closed
Xmas 4hc ⚲ CTV 4P S% B&b£8.10–£8.75
Bdi£11.85–£12.85 W£82.75–£89.75 ⊬ Bar
lunch fr£3.50&alc Dfr£4.50&alc

**GRANGE** *(in Borrowdale)* Cumbria *Map 11
NY21*
**GH Grange** ☎Borrowdale 251 Apr–Oct 7hc
1⇌ 1🛁 (1fb) 7P ⅏ river S% B&b£7.50
Bdi£12.50 W£84 ⊬ D4.30pm

**GRANGE-OVER-SANDS** Cumbria *Map 7
SD47*
**GH Elton Private Hotel** Windermere Rd
☎2838 9hc (3fb) CTV 6P S% B&b£6.50–£7.50
Bdi£9–£9.50 W£60–£65 ⊬ D6pm

**GH Grayrigge Private Hotel** Kents Bank Rd
☎2345 Lic 28hc 3⇌ (A 11hc) (19fb) CTV 60P
6🐾 ⅏ sea S% ✳B&b£7.50–£8.50 Bdi£13
D7pm

**GH Thornfield House** Kents Bank Rd
☎2512 Etr–mid Oct 6hc (2fb) ⚲nc5 CTV 6P
⅏ sea S% B&bfr£6.50 Bdifr£10 Wfr£70 ⊬
D2pm

**GRANSMOOR** Humberside *Map 8 TA15*
**GH Gransmoor Lodge Country House**
☎Burton Agnes 340 Lic 6hc (3fb) ⚲ CTV 12P
S% B&b£10–£12 Bdi£13.50–£15.50
W£84–£98 ⊬ D5pm

**GRANTOWN-ON-SPEY** Highland *Moray
Map 14 NJ02*
**GH Braemoray Private Hotel** Main St
☎2303 Feb–Nov Lic 7hc 3⇌ 🛁 (1fb) CTV 6P
⅏ D7.30pm

**GH Dar-il-Hena** ☎2929 Etr–Oct 7hc (3fb)
CTV 10P ⅏ S% B&bfr£7.75 Bdifr£12 Wfr£80 ⊬
D7pm

**GH Dunachton** off Grant Rd ☎2098 Jan–
Oct 7hc (2fb) ⚲ CTV 8P ⅏ B&b£6.90–£7.40
Bdi£10.25–£10.90 W£65–£72 ⊬ D7pm

**GH Kinross House** Woodside Av ☎2042
Closed Xmas 6hc (2fb) 6P ⅏ S%
✳B&bfr£8.50 Bdifr£12.90 Wfr£87 ⊬ D4.30pm

**GH Pines Hotel** Woodside Av ☎2092 Etr–
Sep 10hc (2fb) ⒸⒽ CTV 4P S% B&bfr£7
Bdifr£11 D7pm

**GH Riversdale** Grant Rd ☎2648 7hc (3fb)
ⒸⒽ CTV 8P ⅏ S% B&b£6.50–£7 Bdi£9.50–£10
W£63–£66.50 D6pm

**GH Umaria** Woodlands Ter ☎2104 7hc (4fb)
TV 10P S% ✳B&b£6.50–£7 Bdi£10.50–£11
Wfr£70 ⊬ D5pm

**GRASMERE** Cumbria *Map 11 NY30*
**GH Beck Steps** College St ☎348 end Mar–6
Nov Lic 10hc 1⇌ (2fb) nc4 8P ⅏ S%
B&b£8.50–£10 Bdi£13–£15 W£96 ⊬ D7pm

**GH Bridge House Hotel** ☎425
Mar–Oct Lic 12hc 4⇌ 🛁 (1fb) 20P D4pm

⋈ **GH Chestnut Villa Private Hotel**
Keswick Rd ☎218 Closed Jan & Feb 8hc
(2fb) 10P ⅏

**GH Dunmail** Keswick Rd ☎256 6hc (2fb) ⚲
nc3 CTV 6P S% B&b£7–£8 Bdi£11–£12 W£75–
£85 ⊬ D5.30pm

**GH Lake View** Lake View Dr ☎384 Mar–
Nov 7hc CTV 10P lake S% B&bfr£9 Bdifr£14
Wfr£93 ⊬ Dnoon

**GH Meadow Brow** ☎275 Mar–Nov Lic 3hc
⚲ 10P ⅏ S% B&b£9 Bdi£16 W£100 ⊬

**GH Titteringdales** Pye Ln ☎439 Apr–Oct
Lic 6hc (2fb) TV 8P ⅏ S% B&b£8.50–£9.50
Bdi£13.50–£14.50 W£92–£100 ⊬ D5pm

**GREAT**
Placenames incorporating the word 'Great',
such as Gt Malvern and Gt Yarmouth, will be
found under the actual placename, *ie*
Malvern, Yarmouth

**GRETNA** Dumfries & Galloway
*Dumfriesshire Map 11 NY36*
**GH Surrone House** Annan Rd ☎341 Lic 6⇌
🛁 (5fb) ⚲ CTV 20P ⅏ ✳B&b£10.35
Bdi£15.35

# "DAR-IL-HENA"

Grant Road, Grantown-on-Spey,
Morayshire PH26 3LA

Telephone Grantown-on-Spey 2929
(STD 0479)

A warm welcome awaits you from the proprietors
Jack and Ann Bairstow in this well situated guest
house standing in approx 1 acre. Good home
cooking, hot and cold in all rooms, centrally heated
throughout, car park, residents' lounge etc. Within
easy reach of the River Spey, golf course and tennis
courts etc. Reasonable terms.

**GRETNA GREEN** Dumfries & Galloway *Dumfriesshire Map 11 NY36*
⊢⊣ **GH Greenlaw** ☎361 Etr–Oct 8hc (1fb) CTV 8P sea S% B&b£5.50–£6

**GRIMSBY** Humberside *Map 8 TA20*
**INN *Wheatsheaf Hotel*** Bargate ☎54729 Closed Xmas Lic 4hc ★ nc10 TV 60P ⅢⅢ

**GUERNSEY** Channel Islands *Map 16*
**See Câtel, St Martin, St Peter Port, St Saviour**

**GUILDFORD** Surrey *Map 4 SU94*
**GH Blanes Court Hotel** Albury Rd ☎73171 Lic 15hc 1⇔ 7⋒ (1fb) CTV in all bedrooms 26P ⅢⅢ S% B&b£9.49–£19.50 Bdi£14.99–£25 D9.30pm

**GUILDTOWN** Tayside *Perthshire Map 11 NO13*
**INN *Angler's Rest*** Main Rd ☎Balbeggie 329 Lic 5hc ★ nc3 CTV 40P ⇏ D9.30pm

**GWBERT-ON-SEA** Dyfed *Map 2 SN15*
**GH Anchor Hotel** ☎Cardigan 612638 Lic 13hc (3fb) CTV 12P ⅢⅢ river sea S% ✱B&bfr£7.50 Bdi fr£11.50 W£50–£60 ⱡ D8pm

**HALESWORTH** Suffolk *Map 5 TM37*
**INN *Angel Hotel*** The Thoroughfare ☎3365 Lic 8hc 2⇔ ⋒ CTV 100P 6⌂ sn D9pm

**HALFORD** Warwicks *Map 4 SP24*
**INN *Halford Bridge*** ☎Stratford-on-Avon 740382 Lic 8hc CTV 50P 2⌂ sn D9pm

**HALTWHISTLE** Northumb *Map 12 NY76*
⊢⊣ **GH Ashcroft** ☎20213 Closed Xmas & New Year 8hc (3fb) [Ch] CTV 12P S% B&b£5.50–£6 Bdi fr£8 D6pm

**HALWELL** Devon *Map 3 SX75*
**GH Stanborough Hundred Hotel** ☎East Allington 236 Lic 7hc 1⇔ (4fb) ★ CTV 10P ⅢⅢ S% B&b£9–£12.50 Bdi£13–£17 W£60–£80 ⱡ D9.30pm

**HAMPTON COURT** Gt London *London plan 4 D2 (page 134)*
**INN Cardinal Wolsey** The Green ☎01-941 3781 18hc 1⇔ CTV 25P ⅢⅢ S% ✱B&b£6.94–£12.50 Bdi£13.01–£18.06 W£43.73–£78.75 M̸ sn L£5.50&alc D9.30£5.50&alc

**HAMPTON HILL** Gt London *London plan 4 D2 (page 134)*
**GH *Jasmin House*** 88–94 High St ☎01-977 2117 9hc 4⇔ ⋒ (A 4hc) (5fb) ★ CTV 5P ⅢⅢ

**HARLECH** Gwynedd *Map 6 SH53*
**GH Cemlyn** ☎780425 Etr–Sep Lic 7hc (3fb) ★ nc10 CTV ⅢⅢ sea S% B&b£10 Bdi£15 D9.30pm

**INN Rum Hole Hotel** ☎780477 8hc 3⋒ CTV 25P ⅢⅢ S% B&b£8–£12 W£56–£70 M̸ Bar lunch75p–£2.50 D9.30pm75p–£2.50

**HARLOW** Essex *Map 5 TL41*
**INN *Green Man Hotel*** Mulberry Green ☎21342 Lic 6hc 50P ⇏ sn D9pm

**HARROGATE** N Yorks *Map 8 SE35*
**GH Alexa House Hotel** 26 Ripon Rd ☎501988 Lic 7hc (2fb) ★ [Ch] CTV 8P 3⌂ ⅢⅢ S% B&b£7.50–£8.50 Bdi£11.45–£13.45 W£72–£84.75 ⱡ D6pm

**GH Alvera Court Private Hotel** 76 Kings Rd ☎55735 6hc 1⇔ 1⋒ (2fb) ★ CTV 4P ⅢⅢ S% B&b£8.50 Bdi£12.50 D6pm

**GH Boston Hotel** 3–7 Swan Rd ☎502918 Lic 20hc (2fb) CTV 10P S% B&b£10 Bdi£15 W£119 D8pm

**GH Carlton Hotel** 98 Franklin Rd ☎64493
Lic 10hc (2fb) ✠ CTV 8P ⬚ S% B&bf9–£9.50
Bdi£13–£13.50 W£82–£85 ⌇

**GH Franklin Private Hotel** 25 Franklin Rd
☎69028 Lic 6hc nc5 CTV S% B&bf7 W£45 Ⓜ

**GH Gillmore Hotel** 98 King's Rd ☎503699
Lic 18hc 2🛏 (7fb) CTV 18P 2🚿 ⬚ S% B&bf8–
£8.25 Bdi£11–£11.25 D6.30pm

**GH Hartington** Franklin Mount ☎69534
14hc 4🛏 (2fb) CTV 8P ⬚ S% B&bf7.20–£7.60
Bdi£11.20–£11.80 W£74.22–£76.96 ⌇ D6pm

**GH Ingleside Hotel** 37 Valley Dr ☎502088
Closed Xmas 9hc 6🛏 (1fb) ✠ CTV ⬚ S%
B&bfr£11.50 Bdifr£16.50 Wfr£112 ⌇ D10am

**GH Manor Hotel** 3 Clarence Dr ☎503916
Lic 16hc (5fb) Ⓒⓗ CTV 6P ⬚ S% B&bf10.92–
£12 Bdi£15.50–£17.50 D8.30pm

**GH Moorland Private Hotel** 34 Harlow
Moor Dr ☎64596 Lic 10hc (2fb) ✠ CTV 3P ⬚
S% B&bf7 Bdi£11.50

**GH Norman Hotel** 41 Valley Dr ☎502171
Lic 14hc 4⇌ 4🛏 (3fb) CTV B&bf10.50–£12.50
Bdi£16–£18 W£116–£130 ⌇ D6pm

**GH Oakbrae** 3 Springfield Av ☎67682
Closed Xmas 6hc (1fb) CTV 4P ⬚ S% B&bf6–
£7 Bdi£9.50–£10.50 D4pm

**GH Prince's** 7 Granby Rd ☎883469 Lic 6hc
1🛏 (1fb) ✠ CTV 4🚿 ⬚ S% B&bf8–£9 Bdi£12–
£13.50 W£80–£90 ⌇ D4pm

**GH Roan** 90 Kings Rd ☎503087 Closed
Xmas 6hc (2fb) ✠ CTV ⬚ S% ✱ B&bfr£7
Bdifr£10.50 D4.30pm

**GH Shelbourne** 78 Kings Rd ☎504390
Closed 25 & 26 Dec Lic 7hc (2fb) ✠ CTV 1P ⬚
S% B&bf9–£10 Bdi£13–£14 W£78–£84 ⌇
D6.30pm

**GH Springfields** 80 Kings Rd ☎67166
Closed Xmas & New Year 6hc (2fb) ✠ CTV
5P ⬚ B&bf9.35–£9.90

**GH Strayend** 56 Dragon View, Skipton Rd
☎61700 6hc (2fb) CTV 6P ⬚ S% B&bf7.50–
£8 Bdi£11–£11.50 D10am

**GH Youngs Private Hotel** 15 York Rd
☎67336 Closed Nov Lic 13hc 7⇌ 3🛏 (3fb)
CTV 11P 2🚿 ⬚ S% B&bf9.75–£10.75
Bdi£16.25–£17.25 W£102.50–£109 ⌇ D6.30pm

**HARROW** Gt London *London plan 4 A2
(page 134)*

**GH Harrow Hotel** 12–18 Pinner Rd ☎01-
427 3435 rsXmas Lic 79hc 11⇌ 35🛏 (A 11hc
3⇌ 8🛏) (12fb) Ⓒⓗ CTV in all bedrooms 46P
⬚ S% ✱ B&bf15–£26.50 Bdi£20.95–£32.45
D9.30pm

**GH Hindes Hotel** 8 Hindes Rd ☎01-427
7468 13hc 1🛏 (2fb) ✠ CTV 6P ⬚ S%
B&bf10–£12.65

**HARTLAND** Devon *Map 2 SS22*
**INN Anchor** Fore St ☎414 11hc 5⇌ ✠ CTV
10P 6🚿 S% ✱ B&bf7.70–£9.20 Bdi£12.20–
£13.70 W£48–£58 ⌇ D9pmf6.10alc

**HARWICH** Essex *Map 5 TM23*
**GH Hotel Continental** 28 Marine Pde,
Dovercourt Bay ☎3454 Lic 8hc (3fb) CTV 6P
sea S% B&bf9.50–£10.50 Bdi£14.50–
£15.50

**HASTINGS & ST LEONARDS** E Sussex
*Map 5 TQ80*
**GH Bryn-y-Mor** 12 Godwin Rd ☎441755 Lic
4rm 1⇌ 1🛏 (A 2rm) (2fb) Ⓒⓗ CTV ⬚ sea

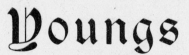

B&b£8.05–£10.93 Bdi£13.23–£17.25 W£69–
£97.75 ⫶ D8pm

**GH Burlington Hotel** 2 Robertson Ter
☎424303 Lic 15hc 1⇔ (2fb) TV in all
bedrooms ▥ sea S% B&b£9.95–£15
Bdi£14.20–£19.25 W£49.95–£95 ⫶ D8pm

**GH Chimes Hotel** 1 St Mathews Gdns
☎434041 Closed Nov Lic 11hc 2⇔ (2fb) CTV
▥ S% B&b£9–£12 Bdi£14.50–£18
W£85–£105 ⫶ D4pm

**GH Eagle House** 12 Pevensey Rd, St
Leonards ☎430535 Lic 14hc 1⇔ 9🏠 (3fb)
nc10 CTV 8P ▥ S% B&b£9.75–£11.50
Bdi£16.75–£18.50 D7.30pm

⊬⊣ **GH Gresford** 12 Devonshire Rd
☎424745 Closed Nov Lic 9hc (3fb) ⚓ CTV 1P
S% B&b£5.95–£6.25 Bdi£8.95–£9.25 W£60–
£63 ⫶ Dnoon

**GH Harbour Lights** 20 Cambridge Gdns
☎423424 8hc (1fb) ⚓ CTV ▥ S% B&b£6.50
Bdi£8.75 W£61.25 ⫶ Dam

**GH Russell Hotel** 35 Warrior Sq ☎431990
Lic 12hc (2fb) CTV S% B&b£9.50–£11.50
Bdi£13.50–£15.50 W£75–£100 ⫶ D6.30pm

**GH *Waldorf Hotel*** 4 Carlisle Pde ☎422185
Lic 12hc (3fb) ⚓ CTV Dnoon

**HATHERLEIGH** Devon *Map 2 SS50*
**INN Bridge** Bridge St ☎357 4hc nc5 20P ▥
S% B&b£7.95 Bdi£13 W£75.90 ⫶ sn
D9.30pm£4.50–£6&alc

**HAVERFORDWEST** Dyfed *Map 2 SM91*
**GH Elliots Hill Hotel** Camrose Rd ☎2383
Lic 21hc 1🏠 (4fb) ⒸⒽ CTV 30P 2☎ ▥ S%
✱B&b£7.47 Bdi£12.65 W£66.70–£69 ⫶

**HAWKSHEAD** Cumbria *Map 7 SD39*
**GH Highfield House** Hawkshead Hill ☎344
Closed Dec Lic 12hc 2⇔ (4fb) nc2 12P ▥
B&b£11–£12.75 Bdi£15.75–£17.50 W£105–
£115 ⫶ D5pm

**GH Ivy House** ☎204 Mar–Nov Lic 6hc 1🏠
(A 5hc) (3fb) CTV 12P ▥ S% B&bfr£8.50
Bdifr£12.50 Wfr£74 ⫶ D5pm

**GH Rough Close Country House** ☎370
Apr–Oct 6hc (2fb) ⚓ CTV 12P ▥ lake S%
B&b£7

**INN King's Arms Hotel** ☎372 6hc ⇎ CTV ▥
✱B&b£8 sn L£3.50alc D9.30pm£4.50alc

**HAYFIELD** Derbys *Map 7 SK08*
**GH Hazel** 1/2 Valley Rd ☎New Mills 43671
9hc 2🏠 (1fb) CTV 9P ▥ S% ✱B&b£8–£13.50

**HAYLING ISLAND** Hants *Map 4 SU70*
**GH Avenue** 5 Wheatlands Av ☎3121 7hc
(2fb) ⚓ CTV 8P ▥ S% B&b£6.50–£7.50
Bdi£10.50–£11.50 W£73.50–£80.50 ⫶

**HEASLEY MILL** Devon *Map 3 SS73*
**GH Heasley House** ☎North Molton 213
Mar–Oct Lic 7hc 1⇔ (2fb) nc6 CTV 11P 1☎
▥ S% B&b£6.50 Bdi£11.50 W£75 ⫶ D7pm

**HEATHFIELD** E Sussex *Map 5 TQ52*
**GH Broadhurst** Swife Ln, Broad Oak (3½m
NE A265) ☎West Burwash 461 4hc 2⇔ (1fb)
nc2 CTV 8P ▥ S% B&b£8–£9.50 Bdi£12–
£13.50 W£80.50–£91 ⫶ D9.30am

**HEDDON'S MOUTH** Devon *Map 3 SS64*
**INN Hunters** ☎Parracombe 230 Mar–Dec
12hc 6⇔ CTV 20P S% B&b£8–£13 Bdi£13–£18
W£48–£78 Ⓜ sn L£2.50–£5 D9pm£5–£7&alc

**HELENSBURGH** Strathclyde *Dunbartons*
*Map 10 NS28*
**GH Aveland** 91 East Princes St ☎3040 6hc
(2fb) nc5 CTV 6P river S% B&b£6–£6.50
Bdi£9.50 W£57–£67 ⫽ D6pm

**HELSBY** Cheshire *Map 7 SJ47*
**GH Poplars Private Hotel** 130 Chester Rd
☎3433 25 Dec–1 Jan 7hc (2fb) ⊁ CTV 10P ▥
S% B&b£8.50 Bdi£12 W£77 ⫽ D4pm

**HELSTON** Cornwall *Map 2 SW62*
**GH Bona Vista** 22 Meneage Rd ☎2579 Lic
6hc TV 10P D6pm

**GH Hillside** Godolphin Rd ☎4788 Closed
Xmas Lic 6hc (2fb) ⊁ CTV 6P S% B&b£6
Bdi£9.50 W£64 ⫽ Dnoon

**HEMEL HEMPSTEAD** Herts *Map 4 TL00*
**GH South Lea Private Hotel** 8 Charles St
☎3061 Closed Xmas 11hc (1fb) ⊁ CTV 8P
1🏠 ▥ S% ✱ B&b£10–£17

**GH Southville Private Hotel** 9 Charles St
☎51387 14hc (3fb) CTV 9P ▥ S% B&b£9
W£63 Ⓜ

**HENLEY-ON-THAMES** Oxon *Map 4 SU78*
**GH Sydney House Hotel** Northfield Rd
☎3412 Lic 10hc 1⇌ (4fb) ⊁ CTV 7P ▥ S%
B&bfr£10

**HENSTEAD** Suffolk *Map 5 TM48*
**GH Henstead Hall Country Hotel**
☎Lowestoft 740345 Lic 14hc (3fb) nc5 CTV
14P D6pm

**HEREFORD** Heref & Worcs *Map 3 SO54*
**GH Ferncroft Private Hotel** 144 Ledbury Rd
☎65538 Jan–Nov Lic 10hc (2fb) ⊁ CTV 8P ▥
S% ✱ B&b£8–£8.50 Bdi£12–£12.50 W£80 ⫽
D7pm

**GH Munstone House** Munstone (2m N
unclass rd off A49) ☎67122 Feb–Nov 6hc
(3fb) ⊁ TV 17P S% B&b£6.50–£7.50

**HERNE BAY** Kent *Map 5 TR16*
**GH Northdown Hotel** 14 Cecil Pk ☎2051
Lic 5hc (A 3hc) (3fb) ☑ CTV 8P ▥ S%
B&b£8–£10 Bdi£13–£15 W£83–£95 ⫽ D8pm

**HERSTMONCEAUX** E Sussex *Map 5 TQ61*
**GH Cleavers Lyng Country Hotel** ☎3131
Feb–23 Dec Lic 8hc ☑ CTV 20P ▥ S%
B&b£8.50–£9 Bdi£11–£12.50 W£70–£79 ⫽
D6pm

**HERTFORD** Herts *Map 4 TL31*
**GH Tower House Private Hotel** 2 Warren
Park Rd, Bengeo ☎53247 Lic 6hc 1⇌ (1fb)
CTV 4P ▥ S% B&b£7

**HEWISH** Avon *Map 3 ST46*
**GH Kara** ☎Yatton 834442 Mar–Oct Lic 7hc
(2fb) ⊁ TV 7P ▥ S% B&b£6–£8.50 Bdi£8–£12
W£52–£75 ⫽ D6.30pm

**HEYSHAM** Lancs *Map 7 SD46*
**GH Carr-Garth** Bailey Ln ☎51175 May–mid
Oct 10hc (5fb) ⊁ CTV 7P S% B&bfr£6.15
Bdifr£8.05 Wfrf£52.33 ⫽

**HIGH WRAY** Cumbria *Map 7 SD39*
**GH Balla Wray Country Hotel** ☎Ambleside
3308 Mar–Oct 8hc (3fb) ⊁ nc5 CTV 10P lake

**HIGH WYCOMBE** Bucks *Map 4 SU89*
**GH Amersham Hill** 52 Amersham Hill
☎40431 Closed 2wks Xmas 7hc (1fb) ⊁ TV
in all bedrooms 9P ▥ S% ✱ B&b£7.75

**GH Clifton Lodge Private Hotel** 210–212
West Wycombe Rd ☎29062 12rm 1⇌ (A
3rm) (1fb) CTV 12P ▥ S% ✱ B&bfr£8.40
Bdifr£12 Dnoon

**GH Drake Court Hotel** London Rd ☎23639
Lic 19hc 2⇌ (5fb) ⊁ CTV 30P ▥ S%
B&b£10.50–£15 Bdi£15.50–£20.50 D8pm

**HILLESLEY** Avon *Map 3 ST78*
**INN Fleece** ☎Wotton-under-Edge 3189 Lic
3hc nc10 TV 30P 🚲 D9pm

**HILL HEAD** Hants *Map 4 SU50*
**GH Seven Sevens Private Hotel** Hill Head
Rd ☎Stubbington 2408 8hc 2⇌ 1🔥 (1fb)
CTV 8P ▥ sea S% B&b£7.50 W£52.50 Ⓜ

**HINCKLEY** Leics *Map 4 SP49*
**GH Cecilia's Private Hotel** 13–19 Mount Rd
☎637193 Closed Xmas Lic 8hc CTV 8P
▥ S% ✱ B&b£8.50

**HINDON** Wilts *Map 3 ST93*
**INN Grosvenor Arms**
☎253 Closed Xmas wk 3hc 8P S% B&b£10
Bdi£13.50 W£85 ⫽ Bar lunch£2–£6 D£4–£9

**HITCHIN** Herts *Map 4 TL12*
**GH Redcoats Farmhouse Hotel** Little
Wymondley ☎Stevenage 3500 Closed 1wk
Xmas Lic 7hc 1🔥 (A 3🔥) (2fb) CTV 40P S%
✱ B&b£16–£19 Bdi£24–£29 D9pm

**HOLMROOK** Cumbria *Map 6 SD09*
**GH Carleton Green** ☎608 Apr–Oct 6hc 1⇌
nc8 TV 6P ▥ S% B&b£10 Bdi£15 W£86 ⫽
D7pm

**HOLNE** Devon *Map 3 SX76*
**INN Church House** ☎Poundsgate 208 5hc
🚲 nc14 TV 7P ▥ S% B&b£11 Bdifr£15.50
Wfrf£55 Ⓜ sn L£4.50alc D10pmf£4.50alc

**HOLNEST** Dorset Map 3 ST61
**GH Manor Farm Country House** Holnest
Park ☎474 Apr–Oct Lic 10hc 5⇔ (2fb) CTV
20P ⚅ B&bf8.50–£9.50 Bdi£13.50–£14.50
W£90–£95 ⌇ D7.30pm

**HOLT** Norfolk Map 9 TG03
**GH Lawns Private Hotel** Station Rd ☎3390
Mar–Nov Lic 9hc 1⇔ (1fb) CTV 9P ⚅
B&bf7.50–£8 Bdi£12–£13 W£84–£91 ⌇
D6pm

**HONITON** Devon Map 3 ST10
**INN Monkton Court** Monkton (2m E A30)
☎2309 9hc 3⇔ ⇌ TV in all bedrooms 150P
⚅ S% ✷ B&bf11.50–£17 Bdi£16.50–£22
W£60–£100 Ⓜ sn L£3alc D£5alc

**HOOK** Hants Map 4 SU75
**GH Oaklea** London Rd ☎2673 Lic 10hc (3fb)
CTV 10P S% ✷ B&bf8.50 Bdi£13 D6.30pm

**HOPE COVE** Devon Map 3 SX63
**GH Fern Lodge** ☎Galmpton 561326 Mar–
Oct 5hc 2⇔ (A 2hc) (2fb) TV 4P 3⚘ ⚅ sea
✷ B&bf5.75–£6.75 Bdi£8.75–£9.50 W£60.95–
£65.95 ⌇ D7pm

**GH Sand Pebbles Hotel** ☎Galmpton
561673 Mar–Nov rsJan & Feb (wknds only)
Lic 10hc 5⇔ 4⋔ (2fb) CTV 10P sea S%
B&bf7.50–£12.50 Bdi£12.50–£17.50 W£89–
£120 ⌇ D8pm

**HOPTON CASTLE** Salop Map 7 SO37
**GH Lower House Country Lodge**
☎Bucknell 352 Mar–Dec Lic 4hc ⚲ nc14
CTV 10P 2⚘ S% B&bf12.90 Bdi£19.90
W£127.50 ⌇ D6pm

**HORNSEA** Humberside Map 8 TA24
**GH Promenade Hotel** Marine Dr ☎2944
Closed Oct & Xmas 12hc (4fb) ⚲ CTV 17P ⚅
sea B&bfr£6.50 Bdi fr£10 Wfr£60 ⌇ D6pm

**GH Hotel Seaforth** Esplanade ☎2616 7hc
(3fb) CTV 4P ⚅ S% B&bf6.50–£8.50 Bdi£10–
£12 W£65 D4pm

**HORRABRIDGE** Devon Map 2 SX56
**GH Overcombe** ☎Yelverton 3501 Lic 7hc
2⋔ (2fb) ⒸⒽ CTV 7P ⚅ S% B&bf8.75–£9.80
Bdi£14–£15.50 W£89–£97.65 ⌇ D7.15pm

**HORSHAM** W Sussex Map 4 TQ13
**GH Wimblehurst Private Hotel** 6
Wimblehurst Rd ☎62319 14hc 2⇔ ⋔ (3fb) ⚲
CTV 14P ⚅ D6pm

**HORSHAM ST FAITH** Norfolk Map 9 TG21
**GH Elm Farm Chalet** Norwich Rd
☎Norwich 898366 Closed Xmas 12hc 4⋔ ⚲
CTV P S% B&bf8–£12 Bdi£12.50–£16.50
W£85.75–£113.75 ⌇ D5pm

**HORTON** Dorset Map 4 SU00
**INN Horton** ☎Witchampton 840252 7hc
3⇔ 4⋔ ⇌ CTV 100P ⚅ ✷ B&bf21.27 sn
L£5.50alc D10pm£7.50alc

**HORTON-IN-RIBBLESDALE** N Yorks Map 7
SD87
**INN Crown** ☎209 10hc ⇌ CTV 20P ⚅
B&bf8.90–£9.80 Bdi£14–£15.45 W£91.40–
£100.60 ⌇ Bar lunch £1.50alc

**HOVE** E Sussex Map 4 TQ20 **See also
Brighton**
**GH Bigwood Lodge Hotel** 40 Old

# Overcombe Hotel

## Horrabridge, Yelverton, Devon

A friendly, family-run hotel on
west Dartmoor between Plymouth and
Tavistock. A comfortable base for exploring
Devon and Cornwall. Conveniently placed
for walking, riding, golf, sea and river
fishing. Children and dogs welcome. Good
home cooking. Licensed. Open all the year
including Christmas. Special walking
week-ends and winter bargain breaks.
Pam & Richard Kitchin.

Tel: Yelverton (082 285) 3501.

# Oaklea Guesthouse

**London Road, Hook, Hampshire. Telephone: Hook 2673; residents 2150**

We are as well placed for the business man
and woman visiting Basingstoke, Reading or
Camberley (London Airport 35 min.) as for
the holidaymaker travelling to London or
the West Country.
We have single, double and family
bedrooms, a TV lounge and a small
comfortable bar; we offer our guests the
very best of home cooking and can by
arrangement cater for small lunch and
dinner parties.
Proprietors: Mr & Mrs T R Swinhoe

Shoreham Rd ☎Brighton 737430 Lic 16hc 4⇔ ⋒ (1fb) CTV 4P 4⌂ ▥ D4pm

**GH Croft** 24 Palmeira Av ☎Brighton 732860 Apr–Nov 12hc (4fb) CTV ▥ S% B&b£7.50–£8.50

**GH *Polonia Hotel*** 36–38 St Aubyns ☎Brighton 733640 Lic 51hc ★ Ch CTV 28P lift ▥ sea D8pm

**GH Tatler Hotel** 26 Holland Rd ☎Brighton 736698 Lic 12hc (3fb) CTV ▥ S% ✻B&b£8 Bdi£11.50 W£80 ℒ Dmidday

**GH Whitehaven Hotel** 34 Wilbury Rd ☎Brighton 778355 rsXmas & New Year (B&b only) Lic 12⋒ (2fb) ★ nc5 CTV in all bedrooms ▥ S% B&b£15–£17.50 Bdi£20.50–£23 W£100–£126 ℒ D7.30pm

**HOWEY** Powys *Map 3 SO05*
**GH Corven Hall Country** Llandrindod Wells ☎Llandrindod Wells 3368 Lic 7rm 6hc (2fb) Ch TV 6P 2⌂ S% B&b£6 Bdi£9.50 W£55 ℒ D6pm

**HOYLAKE** Merseyside *Map 7 SJ28*
**GH *Sandtoft Hotel*** 70 Alderley Rd ☎051-632 2204 Lic 9hc CTV 10P 3⌂ ▥ D6pm

**HUBBERHOLME** N Yorks *Map 7 SD97*
**INN George** ☎Kettlewell 223 3hc ⊠ ★ nc5 10P ▥ S% B&b£9 Bdi£13 Bar lunch£3.35alc D8.30pm£4.50alc

**HUDDERSFIELD** W Yorks *Map 7 SE11*
**GH Cote Royd Hotel** 7 Halifax Rd, Edgerton ☎47588 Closed 3rd wk July, 1wk Xmas Lic 14hc 5⇔ 2⋒ CTV 15P 6⌂ S% ✻B&b£14 Bdi£19 D8.30pm

**GH Dryclough House Hotel** Dryclough Rd, Crossland Moor ☎651731 Closed Xmas Lic 10hc 1⇔ CTV 12P 3⌂ ▥ B&bfr£8 Bdi fr£12 D1pm

**HULL** Humberside *Map 8 TA02*
**GH Ashford** 125 Park Av ☎492849 6hc (1fb) ★ CTV 6P ▥ S% B&b£8.25 Bdi£12.45 D6pm

**INN *Good Fellowship*** Cottingham Rd ☎42858 Lic 7hc CTV 200P 2⌂ ▥ D7.30pm

**HUNA** Highland *Caithness Map 15 NO37*
⊢⊣ **GH Haven Gore** ☎John O' Groats 314 5hc (3fb) CTV 8P ▥ sea S% B&b£5–£6 Bdi£8–£9

**HUNDLETON** Dyfed *Map 2 SM90*
**INN *Corston Guest House*** Axton Hill ☎Castlemartin 242 Lic 12hc ★ TV 30P ▥ ⊠ D6pm

**HUNSTANTON** Norfolk *Map 9 TF64*
**GH Caley Hall Motel** ☎33486 Lic 21hc 16⇔ (6fb) CTV 30P ▥ S% B&b£10.50–£11 Bdi£15.75–£16.25 W£98–£104 ℒ D9pm

**GH Dolphin Private Hotel** 15 Cliff Ter ☎2583 Lic 10hc (6fb) CTV ▥ S% B&b£10 Bdi£14.50 W£91.35 ℒ D9pm

**GH Driftwood Hotel** Lynn Rd ☎2241 Lic 9hc 1⋒ (4fb) CTV 30P S% B&b£10–£11 Bdi£14–£16 W£60–£100 ℒ D9.30pm

**GH Lincoln Lodge Private Hotel** Cliff Pde ☎2948 Mar–5 Nov rs6 Nov–Jan Lic 12rm 4hc (6fb) CTV 8P ▥ sea S% B&b£8–£9.50 Bdi£13–£14.50 W£90–£100 ℒ D8.45pm

**GH *Norfolk Private Hotel*** 32 Kings Lynn Rd ☎2383 Lic 11hc 2⇔ ⋒ (6fb) CTV 14P ▥ ♿ D6.30pm

**GH Sutton House Hotel** 24 Northgate ☎2552 Closed last 3wks Nov Lic 10hc (3fb) CTV 7P ▥ sea S% B&b£7.50–£8.50 Bdi£11–£12 W£52–£56 ℒ D9.30pm

**GH Tolcarne Private Hotel** 3 Boston Sq ☎2359 Etr–mid Oct Lic 11hc (2fb) nc2 CTV 8P ▥ S% B&b£8–£9 Bdi£12–£13.50 W£76–£85 ℒ D5pm

**HUNTINGDON** Cambs *Map 4 TL27*
**INN *Black Bull*** Post St, Godmanchester (1m S B1043) ☎53310 Lic 8hc ★ CTV 30P 6⌂ ⊠ D7pm

**HURN** Dorset *Map 4 SZ19*
**INN *Avon Causeway Hotel*** ☎Christchurch 482714 Lic 9hc TV 50P

**HUTTON-LE-HOLE** N Yorks *Map 8 SE79*
**GH Barn** ☎Lastingham 311 Lic 10hc (1fb) ★ CTV 16P 2⌂ ▥ S% ✻B&b£7.75–£12

**HYTHE** Kent *Map 5 TR13*
**GH Dolphin Lodge** 16 Marine Pde ☎69656 6hc 1⇔ (3fb) ★ nc3 CTV 6P ▥ sea S% B&b£7–£8 Bdi£11–£12.50 W£55–£68 ℒ D6pm

**ICKENHAM** Gt London *London plan 4 B1 (page 134)*
**GH Woodlands** 84 Long Ln ☎Ruislip 34830 9hc ★ nc5 CTV 9P ▥ S% ✻B&b£8.50

**ICKLESHAM** E Sussex *Map 5 TQ81*
**GH Snailham House** Broad St ☎556 Apr–mid Oct Lic 6hc (1fb) ★ CTV 7P ▥ S% B&b£7–£9 Bdi£10.25–£12.25 W£62.50–£77 ℒ D5.30pm

**ILFORD** Gt London *London plan 4 B6 (page 135)*

**GH Blenheim House Hotel** 2 Blenheim Av, Gants Hill ☎01-554 4138 Lic 9hc (2fb) ✻ nc5 CTV 4P 1☎ ▥ S% B&bf13.80 Bdif19.55 D4pm

**GH Cranbrook Hotel** 24 Coventry Rd ☎01-554 6544 Lic 16hc 11♒ (8fb) TV in all bedrooms 11P 2☎ ▥ S% B&bf10.95–£15.50 Bdif13.95–£18.50 Wf97.65–£129.50 ⫽ D9.30pm

**GH Park Hotel** 327 Cranbrook Rd ☎01-554 9616 Lic 20hc 2⇔ 1♒ (2fb) CTV 23P ▥ S% B&bf10.50 Bdif14 D8pm

**ILFRACOMBE** Devon *Map 2 SS54* **See Plan**
**GH Avenue Private Hotel** Greenclose Rd ☎63767 Plan:**1** Apr–Oct Lic 24hc (6fb) ✻

CTV B&bf8–£10.75 Bdif11.75–£14 Wf70–£87 ⫽ D7pm

**GH Blenheim** 5 St James Pl ☎63787 Plan:**3** Etr–Aug Lic 11hc (1fb) nc5 CTV S% B&bf6–£7 Bdif8.50–£10 Wf59–£65 ⫽ D4pm

**GH Briercliffe Hotel** 9 Montpelier Ter ☎63274 Plan:**4** Jan–Oct & Xmas Lic 10hc (4fb) ✻ nc2 CTV 5P sea S% ✱B&bf7–£8.50 Bdif10–£11.50 Wf66.50–£73.50 ⫽ (W only July & Aug) D5pm

⊢⊣ **GH Carbis Private Hotel** 50 St Brannocks Rd ☎62943 Plan:**5** Jan–Nov Lic 10hc (5fb) ✻ CTV 10P S% B&bf5.25–£7 Bdif8–£9.75 Wf54–£65 ⫽

**GH Collingdale Hotel** Larkstone Ter ☎63770 Plan:**6** Closed Nov Lic 9hc (4fb) ✻ CTV sea S% B&bf7–£8.50 Bdif10–£11.50 Wf66–£75 ⫽

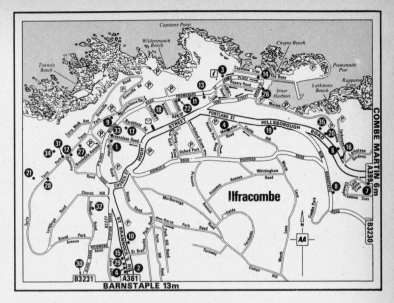

| | | | | |
|---|---|---|---|---|
| **1** | Avenue Private Hotel | **15** | Lantern House Hotel | **27** Southcliffe |
| **3** | Blenheim | **16** | Laston House Private Hotel | **28** South Tor Hotel |
| **4** | Briercliffe | | | **29** Strathmore Private Hotel |
| **6** | Carbis | **17** | Lympstone Private Hotel | **30** Sunny Hill |
| **6** | Collingdale Hotel | **18** | Marlyn | **31** Torrs Private Hotel |
| **7** | Combe Lodge Hotel | **19** | Merrydene Private Hotel | **32** Wentworth House Private Hotel |
| **8** | Craigmillar | **20** | New Cavendish Hotel | **33** Westbourne Private Hotel |
| **9** | Cresta Private Hotel | **21** | Norbury | **34** Westwell Hall Private Hotel |
| **10** | Cromwell Private Hotel | **22** | Queen's Court Hotel | **35** Wilson |
| **11** | Dèdés Hotel | **25** | Rosebank Hotel | |
| **12** | Elmfield Hotel | **26** | Royal Brittania (Inn) | |
| **13** | Glendower | | | |
| **14** | Headlands Hotel | | | |

**GH Combe Lodge Hotel** Chambercombe
Park Rd ☎64518 Plan:**7** Etr–Oct Lic 9hc
(3fb) CTV 7P sea B&b£7 Bdif£11 W£49–£77 ⥮
D6.30pm

**GH Craigmillar** 22 Crofts Lea Pk (New
Barnstaple Rd) ☎62822 Plan:**8** Spr Bank
Hol–end Sep 8hc ⊀ nc1 CTV 5P sea
D4pm

**GH Cresta Private Hotel** Torrs Pk ☎63742
Plan:**9** mid May–mid Oct rsEtr Lic 29hc 20⋒
(12fb) [ch] CTV 30P ▥ S% B&b£9.20–£12.65
Bdif£11.20–£15 W£76.48–£112.70 ⥮ D6.30pm

**GH Cromwell Private Hotel** 20–21 St
Brannocks Rd ☎63829 Plan:**10** Lic 15hc 2⇌
(4fb) CTV 40P 2🏠 ▥ S% B&b£7–£8.75 Bdif£9–
£11 W£60–£73.50 ⥮

**GH** *Dèdés Hotel* 1–2 The Promenade
☎62545 Plan: **11** Etr–mid Oct Lic 17hc 6☞
🛏 (A 5hc) (6fb) CTV sea D9.45pm

**GH Elmfield Hotel** Torrs Pk ☎63377
Plan: **12** Mar–Nov & Xmas Lic 9hc (5fb) 🗶 Ch
CTV 12P sea S% B&b£6–£8 Bdi£8–£10 D4pm

**GH** *Glendower* Sea Front, Wilder Rd
☎62121 Plan: **13** Lic 12hc CTV 22P 🕮 sea
D7.30pm

**GH Headlands Hotel** Capstone Cres
☎62887 Plan: **14** Apr–Oct Lic 26hc (5fb) CTV
12☎ sea S% B&b£8–£11 Bdi£10.50–£14
W£65–£85 ⅃ D6.30pm

**GH Lantern House Hotel** 62 St Brannocks
Rd ☎64401 Plan: **15** Lic 9hc CTV 9P 🕮 S%
B&b£6 Bdi£10 W£63–£72 ⅃

**GH Laston House Private Hotel**
Hillsborough Rd ☎62627 Plan: **16** Lic 12hc
5☞ 2🛏 (5fb) CTV 12P 🕮 sea S% B&b£9–£11
Bdi£12–£15 W£78.50–£92.50 ⅃ D6pm

**GH Lympstone Private Hotel** 14 Cross Pk
☎63038 Plan: **17** Closed Xmas 17hc (6fb)
CTV 6P B&b£6–£7.50 Bdi£8.65–£10 W£55.20–
£64.40 ⅃ D5pm

**GH Marlyn** 7 & 8 Regent Pl ☎63785 Plan: **18**
Mar–Oct Lic 12hc (3fb) CTV 12☎ B&b£6–£7
Bdi£9–£10 W£60–£67 ⅃ D4.30pm

**GH Merrydene Private Hotel** 10
Hillsborough Ter ☎62141 Plan: **19** May–Sep
Lic 13hc (2fb) nc5 CTV 4P 3☎ sea S%
B&b£7.50–£9.50 Bdi£11–£13 W£68–£74 ⅃
D4.30pm

**GH New Cavendish Hotel** 9–10 Larkstone Ter ☎63994 Plan:**20** Etr–Oct & Xmas Lic 21hc 6🛏 (10fb) ✻ CTV sea ✱ B&b£6.90–£8.10 Bdi£10.35–£11.50 W£64–£82.80 D6pm (W only Jul & Aug)

🖼 **GH Norbury** Torrs Park ☎63888 Plan:**21** Apr–Sep Lic 9hc 1🛏 (3fb) CTV 9P sea S% B&b£5.50–£7 Bdi£11–£14 W£63–£73.50 ⅃ D6pm

**GH Queen's Court Hotel** Wilder Rd ☎63789 Plan:**22** Apr–Oct Lic 16hc 1 ⇔ (5fb) CTV 16P sea S% B&b£8.05–£9.20 Bdi£11.65–£12.80 W£73.60–£79.35 D7pm

**GH Rosebank Hotel** 26 Watermouth Rd, Hele Bay ☎62814 Plan:**25** Lic 7hc (2fb) CTV 🏾 S% B&b£7.47–£9.20 Bdi£9.20–£11.50 W£60.37–£74.75 ⅃ D6pm

**GH Southcliffe Hotel** Torrs Park ☎62958 Plan:**27** Apr–Oct Lic 20hc 3🛏 (12fb) Ch CTV 12P S% ✱ B&b£8–£9 Bdi£10–£14 W£55–£75 ⅃ D6.30pm
**See advert on page 114**

**GH South Tor Hotel** Torrs Park ☎63750 Plan:**28** May–Sep Lic 14hc 6🛏 (3fb) nc4 CTV 12P 2🐾 S% B&b£6.50–£8 Bdi£9.50–£11.50 W£67–£78.50 ⅃ D5.30pm

**GH Strathmore Private Hotel** 57 St Brannocks Rd ☎62248 Plan:**29** Lic 10hc (4fb) CTV 9P S% ✱ B&b£6–£7 Bdi£8–£9.25 W£47.50–£59.75 ⅃ D6.30pm

**GH Sunny Hill** Lincombe, Lee ☎62953 Plan:**30** Lic 8hc 2🛏 (3fb) nc5 CTV 6P 🏾 sea S% B&b£8.25–£11 Bdi£12.25–£15.50 W£78.50–£99.75 ⅃ D6pm

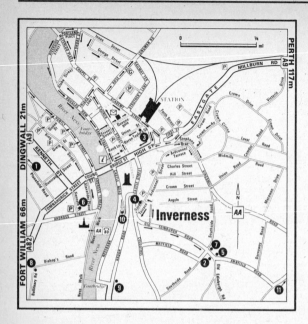

1 Abermar
2 Ardnacoille
3 Arran
4 Craigside
5 Four Winds
6 Glencairn
7 Leinster Lodge
8 Lyndale
9 Moray Park Hotel
10 Riverside Hotel
11 Tigh a' Mhuillinn

**⊬⊣ GH Wentworth House Private Hotel**
Belmont Rd ☎63048 Plan:**32** Apr–Oct 11hc
1⋔ (6fb) CTV 11P S% B&b£5.75–£6.25
Bdi£8–£9 W£52.50–£57.50 ⅃ D5pm

**GH Westbourne Private Hotel** Wilder Rd
☎62120 Plan:**32** Feb–Nov Lic 51hc (7fb)
CTV ▥ lift S% B&b£8–£10 Bdi£10–£12
W£70–£85 D6pm

**GH Westwell Hall Private Hotel** Torrs Park
☎62792 Plan:**34** Apr–Sep Lic 14hc (7fb) nc2
CTV 15P sea S% B&b£6.90–£8.05 Bdi£10.92–
£12.07 W£69–£80.50 ⅃ D2pm

**GH Wilson** 16 Larkstone Ter ☎63921
Plan:**35** Apr–Oct Lic 9hc (6fb) ⊁ CTV sea
S% B&b£6–£7 Bdi£9–£10 W£54.86–£71.30
⅃ D5pm

**INN Royal Britannia** The Quay ☎62939
Plan:**26** 12hc CTV sea S% B&b£9.50–£12
Bdi£14.25–£16.75 W£93.75–£110.20 ⅃
L£2.30alc D8pm£4.75&alc
**See advert on page 113**

**INGHAM** Suffolk Map 5 TL87
**INN Cadogan Arms** ☎Culford 226 4hc CTV
80P S% B&b£9.50

**INGLETON** N Yorks Map 7 SD67
**GH Oakroyd Private Hotel** Main St
☎41258 Feb–Nov Lic 8hc (4fb) Ch CTV 4P
S% B&b£7.50–£8.20 Bdi£11.50–£12 W£75–
£80 ⅃ D5.30pm

**GH Springfield Private Hotel** Main St
☎41280 Closed Nov Lic 6hc (4fb) CTV 12P
river S% B&b£7.50 Bdi£11 W£70 ⅃ D4.30pm

**INSTOW** Devon Map 2 SS43
**GH Anchorage Hotel** The Quay ☎860655
Apr–Oct Lic 10hc (6fb) Ch CTV 9P ▥ sea S%
B&b£10.35–£13 Bdi£14.50–£17.25 W£89–
£104 D7pm (W only mid May–Sep)

**INVERGARRY** Highland Inverness-shire
Map 14 NH30
**GH Graigard** ☎258 Apr–Oct Lic 7hc (2fb) ⊁
nc5 6P D6.30pm

**⊬⊣ GH Lundie View** Aberchalder (3m NE
A82) ☎291 Lic 6hc (3fb) CTV 8P ▥ S%
∗B&bfr£5.50 Bdi fr£9 Wfr£61 ⅃ D7.30pm

**INVERMORISTON** Highland Inverness-
shire Map 14 NH41

**GH Tigh Na Bruach** ☎Glenmoriston 51208 Etr–mid Oct 7rm 5hc (2fb) nc5 12P lake B&bfr£8.05 Bdifr£12.65 Wfr£72.45 ⚡ D7.30pm

**INVERNESS** Highland *Inverness-shire Map 14 NH64* **(See Plan)**

⊬⊣ **GH Abermar** 25 Fairfield Rd ☎39019 Plan:**1** 11hc 3⇌ ⋒ (3fb) CTV 9P ▥ S% B&b£5.50–£6.50 W£38.50–£45.50 ᴍ

⊬⊣ **GH Ardnacoille House** 1A Annfield Rd ☎33451 Plan:**2** Apr–27 Nov Tem 6hc (2fb) ⋇ nc10 CTV 6P ▥ S% B&b£5.50–£6.50 Bdi£9.50–£10.50 W£63–£70 ⚡ D2pm

⊬⊣ **GH Arran** 42 Union St ☎32115 Plan:**3** 7hc (2fb) TV S% B&b£5.50–£6

**GH Craigside House** 4 Gordon Ter ☎31576 Plan:**4** Mar–Oct rsNov & Feb (dinner only if ordered) 6hc 2⋒ (1fb) ⋇ nc13 4P ▥ S%

B&b£7.50–£8.50 Bdi£13–£15 W£88–£92 ⚡ D6pm

**GH Four Winds** 42 Old Edinburgh Rd ☎30397 Plan:**5** 25 Dec & 1 Jan 6hc (2fb) CTV 15P ▥ S% B&b£6–£6.50 W£40 ᴍ

⊬⊣ **GH Glencairn** 19 Ardross St ☎32965 Plan:**6** 11hc (4fb) CTV ▥ & S% B&b£5.50–£6.50

**GH Leinster Lodge** 27 Southside Rd ☎33311 Plan:**7** 6hc (2fb) CTV 8P ▥ S% B&b£6

⊬⊣ **GH Lyndale** 2 Ballifeary Rd ☎31529 Plan:**8** Closed Xmas & New Year 6hc (1fb) CTV 6P B&b£5–£6

**GH Moray Park Hotel** Island Bank Rd ☎33528 Plan:**9** 7hc (4fb) ⋇ CTV 10P ▥ S% B&b£7.70 Bdi£13.60 W£89.50 ⚡ D5pm

**GH Riverside Hotel** 8 Ness Bank ☎31052
Plan: **10** 9hc (3fb) ✶ CTV river S% B&bf7–
£8.50 Bdif12–£13.50 Wf82–£92 ⫽ D7pm

**GH Tigh a' Mhuillinn** 2 Kingsmill Gdns
☎38257 Plan: **11** 6hc CTV 8P P D2pm

**IPPLEPEN** Devon Map 3 SX86
**INN Wellington** Fore St ☎812375 Lic 5hc ✶
CTV 40P D8pm

**IPSWICH** Suffolk Map 5 TM14
**GH Gables Hotel** 17 Park Rd ☎54252 rs
wknds (no dinner) Lic 12hc CTV 10P P S%
B&b£10.35 Bdif13.35 Wf84.45 ⫽ D6.30pm

**ISLAY, ISLE OF** Strathclyde Argyll Map 10
**See Port Ellen**

**ISLE OF MAN** Map 6
Places with AA-listed guesthouses/inns
are indicated on location map 6. Full
details will be found under individual
placenames in the gazetteer section

**ISLE OF SKYE** Highland Inverness-shire
Map 13 NG
**See Broadford, Dunvegan, Isle Ornsay,
Portree, Waterloo**

**ISLE OF WIGHT** Map 4
Places with AA-listed accommodation are
indicated on location map 4. Full details
will be found under individual
placenames within the gazetteer

**ISLE ORNSAY** Isle of Skye, Highland
Inverness-shire Map 13 NG71
⊢⊣ **GH Post Office House** ☎201 Feb–Oct
4rm 3hc TV 10P sea S% B&b£5–£6

**ISLES OF SCILLY** (No map)
**See St Marys**

**IVER HEATH** Bucks Map 4 TQ08
**GH Bridgettine Convent** Fulmer Common
Rd ☎Fulmer 2645 22hc (3fb) nc3 TV 15P P
D2pm

**IVYBRIDGE** Devon Map 2 SX65
⊢⊣ **GH Sunnyside** Western Rd ☎2561
Mar–Oct Lic 8hc (2fb) CTV 3P B&b£5.50–£7
Bdif8.80–£10.30 Wf56–£65 ⫽ D6.15pm

**JEDBURGH** Borders Roxburghs Map 12
NT62
**GH Ferniehirst Mill Lodge** ☎3279 Closed
Nov Lic 11hc 6⇌ 3♠ ✶nc12 16P P river
B&b£9.77–£11.50 Bdif17.25–£18.97
Wf125.92 ⫽ D8.30pm

**GH Kenmore Bank** Oxnam Rd ☎2369 6hc
(2fb) ✶CTV 5P 1♠ P river S% ✳B&b£6
Bdif12.50 Wf80 ⫽ D8.30pm

**JERSEY** Channel Islands Map 16
**See Beaumont, Gorey, La Haule, Rozel
Bay, St Aubin, St Brelade, St Clement, St
Helier, St Martin, St Peter's Valley, St
Saviour, Trinity**

**KEITH** Grampian Banffs Map 15 NJ45
**GH Aultgowrie** 124 Moss St ☎2052 5hc
(1fb) ✶CTV 4P 2♠ P S% B&b£6 Bdi fr£9
Wf58.80 ⫽ D5pm

**KELSO** Borders Roxburghs Map 12 NT73
⊢⊣ **GH Bellevue** Bowmont St ☎2588 8hc
(2fb) ✶CTV 8P S% B&b£5.50 Bdif9 D5pm

**KENILWORTH** Warwicks Map 4 SP27
**GH Enderley** 20 Queens Rd ☎55388 Lic

6hc CTV 2P P S% B&bfr£7.40

**GH Ferndale** 45 Priory Rd ☎53214 Closed
1wk Xmas 7hc (2fb) ✶ CTV 8P P S% B&b£6
Wf38.50 ⫽

**GH Hollyhurst** 47 Priory Rd ☎53882 1 Jan–
12 Dec 9rm 7hc (2fb) CTV 10P B&b£6–£7

**GH Nite Lite** 95 Warwick Rd ☎53594 Lic
12hc (3fb) CTV P S% B&b£8.50 Bdif11.50
D10.30pm

**KENTISBURY** Devon Map 2 SS64
⊢⊣ **GH Homeside** Kentisburyford
☎Combe Martin 3506 Etr–Oct 6hc (2fb) ✶
nc10 CTV P S% B&b£5.50–£6.50 Bdif9–£10
Wf60–£70 ⫽ D5.30pm

**KENTMERE** Cumbria Map 12 NY40
**GH Grove** ☎Staveley (Cumbria) 821548
Mar–Sep rsNew Year Lic 7hc CTV P river
Dnoon

**KESWICK** Cumbria Map 11 NY22
**(See Plan)**
**GH Acorn House Private Hotel** Ambleside
Rd ☎72553 Plan: **1** Apr–Oct 6hc (4fb) CTV
8P P B&b£7.50 Bdif11.70 Wfrf78 ⫽ D3pm

**GH Bay Tree** 1 Wordsworth St ☎73313
Plan: **2** Lic 7hc (3fb) CTV P river B&b£6.95–
£7.95 Bdif9.50–£10.95 Wf65–£73.50 ⫽ D6pm

**GH Burleigh Mead Private Hotel** The
Heads ☎72750 Plan: **3** 1 Apr–10 Nov Lic 8hc
(A 6hc) (9fb) CTV 6P ✳B&b£8.05–£9.20
Bdif11.50–£13.80 D5pm

**GH Clarence House** 14 Eskin St ☎73186
Plan: **4** 8hc (3fb) [Ch] CTV P S% ✳B&b£6
Bdif9.80 Wf66 ⫽ D6pm

**GH Foye House** 23 Eskin St ☎73288 Plan: **5**
Closed Xmas & New Year Lic 6hc ✶nc5 TV
P B&bfrf6.25 Bdi frf10.35 Wf70 ⫽ D9am

**GH Hazeldene Hotel** The Heads ☎72106
Plan: **6** 1 Apr–10 Nov Lic 15hc (6fb) CTV 12P
P ✳B&b£8.05–£9.20 Bdif11.50–£13.80 D5pm

**GH Highfields** The Heads ☎72508 Plan: **7**
Etr–Oct Lic 10hc 1♠ (3fb) nc5 CTV P
B&b£7.50 Bdif11.80 Wf82.60 ⫽ D5pm

**GH Lynwood Private Hotel** 12 Ambleside
Rd ☎72081 Plan: **8** Lic 8hc (5fb) ✶nc5 CTV
P S% B&b£6 Bdif9 Wf62 ⫽ D5pm

**GH Parkfield** 4 Eskin St ☎72324 Plan: **9**
Feb–Dec Lic 8hc (4fb) ✶ CTV P S% B&b£6
Bdif9 D6pm

**GH Ravensworth Private Hotel** Station St
☎72476 Plan: **10** 9hc (2fb) ✶ CTV 4P P S%
B&b£6.50–£8 Bdif10–£12.50 Wf70–£85 ⫽
D4pm

**GH Richmond House** 39 Eskin St ☎73965
Plan: **11** Closed Nov Lic 11hc 2⇌ ♠ (3fb) CTV
P D6pm

**GH Rickerby Grange** Portinscale (1m W
A66) ☎72344 Not on plan Apr–Oct Lic 8hc
2⇌ 1♠ (1fb) CTV 9P P S% B&b£8–£8.80
Bdif11.50–£12.35 Wf74.80–£81 ⫽ D4pm

**GH Silverdale Hotel** Blencathra St ☎72294
Plan: **12** Lic 12hc (4fb) ✶CTV 8P P S%
B&b£8.75 Bdif11.50 Wf73 D5pm

**GH Sunnyside** 25 Southey St ☎72446
Plan: **13** Apr–Oct 8hc (3fb) ✶nc8 CTV 7P
B&b£7 Bdif10.25 Wf68 ⫽ D3pm

**GH Woodlands** Brundholme Rd ☎72399
Plan: **14** Mar–Oct 7hc (2fb) ✶nc6 CTV 10P P
S% ✳B&b£6.50 Bdif10 Wf63–£70 ⫽
D10.30am

**KETTLEWELL** N Yorks Map 7 SD97
**GH Dale House** ☎836 May–Oct 6rm 1♠
CTV P ✳B&b£9.50 Bdif13.50 Wf87.50 D7pm

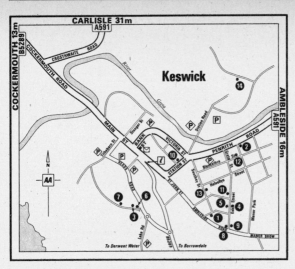

1 Acorn House
   Private Hotel
2 Bay Tree
3 Burleigh Mead
   Private Hotel
4 Clarence House
5 Foye House
6 Hazeldene Hotel
7 Highfields
8 Lynwood Private
   Hotel
9 Parkfield
10 Ravensworth
   Private Hotel
11 Richmond House
12 Silverdale Hotel
13 Sunnyside
14 Woodlands

**KEYNSHAM** Avon *Map 3 ST66*
**GH Uplands Farmhouse** The Wellsway
☎5764 rsXmas 5hc (2fb) CTV 10P ◻️
B&b£7.50–£10 Bdi£12.50–£15 D1pm

**KIDLINGTON** Oxon *Map 4 SP41*
**GH Bowood House** 238 Oxford Rd ☎2839
Lic 9hc 2⇆ 3🏠 (2fb) ✱ CTV 12P ◻️ S%
B&b£7.50–£9.50 D6pm

**KILKHAMPTON** Cornwall *Map 2 SS21*
**INN London** ☎343 3hc nc10 CTV 4P
B&b£7.50 Bdi£10.50 Wfr£65.50 ⅃ Bar lunch
£1.50–£2.50&alc D8.30pm£4alc

**KILLIECRANKIE** Tayside *Perths Map 14
NN96*
**GH Dalnasgadh House** ☎237 Etr–Oct 6hc
(2fb) ✱ CTV 10P ◻️ S% B&b£6.50–£7.50

**KILMARTIN** Strathclyde *Argyll Map 10
NR89*
**INN Kilmartin Hotel** ☎250 5hc ♠ CTV 13P
sea S% B&b£8.25–£8.80 Bdi£11.75–£12.92
Bar lunch£2alc D8.30pm£6alc

**KILNSEY** N Yorks *Map 7 SD96*
**GH Chapel House** ☎Grassington 752654
Mar–Oct Lic 12hc 6⇆ 2🏠 CTV 20P ◻️ river
S% ✱B&b£10.50 Bdi£14 W£90 D6.30pm

**KILVE** Somerset *Map 3 SS14*
**INN Hood Arms** ☎Holford 210 6hc 2⇆ 🚗
nc7 CTV 14P ◻️ S% B&b£9 W£54 M̶ Bar lunch
£1.50alc D9.15pm£5.50alc

**KINGHORN** Fife *Map 11 NT28*
**GH Odin Villa** 107 Pettycur Rd ☎890625 Lic
7🏠 (1fb) CTV 14P ◻️ sea S% B&b£9.50–
£11.50 Bdi£13–£16 W£85–£100 ⅃ D9pm

**KINGSBRIDGE** Devon *Map 3 SX74*
**GH Ashleigh** Westville ☎2893 Mar–Nov
rsDec–Feb 8hc (4fb) Ⓒⓗ CTV 6P S% B&b£7–
£9 Bdi£10–£13 W£63–£80 ⅃ D4pm

**GH Hotel Kildare** Balkwill Rd ☎2451 Lic
12hc (7fb) Ⓒⓗ CTV 12P B&b£12.12 Bdi£18.97
W£90.80–£100.56 ⅃ D7pm

**GH *Westerlands Country Hotel*** Belle
Cross Rd ☎2268 Lic 10hc 6⇆ 🏠 (2fb) ✱ CTV
P 2🚗 ◻️ D7pm

**KINGSDOWN** Kent *Map 5 TR34*
**GH Blencathra Country** Kingsdown Hill
☎Deal 3725 Etr–Oct Lic 5hc (3fb) ✱ nc3 CTV
7P ◻️ S% B&b£7.50 Bdi£11.50 Wfr£69 ⅃

**KINGSKERSWELL** Devon *Map 3 SX86*
**GH Harewood** Torquay Rd ☎2228 Etr–Oct
6hc (3fb) CTV 10P ◻️ S% ✱B&b£5.50–£7
W£38–£42 M̶

**KING'S LYNN** Norfolk *Map 9 TF62*
**GH Runcton House Hotel** 53 Goodwins Rd
☎3098 Lic 8hc 1⇔ (2fb) CTV 14P ▥
B&bfr£10 Bdifr£14.25 D6.30pm

**KINGSTON** Devon *Map 2 SX64*
**GH Trebles Cottage Private Hotel**
☎Bigbury-on-Sea 268 Closed 2wks winter
Lic 5hc 1⇔ ⊁nc6 CTV 10P ▥ S% B&b£7.50–
£8.50 Bdi£11.50–£12.50 W£67.50–£78.75 Ⳑ
D6pm

**KINGSTON UPON THAMES** Gt London
*London plan 4 D2 (page 134)*
**GH Hotel Antoinette** 26 Beaufort Rd ☎01-
546 1044 Lic 55hc 50⇔ (A 55⇔) (40fb) CTV
60P ▥ S% B&b£10.35–£11.25 Bdi£14.95–
£15.85 D9pm

**GH Lingfield House Hotel** 29 Beaufort Rd
☎01-546 1988 8hc 2⇔ (3fb) nc5 CTV 6P ▥
B&b£8–£9

**KINGSWINFORD** W Midlands *Map 7 SO88*
**INN Swan Hotel** Stream Rd ☎287232 5hc
⇔ 54P ▥ S% B&b£8 sn L£1.30alc

**KINGUSSIE** Highland *Inverness-shire Map
14 NH70*
**GH Sonnhalde** East Ter ☎266 Jan–Nov 6hc
(2fb) TV 8P ▥ S% ✳B&b£7–£7.50 Bdi£12–
£12.50 Wfr£84 Ⳑ D8pm

**KINNERSLEY** Heref & Worcs *Map 3 SO34*
**GH Prestegarden** ☎Eardisley 541 4hc 1⇔
1🛉 (2fb) ⊁CTV 10P ▥ S% B&b£6–£9
Bdi£9.50–£14 W£63–£98 Ⳑ D7pm

**KIRBY MUXLOE** Leics *Map 4 SK50*
**GH *Forest Lodge Hotel*** Desford Rd

☎Leicester 393125 Lic 29hc 5⇔ 🛉 (4fb) CTV
60P ▥ D8pm

**KIRKBEAN** Dumfries & Galloway
*Dumfriesshire Map 11 NX95*
**GH Cavens House** ☎234 Closed 15 Dec–15
Jan Lic 6rm 3⇔ 2🛉 (1fb) ᴄʜ CTV P & S%
B&b£9–£9.50 Bdi£15.50–£16

**KIRKOSWALD** Cumbria *Map 11 NY54*
**GH Prospect Hill Hotel** ☎Lazonby 500
Closed Feb Lic 9hc 3🛉 (A 3hc) (2fb) ⊁CTV
12P ▥ B&b£10.45–£18.70 Bdi£16.50–£24.75
W£108.35–£156.88 Ⳑ D8.45pm

**KIRKWALL** Orkney *Map 16 HY41*
**GH *Foveran*** (½m SW A964) ☎2389 Closed
Oct Lic 10hc CTV 12P ▥ D9pm

**KIRTON** Notts *Map 8 SK66*
**GH Old Rectory** Main St ☎Mansfield
861540 Feb–Nov 9hc (1fb) ⊁CTV 10P ▥ S%
B&b£9

**KNAPTON** Norfolk *Map 9 TG33*
**GH Knapton Hall Hotel** ☎Mundesley
720405 Apr–Oct Lic 10hc (A 4hc) (5fb) ⊁
CTV 15P S% B&b£6–£7 Bdi£9–£10.50 W£65–
£70 Ⳑ D7pm

**KNOWSTONE** Devon *Map 3 SS82*
**INN Masons Arms** ☎Anstey Mills 231 3hc
(A 1🛉) ⇔ nc14 CTV 8P ▥ B&b£10–£14.50 Bar
lunch £2alc D9.15pm£6alc

**KNUTSFORD** Cheshire *Map 7 SJ77*
**GH Longview Private Hotel** 55 Manchester
Rd ☎2119 Closed Xmas Lic 14hc 2🛉 (1fb)

# *Guesthouse of the Year 1979 Northern England Winner*

**. . . one of only six chosen from hundreds in Britain . . .**

*A Taste of Rural England in the peace of the Eden Valley.*

## *Prospect Hill Hotel · Kirkoswald*

### *Penrith · Cumbria · CA10 1ER*
### *Telephone Lazonby (std 076883) 500*
*Resident Proprietors: Isa and John M. Henderson*

*. . . so far and yet so near . . .*

**Twenty minute drive from the M6 · Junctions 41 and 42**

Quotes from the AA Guesthouse of the Year article
". . . a wider choice of dishes than the other guesthouses visited . . ."
". . . much of the food is delightfully different . . ."
". . . a syllabub was out of this world . . ."
". . . service by pleasant local girls, is quick and efficient . . ."
". . . it offers extremely good value for money
in a character building in a delightful part of the country . . ."

*The illustration conveys the surroundings of the establishment.
It does not imply such close proximity of the river or the grounds of the hotel.*

CTV 6P ⅢⅢ S% B&bf£9.50–£19.50 Bdi£15–£25.50 D7.30pm

**KYLE OF LOCHALSH** Highland *Ross & Cromarty Map 13 NG72*
**GH Retreat** ☎Kyle 4308 Etr–Oct 14hc (2fb) nc3 TV 14P 2♠ S% B&bf£6.95–£7.50

**LA HAULE** Jersey, Channel Islands *Map 16*
⋈ **GH Au Caprice Private Hotel** Route de la Haule ☎Jersey 22083 mid Feb–Nov Lic 14hc (2fb) ⅂ Ch CTV sea S% B&bf£5–£10 Bdi£6.50–£11.50 W£45.50–£80.50 ⅃ D5pm

**LAIRG** Highland *Sutherland Map 14 NC50*
⋈ **GH Carnbren** ☎2259 Apr–Sep 3hc CTV 4P ⅢⅢ lake S% B&bfr£5.50

**LAMLASH** Isle of Arran, Strathclyde *Bute Map 10 NS03*
**GH Glenisle Hotel** ☎258 Mar–Oct 3⇔ ⋔ (A 3rm) (6fb) CTV 16P sea Dnoon

**GH Marine House Hotel** ☎298 Apr–Sep 19hc 6⋔ (6fb) CTV 16P ⅢⅢ sea S% ✳B&bfr£6.90 Bdi fr£8.63 Wfr£64.40

**LANCASTER** Lancs *Map 7 SD46*
⋈ **GH Belle Vue** 1 Belle Vue Ter, Greaves ☎67751 6hc (3fb) CTV 6P S% B&bf£5.50–£6.50

**LANCING** W Sussex *Map 4 TQ10*
**GH Beach House** 81 Brighton Rd ☎3368 mid Jan–mid Dec 6hc (2fb) CTV 6P ⅢⅢ sea S% B&bf£7–£8 W£45–£50 Ⓜ

**GH Seaways** 83 Brighton Rd ☎2338 8hc (1fb) ⅂ CTV 8P ⅢⅢ S% B&bf£6.50–£7.50 W£40–£45 Ⓜ

**INN Sussex Pad Hotel** Old Shoreham Rd ☎Shoreham-by-Sea 4647 7rm 6⇔ CTV in all bedrooms 50P ⅢⅢ S% B&bfr£20 sn L£6&alc D10pm£12alc

**LANGDALE, GREAT** Cumbria *Map 11 NY30*
**GH New Dungeon Ghyll Hotel** ☎213 mid Mar–Nov Lic 19hc 9⋔ (5fb) CTV 20P ⅢⅢ S% B&bfr£10.94 Bdi fr£16.99 Wfr£111.93 D7pm

**LANGLAND BAY** W Glam *Map 2 SS68*
**GH Wittemberg Hotel** 2 Rotherslade Rd ☎Swansea 69696 Closed Xmas Lic 12hc 8⋔ (2fb) ⅂ nc5 CTV 12P ⅢⅢ S% B&bf£10–£11.50 Bdi£14.50–£16 W£77–£85 ⅃ D6pm

**LANGPORT** Somerset *Map 3 ST42*
**GH Ashley** The Avenue ☎250386 Lic 8hc (2fb) ⅂ Ch CTV 12P ⅢⅢ S% B&bfr£6.50 Bdi fr£10 Wfr£63 ⅃

**GH Brookside** Ducks Hill, Huish Episcopi ☎250259 Lic 6rm 5hc 1⇔ (2fb) ⅂ CTV 12P ⅢⅢ S% B&b£7.50–£8.50 W£45–£51 Ⓜ D9.30pm

**LARGS** Strathclyde *Ayrs Map 10 NS25*
(See Plan)
**GH Aubery** 22 Aubery Cres ☎672330 Plan:**1** Etr–Sep 6hc (2fb) nc3 TV 6P S% ✳B&bf£7 Bdi£7 W£49 ⅃ D5.30pm

**GH Douglas House** 42 Douglas St ☎672257 Plan:**2** Jun–Sep Lic 14hc (2fb) ⅂ CTV 12P ⅢⅢ ✳B&bfr£6.90 Bdi fr£8.62

**GH Gleneldon Hotel** 2 Barr Cres ☎673381 Plan:**3** Mar–Dec Lic 11hc (2fb) ⅂ CTV 12P ⅢⅢ ✳B&b£8.50–£9.50 Bdi£12.50–£14 Wfr£88 ⅃

**GH Holmesdale** 74 Moorburn Rd ☎674793 Plan:**4** Closed Oct, Xmas & New Year 8hc ⅂ CTV 4P ⅢⅢ S% B&bf£6 Bdi£9 W£63 ⅃ Dam

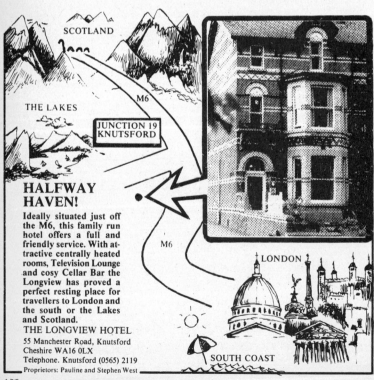

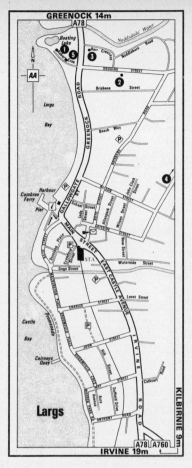

**GREENOCK 14m**

Largs

1 Aubery       4 Holmesdale
2 Douglas House
3 Gleneldon Hotel     5 Sunbury

**GH Sunbury** 12 Aubery Cres ☎673086
Plan:**5** Apr–mid Oct 5hc (3fb) CTV 6P sea
S% B&b£6 Bdi£9.50 W£63 ⫇ D4.30pm

**LAURENCEKIRK** Grampian *Kincardineshire
Map 15 NO77*
**GH** *Eastview Private Hotel* ☎468 8rm 6hc
(2fb) CTV 8P D7.30pm

**LEAMINGTON SPA** Warwicks *Map 4 SP36*
**(See Plan on page 122)**
**GH Beech Lodge Hotel** 28 Warwick New
Rd ☎22227 Plan:**1** Closed Xmas & New
Year Lic 12hc CTV 7P 1🐾 ▥ S% B&b£10.35–
£10.93 Bdi£16.68–£17.25 D7pm

**GH Buckland Lodge Hotel** 35 Avenue Rd
☎23843 Plan:**2** Closed Xmas 8hc (2fb) CTV
12P ▥ S% B&b£7.50–£8.50 Bdi£11.50–£13
D2pm

**GH Glendower** 8 Warwick Pl ☎22784
Plan:**3** Closed Xmas 8hc (2fb) CTV 6P 2🐾 ▥
S% ✳B&b£7.50–£8

**GH Poplars** 1 Milverton Ter ☎28335 Plan:**5**
Lic 11hc (5fb) CTV 11P ▥ S% B&b£8–£8.75
Bdi£12–£12.75 W£78–£87 ⫇ D3pm

**GH Veleta Hotel** 42 Warwick New Rd
☎21380 Plan:**6** Lic 12hc (4fb) CTV 20P ▥
S% B&b£7.50–£8.50 Bdi£12–£12.50 D8pm

**GH** *Victoria Park* 12 Adelaide Rd ☎24195
Plan:**7** 10hc (3fb) CTV 12P Dam

**GH** *Westella Hotel* 26 Leam Ter ☎22710
Plan:**8** Closed Xmas 10hc (2fb) CTV 12P ▥
D4pm

**GH White House** 22 Avenue Rd ☎21516
Plan:**9** Lic 7hc (3fb) TV 10P 2🐾 S% B&bfr£8
Bdifr£12 D9am

**GH York House** 9 York Rd ☎24671 Plan:**10**
7hc (2fb) CTV 3P S% B&b£7–£8 W£45–£56 Ⓜ

**LEEDS** W Yorks *Map 8 SE33*
**GH Ann-Marie House** 47 Cliff Rd, Hyde
Park Cnr ☎758856 Closed Xmas & New
Year Lic 14hc (1fb) CTV 10P ▥ S%
B&b£8.05–£8.57 Bdi£12.57–£13.10 Dam

**GH Aragon Hotel** 250 Stainbeck Ln,
Meanwood ☎759306 Closed Xmas Lic 12hc
2🖂 (2fb) CTV 8P 1🐾 ▥ S% B&bfr£9.87
Bdifr£13.87 D7.30pm

**GH Ash Mount Hotel** 22 Wetherby Rd,
Roundhay ☎658164 Closed Xmas 14hc (2fb)
🐾 CTV 10P ▥ S% ✳B&b£9.20

**GH Budapest Private Hotel** 14 Cardigan
Rd, Headingley ☎756637 Closed Xmas 12hc
(2fb) 🐾 Ⓒⱨ CTV 12P ▥ S% Bdi£12–£13 Dnoon

**Leamington Spa**

1 Beech Lodge
   Hotel
2 Buckland Lodge
   Hotel
3 Glendower
5 Poplars
6 Veleta Hotel
7 Victoria Park
8 Westella Hotel
9 White House
10 York House

**GH Clock Hotel** 317 Roundhay Rd, Gipton Wood ☎490304 Closed Xmas Lic 22hc (6fb) ⊀ ⊀ CTV 12P S% ✱B&b£9.20 Bdi£12.88 D7.30pm

**GH Highfield Hotel** 79 Cardigan Rd, Headingley ☎752193 10hc (1fb) CTV 7P ⅢⅢ ✱B&b£8.50

**GH Oak Villa Hotel** 57 Cardigan Rd, Headingley ☎758439 10hc (2fb) CTV 9P ⅢⅢ S% B&b£10.35 D7pm

**GH Trafford House Hotel** 18 Cardigan Rd, Headingley ☎752034 Closed Xmas 9hc ⊀ Ch CTV 6P ⅢⅢ S% Bdi£12–£13 Dnoon

**LEE-ON-THE-SOLENT** Hants *Map 4 SU50*
**GH Ash House** 35 Marine Parade West ☎550240 6hc CTV 6P ⅢⅢ sea S% ✱B&b£5.50–£7

**LEICESTER** Leics *Map 4 SK50*
**GH Alexandra Hotel** 342 London Rd,

Stoneygate ☎703056 rsEtr Lic 25hc (2fb) ⊀ CTV 18P ⅢⅢ ✱B&b£11.25 Bdi£17.15 D5pm

**GH Daval Hotel** 292 London Rd ☎708234 Closed Xmas Lic 13hc (3fb) nc2 CTV 20P ⅢⅢ S% B&b£10.95 Bdi£15.95 D7.30pm

**GH Old Tudor Rectory** Main St, Glenfield (3m W A50) ☎312214 23hc 3⇔ 6♒ (3fb) nc3 CTV 40P ⅢⅢ S% ✱B&bfr£9.20 Bdi fr£13 D4pm

**GH Scotia Hotel** 10 Westcotes Dr ☎549200 Closed Xmas Lic 9hc (1fb) CTV 4P ⅢⅢ S% B&bfr£9.80 Bdi fr£15 Wfr£64 M̶ D5.45pm

**LELANT** Cornwall *Map 2 SW53*
**GH Ar-Lyn Private Hotel** Vicarage Ln ☎Hayle 753330 Lic 11hc 2♒ (4fb) Ch CTV 16P ⅢⅢ S% B&b£7–£8 Bdi£10–£11.50 W£69–£72 ⅃ D8pm (W only Jul & Aug)

**LEOMINSTER** Heref & Worcs *Map 3 SO45*
**GH Broadward Lodge** ☎2914 Lic 8rm 7hc (3fb) Ch TV 10P ▥ S% B&b£7–£8 Bdi£11–£12 W£68–£73 ⅃ D8pm

**LERWICK** Shetland *Map 16 HU44*
**GH Carradale** 36 King Harald St ☎2890 3hc (2fb) CTV 6P ▥ sea S% B&b£8–£9 Bdi£13–£14 D7pm

**GH Glen Orchy** Lee Knab Rd ☎2031 6hc (1fb) ⅄ CTV ▥ sea ✱ B&b£7–£9 W£49–£63 Ⓜ

**GH Solheim** ☎3613 3hc CTV S% B&bfr£8 Bdi fr£13 D7pm

**LESLIE** Fife *Map 11 NO20*
**GH Rescobie** ☎Glenrothes 742143 Lic 8hc 3♠ CTV 14P ▥ S% ✱ B&b£10.50–£14.75 Bdi£15.75–£20 Dam

**LEVISHAM** N Yorks *Map 8 SE89*
**GH Moorlands** ☎Pickering 60247 5hc (1fb) CTV 5P S% B&bfr£6 Bdi fr£10

**LEWIS, ISLE OF** Western Isles *Ross & Cromarty Map 13* **See Stornoway**

**LEYBURN** N Yorks *Map 7 SE19*
**GH Eastfield Lodge** St Matthews Ter ☎Wensleydale 23196 Apr–Nov Lic 8hc (2fb) CTV 10P ▥ S% B&b£8–£9 W£104–£116 Ⓜ D8.30pm

**LEYSMILL** Tayside *Angus Map 15 NO64*
**GH Spynie** ☎Friockheim 328 Etr–Sep Lic 5hc (2fb) TV 8P ▥ S% ✱ B&bfr£7 Bdi fr£10 Wfr£65 ⅃ D8pm

**LICHFIELD** Staffs *Map 7 SK10*
**GH Oakleigh** 25 St Chads Rd ☎22688 4hc

(A 2hc) (2fb) CTV 20P ▥ lake S% B&b£7.48–£10.35 Bdi£10.93–£13.80 Dnoon
**INN** *Old Crown Hotel* Bore St ☎22879 7hc 10P 2☜

**LIFTON** Devon *Map 2 SX38*
⨝ **GH Mayfield House** Tinhay ☎401 Lic 7rm 6hc (2fb) Ch CTV 10P 1☜ ▥ lake S% B&b£5–£6 Bdi£8–£9 D9.30pm

**LINCOLN** Lincs *Map 8 SK97*
**GH Brierley House Hotel** 54 South Pk ☎26945 Lic 10hc (3fb) CTV ▥ S% B&b£9.20–£10.35 Bdi£13.25–£15 W£86–£98 D4pm

**GH D'Isney Place Hotel** Eastgate ☎38881 12hc 11⇔ 1♠ (2fb) CTV 5P ▥ B&b£13–£19.50

**LISKEARD** Cornwall *Map 2 SX26*
**GH** *Hotel Nebula* 27 Higher Lux St ☎43989 Lic 10hc CTV 20P D5pm

**LITTLEHAM** Devon *Map 2 SS42*
**INN** *Crealock Arms* Shutta Farm ☎Bideford 2791 3hc ⅄ CTV 30P ⇔

**LITTLEHAMPTON** W Sussex *Map 4 TQ00*
**GH Arun Hotel** 42–44 New Rd ☎21206 Lic 10hc (4fb) ⅄ CTV 8P 2☜ ▥ S% B&b£8 Bdi£10.50–£13 W£55–£75 ⅃ D5.30pm

**GH Braemar Private Hotel** Sea Front ☎5487 Closed 2wks Xmas Lic 8hc (2fb) CTV ▥ S% ✱ B&b£8 Bdi£12 W£70 ⅃

**GH Burbridge Hotel** 93 South Ter ☎21606 Lic 6hc (4fb) ⅄ nc5 CTV ▥ river S% ✱ B&b£6.50–£10 W£42–£60 Ⓜ

**GH Harley House Hotel** St Catherines Rd
☎5851 Lic 7hc (6fb) ⚲ CTV 4P ▥ S% B&b£7
Bdi£10.50 D2pm

**GH Regency Hotel** 85 South Ter ☎7707 Lic
8hc (3fb) CTV ▥ sea S% B&b£8 Bdi£12 W£70
⌊ D6pm

**GH The Rowers Hotel** 42 South Ter ☎3940
9hc (2fb) CTV 3P 2☎ sea S% B&bfr£7–£8
Bdi£10.50–£11.50 W£64–£68 ⌊ D6.30pm

**LITTLE HAVEN** Dyfed *Map 2 SM81*
**GH Pendyffryn Private Hotel** ☎Broad
Haven 337 mid Mar–mid Oct Lic 7hc (6fb) ⚲
nc4 CTV 6P ▥ sea S% B&bfr£7.50
Bdi fr£12.10 Wfr£78 ⌊ D6.45pm (W only Jul–
Aug)

**LITTLE LANGDALE** Cumbria *Map 11 NY30*
**INN Three Shires** ☎215 Mar–mid Nov rs
mid Nov–Feb (wknds only) except Xmas 7hc
⇆ nc2 20P ▥ B&b£12 Bdi£22 W£140 ⌊ Bar
lunch£1.20–£2.50 D8.30pm£10

**LIZARD** Cornwall *Map 2 SW71*
**GH Kynance Bay Hotel** ☎The Lizard
290498 Mar–Nov 9hc (3fb) CTV 8P sea S%
B&b£8.50–£9.50 Bdi£10–£12 W£68–£82 ⌊

**GH Mounts Bay Hotel** Penmenner Rd
☎The Lizard 290305 Mar–Nov rsDec–Feb
Lic 10hc (4fb) ₵ĥ CTV 12P sea S%
✳B&b£8.05 Bdi£11.50 Wfr£78.20 ⌊ D7.15pm

**GH Parc Brawse House** ☎The Lizard
290466 Mar–Oct Lic 6hc nc7 CTV 6P sea
✳B&b£7–£7.50 Bdi£11–£12 W£70–£76 ⌊
D7pm

**GH Penmenner House Private Hotel**
Penmenner Rd ☎The Lizard 290370 Apr–

Oct Lic 8hc (2fb) ⚲ ₵ĥ CTV 12P ▥ sea S%
✳B&bfr£8 Bdi fr£10 D6pm

**LLANARTHNEY** Dyfed *Map 2 SN52*
**INN Golden Grove Arms** ☎Dryslwyn 551
Mar–14 Jan 6hc 2ñ 100P ▥ S% B&b£8.50
D10pm£6alc

**LLANBEDROG** Gwynedd *Map 6 SH33*
**GH Glyn Garth Hotel** ☎268 Etr–Oct Lic
10hc (6fb) ⚲ CTV 24P B&b£8–£10.50 Bdi£13–
£15.50 W£75–£105 ⌊ D10pm

**LLANBERIS** Gwynedd *Map 6 SH56*
**GH Lake View** Tan-y-Pant (1m W A4086)
☎422 Lic 7hc (2fb) CTV 7P ▥ D9pm

**LLANDDERFEL** Gwynedd *Map 6 SH93*
**INN Bryntirion Hotel** ☎205 Lic 4hc ⚲ nc8
CTV 50P ▥ river D10pm

**LLANDOGO** Gwent *Map 3 SO50*
**GH Browns Hotel & Restaurant** ☎Dean
530262 Jan–Nov Lic 8hc (A 2hc) 30P S%
B&b£8–£9 D8.30pm

**GH Craiglas** ☎Dean 530348 Mar–Oct 5hc
(3fb) ⚲ TV 20P ▥

**LLANDOVERY** Dyfed *Map 3 SN73*
**GH Llwyncelyn** ☎20566 Closed Xmas 6hc
(3fb) ⚲ CTV 12P ▥ river S% B&b£7.50–£9
Bdi£13–£14.50 W£83–£92 ⌊ D7.30pm

**LLANDRINDOD WELLS** Powys *Map 3
SO06*
**GH Griffin Lodge Hotel** Temple St ☎2432
Lic 11hc (2fb) ⚲ CTV 8P ▥ S% B&b£8.50–
£9.50 Bdi£13.50–£14.50 W£91–£98 ⌊ D8pm

**LLANDUDNO** Gwynedd *Map 6 SH78*
**(See Plan)**
**GH Bella Vista Private Hotel** 72 Church Walks ☎76855 Plan:**1** mid Jan–mid Dec Lic 12hc (9fb) CTV 12P ▥ S% D5.30pm

**GH Braemar Hotel** 5 St Davids Rd ☎76257 Plan:**2** 6hc (3fb) CTV 4P ▥ S% B&b£6.50–£7.50 Bdi£9–£9.50 W£50–£55 ⎩ D6.30pm

**GH Brannock Private Hotel** 36 St Davids Rd ☎77483 Plan:**3** Feb–Oct Lic 8hc (2fb) nc3 CTV 5P ▥ S% B&b£7.25–£8 Bdi£10–£11.20 W£70–£76 ⎩ D5pm

**GH Brigstock Private Hotel** 1 St Davids Pl ☎76416 Plan:**4** Feb–Oct Lic 10hc (3fb) CTV 7P S% B&b£8.05 Bdi£10.87–£11.50 W£72.50–£76.50 ⎩ D6pm

**GH Britannia Hotel** 15 Craig-y-Don Pde ☎77185 Plan:**5** 9hc (6fb) CTV ▥ S% B&b£6.25–£6.95 Bdi£9.25–£9.95

**GH Bryn Rosa** 16 Abbey Rd ☎78215 Plan:**6** 7hc (3fb) nc2 CTV 6P ▥ S% B&b£6–£6.50 Bdi£8.50–£9 W£57–£60 ⎩ D5pm

**GH Bryn-y-Mor Private Hotel** North Pde ☎76790 Plan:**7** Closed Xmas & New Year Lic 19hc (4fb) ⚹ nc3 TV in all bedrooms ▥ sea S% B&b£8.05–£11.50 Bdi£9.20–£12.65 W£57.50–£74.75 ⎩ D7pm (W only Jul–Aug)

**GH Buile Hill Private Hotel** St Mary's Rd ☎76972 Plan:**8** Lic 13hc 1⇌3⋔ (1fb) CTV 6P ▥ S% B&b£6–£8.63 Bdi£9–£12.25 W£63–£79.35 ⎩ D6.30pm
**See advert on page 126**

# LLWYNCELYN GUEST HOUSE

## LLANDOVERY, DYFED, SA20 0EP

### Tel: 0550-20566

*Proprietors:*
*Mr & Mrs D. C. Griffiths.*

Ideal Holiday Centre. Our Guest House with its rural, riverside setting, full central heating and homely atmosphere offers Bed & Breakfast, or Dinner, Bed & Breakfast at moderate rates.

GRIFFIN LODGE
HOTEL & RESTAURANT

**Temple Street, Llandrindod Wells, Powys**
**Telephone: Llandrindod Wells (0597) 2432**

Come and stay in our small hotel and enjoy good food and wine in a friendly atmosphere. We do our own cooking and use local produce as much as possible. From October to May we offer Weekend Breaks for an escape from the rat race—come and be spoilt!

Please contact us, Miles & Pauline Swinburne.

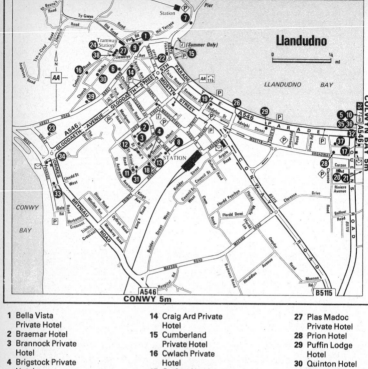

**Llandudno**

| | | |
|---|---|---|
| 1 Bella Vista Private Hotel | 14 Craig Ard Private Hotel | 27 Plas Madoc Private Hotel |
| 2 Braemar Hotel | 15 Cumberland Private Hotel | 28 Prion Hotel |
| 3 Brannock Private Hotel | 16 Cwlach Private Hotel | 29 Puffin Lodge Hotel |
| 4 Brigstock Private Hotel | 17 Grafton Hotel | 30 Quinton Hotel |
| 5 Britannia Hotel | 18 Heatherdale | 31 Rosaire Private Hotel |
| 6 Bryn Rosa | 19 Lynwood Private Hotel | 32 St Hilary Hotel |
| 7 Bryn-y-Mor Private Hotel | 20 Mayfield Private Hotel | 33 Sandilands Private Hotel |
| 8 Buile Hill Private Hotel | 21 Minion Private Hotel | 34 Sandringham Hotel |
| 9 Capri Hotel | 22 Montclare Hotel | 35 Sun Ray Private Hotel |
| 10 Carmel Private Hotel | 23 Morningside Hotel | 36 Tilstone Private Hotel |
| 11 Cleave Court Private Hotel | 24 Nant-y-Glyn | 37 Victoria House |
| 12 Cliffbury Private Hotel | 25 Orotava Private Hotel | 38 Warwick Hotel |
| 13 Cornerways Private Hotel | 26 Penelope Private Hotel | 39 Westdale Private Hotel |

GH *Capri Hotel* 70 Church Walks ☎79177 Plan:**9** Lic 10hc (7fb) CTV D6pm

⊁⊣ **GH Carmel Private Hotel** 17 Craig-y-Don Pde, Promenade ☎77643 Plan:**10** Etr–Oct 10hc 2⋔ (5fb) nc4 7P sea S% B&b£5.95–£6.60 Bdi£7.95–£9 Wf55–£63 ⋮ D4.30pm

**GH Cleave Court Private Hotel** 1 St Seirol's Rd ☎77849 Plan:**11** Etr–Oct 9hc (3fb) ⊁ CTV 10P sea S% B&b£7.50 Bdi£9 D6pm

**GH Cliffbury Private Hotel** 34 St Davids Rd ☎77224 Plan:**12** Etr–Sep 6hc (2fb) ⊁ nc6 CTV 4P S% B&b£6.25–£6.75 Bdi£7.50–£8 Wf48.50–£50.50 ⋮ D5pm

**GH Cornerways Private Hotel** 2 St Davids Pl ☎77334 Plan:**13** Closed Xmas 11hc (4fb) nc5 CTV 6P ⫽ S% B&b£7–£7.50 Bdi£9.50–£10 Wf66.50–£70 ⋮ D4pm

**GH Craig Ard Private Hotel** Arvon Av ☎77318 Plan:**14** Mar–Oct Lic 19hc (5fb) ⌈Ch⌉ CTV 10P ⫽ S% B&b£8.80 Bdi£10.80 Wf74.75 ⋮ D6.30pm

**GH Cumberland Hotel** North Pde ☎76379 Plan:**15** Lic 18hc (8fb) CTV 3P ⫽ sea S% B&b£7.75–£8.75 Bdi£9.75–£10.75 Wf68.25–£75.25 ⋮ D6pm

**GH Cwlach Private Hotel** Cwlach Rd ☎75587 Plan:**16** Lic 11⇔ (4fb) ⊁ CTV sea S% ✳ B&b£5.75–£6 Bdi£6.75–£7.50

**GH Grafton Hotel** 13 Craig-y-Don Pde ☎76814 Plan:**17** Feb–Nov Lic 21hc 4⇔ 11⋔ (14fb) CTV 16P ⫽ ✳ B&b£5.95–£6.90 Bdi£8.95–£9.90 Wf62.65–£69.30 D6pm

**GH** *Heatherdale* 30 St David's Rd ☎77362 Plan:**18** Mar–Oct 6hc CTV D6pm

**GH Lynwood Private Hotel** Clonmel St ☎76613 Plan:**19** Closed Xmas Lic 12hc (8fb) ⊁ CTV sea B&b£7–£8.90 Bdi£8–£10.50 D6pm

**GH Mayfield Private Hotel** 19 Curzon Rd, Craig-y-Don ☎77427 Plan:**20** Apr–Oct 8hc (5fb) CTV B&b£6–£7 Bdi£8–£9 Wf50–£55 ⋮

⊁⊣ **GH Minion Private Hotel** 21–23 Carmen Sylva Rd, Craig-y-Don ☎77740 Plan:**21** Etr & mid May–4 Oct Lic 14hc (4fb) CTV 8P S% B&b£5.75 Bdi£7.47–£9.20 D5pm

**GH Montclare Hotel** North Pde ☎77061 Plan:**22** Mar–Oct Lic 19hc (5fb) ⊁ CTV 4P sea S% ✳ B&b£5.50–£7.50 Bdi£7.50–£10 Wf52–£70 ⋮ D6pm

**GH Morningside Hotel** Gogarth Rd ☎79858 Plan:**23** Mar–Oct Lic 13hc 1⇔ 2⋔ (4fb) CTV 9P ⫽ S% B&b£8.50–£9 Bdi£11–£12 Wf75–£80 ⋮ D6.45pm

**GH Nant-y-Glyn** 59 Church Walks ☎75915 Plan:**24** Apr–Oct 10hc (4fb) ⊁ nc5 CTV ⫽ sea S% B&b£6–£6.50 Bdi£8–£9 Wf56–£63 D6pm

**GH Orotava Private Hotel** 105 Glan-y-Mor Rd, Penrhyn Bay ☎49780 Plan:**25** Etr–Oct 6hc (1fb) ⊁ nc4 CTV 6P sea S% B&bfr£7.65 Bdifr£11.60 Wfr£81.20 ⋮ D6.30pm

**GH Penelope Private Hotel** Central Prom ☎76577 Plan:**26** Apr–Sep Lic 24hc ⊁ CTV 10P sea S% B&b£6.64–£8.22 Bdi£9.17–£11.38 Wf61.35–£78.43 ⋮ D4pm

**GH Plas Madoc Private Hotel** 60 Church Walks ☎76514 Plan:**27** Etr–Oct Lic 9hc (3fb) ⊁ nc5 CTV 5P sea S% B&b£6–£7.25 Bdi£8–£9.50 Wf42–£66.50 ⋮ D6pm

**GH** *Prion Hotel* 8 Mostyn Av, Craig-y-Don ☎75050 Plan:**28** Mar–Oct 9hc (4fb) CTV ⫽ D6pm

**GH Puffin Lodge Hotel** ☎77713 Plan:**29**
Mar–Sep Lic 14hc 1🛏 (8fb) ✠ CTV 14P sea
S% B&bf7.75–£8.75 Bdi£10.75–£11.75
W£75.25–£82.25

**GH Quinton Hotel** 36 Church Walks
☎76879 Plan:**30** Mar–Oct & 1wk Xmas Lic
16hc 3⇔ CTV P 🎜 ✱ B&bfr£6.90 Bdi fr£8.62
D6.30pm

**GH Rosaire Private Hotel** 2 St Seiriols Rd
☎77677 Plan:**31** Lic 12hc (5fb) ✠ CTV 5P
S% B&b£6.50–£7.50 Bdi£8–£8.50 W£52–
£55 ⅃ D5pm
**See advert on page 127**

**GH St Hilary Hotel** Promenade, Craig-y-Don
☎75551 Plan:**32** Mar–Nov 11hc 1🛏 (5fb)
CTV sea S% B&b£6.25 W£43.75 Ⓜ

**GH Sandilands Private Hotel** Dale Rd,
West Shore ☎75555 Plan:**33** May–Sep Lic
11hc (5fb) CTV 11P 🎜 sea B&b£6.65–£7.10
Bdi£9.90–£10.35 W£66.25–£69.50 ⅃ D6pm

**GH Sandringham Hotel** West Pde ☎76513
Plan:**34** Etr–Nov Lic 18hc 2⇔ (4fb) ✠ CTV TV
in all bedrooms 6P 🎜 sea B&b£9–£10
Bdi£11.50–£12.50 W£80–£87.50 ⅃ D7pm

**GH *Sun Ray Private Hotel*** 13 Carmen Sylva
Rd, Craig-y-Don ☎77828 Plan:**35** Lic 9hc
(2fb) ✠ nc5 CTV D5pm

**GH Tilstone Private Hotel** Carmen Sylva
Rd, Craig-y-Don ☎75588 Plan:**36** Lic 8hc
(1fb) ✠ nc5 CTV 🎜 S% B&b£8.25 Bdi£10.50
W£71.75 D6pm

⊨⊣ **GH Victoria House** 4–5 Victoria St
☎79920 Plan:**37** 9hc (3fb) ✠ CTV 3P 🎜 S%
B&b£5.25–£6.05 Bdi£7.25–£8.35 W£50.75–
£58.45 D8pm

**GH Warwick Hotel** 56 Church Walks
☎76823 Plan:**38** Apr–Oct Lic 17hc (11fb)
CTV 🎜 sea B&b£7.50–£8 Bdi£9.75–£10.35
W£64.40–£70.15 ⅃ D6.45pm

**GH Westdale Private Hotel** 37 Abbey Rd
☎77996 Plan:**39** Apr–Oct Lic 12hc 1⇔ (5fb)
CTV 6P sea S% B&b£6.35–£6.75 Bdi£8.35–
£8.75 W£58–£61 ⅃ D6pm

**LLANELLI** Dyfed *Map 2 SN50*
**GH *Croft*** 89 Queen Victoria Rd ☎4539
Closed Etr & Xmas Lic 18hc (4fb) ✠ CTV 20P
🎜 D6pm

**LLANFAIRFECHAN** Gwynedd *Map 6 SH67*
**GH Plas Menai Hotel** Penmaenmawr Rd
☎680346 Mar–Oct & Xmas 29hc 1⇔ 1🛏
(16fb) ✠ CTV 15P S% ✱ B&b£6.50–£8
Bdi£8.75–£9.75 W£56.50–£67.85 ⅃ Dam (W
only mid Jul–Aug)

**GH Queens House** ☎680509 10rm 8hc
(3fb) CTV 30P S% B&b£6–£7

**GH Rhiwiau Riding Centre** Gorddinog
☎680094 Lic 3hc (A 4hc) (1fb) ✠ CTV 8P S%
B&b£7.50 Bdi£10.50

**LLANGATTOCK** Powys *Map 2 SO21*
**GH Park Place** The Legar ☎Crickhowell
810562 May–Oct 7hc (4fb) ✠ CTV 10P 🎜
river S% B&b£6–£7

**LLANGRANOG** Dyfed *Map 2 SN35*
**INN Pentre Arms Hotel** ☎229 Apr–Sep
rsMar & Oct 11hc 🚿 nc5 CTV 6P 4🏠 🎜 sea
S% B&b£8.60–£9.50 Bdi£13.20–£14.40
W£82–£86 ⅃ Bar lunch£1.50–£2.50
D6pmf4–£5.50

**LLANSANTFFRAID YM MECHAIN** Powys
*Map 7 SJ22*
**GH** *Bryn Tanat Hall Hotel* ☎Llansantffraid
259 mid May–Sep Lic 12hc ✝ CTV 12P 2🐎
river D7pm

**LLANWRTYD WELLS** Powys *Map 3 SN84*
**GH** *Lasswade House* ☎515 Lic 6hc (2fb) Ch
CTV 6P ⅢⅢ S% B&bfr£7 Bdifr£12 Wfr£75 ⅃
D8.30pm

**LLANYSTUMDWY** Gwynedd *Map 6 SH43*
**GH** *Gwyndy* ☎Criccieth 2720 Closed 2wks
Oct Lic 6hc 2🛁 (1fb) CTV 20P ⅢⅢ B&b£6.25–
£6.50 Bdi£10.25–£10.50 W£42–£45 Ⓜ
D8.30pm

**LLWYNGWRIL** Gwynedd *Map 6 SH50*
**GH** *Gwelfor* ☎Fairbourne 250343 Etr–Sep
Lic 5hc ✝nc CTV 6P ⅢⅢ sea S% B&b£7 Bdi£10
W£60 ⅃ D6pm

**LOCHINVER** Highland *Sutherland Map 14
NC02*
**GH** *Ardglas* ☎257 Mar–Oct 8hc (4fb) CTV
20P ⅢⅢ sea S% ✳ B&b£5.50–£6

**GH** *Hillcrest* Badnaban (2m S on unclass rd)
☎391 4hc CTV 4P ⅢⅢ sea S% ✳ B&b£6–£7
Bdi£11.50–£12 D6.30pm (W only Oct–Apr)

**GH** *Park House Hotel* Main St ☎259 Lic 4hc
CTV 20P ⅢⅢ river S% B&bfr£9.20 D9pm

**LOCHRANZA** Isle of Arran, Strathclyde *Bute
Map 10 NR95*
**GH** *Kincardine Lodge* ☎267 Apr–Oct 8hc
(4fb) 6P sea D7pm

**LOCKERBIE** Dumfries & Galloway
*Dumfriesshire Map 11 NY18*

**GH** *Rosehill* Carlisle Rd ☎2378 6hc (3fb)
CTV 4P ⅢⅢ S% B&bf£6

**LONDON** Greater London *Map 4 & 5* **See
plans 1–4 pages *131–135***
**A map of the London postal area appears
on pages *136 & 137***
Places within the London postal area are
listed below in postal district order
commencing North, then South and West,
with a brief indication of the area covered.
Detailed plans **1–3** show the locations of AA-
listed hotels within the Central London
postal districts which are indicated by a
number. Plan **4** highlights the districts
covered within the outer area keyed by a grid
reference eg A3. **Other places within the
county of London are listed under their
respective placenames and are also
keyed to this plan or the main map
section**

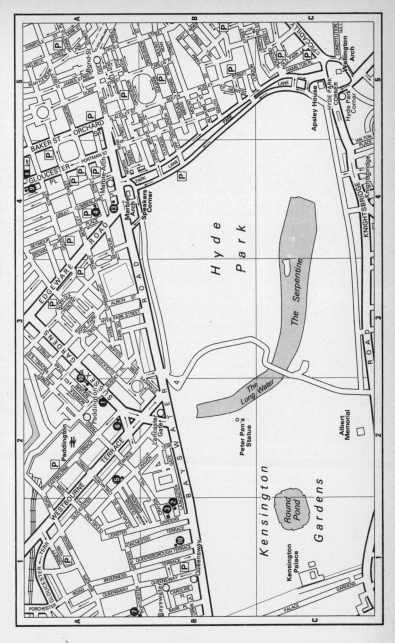

1 Ashley Hotel
2 Caring Hotel
3 Century Hotel
4 Concorde Hotel
5 Dylan Hotel

6 Edward Hotel
7 Garden Court
   Hotel
8 Georgian House
   Hotel

9 Hart House Hotel
10 King's Hotel
10A Nayland Hotel
13 Rose Court Hotel

# London Plan 2

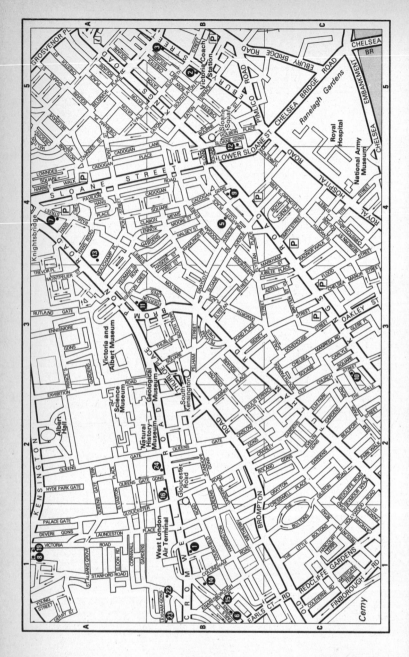

| | | |
|---|---|---|
| **1** Adelphi Hotel | **9** Culford Hall Hotel | **16** Milton Court Hotel |
| **5** Blair House Hotel | **10** Eden House Hotel | **19** Prince's Lodge |
| **6** Burns Hotel | **11** Garden House Hotel | **22** Silver Star Hotel |
| **7** Campden Court | **12** Willet Hotel | **23** Suncourt Hotel |
| **3** Chesham House | **13** Knightsbridge | **24** Tudor Court Hotel |
| **2** Chester House Hotel | **14** Manor Court Hotel | |
| **8** Clearlake Hotel | **15** Merlyn Court Hotel | |

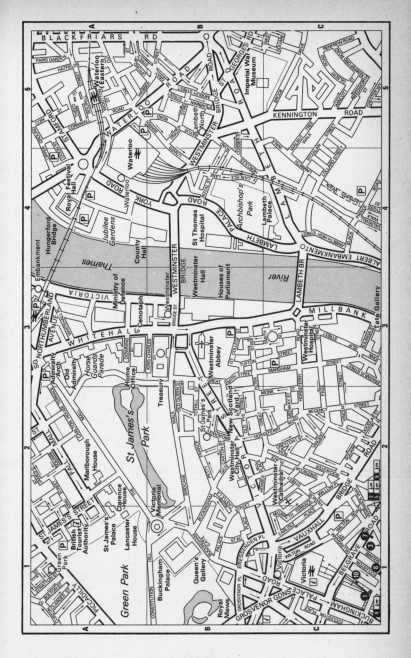

1 Arden House
2 Beverley Towers
  Hotel
5 Corbigoe Hotel

6 Corona Hotel
7 Easton Hotel
8 Elizabeth
3 Franterre

9 Hanover Hotel
10 Holly House

# London Plan 4

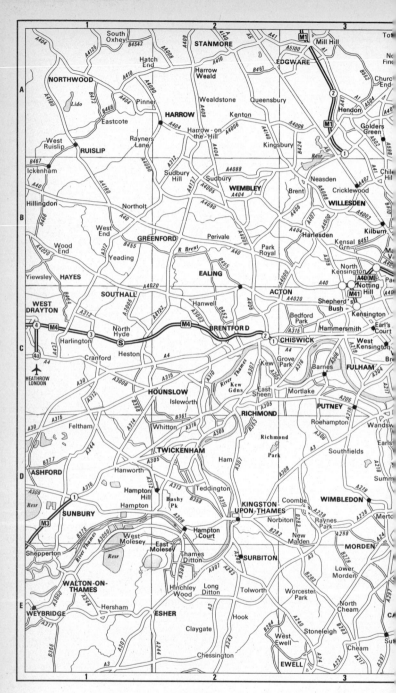

● locations with AA listed establishments

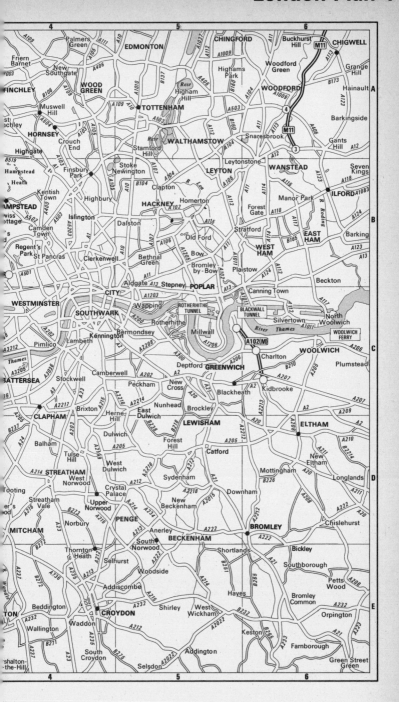

# London Postal Districts and ways in & out of London

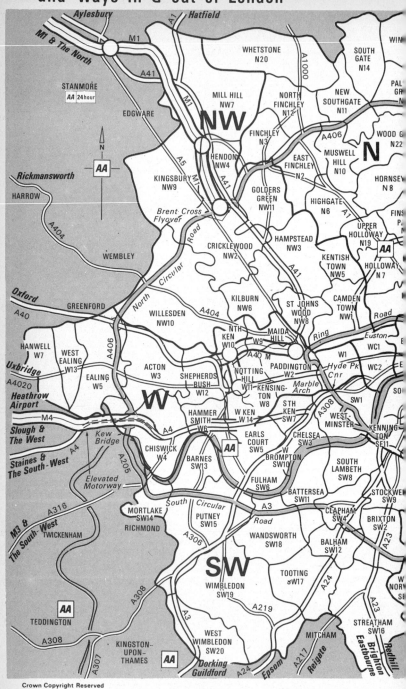

London Postal Area Boundary
London Postal District Boundaries
Main Roads into and out of London
Signposted North and South Circular
Roads & Ring Road
Other Main Roads

Service Centre **AA**

Scale of Miles
0  1  2  3  4

Cambridge
A10

LOWER
EDMONTON
N9

CHINGFORD
E4

UPPER
EDMONTON N18

TOTTENHAM
N17

Epping
Bishops Stortford

WOODFORD
E18

A104

M11

A406

Chelmsford
Southend

SOUTH
TOTTENHAM
N15

A503

WALTHAMSTOW
E17

GANTS HILL

A12

A12
Romford

STOKE
NEWINGTON
N16

A114

LEYTONSTONE
E11

A10

CLAPTON
E5

LEYTON
E10

E

ILFORD

FOREST
GATE
E7

MANOR
PARK
E12

HACKNEY
E8

HOMERTON
E9

A11

A117

BARKING

Tilbury
A13

BETHNAL
GREEN
E2

BOW
E3

STRATFORD
E15

PLAISTOW
E13

EAST HAM
E6

EC3

A13

R THAMES

STEPNEY
E1

POPLAR
E14

NORTH WOOLWICH
E16

THAMESMEAD
SE28

Free Ferry

ABBEY
WOOD
SE2

ROTHERHITHE
SE16

Ring Road

DEPTFORD
SE8

CHARLTON
SE7
A102M

A205

WOOLWICH
SE18

Erith
A206

NEW
CROSS
SE14

GREEN
WICH
SE10

A2

SE

A202

PECKHAM
SE15

BLACKHEATH
SE3

WELLING

A207

EAST
DULWICH
SE22

BROCKLEY
SE4

A21

LEWISHAM
SE13

A20

South

ELTHAM
SE9

A2

ULWICH
SE21

FOREST
HILL
SE23

A205

LEE
SE12

A20

Rochester
Motorway
Dover

CATFORD
SE6

SYDENHAM
SE26

SIDCUP

A20

WOOD
E19

ANERLEY
SE20

Maidstone
Folkestone

SOUTH
NORWOOD
SE25

A21

BROMLEY
Sevenoaks

BECKENHAM

Sevenoaks
Hastings

A224

© The Automobile Association 1981

137

**N4** Finsbury Park *London plan 4 B4*
**Redland Hotel** 418 Seven Sisters Rd ☎01-800 1826 24rm 23hc (5fb) ⚊ nc2 CTV 10P B&b£8–£10

**N8** Hornsey *London plan 4 A4*
**Aber Hotel** 89 Crouch Hill ☎01-340 2847 8hc (4fb) ⚊ CTV ⫿ S% B&b£6–£7 W£40 M̶ (W only Oct–Etr)

**Highgate Lodge Hotel** 9 Waverley Rd ☎01-340 5601 20hc (2fb) CTV 4P S% B&b£8.40–£9.60 Bdi£9.80–£11.90 W£57–£71 Ł D7.30pm

**N10** Muswell Hill *London plan 4 A4*
**Princes Hotel** 36–38 Princes Av, ☎01-883 5676 12hc (A 8hc) (4fb) ⚊ TV 4P ⫿ S% ✻ B&b£6.25–£7.25 W£39.10–£43.70 M̶

**N15** Tottenham *London plan 4 A5*
**Granham House** 97 Philip Ln ☎01-801 2244 Lic 15hc (1fb) CTV 12P ⫿ S% ✻ B&b£12.07–£17.25 Bdi£18.06–£23.24

**NW2** Cricklewood *London plan 4 B3*
⋈ **Clearview House** 161 Fordwych Rd ☎01-452 9773 6hc (1fb) ⚊ nc5 CTV P ⫿ S% B&b£5.50

**Garth Hotel** 72–76 Hendon Way ☎01-455 4742 Lic 36hc 27⇔ ⋔ (A 5hc) (15fb) ⚊ CTV 31P ⫿ S% ✻ B&b£15–£21 D8pm.

**NW3** Hampstead and Swiss Cottage *London plan 4 B4*
**Langorf Hotel** 20 Frognal ☎01-794 4483 32hc (2fb) CTV ⫿ S% B&b£6.50–£8

**NW6** Kilburn, West Hampstead *London plan 4 B3*

**Dawson House Hotel** 72 Canfield Gdns ☎01-624 0079 15hc ✶ CTV ▥ S% B&bf£7.50–£8.50 Wf£37.50–£49 ⋈

**Hazlewood House Hotel** 109 Broadhurst Gdns ☎01-624 8443 13hc (3fb) nc2 TV ▥ S% B&bf£8–£9 Wf£30 ⋈ (W only Oct–1 May)

*Mowbray House Hotel* 5 Mowbray Rd ☎01-459 4481 10hc (7fb) CTV ▥

**GH Mulroy** 4–6 Burton Rd ☎01-624 0727 12hc (4fb) ✶ CTV 6P ▥ S% B&bf£6–£8

**NW11** Golders Green *London plan 4 A3*

**Central Hotel** 35 Hoop Ln ☎01-458 5636 18hc (A 18⇆) (6fb) ✶ CTV 12P ▥ S% B&bf£10–£22 D6pm

**GH Croft Court Hotel** 44 Ravenscroft Av ☎01-458 3331 20hc 5⇆ 1🛆 (4fb) CTV 3P ▥ S% B&bf£11.50–£13.50 Bdi£16–£18 Wf£70–£80 ⋈ D6pm

**Ridgeway House Hotel** 59 The Ridgeway ☎01-458 4146 6hc ✶ nc4 CTV ▥ S% B&bfrf£6–£8

**SE3** Blackheath *London plan 4 C5*

**Bardon Lodge** 15 Stratheden Rd ☎01-853 4051 Closed Xmas 6hc 4🛆 (2fb) ✶ CTV 10P ▥ S% B&bf£8.75–£11

**SE9** Eltham *London plan 4 D6*

**Yardley Court** 18 Court Yard ☎01-850 1850 7hc 1⇆ (2fb) ✶ nc3 CTV 6P S% B&bf£8.80

**SE19** Norwood *London plan 4 D4*

**Crystal Palace Tower Hotel** 114 Church Rd ☎01-653 0176 13hc (5fb) CTV 12P ▥ S% B&bf£7–£9

**SE25** South Norwood *London plan 4 D4*

**Toscana** 19 South Norwood Hill ☎01-653 3962 Lic 8hc (2fb) ✶ CTV 8P ▥ S% B&bf£10 Wf£62 ⋈

**SW1** West End–Westminster; St James's Park, Victoria Station

**Arden House** 12 St Georges Dr ☎01-834 2988 Plan3:**1** 34hc 6⇆ 2🛆 (A 14hc) (12fb) ✶ CTV ▥ S% B&bf£11–£12

*Beverley Towers Hotel* 106–108 Belgrave Rd ☎01-828 6767 Plan**3:** 2 Lic 53hc CTV ▥ D9.30pm

**Chesham House** 64–66 Ebury St, Belgravia ☎01-730 8513 Plan 2:**3** TV in all bedrooms ▥ S% ✻B&bf£8.75–£9.75

*Chester House Hotel* 134 Ebury St, Belgravia ☎01-730 3632 Plan2:**2** 12hc 8⇆ ✶ CTV ▥

**Corbigoe Hotel** 101 Belgrave Rd, Victoria ☎01-828 6873 Plan3:**5** 17hc 1⇆ 1🛆 (6fb) ✶ CTV ▥ S% B&bf£6–£10 (w only Nov–Mar)

**Corona Hotel** 87–89 Belgrave Rd, Victoria ☎01-828 9279 Plan3:**6** Closed Xmas Lic 31hc 8⇆ 10🛆 (2fb) CTV ▥ S% ✻B&bf£12–£15 Wf£70 ⋈

**Easton Hotel** 36–40 Belgrave Rd ☎01-834 5938 Plan3:**7** Lic 42hc (A 12hc) (13fb) ✶ nc3 CTV ▥ S% ✻B&bf£9–£11

**Elizabeth Hotel** 37 Eccleston Sq, Victoria ☎01-828 6812 Plan3:**8** 24hc 1⇆ 2🛆 (6fb) ✶ CTV ▥ S% B&bf£9.50–£17.50

**Franterre Hotel** 142 Warwick Way, Victoria ☎01-834 5163 Plan3:**3** 8hc (4fb) nc10 CTV ▥ B&bf£10 (W only Jan–1 Mar)

**Hanover Hotel** 30 St Georges Dr ☎01-834 0134 Plan3:**9** 34hc 6⇌ 12🛏 (8fb) CTV in all bedrooms ▥ S% B&bf£10–£16 W£56–£84 M (W only Oct–Mar)

**Holly House** 20 Hugh St ☎01-834 5671 Plan3:**10** 11hc (2fb) ✟ ▥ S% B&bf£10–£11

**Willet Hotel** 32 Sloane Gdns, Sloane Sq ☎01-730 0634 Plan2:**12** 17hc 14⇌ (6fb) ✟ ▥ S% B&bf£11.25–£13.25

**SW3** Chelsea
*Blair House Hotel* 34 Draycott Pl ☎01-581 2323 Plan2:**5** 17hc 10⇌ (4fb) ✟ CTV ▥

**Campden Court Hotel** 28 Basil St ☎01-589 6286 Plan2:**7** Lic 16hc 8⇌ (3fb) CTV in all bedrooms ▥ lift S% ✳ B&bf£20

**GH Culford Hall Hotel** 7 Culford Gdns

☎01-581 2211 Plan2:**9** 30hc 6⇌ 6🛏 (4fb) CTV ▥ S% B&bfr£8.50 (W only Nov–Apr)

**Eden House Hotel** 111 Old Church St ☎01-352 3403 Plan2:**10** 14hc 4⇌ 3🛏 (4fb) 🄲🄷 CTV ▥ S% B&bf£9.20–£16.10 W£70 M

**Garden House Hotel** 44–46 Egerton Gdns ☎01-584 2990 Plan2:**11** 27hc 4⇌ 4🛏 (2fb) TV in all bedrooms ▥ lift B&bf£7.50–£10.50

**Knightsbridge** 10 Beaufort Gdns ☎01-589 9271 Plan2:**13** Lic 20hc 9⇌ (2fb) CTV ▥ D10.30pm (W only Nov–Mar)

**SW4** Clapham *London plan 4 D4*
⋈ **GH Edwards** 91 Abbeville Rd, Clapham Common ☎01-622 6347 9hc (3fb) ✟ nc5 TV winter only S% B&bf£5–£7

*Regency Lodge Hotel* 5 Crescent Gv, South Side, Clapham Common ☎01-622 2684 Lic 30hc nc4 CTV 6P ▥ D7.30pm

**SW5** Earls Court *London plan 4 C3*
**Arlanda Hotel** 17 Longridge Rd ☎01-370 5213 15hc 2⇌ (4fb) ✹ nc14 CTV ▥ S% B&b£7.50–£10 W£35–£49 ℳ

**Burns Hotel** 18–24 Barkston Gdns, Earls Court ☎01-373 3151 Plan2:**6** Lic 104hc 100⇌ 4⋔ (A 17hc 5⇌) (14fb) ✹ CTV ▥ lift S% ✳B&b£8–£20 Bdi£12–£24 W£65–£125 ⱔ D9.15pm

**Kensington Court Hotel** 33–35 Nevern Pl ☎01-370 5151 Lic 35⇌ (11fb) CTV in all bedrooms 10P 1☎ ▥ lift S% B&b£14–£16 W£95–£105 ℳ

*Manor Court Hotel* 35 Courtfield Gdns ☎01-373 8585 Plan2:**14** Lic 88rm 20hc 53⇌ (15fb) CTV ▥ lift

*Merlyn Court Hotel* 2 Barkston Gds ☎01-370 1640 Plan2:**15** 18hc 2⇌⋔ (4fb) ✹ CTV ▥

**Nevern Hotel** 29–31 Nevern Pl ☎01-370 4827 Lic 32hc 6⇌ 3⋔ (10fb) ✹ CTV ▥ lift S% B&b£7–£8.50

**SW7** South Kensington
**Adelphi Hotel** 127–129 Cromwell Rd ☎01-373 7177 Plan2:**1** Lic 57hc 54⇌ CTV ▥ lift S% ✳B&b£14.50

**Milton Court Hotel** 68–74 Cromwell Rd ☎01-584 7851 Plan2:**16** 102hc 17⇌ 1⋔ (5fb) CTV ▥ lift S% B&b£12.50–£21

**Tudor Court Hotel** 58–66 Cromwell Rd ☎01-584 8273 Plan2:**24** 83hc 39⇌ 2⋔ (13fb) CTV ▥ lift S% B&b£12.50–£21

**SW13** Barnes *London plan 4 C3*
**Arundel Hotel** Arundel Ter ☎01-748 8005 rsXmas 30hc 5⇌ (2fb) ▥ S% B&b£8.63–£10.93 W£33.93–£51.38 ℳ

**SW15** Putney *London plan 4 C3*
GH *Lodge Hotel* 52 Upper Richmond Rd ☎01-874 1598 rsXmas Lic 30hc 22⇌ (4fb) CTV 14P ▥ ⅋

**Wilton House Hotel** 2 Ravenna Rd ☎01-789 3768 10hc (2fb) CTV 2P ▥ S% B&b£6.50–£9

**SW19** Wimbledon *London plan 4 D3*
**Hatherley Hotel** 87 Worple Rd ☎01-946 5917 9hc 1⇌ 1⋔ (4fb) CTV 9P ▥ S% B&b£11

**Trochee** 21 Malcolm Rd ☎01-946 1579 17hc (2fb) CTV 6P ▥ S% B&b£12.50 (W only Oct–Apr)

**Wimbledon Hotel** 78 Worple Rd ☎01-946 9265 9hc (4fb) CTV 9P ▥ S% B&b£11

*Worcester House* 38 Alwyne Rd ☎01-946 1300 7hc 4⇌ ⋔ (1fb) ✹ CTV ▥

**W1** West End, Piccadilly Circus, St Marylebone and Mayfair *London plan 4*
*Concorde Hotel* 50 Gt Cumberland Pl ☎01-402 6169 Plan1:**4** Lic 28⇌ CTV ▥ lift

**Eros Hotel** 67 Shaftesbury Av ☎01-734 8781 Lic 63rm 40hc 23⇌ (13fb) TV in all bedrooms B&b£15.15

**Georgian House Hotel** 87 Gloucester Pl, Baker St ☎01-935 2211 Plan1:**8** Lic 19hc 15⇌ 4⋔ (3fb) ✹ nc5 CTV ▥ lift S% B&b£11–£13

**Hart House Hotel** 51 Gloucester Pl, Portman Sq ☎01-935 2288 Plan1:**9** Closed Xmas 15hc 9⇌ (4fb) ✹ CTV ▥ S% B&b£10–£16

**Milford House** 31 York St ☎01-935 1935 6hc 1⇌ (2fb) ✹ CTV ▥ S% B&b£7–£10 (W only Nov–Mar)

*Rose Court Hotel* 35 Gt Cumberland Pl ☎01-262 7241 Plan1:**13** Lic 60hc CTV lift ▥

**W2** Bayswater, Paddington *London plan 4*
**Ashley Hotel** 15 Norfolk Sq, Hyde Pk ☎01-723 3375 Plan1:**1** rsXmas (no breakfast) 16hc 2⋔ (1fb) ✹ CTV ▥ S% B&b£7.70

**Caring Hotel** 24 Craven Hill Gdns, Leinster Ter, Hyde Pk ☎01-262 8708 Plan1:**2** 26hc 11⇌ (8fb) ✹ ▥ S% B&b£11.50 (W only Nov–Mar)

*Century Hotel* 18–19 Craven Hill Gdns ☎01-262 6644 Plan1:**3** Lic 60⇌ ✹ CTV 2P ▥ lift

*Dylan Hotel* 14 Devonshire Ter ☎01-723 3280 Plan1:**5** 15hc CTV

**Edward Hotel** 1A Spring St ☎01-262 2671 Plan1:**6** Lic 58hc (10fb) CTV 8P ▥ lift S% ✳B&b£8–£12 Wfr£50 ℳ D9.45pm (W only Nov–Mar)

**Garden Court Hotel** 30–31 Kensington Gardens Sq ☎01-727 8304 Plan1:**7** Lic 37hc 6⇌ 4⋔ (4fb) ✹ CTV ▥ S% B&b£10.35–£13.80

*King's Hotel* 60–62 Queensborough Ter ☎01-229 7055 Plan1:**10** 29hc CTV ▥

**Nayland Hotel** 134 Sussex Gdns ☎01-723 3380 Plan1:**10A** 15hc 1⇌ (4fb) ✹ CTV P ▥ S% B&b£8.40

**Pembridge Court Hotel** 34 Pembridge Gdns ☎01-229 9977 Lic 27hc 18⇌ 8⋔ ✹ CTV 2☎ ▥ S% ✳B&b£23.50 D11pm (W only Nov–Feb)

**Slavia Hotel** 2 Pembridge Sq ☎01-727 1316 Lic 31rm 1⇔ 30⋒ (8fb) CTV 2P ⊞ *B&b£7.75–£12.50 W£65–£90 M̸

**W5** Ealing *London plan 4 B2*
**Grange Lodge** 50 Grange Rd ☎01-567 1049 Lic 14hc 4⋒ (5fb) ✱ CTV 5P ⊞ S% B&b£7–£8 Bdi£11.50 W£49 M̸ D5.30pm

**22 Grange Park** ☎01-567 6984 12rm 11hc 2⇔ CTV available on request 4P ⊞ S% B&b£12.65 W£75 M̸

**W8** Kensington *London plan 4 C3*
***Alexa Hotel*** 71–75 Lexham Gdns ☎01-373 7272 49hc 6⇔ ✱ nc3 CTV ⊞ lift

**Clearlake Hotel** 18–19 Prince of Wales Ter ☎01-937 3274 Plan2: **8** Lic 15hc 3⇔ 6⋒ (3fb) CTV in all bedrooms ⊞ lift S% B&b£9.20–£18.40 Bdi£14.95–£23 W£64.40 M̸ D10.30pm

**Observatory House Hotel** Observatory Gdns ☎01-937 1577 24hc (2fb) ✱ CTV ⊞ S% B&b£12–£13

**Prince's Lodge** 6–8 Prince of Wales Ter ☎01-937 6306 Plan2: **19** Lic 36hc 17⇔ 4⋒ (7fb) ✱ CTV ⊞ lift S% B&b£8–£20

**Silver Star Hotel** 13 Lexham Gdns ☎01-373 9426 Plan2: **22** 20hc 4⇔ 16⋒ (3fb) ✱ CTV ⊞ S% B&b£10–£16 (W only Oct–Mar)

**Suncourt Hotel** 57–67 Lexham Gdns ☎01-373 7242 Plan2: **23** 100hc 27⇔ (12fb) CTV ⊞ lift S% B&b£12.50–£21

**W14** West Kensington *London plan 4 C3*
**Avonmore Hotel** 66 Avonmore Rd ☎01-603 4296 Lic 9hc ✱ CTV in all bedrooms ⊞ S% B&b£12 W available M̸

**WC1** Bloomsbury, Holborn *London plan 4*
***Mentone Hotel*** 54–55 Cartwright Gdns ☎01-387 3927 27hc (10fb) ✱ CTV ⊞

**Mount Pleasant Hotel** 53 Calthorpe St ☎01-837 9781 Lic 405hc 30⇔ 39⋒ (23fb) ✱ CTV ⊞ lift D8.45pm

**LONGDOWNS** Cornwall *Map 2 SW73*
**GH Marrack House** ☎Stithians 860231 6rm 5hc CTV 6P S% B&b£6 Bdi£10 W£63 Ł D10am

**LONG EATON** Derbys *Map 8 SK43*
**GH Camden Hotel** Nottingham Rd ☎62901 rs wknds Lic 7hc (A 9hc) (3fb) CTV 16P ⊞ B&b£11.39–£12.65 Bdi£16.45–£17.71 D7.30pm

**LONGFRAMLINGTON** Northumb *Map 46 NU10*
**INN Granby** ☎228 3hc 1⇔ ⇎ ✱ nc12 30P ⊞ S% *B&b£8.75–£10 Bdi£14.75–£16 Bar lunch £3.10–£7.90 D9pm£7alc

**LOOE** Cornwall *Map 2 SX25* **(See Plan)**
**GH Annaclone Hotel** Marine Dr, Hannafore ☎4177 Plan: **1** May–Sep 7rm 3hc 3⇔ 1⋒ (3fb) ✱ nc12 CTV 2P sea S% *B&b£6–£8 W£40–£53 M̸

**GH Commonwood Hotel** St Martin's Rd ☎2929 Plan: **2** Etr–Oct Lic 18hc 1⋒ (3fb) Ch CTV 20P river sea B&b£7–£9 Bdi£10–£13 W£68–£89 Ł D8pm

**GH Deganwy Hotel** Station Rd ☎2984 Plan: **3** Etr–Oct Lic 9hc (3fb) ✱ nc5 CTV 6P river sea S% B&b£7.75–£9.80 Bdi£12.35–£14.40 W£69–£92 Ł

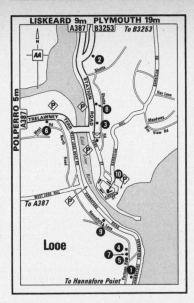

1  Annaclone Hotel
2  Commonwood Hotel
3  Deganwy Hotel
4  Fieldhead Hotel
5  Hillingdon
6  Kantara
7  Lemain Hotel
8  Riverside Hotel
9  Rockwell Hotel
10 Smugglers' House Hotel

**GH Fieldhead Hotel** Portruan Rd, Hannafore ☎2689 Plan:**4** Mar–mid Nov Lic 17hc 6⇔ (3fb) ✻ CTV 13P 12☎ sea B&bf£9.20–£14.95 Bdi£15.55–£21.30 Wf£56.35–£96.60 M D8.30pm
**See advert on page 144**

**GH Hillingdon** Portruan Rd, Hannafore ☎2906 Plan:**5** Mar–Oct Lic 8hc (3fb) ✻ CTV 2☎ ⬛ sea S% B&bf£6.50–£8.50 Bdi£9.50–£11 Wf£65–£75 ⱡ D5pm

⋈ **GH Kantara** 7 Trelawney Ter ☎2093 Plan:**6** Mar–Oct 6hc (2fb) TV river S% B&bf£5–£6.50 Wf£35–£45.50 M

**GH Lemain Hotel** Hannafore Ln, Hannafore ☎2073 Plan:**7** Etr–Sep Lic 9hc (4fb) CTV 14P ⬛ S% ✳B&bf£7.95–£11 Bdif£11.90–£15.22 Wf£68.10–£90.60 ⱡ D4.30pm

**GH Riverside Hotel** Station Rd ☎2100 Plan:**8** Etr–Oct Lic 13hc (5fb) ✻ CTV river S% B&bf£6.75–£8 Bdif£10.50–£11.75 Wf£58–£75 ⱡ D4pm

**GH Rockwell Hotel** Hannafore Rd, Hannafore ☎2123 Plan:**9** Lic 12hc (4fb) CTV 9P 1☎ ⬛ river sea S% B&bf£8–£11.50 Bdif£13–£16.50 Wf£75–£105 ⱡ D7.30pm
**See advert on page 144**

**GH Smugglers House Hotel** Middle Market St ☎2397 Plan:**10** Lic 7hc 3⇔ (1fb) ✻ CTV ⬛ D10.30pm

**LOSTWITHIEL** Cornwall *Map 2 SX15*
**GH Trevone Hotel** ☎Bodmin 872528 Feb–Nov Lic 8hc (2fb) CTV 15P ⬛ S% B&bf£9.50–£11 Bdif£11–£13.50 Wf£75–£80 ⱡ D7pm

**LOUGHBOROUGH** Leics *Map 8 SK51*
**GH De Montfort Hotel** 88 Leicester Rd

☎216061 Lic 9hc (1fb) CTV ▥ S% B&b£8.50 D8pm

**GH Sunnyside Hotel** The Coneries ☎216217 8hc ★ CTV 8P 3⌂ ▥ S% B&b£8 Bdi£11 W£77 D4pm

**LOUTH** Lincs *Map 8 TF38*
**INN King's Head** ☎602965 Closed Xmas 17hc 1⇔ ★ CTV 30P 10⌂ ▥ S% B&b£9.50–£11.50 Bdi£15–£20 sn L£1.25–£2.60&alc D10pm£4.50–£6.50&alc

**INN Lincolnshire Poacher** 211 Eastgate ☎603657 5hc 2⋒ ★ CTV 20P ▥ S% B&b£8.05 W£56.35 M̸

**LOWESTOFT** Suffolk *Map 5 TM59*
**GH Amity** 396 London Rd South ☎2586 Lic 6hc (4fb) ★ CTV 3P ▥ S% ✱B&b£5–£5.50 Bdi£7–£7.50 W£42–£45 ⱡ D4pm

⊢⊣ **GH Cleveland House** 9 Cleveland Rd ☎62827 Closed Xmas 6hc (2fb) CTV 1P ▥ S% B&b£5.50 Bdi£7.75 W£35–£37 M̸ D6pm

**GH Kingsleigh** 44 Marine Pde ☎2513 Closed Xmas 6hc (2fb) nc4 CTV 6P sea S% B&b£6.50–£7

**GH Westview House Hotel** Lyndhurst Rd ☎64616 Lic 13hc 3⋒ (2fb) CTV 9P ▥ S% B&b£9.20–£10.35 Bdi£12.65 W£63.25–£75.90 ⱡ D6pm

**LUCKWELL BRIDGE** Somerset *Map 3 SS93*
**GH Brook Farm Hotel** ☎Timberscombe 263 Closed Xmas wk rs2wks Oct (B&b only) Lic 6hc (2fb) ★ Ch CTV 6P 1⌂ ▥ S% B&b£6.50–£8.45 Bdi£10–£13 W£63–£82 ⱡ D5pm (W only Aug)

**LUDLOW** Salop *Map 7 SO57*
**GH Cecil Private Hotel** Sheet Rd ☎2442 Lic 11hc (1fb) CTV 11P ▥ S% B&b£7–£8 Bdi£11–£12.50 W£66–£75 ⱡ D9am

**GH Croft** Dinham ☎2076 8hc (3fb) CTV S% B&b£6 W£40 M̸

**LULWORTH** Dorset *Map 3 SY88*
**GH Gatton House Hotel** ☎West Lulworth 252 Closed Xmas rsJan Lic 10hc (2fb) CTV 10P ▥ S% B&b£8–£12 Bdi£12.50–£17 W£80–£95 ⱡ D6.30pm

**GH *Lulworth Hotel*** Main Rd ☎West Lulworth 230 Mar–Oct rsNov–Feb Lic 12hc ★ nc5 CTV 12P

**GH Shirley Hotel** ☎West Lulworth 358 Jun–Sep rsMar–May & Oct Lic 15hc 6⇔ 3⋒ (4fb) CTV 20P ▥ B&b£7.80–£10.50 Bdi£11.40–£14.50 W£79.80–£101.50 ⱡ D9pm

**LUTON** Beds *Map 4 TL02*
**GH Albany House Hotel** 9 Marsh Rd ☎591033 Closed Xmas Lic 10hc (1fb) ★ CTV 14P ▥ S% ✱B&b£9.28–£14.95 W£95–£125 ⱡ D7pm

**GH Arlington Hotel** 137 New Bedford Rd ☎419614 Lic 17hc (2fb) ★ 20P ▥ S% ✱B&bfr£15 Bdifr£16 Wfr£100 ⱡ D6.30pm

**GH Humberstone Private Hotel** 618 Dunstable Rd ☎54399 rs wknds Lic 10hc 2⋒ (4fb) ★ nc7 TV in all bedrooms 14P ▥ S% ✱B&b£9.20–£18.40 Bdi£13.20–£17.50 D8pm

**GH *Lansdowne Lodge Private Hotel*** 31 Lansdowne Rd ☎31411 Lic 12hc 2⇔ (4fb) CTV 20P ▥ D7.45pm

**LYDFORD** Devon *Map 2 SX58*
**GH *Moor View*** Vale Down ☎220 Apr–Oct 7hc TV 6P 1⌂ D4pm

**INN Castle** ☎242 Closed Xmas day 5hc nc8 50P ▥ S% B&bf£9 sn L£2.50alc D9.30pm£5alc

**LYME REGIS** Dorset *Map 3 SY39*
**GH Coverdale** Woodmead Rd ☎2882 Etr & May–Oct 8hc (3fb) CTV 10P ▥ sea S% ✱B&b£5.95–£7.50 Bdi£7.95–£10.95 W£54.75–£69.75 Ł D5pm

**GH *Kent House Hotel*** Silver St ☎2020 Lic 10hc CTV 9P ▥ lift D7pm

**GH Kersbrook Hotel** Pound Rd ☎2596 Mar–mid Nov Lic 13hc 2⇌ 5⋒ (3fb) [Ch] CTV 14P ▥ S% B&b£8.50–£10.56 Bdi£13.80–£15.87 W£92–£106 Ł D7.15pm

**GH Old Monmouth Hotel** Church St ☎2456 Lic 7hc 3⋒ (2fb) ✯ CTV 6P S% B&b £6–£8 Bdi£9.50–£12 W£56–£74 Ł D7.30pm

**GH *Rotherfield*** View Rd ☎2811 Apr–Oct 7hc (4fb) nc3 CTV 7P sea D6.50pm

**GH White House** 47 Silver St ☎3420 Mar–Nov Lic 6hc (3fb) nc3 CTV ▥ S% B&bfr£6 Bdi fr£9.50 Wfr£59.50 Ł Dnoon

**LYNDHURST** Hants *Map 4 SU30*
**GH Bench View** Southampton Rd ☎2502 Jan–Nov 9rm 8hc (6fb) ✯ CTV 9P S% B&b£7–£8 Bdi£11–£13 W£70–£75 Ł D4pm

**GH Ormonde House Hotel** Southampton Rd ☎2806 Lic 16hc 4⋒ (4fb) [Ch] CTV 12P ▥ B&b£10 Bdi£15.50 W£88 Ł D7pm

**GH Whitemoor House Hotel** Southampton Rd ☎2186 Lic 5hc (2fb) [Ch] CTV 10P ▥ S% B&b£7.50–£8 Bdi£11.25–£12 W£75–£80 Ł D6.30pm

**LYNMOUTH** Devon *Map 3 SS74* **(See Plan)**
**See also Lynton**
**GH Bonnicott Hotel** Watersmeet Rd ☎Lynton 3346 Plan:**2** Mar–Dec Lic 9hc 1⋒ (2fb) CTV sea S% B&b£7–£9.50 Bdi£12–£14 W£69–£86 Ł D9pm
**See advert on page 146**

**GH Countisbury Lodge Hotel** Tors Park ☎Lynton 2388 Plan:**5** Feb–Nov Lic 8hc 2⇌ (2fb) CTV 10P ▥ river sea S% B&b£8.50–£9.50 Bdi£12–£13.50 W£79.35–£86 Ł D6pm

**GH East Lyn** Watersmeet Rd ☎Lynton 2540 Plan:**6** Lic 8hc (3fb) CTV 4P 2⌂ river sea S% ✱B&b£6.90–£8.25 Bdi£10.90–£12.25 W£69–£74 Ł D4pm

**GH Glenville Hotel** 2 Tors Rd ☎Lynton 2202 Plan:**8** Feb–Nov Lic 7hc (2fb) ✯ (guide dogs only) nc5 CTV 8P river S% B&b£6.90–£9.20 Bdi£10.35–£12.65 W£69–£80.50 Ł

**GH Heatherville** Tors Park ☎Lynton 2327 Plan:**9** Feb–Nov Lic 8hc 2⋒ (2fb) ✯ CTV 7P ▥ river S% ✱B&b£7.50–£8.50 Bdi£10.50–£11.50 W£65–£72 Ł D6pm
**See advert on page 147**

**GH Rock House** ☎Lynton 3508 Plan:**20** Mar–Oct rs mid Nov–Feb Lic 6hc (2fb) ✯ CTV 6P ▥ river S% B9b£8.50–£9.50 Bdi£13–£14.50 W£82.50–£92 Ł D6.30pm
**See advert on page 147**

**INN Rising Sun** Mars Hill, The Harbour ☎Lynton 3223 Plan:**19** Feb–mid Dec 16hc 1⋒ CTV ▥ sea S% B&b£11.82–£13 W£110.68–£121.74 Ł Bar lunch £1–£5&alc D9pm£3–£8.50&alc
**See advert on page 147**

**LYNTON** Devon *Map 3 SS74*
**(See Plan.) See also Lynmouth**

1 **Alford House** *(see under Lynton)*
2 **Bonnicott Hotel** *(see under Lynmouth)*
3 **Channel View** *(see under Lynton)*
5 **Countisbury Lodge** *(see under Lynmouth)*
6 **East Lyn** *(see under Lynmouth)*
7 **Gable Lodge Hotel** *(see under Lynton)*
8 **Glenville Hotel** *(see under Lynmouth)*
9 **Heatherville** *(see under Lynmouth)*
10 **Ingleside Hotel** *(see under Lynton)*
11 **Kingford House Private Hotel** *(see under Lynton)*
12 **Longmead House** *(see under Lynton)*
14 **Lynhurst** *(see under Lynton)*

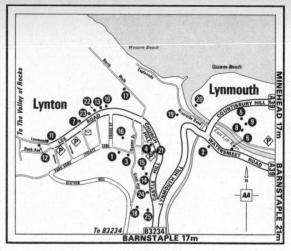

15 **Mayfair Hotel** *(see under Lynton)*
17 **North Cliff Private Hotel** *(see under Lynton)*
18 **Pine Lodge** *(see under Lynton)*
19 **Rising Sun** *(Inn)*
*(see under Lynmouth)*
20 **Rock House** *(see under Lynmouth)*
21 **St Vincents** *(see under Lynmouth)*
22 **South View** *(see under Lynton)*
23 **Turret** *(see under Lynton)*
24 **Valley House Hotel** *(see under Lynton)*
25 **Woodlands Hotel** *(see under Lynton)*

---

**GH Alford House** 3 Alford Ter ☎2359
Plan:**1** Apr–Oct Lic 8hc (1fb) ✻nc5 CTV ⬛ river sea S% B&bf7–£9 Bdif£13–£15 Wf£80–£95 ⌇ D6pm

**GH *Channel View*** 2 Alford Ter ☎3379
Plan:**3** Mar–Oct Lic 7hc ✻CTV sea D6.45pm

**GH Gable Lodge Hotel** Lee Rd ☎2367
Plan:**7** Mar–Nov rsFeb Lic 9hc 2⇔4⋔ (2fb) CTV 4P 5♨⬛ S% B&bf£8.85–£9.50 Bdif£13.90–£14.50 Wf£91.70–£96.80 ⌇ D7pm

**GH Ingleside Hotel** Lee Rd ☎2223 Plan:**10** Apr–9 Oct 7rm 4⇔3⋔ (3fb) ✻ Ⓒ CTV 9P ⬛ S% B&bf£8–£12 Bdif£13.50–£17 D6pm

**GH Kingford House Private Hotel** Longmead ☎2361 Plan:**11** Mar–Oct Lic 8hc 2⋔ (2fb) ✻nc5 CTV 8P S% B&bf£6–£7 Bdif£9.50–£10.50 Wf£64–£68 ⌇ D5.30pm

**GH Longmead House** 9 Longmead ☎2523
Plan:**12** Mar–Oct Lic 9hc (1fb) ✻nc5 CTV 9P ⬛ S% B&bf£6–£7 Bdif£10–£11 Wf£68–£75 ⌇ D4pm

◄►◄ **GH Lyndhurst Hotel** Lynway ☎2241
Plan:**14** Mar–Oct Lic 7hc 4⇔3⋔ (1fb) CTV 7P S% B&bf£6–£6.50 Bdif£7–£8 Wf£50.50–£56.50 ⌇ D6pm

**GH Mayfair Hotel** Lynway ☎3227 Plan:**15** Mar–Oct Lic 13hc 2⇔ (2fb) nc2 CTV 12P ⬛ sea S% B&bf£8.63–£10.07 Bdif£11.16–£12.77 Wf£67.70–£82.80 ⌇ D7pm

**GH *North Cliff Private Hotel*** North Walk ☎2357 Plan:**17** Etr–Oct 24hc (5fb) CTV 19P sea D6.30pm
**See advert on page 148**

**GH Pine Lodge** Lynway ☎3230 Plan:**18** Etr–early Oct 10hc 1⇔ (1fb) nc5 TV 9P S% B&bf£8.33–£9.20 Bdif£12.07–£13.23 Wf£83.95–£88.55 ⌇
**See advert on page 148**

---

**GH St Vincents** Castle Hill ☎2244 Plan:**21**
Apr–Oct Lic 6hc (2fb) ✻ CTV 5P S% B&bfr£7
Bdi£10.50–£11.50 W£63–£69 ⅃ D5pm

⤫⤫ **GH South View** Lee Rd ☎2289
Plan:**22** Feb–Nov 8hc (2fb) ✻ nc7 CTV 6P
S% B&bf£5.50–£6 W£37–£41 M̶

⤫⤫ **GH Turret** Lee Rd ☎3284 Plan:**20**
Mar–Oct 6hc 2⇩ (1fb) ✻ nc5 CTV 5☎ S%
B&bf£5.50–£6.25 Bdi£8.75–£9.50 W£56–
£61.25 ⅃ D5pm

**GH Valley House Hotel** Lynbridge Rd
☎2285 Plan:**24** Lic 9hc 2⇩ (2fb) CTV 9P sea
S% ✻B&bf£8.63–£9.78 Bdi£12.08–£13.23
W£82.80–£89.70 ⅃ D6pm

**GH Woodlands** Lynbridge ☎2324 Plan:**25**
Mar–Nov Lic 10hc (3fb) nc5 CTV 11P ⅢⅢ S%
B&bf£7.45–£9.80 Bdi£9.80–£12.10 W£63.95–
£75.90 ⅃ D5pm

**LYTHAM ST ANNES** Lancs Map 7 SD32
Telephone exchanges Lytham & St Annes
**GH Beaumont Private Hotel** 11 All Saints
Rd ☎723958 Lic 9hc (4fb) ✻ CTV ⅢⅢ S%
✻B&bfr£6 Bdifr£8 W£56 ⅃

**GH Gables Hotel** 35 Orchard Rd ☎729851
Apr–Oct Lic 17hc (7fb) ✻ CTV 17P ⅢⅢ S%
✻B&bf£8.05 Bdi£9.77 W£68.42 ⅃
D5.45pm

**GH Harcourt Hotel** 21 Richmond Rd, St
Annes ☎722299 10 Jan–18 Dec Lic 10hc
(3fb) ✻ CTV 6P ⅢⅢ B&bf£6.90–£8.05 Bdi£9.20–
£10.35 W£64.40–£72.45 ⅃ D4pm

**GH Lyndhurst Private Hotel** 338 Clifton
Drive North ☎724343 Apr–Oct 12hc 1⇩
(2fb) ✻ CTV 11P S% B&bf£7–£7.50 Bdi£9.50–
£11 W£59–£63 ⅃ D6pm

**GH Orchard Hotel** 34–36 Orchard Rd, St
Annes ☎728840 Lic 18hc (5fb; CTV 8P
Dnoon

**GH Westbourne Hotel** 10–12 Lake Rd,
Fairhaven ☎734736 Closed Xmas & New
Year 19hc 1⇩ ✻ CTV 7P ⅢⅢ S% B&b£8.25–
£9.50 Bdi£11.25–£12.50 W£75–£85
⅃ D am

**MAIDSTONE** Kent Map 5 TQ75
**GH Howard Hotel** 22–24 London Rd
☎58778 Closed Xmas Lic 16hc CTV 12P ⅢⅢ
S% B&bfr£9 Bdifr£14 D am

**GH Rock House Hotel** 102 Tonbridge Rd
☎51616 12hc (1fb) ✻ CTV 6P ⅢⅢ S%
B&b£10.35 W£70 M̶

**MALDON** Essex Map 5 TL80
**INN Swan Hotel** Maldon High St ☎53170
Lic 6hc ✻ CTV 40P ⅢⅢ ⇙

**MALHAM** N Yorks Map 7 SD96
**GH Sparth House Hotel** ☎Airton 315 Lic
10rm 9hc 1⋔ (3fb) ✻ CTV 6P S% B&b£9.20–
£11.50 Bdi£14.50–£17.75 W£82.80–£97.75
⅃ D5.30pm

**MALVERN, GT** Heref & Worcs Map 3
SO74
**GH Bredon House** 34 Worcester Rd ☎5323
Lic 9rm (2fb) CTV 8P ⅢⅢ S% B&bfr£7.50
Bdifr£11 D4pm

**GH Fromefield** 147 Barnards Green Rd
☎62466 Lic 7hc 1⇩ (2fb) ✻ CTV 3P ⅢⅢ S%
B&b£8–£10 Bdi£12.75–£14.75 W£86–£100
⅃ D5pm

**MANCHESTER** Gt Manchester *Map 7 SJ89*
**GH Kempton House Hotel** 400 Wilbraham Rd, Chorlton-cum-Hardy ☎061-881 8766 Lic 14hc (1fb) ✱ CTV 9P ⅏ S% B&b£9.05 Bdi£13

**GH Hotel Tara** 10–12 Oswald Rd, Chorlton-cum-Hardy ☎061-861 0385 Lic 14hc (6fb) CTV 8P ⅏ S% B&bfr£9.78 Bdi fr£14.38 D7pm

**GH White House Hotel** 17 Whitelow Rd, Chorlton-cum-Hardy ☎061-861 0890 Lic 28hc 10⋔ CTV 28P ⅏ S% B&b£8 Bdi£10 W£56 ⌊

**MAN, ISLE OF** *Map 6*
Places with AA-listed guesthouses/inns are indicated on location map 6. Full details will be found under individual placenames in the gazetteer section

**MARGATE** Kent *Map 5 TR37*
⋈ **GH Alice Springs Private Hotel** 6–8 Garfield Rd ☎Thanet 23543 Lic 18hc 10⋔ (5fb) ✱ nc6 CTV ⅏ S% B&b£5–£6 Bdi£8–£9 W£38–£46 D4pm

**GH Beachcomber Hotel** 3–4 Royal Esp, Westbrook ☎Thanet 21616 Apr–Oct Lic 16hc (4fb) ✱ nc4 CTV sea S% B&b£8.05–£9.20 Bdi£10.35–£11.50 W£51.75–£59.80 ⌊ D6pm

**GH Charnwood** 20 Canterbury Rd ☎Thanet 24158 Lic 15hc (8fb) ✱ CTV S% B&b£7–£8 Bdi£9–£10 W£45–£55 ⌊ D6pm

**GH** *Lancelot* 39 Edgar Rd, Cliftonville ☎Thanet 22944 Lic 8hc 1⇆ ⋔ ✱ CTV ⅏ D4.30pm

**GH Tyrella Private Hotel** 19 Canterbury Rd ☎Thanet 22746 Closed Xmas Lic 8hc (5fb) ✱ nc6 CTV ⅏ sea S% ✱ B&b£6 Bdi£8 W£38–£45 ⌊ D5pm

**MARLOW** Bucks *Map 4 SU88*
**GH Glade Nook** 75 Glade Rd ☎4677 7hc 1⋔ (1fb) nc7 CTV 7P ⅏ S% ✱ B&b£10–£16.50

**MARNHULL** Dorset *Map 3 ST71*
**INN Crown Hotel** ☎820224 3hc ⌷ ✱ 70P ⅏ B&b£7.50–£8.50 L50p–£4&alc D9.30pm£8alc

**MARSDEN** W Yorks *Map 7 SE01*
**INN Coach & Horses** Standage ☎Huddersfield 844241 10hc 1⇆ TV 200P 5⌷ ⅏ S% B&b£12–£15 Bar lunch £3.50alc D10pm£6.50alc

**MARSHBROOK** Salop *Map 7 SO48*
**INN** *Wayside* ☎208 Lic 4hc nc10 30P ⅏

**MARYTAVY** Devon *Map 2 SX57*
**GH Moorland Hall** Brentor Rd ☎466 Lic 10hc 1⇆ 1⋔ (4fb) ⌷Ch⌷ CTV 15P ⅏ B&b£8.50–£14.50 Bdi£12–£19.50 W£84–£126 ⌊ D8.30pm

**MASHAM** N Yorks *Map 8 SE28*
**GH Bank Villa** ☎605 Lic 7hc nc5 CTV 7P ⅏ river S% B&b£7.50–£8 Bdi£13–£13.50 W£80–£85 ⌊ Dnoon
See advert on page 150

**GH Sutton Grange Country** Leyburn Rd ☎400 Mar–Dec Lic 12hc (2fb) nc4 CTV 20P ⅏ S% ✱ B&b£8–£9.50 Bdi£12–£14 W£70–£85 ⌊ D7pm

**MATLOCK** Derbys *Map 8 SK36*
**GH Cavendish** 26 Bank Rd ☎2443 Closed Xmas 8hc (4fb) CTV 4P S% B&b£7.50–£9 Bdi£11–£13 W£68–£87.50 Dnoon

**MAWGAN PORTH** Cornwall *Map 2 SW86*
⋈ **GH Pandora** Tredragon Rd ☎St
Mawgan 412 May–Sep Lic 7rm 6hc (1fb)
CTV 8P ⬜ sea S% B&bf£5.50–£7.50 Bdi£8–
£9.50 W£56.50–£63.50 ⌧ D4.30pm

**GH** *Seavista Hotel* ☎St Mawgan 276 10hc
(4fb) [Ch] CTV 8P sea D5pm

**GH Surf Riders Hotel** Tredragon Rd ☎St
Mawgan 383 Etr–Sep Lic 11hc (5fb) ✸ CTV
15P sea S% B&bf£8.22–£9.49 Bdi£10.12–
£11.92 W£70.85–£83.50 ⌧ D6pm

**GH** *Thorncliff Hotel* Trenance ☎St Mawgan
428 Lic 14hc CTV 18P sea D8pm

**GH Trenance Farm House** ☎St Mawgan
515 Closed Xmas 6hc (2fb) 8P sea S%
B&bf£7.50–£9 Bdi£11.35–£14.80 W£84–£94
⌧ D6pm

**GH White Lodge Hotel** ☎St Mawgan 512
Mar–Oct Lic 16hc 9⇌ 9⋔ (6fb) nc3 CTV 18P
⬜ sea S% B&bf£8–£11.50 Bdi£11.50–£15.50
W£62.50–£98 ⌧ D7.30pm

**MAYFIELD** Staffs *Map 7 SK14*
**INN Queens Arms** ☎Ashbourne 42271 7rm
5hc TV 12P B&bf£7.48

**MELBOURNE** Derbys *Map 8 SK32*
**INN** *Melbourne Hotel* ☎2134 Lic 8hc CTV
50P ⬜ D10pm

**MELKSHAM** Wilts *Map 3 ST96*
**GH Regency Hotel** 10–12 Spa Rd ☎702971
12hc 1⋔ (1fb) CTV ⬜ ✱B&bf£8.63 Bdi£13.23
W£92.61 ⌧ D6.30pm

**GH Shaw Farm** Shaw (1½ NW off A365)
☎702836 Closed Xmas Lic 10hc 1⇌ (4fb) ✸
CTV 12P S% B&bf£9.50–£10 Bdi£14.50–
£15.25 W£95.50–£100 ⌧ D7.30pm

**GH York** Church Walk ☎702063 9hc (3fb)
CTV 2☎ ⬜ S% B&bfr£6.50 Bdi fr£10 W£70 ⌧

**MELTON MOWBRAY** Leics *Map 8 SK71*
**GH Sysonby Knoll Hotel** 225 Asfordby Rd
☎63563 Closed Xmas Lic 15hc 2⇌ 2⋔ (1fb)
CTV 16P ⬜ river S% B&b£7.50–£9 Bdi fr£11
D8pm

**GH Westbourne House** 11A Nottingham Rd
☎69456 17hc (3fb) CTV 18P ⬜ S%
✱B&bf£6.50–£7 D7pm

**MENHENIOT** Cornwall *Map 2 SX26*
**INN Sportsman's Arms** Station Rd
☎Widegates 249 5hc 50P S% B&bf£6–£8 Bar
lunch 95p–£3 D9.30pm£3–£7&alc

**INN** *White Hart Hotel* ☎Liskeard 42245 Lic
6hc 3⇌ ⋔ ✸nc16 CTV 30P ⬜ D9.30pm

**MERIDEN** W Midlands *Map 4 SP28*
**GH Meriden Hotel** Main Rd ☎22005 8rm
6hc (2fb) CTV 20P ⬜ S% ✱B&bf£10–£12.50
Bdi£13.75–£16.25 D7pm

**MEVAGISSEY** Cornwall *Map 2 SX04*
**GH Headlands Hotel** Polkirt Hill ☎843453
Mar–Nov & Xmas Lic 12hc 6⋔ (2fb) nc5 CTV
10P ⬜ sea S% B&bf£8.60–£9.70 Bdi£12.60–
£13.75 D7pm

**GH Polhaun Hotel** Polkirt Hill ☎3222 Etr–
Oct Lic 8hc ✸nc10 TV in all bedrooms 10P ⬜
sea S% ✱B&bfr£9 Bdi fr£12 Wfr£80 ⌧
D6.30pm

**GH Spa Private Hotel** Polkirt Hill ☎2244
Etr–Oct Lic 10hc 4⇌ (1fb) ✸nc3 CTV 10P 2☎
⬜ sea S% B&bf£10.12–£11.40 Bdi£15.30–
£16.56 W£87.23–£98.73 ⌧ D6pm

**GH** *Valley Park* Tregoney Hill ☎2347

Closed Xmas & New Year Lic 8hc (2fb) ✻
CTV 10P D6pm

**INN Ship** ☎3324 Lic 5hc CTV 🚗

**MIDDLESBROUGH** Cleveland *Map 8 NZ42*
**GH Chadwick Private Hotel** 27 Clairville Rd
☎245340 rsXmas 6hc (1fb) ✻ CTV ⅏ S%
✱ B&b£7 Bdi£9.50 D4pm

**GH Longlands Hotel** 295 Marton Rd
☎244900 Lic 7hc (3fb) ✻ CTV 6✿ ⅏ S%
✱ B&b£10 Bdi£13.50 Dnoon

**MIDDLETON-ON-SEA** W Sussex *Map 4
SU90*
**GH Ancton House Hotel** Ancton Ln ☎2482
Lic 8hc 2⇨ (2fb) Ⓒⓗ CTV 6P 5✿ ⅏ S%
B&b£10 Bdi£13.50 W£82 Ⅼ D7pm

**MILFORD-ON-SEA** Hants *Map 4 SZ29*

**GH La Charmeuse** 9 Hurst Rd ☎2646 Apr–
Oct 4hc (1fb) ✻ TV 8P ⅏ sea S% B&b£9.25–
£18

**GH Kingsland Hotel** Westover Rd ☎2670
Lic 18hc 7⇨ ⌂ (4fb) ✻ nc6 CTV 14P ⅏ lift

**GH Seaspray** 8 Hurst Rd ☎2627 Mar–Oct
Lic 6hc 2⌂ (2fb) ✻ nc3 CTV 10P ⅏ sea S%
B&b£8 Bdi£12 W£75 Ⅼ D7pm

**MILLPOOL** Cornwall *Map 2 SW53*
**GH Chyraise Lodge Hotel** ☎Germoe 3485
Lic 9hc (1fb) ✻ Ⓒⓗ CTV 10P S% B&b£7.25–
£8.25 Bdi£9.50–£10.50 W£65–£72 Ⅼ
Dnoon

**MINCHINHAMPTON** Glos *Map 3 SO80*
**GH Sherrards** ☎Brimscombe 882742 Lic
8hc 1⇨ (2fb) CTV 7P ⅏ S% B&b£9.50
Bdi£14.75 W£99.25 Ⅼ D7pm

---

# KILBOL HOUSE

**Tom and Carole Berry**
Kilbol has a long history as a farm, and
has been converted to a luxurious hotel,
with extensive lawns and grounds.
Cornwall Tourist Board approved. Ideally
placed for touring Cornwall. Open all year.
Ample parking. Family rooms, double
rooms and single rooms, some with
bathrooms en suite, private bathrooms or
showers. Lounge and dining room. Also
16th Century lounge with bar. Central
heating. Bed and breakfast, optional
dinner — terms on request. Licensed.
Heated swimming pool. Kilbol has
exceptional peace and quiet, yet we are
located just 3-4 miles from 5 beaches.

**Kilbol House, Polmassick, Nr. Mevagissey. Tel: Mevagissey 2481**

---

## The Spa Hotel

**AA LISTED**    **MEVAGISSEY CORNWALL**    Telephone: **0726-842244**

* Detached in own grounds
* Traffic free position
* Private car park
* Cocktail lounge    • Tennis Court
* Private bathrooms    • Colour TV lounge
* Excellent cuisine    • Sea Views
* Full central heating    • Licensed
* Open Easter to October
* Bargain breaks early & late season
* Accommodation, breakfast & dinner from
  £75.90 (+VAT) per person per week
* The Spa offers the highest standard, warm
  welcome & hospitality

*Proprietors:* Mr. & Mrs. J. Evans
Brochure on request

---

AA Listed

# Van Ruan House

## Boswinger, Gorran, Nr. Mevagissey, Cornwall

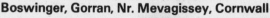

"Van Ruan" is a select guest house set in
peaceful surroundings offering every comfort
and good food. Situated in its own grounds of
over an acre, overlooking the sea and a
National Trust beauty area. Six sandy beaches
are within 2 miles, the nearest is less than ½
mile.
Full central heating, most bedrooms have
unrivalled sea views, all with H&C. Some
ground floor bedrooms. Comfortable lounge
with colour TV. Licensed Bar. Own car park.
Bed, Breakfast and evening dinner. Stamp
please for colour brochure and terms to:—
**Resident proprietors Mr & Mrs R Bulled
Telephone Mevagissey (0726) 842425**

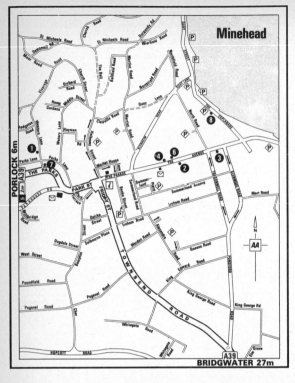

1 Carbery
2 Dorchester Hotel
3 Gascony Hotel
4 Glen Rock Hotel
5 Higher
  Woodcombe
  Hotel
6 Mayfair Hotel
8 Red Lion Hotel
  (Inn)

**MINEHEAD** Somerset *Map 3 SS94* **(See Plan)**

**GH Carbery** Western Ln, The Parks ☎2941
Plan:**1** Apr–Oct Lic 6hc ⊀ nc16 CTV 8P ▥
S% B&b£7–£8 Bdi£10.50–£12
W£73.50–£84 ⫨ D4pm

**GH Dorchester** 38 The Avenue ☎2052
Plan:**2** Lic 13hc (3fb) nc3 CTV 10P ▥ S%
B&b£7.25 Bdi£10.50 W£60 ⫨ D8.30pm

**GH Gascony Hotel** The Avenue ☎2817
Plan:**3** Mar–Oct Lic 15hc 2⇌ 2⋔ (6fb) ⊀ Ch
CTV 10P S% B&b£8.50–£9.50 Bdi£12–£13
W£58–£79 ⫨ D8pm

**GH Glen Rock Hotel** 23 The Avenue ☎2245
Plan:**4** Mar–Nov Lic 12hc (2fb) nc2 CTV 10P
1✍ S% B&b£7.50–£9 Bdi£11–£12.50
W£62–£70 ⫨ D7.30pm

**GH Higher Woodcombe Hotel** Bratton Ln
☎2789 Plan:**5** Apr–mid Oct Lic 9hc (1fb) nc9
CTV 9P ▥ S% Bdi£11–£11.50 W£102–£110
⫨ D6.30pm

**GH Mayfair Hotel** 25 The Avenue ☎2719
Plan:**6** Mar–Oct Lic 18hc (6fb) CTV 12P ▥
B&b£8–£8.75 Bdi£11.50–£12.50 W£66–£71
⫨ D7pm

**INN Red Lion Hotel** The Esplanade ☎2653
Plan:**8** Lic 7hc CTV 6P sea

**MODBURY** Devon *Map 3 SX65*
**GH Modbury** Brownston St ☎830275 7hc
1⇌ ⊀ 10P ▥ S% B&bfr£8.50 D10pm

**MOFFAT** Dumfries & Galloway
*Dumfriesshire Map 11 NT00*
**GH Arden House** High St ☎20220 Jan–Oct
8hc 4⋔ (2fb) CTV 10P ▥ S% ✳B&b£5.50–£7
Bdi£8.50–£9 W£59–£65 ⫨ D6.45pm

⊦⊣ **GH Buchan** 13 Beechgrove ☎20378
8hc (2fb) CTV 7P ▥ S% B&b£4.50–£5
Bdi£7.50–£8 W£52–£56 ⫨ D7pm

**GH Hartfell House** Hartfell Cres ☎20153
Mar–Dec 9hc (3fb) TV 10P ▥ B&b£6.90
Bdi£11.50 W£40 ⫨ D7pm

**GH Robin Hill** Beechgrove ☎20050 Etr–Oct
6hc (2fb) CTV 6P ▥ S% ✳B&b£6–£7

**GH Rockhill** 14 Beechgrove ☎20283 Mar–
Oct 10hc (3fb) CTV D6.15pm

**GH St Olaf** Eastgate, off Dickson St
☎20001 Apr–early Oct 7hc (3fb) 4✍ ✳B&b£5
Bdi£8.50 D6.15pm

**MOLESWORTH** Cambs *Map 4 TL07*
**INN Cross Keys** ☎Bythorn 283 3hc 1⇌ 1⋔
🚗 nc10 50P ▥ S% B&b£10 Bdif£14 W£70 Ⓜ
sn L£7alc D10pm£8alc

**MONMOUTH** Gwent *Map 3 SO51*
**INN Queens Head** St James Street ☎2767
5hc 2⋔ CTV 8P ▥ river S% B&b£8.50–£9.50
Bdi£11–£12 W£60–£70 ⫨ sn L£2.50–£3.50&alc
D9.30pm£3–£4&alc

**MONTROSE** Tayside *Angus Map 15 NO75*
**GH Linksgate** 11 Dorward Rd ☎2273 6hc
(3fb) CTV 6P D9am

**MOODIESBURN** Strathclyde *Lanarks Map
11 NS67*
**GH El Ranchero Western** 6 Cumbernauld
Rd (On A80) ☎Glenboig 874769 rs25 Dec–1
Jan (B&b only) 5hc (2fb) CTV 30P D6.45pm

**MORECAMBE** Lancs *Map 7 SD46*
**GH Ashley Private Hotel** 371 Marine Rd
East ☎412034 Lic 13hc (4fb) ⊀ CTV 4P sea

✳B&b£7.50–£9.20 Bdi£9.80–£10.95 W£63–£68 ⌊ D4pm (W only 1 Jul–18 Aug)

**GH Beach Mount** 395 Marine Rd East ☎420753 Mar–Nov Lic 25hc 14⇔ (5fb) CTV ▥ S% B&b£7.48 Bdi£10.64 W£72.45 ⌊ D4pm

**GH** *Channings Private Hotel* 455 Marine Rd East ☎417925 Lic 24hc TV sea

⊢⊣ **GH Ellesmere Private Hotel** 44 Westminster Rd ☎411881 May–Oct 5hc (2fb) ✝ CTV S% B&b£5.50–£6.50 Bdi£7.50–£8.50 W£43–£46 D5.15pm

**GH** *Elstead Private Hotel* 72 Regent Rd ☎412260 12hc ✝ D3pm

⊢⊣ **GH Glendene** 42 Westminster Rd ☎416358 Apr–20 Oct 6hc (1fb) ✝ CTV ▥ S% B&b£4 Bdi£7 W£40–£45 ⌊

**GH New Hazlemere Hotel** 391 Marine Rd, East Promenade ☎417876 Etr–early Nov Lic 21hc (4fb) CTV 3P sea S% ✳B&b£8–£9 Bdi£10–£11 W£58–£65.50 ⌊ D5.30pm

**GH Hotel Prospect** 363 Marine Rd, East Promenade ☎417819 Etr–Oct Lic 15hc 8⇔ (5fb) CTV 6P ▥ sea S% B&b£6.25–£7.40 Bdi£9.20–£10.20 D3pm

**GH Rydal Mount Private Hotel** 361 Marine Rd East ☎411858 Etr–Oct Lic 14hc (6fb) CTV 15P ▥ sea S% ✳B&b£8.05 Bdi£9.78 W£66.70 ⌊ D3.30pm

**GH Hotel Warwick** 394 Marine Rd East ☎418151 Lic 21hc 3⋔ (5fb) CTV ▥ lift sea S% B&b£7.47–£8.62 Bdi£10.50–£11.62 D6pm

**GH Wilmslow Private Hotel** 374 Marine Rd East ☎417804 Apr–Oct rsFeb–Apr (B&b only) Lic 15hc (4fb) ✝ CTV 4P sea B&bfr£8.05 Bdifr£10.35 Wfr£67.85 ⌊ D4.30pm

**MORETONHAMPSTEAD** Devon *Map 3 SX78*

**GH Cookshayes** 33 Court St ☎374 15 Mar–5 Nov Lic 8hc 5⇔ (1fb) nc10 CTV 15P ▥ B&b£7.50–£9 Bdi£12.50–£14 W£78–£90 ⌊ D6pm

**GH Elmfield** Station Rd ☎327 Etr–Oct Lic 6hc (2fb) CTV 8P ▥ S% B&b£6.50 Bdi£10.50 W£65 ⌊ D6pm

**GH Wray Barton Manor** ☎246 10 Jan–20 Dec 9hc 2⇔ 1⋔ ✝ nc12 CTV 12P ▥ S% B&b£7 Bdi£11 Wfr£75 ⌊

**INN Ring of Bells** North Bovey ☎375 3⇔ ✝ 8P 4🐾 B&b£12.93 Bdi£17.53 W£122.76 ⌊ Bar lunch 95p–£2.25 D8.30pm£6.60

**MORFA NEFYN** Gwynedd *Map 6 SH23*

**GH Erw Goch** ☎Nefyn 720539 Etr–Sep Lic 15hc (5fb) [ch] CTV 20P ▥ ✳B&b£6.90 Bdi£11.21 W£56.93–£60.95 ⌊ D5pm (W only Jul & Aug)

**MORTEHOE** Devon *Map 2 SS44*

**GH Baycliff** Chapple Hill ☎Woolacombe 870393 Mar–Nov Lic 10hc 1⇔ (2fb) CTV 9P ▥ sea S% B&b£8–£11 Bdi£12.50–£15.50 W£75–£95 ⌊ D4.30pm

**GH Haven** ☎Woolacombe 870426 Mar–Oct Lic 17rm 2hc 15⇔ (9fb) [ch] CTV 20P 1🏠 ▥ sea B&b£8.50–£10.50 Bdi£12.50–£14.50 W£80–£100 ⌊ D8pm

**GH Sunnycliffe Hotel** ☎Woolacombe 870597 Lic 8hc 4⇔ 4⋔ (2fb) ✝ nc10 CTV 11P ▥ sea S% ✳B&bfr£9.20 Bdifr£14.38 Wfr£98.90 ⌊ D6.30pm

**MOUNT HAWKE** Cornwall *Map 2 SW74*
**GH Tregarthen** ☎Porthtowan 890399 Lic
7hc 4⇌ (2fb) ⊁ CJV 12P ▥ S% B&b£9.20
Bdi£13.80 W£74.75 ⅃

**MOUSEHOLE** Cornwall *Map 2 SW42*
**GH Tavis Vor** ☎73306 Closed Xmas Lic 7hc
(3fb) CTV 7P ▥ sea S% B&b£7.95–£9.95
Bdi£12.50–£13.50 W£84–£91 ⅃ D7pm

**MOY** Highland *Inverness-shire Map 14
NH73*
⊬⊣ **GH Invermoy House** Tomatin ☎271
Lic 7hc 1⋔ ⊁ ⒸⒽ CTV 10P ▥ lake S%
B&b£5.75–£6.33 Bdi£9.20–£9.78 W£59.80–
£64.40 ⅃ D6pm

**MULL, ISLE OF** Strathclyde *Argyll Map 10 &
13 See Salen, Tobermory*

**MULLION** Cornwall *Map 2 SW61*
⊬⊣ **GH Belle Vue** ☎240483 Apr–Sep 8hc
(1fb) ⊁ CTV 10P S% B&b£5.50–£6.50
Bdi£8.50–£9.50 W£55–£60 D4pm

**GH** *Henscath House* Mullion Cove
☎240537 Feb–Nov Lic 6hc ⊁ nc5 CTV 6P
sea

**GH** *Trenowyth House Private Hotel*
Mullion Cove ☎240486 Lic 5hc CTV 10P ▥
sea D6.30pm

**GH Trevelyan** ☎240378 Etr–Oct 5hc (A 2rm
1hc 1⇌) (1fb) CTV 20P ⅃ S% B&b£6.25–
£6.50 Bdi£9–£9.25 W£60–£62 ⅃

**INN** *The Old Inn* Church Town ☎240240
rsXmas (no accommodation) Lic 7hc 4⇌ ⊁
nc14 TV 10P ⇼ sea D9pm

**MUMBLES** W Glam *Map 2 SS68*
**GH Harbour Winds Private Hotel** Overland

Rd, Langland ☎Swansea 69298 Jan–Nov
8hc 1⇌ 1⋔ (3fb) ⒸⒽ CTV 16P ▥ S%
B&bfr£10 Bdi£15–£20 W£83–£91 ⅃ D6.30pm
⊬⊣ **GH Southend Hotel** 724 Mumbles Rd
☎Swansea 66329 rs Jan & Feb Lic 11hc
(4fb) ⒸⒽ CTV 2P sea S% B&b£6–£8 Bdi£9–£11
Wfr£42 ⓜ D9.30pm

**MUNDESLEY-ON-SEA** Norfolk *Map 9 TG33*
**INN** *Ingleside Hotel* Cromer Rd ☎720530
Lic 11hc TV ▥ D9.30pm

**MUNGRISDALE** Cumbria *Map 11 NY33*
**GH Mill Guest House** ☎Threlkeld 659 mid
Mar–Oct Lic 9hc (2fb) ⊁ CTV 12P B&b£9.50–
£10 Bdi£13–£14.50 W£90–£100 ⅃ D5pm

**INN** *Mill* ☎Threlkeld 632 Mar–Oct Lic 8hc ⊁
30P D9pm

**MUSBURY** Devon *Map 3 SY29*
**GH Barley Close** ☎Colyton 52484 6hc
(2fb) ⊁ nc12 CTV 7P ▥ S% ✳B&b£5 Bdi£8
D3pm

**MUSSELBURGH** Lothian *Midlothian Map
11 NT37*
**GH Parsonage** 15 High St ☎031-665 4289
Jan–Nov 7hc 2⇌ (2fb) CTV TV in 3
bedrooms 10P ▥ S% B&b£6.50–£8 W£40–
£55 ⓜ

**MYLOR BRIDGE** Cornwall *Map 2 SW83*
**GH Penmere** Rosehill ☎Penryn 74470 Mar–
Oct 6hc (3fb) ⒸⒽ CTV P ▥ river S% B&b£6
Bdi£9.75 W£54 ⅃ D5pm

**NAILSWORTH** Glos *Map 3 ST89*
**GH Gables Private Hotel** Tiltups End, Bath
Rd ☎2265 Lic 6rm 5hc (2fb) CTV 10P S%
B&b£7.50 D9pm

**NAIRN** Highland *Nairns Map 14 NH85*
**GH** *Greenlawns* 13 Seafield St ☎52738
Apr–Oct 6hc 2⇔ (3fb) CTV 8P D5pm
**GH** *Lothian House Private Hotel* 10
Crescent Rd ☎53555 Lic 9hc CTV 10P sea
D7pm

**NARBERTH** Dyfed *Map 2 SN11*
**GH Blaenmarlais** ☎860326 Spr Bank Hol–
Sep Lic 11hc 1⇔ (A 3hc) (5fb) ⅍ CTV 30P
8🅐 B&b£8 Bdi£11 W£60–£66 Ⱡ
D6.30pm

**GH** *Parc Glas Country House Hotel* Parc
Glas ☎860947 Etr–Oct Lic 6hc 2⇔ (2fb) ⅍
CTV 10P ▦ D7pm

**NEAR SAWREY** Cumbria *Map 7 SD39*
**GH High Green Gate** ☎Hawkshead 296
Apr–Oct 7hc (2fb) TV 7P ▦ S% B&bfr£8
Bdi fr£12.50 Wfr£80 Ⱡ D5pm

**GH Sawrey House Private Hotel**
☎Hawkshead 387 Closed Xmas Lic 12hc
1⇔ 1🛁 (3fb) CTV 20P ▦ lake S% B&b£8–£9
Bdi£12.50–£14 W£85–£95 Ⱡ D7pm

**NEATISHEAD** Norfolk *Map 9 TG32*
**GH Barton Angler Hotel** ☎Horning 630740
Lic 8hc 3🛁 (1fb) nc7 CTV 16P ▦ B&bfr£8.50
Bdi fr£13.50 Wfr£80 Ⱡ
**See advert on page 156**

**NESSCLIFF** Salop *Map 7 SJ31*
**INN Nesscliff Hotel** ☎253 5🛁 TV 75P 2🅐
B&b£8.68 Bdi£12.68 sn L£3.50&alc
D10.30pm£5alc

**NEWBURY** Berks *Map 4 SU46*
**GH The Guest House** 133 Andover Rd
☎41359 11hc (1fb) ⅍ nc10 TV in all
bedrooms 12P ▦ S% B&b£8 W£56 Ⱦ

**NEWCASTLE-UNDER-LYME** Staffs *Map 7
SJ84*
**GH Grove Court Hotel** 100 Lancaster Rd
☎614406 Lic 10hc (2fb) (A2⇔) CTV 12P ⊪
B&b£9.97 Bdi£13.23

**NEWCASTLE UPON TYNE** Tyne & Wear
*Map 12 NZ26*
**GH Chirton House Hotel** 46 Clifton Rd
☎730407 Lic 12hc (2fb) ⊁ CTV 12P ⊪ S%
B&b£11 Bdi£16.75 W£70 ⋈ D6pm

**NEWHAVEN** Derbys *Map 7 SK16*
**INN Newhaven Hotel** ☎Hartington 217
13rm CTV 200P ⊪ S% ✻B&b£9.50 Bdi£13.75
sn L£3.50&alc D1am£3.50&alc

**NEWNHAM-ON-SEVERN** Glos *Map 3
SO61*
**INN** *Victoria* ☎221 Lic 16hc 3⇔ CTV 50P
3♨ ⊪ D9.30pm

**NEWPORT** Dyfed *Map 2 SN03*
**GH Gellifawr** Pontfaen (4m S on unclass rd)
☎820343 Mar–Oct Lic 9rm 8hc (3fb) CTV
50P S% B&b£10 Bdi£15 W£100 ⋈ D5pm

**INN Golden Lion Hotel** East St ☎820321
10rm 9⇔ ⋒ ⊁ CTV 40P ⊪ B&b£8–£9
Bdi£14–£15 W£55 ⋈ sn L£4alc
D10pm£6alc

**NEWPORT** Gwent *Map 3 ST38*
**GH Caerleon House Hotel** Caerau Rd
☎64869 Lic 8hc (2fb) CTV 8P ⊪ S% B&b£9–
£10 D9.30pm

**NEWPORT** Isle of Wight *Map 4 SZ48*
**GH Clatterford House Hotel** Clatterford
Shute, Carisbrooke (1m W B3323) ☎526939
Lic 9hc 1⇔ 1⋒ (2fb) ⊁ nc8 TV 15P ⊪ S%

B&b£7.50–£10 Bdi£12–£14 W£68–
£74 ⋈ D9.30pm

**NEWPORT Salop** *Map 7 SJ71*
**INN Barley Mow Hotel** High St ☎810146
6hc ♨ ⊁ CTV 12P S% B&bfr£9.20 Bar lunch
£1.50–£2.50 D8pm£2.50–£3.50

**NEWQUAY** Cornwall *Map 2 SW86* **(See
Plan)**
⊦⊣ **GH Arundell Hotel** Mount Wise
☎2481 Plan:**1** mid May–mid Sep Lic 43hc
4⇔ (6fb) ⊁ [Ch] CTV 30P sea S% B&b£5.75–
£9.20 Bdi£8.60–£12 W£60.95–£83.95 ⋈
D7pm (W only Jul & Aug)

⊦⊣ **GH Castaways Hotel** 39 St Thomas
Rd ☎5002 Plan:**2** Mar–Nov Lic 13hc (3fb)
[Ch] CTV 14P sea S% B&b£5.50–£8 Bdi£8–
£11.50 W£49.45–£79.35 ⋈ D9pm (W only Jul
& Aug)

**GH Cherington** 7 Pentire Av ☎3363 Plan:**3**
Etr–Sep 22hc 1⇔ 4⋒ (A 6hc) (5fb) CTV 16P
sea B&b£7.50 Bdi£8.50 W£62 ⋈ D7.30pm

**GH Copper Beech Hotel** 70 Edgcumbe Av
☎3376 Plan:**4** Etr–Oct 16hc (5fb) CTV 16P ⊪
S% B&b£6.90–£8.05 Bdi£9.20–£10.93
W£64.40–£73.60 ⋈ D6pm (W only Jul & Aug)

⊦⊣ **GH Fairlands** 107 Tower Rd ☎2917
Plan:**5** Closed Xmas & New Year 8hc (3fb) ⊁
CTV 10P S% B&b£5–£7 Bdi£6.50–£8.50
W£48–£59 ⋈ D5pm

**GH La Felica Hotel** Henver Rd ☎2129
Plan:**6** Lic 24hc (6fb) nc3 CTV 16P sea
B&bfr£8.05 Bdi£10.35–£12 W£63.25–£90.85
⋈ D6pm (W only Jul & Aug)

**GH Fistral Beach Hotel** Esplanade Rd,
Pentire ☎3993 Plan:**7** Etr–Oct Lic 16hc 3⋒
(4fb) CTV 12P ⊪ sea S% B&b£6.90–£9.78
Bdi£9.78–£13.80 W£59.80–£89.70 ⋈ D6.45pm

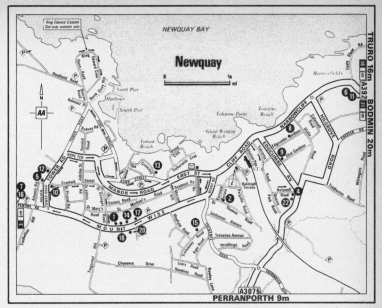

| | | | |
|---|---|---|---|
| **1** Arundell Hotel | **7** Fistral Beach Hotel | **12** Long Beech Hotel | **17** Priory Lodge Hotel |
| **2** Castaways Hotel | **8** Gluvian Park Hotel | **13** Minerva Hotel | **18** Quies Hotel |
| **3** Cherington | | **14** Mount Wise Hotel | **19** Ranelagh Court Hotel |
| **4** Copper Beech Hotel | **9** Hepworth Hotel | **15** Ocean Hill Lodge Private Hotel | **21** Viewpoint Hotel |
| **5** Fairlands | **10** Jonel Hotel | | **22** Wheal Treasure |
| **6** La Felica Hotel | **11** Kellesboro Hotel | **16** Philema | |

(W only mid Jul–mid Aug)

**GH Gluvian Park Hotel** 12 Edgcumbe Gdns
☎3133 Plan:**8** Apr–mid Oct Lic 24hc 7ﬁ
(4fb) ✠ nc3 CTV 12P B&b£7.50–£12
Bdif£10.50–£15.50 Wf66.50–£87.50 ⅃
D6.30pm

**GH Hepworth Hotel** 27 Edgcumbe Av
☎3686 Plan:**9** Etr–Oct Lic 13hc 4ﬁ (4fb) ✠
CTV 12P ⬚ ✳ B&bf£6.90–£9.20 Bdif£10.35–
£14.38 Wf50–£79 ⅃ D6.30pm (W only 17 Jul–
21 Aug)

**GH Jonel** 88–90 Crantock St ☎5084
Plan:**10** Jan–Oct Lic 11hc (3fb) ✠ CTV 7P
S% ✳ B&bf£6–£10 Bdif£8–£12 Wf51.75–
£78.20 ⅃ D4pm

**GH Kellesboro Hotel** 12 Henver Rd ☎4620
Plan:**11** Mar–Dec Lic 14hc 4 3ﬁ (7fb) CTV
16P ⬚ & S% B&bf£9.20–£10.35 Bdif£11.50–
£13.80 Wf69–£80.50 ⅃ D7pm

⊢✠⊣ **GH Long Beech Hotel** 11 Trevose Av
☎4751 Plan:**12** Etr–Oct Lic 8hc (4fb) CTV 7P
sea S% B&bf£5.50–£6.50 Bdif£8–£10 Wf55–
£65 ⅃ (W only Jul–Aug)

**GH Minerva Hotel** The Crescent ☎3439
Plan:**13** Apr–Oct Lic 26hc (12fb) CTV 5P sea
S% B&bf£8.50–£12.50 Bdif£10.50–£15
Wf49.50–£76 ⅃ D6.30pm (W only Jul & Aug)

**GH Mount Wise Hotel** Mount Wise ☎3080
Plan:**14** Apr–Nov Lic 36hc 8 1ﬁ (10fb) CTV
30P lift sea S% B&bf£7–£11.16 Bdif£9.35–
£13.46 Wf57.50–£86.25 ⅃ D7pm

⊢✠⊣ **GH Ocean Hill Lodge Private Hotel**
Trelawney Rd ☎4595 Plan:**15** May–Sep Lic
16hc (6fb) CTV 12P S% B&bf£5.50–£7.50
Bdif£7–£9.25 Wf48–£63.50 ⅃ D10am (W only
18 Jul–22 Aug)

**GH Philema Hotel** 1 Esplanade Rd, Pentire

☎2571 Plan:**16** Etr–mid Oct Lic 23hc 6
(7fb) CTV 25P D6.30pm

**GH Priory Lodge Hotel** Mount Wise ☎4111
Plan:**17** Lic 12hc 1 2ﬁ (4fb) CTV 20P ⬚
S% B&bf£9–£10 Bdif£12.50–£13.90 D7pm (W
only Jul & Aug)

⊢✠⊣ **GH Quie's Hotel** 84 Mount Wise
☎2924 Plan:**18** Etr–Oct Lic 10hc (6fb) ✠ CTV
8P ⬚ S% B&bf£4.50–£7 Bdif£6–£9
Wf46–£65 D4.30pm

**GH Ranelagh Court Hotel** 101A Henver Rd
☎4922 Plan:**19** Lic 8hc (1fb) nc8 CTV 12P ⬚
sea D6.30pm

**GH Viewpoint Hotel** 89 Henver Rd ☎2170
Plan:**21** Lic 17hc 8 1ﬁ (2fb) ✠ CTV 12P ⬚
sea B&bf£13–£15 Bdif£17.50–£19.50 D10pm

⊢✠⊣ **GH Wheal Treasure** 72 Edgcumbe Av
☎4136 Plan:**22** Apr–Oct Lic 11hc (3fb) ✠
nc4 CTV 9P ⬚ S% B&bf£5.75–£8.50 Bdif£8.75–
£12 Wf60–£80.50 ⅃ D5pm (W only Jul & Aug)

**NEW QUAY** Dyfed *Map 2 SN35*
**INN** *Queens Hotel* Church St ☎560678
Mar–Oct Lic 8hc CTV 8P ⬚ sea D9.30pm

**NEW ROMNEY** Kent *Map 5 TR02*
**GH Blue Dolphin Hotel** Dymchurch Rd
☎3224 Closed Xmas wk Lic 6rm 5hc 1
CTV P ⬚ ✳ B&bfr£12.50

**NEWTON ABBOT** Devon *Map 3 SS87*
**GH Berwyn Hotel** 33a Torquay Rd ☎66130
Lic 8hc (3fb) ✠ CTV 6P S% B&bf£9.75–£10.95
Bdif£14–£15.80 Wf89.50–£99.50 ⅃ D8.30pm

**GH Lamorna** Exeter Rd, Coombe Cross,
Sandygate (3m N A380) ☎5627 Lic 7hc (2fb)
✠ CTV 20P ⬚ S% ✳ B&bf£7–£8 Bdif£10.50–
£11.50 Wf73.50–£80.50 ⅃ D8pm

**NEWTONMORE** Highland *Inverness-shire*
*Map 14 NN79*
**GH Alder Lodge** ☎376 Lic 7rm 6hc (3fb)
CTV 10P ⦿ S% B&b£7 Bdi£11 W£70 ⽚
D8.30pm

**GH Alvey House Hotel** Golf Course Rd
☎260 20 Dec–Oct Lic 7hc (2fb) CTV 12P S%
B&b£7–£8 Bdi£10–£11.25 W£66–£74
⽚ D7pm

**GH Ard-na-Coille Hotel** ☎214 Jan–Oct Lic
12hc 1⇌ 4⣳ (3fb) CTV 20P ⦿ S%
B&b£10.50–£11 Bdi£15.50–£16.50 D7.30pm

**GH Cairn Dearg** Station Rd ☎398 6hc (2fb)
Ⓒⓗ CTV 8P S% B&b£6–£7 Bdi£10–£11.50
W£67–£77 ⽚ D5pm

**GH Coig-na-Shee** Fort William Rd ☎216
Apr–Oct rsFeb & Mar 6hc (1fb) CTV 8P ⦿
S% B&b£8.50–£9.50 Bdi£13.50–£15 W£85–
£95 ⽚ D6.30pm

**GH Glenquoich** Glen Rd ☎461 Closed
Xmas 6rm 5hc (3fb) Ⓒⓗ CTV 6P S%
B&bfr£7.50 Bdifr£12.50 Wfr£50 Ⓜ D7pm

**NEWTON STEWART** Dumfries & Galloway
*Wigtowns Map 10 NX46*
**GH Duncree House Hotel** Girvan Rd ☎2001
Lic 6hc (5fb) Ⓒⓗ CTV 25P S% B&b£6 Bdi£9
Wfr£63 D5pm ⌡

**NITON** Isle of Wight *Map 4 SZ57*
**GH Windcliffe House Hotel** Sandrock Rd
☎730215 Etr–Oct Lic 12hc (7fb) CTV 18P
sea S% B&b£8–£11.50 Bdi£12–£15
W£82.80–£108.10 ⽚ D6pm

**NORTHALLERTON** N Yorks *Map 8 SE39*
**GH Windsor** 56 South Pde ☎774100 Closed
1st 2wks Jun & 24 Dec–2 Jan 6hc (3fb) CTV
⦿ S% B&bfr£8

**INN Station Hotel** 2 Boroughbridge Rd
☎2053 Lic 9hc CTV 30P ⦿ D6pm

**NORTHAMPTON** Northants *Map 4 SP76*
**GH Poplars Hotel** Cross St, Moulton
☎43983 Closed Xmas wk Lic 22hc 2⇌ 5⣳
(4fb) Ⓒⓗ CTV 22P ⦿ S% B&bfr£11 Bdifr£15
D6.30pm

**NORTH BERWICK** Lothian *E Lothian Map
12 NT58*
**GH Belhaven Private Hotel** Westgate
☎2573 mid Mar–Sep 6hc (2fb) sea

**GH Cragside Private Hotel** 16 Marine Pde
☎2879 Apr–Oct 6hc (1fb) CTV P ⦿ sea S%
✻B&b£6 Bdi£10 W£65 ⽚ D7pm

**NORTH HYKEHAM** Lincs *Map 8 SK96*
**GH Loudor Hotel** 37 Newark Rd ☎Lincoln
680333 Lic 10hc 3⣳ (A 2hc 1⇌ 1⣳) (1fb) ✸
CTV 14P ⦿ S% B&b£9.78–£11.50 Bdi£13.80–
£15.87 D7.30pm

**NORTH WALSHAM** Norfolk *Map 9 TG23*
**GH Beechwood Private Hotel** 20 Cromer
Rd ☎403231 Closed Xmas Lic 11hc 2⇌ 2⣳
(8fb) Ⓒⓗ CTV 12P ⦿ B&b£9.80–£10.40
Bdi£13.80–£14.40 W£82–£96 ⽚ D6pm

**NORTHWOOD** Salop *Map 7 SJ43*
**GH Woodlands Country House** (1m S off
B5063) ☎Wem 33268 Closed Xmas Lic 8hc
1⇌ 2⣳ (3fb) ✸ CTV 12P ⦿ B&b£6.50–£7.75
Bdi£10.50–£11.75 D6.30pm

**NORWICH** Norfolk *Map 5 TG20*
**GH Argyle House Hotel** 10 Stracey Rd

☎27493 11hc (1fb) ⊁nc6 CTV ▥ S%
✱B&b£8 Bdi£11.50 W£80.50 ⅃ D3pm

**GH** *Gables* 240 Thorpe Rd ☎34475 12hc (A
4hc) (3fb) CTV 11P ▥

**GH Grange Hotel** 230 Thorpe Rd ☎34734
Lic 37hc 34⇔ 10♒ (1fb) CTV 48P 3☎ ▥ &
S% B&b£12–£24 Bdi£14–£24 D8pm

**GH** *Marlborough House Hotel* 22 Stracey
Rd, Thorpe Rd ☎28005 Lic 11hc 3⇔ ♒ CTV
5P ☎ ▥

**NOTTINGHAM** Notts *Map 8 SK53*
**GH Crantock Hotel** 480 Mansfield Rd
☎623294 Lic 9hc CTV 9P ▥ S% ✱B&b£10–
£12.65 Bdi£15.50–£18.40 D8pm

**GH Rufford Hotel** Melton Rd, West
Bridgford (1m S on A52) ☎814202 Closed
Xmas Lic 30hc 22♒ ⊁ CTV 35P 2☎ ▥ S%

✱B&b£9.20–£11.50 Bdi£14.95–£17.25
D7.45pm

**GH Waverley** 107 Portland Rd, Waverley St
☎786707 17hc (2fb) CTV 1☎ S% B&b£6
Bdi£9 D4pm

**GH** *Windsor* 4 Watcombe Circus ☎621317
Closed Xmas 8hc (1fb) CTV 6P ▥

**GH Windsor Lodge** 116 Radcliffe Rd, West
Bridgford (1m S on A52) ☎813773 Lic 42hc
20♒ (10fb) ⊁ CTV 48P ▥ S% B&b£10.90
Bdi£16 D7.15pm

**NUNEATON** Warwicks *Map 4 SP39*
**GH Abbey Grange Hotel** 100 Manor Court
Rd ☎385535 Lic 9hc ⊁ TV 30P ▥ S%
B&b£12.65–£13.91 D9pm

**GH Drachenfels Hotel** 25 Attleborough Rd
☎383030 Lic 6hc CTV in all bedrooms 8P ▥

S% ✻B&bfr£12.50 Bdifr£16.50 D8.30pm

**INN *Bull Hotel*** Market Pl ☎386599 Lic 12hc CTV 18P 2🚗 ♨ D8pm

**NUNNEY** Somerset *Map 3 ST74*
**INN George** Church St ☎458 6rm 1hc 3🛁 2🚿 🚐 CTV 20P S% ✻B&b£11–£19 sn L£3–£4&alc D9pm£7alc

**OAKS, THE, Charnwood Forest** Leics *Map 8 SK31*
**INN Belfry Hotel** Oaks Rd ☎Shepshed 3247 Lic 16hc 6🛁 3🚿 CTV 150P 2🚗 ♨ S% B&b£14.75–£19 Bdi£19.75–£27 W£133–£175 L£2.25–£3&alc D10pm£5.50–£6.50&alc

**OBAN** Strathclyde *Argyll Map 10 NM83*
**(See Plan)**
⊢⊣ **GH Ardblair** Dalriach Rd ☎62668 Plan:**1** 5 May–27 Sep 15hc (A 7hc) (4fb) ✋ CTV 12P sea S% B&b£5.50–£6.50 Bdi£9.50–£10.50 D6.30pm

**GH Barriemore Private Hotel** Esplanade ☎62197 Plan:**2** wk before Etr–mid Oct 14hc (4fb) nc6 CTV 17P sea B&b£6.67–£8.75 Bdi£10.93–£12.08 D6.45pm

**GH *Crathie*** Duncraggen Rd ☎62619 Plan:**4** May–Oct 9hc nc3 CTV 12P sea

**GH Glenburnie Private Hotel** Esplanade ☎62089 Plan:**5** May–Sep 13hc (3fb) ✋ nc5 CTV 12P 1🚗 sea ✻B&b£6.95–£8.22

**GH Heatherfield Private Hotel** Albert Rd ☎62681 Plan:**6** Apr–Oct 10hc (3fb) nc5 CTV 10P sea S% B&b£6.33 Bdi£10.50 W£73 Ⱡ D6pm

⊢⊣ **GH Kenmore** Soraba Rd ☎63592 Plan:**7** 7hc (4fb) CTV 20P ♨ S% B&b£5.50–£6

⊢⊣ **GH Roseneath** Dalriach Rd ☎64262 Plan:**8** 10hc (2fb) CTV 9P ♨ sea ✻B&b£5.75–£7.50 Bdi£8.50–£12 W£76 Ⱡ D6pm

**ODDINGTON** Glos *Map 4 SP22*
**INN Fox** ☎Stow-on-the-Wold 30446 3hc 🚐 CTV 30P S% B&b£8 Bdi£12 W£84 Bar lunch 95p–£3.20 D9pm£3.75–£6.50

**ODIHAM** Hants *Map 4 TQ75*
**INN King's Arms Hotel** High St ☎2559 4hc CTV 6P S% B&bfr£14 sn Lfr£3.50&alc D9.30pm£5alc

**OKEHAMPTON** Devon *Map 2 SX59*
**INN *Fountain*** Fore St ☎2828 Etr–Sep Lic 6hc ✋ nc11 TV 6P 4🚗 🚐 D7pm

**ONICH** Highland *Inverness-shire Map 14 NN06*

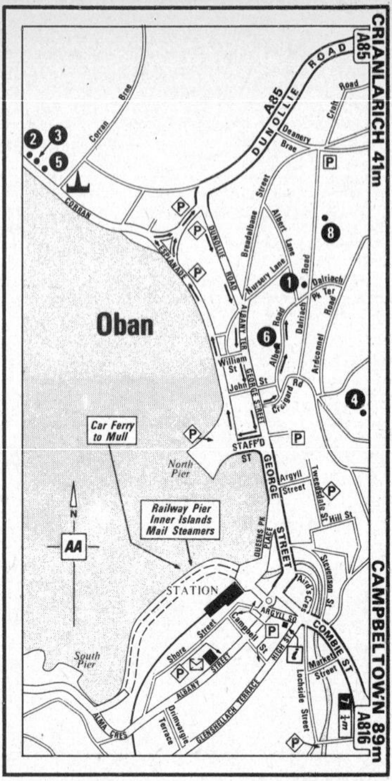


**1** Ardblair
**2** Barriemore Private Hotel
**4** Crathie
**5** Glenburnie Private Hotel
**6** Heatherfield Private Hotel
**7** Kenmore
**8** Roseneath

**GH Glenmorven House** ☎247 Etr–Oct 7rm 6hc (2fb) 20P ♨ lake S% Bdifr£12.25 Wfr£85.75 Ⱡ D8pm

**GH *Tigh-a-Righ*** ☎255 Closed 22 Dec–7 Jan Lic 5hc (2fb) CTV 20P ♨ D8.30pm

**ORFORD** Suffolk *Map 5 TM44*
**INN King's Head** Front St ☎271 Closed Jan rsSun & Mon 5hc 🚐 ✋ 100P 1🚗 B&b£13.20 sn L£4.50alc D9pm£8alc

**ORKNEY** *Map 16* **See Kirkwall, Stromness**

**OSWESTRY** Salop *Map 7 SJ22*
**GH Ashfield Country House** Llwyn-y-Maen, Trefonen Rd ☎5200 Mar–Nov Lic 14hc 6⇆ (2fb) ⚹ CTV 20P ⅏ S% B&bf£10–£15 Bdi£14–£16 Wf£80–£95 ⅃ D9pm

**OXFORD** Oxon *Map 4 SP50*
**GH Brown's** 281 Iffley Rd ☎46822 7hc (2fb) CTV 3P ⅏ S% B&bf£6–£7
**See advert on page 162**

**GH Combermere** 11 Polstead Rd ☎56971 Feb–Nov 6hc (2fb) ⚹ nc8 3P S% B&bf£6.50–£8

**GH Conifer** 116 The Slade, Headington ☎63055 8hc 1⇆ 2🛁 (1fb) ⚹ CTV 8P ⅏ S% B&bf£6–£7.50

**GH Earlmont** 322–324 Cowley Rd ☎40236 (due to be prefixed by 2) 4hc (A 6hc) (2fb) ⚹

CTV 10P 1🐾 ⅏ S% B&bf£6–£7.50

**GH Falcon** 88–90 Abingdon Rd ☎722995 10hc (2fb) ⚹ CTV 8P ⅏ S% B&bf£6–£6.50 Wf£40 Ⓜ (W only Sep–Mar)

**GH Galaxie Private Hotel** 180 Banbury Rd ☎55688 27hc 4🛁 (4fb) CTV 25P ⅏ S% B&bf£11.50–£15

**GH Melcombe House** 227 Iffley Rd ☎49520 Closed Xmas 7hc (2fb) nc3 CTV 5P ⅏ S% B&bf£6–£7.50
**See advert on page 162**

**GH Micklewood** 331 Cowley Rd ☎47328 6hc (3fb) ⚹ CTV 6P ⅏ S% ✳ B&bf£6–£6.50

**⋈ GH Pine Castle** 290 Iffley Rd ☎41497 7hc (3fb) CTV 4P ⅏ S% B&bf£5.50–£7 Bdi£8.50–£10 D8pm (W only Apr–Sep)

**GH St Giles Hotel** 86 St Giles ☎54620 10hc ⅓ CTV

**GH Victoria Hotel** 180 Abingdon Rd ☎724536 Lic 16hc 4⇔ 2↥ (3fb) CTV 20P ⅏ S% B&bf£11.50–£12.50 D8.30pm

**GH Westwood Country Hotel** Hinksey Hill Top ☎735408 16hc 6⇔ 10↥ (3fb) ⅓ CTV 16P 1🎱 ⅏ ⅙ S% ✱B&bf£23 Bdif£29.50 D2pm

**GH Willow Reaches Private Hotel** 1 Whytham St ☎721545 Lic 6hc 2⇔ 2↥ (3fb) ⅓ CTV 3P 3🎱 ⅏ S% B&bf£8–£11.50 Bdif£12.50–£15 Wf£84–£98 ⅃ D6pm

**OXWICH** W Glam *Map 2 SS58*
**GH Oxwich Bay Hotel** Gower ☎Gower 329 Etr–Sep rsOct–mid Apr Lic 19hc (2fb) ⅓ CTV 40P ⅏ sea D10pm

**PADSTOW** Cornwall *Map 2 SW97*
**GH Cross House** Church St ☎532391 9hc (4fb) ⅓ CTV river B&bf£6.90–£8.63 Bdif£9.20–£11.50 Wf£62.10–£80 ⅃ D5.30pm

**GH Duke House** 48–50 Duke St ☎532372 8hc (6fb) S% B&bf£6–£8.50 Wf£40–£56

**GH Nook** Fentonula Ln ☎532317 Apr–Oct Lic 10hc (3fb) nc3 CTV 10P ⅏ lake S% B&bf£7.50–£10 Bdif£12–£14.50 Wf£39–£49.50 M D6pm

**GH Tregea** High St ☎532455 Etr–Sep 8hc ⅓ CTV 8P ⅏ S% B&bf£10 Bdif£14

**PAIGNTON** Devon *Map 3 SX86* **(See Plan)**
**GH Amaryllis Hotel** 14 Sands Rd ☎559552 Plan:**1** Mar–Oct & Xmas 10hc (6fb) nc3 CTV 10P S% B&bf£8.05–£10.35 Bdif£11.50–£14.95 Wf£63.25–£78.20 ⅃ D6pm

---

# Brown's Guest House

### 281 Iffley Road, Oxford OX4 4AQ
### Tel: Oxford 46822 (STD 0865)

Open twelve months a year.
All 6 bedrooms have hot and cold water—Showers are available.
A colour television is available for the use of guests.
Central heating throughout. Baby sitting/watching service and special meals for children.
Fire certificate granted.
Please see the gazetteer entry for further details.

---

# Bowood House Kidlington

Situated on the A423 4½ miles north of Oxford city centre. Bowood House offers accommodation of a very high standard all of the 9 bedrooms have radio, intercom, H&C. (Most have private facilities.) Full central heating throughout, TV lounge and residential license. Evening meals are available. More than ample parking on the premises.
British Tourist Authority commendation.
Local amenities include swimming baths, squash, tennis courts and golf course.

**238 Oxford Rd, Kidlington, Oxon.**
**Tel: Kidlington 2839 (STD 08675)**

---

## MELCOMBE HOUSE

*Proprietors:* Mr & Mrs P H Butler
AA Listed

*Full English breakfast*
*Tea making facilities*
*Colour TV lounge*
*Car parking space*

**227 Iffley Road**
**Oxford OX4 1SQ**
**Tel: Oxford 49520**

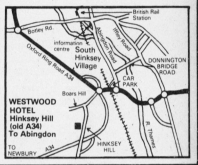

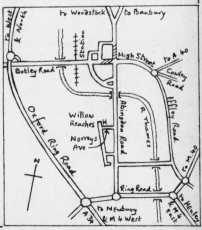

1 Amaryllis Hotel
2 Clennon Valley Hotel
3 Cornerways Hotel
4 Nevada Private Hotel
5 Orange Tubs Hotel
6 Preston Sands Hotel
7 Redcliffe Lodge Hotel
8 Roseville Private Hotel
9 St Weonard Private Hotel
10 San Remo Hotel
11 Sea Verge Hotel
12 Shorton House
13 Sunnybank Private Hotel
14 Torbay Sands Hotel

**GH Clennon Valley Hotel** 1 Clennon Rise
☎557736 Plan:**2** Closed Dec Lic 12hc (5fb)
CTV 12P ▥ S% B&bf6.90–£8.05 Bdif11.50–
£13.23 Wf72.45–£78.20 ⅃ D5pm

**GH Cornerways Hotel** 16 Manor Rd
☎551207 Plan:**3** Etr–Oct 29hc 14⋔ (10fb)
CTV 25P ▥ S% B&bf8–£13 Bdif12–£15.50
Wf80.50–£104.65 ⅃ D7pm

**GH Nevada Private Hotel** 61 Dartmouth Rd
☎558317 Plan:**4** Lic 13hc (3fb) ✻ CTV 10P ▥
S% B&bf7.50 Bdif12.50 Wf55–£66 ⅃

**GH Orange Tubs Hotel** 14 Manor Rd,
Preston ☎551541 Plan:**5** Apr–Sep Lic 11hc
3⋔ (3fb) ✻ CTV 6P ▥ S% B&bf7–£10
Bdi fr£9.50

**GH Preston Sands Hotel** 12 Marine Pde,
Preston ☎558718 Plan:**6** Lic 15hc (6fb) CTV
12P ▥ sea B&bf8.50–£8.50 Bdif8.50–£11
Wf57–£77 ⅃ D3pm

**GH Redcliffe Lodge Hotel** 1 Marine Dr
☎551394 Plan:**7** Lic 19hc 6⇔ (4fb) ✻ Ch
CTV 20P ▥ sea B&bf8.50–£12 Bdif12.50–£16
D6.30pm

**GH *Roseville Private Hotel*** Marine Gdns
☎550530 Plan:**8** Lic 11hc CTV 12P

**I✝I GH St Weonard Private Hotel**
12 Kernou Rd ☎558842 Plan:**9** Lic 9hc (4fb)
✻ CTV 2P S% B&bf5–£8 Bdif8.50–£10.50
Wf55–£72 ⅃ D4pm (W only Jul & Aug)

**GH San Remo Hotel** 35 Totnes Rd
☎557855 Plan:**10** Feb–Nov Lic 18hc (8fb)

CTV 8P S% B&bf7.50–£8.50 Bdif9–£10
Wf66–£77 D6.30pm (W only Jul & Aug)

**GH Sea Verge Hotel** Marine Dr, Preston
☎557795 Plan:**11** Mar–Oct Lic 12hc 4⋔
(3fb) ✻ CTV 18P ▥ sea S% ✻ B&bf7–£7.50
Bdif11–£12 Wf72.45–£80.50 ⅃ D6.30pm
**See advert on page 166**

**GH Shorton House** 17 Roundham Rd
☎557722 Plan:**12** Mar–Oct Lic 20hc (8fb)
CTV 20P ₺ B&bf8–£10 Bdif11–£13 Wf70–
£75 D6pm

**GH Sunnybank Private Hotel** 2 Cleveland
Rd ☎525540 Plan:**13** Mar–Oct Lic 12hc
(5fb) ✻ CTV 10P sea S% ✻ B&bf7–£8.50
Bdif10.35–£11.50 Wf63.25–£73.60 ⅃
D6pm

**GH Torbay Sands Hotel** Sea Front, 16
Marine Pde ☎522012 Plan:**14** Lic 12hc (4fb)
CTV 5P sea S% B&bf6.50–£11 Bdif9.50–
£14 D4pm
**See advert on page 166**

**PAISLEY** Strathclyde *Renfrews* Map 11
**NS46 For accommodation details see
under Glasgow Airport**

**PATCHWAY** Avon *Map 3 ST68*
**GH Willow** 209 Gloucester Rd
☎Almondsbury 612276 Bristol plan:**14** 6hc
(3fb) CTV 6P 2☎ ▥ S% B&bf8 Bdif10.50
D4pm

**PATELEY BRIDGE** N Yorks Map 7 SE16
**GH Grassfields Country House Hotel**
☎Harrogate 711412 mid Mar–Oct Lic 9hc
3⇔ 2♒ (3fb) CTV 12P 1☎ ▥ S% B&b£10.50
Bdi£16.80 W£71.30–£112.70 D7pm

**PEACEHAVEN** E Sussex Map 5 TQ40
**INN Peacehaven Hotel** South Coast Rd
☎4555 14hc 3⇔ 1♒ CTV 50P ▥ & S%
B&bfr£14 W£150 sn Lfr£3.70
D9.45pmfr£6.50&alc

**PEEBLES** Borders Peebles Map 11 NT24
**GH 'Lindores'** Old Town ☎20441 Closed
Nov 5hc (2fb) CTV 3P ▥ S% B&b£6–£6.50
W£42–£45.50 M

**PEMBROKE** Dyfed Map 2 SM90
⊢⊣ **GH Camrose Hotel** 106 St Michael's
Sq ☎5383 7hc (1fb) ⃣Ch⃣ CTV 6P ▥ S%
B&b£5–£7 Bdi£7–£8 W£42–£56 ⌀ D7pm

**PENARTH** S Glam Map 3 ST17
**GH Alanleigh Hotel** 14 Victoria Rd ☎Cardiff
701242 Lic 10hc 1⇔ (3fb) CTV 8P ▥ S%
✳B&b£9 Bdi£13 W£85 D6.45pm

**GH** *Westbourne Hotel* 8 Victoria Rd
☎Cardiff 707268 Lic 11hc (1fb) ✱ CTV 6P ▥
D10pm

**PENMAENMAWR** Gwynedd Map 6 SH77
**GH Crescent Hotel** 1 Paradise Cres
☎622079 Lic 10hc 4♒ CTV ▥ B&bfr£8.50
Bdifr£12.50 D8pm

**PENNAN** Grampian Aberdeens Map 15
NJ86
**INN Pennan** ☎New Aberdour 201 8hc ⇔

CTV 6P ▥ S% ✳B&b£10.50 Bdi£17.50 Bar
lunch90p–£2.75 D9.30pmf£6.50&alc

**PENRITH** Cumbria Map 12 NY53
⊢⊣ **GH Brandelhow** 1 Portland Pl
☎64470 6hc (4fb) CTV 4P S% B&b£5.50–
£6.50 Bdi£7.50–£9 W£52–£56 ⌀
D5.30pm

**GH** *Kinsale* 24 Wordsworth St ☎63265 6hc
✱ CTV

⊢⊣ **GH Pategill Villas** Carleton Rd
☎63153 Lic 12hc (5fb) ⃣Ch⃣ CTV 18P ▥ S%
B&b£5.50–£7.50 D6pm

**GH Woodland House Private Hotel**
Wordsworth St ☎64177 Lic 8hc (2fb) CTV
12P 1☎ ▥ S% B&b£6.75–£7 Bdi£10.90–£11.15
W£76.30–£78.05 D7pm

**PENZANCE** Cornwall Map 2 SW43
**(See Plan)**
**GH** *Alverton Court Hotel* Alverton Rd
☎2306 Plan:**1** Apr–Oct Lic 15hc 6⇔ ♒ (3fb)
✱nc5 CTV 12P 1☎ sea D6pm

**GH Bella-Vista Private Hotel** 7 Alexandra
Ter, Lariggan ☎2409 Plan:**2** Apr–Oct 10hc
(6fb) ✱nc3 CTV 8P sea S% B&b£8–£8.63
Bdi£10.07–£12.37 W£59.80–£77.05 ⌀
D5pm
**See advert on page 168**

⊢⊣ **GH Camilla Hotel** Regent Ter ☎3771
Plan:**3** Closed Xmas 9hc (3fb) CTV 3P sea
S% B&b£5–£6.50 Bdi£7.50–£9

**GH Carlton Private Hotel** ☎2081 Plan:**4**
Mar–Oct Lic 12hc 3♒ (3fb) ✱nc10 CTV sea
B&b£7.50–£9.50 Bdi£13–£15.50 W£75–£85
⌀ D5pm

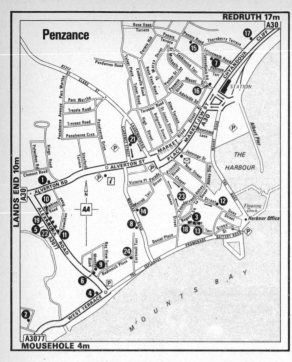

Penzance

REDRUTH 17m

1 Alverton Court Hotel
2 Bella-Vista Private Hotel
3 Camilla Hotel
4 Carlton Private Hotel
5 Dunedin
6 Duporth Private Hotel
7 Essex
8 Estoril Private Hotel
9 Glancree Private Hotel
10 Hansord Private Hotel
11 Holbein Hotel
12 Hopedale
13 Killindini Private Hotel
14 Kimberley House
15 Kirkstowe
16 Longboat *(Inn)*
17 Mount Royal Hotel
18 Old Manor House Private Hotel
19 Penmorvah Hotel
21 Tarbert Hotel
22 Trenant Private Hotel
23 Trevelyan Hotel
24 Willows

**GH Dunedin** Alexandra Rd ☎2652 Plan:**5** Mar–Dec Lic 9hc (4fb) nc3 CTV ⬚ B&b£7–£8 Bdi£11–£12 W£70–£78 ⓛ D4.30pm

**GH Duporth Private Hotel** 1 Mennaye Rd ☎2689 Plan:**6** Apr–Oct 9hc (3fb) CTV sea B&b£6.95–£7.50 Bdi£10.35–£12.07 W£63.25–£72.45 ⓛ D4pm

⊁⊣ **GH Essex** 23 Lannoweth Rd ☎5129 Plan:**7** Closed Nov–Dec rsJan–Feb (B&b only) Lic 10hc ✦ nc12 CTV 4P sea S% B&b£5.50–£7 Bdi£8–£9.50 W£52–£62 ⓛ D4pm

**GH Estoril Private Hotel** 46 Morrab Rd ☎2468 Plan:**8** Jan–Oct Lic 10rm 5⇔ 5⋔ (1fb) CTV 4P ⬚ S% B&b£11–£11.50 Bdi£16.50 W£95–£109 ⓛ D7pm

**GH Glancree Private Hotel** 2 Mennaye Rd ☎2026 Plan:**9** Apr–Sep rsMar 9hc (3fb) ✦ CTV sea S% B&b£6.75–£7.25 Bdi£10–£10.50 W£55–£70 ⓛ D10am

**GH Hansord Private Hotel** Alexandra Rd ☎3311 Plan:**10** Mar–Nov Lic 12hc (3fb) nc3 CTV ⬚ S% B&b£6.50–£7.50 Bdi£10–£11.50 W£65–£72 ⓛ D4pm

**GH Holbein House** Alexandra Rd ☎5008 Plan:**11** Lic 8hc 1⇔ (2fb) ✦ nc3 CTV ⬚ S% B&b£6.50–£8.50 Bdi£10–£12 W£60–£77 ⓛ D5.30pm

**GH Hopedale** 29 Chapel St ☎3277 Plan:**12** 6hc (2fb) CTV sea S% ✳B&b£6.50–£8

**GH Kilindini Private Hotel** 13 Regent Ter ☎4744 Plan:**13** Closed Dec Lic 11hc 3⋔ (2fb) ✦ nc3 CTV 12P ⬚ sea B&b£7.48–£8.63 Bdi£9.78–£10.93 W£66.70–£75.90 ⓛ D3.30pm

**GH Kimberley House** 10 Morrab Rd ☎2727 Plan:**14** Mar–Dec Lic 9hc (2fb) ✦ nc5 CTV 4P ⬚ S% B&b£7.75–£9.75 Bdi£12–£14 W£75–£91 D5.30pm

**GH Kirkstowe** Penare Rd ☎3115 Plan:**15** Lic 9hc (1fb) ✸ nc5 CTV 5P Ⅲ sea S% B&b£8 Bdi£11 W£70 D4pm

**GH Mount Royal Hotel** Chyandour Cliff ☎2233 Plan:**17** Mar–Oct 9hc 1⇌ (1fb) CTV 12P 4⊛ Ⅲ sea S% B&b£8–£9.50 Bdi£13–£14.50 W£87.50–£98 ⌁ Dnoon

**GH Old Manor House Private Hotel** Regent Ter ☎3742 Plan:**18** Lic 12hc (4fb) ✸ Ⅺ CTV 12P Ⅲ sea S% B&b£8.50–£12.50 Bdi£12.50–£15 W£70–£105 ⌁ D7.30pm

**GH Penmorvah Hotel** Alexandra Rd ☎3711 Plan:**19** Lic 9hc 1⇌ 1Ⅺ (4fb) CTV 2P Ⅲ S% B&b£7–£10 Bdi£10.50–£13.50 W£60–£87 ⌁ D6pm

**GH Tarbert Private Hotel** 11 Clarence St ☎3758 Plan:**21** Lic 14hc 3Ⅺ (5fb) CTV 2P B&b£6.75–£8.50 Bdi£10.25–£12 W£66.50–£80 ⌁ D4.30pm

**⊢⊣ GH Trenant Private Hotel** Alexandra Rd ☎2005 Plan:**22** 1 May–6 Oct 7hc nc7 TV S% B&b£5.90–£6.50 Bdi£9–£9.60 W£56–£62 ⌁ D5pm

**⊢⊣ GH Trevelyan Hotel** 16 Chapel St ☎2494 Plan:**23** Closed Xmas Lic 7hc (4fb) CTV 9P sea B&b£5–£6 Bdi£8–£9 W£56–£63 ⌁ Dnoon

**GH Willows** Cornwall Ter ☎3744 Plan:**24** Closed Oct 6hc (1fb) nc5 CTV 6P Ⅲ S% B&b£6.50–£9 Bdi£9.50–£10.50 W£62–£68 ⌁ D3pm

**INN** *Longboat* Market Jew St ☎4137 Plan:**16** Lic 15hc 2⇌ Ⅺ ✸ CTV 4⊛ Ⅲ D9pm

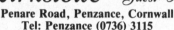

**PERRANPORTH** Cornwall *Map 2 SW75*
**GH** *Beach Dunes Hotel* Ramoth Way, Reen Sands ☎2263 Apr–Oct Lic 8hc 1⇌ 🖾 (2⇌ 🖾) (3fb) 🖾 CTV 14P 🖾 sea D6pm

**GH** *Boscawen Private Hotel* ☎3472 Etr–5 Oct Lic 15hc CTV 10P 1🅰

**GH Cellar Cove Hotel** Droskyn Point ☎2110 Lic 14hc (4fb) CTV P 🖾 sea S% B&bf£10.50 Bdif£15 Wf£90–£105 D6pm

**⋈ GH Fairview Hotel** Tywarnhayle Rd ☎2278 Apr–Oct Lic 15hc (5fb) ✶ CTV 4P 🖾 sea S% B&bf£5.50–£7.50 Bdif£7–£11.50 Wf£49–£80 ⱔ D4pm (W only late Jul & Aug)

**GH Lake House Private Hotel** Perrancombe ☎3202 Mar–Sep Lic 10hc (3fb) 🖾 CTV P 1🅰 B&bf£6.90–£8.05 Bdif£8.05–£9.20 Wf£52.90–£73.60 ⱔ D6.30pm

**GH Lamorna Private Hotel** Tywarnhayle Rd ☎3398 Closed Xmas Lic 9hc (4fb) CTV 3P S% B&bf£9.20–£10.35 Bdif£12.65–£13.80 Wf£80.50–£88.55 ⱔ D6pm (W only Jul & Aug)

**⋈ GH Lynton** Cliff Rd ☎3457 Lic 8hc (3fb) CTV 6P 🖾 sea S% B&bf£5.50–£7.50 Bdif£8–£10 Wf£48–£61 ⱔ D6pm

**GH Park View Private Hotel** 42 Tywarnhayle Rd ☎3009 Mar–Oct Lic 10hc (4fb) CTV 10P S% B&bf£7–£8.50 Bdif£9.50–£11 Wf£63–£70 ⱔ D6pm (W only end Jul–Aug)

**PERRANUTHNOE** Cornwall *Map 2 SW52*
**GH Ednovean House** ☎Penzance 711071 Dec–Oct Lic 8hc 3🖾 (2fb) nc7 CTV 12P 🖾 sea S% B&bf£7–£12.50 Bdif£10.50 Wf£66–£99 ⱔ D5.30pm

**PERTH** Tayside *Perths Map 11 NO12*
**GH Clunie** 12 Pitcullen Cres ☎23625 7hc 1⇌ 1🖾 (2fb) ✶ CTV 7P 🖾 S% B&bf£6.50 Bdif£10 Wf£70 ⱔ D5pm

**GH Darroch** 9 Pitcullen Cres ☎36893 7hc (3fb) CTV 12P 🖾 S% B&bf£6.50–£7.50 D9.15pm

**GH Gables of Perth** 24–26 Dunkeld Rd ☎24717 8hc (4fb) CTV 6P 🖾 S% ✳ B&bf£6

**⋈ GH Garth** Dundee Rd ☎22368 6hc (3fb) CTV 3P 3🅰 🖾 river S% B&bf£5.50–£6.50

**GH Pitcullen** 17 Pitcullen Cres ☎26506 10hc (2fb) CTV 12P 🖾 S% B&bfr£6 Bdifr£9.50

**PETERSFIELD** Hants *Map 4 SU72*
**GH** *Malva Hotel* 3 Church Rd, Steep (2m NW unclass) ☎2657 Lic 5hc ✶ CTV 12P

**PICKERING** N Yorks *Map 8 SE88*
**GH Bramwood** 19 Hall Garth ☎74066 Closed Xmas 6hc (4fb) ✶ nc6 CTV 6P 🖾 S% B&bf£6–£8 Bdif£9.20–£12.60 Wf£64.40–£88.20 ⱔ D4pm

**PILTON** Somerset *Map 3 ST54*
**GH Long House** ☎283 rsDec–Feb Lic 7hc 3⇌ 1🖾 (1fb) 10P 2🅰 🖾 S% B&bf£9.75–£10.60 Bdif£15.10–£16.60 Wf£89.60–£100.40 ⱔ D7pm

**PITLOCHRY** Tayside *Perths Map 14 NN95* **(See Plan)**
**GH Adderley Private Hotel** 23 Toberargan Rd ☎2433 Plan:**1** 14 Apr–14 Oct 10hc (1fb) ✶ nc10 CTV 9P S% Bdif£11.50–£12.25 Wf£77.20–£80.50 ⱔ D6.30pm

**GH Balrobin Private Hotel** Higher Oakfield ☎2901 Plan:**2** late May–late Sep 7hc 1⇌ 1🖾 (2fb) 10P S% B&bf£10 Bdif£15 Wf£55 ⱔ D7pm

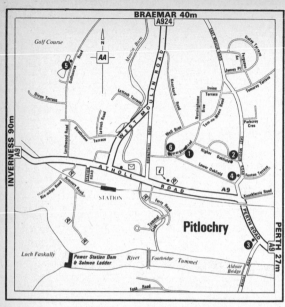

1　Adderley Private Hotel
2　Balrobin Private Hotel
3　Fasganeoin Hotel
4　Poplars Private Hotel
5　Torrdaroch Hotel
6　Well House Private Hotel

**GH Duntrune** 22 East Moulin Rd ☎2172 Not on plan mid Mar–mid Oct 7hc (1fb) ⊁ nc5 8P S% B&bf7–£7.50 Bdif11–£11.50 Wf71.50–£75.25 ⌊ D6.30pm

**GH Fasganeoin Hotel** Perth Rd ☎2387 Plan:**3** Apr–Sep Lic 9hc (4fb) ⊁ TV 20P ⠀⠀⠀ river S% B&bf9.50–£10.50 Bdif14.50–£15.50 Wf99–£106 ⌊ D7.30pm

**GH Poplars Private Hotel** Lower Oakfield ☎2129 Plan:**4** Mar–Oct 9hc 7⅍ (2fb) CTV 14P ⠀⠀⠀ S% B&bf6.50–£7.50 Bdif11.50–£13 D6.30pm

**GH Torrdarach Hotel** Golf Course Rd ☎2136 Plan:**5** 7hc 1⅍ (1fb) CTV 9P ⠀⠀⠀ S% B&bf8.25–£8.75 Bdif13.50–£14 Wf89.50–£93 ⌊ D6pm

**GH Well House Private Hotel** Toberargan Rd ☎2239 Plan:**6** Lic 8hc (3fb) CTV 10P S% B&bf6.75–£7.75 Bdif10.75–£12 D6.30pm

**PLOCKTON** Highland *Ross & Crom Map 14 NG83*
**GH Haven** ☎223 mid Jan–mid Dec 15hc 1⇌ (4fb) CTV 11P ⠀⠀⠀ ✻ B&bfrf7 Bdifrf12 Wfrf80 D8pm

**PLYMOUTH** Devon *Map 2 SX45* **(See Plan)**
**GH Bowling Green Hotel** Lockyer St, The Hoe ☎667485 Plan:**1** 10hc (2fb) CTV ⠀⠀⠀ S% B&bf10.35–£13.80

⊁⊣ **GH Burgoyne Villa** 70 Alma Rd, Mile House ☎662624 Plan:**2** 6hc (3fb) ⊁ CTV 4P ⠀⠀⠀ S% B&bf5.50–£6.50

**GH Cadleigh** 36 Queens Rd, Lipson ☎665909 Plan:**3** 9hc (4fb) CTV ⠀⠀⠀ S% ✻ B&bf9.25 Bdif13.25 D4pm

**GH Carnegie Hotel** 172 Citadel Rd, The Hoe ☎25158 Plan:**3A** Lic 10hc (3fb) ⊁ CTV ⠀⠀⠀ sea S% B&bf8.95–£11.95 Bdif13.90–£17.90 Wf92.60–£118 ⌊ D7pm

**GH Chester** 54 Stuart Rd, Pennycomequick ☎663706 Plan:**4** 7hc (2fb) nc5 CTV 8P 1✿ ⠀⠀⠀ S% B&bfrf6 Bdifrf10 D4pm

**GH *Dudley*** 42 Sutherland Rd, Mutley ☎668322 Plan:**5** 7hc (3fb) CTV 3P ⠀⠀⠀ Dnoon

**GH Eddystone** 16 Woodland Ter, Greenbank ☎668672 Plan:**6** Closed Xmas wk Lic 9hc (3fb) CTV 6P S% ✻ B&bf5.50 Bdif8.50 D6.30pm

**GH Gables End Hotel** 29 Sutherland Rd, Mutley ☎20803 Plan:**7** 7hc (4fb) ⊁ CTV

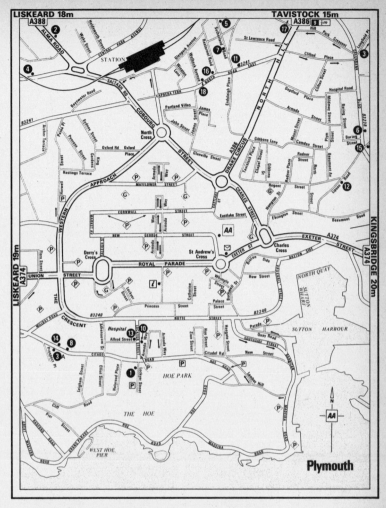

| | | | |
|---|---|---|---|
| **1** Bowling Green Hotel | **5** Dudley | **10** Imperial Hotel | **15** Trenant House |
| **2** Burgoyne Villa | **6** Eddystone | **11** Kildare | **16** Welbeck House |
| **3** Cadleigh | **7** Gables End Hotel | **12** Lagos Hotel | **17** York |
| **3A** Carnegie Hotel | **8** Georgian House Hotel | **13** Lockyer House Hotel | **18** Yorkshireman Hotel |
| **4** Chester | **9** Glendevon Hotel | **14** St James Hotel | |

S% B&b£8–£8.50 Bdi£12.50–£13 W£82–
£85 ⅃ D3pm

**GH Georgian House Hotel** 51 Citadel Rd,
The Hoe ☎663237 Plan:**8** Lic 10hc 2🛏 (1fb)
CTV 1P 🎵 S% B&b£10–£12 D9pm

**GH Glendevon Hotel** 20 Ford Park Rd,
Mutley ☎663655 Plan:**9** Lic 8hc (2fb) 🛏 CTV
🎵 S% B&b£7.48–£8.65 Bdi£11.51–£13.26
W£75–£85 ⅃ D9pm

**GH Imperial Hotel** 3 Windsor Villas, Lockyer
St, The Hoe ☎27311 Plan:**10** Closed Xmas
& New Year Lic 24hc 2⇌ 8🛏 (7fb) CTV 20P
1🐾 🎵 S% B&b£10–£11.50 Bdi£15–£16.50
W£83–£109 ⅃ D7.30pm

**GH Kildare** 82 North Rd East ☎29375
Plan:**11** Closed Xmas & New Year 9hc (2fb)
🛏 CTV 🎵 S% B&b£6.50–£8

⊢⊣ **GH Lagos Hotel** 46 Lipson Rd
☎669145 Plan:**12** Lic 8hc (2fb) CTV S%
B&b£5.50–£6 Bdi£9–£9.50 D4pm

**GH Lockyer House Hotel** 2 Alfred St, The
Hoe ☎665755 Plan:**13** Lic 6hc (1fb) CTV 🎵
B&b£8.20 Bdi£12.94 W£80–£85 ⅃ Dnoon

⊢⊣ **GH Norway** 70 Normandy Way, St
Budeaux ☎361979 Not on plan 6hc (1fb) 🛏
CTV river S% B&b£5–£5.50 Bdi£8–£8.50
D4pm

**GH St James Hotel** 49 Citadel Rd, The Hoe
☎661950 Plan:**14** Closed Xmas & Jan Lic
9🛏 (3fb) nc7 CTV 🎵 S% B&b£8.25–£10.75
Bdi£13.75–£15.25 W£96.25–£106.75 ⅃

**GH Trenant House** Queens Rd, Lipson
☎663879 Plan:**15** Lic 21hc (1fb) CTV 20P 🎵
S% B&b£9.50–£10.50 Bdi£13.50–£14.50
D4pm

**GH Welbeck Hotel** North Rd East ☎661350
Plan:**16** Closed Xmas wk 8hc (2fb) CTV P
S% ✱B&b£5–£5.50

⊢⊣ **GH York** 23 Wilderness Rd,
Mannamead ☎266129 Plan:**17** 6hc (2fb)
CTV sea S% B&b£5.50–£6 Bdi£8.25–£8.50
W(5dys)£45 ⅃ D4pm

**GH Yorkshireman Hotel** 64 North Rd East
☎668133 Plan:**18** Closed Xmas 12hc (6fb) 🛏
CTV 7P S% ✱B&b£6.25–£7 Bdi£10–£10.50
Dnoon

**POLMASSICK** Cornwall Map 2 SW94
**GH Kilbol House** ☎Mevagissey 2481 Feb–
Oct Lic 7hc 1⇌ (3fb) (A2rm) 🛏 CTV P 1🐾 🎵
S% B&b£9–£10.50 Bdi£13.50–£14.50 D5pm

**POLPERRO** Cornwall Map 2 SX25
**GH Atlantis Hotel** Polperro Rd ☎72243 Lic
10hc (2fb) 🅲🅷 CTV 15P S% B&b£8.05–£11.50
Bdi£11.50–£16.10 W£74.75–£109.25 ⅃

**GH Kit Hill** Talland Hill ☎72369 Lic 8rm 7hc
1⇌ (1fb) 🛏 nc6 CTV 10P 🎵 sea S% B&b£6–
£10.50 Bdi£15.50 Dnoon

**GH Landaviddy Manor** Landaviddy Ln
☎72210 Mar–Oct Lic 11hc 2🛏 🛏 nc12 CTV
12P 🎵 sea S% B&b£8–£11 Bdi£13.75–
£16.75 W£82.50–£94.50 ⅃ D4pm

**GH Lanhael House** ☎72428 Feb–Nov 6hc
1🛏 🛏 nc15 CTV 8P 1🐾 🎵 S% B&b£8.50–£10

⊢⊣ **GH Sleepy Hollow Private Hotel**
Brentfields ☎72288 Apr–Sep 7hc 2🛏 🛏
nc12 CTV 7P sea S% B&b£5.50–£7 Bdi£8.50–
£11 W£59.50–£77 ⅃ (W only Jul & Aug)

**POLRUAN** Cornwall Map 2 SX15
**GH Florizel** Fore St ☎208 Mar–Oct 12hc
2⇌ 2🛏 nc8 CTV 4P 8🐾 sea S% ✱B&b£9–£10
Bdi£13–£14 W£80–£85 ⅃

**POLYPHANT** Cornwall Map 2 SX28
**GH Bowden Derra Country House**
☎Pipers Pool 230 Lic 7hc 2⇌ (3fb) 🛏 CTV
10P 🎵 S% ✱B&b£9.20 Bdi£15.15–£16.30
W£92.05–£107.10 ⅃ D8.30pm

**POLZEATH** Cornwall Map 2 SW97
**GH White Lodge** Old Polzeath
☎Trebetherick 2370 Lic 9hc (2fb) CTV 9P 🎵
S% B&b£6–£7.50 Bdi£9–£10.50 W£55–
£70 ⅃ D9.30am

**PONTLYFNI** Gwynedd Map 6 SH45
**GH Bron Dirion Hotel** ☎Clynnogfawr 346
Mar–Oct Lic 9hc (4fb) CTV 10P 🎵 sea S%
B&b£8–£9 Bdi£11–£12.50 W£70–£80 ⅃
D6.30pm

**POOLE** Dorset Map 4 SZ09
For locations and additional guesthouses see
**Bournemouth**
**GH Avalon Private Hotel** 14 Pinewood Rd,
Branksome Park ☎760917 Bournemouth
district plan:**60** Lic 9hc 3⇌ (2fb) nc6 CTV
14P 🎵 S% B&b£6.50–£7 Bdi£9.50–£10.50
W£56–£68 ⅃

**GH Blue Shutters Hotel** 109 North Rd,
Parkstone ☎748129 Bournemouth district
plan:**65** Lic 11hc (1fb) 🅲🅷 CTV 10P 🎵 sea S%
B&bfr£6 Bdifr£9

**GH Dene Hotel** 16 Pinewood Rd,
Branksome Park ☎761143 Bournemouth
district plan:**73** Lic 16hc 1⇌ 6🛏 (5fb) 🛏 CTV
20P 🎵 S% B&b£10.35–£17.25 Bdi£14.95–
£22.43 W£71.88–£98.63 ⅃ D7.30pm

⊢⊣ **GH Lewina** 225 Bournemouth Rd,
Parkstone ☎742295 Bournemouth district
plan:**86** 6hc (2fb) 🅲🅷 TV 8P S% B&bfr£5
Wtrf£30 Ⓜ

**↦ GH Ormonde House** 18 Ormonde Rd,
Branksome Park ☎761093 Bournemouth
district plan:**96** Lic 8hc (4fb) [CH] CTV 8P S%
B&b£5.75–£7.75 Bdi£8.50–£10.50
W£60–£73 ₺ D7pm

**GH Redcroft Private Hotel** 20 Pinewood
Rd, Branksome Park ☎763959
Bournemouth district plan:**100** Lic 10hc (4fb)
↦nc5 CTV 12P ﷯ S% B&b£9.20 Bdi£13.80
W£63.25–£74.75 ₺ D5pm

**GH Sandbourne Hotel** 1 Sandecotes Rd,
Parkstone ☎747704 Bournemouth district
plan:**103** 7hc (3fb) ↦ CTV 8P ﷯ S% B&b£7–
£8 Bdi£9.50–£10.50 W£63–£70 ₺ D4pm

**GH Sheldon Lodge** 22 Forest Rd,
Branksome Park ☎761186 Bournemouth
district plan:**105** Etr–20 Oct Lic 15hc 4⇨ 4🛆
(2fb) ↦nc8 CTV 15P ﷯ S% B&b£7.35–£8.35
Bdi£9.50–£10.50 Wfr£68 ₺ D6pm

**GH Teesdale Hotel** 3 De Maulley Rd,
Canford Cliffs ☎708707 Bournemouth
district plan:**110** Lic 14hc 1⇨ 4🛆 (3fb) [CH]
CTV 12P ﷯ S% B&b£12–£14 Bdi£15–£17
W£80.50–£98 ₺ D7pm

**GH Twin Cedars Hotel** 2 Pinewood Rd,
Branksome Park ☎761339 Bournemouth
district plan:**112** Lic 9rm 5hc 3⇨ 1🛆 (8fb) nc6
CTV 15P ﷯ S% B&b£11.50–£14.95 Bdi£14.95–
£18.40 W£97.75–£120.75 ₺ D10pm

**GH Wayside Lodge Hotel** 179
Bournemouth Rd, Parkstone ☎732328 Not
on plan Lic 12hc (3fb) CTV 15P 2🏠 ﷯ S%
✱B&b£6.50–£7.50 Bdi£8.50–£9.50 W£56–
£59.50 ₺ D8pm

**GH *Westminster Cottage Hotel***
3 Westminster Rd East, Branksome Park
☎765265 Bournemouth district plan:**115** Lic
12hc 4⇨ 🛆 CTV 14P

**PORLOCK** Somerset *Map 3 SS84*
**GH *Gables*** ☎862552 Etr–Oct 8hc ↦nc12
CTV ﷯ D4pm

**GH Lorna Doone Hotel** ☎862404 Feb–Nov
Lic 11hc 2⇨ 2🛆 (1fb) ↦ CTV 8P ﷯
B&bfr£11.50 Bdifr£16.50 Wfr£106.50 ₺

**GH Overstream** Parson St ☎862421 Closed
Xmas 7hc (3fb) nc3 10P sea S% B&b£7
Bdi£10.50 W£68 ₺ D3pm

**PORT ELLEN** Isle of Islay, Strathclyde *Argyll
Map 10 NR34*
**GH *Tighcargaman*** ☎2345 Lic 3hc 1⇨ 🛆
(A 6rm 4hc 1⇨ 🛆) (2fb) [CH] 9P ﷯ sea D8pm

**PORT ERIN** Isle of Man *Map 6 SC26*
**GH *Golf Links Hotel*** ☎832270 May–29 Sep
Lic 64hc ↦ [CH] CTV 35P sea D8pm

**GH Regent Hotel** ☎833454 May–Sep 12hc
1🛆 (3fb) ↦ CTV 20P sea S% B&b£6–£6.50
Bdi£8–£8.50 W£56–£59.50 ₺ D5pm

**GH *Snaefell*** The Promenade ☎832273
May–Sep Lic 54hc [CH] CTV 40P sea D7pm

**PORTESHAM** Dorset *Map 3 SY68*
**GH Millmead Country** Goose Hill
☎Abbotsbury 432 7hc (2fb) ↦nc12 CTV in all
bedrooms 10P ﷯ S% ✱B&bfr£9 Bdifr£14
D5.30pm

**PORTHCAWL** Mid Glam *Map 3 SS87*
**GH Collingwood Hotel** 40 Mary St ☎2899
Closed 24–31 Dec Lic 6hc (3fb) ↦ CTV ﷯ S%
B&b£7 Bdi£10.50 W£73.50 ₺ D2pm

**GH Craig-y-Don Private Hotel** 30 The
Esplanade ☎3259 9hc (2fb) CTV ﷯ sea S%

B&b£6.50–£8.50 Bdi£12–£13 W£55–£60 ₺
D7pm

**GH Gwalia Private Hotel** 40 Esplanade Av
☎2751 7hc (2fb) ↦ CTV ﷯ S% ✱B&b£6

**GH Seaways Hotel** 28 Mary St ☎3510 Lic
13hc 1⇨ (1fb) ↦nc3 CTV 2P ﷯ S%
B&b£13.25 Bdi£18 W£90 ₺ D9.30pm

**PORTHCOTHAN BAY** Cornwall *Map 2
SW87*
**GH Bay House** ☎Padstow 520472 Etr–Oct
Lic 17hc (1fb) CTV P sea S% B&b£9.41–
£12.36 Bdi£12.14–£16.33 W£81.21–£97.80 ₺

**PORTHCURNO** Cornwall *Map 2 SW32*
**GH Corniche Trebehor Farm** ☎Sennen 424
Feb–Nov Lic 4hc (1fb) ↦nc7 CTV 5P ﷯ sea
B&b£6.50–£7 Bdi£10–£10.50 W£73–£74 ₺
D5.50pm (W only Jul & Aug)

**GH Mariners Lodge** ☎St Buryan 236 Feb–
Oct Lic 7hc 2🛆 (1fb) ↦nc7 CTV 16P ﷯ sea
S% ✱B&b£7.50–£12 Bdi£15–£19.50 D7.30pm

**PORTHMADOG** Gwynedd *Map 6 SH53*
**GH Oakleys** The Harbour ☎2482 Apr–Oct
Lic 8hc 1⇨ (2fb) CTV 12P S% B&b£7–£8
Bdi£12–£14 W£65–£75 ₺ D6pm

**GH Owen's Hotel** High St ☎2098 Closed
Xmas 12hc 1🛆 (4fb) CTV 4P 5🏠 ﷯ S%
B&bfr£9 Bdifr£14 Wfr£90 ₺ D7pm

**GH *Tan-yr-Onnen Hotel*** Penamser Rd
☎2443 Closed Dec rsNov & Feb Lic 11hc
1⇨ 🛆 (1fb) ↦ CTV 10P ﷯ D9am

**PORT ISAAC** Cornwall *Map 2 SW98*
**GH *Archer Farm*** Trewetha (1m E B3267)
☎522 Apr–Dec Lic 9rm 8hc 3⇨ 🛆 (1fb) nc3
CTV 8P ﷯ D7.30pm

**GH Bay Hotel** 1 The Terrace ☎380 Etr–Oct
& Xmas Lic 11hc (5fb) CTV 10P sea S%
B&b£7.50–£9.50 Bdi£10.50–£13.75 W£66–
£86.25 ₺ D8pm

**↦ GH Fairholme** 30 Trewetha Ln ☎397
6hc (2fb) ↦ CTV 8P ﷯ S% B&b£5–£6 Bdi£9–
£10 W£60–£70 ₺ D10am

**GH Trethoway Hotel** 98 Fore St ☎214 Apr–
mid Nov Lic 12hc (2fb) CTV 1🏠 sea
B&b£8.75–£11.95 Bdi£11.30–£15
W£78–£102 ₺ D5pm

**PORTPATRICK** Dumfries & Galloway
*Wigtowns Map 10 NX05*
**GH Blinkbonnie** School Brae ☎282 Apr–
Sep 6hc (1fb) CTV 8P ﷯ B&b£6.25 Bdi£10.50
W£73 ₺ D5.30pm

**GH Carlton** 21 South Cres ☎253 Mar–Oct
8hc nc CTV sea S% B&b£8 Bdi£12 D6pm

**GH Melvin Lodge** Dunskey St ☎238 Etr–
Sep Tem 13hc (4fb) CTV 8P sea B&b£7.50
Bdi£9.50 D6.30pm

**GH South Cliff House Hotel** ☎441 Lic 6hc
(2fb) CTV 8P ﷯ sea S% B&b£9 Bdi£12.50
W£75 ₺ D7pm

**PORTREE** Isle of Skye, Highland *Inverness-
shire Map 13 NG44*
**GH Bosville** Bosville Ter ☎2846 Apr–Oct
13hc 1⇨ 1🛆 (3fb) CTV 8P sea S%
✱B&b£6.50–£7.50 Bdi£9.50–£11.50
W£52–£60 D7.45pm

**GH Craiglockhart** Beaumont Cres ☎2233
Closed Dec rsJan & Feb 4hc (A 5hc) TV 4P ﷯
sea S% B&b£6.90–£7.48 Bdi£10.35–£11.51
W£68–£75 ₺ D7pm

**PORTSMOUTH & SOUTHSEA** Hants *Map 4 SZ69*

**Telephone Exchange 'Portsmouth' (See Plan)**

**GH Astor** 4 St Andrews Rd, Southsea ☎755171 Plan:**1** 6hc (3fb) CTV ▥ S% B&b£6.50–£7.50 W£36–£42 ⋈

**GH Averano** 65 Granada Rd, Southsea ☎820079 Plan:**2** 13hc (5fb) ✠ CTV 8P 2⩔ ▥ ✷ B&b£6.90–£8.05 Bdi£10.35–£11.50 W£64.40–£69 ⋏ D2.30pm

**GH Beaufort Hotel** 71 Festing Rd, Southsea ☎823707 Plan:**3** 15hc (4fb) CTV 8P sea S% B&b£10–£12 Bdi£15–£18 W£68–£75 ⋏ D6pm

**GH Birchwood** 44 Waverley Rd, Southsea ☎811337 Plan:**4** Closed Xmas 6hc (4fb) ✠ nc3 CTV ▥ S% B&b£6–£6.50 Bdi£9.50–£10 W£49.50–£52 ⋏ D4pm

**GH Bristol Hotel** 55 Clarence Pde, Southsea ☎821815 Plan:**5** Closed Xmas Lic 14hc 4⋔ (7fb) ✠ CTV 7P B&b£9–£10 Bdi£13–£14 W£60–£75 ⋏ D5pm

**GH Chequers Hotel** Salisbury Rd, Southsea ☎8735277 Plan:**6** Lic 13hc (3fb) Ch CTV 10P ▥ B&b£11.50 Bdi£16 W£65–£83 ⋏ D6pm

**GH Elms** 48 Victoria Rd South, Southsea ☎823924 Plan:**7** Closed Xmas 7hc (2fb) ✠ nc CTV 2P D4pm

**GH Gainsborough House** 9 Malvern Rd, Southsea ☎822604 Plan:**8** Closed Xmas 6hc (2fb) CTV ▥ S% B&b£6.50–£7 Bdi£8–£9 W£50–£56 ⋏ D4pm

**GH Grosvenor Court Hotel** 37 Granada Rd ☎821653 Plan:**9** Apr–Nov Lic 15hc (4fb) nc5 CTV 10P S% B&b£8–£8.50 Bdi£9.50 W£55.20 ⋏ Dnoon

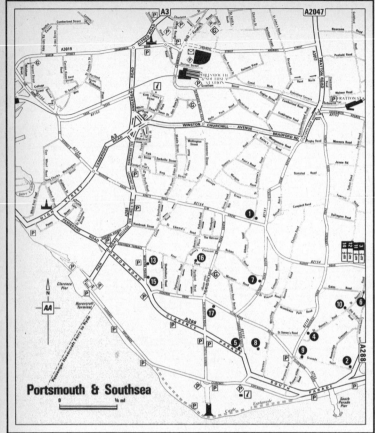

**Portsmouth & Southsea**

| | | | |
|---|---|---|---|
| 1 Astor House | 7 Elms | 11 Homeleigh | 16 Tudor Court |
| 2 Averano | 8 Gainsborough | 12 Lyndhurst | Hotel |
| 3 Beaufort | House | 13 Ryde View | 17 Upper Mount |
| 4 Birchwood | 9 Grosvenor Court | 14 Salisbury Hotel | House |
| 5 Bristol | Hotel | 15 Somerset Private | |
| 6 Chequers Hotel | 10 Harwood Hotel | Hotel | |

**GH Harwood Hotel** 47–49 St Ronans Rd, Southsea ☎823104 Plan:**10** Lic 15hc (5fb) ✶ CTV ⅢⅢ S% B&b£8–£9.20 Bdi£11.50–£12.65

**GH Homeleigh** 42–44 Festing Gv, Southsea ☎823706 Plan:**11** 10hc CTV

**GH Lyndhurst** 8 Festing Gv, Southsea ☎735239 Plan:**12** Closed Xmas 7hc (2fb) CTV ⅢⅢ S% B&b£6.50 Bdi£8 Dnoon

**GH Ryde View** 9 Western Pde, Southsea ☎820865 Plan:**13** Closed Xmas Lic 15hc (7fb) CTV ⅢⅢ sea S% ✶B&b£7.50–£8.50 Bdi£12–£13 D3pm

**GH Salisbury Hotel** 57–59 Festing Rd, Southsea ☎823606 Plan:**14** Lic 25hc (6fb) CTV 50P D5pm

**GH Somerset Private Hotel** 16 Western Pde, Southsea ☎822495 Plan:**15** Closed Xmas 15hc (7fb) ✶nc3 CTV sea S% B&b£7.50–£8.50 W£52.50–£59.50 M

**GH Tudor Court Hotel** 1 Queens Gv, Southsea ☎820174 Plan:**16** Lic 9hc (4fb) nc3 CTV 9P D3pm

**GH Upper Mount House** The Vale, Clarendon Rd, Southsea ☎820456 Plan:**17** Lic 12hc 2⇌ 4⋔ (2fb) ✶ CTV in all bedrooms 7P ⅢⅢ S% B&b£11–£12 Bdi£16.50  £18.50 W£80–£90 D7.30pm

**PORT ST MARY** Isle of Man *Map 6 SC26*
**GH Mallmore Private Hotel** The Promenade ☎833179 Apr–Sep 47hc (12fb) Ⓒⓗ CTV P sea S% B&b£6.50–£7 Bdi£8–£8.50

**POSTBRIDGE** Devon *Map 3 SX67*
**GH Lydgate House Hotel** ☎88209 Closed Xmas Lic 9hc (1fb) CTV 11P ⅢⅢ river D7.30pm

**POTTER HEIGHAM** Norfolk *Map 9 TG41*
**GH Broadland House** Bridge Rd ☎632 Closed Xmas 7hc (2fb) Ⓒⓗ CTV 25P S% ✶B&b£6 Bdi£9 W£50 ⅃ Dnoon

**POULTON-LE-FYLDE** Lancs *Map 7 SD33*
**For location see Blackpool Plan**
**GH Breck Hotel** 28A Breck Rd ☎885702 Blackpool plan:**4** Lic 12hc ✶nc14 TV in all

Blackpool plan: **4** Lic 12hc ★ nc14 TV in all bedrooms 12P ▥ B&b£7.50 Bdi£11.25 Dnoon

**POUNDSGATE** Devon *Map 3 SX77*
**GH Leusdon Lodge** ☎304 Lic 8hc 2⇌ (2fb) CTV 24P ▥ S% ✱B&b£8.50–£9.20 Bdi£12.50–£13.80 W£89.35 D9pm

**PRAA SANDS** Cornwall *Map 2 SW52*
**GH La Connings** ☎Germoe 2380 Etr–Oct Lic 8hc (3fb) TV 12P ▥ S% ✱B&b£6.50–£7.50 Bdi£8.50–£10 W£59.50–£70 ⱡ D6pm

**PRESTATYN** Clwyd *Map 6 SJ08*
**GH Bryn Gwalia Hotel** 17 Gronant Rd ☎2442 Lic 9hc (1fb) ★ TV 12P ▥ S% ✱B&b£9 Bdi£13 W£85 ⱡ D9pm

**PRESTON** Lancs *Map 7 SD52*
**GH Beech Grove Hotel** 12 Beech Gv, Ashton ☎729969 Closed Xmas Lic 7hc (2fb) ★ nc2 CTV 6P ▥ S% B&b£11.50–£12 Bdi£16–£16.50 W£100 ⱡ D6.30pm

**GH Fulwood Park Hotel** 49 Watling Street Rd ☎718067 rs25 & 26 Dec 22hc 8⇌ 4⋔ (A 4hc 1⇌ ⋔) (2fb) CTV 24P 1⌂ ▥ S% B&b£10–£12 Bdi£13.75–£15.75 D7.15pm

**GH Lauderdale Hotel** 29 Fishergate Hill ☎55460 Lic 18hc (3fb) CTV 8P 6⌂ ▥ S% ✱B&b£8.60–£9.80 Bdi£12.10–£12.70 D6pm

**GH Tulketh House** 209 Tulketh Rd, Ashton ☎728096 Lic 7hc 1⋔ (1fb) ★ Ch CTV 20P ▥ S% ✱B&b£14.42 Bdi£20.63 D6.30pm

**GH Withy Trees** 175 Garstang Rd, Fullwood (2m N on A6) ☎717693 10hc (2fb) ★ CTV 30P ▥ S% B&b£8–£10

**PRESTWICH** Gt Manchester *Map 7 SD80*
**GH *Oak Lodge Hotel*** 514 Bury New Rd ☎061-773 1329 13hc 10⇌ ⋔ (13fb) ★ CTV 15P ▥

**PRESTWICK** Strathclyde *Ayrs Map 10 NS32*
**GH Kingcraig Private Hotel** 39 Ayr Rd ☎79480 Lic 7hc (1fb) ★ nc3 CTV 8P ▥ S% B&b£6.25–£6.50 Bdi£10.25–£10.50 Wfr£65 ⱡ D5.30pm

**PWLLHELI** Gwynedd *Map 6 SH33*
**GH Seahaven Hotel** West End Pde ☎2572 Mar–Sep rsOct, Nov & Feb Lic 10hc (3fb) CTV ▥ sea S% B&b£7.75–£12.50 Bdi£10.75–£15.50 W£55–£72 ⱡ D6pm

**QUEEN CAMEL** Somerset *Map 3 ST52*
**INN Mildmay Arms** ☎Marston Magna 850456 3hc ★ nc14 50P S% B&b£10–£12 sn L£1.50–£2.50&alc D£5–£10

**QUORNDON** Leics *Map 8 SK51*
**INN *Hurst Hotel*** 23 Loughborough Rd ☎Quorn 42541 Lic 7hc 1⇌ ⋔ CTV P D7.30pm

**RAGLAN** Gwent *Map 3 SO40*
**GH Grange** Abergavenny Rd ☎690260 Lic 4hc 1⇌ CTV 10P ▥ S% B&bfr£14 Bdifr£20 D9pm

**RAMSGATE** Kent *Map 5 TR36*
**GH Abbeygail** 17 Penshurst Rd ☎Thanet 54154 Closed Xmas 10hc (2fb) ★ nc2 CTV 1P S% B&b£6.50–£7.50 Bdi£8–£9.50 W£49–£58 ⱡ D2pm

**GH Jalna Hotel** 49 Vale Sq ☎Thanet 53848 Lic 10hc 1⇔ 3🛏 (5fb) ⊁ CTV 4P 1�її S% B&b£6.50–£10 Bdi£10–£13.50 W£49–£63 ⅃ D4.30pm

**GH St Hilary Private Hotel** 21 Crescent Rd ☎Thanet 51427 Lic 7hc (4fb) ⊁ nc4 CTV її S% B&b£6.50–£8 Bdi£9.50–£10.50 W£49–£60 ⅃ D4pm

**GH Westcliff Hotel** 9 Grange Rd ☎Thanet 581222 Closed Nov Lic 10hc (3fb) nc5 CTV 13P 1� sea S% B&b£9–£10

**RAVENSTONEDALE** Cumbria *Map 12 NY70*
**INN Fat Lamb** ☎Newbiggin-on-Lune 242 6hc CTV 40P її ✱B&b£8 Bdi£13 W£91 ⅃ sn L£3.75–£7 D9.30pm£3.75–£7

**READING** Berks *Map 4 SU77*
**GH Aeron** 191 Kentwood Hill, Tilehurst (3m W off A329) ☎24119 Closed Xmas 9hc (A 9rm) (3fb) CTV in all bedrooms 18P її S% ✱B&b£9.50 Bdi£13 D7pm
**See advert on page 179**

**GH Private House Hotel** 98 Kendrick Rd ☎84142 Closed Xmas 7hc ⊁ nc12 CTV 6P її S% ✱B&b£8.45 Bdi£12.75 Dnoon

**REDCAR** Cleveland *Map 8 NZ62*
**GH Claxton House Private Hotel** 196 High St ☎486745 Closed 24 Dec–2 Jan Lic 14hc 5🛏 (1fb) ⊁ CTV 8P її sea S% B&b£7.25–£8.75 Bdi£10.25–£11.75 D6.30pm

**REDHILL** Surrey *Map 4 TQ25*
**GH Ashleigh House Hotel** 39 Redstone Hill ☎64763 Closed Xmas 10hc (2fb) ⊁ CTV 12P її S% B&bfr£13.80 D10.15pm

**REDRUTH** Cornwall *Map 2 SW64*
**GH Foundry House** 21 Foundry Row, Chapel St ☎215143 Closed Xmas & Etr 6hc nc2 CTV 5P S% B&b£6 Bdi£7.50 D4pm

⊬⊣ **GH Lyndhurst** 80 Agar Rd ☎215146 8hc (2fb) CTV 8P S% B&b£5 Bdi£7.50 W£49–£52 ⅃ D4pm

**REIGATE** Surrey *Map 4 TQ25*
**GH Cranleigh Hotel** 41 West St ☎40600 Lic 12hc 4⇔ (3fb) Ⓒⓗ CTV 6P її S% B&b£16–£22 Bdi£22–£28 D9pm

**GH Priors Mead** Blanford Rd ☎48776 9hc 1⇔ (2fb) CTV 6P 1🌞 її S% B&b£10–£11 Bdi£14.50–£15.50

**RHES-Y-CAE** Clwyd *Map 7 SJ17*
**INN Miners Arms** ☎Halkyn 780567 10hc TV 150P 3🌞 її S% B&b£6.50  £7 Bdi£13.50–£14 Wfr£78 sn L£4.50–£5&alc D10pm£5.50–£6&alc

**RHOS-ON-SEA** Clwyd *Map 6 SH88*
**See Colwyn Bay**

**RHUALLT** Clwyd *Map 6 SJ07*
**INN White House** ☎St Asaph 582155 5hc CTV 100P її ✱B&b£6 W£42 M sn L£2.25–£2.50&alc D9.30pm£5alc

**RHYL** Clwyd *Map 6 SJ08*
**GH Ashurst Private Hotel** 7 Seabank Rd ☎50417 Jun–Sep Lic 7hc (3fb) ⊁ nc6 TV S% B&b£6 Bdi£8 W£45 ⅃

**GH Ingledene Hotel** 6 Bath St ☎4872 Closed Xmas & New Year Lic 11hc (5fb) CTV S% ✱B&b£6.50–£7 Bdi£9 W£51.75–£56.35 ⅃ D6pm (W only Jul & Aug)

**GH Pier Hotel** 23 East Pde ☎50280 Closed Xmas Lic 12hc 3⋔ (3fb) CTV 2P ▥ sea S% B&b£9–£12 Bdi£10–£15 W£56–£70

**GH** *Toomargoed Private Hotel* 31–33 John St ☎4103 Etr–Sep Lic 15hc (8fb) ⊁ CTV

**RICKINGHALL** Suffolk *Map 5 TM07*
**INN Hamblyn House** The Street ☎Botesdale 292 Lic 4hc ⊁ CTV in 2 bedrooms 12P 2⊛ ▥ S% B&b£8.50–£10 Bdi£12.50–£14 W£50–£60 M D9.45pm

**RINGWOOD** Hants *Map 4 SU10*
**GH Little Moortown House Hotel** ☎3325 Closed Dec & Jan Lic 6hc 4⋔ ⊁ nc8 CTV P ▥ B&bfr£10.50 Bdifr£15.45 Wfr£92.70 ⑮ D7pm

**RIPON** N Yorks *Map 8 SE37*
**GH Crescent Lodge** 42–42A North St ☎2331 14hc (3fb) CTV 10P 1⊛ S% B&b£6.50–£6.90 Bdi£10–£10.50 W£65–£70 ⑮ D6.30pm

**GH Nordale** 2 North Pde ☎3557 12hc (3fb) CTV 14P B&b£7.50–£8.50 Bdi£11–£12.50 W£66–£80 ⑮ D5pm

⊬⊢⊣ **GH** *Old Country* 1 The Crescent ☎2162 7hc (4fb) ⊁ TV 10P 2⊛ ▥

**ROBIN HOOD'S BAY** N Yorks *Map 8 NZ90*
⊬⊢⊣ **GH Storra Lee** ☎Whitby 880593 Feb–Nov 6hc (1fb) ⊁ 4P sea S% B&b£5–£7 Bdi£8–£10 W£70 ⑮ D6pm

**ROCHESTER** Kent *Map 5 TQ76*
**GH Greystones** 25 Watts Av ☎Medway 47545 Closed Xmas 6hc (2fb) ⊁ CTV 3P 1⊛ ▥ S% B&b£7.50–£9

**ROMFORD** Gt London *Map 5 TQ58*
**GH Repton Private Hotel** 18 Repton Dr, Gidea Pk ☎45253 8hc ⊁ CTV

**ROMSEY** Hants *Map 4 SU32*
**GH Adelaide House** 45 Winchester Rd ☎512322 6hc (1fb) ⊁ TV 6P ▥ S% B&b£6.50–£7.50

**GH Chalet** Botley Rd, Whitenap ☎514909 4hc (2fb) ⊁ CTV 6P ▥ S% B&b£6–£6.50

**ROSSETT** Clwyd *Map 7 SJ35*
**INN** *Golden Lion* ☎Chester 570316 Lic 4hc ⊁ CTV 50P ▥ D9.15pm

**ROSS-ON-WYE** Heref & Worcs *Map 3 SO52*
**GH** *Bridge House* ☎2655 Lic 9hc (2fb) ⊁ CTV 15P ▥ river D9.15pm

**GH** *Orles Barn Hotel* ☎2155 Lic 6hc CTV 12P ▥

**GH Ryefield House** Gloucester Rd ☎63030 Closed Xmas Lic 7hc 1⇨ (3fb) CTV 10P ▥ S% B&b£6.75–£7.25 Bdi£10.65–£11.45 W£69.50–£72.50 ⑮ D5pm

**ROTHERFIELD** E Sussex *Map 5 TQ52*
**INN King's Arms** ☎2465 4hc ⊛⊛ ⊁ nc14 CTV 50P ▥ S% B&b£9.50 sn L£6alc D9.15pm £6alc

**ROTHESAY** Isle of Bute, Strathclyde *Bute Map 10 NS06*
**GH Alva House Private Hotel** 24 Mountstuart Rd ☎2328 May–Sep 6hc (1fb) ⊁ CTV sea S% B&b£7–£8 Bdi£8–£9 W£56–£63 D4pm

**GH Morningside** Mount Pleasant Rd ☎3526 Apr–mid Oct 6hc (A 3hc) (2fb) CTV sea S% B&b£6.75 Bdi£9.25 W£54–£58 ⑮ D6pm

**GH St Fillans** 36 Mountstuart Rd ☎2784 Apr–Sep 6hc (2fb) ⊁ CTV 6P ▥ sea S% B&b£6–£7 Bdi£7.50–£8.50

**ROTHLEY** Leics *Map 8 SK51*
**GH Rothley** 35 Mountsorrel Ln ☎Leicester 302531 Lic 9hc ⊁ CTV 10P ▥ S% B&b£7.50–£8.50 Bdi£12–£13 Dnoon

**ROTTINGDEAN** E Sussex *Map 5 TQ30*
**GH Braemar House** Steyning Rd ☎Brighton 34263 15hc (2fb) CTV ▥ B&b£6.90–£9.20

**GH Corner House** Steyning Rd ☎Brighton 34533 6hc (1fb) nc6 TV in all bedrooms ▥ sea S% B&b£7–£8

**ROWLEY REGIS** W Midlands *Map 7 SO98*
**For location see Birmingham Plan**
**GH Highfield House Hotel** Waterfall Ln ☎021-559 1066 Birmingham plan:**2** Lic 12hc ⊁ nc12 CTV 12P ▥ S% B&b£9 Bdi£12.50 D10am

**ROZEL BAY** Jersey, Channel Islands *Map 16*
**GH** *Château la Chaire* ☎Jersey 63354 Mar–Oct Lic 17hc 9⇨ ⋔ 20P ▥

**RUGBY** Warwicks *Map 4 SP57*
**GH Grosvenor House Hotel** 81 Clifton Rd ☎3437 Lic 9hc (1fb) ⒸⒽ CTV 9P 3⊛ ▥ S% B&b£12 Bdi£16

**GH Mound Hotel** 17–19 Lawford Rd ☎3486 Closed Xmas Lic 18hc 4⋔ (5fb) TV 17P ▥ S% B&b£10.60–£16 Bdi£15.30–£20.60 D4.30pm

# Little Moortown House Hotel

## 244 CHRISTCHURCH ROAD · RINGWOOD · HAMPSHIRE
### Telephone: (042 54) 3325

A 6 bedroom family hotel under personal supervision of Mr. & Mrs. R. Morris. We offer a high standard of comfort, with good English cooking. Ideally situated for the New Forest, Bournemouth and Hurn Airport.
*Please send for brochure.*

**RUISLIP** Gt London *London plan 4 A1 (page 134)*
**GH 17th Century Barn Hotel** West End Rd ☎36057 Closed Xmas wk Lic 60hc 43⇐ ⋔ (6fb) CTV 70P ⅏ S% ✳ B&bf£18.97–£22.77 Bdif£25.50–£29.50 D8.30pm

**RUSTINGTON** W Sussex *Map 4 TQ00*
**GH Kenmore** Claigmar Rd ☎4634 5hc 1⇐ (3fb) TV 6P ⅏ B&b£6.87–£9.07 Wf£43.14–£56.34 Ⓜ

**GH Mayday Hotel** 12 Broadmark Ln ☎71198 Closed Oct Lic 8hc (2fb) ✝nc6 CTV 12P ⅏ S% B&bf£10–£12 Bdif£15–£17 Wf£80–£95 ⚟ D7pm

**RUTHIN** Clwyd *Map 6 SJ15*
**INN Wynstay Arms Hotel** Well St ☎3147 Lic 8hc 2⇐ ⋔ ✝ CTV 12P ⅏ ⇔ D8.30pm

**RYDAL** Cumbria *Map 11 NY30*
**See Ambleside**

**RYDE** Isle of Wight *Map 4 SZ59*
**GH Dorset Hotel** Dover St ☎64327 Etr–Oct Lic 26hc 1⇐ 7⋔ (7fb) ✝nc5 CTV 25P sea B&b£8.50 Bdif£11.50 Wf£69–£74 ⚟ D7pm

**GH Teneriffe** 36 The Strand ☎63841 Lic 16hc 6⇐ (6fb) ✝ CTV 6P ⅏ S% ✳ B&bf£6.90 Bdif£9.20 D3pm

**RYE** E Sussex *Map 5 TQ92*
**GH Little Saltcote** 22 Military Rd ☎3210 6hc 1⇐ (2fb) CTV 3P ⅏ river S% B&bf£6–£6.50

**GH Mariner's Hotel** High St ☎3480 Lic 19hc 6⇐ 1⋔ (4fb) CTV ⅏ B&bf£12.50

**GH Monastery Hotel & Restaurant**

6 High St ☎3272 Closed Xmas & New Year Lic 7hc ✝ nc7 CTV ⅏ S% B&bf£8.50–£9 D9.15pm

**GH Old Borough Arms** The Strand ☎2128 Closed end Jan–mid Mar 9⋔ (4fb) CTV 3P 3☎ ⅏ S% B&bf£9.20–£10 Wf£64.40–£70 Ⓜ

**GH Playden Oasts Hotel** Playden ☎3502 Lic 6⇐ (2fb) CTV P ⅏ S% ✳ B&bf£10.50 Bdif£15 Wf£90–£95 ⚟ D9.30pm

**ST ALBANS** Herts *Map 4 TL10*
**GH Grange Hotel** 276 London Rd ☎51232 Closed Xmas wk Lic 15hc 1⇐ 2⋔ nc3 CTV 15P ⅏ S% ✳ B&bf£12 D9pm

**GH Melford** 24 Woodstock Rd North ☎53642 Lic 12hc (2fb) CTV 12P ⅏ S% B&bf£9.78–£13.80

**ST ANDREWS** Fife *Map 12 NO51*
**GH Argyle House Hotel** 127 North St ☎73387 Apr–Oct Lic 18hc (4fb) nc2 CTV ⅏ S% B&bf£6.50–£9.50 Bdif£11–£14 Wf£60–£90 ⚟ D4pm

**GH Beachway House** 4–6 Murray Pk ☎73319 Mar–Oct rsNov–Feb 11hc (4fb) CTV ⅏ ✳ B&bf£5.50–7.95 Bdif£9.75–£12.20 Wf£65–£80 D2pm (W only Jul–early Aug)

**GH Clevedon House** 3 Murray Pl ☎74212 6hc (1fb) CTV 20P S% B&bf£7–£7.50

**GH Craigmore** 3–5 Murray Pk ☎72142 Apr & Jun–Oct rsJan–Mar & May 12hc (5fb) CTV ⅏ B&bfr£6.95 Bdifr£11.25 Wfrf£75 ⚟ D6pm

**GH Hazelbank Private Hotel** The Scores ☎72466 Mar–Nov 10hc ✝ CTV ⅏ sea

**GH Lorimer House** 19 Murray Pk ☎76599 Apr–Oct 4hc (3fb) ✝ nc3 CTV ⅏ B&bf£7–£8

**GH** *Nithsdale Hotel* The Scores ☎75977
Mar–Nov Lic 9hc CTV ▥ sea

**GH Number Ten** 10 Hope St ☎74601 10hc
(4fb) CTV ▥ S% B&b£6–£7.50 Bdi£9.95–
£11.45 W£65–£73.25 ⅃ D4.30pm

**GH Yorkston Hotel** 60–70 Argyle St
☎72019 Lic 12hc (2fb) ✻ CTV ▥ B&b£7.50–£9
Bdi£12.30–£13.80 W£86–£93 ⅃ D6.30pm

**ST AUBIN** Jersey, Channel Islands *Map 16*
**GH Panorama Private Hotel** High St
☎Jersey 42429 Feb–Nov 17rm 15hc 2⌲
(2fb) ✻nc5 CTV sea B&b£6–£14.50

**ST AUSTELL** Cornwall *Map 2 SX05*
**GH Alexandra Hotel** 52–54 Alexandra Rd
☎4242 Lic 14hc 4♨ (6fb) CTV 16P ▥ sea S%
B&b£7–£8 Bdi£10–£11 W£64.40–£71.30 ⅃
D5pm

**GH Copper Beeches** Truro Rd, Trevarrick
☎4024 Lic 8hc 1♨ (2fb) CTV 8P ▥
B&b£6.50–£7.50 Bdi£9.50–£10.50 Wfr£59
⅃ D6.30pm

**GH** *Cornerways* Penwinnick Rd ☎61579
Closed Xmas wk Lic 6hc (2fb) ✻nc2 CTV 8P
▥ D6.30pm

**GH Lynton House Hotel** 48 Bodmin Rd
☎3787 Lic 6hc (2fb) ✻ CTV 6P S%
B&b£6.32–£7.15 Bdi£9.07–£9.90 W£53.90–
£63.80 ⅃ Dnoon (W only Jul & Aug)

**GH Treskillon** 26 Woodland Rd ☎2920 Lic
10hc (2fb) ✻ CTV 10P ▥ S% ✻ B&b£5.90–
£6.90 Bdi£8.80–£10.12 W£48.96–£60.72 ⅃
D6.15pm

**GH Wimereux** 1 Trevanion Rd ☎2187 Lic
14hc 4♨ (3fb) ✻ CTV 14P ▥ S% ✻ B&bfr
£6.90 Bdifr£10.35 W£56–£65 ⅃ D6pm

**INN Holmbush** 101 Holmbush Rd ☎3217
3hc 50P S% B&b£5–£6 Bar lunch60p–£1.50

**ST BLAZEY** Cornwall *Map 2 SX05*
**GH Moorshill House Hotel** Rosehill ☎Par
2368 Lic 5hc (2fb) ✻ [Ch] CTV 6P ▥ S%
B&b£7.25–£7.75 Bdi£10–£11.25 W£58–£62
⅃ D9.30pm

**ST BRELADE** Jersey, Channel Islands *Map 16*
**GH Arnewood Lodge** Route des Genets
☎Jersey 41516 Apr–Oct Lic 14hc 2⌲ 6♨
(2fb) ✻nc3 CTV S% ✻ B&b£5–£6.50
Bdi£9.75–£11.25 W£68.25–£78.75 ⅃ D11am
(W only mid Jun–mid Sep)

**ST CATHERINE'S** Strathclyde *Argyll Map 10
NN00*
**GH Thistle House** ☎209 6hc (1fb) 6P ▥ sea
✳ B&bfr£8 Bdifr£13.90 Wfr£93.80 ⅃ D7pm

**ST CLEARS** Dyfed *Map 2 SN21*
**INN Black Lion Hotel** ☎230700 7hc CTV
20P ▥ S% B&b£6 W£40 Ⓜ sn L£3–£5
D9.30pm£3–£5

**ST CLEMENTS** Jersey, Channel Islands
*Map 16*
**GH Belle Plage Hotel** Green Island ☎Jersey
53750 15 Apr–Oct Lic 19hc 3⌲ 16♨ (2fb) ✻
nc8 CTV 25P sea ✳ B&b£9–£13 Bdi£11–£15
W£77–£109 ⅃ D7.30pm

**ST DAVIDS** Dyfed *Map 2 SM72*
**GH** *Pen-y-Daith* 12 Millard Park ☎720 Lic
8hc (3fb) ✻ CTV 8P ▥

**GH Y Glennydd** 51 Nun St ☎576 (due to
change to 720576) Closed Xmas Lic 10hc

(3fb) ✦ Ch CTV ▥ S% B&bfr£6.25 Bdifr£9.75 Wfr£66 Ⳡ D5pm

**ST DOGMAELS** Dyfed *Map 2 SN14*
**GH *Glanteifi*** ☎Cardigan 612353 Mar–Oct Lic 11hc 3⇨ ♒ (2fb) CTV 20P ▥ sea D5pm

**ST ERVAN** Cornwall *Map 2 SW87*
**GH St Ervan Country House Hotel**
☎Rumford 255 Mar–Dec Lic 6⇨ ♒ ✦ nc10 Ch CTV 24P ▥ S% B&bf£8.50–£10 Bdif£16–£17.25 W£112–£120.75 Ⳡ D6.15pm

**ST FLORENCE** Dyfed *Map 2 SN00*
**GH *Flemish Court*** ☎Manorbier 413 5hc (3fb) CTV 6P ▥ D7.30pm

**GH *Greenhills Hotel*** ☎Manorbier 291 Lic 11hc (7fb) CTV D8pm

**GH Ponterosa** Eastern Ln ☎Manorbier 378 May–Sep Lic 6hc (2fb) ✦ CTV 6P S% B&bf£6.50–£8 Bdif£11–£12.50 W£60–£70 Ⳡ D6.30pm

**INN *Parsonage Farm*** ☎Manorbier 436 Mar–Oct, Xmas & New Year Lic 11hc CTV 25P ▥ D9pm

**ST HELIER** Jersey, Channel Islands *Map 16*
**GH Almorah Hotel** La Pouquelaye ☎Jersey 21648 mid Apr–mid Oct Lic 16rm 5hc 11⇨ (4fb) ✦ nc3 CTV 10P ▥ S% B&bf£7.50–£11 Bdif£9–£13.50

**⤗ GH Runnymede Court Hotel** 48 Roseville St ☎Jersey 20044 mid Mar–mid Nov Lic 46hc 15⇨ 10♒ (6fb) ✦ CTV S% B&bf£5.50–£10.50 Bdif£8–£13.20 D6.30pm

**GH Sandy Bay** 74 Roseville St ☎Jersey 23982 Apr–Oct Lic 9hc (4fb) ✦ nc4 CTV S% B&b£6.90–£7.50 Bdif£9.60–£10.35 W£67.20–£72.45 Ⳡ (W only last wk May–last wk Sep)

**ST ISSEY** Cornwall *Map 2 SW97*
**INN *Ring O'Bells*** ☎Rumford (Bodmin) 251 Lic 3hc CTV 40P D10pm

**ST IVES** Cambs *Map 4 TL37*
**GH Firs Hotel** 50 Needingworth Rd ☎63252 Lic 5rm 4hc (1fb) TV in all bedrooms 8P 2⌂ ▥ B&b£12.50–£13.50 D9.30pm

**ST IVES** Cornwall *Map 2 SW54* **(See Plan)**
**GH Bay View** Headland Rd, Carbis Bay ☎796469 Not on plan Lic 8hc 2♒ (3fb) ✦ CTV 6P ▥ sea S% B&b£6–£9.20 Bdif£9.50–£12 W£66.50–£84 Ⳡ D4pm (W only end Jul & Aug)

**GH Boskerris Lodge** ☎797700 Not on plan 7hc 1⇨ 4♒ (2fb) ✦ Ch CTV 10P sea S% B&b£6.50–£8 Bdif£8.50–£9.50 W£58–£68 Ⳡ D6pm

**GH Channings Private Hotel** 3 Talland Rd ☎795681 Plan:**1** Mar–Oct Lic 12hc 2⇨ 2♒ (6fb) Ch CTV 12P sea S% B&b£6–£8 Bdif£8.50–£10.50 D6pm

**GH Chy-An-Creet Private Hotel** Higher Stennack ☎796559 Plan:**2** Mar–Oct Lic 12hc (4fb) ✦ CTV 12P ✳ B&b£7.48–£7.99 Bdif£10.64–£11.21 W£63.25–£74.75 Ⳡ D7pm

**GH Cortina & Kandahar** 26 The Warren ☎796183 Plan:**3** Closed Xmas 11hc 1⇨ (1fb) CTV sea B&b£6–£9

**GH Cottage Hotel** Carbis Bay ☎796351 Not on plan 7 May–Sep Lic 60⇨ (54fb) ✦ Ch CTV 100P ▥ lift sea S% B&b£9.50–£12.50

Bdi£12.65–£16.50 W£88.55–£115 ⅃ (W only mid Jun–Aug)

**GH Dean Court Hotel** Trelyon Av ☎796023 Plan:**4** Lic 12hc 5⇔ 7🏠 ⊁ nc15 CTV 12P ⊞ sea S% B&b£12–£15 Bdi£15–£19 W£93–£103 ⅃ D4pm (W only Jun–Aug)

**GH Grey Tyles** Carbis Bay ☎796408 Not on plan Apr–Oct Lic 17hc (4fb) CTV 14P sea S% B&b£6–£7 Bdi£8.50–£11

**GH Hollies Hotel** Talland Rd ☎796605 Plan:**5** Lic 12hc (7fb) ⊁ Ch CTV 12P ⊞ sea S% B&b£7.47–£10.92 Bdi£9.77–£13.23 W£59.51–£89.70 ⅃ D6.30pm (W only Jul & Aug)

**GH Island View** 2 Park Av ☎795111 Plan:**6** Mar–Oct 10hc (4fb) ⊁ CTV sea S% ✱B&bfr£6 Bdifr£8 Wfr£49 ⅃

**GH Longships** 2 Talland Rd ☎798180 Plan:**7** Etr–Oct & Xmas Lic 24hc 3⇔ 12🏠 (11fb) CTV 20P sea S% B&b£6–£10 Bdi£9.50–£15 D6pm

**GH Lyonesse Hotel** 5 Talland Rd ☎796315 Plan:**8** Mar–Oct Lic 15hc (5fb) ⊁ CTV 4P ⊞ sea B&b£7.50–£8.62 Bdi£10.35–£12.65 W£61–£80.50 ⅃ D7pm

**GH Monowai Private Hotel** Headland Rd, Carbis Bay ☎795733 Not on plan May–Oct Lic 10hc (2fb) nc5 CTV 8P ⊞ sea S% B&bfr£6.50 Bdifr£8.75 Wfr£60 ⅃ D6.30pm

⊩⊣ **GH Pondarosa** 10 Porthminster Ter ☎795875 Plan:**9** Mar–Oct 10hc 1⇔ (2fb) ⊁ nc3 CTV 8P ⊞ S% B&b£5.50–£7.70 Bdi£8.80–£11 W£55–£75 ⅃ D6pm

**GH Primrose Valley Hotel** Primrose Valley ☎795564 Plan:**10** Apr–Oct Lic 10hc 5⇔ (5fb) ⊁ CTV 10P sea S% B&b£7.50–£10.90 Bdi£8.30–£16 W£57.50–£104.88 ⅃ D6pm

**GH Rosemorran Private Hotel** The Belyars ☎796359 Plan:**11** Lic 12hc (5fb) CTV 9P sea S% B&b£6.50–£9.50 Bdi£10–£13 W£69–£92 ⅃ D7pm

**GH Hotel Rotorua** Trencrom Ln, Carbis Bay ☎795419 Not on plan Etr–Oct Lic 14hc 8⇔ (6fb) ⊁ CTV 14P ⊞ S% B&b£8.40–£10.06 Bdi£10.78–£12.94 W£82.46–£90.51 ⅃ D7pm (W only Jul & Aug)

**GH St Margarets** 3 Park Av ☎795785 Plan:**12** Closed Xmas Lic 6hc (3fb) ⊁ CTV ⊞ sea B&b£6–£7 Bdi£9–£10 W£63–£70 ⅃ D3pm

**GH St Merryn Hotel** Trelyon ☎795767
Plan:**13** Mar–Nov Lic 12hc 1🚻 1🏠 (5fb) 🐾
CTV 20P 🎱 sea S% B&bf£7.48–£9.20
Bdi£10.43–£13.80 Wf£57.50–£90.85 ₺

🟦🟦 **GH Sherwell** St Ives Rd, Carbis Bay
☎796142 Not on plan Closed Dec 8hc (2fb)
🐾 CTV 8P sea S% B&bf£5.60–£6
Bdi£8.35–£8.95 Wf£56–£62.50 ₺ D6.30pm

**GH Shun Lee Private Hotel** Trelyon Av
☎796284 Plan:**14** Mar–Sep Lic 11hc 2🚻 1🏠
(4fb) 🐾nc5 CTV 13P 🎱 sea S% B&bf£8.25–
£8.75 Bdi£13–£13.50 Wf£70–£90 ₺ D5pm
(W only Aug)

**GH Skidden House Hotel** Skidden Hill
☎796899 Plan:**15** Lic 7hc 🐾 CTV 4P 🎱
Dnoon

**GH Sunrise** 22 The Warren ☎795407
Plan:**16** Whit–Oct 8hc 🐾 CTV 4P S% B&bf£6–
£8 Wf£42–£56

**GH Trelissick Hotel** Bishops Rd ☎795035
Plan:**17** mid Mar–mid Oct Lic 15hc 3🚻 1🏠
(3fb) CTV 12P sea B&bf£7–£11 Bdi£9.50–
£13.50 Wf£65–£90 ₺ D6.45pm

**GH Verbena** Orange Ln ☎796396 Plan:**18**
Etr–Oct 7hc (2fb) 🐾nc3 CTV 8P sea S%
B&bfr£6 Bdifr£8.50 Wfr£56 ₺ D4pm (W only
Jul & Aug)

**GH Windsor Hotel** The Terrace ☎798174
Plan:**18A** Closed Xmas Lic 9hc (4fb) 🐾 🅒🅗
CTV 4🏠 B&bf£7.50–£9.20 Bdi£11.50–£13.80
Wf£78–£88.50 ₺ D5pm

**GH Woodside Hotel** The Belyars ☎796282
Plan:**19** Lic 11hc (5fb) 🐾 🅒🅗 CTV 30P sea S%
B&bf£7.50–£9.50 Bdi£10.84–£14.09
Wf£75.90–£98.67 ₺ D6.30pm
(W only Jul & Aug)

**GH York Hotel** ☎796586 Plan:**20** Lic 29hc
(4fb) CTV 10P 16🏠 🎱 sea S% B&bf£6–£10
Bdi£10–£14 Wf£87.50–£115.50 D5pm

**ST IVES** Dorset *Map 4 SU10*
**GH Foxes Moon Hotel** 40 Ringwood Rd
☎Ringwood 4347 Lic 8rm 7hc (1fb) CTV
20P 🎱 S% B&bf£7.95–£8.95 Bdi£11.75–
£12.75

**ST JUST** Cornwall *Map 2 SW33*
**GH Boscean Country Hotel** ☎788748 Lic
9hc (4fb) 🐾 🅒🅗 CTV 12P 2🏠 sea S% B&bf£6–
£8 Bdi£10–£13 Wf£70–£90 ₺ D8pm

**GH Boswedden House Private Hotel** Cape
Cornwall ☎788733 Mar–Oct Lic 8rm 7hc 2🏠
(5fb) 🐾nc7 CTV 7P 1🏠 🎱 sea ✳B&bf£8.25
Bdi£13.25 (W only late Jul–Aug)

**ST JUST-IN-ROSELAND** Cornwall *Map 2
SW83*
**GH Rose-Da-Mar Hotel** ☎St Mawes
270450 Etr–Oct Lic 9hc 4🚻 1🏠 (2fb) 🐾nc7
CTV 10P 🎱 sea S% Bdi£17–£20

**ST LAWRENCE** Isle of Wight *Map 4 SZ57*
**GH Woody Bank Hotel** Undercliff Dr
☎Ventnor 852610 Etr–mid Oct Lic 10hc
(2fb) CTV 10P sea S% B&bf£9 Bdi£15 Wf£105
D7pm

**ST MARTIN** Guernsey, Channel Islands
*Map 16*
**GH Triton** Les Hubits ☎Guernsey 38017
mid May–mid Sep 14hc 4🚻 (1fb) 🐾nc4 CTV
12P S% B&bf£6.75 Bdi£9.50 D6.30pm

**ST MARTIN Jersey,** Channel Islands *Map 16*
**GH St Martin's House** ☎Jersey 53271
Closed Xmas rsNov, Feb & Mar (no evening meal) Lic 11hc 2⇔ 2🛏 (2fb) ⊁ Ch CTV 10P �🏨 ⎘ ✻ B&b£6.50–£9 Bdi£8.50–£12.75

**ST MARY CRAY** Gt London *Map 5 TQ46*
**GH Sheepcote Farmhouse** Sheepcote Ln
☎Orpington 70498 Apr–Oct 4hc ⊁ CTV P �🏨 D7.30pm

**ST MARY'S** Isles of Scilly *(No map)*
**GH Evergreen Cottage** ☎Scillonia 22711 Feb–mid Nov 5hc ⊁ nc6 CTV �🏨 B&b£7 Bdi£11.75 W£82.25 Dnoon (W only Jul & Aug)

**GH Hanjague** ☎Scillonia 22531 Etr–Sep Lic 5hc ⊁ nc10 CTV �🏨 sea B&b£11.38 Bdi£18.97 D6.15pm

**GH Tremellyn Private Hotel** ☎Scillonia 22656 Mar–Oct Lic 9hc 1🛏 (3fb) ⊁ CTV available in bedrooms 12P B&b£11.65 Bdi£16 W£112 ⎘ D7.15pm

**ST MAWES** Cornwall *Map 2 SW83*
**GH Waterloo House** Upper Castle Rd
☎270570 Etr–Oct Lic 5hc 1fb) nc5 CTV 8P �🏨 sea S% B&b£9.50 Bdi£14 W£91 ⎘

**ST NEWLYN EAST** Cornwall *Map 2 SW85*
**GH Trewerry Mill** Trerice (2m W of A3058 midway between Summercourt and Quintrell Downs) ☎Mitchell 345 Etr–Oct Lic 6hc (2fb) ⊁ CTV 12P S% ✻ B&b£5–£8.30 Bdi£8–£11.30 W£49–£72 ⎘ D6pm (W Jul & Aug)

**ST PETER PORT** Guernsey, Channel Islands *Map 16*

**GH Changi Lodge Private Hotel** Les Baissieres ☎Guernsey 56446 Lic 14hc 2⇔🛏 (8fb) ⊁ nc7 CTV 20P �🏨 Dnoon

**GH Maison Du Guet Private Hotel**
Amhurst ☎Guernsey 22007 Feb–Nov Lic 18hc 3⇔ 🛏 ⊁ CTV 10P �🏨

**ST PETER'S VALLEY** Jersey, Channel Islands *Map 16*
**GH Midvale Private Hotel** ☎Jersey 42498 Etr–Oct Lic 21hc 7⇔ 🛏 (3fb) ⊁ CTV 18P D6.30pm

**ST SAVIOUR Guernsey,** Channel Islands *Map 16*
**GH La Girouette Country House Hotel**
☎Guernsey 63269 Feb–Nov Lic 14hc 1⇔ 6🛏 (6fb) ⊁ nc3 CTV in all bedrooms 14P S% ✻ B&b£8–£10.50 Bdi£10–£14 W£70–£98 ⎘ D7.30pm

**ST SAVIOUR Jersey,** Channel Islands *Map 16*
**GH Talana Private Hotel** Bagot Rd ☎Jersey 30317 Lic 36hc 15⇔ 2🛏 (3fb) ⊁ CTV 20P �🏨 S% B&b£8–£12 Bdi£9–£13 W£63–£91 D7pm (W only Jul & Aug)

**SALCOMBE** Devon *Map 3 SX73*
**GH Bay View Hotel** Bennett Rd ☎2238 Etr–Sep Lic 11hc 1⇔ (1fb) ⊁ nc6 CTV 8P �🏨 sea B&b£9.50–£11.50 Bdi£14.50–£16.50 W£95–£105 ⎘ D7pm

**GH Charborough House Hotel** Devon Rd ☎2260 Apr–Oct Lic 10hc 1⇔ 1🛏 (1fb) ⊁ CTV �🏨 sea B&b£8.50–£10 Bdi£13–£14.50 W£72–£92 ⎘

**GH Lyndhurst Hotel** Bonaventure Rd ☎2481 Closed Xmas Lic 8hc 2⋒ (3fb) ✱ nc7 CTV 8P ▥ sea S% B&b£8 Bdi£12 W£74.50 Ɫ D7pm

**GH Melbury Hotel** Devon Rd ☎2883 Etr & 15 May–24 Sep Lic 14hc 3⌓ 3⋒ (2fb) ✱ nc5 CTV 18P sea B&b£9.50–£12 Bdi£12.65–£15.40 W£76–£93.50 Ɫ D7.30pm

**GH Stoneycroft Hotel** Devon Rd ☎2218 Etr–Sep Lic 10hc (5fb) nc5 CTV 15P ▥ sea S% B&b£9.20–£10.35 Bdi£13.18–£14.95 W£82.80–£87.40 Ɫ

**GH Trennels Private Hotel** Herbert Rd ☎2500 Apr–Oct 11hc ✱ nc12 CTV 8P 1⛟ ▥ sea S% B&b£9.50 Bdi£14 W£70 Ɫ D9am

**GH Woodgrange Private Hotel** Devon Rd ☎2439 Apr–Sep Lic 8hc 5⌓ (1fb) [ch] CTV in all bedrooms 11P ▥ river sea S% B&b£9–£12 Bdi£14–£17 W£80–£99 Ɫ D6pm

**SALEN** Isle of Mull, Strathclyde *Argyll Map 10 NM54*
**GH Craig Hotel** ☎Aros 347 Closed Xmas & New Year Lic 7hc [ch] 8P sea S% B&b£8.50–£11.50 Bdi£13–£14.50 W£90–£100 Ɫ D8pm

**SALFORD** Gt Manchester *Map 7 SJ89*
**GH Hazeldean Hotel** 467 Bury New Rd ☎061-792 6667 Lic 21rm 10⌓ 6⋒ (A 4rm 1⌓) (2fb) [ch] CTV 26P ▥ *B&b£16.45–£20.24 D8pm

**SALISBURY** Wilts *Map 4 SU12*
**GH Byways House** 31 Fowlers Rd ☎28364 11hc (3fb) CTV 10P ▥ S% B&b£7.50–£8.50 W£49–£56 Ⅿ

**GH Hayburn Wyke** 72 Castle Rd ☎24141 6hc (2fb) ✱ CTV 5P 1⛟ ▥ S% B&b£6–£7

⋈ **GH Holmhurst** Downtown Rd ☎23164 7hc 7P ▥ S% B&b£5.50–£6.50 W£35–£42 Ⅿ

**GH Westmead** 41–43 Hulse Rd ☎22930 6rm 5hc 1⌓ 3⋒ (3fb) ✱ CTV 6P ▥ S% B&b£7.50–£8.50

**INN White Horse Hotel** Castle St ☎27844 13hc ⛟ CTV 6P 8⛟ S% B&b£11.50–£14.50 Bdi£16.50–£20 sn Lfr£3.50 D8.45pmfr£5

**SALTDEAN** E Sussex *Map 5 TQ30*
**GH Linbrook Lodge** 74 Lenham Av ☎Brighton 33775 Lic 7hc (2fb) [ch] CTV 8P ▥ sea B&b£7–£8.50 Bdi£10.50–£12 W£56–£65 Ɫ D4pm

**SANDOWN** Isle of Wight *Map 4 SZ58*
**GH Chester Lodge Hotel** Beachfield Rd ☎402773 May–Sep 18hc (6fb) CTV 15P B&b£9.20–£10.35 Bdi£12.65–£13.80 W£63.25–£71.30 D6.15pm

**GH Cliff House Hotel** Cliff Rd ☎403656 May–Sep Lic 16hc 8⋒ (5fb) [ch] CTV 20P ▥ sea S% B&b£15–£17.25 Bdi£17.80–£21.55 W£86.25–£91.25 Ɫ D6.30pm

**GH Rosetrevor Private Hotel** 96 Sandown Rd ☎402775 Etr–Oct Lic 17hc (4fb) ✱ nc2 CTV 14P sea S% B&b£8–£9.50 Bdi£10.50–£11.50 W£55.20–£69 Ɫ D6pm

**GH St Catherine's Hotel** 1 Winchester Pk ☎402392 Closed 18 Dec–5 Jan Lic 18hc 3⌓ 4⋒ (2fb) ✱ nc3 CTV 8P ▥ S% B&b£10–£14.50 Bdi£14.25–£18.50 W£95–£129.50 Ɫ D7pm
**See advert on page 190**

**GH Trevallyn** 32 Broadway ☎402373 Etr–Oct & Xmas Lic 23hc (5fb) ✱ [ch] CTV 20P S% B&b£8.50 Bdi£11.50 W£66.70–£74.75 Ɫ D6.30pm

**SANDPLACE** Cornwall *Map 2 SX25*
**GH Polraen Country Hotel Hotel** ☎Looe
3956 mid Jan–mid Dec Lic 7hc 4🏠 (1fb) ⚹
CTV 12P 🏭 S% B&bf10–£14 Bdi£15–£22.50
W£96–£130 D8pm

**SANDWICH** Kent *Map 5 TR35*
**INN Fleur de Lis** Delf St ☎611131 5hc 2🏠
CTV S% B&bf9–£12 sn L£2.50alc D10.30pm
£6.50alc

**SANDY** Beds *Map 4 TL14*
**GH Fairlawn Hotel** 70 Bedford Rd ☎80336
rsSun & public hols Lic 10rm 9hc ⚹ CTV 10P
🏭 S% B&bf11.50 Bdifrf15.27 Wfrf106.89 ⎬
D8pm

**SANNOX** Isle of Arran, Strathclyde *Bute
Map 10 NS04*

**⊢⊣ GH Cliffdene** ☎Corrie 224 Dec–Sep
5hc (3fb) ⚹ TV 6P river S% B&bf4.90
Bdi£7.20 W£50.40 ⎬ D4.30pm

**SANQUHAR** Dumfries & Galloway
*Dumfriesshire Map 11 NS71*
**GH Blackaddie House Hotel** Blackaddie Rd
☎270 Lic 6rm 4hc 1⟲ (2fb) CTV 15P 🏭 river
B&bf8 Bdif12.50 W£48 🅜 D8.30pm

**INN Nithsdale Hotel** High St ☎506 6hc CTV
🏭 S% B&bf8.75–£9.50 W£100–£115
Bar lunch frf1 D8pmfrf5

**SAUNDERSFOOT** Dyfed *Map 2 SN10*
**GH** *Harbour Lights Private Hotel* 2 High St
☎813496 Mar–Nov rsDec–Feb Lic 12hc
(5fb) ⚹ CTV 8P sea D4.30pm

**GH Jalna Hotel** Stammers Rd ☎812282

Etr–Oct Lic 14hc 7⇔ 3♒ (8fb) CTV 16P Ⅲ
✻B&b£7.50–£8.65 Bdi£11.50–£12.60
D6.30pm

**GH Malin House** St Bride's Hill ☎812344
May–Sep Lic 11hc 5⇔ 6♒ (6fb) ⊁ Ch CTV
80P Ⅲ S% B&b£6–£11.50 Bdi£8.50–£14
W£59.50–£98 Ŀ D7pm (W only Jul–Aug)

**GH Merlewood Hotel** St Bride's Hill
☎812421 Closed Nov Lic 21hc (15fb) ⊁ Ch
CTV 30P Ⅲ sea S% B&b£7.50–£9 Bdi£11–£13
W£77–£90 Ŀ D6.30pm (W only Jul–Aug)

**GH Rhodewood House** St Bride's Hill
☎812200 Lic 27hc 9⇔ (8fb) CTV 30P sea S%
B&b£7–£10 Bdi£9–£12 W£63–£84 Ŀ D6pm

**SCARBOROUGH** N Yorks Map 8 TA08
**(See Plan)**
**GH Avoncroft Hotel** Crown Ter ☎72737
Plan:**1** Closed Nov rsDec–Feb (wknds only)
Lic 31hc 1⇔ (13fb) CTV 8P Ⅲ S% B&b£8.50–
£9.80 Bdi£10.60–£12.20 W£70.50–£81.20 Ŀ

**GH Bay Hotel** 67 Esplanade, South Cliff
☎73926 Plan:**2** Lic 19hc 4♒ (5fb) CTV 12P
sea S% B&b£10.93–£12.08 Bdi£14.38–£15.53
W£96.60–£104.65 Ŀ D5.30pm

**GH** *Burghcliffe Hotel* 28 Esplanade, South
Cliff ☎61524 Plan:**3** Mar–Nov Lic 15hc
(10fb) CTV sea

**GH Church Hills Private Hotel** St Martins
Av, South Cliff ☎63148 Plan:**4** Dec–Oct Lic
16hc (1fb) ⊁nc12 CTV S% ✻B&b£9.78–
£10.93 Bdi£10.93–£12.08 W£76.48–£84.53 Ŀ
D6pm

**GH Geldenhuis** 145–147 Queens Pde
☎61677 Plan:**4A** Etr–Oct Lic 15hc ⊁ nc5
CTV 16P Ⅲ sea S% ✻B&b£9.78 Bdi£12.08
D5.30pm

**GH** *Green Park Hotel* 15 Prince of Wales
Ter, South Cliff ☎65770 Plan:**5** Etr–Oct Lic
20hc 7⇔ ♒ CTV lift

**GH Ridbech Private Hotel** 8 The Crescent
☎61683 Plan:**6** May–Oct 25hc (3fb) CTV
S% B&b£6.90–£7.50 Bdi£9.80–£10.35
D5.45pm

**GH Sefton Hotel** 18 Prince of Wales Ter
☎72310 Plan:**7** Lic 16hc (7fb) nc4 CTV Ⅲ lift
S% B&b£8.05–£9.20 Bdi£10.35–£11.50
W£80.50–£96.60

**SCILLY, ISLES OF** *(No map)* **See St Mary's**

**SEAFORD** E Sussex Map 5 TV49
**GH Avondale Hotel** Avondale Rd ☎890008
6hc (1fb) ⊁ nc4 CTV Ⅲ S% B&b£7–£8
Bdi£10.25–£11.50 W£63.50–£69 Ŀ D4pm

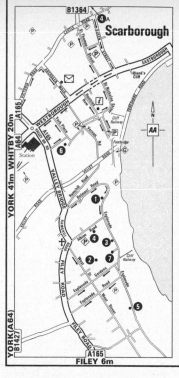

**1** Avoncroft Hotel
**2** Bay Hotel
**3** Burghcliffe Hotel
**4** Church Hills
Private Hotel
**4A** Geldenhuis
**5** Green Park Hotel
**6** Ridbech Private
Hotel
**7** Sefton Hotel

**SEATON** Devon Map 3 SY29
**GH Eyre House** Queen St ☎21455 Mar–Oct
Lic 8hc (3fb) CTV 8P Ⅲ S% ✻B&b£7–£7.50

**GH Glendare** Fore St ☎20542 Jun–Sep Lic
6hc (3fb) ⊁ nc3 CTV Ⅲ S% B&b£6.50–£7.50
Bdi£9.50–£10.50 W£43.50 Ⅾ D5pm

**GH Harbourside** 2 Trevelyan Rd ☎20785
7hc (4fb) ⊁ CTV 10P Ⅲ sea S% B&b£6–£6.50
Bdi£9.50–£10.50 Wfr£66 Ŀ

**GH Mariners Homestead** Esplanade
☎20560 Feb–Nov Lic 11hc (1fb) nc3 CTV
11P 🏛 sea S% B&bf£9.60–£10.50 Bdif£14.25–
£15 Wf£86.75–£94 ⅃ D1pm

**GH Netherhayes** Fore St ☎21646 Etr–Oct
Lic 10hc (3fb) ⊁ nc3 CTV 10P B&bf£8–£9.50
Bdif£11.50–£13.75 Wf£63–£82.50 ⅃

**GH St Margarets** 5 Seafield Rd ☎20462
Apr–Oct Lic 9hc (5fb) CTV 7P 🏛 sea S%
B&bf£6–£7 Bdif£10.75–£11.75 Wf£71.75–
£78.75 ⅃ D6pm

**GH Thornfield** 87 Scalwell Ln ☎20039 Jan–
Nov Lic 8hc (A 3hc) (3fb) CTV 12P S%
B&bf£7–£9 Bdif£11–£13 Wf£70–£84 ⅃ D5.30pm

**SEAVIEW** Isle of Wight *Map 4 SZ69*
**GH Northbank Hotel** ☎2227 Etr–Oct Lic
18hc (6fb) CTV 16P 5🅰 🏛 sea S% B&bf£10
Bdif£14 Wf£90–£95 D8pm

**INN Seaview Hotel** High St ☎2278 15hc
4⇌ 🖝 CTV 12P 🏛 B&bf£8.50–£13.50
Bdif£11.50–£18.50 sn Lf£4.95&alc
D9.30f£4.95&alc

**SELBY** N Yorks *Map 8 SE63*
**GH Hazeldene** 34 Brook St (A19) ☎704809
Closed Xmas wk 7hc (2fb) ⊁ CTV 5P S%
B&bf£6.50–£7.50

**SELSEY** W Sussex *Map 4 SZ89*
**GH Fairbrook** 71 Hillfield Rd ☎2914 Lic
6hc(2fb) ⊁ TV 6P S% ✳ B&bf£6 Wf£42 ꙥ

**GH *White Waves Private Hotel*** Seal Rd
☎2379 Lic 7hc (A 2hc) (1fb) ⊁ CTV 3P 🏛 sea
Dnoon

**SEMLEY** Wilts *Map 3 ST82*
**INN *Bennett Arms*** ☎East Knoyle 221 Lic
A 3⇌ 🏛 CTV P 🏛 ⇌ D10pm

**SEVENOAKS** Kent *Map 5 TQ55*
**GH Moorings Hotel** 97 Hitchin Hatch Ln
☎52589 (due to change to 452589) Lic 9hc
1🏛 (A 2🏛) (1fb) CTV 25P 🏛 S% B&bf£9.78–
£19.55

**GH *Sevenoaks Park Hotel*** 4 Seal Hollow
Rd ☎54245 Lic 15hc 4⇌ 🏛 (A 3hc 1⇌ 🏛)
25P 3🅰 🏛

**SHANKLIN** Isle of Wight *Map 4 SZ58*
**(See Plan)**
**GH Afton Hotel** Clarence Gdns ☎3075
Plan:**1** Mar–Nov Lic 9hc 6🏛 (A 4hc) (2fb) ⊁
nc5 CTV 8P 🏛 sea S% B&bf£12.37–£14.37
Bdif£12.96–£14.95 Wf£81.19–£91.54 ⅃ D6pm

**GH Aqua Hotel** The Esplanade ☎3024
Plan:**2** Mar–Oct Lic 23hc 2⇌ (8fb) ⊁ nc2

SANDOWN 2m

Shanklin

VENTNOR 3m

1 Afton Hotel
2 Aqua Hotel
3 Berry Brow Hotel
4 Culham Private
  Hotel
5 Culver Lodge
  Hotel
6 Fern Bank
7 Langthorne
  Private Hotel
8 Leslie House
  Hotel
9 Meyrick Cliffs
10 Monteagle Hotel
11 Ocean View
12 Overstrand Hotel
13 Sandringham

CTV sea B&bf£8.05–£10.35 Bdif£11.50–£13.23
Wf£65.55–£90.85 ⅃ D6pm

**GH Berry Brow Hotel** Popham Rd ☎2825
Plan:**3** May–Nov Lic 21hc (4fb) CTV 10P 🏛
S% B&bf£7.25 Bdif£14.50 Wf£80 ⅃ D6.30pm

**GH Culham Private Hotel** 31 Landguard
Manor Rd ☎2880 Plan:**4** Closed Xmas 10hc
1⇌ 1🏛 (1fb) nc9 CTV 5P 🏛 S% B&bf£6.50–£8
Bdif£8.50–£10 Wf£49–£59 ⅃ D4pm

**GH Culver Lodge Hotel** Culver Rd ☎3515
Plan:**5** Lic 8rm 2⇌ 6🏛 (1fb) nc8 CTV in all
bedrooms 8P 🏛 S% ✳ B&bf£9.50 Bdif£10–£15
Wf£70–£105 ⅃ D8.30pm

**GH Fern Bank** Highfield Rd ☎2790 Plan:**6**
Closed Xmas Lic 22hc 4⇌ 5🏛 (5fb) ⊁ nc3
CTV 17P S% B&bf£7.25–£8.45 Bdif£10.85–
£12.65 Wf£76–£88.50 ⅃ D6.30pm

⋈ **GH Langthorne Private Hotel** 3 Witbank
Gdns ☎2980 Plan:**7** Apr–Oct 12hc 1⇌ (3fb)
⊁ nc5 CTV 12P 🏛 S% B&bf£5.53–£6.61

Bdi£7.78–£8.83 W£40–£57 Ł D7pm (W only Jun–Aug)

**GH Leslie House Hotel** 10 Hope Rd ☎2798 Plan: **8** Jan–Oct Lic 10hc (4fb) ★ nc5 CTV 5P ▥ S% B&b£6.50–£7 Bdi£9.50–£10.50 W£66–£80 D6.15pm

**GH Meyrick Cliffs** The Esplanade ☎2691 Plan: **9** May–Oct Lic 20hc 1⇔ (4fb) ★ nc7 CTV 5P B&b£7.50–£8.50 Bdi£10.50–£11.50 W£69–£74 Ł D6.30pm

**GH Monteagle Hotel** Priory Rd ☎2854 Plan: **10** Apr–Oct Lic 40hc 12⇔ 8⋔ (3fb) ★ nc9 CTV 30⌂ ▥ S% B&b£10–£15 Bdi£15–£20 W£70–£106 Ł D7.30pm

**GH Ocean View Hotel** 38 The Esplanade ☎2602 Plan: **11** Apr–Oct Lic 36hc 4⇔ 9⋔ (12fb) CTV 25P sea S% B&b£9.22–£10.95 Bdi£13.22–£14.95 W£86.25–£99.47 Ł D8.45pm

**GH Overstrand Private Hotel** Howard Rd ☎2100 Plan: **12** Etr–Oct Lic 15hc 4⇔ 1⋔ (8fb) ★ [Ch] CTV 20P ▥ sea B&b£10.80–£14.20 Bdi£13.80–£17.20 W£72–£103.50 Ł D6pm

**GH Sandringham Hotel** Hope Rd ☎3189 Plan: **13** early May–mid Oct Lic 30hc 8⇔ 3⋔ (11fb) [Ch] CTV 20P sea S% B&bfr£9 Bdifr£11.75 W£71.30–£92 Ł D6.30pm

**SHAP** Cumbria *Map 12 NY51*
**GH Brookfield** ☎397 Closed Jan Lic 5hc (3fb) ★ CTV 25P 5⌂ ▥ S% B&b£6.50–£7 Bdi£11.50–£12.50 D8.15pm

**SHEERNESS** Kent *Map 5 TQ97*
**GH Victoriana** 107 Alma Rd ☎665555 Lic 20hc 2⇔ 5⋔ (4fb) [Ch] CTV 12P 2⌂ ▥ S% B&b£11–£15 Bdi£15–£20 D10pm

**SHEFFIELD** S Yorks *Map 8 SK38*
**GH *Millingtons*** 70 Broomgrove Rd (off A625 Ecclesall Rd) ☎669549 Closed New Year 7hc 3⇔ ⋔ CTV 4P ▥
**See advert on page 194**

**GH Sharrow View Hotel** 13 Sharrow View ☎51542 Lic 20hc 8⇔ (A 5hc 3⇔) (4fb) CTV 25P ▥ S% *B&b£8–£12 Bdi£12.50–£16.50 W£50–£75 D8pm
**See advert on page 195**

**SHERFIELD ON LODDON** Hants *Map 4 SU65*
**GH Wessex House Hotel** ☎882243 Closed 10 days Xmas & New Year Lic 8⇔ CTV in all bedrooms 12P ▥ S% B&b£17–£23 D9.30pm

**SHERIFF HUTTON** N Yorks *Map 8 SE66*
**GH Ranger's House** Sheriff Hutton Park ☎397 6hc 1⇔ (1fb) ★ CTV 20P ▥ S% B&b£8.50–£9.50 Bdi£14–£16 W£100 Ł D8.30pm

**SHERINGHAM** Norfolk *Map 9 TG14*
**GH Beacon Hotel** Nelson Rd ☎822019 Apr–Oct Lic 8hc ★ nc12 CTV 10P ▥ sea S% Bdi£14.50 W£92 Ł D7pm

**GH Beeston Hills Lodge** 64 Cliff Rd ☎822615 May–Sep 7hc 2⇔ (1fb) ★ nc8 CTV 7P ▥ sea S% B&bfr£7 Bdifr£9.75 Wfr£64 Ł

**GH Camberley House Hotel** 62 Cliff Rd ☎823101 May–Oct Lic 9hc (3fb) [Ch] CTV 12P ▥ sea S% B&b£7–£8 Bdi£10.50–£11.50 W£73.50–£80.50 Ł D7pm

**GH Melrose Hotel** 9 Holway Rd ☎823299 Mar–Nov 10hc (1fb) nc10 TV 10P S% B&b£7.50–£8.50 Bdi£9–£9.50 W£55–£60 Ł D6pm

**SHETLAND** *Map 16* **See Lerwick**

**SHIPSTON-ON-STOUR** Warwicks *Map 4 SP24*
**INN Ye Olde White Bear Hotel** High St
☎61558 9hc 4⇨ 20P B&b£8–£11 Bdi£12–
£21 W£50–£70 ⋈ sn L£9alc D9.30pm£9alc

**SHOREHAM-BY-SEA** W Sussex *Map 4 TQ20*
**GH Pende-Shore Hotel** 416 Upper
Shoreham Rd ☎2905 Closed Xmas wk Lic
12hc 1⇨ (3fb) ⚁ CTV 8P ▥ S% B&b£10–
£11.50 Bdi£16–£18 W£100–£113.70 ⅃
D6.30pm

**SHOTTENDEN** Kent *Map 5 TR05*
**GH Cona** Goldups Ln ☎Chilham 405 Lic
10hc 4⌂ (2fb) ⒸⒽ CTV 12P ▥ B&b£7.48–
£8.05 Bdi£12.66–£13.23 W£88.62–£92.61 ⅃

**SHOTTLE** Derbys *Map 8 SK34*
**GH Shottle Hall Farm** ☎Cowers Lane 276
Closed Dec & last 2wks July Lic 8hc (3fb)
24P ▥ B&bfr£11 Bdifr£15.50

**SHREWSBURY** Salop *Map 7 SJ41*
**GH Cannock House Private Hotel** 182A
Abbey Foregate ☎56043 7hc (2fb) nc5 CTV
4P 2⍥ ▥ S% ✱B&b£5.50

**GH Leagrove Hotel** 29 Hereford Rd
☎52078 Lic 8hc (3fb) ⒸⒽ CTV 8P S% B&b£9
Bdi£13.50 D5.30pm

**GH Shelton Hall Hotel** ☎3982 Feb–Dec
rsJan (no evening meals) Lic 10hc 1⇨ 3⌂
(3fb) ⚁ CTV 50P ▥ S% ✱B&b£9–£11 Bdi£14–
£16 D9pm

**SIDMOUTH** Devon *Map 3 SY18*
**GH Canterbury** Salcombe Rd ☎3373 May–
Sep 6hc 1⇨ 3⌂ (1fb) ⚁ nc8 CTV 5P 1⍥ ✱
B&b£7–£9 Bdi£9.50–£12 W£50–£59 ⅃ D7pm

**GH Mount Pleasant Hotel** Salcombe Rd
☎4694 Etr–Oct Lic 13hc 3⇨ 6⌂ (3fb) CTV
20P ▥ B&bfr£9 Bdifr£12 Wfr£80 D6.30pm

**GH Ryton House** 52–54 Winslade Rd
☎3981 9hc (4fb) CTV 9P ▥ ✱Bdi£8–£10
W£53–£58 ⅃ D3pm

**GH Southernhay** 3–4 Fortfield Ter ☎3189
18hc (2fb) CTV sea S% B&b£9.06–£10
Bdi£13.58–£15 W£90.56–£100 ⅃ D5pm

**GH Westbourne Hotel** Manor Rd ☎3774
Closed Oct–Apr Lic 14hc 8⇨ (2fb) CTV 14P
▥ B&b£14–£16.50 Bdi£16–£19.50 W£90.29–
£100.82 ⅃ D7pm

**INN Bowd** (2m NW junc A3052/B376)
☎3328 late Mar–Oct 4hc ⚁ nc5 CTV 130P ▥
S% B&b£12 Bdi£16–£17 W£75–£80 ⅃ sn

L£3.50–£6&alc D10pm£3.50–£6&alc

**SKEGNESS** Lincs *Map 9 TF56*
**GH Crawford Hotel** South Pde ☎4215 Etr–
Oct & Xmas Lic 20hc 7⇨ 1⌂ (8fb) CTV sea
S% B&b£9.32–£10.35 Bdi£12.42–£13.80
W£77.62–£96.60 ⅃ D6pm

**SKIPTON** N Yorks *Map 7 SD95*
**GH Fairleigh** 24 Belle Vue Ter, Broughton
Rd ☎4153 Closed Xmas 5hc (2fb) ⚁ CTV ▥
S% B&b£6–£8 Bdi£9.25–£11.25 W£61.25–
£75.25 ⅃ D7.30pm

**GH Highfield Hotel** 58 Keighley Rd ☎3182
Closed Xmas & New Year Lic 10hc 1⇨ CTV
S% B&b£8–£9 Bdi£13.50–£14.50 D7pm

**GH Unicorn Hotel** Keighley Rd ☎4146
*Continental breakfast only; provided in
bedrooms* Closed Xmas & New Year 9⇨
(7fb) ⚁ CTV in all bedrooms ▥ S% B&b£16–
£17.50

**SKYE, ISLE OF** Highland *Inverness-shire
Map 13 NG* **See Broadford, Dunvegan, Isle
Ornsay, Portree, Waterloo**

**SLOUGH** Berks *Map 4 SU97*
**GH Francis House** 21 London Rd, Langley
☎22286 Closed 25–28 Dec Lic 13hc nc10
CTV 16P ▥ ✱B&b£13.80 Bdi£18.97 D5.30pm

**GH Parkside** 1 Upton Court Rd ☎22533
Closed Xmas wk Lic 19hc (4fb) CTV 15P ▥
S% B&bfr£10.35 Bdifr£14.95 Wfrfr£88.55 ⅃
D4pm

**SNAPE** Suffolk *Map 5 TM35*
**INN Crown** ☎324 rsXmas 4hc 2⌂ ⚁ nc14
TV 50P ▥ S% B&b£15–£18 sn L£3alc
D8.30pm £7alc

**SOMERTON** Somerset *Map 3 ST42*
**GH Church Farm** School Ln, Compton
Dundon ☎72927 Closed Xmas & last 2wks
Oct Lic 4rm 3hc (A 2hc 1⇨ 2⌂) (1fb) nc4 CTV
5P 2⍥ B&b£8–£10 Bdi£14–£16 W£84–£96
⅃ D3pm

**SOUTHAMPTON** Hants *Map 4 SU41*
(See Plan)
**GH** *Amberley* 1 Howard Rd ☎23789 Plan:**1**
8hc nc6 CTV 8P ▥

**GH Banister** 11 Brighton Rd ☎21279 Plan:**2**
Closed Xmas Lic 20hc 1⇨ (4fb) CTV 13P ▥
S% B&b£11.10 D7.30pm

**GH Beacon** 49 Archers Rd ☎25910 Plan:**3**
6hc (1fb) ⚁ nc1 CTV 4P ▥ S% B&b£6 Bdi£10
D1pm

# Sharrow View Hotel

**Sharrow View, Sheffield, S7 1ND**

Warm friendly atmosphere, excellent food and cosy cocktail bar.

In a quiet district 1 mile from city centre. Bus service nearby.

20 Bedrooms, all H & C. Lounge with Colour TV. Central Heating throughout. Large car park. Moderate terms.

**Michael F. Morris MHCIMA**
**RESERVATIONS: 0742-51542**

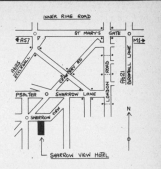

# Mount Pleasant Private Hotel

**Salcombe Road, Sidmouth, Devon. Tel: Sidmouth (STD 03955) 4694**

An early Georgian residence standing in ¾ acre of tree-surrounded lawn providing a homely and relaxing atmosphere. Centrally heated throughout; there are two Lounges tastefully decorated and comfortably furnished, one having Colour TV. A short walk from the Sea and Shopping Centre, yet ideally situated for interesting country walks. The Dining Room is licensed and the Menu is varied daily providing appetizing and wholesome food. Most bedrooms with private Toilet and Shower/Bath. Ample parking in the grounds, and the Hotel holds a Fire Certificate. 1981 Tariff applies to reservations made in Dec '81 and Jan & Feb '82. Special Terms for early and late season holidays.
Resident Proprietors: Mr & Mrs D J Morgan.

# Southernhay Hotel

**Fortfield Terrace, Sidmouth, Devon EX10 8NT. Tel: 3189 (STD 03955)**

The Hotel is part of a regency terrace built in 1790. Situated in an excellent position overlooking cricket field, tennis courts and the sea front. A few yards from bus terminus, town and public gardens. A family run hotel with plenty of good food. All rooms have H & C, electric fires and tea making facilities. SAE for brochure to Ann Forth.

# The Crown Inn

*Fifteenth century*

### SNAPE SAXMUNDHAM SUFFOLK
Tel: Snape (072 888) 324

Local fish and game in season
Crab & Lobster. Pheasant, Partridge & Wild Duck
Wide range of hot and cold snacks.

Hosts: Louise and Stuart Pakes.
Pleasant Inn type accommodation.

Hot and Cold water. Central Heating.
Razor points. Showers in some rooms.
Television in all rooms. No Deep Fry.
No Juke Box. No Fruit Machine.

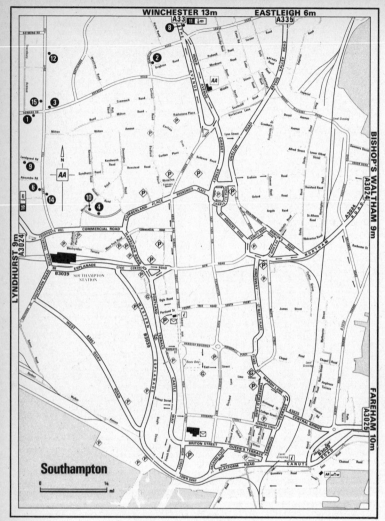

Southampton

| | | | |
|---|---|---|---|
| **1** Amberley | **6** Eaton Court Hotel | **10** Linden | **14** Rosida Hotel |
| **2** Banister | **8** Elizabeth House | **11** Lodge | **15** St Andrews |
| **3** Beacon | Hotel | **12** Madison House | **16** La Valle |
| **4** Claremont | **9** Hunters Lodge | | |

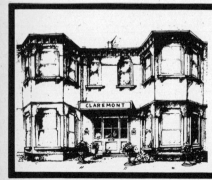

**GH Claremont** 33 The Polygon ☎23112
Plan:**4** 14hc (6fb) CTV 10P Ⅲ S% B&b£6–
£6.50 W£35–£42 ⋈

**GH Eaton Court Hotel** 32 Hill Ln ☎23081
Plan:**6** Closed Xmas wk Lic 12hc 2♔ (2fb) ⊁
CTV 12P ⅢⅢ S% B&b£9.75–£11.75 D9pm

**GH Elizabeth House Hotel** 43/44 The
Avenue ☎24327 Plan:**8** Lic 25hc 5⇔ 8♔
(2fb) CTV 22P ⅢⅢ S% B&b£11.50 Bdi£16.50
W£70 ⋈ D8.30pm

**GH Hunters Lodge Hotel** 25 Landguard Rd,
Shirley ☎27919 Plan:**9** Closed Xmas
rswknds Lic 14hc (1fb) ⊁ CTV 15P 4⌂ ⅢⅢ
✱B&bfr£9.50 Bdi fr£13 Wfr£80.50 ⅃ Dnoon

**GH Linden** 51 The Polygon ☎25653 Plan:**10**
12hc (4fb) ⊁ CTV 6P ⅢⅢ S% B&b£6–£7.50

**GH Lodge** 1 Winn Rd, The Avenue
☎557537 Plan:**11** 12hc (1fb) ⊁ CTV 12P ⅢⅢ
S% B&b£9

**GH Madison House** 137 Hill Ln ☎22374
Plan:**12** 9hc (4fb) ⊁ TV 10P ⅢⅢ S% B&b£6.50–
£8.50

**GH Rosida Hotel** 25–27 Hill Ln ☎28501
Plan:**14** 3 Jan–23 Dec Lic 36hc 4⇔ 3♔ (8fb)
CTV 26P ⅢⅢ B&b£12–£16.50 Bdi£15–£19.50
D7.30pm

**GH St Andrews** 128 Hill Ln ☎21140
Plan:**15** Lic 11hc (4fb) ⊁ nc8 TV 7P ⅢⅢ S%
✱B&b£6.50–£7 Bdi£9.50–£11.50 D8pm

**GH La Valle** 111 Millbrook Rd ☎27821
Plan:**16** Closed Xmas 6hc (2fb) CTV 6P ⅢⅢ
S% B&b£6 W£42 ⋈

**SOUTHEND-ON-SEA** Essex *Map 5 TQ88*
**GH Argyle Hotel** 12 Clifftown Pde
☎339483 Lic 10hc (3fb) nc5 CTV ⅢⅢ sea S%
✱B&b£6.50–£7 Bdi£8.50–£9 W£59–£62.50 ⅃
D4pm

**GH *Camelia Hotel*** 178 Eastern Esplanade,
Thorpe Bay ☎587917 Lic 12hc 1⇔ ♔ ⊁ CTV
ⅢⅢ sea D10pm

**GH Cobham Lodge Private Hotel**
2 Cobham Rd, Westcliff-on-Sea ☎46438 Lic
24hc (3fb) Ⓒⓗ CTV ⅢⅢ sea S% B&b£9–£10
Bdi£13–£14 W£70 ⅃ D6.30pm

**GH Ferndown Hotel** 136 York Rd ☎68614
Lic 17hc (3fb) ⊁ nc5 CTV 12P ⅢⅢ sea B&b£9
Bdi£14

**GH Gladstone Hotel** 40 Hartington Rd
☎62776 Lic 7hc (A4hc) (2fb) ⊁ nc3 CTV ⅢⅢ
sea S% B&b£7–£8.50 W£45–£55 ⋈

**GH Haven Private Hotel** 32–34 Burgess
Rd, Thorpe Bay ☎585085 Lic 18hc 6⇔ 1♔
(1fb) Ⓒⓗ CTV 12P ⅢⅢ S% ✱B&b£12.42
Bdi£15.40 W£92.40 ⅃ D9.30pm

**GH Hudson's Regency Hotel** 18 Royal
Ter ☎40747 11hc (5fb) CTV TV in all
bedrooms 3P 2⌂ ⅢⅢ sea S% B&b£9.78
Bdi£13.80 W£86.25 D7pm

**GH Maple Leaf Private Hotel** 9–11 Trinity
Av, Westcliff-on-Sea ☎46904 Lic 16hc (2fb)
⊁ CTV ⅢⅢ S% B&b£9–£9.50 Bdi£11.25–£12
W£65.50–£72 ⅃ D6pm

**GH *Marine View*** 4 Trinity Av, Westcliff-on-
Sea ☎44104 6hc (2fb) nc5 CTV ⅢⅢ

**GH Mayfair** 52 Crowstone Av, Westcliff-on-
Sea ☎40693 Closed Xmas 6hc (1fb) ⊁ nc5
CTV 4P ⅢⅢ B&b£6–£6.50 Bdi£8.50–£9.50
W£45–£48 ⅃ D4pm

**GH Mayflower Hotel** 5–6 Royal Ter
☎40489 21hc (5fb) CTV ⅢⅢ S% B&b£7.48
W£45 ⋈

**GH Miramare Hotel** 84 Station Rd,
Westcliff-on-Sea ☎44022 Lic 8hc 2♔ (2fb)
Ⓒⓗ CTV 2P 1⌂ ⅢⅢ B&b£9–£10
Bdi£13–£14 W£72–£75 ⅃ D4.30pm

**GH Pavilion** 1 Trinity Av, Westcliff-on-Sea
☎41007 Closed Xmas 8hc (1fb) CTV ⅢⅢ S%
B&b£8–£8.50 Bdi£11.50 W£68 ⅃ Dnoon

**GH Terrace Hotel** 8 Royal Ter ☎48143
mid Jan–mid Dec Lic 9hc (3fb) nc10 CTV ⅢⅢ
sea B&b£8.50

**GH Trinity Lodge Hotel** 6–8 Trinity Av,
Westcliff-on-Sea ☎46066 Lic 16hc (1fb) ⊁
CTV ⅢⅢ S% ✱B&b£8 Bdi£10 W£65 ⅃ D3.15pm

**GH West Park Private Hotel** 11 Park Rd,
Westcliff-on-Sea ☎330729 Lic 12hc 4⇔ 4♔
(3fb) CTV 15P 1⌂ ⅢⅢ D4pm

**SOUTH LAGGAN** Highland *Inverness-shire
Map 14 NN29*
**GH *Forest Lodge*** ☎Invergarry 219 Apr–Oct
6hc ⊁ nc3 CTV 8P ⅢⅢ lake

**SOUTH LUFFENHAM** Leics *Map 4 SK90*
**INN *Boot & Shoe*** ☎Stamford 720177
Lic 4rm 3hc ⊁ TV 20P ⅢⅢ sn D9.30pm

**SOUTHPORT** Merseyside *Map 7 SD31*
**(See Plan)**
**GH Abbey Hotel** 6 Lathom Rd ☎38430
Plan:**1** 11hc (3fb) ⊁ CTV 12P ⅢⅢ lake sea S%
B&b£6.50–£7 Bdi£8.50–£9 W£58–£62 ⅃
D4pm

**GH Balmoral Lodge** 41 Queens Rd ☎30751
Plan:**1A** Lic 11hc 1♔ (3fb) Ⓒⓗ CTV 10P ⅢⅢ
S% ✱B&b£8.05 Bdi£11.50 D7.45pm

**GH Crimond Hotel** 28 Knowsley Rd
☎36456 Plan:**2** Lic 12hc (3fb) CTV 15P ⅢⅢ
S% B&b£8.25–£9.50 Bdi£11.25–£13
W£72.45–£83.50 ⅃ D6pm

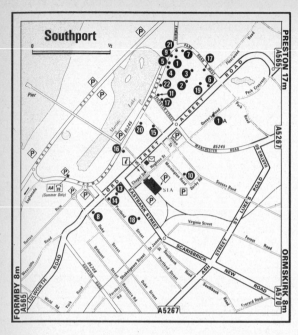

1 Abbey Hotel
1A Balmoral Lodge
2 Crimond Hotel
3 Fairway Private Hotel
4 Fernley Private Hotel
5 Franklyn Hotel
6 Fulwood Private Hotel
7 Garden Hotel
8 Glenwood Private Hotel
9 Golf Links Hotel
10 Hollies Private Hotel
11 Knowsley Private Hotel
13 Newnholme
14 Oakwood Private Hotel
15 Ocean Bank
16 Richmond Hotel
17 Savoia Hotel
18 Sidbrook Hotel
19 Sunningdale Hotel
20 Westhaven
21 Whitworth Falls Hotel
22 Windsor Lodge Hotel

**GH Fairway Private Hotel** 106 Leyland Rd ☎42069 Plan:**3** Apr–Oct Lic 9hc 2⋔ (4fb) ⊁ CTV 20P ⠩ S% B&bf6–£7 Bdif£9–£10 Wf63–£70 ⫢ D6pm

**GH Fernley Private Hotel** 69 The Promenade ☎35610 Plan:**4** Lic 22hc (4fb) CTV 16P ⠩ lake sea D6pm

**GH Franklyn Hotel** 65 The Promenade ☎40290 Plan:**5** Lic 28hc (6fb) CTV 20P ⠩ lake sea B&bf£7.76–£8.40 Bdif£11.50–£12.13 Wf96.83–£101.25 D7pm

**GH Fulwood Private Hotel** 82 Leyland Rd ☎30993 Plan:**6** Lic 12hc (1fb) CTV 7P ⠩ S% B&bf7.48 Bdif11.50 Wf80.50 ⫢ D6pm

**GH Garden Hotel** 19 Latham Rd ☎30244 Plan:**7** Jan–Oct Lic 10hc (2fb) CTV 2P ⠩ sea S% B&bf7.50–£9 Bdif10–£12 Wf65–£78 ⫢ D6pm (W only Jun–Aug)

**GH Glenwood Private Hotel** 98/102 King St ☎35068 Plan:**8** Lic 16hc (2fb) ⊁ CTV 6P ⠩ B&bf9–£10 Bdif12–£13 Wf80–£87 ⫢ D4pm

**GH Golf Links Hotel** 85 The Promenade ☎30405 Plan:**9** Mar–Dec Lic 12hc (3fb) ⊁ nc5 CTV 11P D10pm

**GH Hollies Hotel** 7 Mornington Rd ☎30054 Plan:**10** 17hc 3⇔ 1⋔ (3fb) ⊁ CTV TV available in some bedrooms 17P ⠩ S% B&bf8–£9.50 Bdif11–£13 Wf48–£53 ⫢ D1pm

**GH Knowsley Private Hotel** Promenade, 2 Knowsley Rd ☎30190 Plan:**11** Closed Oct rsNov–May (B&b only) Lic 12hc (5fb) CTV 15P ⠩ lake S% B&bfr£7.47 Bdifr£10.35 Wfr£69 ⫢ D5.45pm

**GH Newnholme** 51 King St ☎30425 Plan:**13** 6hc (2fb) ⊁ nc3 CTV 2P ⠩ S% B&bf7–£8 Bdif£9.50–£10.50 Wf65–£70 ⫢ D5pm

**GH Oakwood Private Hotel** 7 Portland St ☎31858 Plan:**14** Etr–Sep 8hc (2fb) ⊁ nc5 CTV 2P ⠩ D6pm

⊬⊣ **GH Ocean Bank** 16 Bank Sq, Central Promenade ☎30637 Plan:**15** 9hc (2fb) ⊁ nc CTV 2P ⠩ lake sea S% B&bf5.50–£6.50 Bdif7–£8 Wf45–£52 ⫢ D4pm

**GH Richmond Hotel** 31 The Promenade ☎30799 Plan:**16** Jan–Oct Lic 9hc (3fb) CTV

8P ▥ S% B&b£7–£8 Bdi£9–£10.50 W£55–£63 ⌇ D5.30pm

**GH Savoia Hotel** 37 Leicester St ☎30559
Plan:**17** Lic 16hc (4fb) ⊁ nc4 CTV 10P ▥ lake
S% B&b£8.25–£9.25 Bdi£11.25–£12.50
W£77–£84 ⌇ D4pm

**GH Sidbrook Hotel** 14 Talbot St ☎30608
Plan:**18** Lic 9hc (6fb) CTV 10P S% B&b£6–
£8.50 Bdi£8.50–£10 W£50–£65 ⌇ D6pm (W
only Jul & Aug)

**GH Sunningdale Hotel** 85 Leyland Rd
☎30042 Plan:**19** Lic 15hc 5🛋 (7fb) ⊁ CTV
10P ▥ S% ✳ B&b£7.71–£8.63 Bdi£11.16–
£12.08 W£50.60–£81.65 ⌇ D4.30pm

**GH Westhaven** 22 Bank Sq ☎30219
Plan:**20** Lic 7hc (1fb) ⊁ nc5 CTV 2P sea

**GH Whitworth Falls Hotel** 16 Lathom Rd
☎30074 Plan:**21** Lic 14hc (3fb) ⊁ CTV 9P ▥
D6pm

**GH Windsor Lodge Hotel** 37 Saunders St
☎30070 Plan:**22** Lic 12hc 1🖛 (2fb) ⊁ CTV 9P
▥ lake sea S% ✳ B&bfr£8.50 Bdi fr£10.75
Wfr£63.50 ⌇ D5.30pm

**SOUTHSEA** Hants see **Portsmouth &
Southsea**

**SOUTH TAWTON** Devon *Map 3 SX69*
**INN Seven Stars** ☎Sticklepath 292 4hc 20P
▥ S% B&b£6.90–£8.05 Bdi£11.50 W£43.47–
£72.45 ⌇ Bar lunch£1–£1.50
D10pm£1.80–£5

**SOUTHWOLD** Suffolk *Map 5 TM57*
**GH Mount** North Pde ☎722292 Closed
Xmas 7hc (5fb) ⊁ CTV ▥ sea B&b£7.28–£8.49
W£46.96–£55.43 M

**SOUTH ZEAL** Devon *Map 3 SX69*
**GH Poltimore** ☎Sticklepath 209 Lic 7hc
(2fb) nc7 CTV 15P ▥ S% B&b£9–£9.50
Bdi£14–£14.50 W£87–£92 ⌇ D2pm

**SPEAN BRIDGE** Highland *Inverness-shire
Map 14 NN28*
⊢⊣ **GH Coire Glas** ☎272 Feb–Nov Lic
15hc 3🛋 (2fb) TV 15P ▥ S% B&bfr£5.25
Bdi fr£9.50 D7.30pm

**GH Druimandarroch** ☎335 Mar–Dec Lic
8hc (3fb) TV 9P 3🛋 river ✳ B&b£6.50
Bdi£11.10 W£97.75 D7pm

⊢⊣ **GH Lesanne** ☎231 5hc (1fb) ⊁ CTV 6P
S% B&bfr£5.50 Bdi fr£9.50 Wfr£65 ⌇

**STAFFORD** Staffs *Map 7 SJ92*
**GH Abbey** 65–68 Lichfield Rd ☎58531
Closed 2wks Xmas & New Year 6hc (A 9hc)

(4fb) ⊁ CTV 15P ▥ B&b£6.50 Bdi£8.80
D6.45pm

**GH Leonards Croft Hotel** 80 Lichfield Rd
☎3676 Closed Xmas 12hc (A 6hc) (1fb) CTV
14P ▥ S% ✳ B&b£5.75–£6.90

**INN Royal Oak** Rising Brook ☎58402 Lic
10hc CTV 200P ▥ D10pm

**STAINTON** Cumbria *Map 12 NY42*
**GH Limes Country Hotel** Redhills ☎Penrith
63343 8hc (3fb) ⊁ CTV 12P ▥ B&bfr£6.90
Bdi fr£10.35 Wfr£69 ⌇ D6pm

**STAMFORD** Lincs *Map 4 TF00*
**GH St Martin's** ☎3359 Feb–Dec Lic 10rm
9hc (3fb) 🔲 CTV 3P 7🛋 ▥ ✳ B&b£11.50–
£15 D9pm

**STAMFORD** Northumb *Map 12 NU21*
**INN Masons Arms** ☎Longhoughton 275
6hc nc10 30P ✳ B&b£5.75

**STANFORD LE HOPE** Essex *Map 5 TQ68*
**GH Homesteads** 216 Southend Rd ☎2372
rsXmas Lic 11hc (2fb) 🔲 CTV 8P ▥ D6pm

**STEPASIDE** Dyfed *Map 2 SN10*
**GH Bay View** Pleasant Valley
☎Saundersfoot 813417 Lic 12hc ⊁ 🔲 CTV
20P ▥ W only Spring Bank Hol–Sep

**STEVENAGE** Herts *Map 4 TL22*
**GH Northfield Private Hotel** Stevenage Old
Town ☎4537 Lic 10hc 1🛋 (2fb) ⊁ CTV 10P ▥
S% B&b£10–£12 Bdi£15–£17 D6pm

**STEYNING** W Sussex *Map 4 TQ11*
**GH Down House** King's Barn Villas
☎812319 Closed Xmas 6hc (1fb) nc5 CTV 8P
▥ S% B&b£8–£10 Bdi£13.50–£15.50 W£81–
£93 ⌇ D9.30am

**GH Lands Down** ☎812065 5hc (1fb) nc5
CTV 6P ▥ S% ✳ B&b£8 Bdi£13 W£51 M D am

**STOCKBRIDGE** Hants *Map 4 SU33*
**GH Carbery** Salisbury Hill ☎771 Closed
Xmas Lic 11hc (3fb) ⊁ CTV 12P ▥ S%
B&b£8.62 Bdi£13.22 W£89.70 ⌇ D6pm

**GH Old Three Cups** ☎527 Lic 7hc 2🖛 (2fb)
⊁ TV available on request 12P ▥ ✳ B&b£8–
£14 D9.30pm

**STOCKTON-ON-TEES** Cleveland *Map 8
NZ41*
**GH Clairville Hotel** 517–519 Yarm Rd,
Eaglescliffe (3m S A19) ☎780378 Closed
Xmas & New Year Lic 21hc (1fb) CTV 30P ▥
✳ B&b£8.63 Bdi£12.08 D7pm

**STOKEINTEIGNHEAD** Devon *Map 3 SX97*
**GH Bailey's Farm** ☎Shaldon 3361 Apr–Sep
10hc (3fb) CTV 10P S% B&bf£6–£7 Bdi£8.50–
£10 W£58.50–£65 ⫼ D7pm

⋈ **GH Santa Rosa** ☎Shaldon 2607 6hc
(1fb) CTV 10P ▥ S% B&bf£5.50–£6.50
Bdi£9.50–£10.50 W£57–£62.50 ⫼ D6.30pm

**STOKE ST GREGORY** Somerset *Map 3
ST32*
**GH Meare Green** ☎North Curry 490250
Mar–Oct Lic 6hc ⊁ nc12 TV 6P 2☂ ▥ S%
✶ B&bf£6.50–£7.50 Bdi£10.50–£11.50
W£37.50–£42.50 Ⓜ

**STONE** Glos *Map 3 ST69*
**GH Elms** ☎Falfield 260279 Lic 10hc (2fb) Ⓒⓗ
CTV 20P ▥ S% ✶ B&bf£9.20 Bdi£13.25
D2.30pm

**STONETHWAITE** *(Borrowdale)* Cumbria
*Map 11 NY21*
**GH Langstrath Hotel** Borrowdale
☎Borrowdale 239 mid Mar–Oct & New Year
Lic 14hc (3fb) 20P ▥ S% B&bf£10 Bdi£14.50
W£94 ⫼ D3pm

**STORNOWAY** Isle of Lewis, Western Isles
*Ross & Crom Map 13 NB43*
**GH Ardlonan** 29 Francis St ☎3482 Closed
Xmas & New Year 5rm 3hc (1fb) ⊁ CTV ▥
S% ✶ B&bf£6

**GH Park** 30 James St ☎2485 7rm 6hc CTV
▥ S% ✶ B&bf£7

**STOURBRIDGE** W Midlands *Map 7 SO98*
**GH Limes** 260 Hagley Rd, Pedmore

☎Hagley 882689 10hc (1fb) CTV 12P ▥ S%
B&bfr£10.50 Bdi fr£14 D7pm

**STOURPORT-ON-SEVERN** Heref & Worcs
*Map 7 SO87*
**INN *Angel Hotel*** Severnside ☎2661 Lic 5hc
CTV 40P ▥ river D9pm

**STOW-ON-THE-WOLD** Glos *Map 4 SP12*
**GH Old Farmhouse Hotel** Lower Swell (1m
W B4068) ☎30232 mid Jan–24 Dec Lic 5hc
1⇌ (1fb) ⊁ TV 25P ▥ S% B&bfr£12.75
Bdi fr£20.75 Wfr£139.79 ⫼ D8.45pm

**GH Parkdene Hotel** Sheep St ☎30344
Closed Xmas & New Year Lic 11hc 2⇌ (2fb)
CTV ▥ B&bf£10.50 Bdi£10.75–£14.35
W£85.75–£110.95 D8.30pm

**STRANRAER** Dumfries & Galloway
*Wigtowns Map 10 NX05*
**GH Lochview** 52 Agnew Cres ☎3837 6hc
(2fb) CTV 6P sea S% B&bf£6 Bdi f£9 W£60 ⫼
Dnoon

**STRATFORD-UPON-AVON** Warwicks *Map
4 SP25* **(See Plan)**
**GH Argos Hotel** 5 Arden St ☎4321 Plan: **1**
Jan–Nov 9hc (1fb) ⊁ nc10 CTV ▥ S%
B&bf£6.50–£7.50

**GH *Avon House*** 8 Evesham Pl ☎293328
Plan: **2** 9hc (2fb) ⊁ CTV ▥ D am

**GH Coach House** 17 Warwick Rd ☎4109
Plan: **2A** 11hc 1⇌ 1🛏 (3fb) ⊁ TV in all
bedrooms 12P S% B&bf£7–£9.50 Bdi£10–
£12.50 W£49–£66.50 Ⓜ

**GH Glenavon Private Hotel** Chestnut Walk
☎292588 Plan: **3** Closed Xmas 11hc (1fb) TV
▥ S% B&bf£6–£15

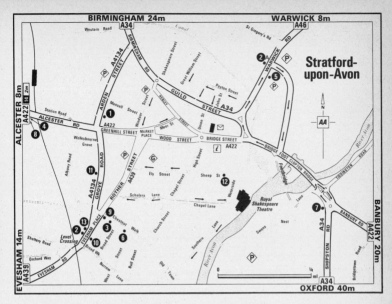

1 Argos Hotel
2 Avon House
2A Coach House
3 Glenavon Private
  Hotel

4 Hunter's Moon
5 Hylands Hotel
6 Marlyn
7 Melita

8 Moonraker
  House
9 Nando's
10 Penshurst
11 Salamander

12 Stratford House
   Hotel
13 Virginia Lodge
14 Wildmoor

# HUNTERS MOON
## GUEST HOUSE
### 150 ALCESTER ROAD
### STRATFORD-ON-AVON
### WARWICKSHIRE
### (0789) 292888

Family, double, twin or single bedrooms with central heating, shaver points
and tea and coffee making facilities. Shower rooms with fitted hair driers are
available to all bedrooms and some have private showers. TV lounge,
car park, evening meal by arrangement. Free lift usually available from bus or
rail station on receipt of phone call. Terms on request.

# HYLANDS HOTEL

**Warwick Road, Stratford-upon-Avon, Warwickshire CV37 6YW.
Telephone: Stratford-upon-Avon 297962.**

Distinguished private hotel, five minutes walk
to theatre, town centre and river. About 400
yards to indoor swimming pool, sauna,
solarium and squash courts. Attractive garden.
Large enclosed car park. Charming small bar
and pine furnished dining room. Rooms with
private toilet and shower; also family rooms
with shower. All rooms with colour TV.

*The sort of place one is always hoping to find
and so rarely does. A warm welcome awaits you.*

**Proprietors: Anna & Hamish Barton.**

⊁⊣ **GH Hunters Moon** 150 Alcester Rd
☎292888 Plan:**4** 6hc (2fb) CTV 5P ⫿⫿⫿ S%
B&b£5.50–£7

**GH Hylands Hotel** Warwick Rd ☎297962
Plan:**5** Lic 12hc 5⋔ (3fb) ⁑ CTV in all
bedrooms 20P ⫿⫿⫿ S% ✳B&b£8–£11.50
Bdi£13–£19 W£82–£120 ⫽ D8.30pm

**GH Marlyn** 3 Chestnut Walk ☎293752
Plan:**6** Closed Xmas 8hc (2fb) ⁑ TV ⫿⫿⫿ S%
B&b£6.90–£8.75 W£41.40–£52.50 Ṁ

**GH Melita** 37 Shipston Rd ☎292432
Plan:**7** Closed Xmas–New Year & Feb Lic
13hc 5⇨ 1⋔ (5fb) ⁑ CTV 12P 2⊯ ⫿⫿⫿ S%
B&b£8–£10

⊁⊣ **GH Moonraker House** 40 Alcester Rd
☎67115 Plan:**8** 7hc 3⋔ (2fb) CTV 7P ⫿⫿⫿ S%
B&b£5–£7.50 Bdi£9–£11.50 D2pm

**GH Nando's** 18–19 Evesham Pl ☎4907
Plan:**9** 12hc 1⇨ 1⋔ (2fb) ⁑ CTV ⫿⫿⫿ S%
B&bfr£6.50

**GH Penshurst** 34 Evesham Pl ☎5259
Plan:**10** Apr–Dec Lic 8hc (2fb) ⁑ CTV 3P 1⊜
⫿⫿⫿ S% ✳B&b£5.50–£6.50

⊁⊣ **GH Salamander** 40 Grove Rd ☎5728
Plan:**11** 7hc (2fb) CTV 1⊜ ⫿⫿⫿ S% B&b£5.75–
£7.50

**GH Stratford House Hotel** Sheep St
☎68288 Plan:**12** Closed Xmas Lic 10hc 8⇨
(1fb) ⁑ nc9 CTV ⫿⫿⫿ S% B&b£14–£17

⊁⊣ **GH Virginia Lodge** 12 Evesham Pl
☎292157 Plan:**13** Closed Xmas Lic 7hc (3fb)
CTV 10P S% B&b£5.50–£6.50 Bdi£8.50–
£9.50 W£59.50–£66.50 ⫽

**INN Wildmoor** Alcester Rd ☎67063
Plan:**14** 6rm 5⇨ 1⋔ CTV in all bedrooms
100P 50⊜ ⫿⫿⫿

**STRATHAVEN** Strathclyde *Lanarks Map 11
NS74*
**GH Springvale Hotel** 18 Letham Rd
☎21131 Lic 6hc 1⋔ (A 8hc) (3fb) ℂℎ CTV 8P
⫿⫿⫿ ✳B&b£7.50 Bdi£11 W£90 D7pm

**STRATHPEFFER** Highland *Ross & Crom
Map 14 NH45*
**GH *Kilvannie Manor*** Fodderty ☎389 Lic
8hc (2fb) ⁑ CTV 15P D7pm

**GH *Rosslyn Lodge Private Hotel*** ☎281
Feb–Nov 15rm 14hc (5fb) ℂℎ CTV 15P ⫿⫿⫿
D6.30pm

**STRATHYRE** Central *Perths Map 11 NN51*
**INN Strathyre** ☎224 8⇨ ⇶ CTV 30P ⫿⫿⫿ S%
B&b£8.50–£11 Bdi£12.50–£17
W£100–£110 sn L£5alc D9pm£5alc
**See advert on page 204**

**STRETE** Devon *Map 3 SX84*
**GH Highcliff** ☎Stoke Fleming 307 Mar–Oct
Lic 10hc 1⇨ (2fb) ℂℎ CTV 10P sea S%
B&b£6.32–£6.90 Bdi£9.20–£9.90 W£64.40–
£69.20 ⫽ D7pm

**GH Tallis Rock Private Hotel** ☎Stoke
Fleming 370 May–Sep 10hc (2fb) CTV 8P 1⊜
sea B&b£6–£7 Bdi£9–£10 W£60–£65 ⫽
D7pm

**STRETTON** Leics *Map 8 SK91*
**INN *Olde Greetham*** ☎Castle Bytham 365
Lic 5hc 60P ⫿⫿⫿ D9.30pm

**STROMNESS** Orkney *Map 16 HY20*
**GH *Oakleigh Private Hotel*** Victoria St
☎850447 Closed New Year Lic 7hc (A 1hc)
(3fb) ⁑ CTV 2P D5pm

**STROUD** Glos Map 3 SO80
**GH Downfield Private Hotel** Caincross Rd
☎4496 5 Jan–19 Dec Lic 18rm 15hc 3⇔
(3fb) CTV 26P 🅟 S% B&bf£9.50–£12 Bdif£11–
£17 Wf£50–£55 ⋈ D8pm

**STUKELEY, GREAT** Cambs Map 4 TL27
**GH The Stukeleys** ☎Huntingdon 56927 Lic
8rm 7hc (5fb) CTV 20P 🅟 S% B&bf£12
D8.30pm

**STURRY** Kent Map 5 TR16
**GH Whatmer House** ☎Canterbury 710883
Lic 7hc (2fb) CTV 8P 🅟 lake & S%
B&bfrf£9.20 Bdifrf£13 D9pm

**SUDBURY** Suffolk Map 5 TL84
**GH Hill Lodge Private Hotel** 8 Newton Rd
☎77568 Closed Xmas wk 12hc (1fb) ⋇ CTV
20P 2🚗 🅟 S% B&bf£8.05 Bdif£11.50

**GH Oriel Lodge Hotel** 21 Kings Hill,
Cornard Rd ☎72456 Lic 11hc (3fb) Ch CTV
10P 🅟 & S% B&bf£9.95 Bdif£13.45 Wf£60 ⋈
D7.30pm

**SUNDERLAND** Tyne & Wear Map 12 NZ35
**GH St Annes Private Hotel** 1 Northcliff,
Roker Ter ☎72649 Lic 12hc 1🎇 (2fb) CTV
12P 🅟 sea B&bf£8.50–£10.50 D9pm

**SURBITON** Gt London London plan 4 E2
(page 134)
**GH Dalton Private Hotel** 317 Ewell Rd,
Tolworth ☎01-399 8663 18hc 12⇔ 🎇 (4fb)
nc10 CTV 10P 🅟

**GH Holmdene** 23 Cranes Dr ☎01-399 9992
Closed Xmas 6hc (1fb) nc5 CTV P 🅟 S%
B&bf£8–£11 Wf£52.50–£64 ⋈

**GH Villiers Lodge** 1 Cranes Pk ☎01-399
6000 6hc ⋇ CTV 6P

**GH Warwick** 321 Ewell Rd ☎01-399 5837
9hc 1⇔ 🎇 (3fb) CTV 5P 🅟

**SUTTON** Gt London London plan 4 E3 (page
134)
**GH Dene Private Hotel** 39 Cheam Rd ☎01-
642 3170 17rm 16hc 2⇔ (3fb) ⋇ nc5 CTV in
all bedrooms 8P 🅟 S% B&bf£10.35–£23

**GH Eaton Court Hotel** 49 Eaton Rd ☎01-
642 4580 Closed 24 Dec–3 Jan Lic 12rm
11hc (3fb) nc3 CTV 6P 🅟 S% B&bf£11–£12

**GH Thatched House Hotel** 135 Cheam Rd
☎01-642 3131 Lic 18hc 7🎇 (1fb) CTV 12P 🅟
S% B&bfrf£15 Bdifrf£21 D8pm

**SUTTON COLDFIELD** W Midlands Map 7
SP19
**For location see Birmingham Plan**
**GH Cloverley Hotel** 17 Anchorage Rd
☎021-354 5181 Not on plan Lic 17🎇 (2fb) ⋇
CTV 14P 🅟 ✱ B&bfrf£13.28 D8pm

**GH Standbridge Hotel** 138 Birmingham Rd
☎021-354 3007 Birmingham plan:**8** Lic 8hc
(A 1hc) CTV 11P 🅟 S% B&bf£12–£13.50
Bdif£15.60–£17.10 Dnoon

**SWANAGE** Dorset Map 4 SZ07
**GH Boyne Hotel** Cliff Av ☎2939 Lic 15hc
1⇔ (3fb) CTV 7P S% ✱ B&bf£8.05–£8.50
Bdif£10.35–£10.75 Wf£55.20–£70.15 ⋈
D6.30pm

**GH Burlington Hotel** 7 Highcliffe Rd ☎2422
(liable to change to 422422) Lic 9hc 1⇔ 3🎇
(3fb) CTV 9P 🅟 sea B&bf£6–£9.50 Bdif£9–
£12.50 Wf£58–£86.25 ⋈ D6.30pm

**GH Byways** 5 Ulwell Rd ☎2322 mid May–mid Sep 11hc (3fb) nc5 CTV 3P S% B&b£7 Bdi£9 W£63.25–£67.85 D6.30pm (W only Jun–Aug)

**GH Castleton Private Hotel** Highcliffe Rd ☎3972 Feb–Oct Lic 12hc (4fb) ⌖ nc3 CTV 8P S% B&b£7.48–£8.63 Bdi£10.35–£11.50 W£63.25–£74.75 ⌖ D5pm

**GH Eversden Private Hotel** Victoria Rd ☎3276 Lic 12hc 2⇩ 3⋔ (4fb) ⌖ CTV 12P ▥ S% ✳ B&b£7.50–£8.05 Bdi£10–£10.92 W£59–£69 D6pm

**GH Golden Sands Private Hotel** 10 Ulwell Rd ☎2093 14 Jan–14 Dec Lic 15hc 1⇩ 2⋔ (10fb) ⌖ CTV 14P ▥ S% B&b£6–£8 Bdi£9–£12.50 W£60–£84 ⌖ D6.30pm

**GH Havenhurst Hotel** 3 Cranbourne Rd ☎4224 Mar–Oct Lic 16hc 1⇩ 1⋔ (6fb) CTV 16P ▥ S% B&b£8–£11 Bdi£11.50–£14.50 W£75–£92.50 ⌖ D6.30pm (W only mid Jun–Aug)

**GH Horseshoe House Hotel** Cliff Av ☎2194 May–Sep 10hc nc10 CTV 5P ▥ D9pm

**GH Ingleston Private Hotel** 2 Victoria Rd ☎2391 Apr–Oct Lic 8hc (4fb) ⌖ nc3 CTV 10P ▥ S% B&b£6.50–£7.50 Bdi£9–£10.50 W£75–£77 ⌖ D5pm

**GH Kingsley Hall Hotel** 8 Ulwell Rd ☎2872 rsOct–Mar Lic 18hc 1⇩ 3⋔ (7fb) ⌖ CTV 20P ▥ sea B&bfr£6 Bdifr£8 Wfr£56 (W only Jul–Aug)

**GH Oxford Hotel** 3 & 5 Park Rd ☎2247 (liable to change to 422247) Apr–Oct Lic 14hc (5fb) ⌖ nc2 CTV S% B&bfr£7.50 Bdifr£10 D6.30pm

**GH Tower Lodge Private Hotel** 17 Ulwell Rd ☎2887 Mar–Nov Lic 11hc 4⋔ (7fb) ⌖ Ch CTV 9P S% B&b£9.92–£11.76 Bdi£12.12–£13.96 W£72.45–£83.81 ⌖ D5pm

**GH Westbury Hotel** 6 Rempstone Rd ☎2345 Etr–Oct Lic 20hc CTV 12P sea

**SWANSEA** W Glam *Map 3 SS69*
**GH Avion Hotel** 12 Gore Ter ☎53407 Lic 12hc (4fb) CTV TV in all bedrooms P ▥ S% ✳ B&b£9.20 Bdi£13.23

**GH '57' Bed & Breakfast** Bryn Rd, Brynmill ☎466948 7hc (2fb) CTV ▥ sea S% B&b£6–£6.50 (W only Oct–Mar)

⋈ **GH Channel View** 17 Bryn Rd, Brynmill ☎466834 Closed Xmas wk 6hc CTV ▥ S% B&b£5.50–£6.50 Bdi£8–£8.50 W£48–£52 ⌖ D4pm

**GH Crescent** 132 Eaton Cres ☎466814 6hc (2fb) ⌖ CTV 4P ▥ sea S% B&b£6–£6.50 W£38.50–£42 ▯

**GH Mount Vernon** 18 Uplands Cres ☎466790 6hc 1⋔ (1fb) ⌖ CTV ▥ S% B&b£8–£8.50 W£49–£54 ▯

**GH Parkway Hotel** 253 Gower Rd, Sketty ☎201632 Lic 14hc 2⋔ (1fb) nc12 CTV 20P ▥ sea S% ✳ B&b£9.77 Bdi£14.95 W£60.37 ▯ D5pm

**GH St Anne's Hotel** 6 Gore Ter ☎50914 rsXmas Lic 8hc (3fb) ⌖ CTV S% B&b£6–£7 Bdi£9–£10 W£57–£65 ⌖ D5.30pm

**GH St Davids Private Hotel** 15 Sketty Rd, Uplands ☎473814 Lic 12hc 2⇩ 2⋔ (4fb) CTV ▥ S% B&b£6.50–£8 Bdi£10.50–£12 W£63–£84 ⌖ D5.30pm

**GH St Helen's House** St Helen's Cres
☎460065 rsXmas wk 7hc (2fb) CTV 6P 3🐕 ▥
S% B&bf7.50–£8.50 Bdi£11–£12 D am

**GH Tregare Hotel** 9 Sketty Rd, Uplands
☎56608 Lic 11hc 8🍴 🛁 (3fb) CTV 6P ▥
D4.30pm

**GH Uplands Court** 134 Eaton Cres
☎473046 Closed Xmas wk Lic 8hc (1fb) 🕯
CTV 2P 2🐕 ▥ sea S% B&bf7.50–£8 Bdi£11–
£12 W£77–£84 ⚊ D4pm

⨯ **GH Westlands** 34 Bryn Rd, Brynmill
☎466654 6hc (2fb) CTV ▥ S% B&bf5.50–£6
Bdi£8–£9 W£54–£56 ⚊ D6pm

**SWINTON** Borders Berwicks Map 12 NT84
**INN Wheatsheaf** Main St ☎257 4hc 10P ▥
S% ✳B&bf7 Bar lunch 80p–£1.50
D9pm£5alc

**SWYNNERTON** Staffs Map 7 SJ83
**INN Fitzherbert Arms** ☎241 5hc (A 7hc 2🍴
3🛁) CTV 40P 3🐕 ▥ S% B&bfr£10
Bdifr£13.75 Wfr£70 ⚊ sn L£7.99alc
D9.30pmfr£3.75

**SYMONDS YAT, EAST** Heref & Worcs Map
3 SO51
**GH Garth Cottage Hotel** ☎890364 Feb–
Oct Lic 7hc 1🛁 (1fb) CTV 8P ▥ river S%
B&bf9.25–£9.75 Bdi£14–£14.95 W£95–£98
⚊ D6pm

**SYMONDS YAT, WEST** (Nr Ross-on-Wye)
Heref & Worcs Map 3 SO51
**GH Woodlea** ☎890206 Closed Xmas wk Lic
10hc 2🛁 (4fb) CTV 10P ▥ river B&bf8 Bdi£13
W£85–£87 ⚊ D6pm

**TADCASTER** N Yorks *Map 8 SE44*
**GH Shann House** 47 Kirkgate ☎833931 8hc
5⇌ 3🛏 (2fb) CTV in all bedrooms 12P ▥ S%
✷B&bfr£13.50

**TAL-Y-LLYN** Gwynedd *Map 6 SH70*
**GH** *Minffordd Hotel* (2m E on A487)
☎Corris 665 Mar–Oct rsNov–Xmas & 2
Jan–Feb Lic 6hc (2fb) ✻nc3 15P ▥ D8.30pm

**TARPORLEY** Cheshire *Map 7 SJ56*
**GH Perth Hotel** High St ☎2514 Lic 8hc 2⇌
1🛏 nc5 CTV 10P ▥ S% B&bf£14.50–£15.70
Bdif£17.20–£18.90 D9.30pm

**TAUNTON** Somerset *Map 3 ST22*
**GH Brookfield House** 16 Wellington Rd
☎72786 Lic 8hc (1fb) CTV 6P ▥ S%
B&bf£10.35 Bdif£14.95 W£56.35 ⅃ D5pm

**GH Meryan House Hotel** Bishop's Hull
☎87445 Lic 8hc (4fb) 🄲🄷 CTV 15P ▥ S%
✷B&bf£8.50–£9.50 Bdif£11.50–£13 D6.30pm

**GH St Georges** 17 Wilton St ☎70584 Lic
9hc (1fb) CTV 10P ▥ S% B&bfr£8
Bdifr£12.50 D6.30pm

**GH White Lodge Hotel** 81 Bridgwater Rd
☎73287 Lic 10hc (2fb) ✻CTV 12P ▥ S%
B&bfr£10 Bdifr£14.50 Wfr£84 ⅃ D7pm

**TAVISTOCK** Devon *Map 2 SX47*
**GH Cherry Trees** 40 Plymouth Rd ☎3070
5hc (1fb) ✻CTV 1P 4🛱 river S% B&bf£6.50–£8

**GH Dulverton** 13 Plymouth Rd ☎2964 Lic
8hc (5fb) CTV 10P ▥ B&bf£6–£12 Bdi fr£10
Wfr£60 ⅃ D7.30pm

**TEIGNMOUTH** Devon *Map 3 SX97*
**GH Bay Cottage Hotel** 7 Marine Pde,

Shaldon ☎Shaldon 2394 Mar–Oct 8hc (2fb)
✻ CTV 3P ▥ river sea D4.30pm
**GH Bay Hotel** Sea Front ☎4123 Etr–
Oct & Xmas Lic 20hc 6⇌ 4🛏 (4fb) CTV 16P
▥ sea S% B&bf£10–£12 Bdif£14–£16
W£75–£85 ⅃ D7pm

**GH Glen Devon** 3 Carlton Pl ☎2895 Lic 8hc
(4fb) ✻CTV 6P ▥ S% B&bf£6.50–£8 Bdif£8–£11
W£55–£75 ⅃ D5.30pm

**GH Hillsley** Upper Hermonsa Rd ☎3878
May–Sep Lic 7hc (4fb) nc3 CTV 10P river sea
S% B&bf£8.62–£9.20 Bdif£11.50–£12.65
W£56.35–£63.25 ⅃ D6.30pm

⊩⊣ **GH Leafield** 61 Dawlish Rd ☎2986
May–Sep 6hc (2fb) nc5 CTV 6P ▥ river sea
S% B&bf£5–£7 W£30–£45 Ⓜ

**GH Lyme Bay House Hotel** Den
Promenade ☎2953 Lic 10hc 3🛏 (6fb) CTV ▥
lift sea S% B&bf£8–£10.30 Bdif£11–£13.60
W£67.50–£82.25 ⅃ D4pm

**GH** *New Strathearn Hotel* Bitton Park Rd
☎2796 Closed Xmas Lic 11hc ✻ CTV 10P
sea S% D6.30pm

**GH Thornhill Hotel** Sea Front ☎3460 Etr–
mid Oct Lic 14hc (4fb) nc2 CTV 4P ▥ sea S%
B&bf£8.25–£9.25 Bdif£11–£12.75
W£58.75–£73.50 D6.30pm (W only Jul–Aug)

**GH** *Westlands Hotel* Reed Vale ☎3007 Lic
16hc 5⇌ 🛏 (3fb) ✻CTV 16P river D7pm

**TENBY** Dyfed *Map 2 SN10*
**GH Belvedere Private Hotel** Serpentine Rd
☎2549 Lic 16hc 1⇌ (11fb) CTV 20P S%
B&bf£7.50–£10.50 Bdif£10–£13.50 W£70–
£95 ⅃ D6.30pm

**GH Hotel Doneva** The Norton ☎2460 Lic
14hc 3⇔ (7fb) CTV 18P S% B&bf8–£9
Bdif9.50–£11 Wf65–£78 (W only Jul–Aug)

**GH Harbour Heights Hotel** 11 The Croft
☎2264 Etr–mid Nov Lic 10hc 2⇔ (8fb) ✻ nc3
TV in all bedrooms sea ✱ B&bf8.25–£10.45
Bdif11.50–£13.75 Wf82.50–£90.50 ⫽

**GH Heywood Lodge** Heywood Ln ☎2684
Etr–Oct Lic 14hc 3⇔ (4fb) ⒸⒽ CTV 20P ⩗
S% B&bf6.90–£8.05 Bdif11.50–£12.60
Wf78.20–£82.80 ⫽ D7pm

**GH Myrtle House Hotel** St Marys St ☎2508
Apr–Sep Lic 9hc (3fb) CTV ⩗ S% B&bf8–£12
Bdif11–£14 Wf69–£88 D6.30pm

**GH Pembroke Hotel** Warren St ☎3670
Closed Xmas & New Year Lic 15hc (6fb) CTV
5P ⩗ D6.30pm

**GH Sea Breezes Hotel** 18 The Norton
☎2753 Mar–Oct Lic 18hc 4⇔ (3fb) ✻ nc3
CTV ⩗ sea S% B&bf6–£8.50 Bdif9.50–
£11.50 Wf68–£82 ⫽

**TEWKESBURY** Glos Map SO83
**GH South End House** 67 Church St
☎294097 Lic 10hc 2⇔ (3fb) CTV 3P ⩗ S%
B&bf10–£12.50

**THAXTED** Essex Map 5 TL63
**INN Fox & Hounds Hotel** Walden Rd
☎830129 10hc 4🏠 P ⩗ ✱ B&bf12.50–£14
Lf4.50–£5&alc D10pm£8.75alc

**THORNTHWAITE** (Nr Keswick) Cumbria
Map 11 NY22
**GH Ladstock Country House Hotel**
☎Braithwaite 210 Mar–Oct Lic 17hc 1⇔
(1fb) ✻ CTV 30P ⩗ S% B&bf10–£12 Bdif15–
£17 Wfrf90 ⫽ D6pm

**THORNTON CLEVELEYS** Lancs Map 7
SD34
**GH Lyndhope** 2 Stockdove Way, Cleveleys
☎Cleveleys 852531 rs winter (B&b only)
6hc (2fb) ✻ nc3 CTV 12P ⩗ S% B&bf6–£7
Bdif7.50–£8.50 D3pm

**THORNTON HEATH** Gt London
London plan 4 E4 (page 135)
**GH Clock House Hotel** 47 Brigstock Rd
☎01-684 8480 Tem 12hc CTV 7P ⩗ S%
B&bf8–£8.50

**THORPE BAY** Essex **See Southend-on-Sea**

**THORPENESS** Suffolk Map 5 TM45
**INN Dolphin** ☎Aldeburgh 2681 9hc 1⇔
(A 8hc 4⇔) (1fb) CTV ⩗ ✱ B&bf14–£13.50
Bdif15.50–£19 Wf104–£129 ⫽ D9pm

**THURLESTONE SANDS** Devon Map 3
SX64
**GH La Mer** ☎Galmpton 561207 May–Sep
Lic 10hc (6fb) nc4 CTV 10P sea S% B&bf10–
£13 Bdif11–£14 Wf80–£90 ⫽ D7pm

**TICEHURST** E Sussex Map 5 TQ63
**INN Bell Hotel** The Square ☎200234 3hc ✻
nc5 25P ⩗ S% B&bf8 sn Lf4alc
D9.30pm£4alc

**TICKENHAM** Avon Map 3 ST47
**INN Star** ☎Nailsea 852071 4hc ✻ nc12 CTV
60P S% B&bf8 Bdif10 sn Lf1.80–£2.50
D7.30pm£2–£3

**TIMSBURY** Avon Map 3 ST65
**GH Old Malt House** ☎70106 Lic 6hc 3⇔
(1fb) ✻ nc3 CTV 16P ⩗ B&bf10–£15 Bdi frf17
Wfrf67.50 Ⓜ D8.30pm

**TINTAGEL** Cornwall *Map 2 SX08*
⊶† **GH Belvoir** ☎265 (due to change to
Camelford 770265 in autumn 81) Closed
Xmas Lic 7hc 1🛏 (2fb) TV 12P sea S%
B&b£5.95–£7.25 Bdi£9.20–£10.50 W£49.75–
£69.75 ⅃ D5pm

**GH Halgabron House** ☎667 (due to change
to Camelford 770667 in autumn 81) Etr–Sep
Lic 5hc (3fb) CTV 5P sea S% *B&b£8.63
Bdi£13.23 W£69–£82.80 ⅃ D3pm (W only Jul–
Aug)

**GH Penallick Hotel** Treknow ☎296 Lic 10hc
1🛏 (3fb) CTV 12P 🕮 sea S% B&b£9–£10.50
Bdi£11–£12.50 W£67–£78 ⅃ D6pm

**GH Trebrea Lodge** Trenale ☎410 (due to
change to Camelford 770410 in autumn 81)
Etr–Oct rsNov–Etr Lic 7hc (3fb) CTV in all
bedrooms 10P 🕮 sea S% *B&b£11.50

Bdi£14.38 W£82.80–£88.55 ⅃ D6pm
(W only mid Jun–mid Sep)

**TINTERN** Gwent *Map 3 SO50*
**GH Parva Farmhouse** ☎411 Lic 5hc (2fb)
CTV 8P 2🚗 🕮 river S% B&b£8–£8.50 Bdi£13–
£13.50 W£75–£78 ⅃ D7pm

**INN Fountain** Trellech Grange (2m W of
Tintern on unclass rd) ☎303 4hc 50P 🕮 S%
B&b£8.50 Bdi£12.35 sn L£4.20–£6&alc
D10pm£4.20–£6&alc

**TIVETSHALL ST MARGARET** Norfolk *Map
5 TM18*
**GH Glenhaven** ☎238 5hc (1fb) TV 8P 🕮 S%
B&bfr£8 Bdifr£10.50

**TOBERMORY** Isle of Mull, Strathclyde *Argyll Map 13 NM55*
**GH Suidhe Hotel** 59 Main St ☎2209 Mar–Oct Lic 9hc 1🛁 (2fb) ✱ CTV 5P ▥ sea S% B&b£9–£10 Bdi£14–£15 W£90.65–£97.12 ⊾ D8.30pm

**GH Tobermory** 53 Main St ☎2091 Closed Xmas & New Year Lic 13hc (2fb) CTV 10P ▥ sea S% B&b£9.20–£10 Bdi£13.23–£14.50 W£86.25–£98 ⊾ D6.30pm

**TORBAY** Devon **See under Brixham, Paignton and Torquay**

**TORCROSS** Devon *Map 3 SX84*
**GH Cove House** ☎Kingsbridge 580448 Feb–Nov Lic 12hc 4🛁 4🚿 (1fb) ✱ nc9 TV in all bedrooms 12P sea S% B&b£10–£12 Bdi£15–£17 Wfr£95 Dnoon (W only Jul–Aug)

**GH Shingle** ☎Kingsbridge 508782 Closed Xmas & 2wks in winter Lic 6hc 1🚿 (2fb) ✱ nc3 TV in all bedrooms 4P sea S% B&b£7.20–£8 Bdi£10.80–£12 W£71–£79 ⊾ D6pm

**TORMARTON** Avon *Map 3 ST77*
**INN Compass** ☎Badminton 242 11hc CTV 160P ▥ B&b£14–£18 sn L£2–£3.75 D10pm£2.50–£4&alc

**TORPOINT** Cornwall *Map 2 SX45*
**GH Elms Private Hotel** 16 St James Rd ☎Plymouth 812612 Lic 7rm 6hc (4fb) CTV 4P ▥ S% B&bfr£8.05 Bdifr£12.65 Wfr£85 D9pm

**TORQUAY** Devon *Map 3 SX96* **(See Central & District plans)**
**GH Braddon Hall Hotel** Braddons Hill Rd East ☎23908 Central plan: **1** Lic 13hc 1🛁 (5fb) CTV 10P 1⛟ ▥ S% B&b£6–£9.50 Bdi£7.50–£11.50 W£49–£79 ⊾ D7pm

**GH Brandize Hotel** Avenue Rd ☎27798 Central plan: **2** Etr–Sep 12hc (4fb) CTV 12P S% ✱B&b£6–£6.50 Bdifr£8.72 D6pm

**GH Brookesby Hall Hotel** Hesketh Rd ☎22194 Central plan: **3** 12hc (3fb) CTV ▥ sea S% B&b£6.90–£8.63 Bdi£12–£13.80 W£73.60–£82.80 ⊾ D4.30pm

**GH *Burley Court Hotel*** Wheatridge Ln, Livermead ☎607879 District plan: **44** Apr–Sep Lic 22hc 10🛁 🚿 ✱ CTV 30P sea

**GH Carn Brea** 21 Avenue Rd ☎22002 Central plan: **4** Closed Etr Lic 22rm 21hc 3🚿 (5fb) CTV 14P 1⛟ S% B&b£8.22–£9.48 Bdi£13.15–£15.10 D7pm

⊢⊣ **GH Casey's Court Motel** 127 Newton Rd ☎63909 District plan: **45** Apr–Oct 6hc (2fb) ✱ nc2 TV in some bedrooms S% B&b£4.75–£6

**GH Castle Mount Hotel** 7 Castle Rd ☎22130 Central plan: **5** Feb–Nov 9hc nc7 CTV 6P S% B&bfr£6.90 Bdifr£10.35 Wfr£59.80 ⊾ D6pm

**GH *Castleton Private Hotel*** Castle Rd ☎24976 Central plan: **6** 17 Mar–Dec 13hc ✱ nc3 CTV 7P ▥ sea D5pm

**GH Chelston House Hotel** Chelston Rd ☎605200 Central plan: **7** Etr–Sep Lic 18hc (3fb) CTV 18P ▥ sea S% B&b£7.50–£9.50 Bdi£10.50–£13 W£71.50–£90 ⊾ D5.30pm

**GH Clevedon Private Hotel** Meadfoot Sea
Rd ☎24260 District plan:**46** Lic 16hc (4fb)
nc5 CTV 10P B&b£8.75–£9.75 Bdi£13–
£14.25 W£91–£99.75 ⱠD7.30pm

⊨⊣ **GH Clovelly Hotel** 89 Avenue Rd
☎22286 Central plan:**8** Lic 12hc (6fb) ⊁ Ch
CTV 7P ⊯ S% B&b£5–£6.50 Bdi£8–£10.50
W£48–£70 ⱠD5.30pm

**GH Hotel Concorde** 26 Newton Rd ☎22330
Central plan:**9** Lic 16hc 2⋔ (8fb) CTV 17P
S% B&b£6.50–£9.20 Bdi£10–
£12.70 D6pm

⊨⊣ **GH Craig Court Hotel** 10 Ash Hill Rd,
Castle Circus ☎24400 Central plan:**10** Mar–
Oct Lic 10hc 2⋔ (3fb) ⊁ Ch CTV 8P sea S%
B&b£5.50–£8 Bdi£8–£10.50 W£51.75–
£81.50 D5pm (W only Jul–Aug)

**GH Devon Court Hotel** Croft Rd ☎23603
Central plan:**11** Apr–Oct Lic 15hc 1⇔ 2⋔
(3fb) ⊁CTV 14P ⊯ S% B&b£10.50–£14.50
Bdi£12.50–£17.50 W£80–£110 Ⱡ

**GH Elm Court** Cary Av, Babbacombe
☎37828 District plan:**47** Etr–Nov Lic 16hc
2⋔ (4fb) nc4 CTV 12P ⊯ S% B&b£6–£8
Bdi£7.50–£11.50 W£54–£78 ⱠD6pm

**GH Exmouth View Hotel** Bedford Rd,
Babbacombe Downs ☎37307 District
plan:**48** Etr–Sep Lic 18hc 4⋔ (4fb) CTV 12P
sea S% ✱B&b£8.50–£10.46 Bdi£11.39–
£13.34 W£79.35–£93.15 ⱠD5.30pm

**GH Fluela Hotel** 17 Hatfield Rd ☎27512
Central plan:**12** Mar–Dec Lic 12hc 9⋔ (3fb)
⊁CTV 16P ⊯ S% B&b£7–£8 Bdi£10.50–
£13.20 W£73–£92 D7pm

⊨⊣ **GH Forest Hotel** Haldon Rd ☎24842
District plan:**49** Etr & mid May–mid Oct Lic
34hc 12⇔ (7fb) CTV 20P B&b£5.75–£11.50

Bdi£8.50–£13.50 W£57.50–£103.50 Ⱡ
D7.30pm

**GH Fretherne Hotel** St Lukes Rd South
☎22594 Central plan:**13** Etr–Sep Lic 24hc
(7fb) CTV 24P sea S% ✱B&b£6.90–£8.05
Bdi£10.35–£10.92 Wfr£82.80 Ⱡ D6pm

**GH** *Glendon Hotel* St Marychurch Rd
☎23117 Central plan:**14** Lic 12hc 6⇔ ⋔ (5fb)
⊁CTV 14P sea

**GH Glenorleigh Hotel** 26 Cleveland Rd
☎22135 Central plan:**15** Xmas & Mar–Oct
Lic 16hc 3⋔ (6fb) CTV 12P S% B&b£6.90–
£10.35 Bdi£11.50–£13.80 W£57.50–£92 Ⱡ
D6pm

**GH Hatherleigh Hotel** 56 St Marychurch Rd
☎25762 Central plan:**16** Apr–Sep Lic 19hc
(4fb) CTV 18P S% B&b£8–£11.50 Bdi£10–£13
W£60–£80 Ⱡ

**GH Holly House Hotel** York Rd,
Babbacombe ☎311333 District plan:**50**
Apr–Oct Lic 13hc 1⋔ (3fb) CTV 10P 2⋧ ⊯
S% ✱B&b£6.50 Bdi£8–£10 W£55–£70
Ⱡ Dnoon

**GH** *Ilsham Valley* Ilsham Marine Dr
☎22075 District plan:**51** Mar–Oct rsFeb Lic
19hc (A 3hc) CTV 20P D6pm

**GH Ingoldsby Hotel** 1 Chelston Rd
☎607497 Central plan:**17** Mar–Oct Lic 16hc
(7fb) CTV 16P ⊯ sea S% B&b£8–£12.65
Bdi£11–£15 W£57.50–£88.55 D5.30pm

**GH Kilworthy Hotel** Westhill Rd,
Babbacombe ☎37236 District plan:**52** Apr–
Sep Lic 14hc 2⇔ (4fb) Ch CTV 10P S%
B&b£6–£7.50 Bdi£8.50–£11
W£58–£80 D5pm

**GH Lindum Hotel** Abbey Rd ☎22795
Central plan:**18** Mar–Oct 21hc 6⋔ (3fb) CTV

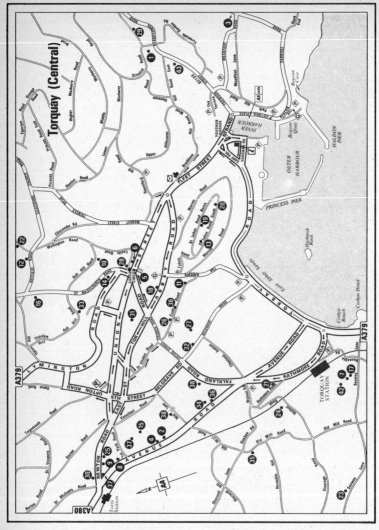

Torquay (Central)

1  Braddon Hall Hotel
2  Brandize Hotel
3  Brookesby Hall
4  Carn Brea
5  Castle Mount
6  Castleton Private Hotel
7  Chelston House Hotel
8  Clovelly Hotel
9  Hotel Concorde
10  Craig Court Hotel
11  Devon Court Hotel

12  Fluela Hotel
13  Fretherno Hotel
14  Glendon Hotel
15  Glenorleigh Hotel
16  Hatherleigh Hotel
17  Ingoldsby
18  Lindum Hotel
19  Mapleton Hotel
20  Mount Nessing Hotel
21  Normanhurst Hotel
22  Pencarrow Hotel
23  Rawlyn House Hotel

24  Red House Hotel
25  Richwood Hotel
26  Riva Lodge
27  Rothesay Hotel
28  St Bernard's Private Hotel
29  Sea Point Hotel
30  Silverlands Hotel
31  Skerries Private Hotel
32  Southbank Hotel
33  Stephen House Hotel
34  Sun Court Private Hotel

35  Torbay Rise Hotel
36  Torcroft Hotel
37  Tormohun Hotel
38  Trafalgar House Hotel
39  Tregantle Hotel
40  Tregenna Hotel
41  Westgate Hotel
42  Westowe Hotel
43  Four Seasons Hotel (Inn)

15P ▥ S% B&b£7–£9 Bdi£9.20–£13 W£64.50–£91 ⌧ D6pm

**GH Mapleton Hotel** St Luke's Rd North ☎22389 Central plan:**19** Apr–Oct Lic 9hc (3fb) ✹ CTV 8P sea S% B&b£7.50–£11 Bdi£10–£14 W£62–£84 ⌧ D5pm

**GH Mount Nessing Hotel** St Luke's Rd North ☎22970 Central plan:**20** Xmas & Etr–Oct Lic 14hc (6fb) CTV 12P sea S% B&b£7.50–£10 Bdi£10.75–£13.75 W£65–£88 ⌧ D4.30pm

**GH Normanhurst Hotel** Rathmore Rd ☎22420 Central plan:**21** Etr–mid Oct Lic 14hc (6fb) CTV 8P ✱ B&b£6.50–£7.50 Bdi£8.50–£11.25 W£66.12–£79 D4pm

**GH Overdale Hotel** Great Hill, Barton ☎311280 District plan:**53** mid Apr–mid Oct Lic 10hc (3fb) CTV 16P 2🏖 sea S%

B&b£7.50–£9 Bdi£10–£12 W£50–£80 ⌧

**GH Pembroke Hotel** Meadfoot Sea Rd ☎22837 District plan:**54** Apr–Nov Lic 19hc 2🛏 (6fb) ✹ CTV 12P 3🏖 B&b£6.50–£12.50 Bdi£10.50–£16.50 W£58–£92 ⌧ D6pm

**⋈ GH Pencarrow Hotel** 64 Windsor Rd ☎23080 Central plan:**22** May–9 Oct Lic 13hc 4🛏 (2fb) CTV 8P S% B&b£5.50–£6.50 Bdi£7.50–£9 W£58–£68 ⌧ (W only Jul–Aug)

**GH Pines Hotel** St Marychurch Rd ☎38384 District plan:**55** Apr–Oct Lic 22hc 1⇔ (6fb) Ⓒⱨ CTV 20P S% B&b£6.33–£9.78 Bdi£8.62–£11.10 W£60.34–£77.70 ⌧ D5pm

**GH Rawlyn House Hotel** Rawlyn Rd, Chelston ☎605208 Central plan:**23** Lic 15hc 5🛏 (A 4hc) (5fb) ✹ Ⓒⱨ CTV 15P S% B&bfr£6.50 Bdi fr£9.30 Wfr£66 ⌧ D6.45pm

---

# MAPLETON HOTEL, TORQUAY
### St Luke's Road North.     Tel. 0803 22389

A fine detached private hotel offering first class food, service and accommodation. Centrally situated in a quiet, elevated position with open views from most bedrooms.

Ample free parking space in own grounds.

**Take advantage of specially attractive terms for a relaxing early or late season holiday in southern Devon.**

**BB & EM from £59.00 per week (inc VAT)**

RESIDENTIAL AND RESTAURANT LICENCE

Colour brochure with pleasure from resident proprietors Mr and Mrs D J Banks.

---

# Mount Nessing Hotel

**St Lukes Road, North Torquay, TQ2 5PD.**
**Telephone: 0803 22970**

A small, friendly hotel standing on Waldon Hill in quiet position facing south with panoramic views over the bay and town. Steps from hotel to promenade and town (approx 600 yds). Bar, TV and sun lounges. Car park.

Resident proprietors (7 years) have a reputation for good food and service as well as comfort. Inspection of kitchen welcomed. No service charge. Summer bus service. Fire Certificate granted. OPEN CHRISTMAS:

---

# PENCARROW HOTEL
### 64 WINDSOR ROAD, TORQUAY.

Mr & Mrs Templeman are often complimented on the excellence of the food and the cleanliness of the hotel. Conveniently situated for town centre, beaches and all places of interest. All rooms have teasmades, most have showers. Near tennis courts, bowls, swimming pool. Free car park at rear. Sun-trap patios in front. Our terms are very moderate.
**Send for brochure or telephone: Torquay (0803) 23080.**

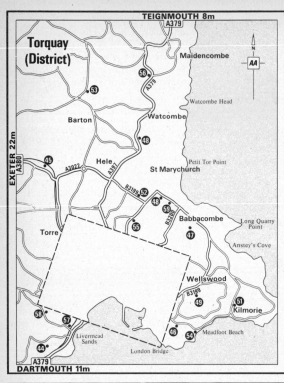

44 Burley Court Hotel
45 Casey's Court
46 Clevedon Private Hotel
47 Elm Court
48 Exmouth View Hotel
49 Forest Hotel
50 Holly House Hotel
51 Ilsham Valley
52 Kilworthy Hotel
53 Overdale Hotel
54 Pembroke Hotel
55 Pines Hotel
56 Rosewood
57 Sunleigh Hotel
58 Villa Marina Hotel
59 Watcombe View Hotel

**GH Red House Hotel** Rousdown Rd
☎605687 Central plan:**24** Apr–Oct Lic 12hc
2♒ (5fb) ❀ CTV 12P ▥ sea S% B&b£6–£8.50
Bdi£8.60–£11.50 W£60–£79.50 ⅃ D10am

**GH Richwood Hotel** 20 Newton Rd
☎23729 Central plan:**25** Apr–Oct Lic 23hc
(6fb) CTV 12P S% ✳B&b£5.75–£8.62
Bdi£8.05–£11.25 W£56.35–£78.77 ⅃ D5pm

**GH** *Riva Lodge* Croft Rd ☎22614 Central
plan:**26** Mar–Oct Lic 18hc 7❤ ♒ (5fb) ❀
nc10 CTV 18P

**GH Rosewood** Teignmouth Rd,
Maidencombe ☎38178 District plan:**56** 8hc
1♒ (3fb) ❀ nc12 CTV 14P ▥ sea S% B&b£6–
£8 Bdi£9.50–£10.50 W£39.90–£53.20 Ⓜ
D4.30pm

**GH Rothesay Hotel** Scarborough Rd
☎23161 Central plan:**27** Apr–Oct Lic 18hc

(7fb) ❀ Ⓒₕ CTV 12P B&b£6.80–£11 Bdi£10–
£14 W£68–£97 ⅃ D3pm

**GH St Bernards Private Hotel** Castle Rd
☎22508 Central plan:**28** Lic 13hc 3♒ (3fb)
Ⓒₕ CTV 8P ▥ sea S% B&b£7.50–£10.06
Bdi£12–£14 W£74.45–£85.25 ⅃

**GH Sea Point Hotel** 5 Clifton Gr ☎28012
Central plan:**29** Lic 8hc (3fb) CTV 2P S%
✳B&b£5–£7 Bdi£7–£9 W£42–£65 ⅃
(W 18 Jul–8 Aug)

**GH Silverlands Hotel** 27 Newton Rd
☎22013 Central plan:**30** Closed Xmas 12hc
(1fb) nc2 CTV 12P ▥ S% ✳B&b£5–£6

 **GH Skerries Private Hotel** 25 Morgan
Av ☎23618 Central plan:**31** 13hc (3fb) CTV
8P ▥ S% B&b£5.50–£7.50 Bdi£7.50–£9.25
W£49–£65 ⅃ D6pm
(W only 20 Jul–20 Aug)

**GH Southbank Hotel** 15/17 Belgrave Rd
☎26701 Central plan:**32** Mar–Dec Lic 20hc
(6fb) ⚲ CTV 14P S% B&b£7.50–£10 Bdi£10–
£14 W£68–£98 ⓛ D6pm (W only Jul–Aug)

⋈⋈ **GH Stephen House Hotel** 50 Ash Mill
Rd ☎25796 Central plan:**33** Apr–Oct &
Xmas Lic 11hc (5fb) CTV 11P sea S%
B&b£5–£7.50–£15 W£45–£90 ⓛ
D5pm (W only mid Jul–mid Aug)

⋈⋈ **GH Sun Court Private Hotel**
Rowdens Rd ☎27242 Central plan:**34** mid
Mar–Oct 11hc (2fb) CTV 12P S% B&b£5–£7
Bdi£7.50–£10.50 W£60–£75 D6pm

**GH Sunleigh Hotel** Livermead Hill
☎607137 District plan:**57** Etr–last wknd Sep
Lic 19hc 10ⓕ (4fb) ⚲ CTV 17P ⬛ sea S%
B&b£8.25–£9 Bdi£10.70–£14.75 W£58.32–
£84.78 ⓛ

**GH Torbay Rise** Old Mill Rd ☎605541
Central plan:**35** Etr & May–Oct Lic 16hc (5fb)
⚲ CTV 10P sea S% ✳B&b£6.90–£10
Bdi£10.40–£13.50 W£59–£87.40 ⓛ D6.30pm
(W only last wk Jul & 1st 2wks Aug)

**GH Torcroft Hotel** Croft Rd ☎28292 Central
plan:**36** Apr–Sep Lic 22hc 6ⓕ (4fb) CTV 22P
sea B&b£6–£11 Bdi£8.50–£13.50 W£65–£90 ⓛ
D6.45pm

**GH Tormohun Hotel** 28 Newton Rd
☎23681 Central plan:**37** Lic 24hc 13⊟ 6ⓕ
(12fb) CTV 26P ⬛ S% B&b£6.90–£12.20
Bdi£11–£14 D7.30pm (W only Jul–Sep)

**GH Trafalgar House Hotel** Bridge Rd
☎22486 Central plan:**38** Lic 11hc 1ⓕ (2fb)
CTV 9P B&b£7.25–£10 Bdi£10.50–£13.25
W£64–£86 ⓛ D6.45pm

**GH Tregantle Hotel** 64 Bampfylde Rd
☎27494 Central plan:**39** Lic 11hc (2fb) ⒸⒽ
CTV 11P ⬛ S% B&b£6–£8 Bdi£8–£12 W£50–
£80 ⓛ D7pm

**GH Tregenna Hotel** 20 Cleveland Rd
☎23578 Central plan:**40** Closed Xmas Lic
11hc (3fb) CTV 10P S% B&b£6.50–£8.50
Bdi£9.50–£12 W£57–£72 ⓛ D5pm

**GH Villa Marina Hotel** Cockington Ln,
Livermead ☎605440 District Plan:**58** May–
.Oct 26hc 18⊟ 1ⓕ (4fb) CTV 26P ⬛ sea S%
✳B&b£6.50–£9.50 Bdi£9–£12 W£61–£84 ⓛ
D6.15pm

**GH Watcombe View Hotel** St Albans Rd,
Babbacombe ☎39967 District plan **56** Etr–
Sep Lic 18hc 5⊟ⓕ (3fb) ⚲ CTV 10P ⬛ sea

**GH Westgate Hotel** Falkland Rd ☎25350
Central plan:**41** Etr–mid Oct Lic 14hc (6fb)
ⒸⒽ CTV 12P S% B&b£6–£8.50 Bdi£8.25–
£11.50 W£57–£80 ⓛ D6.30pm (W only 18 Jul–
5 Aug)

**GH Westowe Hotel** Chelston Rd ☎605207
Central plan:**42** Mar–Oct Lic 13hc (1fb) ⚲
nc5 CTV 8P ⬛ sea S% B&b£7.56–£8.69
Bdi£9.56–£10.69 W£52.92–£74.83 ⓛ

**INN Four Seasons Hotel** 547 Babbacombe
Rd ☎25292 Central plan:**43** Lic 34hc ⚲ TV
10P

**TORRINGTON, GREAT** Devon Map 2 SS41
**GH Smytham** ☎2110 rsNov–Apr Lic 12hc
(2fb) CTV 12P S% B&b£6.50 Bdi£10 D4pm

**TOTLAND BAY** Isle of Wight Map 4 SZ38
**GH Garrow Hotel** Church Hill ☎Freshwater
753174 Apr–Sep Lic 18hc 4ⓕ (7fb) nc3 CTV
18P ⬛ sea B&b£8.25–£9.25 Bdi£11–£13
W£73.50–£83.50 ⓛ D7pm

**GH Hermitage Hotel** Cliff Rd ☎Freshwater
2518 Apr–Oct Lic 12hc (2fb) ⒸⒽ CTV 12P
D7pm

**GH Lismore Private Hotel** 23 The Avenue
☎Freshwater 752025 Lic 8hc (4fb) ⚲ nc3
CTV 8P S% B&bfr£7 Bdi fr£10.50 Wfr£63 ⓛ
Dnoon

**GH Randolph Private Hotel** Granville Rd
☎Freshwater 2411 May–Sep 8hc (2fb) CTV
6P ⬛ D6.50pm

**GH Sandy Lane** Colwell Common Rd,
Colwell Bay ☎Freshwater 753330 Lic 9hc
(6fb) CTV 5P sea S% B&b£7.30–£7.77
Bdi£10.30–£10.55 W£65.69–£69.34 ⓛ
D6.30pm

**TOTTENHILL** Norfolk Map 9 TF61
**GH Oakwood House Private Hotel** ☎Kings
Lynn 810256 Closed 24–26 Dec Lic 9hc (3fb)
CTV in all bedrooms 20P S% B&b£11.25
Bdi fr£17.25 W£70.90 Ⓜ D6.30pm

**TOWCESTER** Northants Map 4 SP64
**INN Brave Old Oak** Watling St ☎50533 Lic
9hc 1⊟ ⓕ CTV 10P D6.30pm

**TREARDDUR BAY** Gwynedd Map 6 SH27
**GH Fairway Private Hotel** ☎860255 Lic
7hc (2fb) ⚲ CTV 7P ⬛ sea S% B&bfr£9.20
Bdi fr£12.65 Wfr£80.50 ⓛ (W only Jul–Aug)

**GH High Ground** Lon Penrhyn Garw,
Ravenspoint Rd ☎860078 8rm 7hc (3fb) ⒸⒽ
CTV 10P 2☎ ⬛ sea S% B&b£7 Bdi£11
Wfr£77 ⓛ D7pm (W only Aug)

**GH Towyn Capel Hotel** ☎860227 Lic 8hc
1⊟ (3fb) CTV P ⬛ B&b£8.63 Bdi£14.38
W£96.60 ⓛ D am

**TREBARWITH** Cornwall Map 2 SX08
**INN Mill House** ☎Tintagel 200 Closed Xmas
wk 5hc 2⊟ 3ⓕ nc6 CTV in all bedrooms 60P

▥ ✳B&bf£9.20–£12.19 Bdi£14.45–£17.44
Bar lunch50p–£3.50 D9.30pmf£8.50alc

**TREGARON** Dyfed *Map 3 SN65*
**GH Aberdwr** Abergwesyn Rd ☎255 Apr–
Sep 7hc (1fb) TV 20P river S% B&bf£7 Bdi£11
Wfrf£77 ⅃

**TREGONY** *(Nr Truro)* Cornwall *Map 2 SW94*
**GH Tregony House** 15 Fore St ☎671 Lic
6hc ✶nc6 CTV 6P S% B&bf£8.50–£10 Bdi£13–
£15 Wf£85–£99 ⅃

**TRESILLIAN** Cornwall *Map 2 SW84*
**GH Manor Cottage** ☎212 Apr–Oct Lic 7hc
(1fb) nc4 CTV 10P ▥ S% B&bf£7.50–£9.25
Wf£50–£55 Ⓜ

**TRETOWER** Powys *Map 3 SO12*
**INN Tretower Court** ☎Bwlch 730204 4hc
✶100P ▥ S% B&bfr£7.50 sn L£1–£2.60
D9.30pmf£8alc

**TREVONE** Cornwall *Map 2 SW87*
**GH Bowen House Hotel** ☎Padstow
520389 Etr–Sep Lic 15hc (3fb) nc4 CTV 16P
sea S% B&bf£8 Bdi£8–£10 Wf£48–£63 ⅃
D4.30pm

**GH Coimbatore Hotel** ☎Padstow 520390
May–Sep Lic 11hc (3fb) ✶ CTV 6P 6🅰 sea
S% ✳B&bf£7 Bdi£9.50 Wf£57.50–£62.79 ⅃
D6.30pm (W only Jul & Aug)

⤝⤞ **GH Green Waves Private Hotel**
☎Padstow 520114 Closed Xmas Lic 16hc (A
7hc) (8fb) nc2 CTV 16P 6🅰 sea S% B&bf£5–£6
Bdi£10 Wf£65–£70 ⅃ D6pm

**GH Newlands Hotel** ☎Padstow 520469
May–Sep Lic 12hc 1⋔ (2fb) nc4 CTV 15P

✳B&bf£8.05 Bdi£10.35–£12.65 Wf£61.10–
£78.20 ⅃ D6.30pm (W only Jun–Aug)

**GH** *Sea Spray Hotel* Trevone Bay
☎Padstow 520491 Mar–Nov Lic 6➛ ⋔ (3fb)
nc3 CTV 8P sea

**TREWARMETT** Cornwall *Map 2 SX08*
**GH Trevervan Hotel** ☎Tintagel 486 (due to
change to Camelford 770486) Lic 6hc (4fb)
CTV 10P sea S% B&bf£8.65–£9.20
Bdi£11.50–£12.65 Wf£69–£75.90 ⅃ D8pm

**TRINITY** Jersey, Channel Islands *Map 16*
**GH Highfield Country Hotel** Route du
Ebenezer ☎Jersey 62194 Lic 25hc 14➛
(4fb) Ⓒⓗ CTV 24P 1🅰 sea S% B&bf£12–
£16.35 Bdi£12.50–£16.85 (W only Oct–Apr)

**TRURO** Cornwall *Map 2 SW84*
**GH Colthrop** Tregolls Rd ☎2920 7rm 6hc
(3fb) nc7 CTV 8P ▥ S% B&bf£6–£8 Bdi£9–
£11 Wf£63–£70 ⅃ D6pm

**GH Farley Hotel** Falmouth Rd ☎3680 23hc
(4fb) CTV 18P 1🅰 ▥ S% ✳B&bf£9.15
Bdi£12.99 D6.30pm

**INN Globe** Frances St ☎3869 Closed Xmas
4hc ✶nc12 CTV 4P S% B&bf£7–£8 Bdi£10–
£11 Wf£60–£70 ⅃ Bar lunch 50p–£1.50

**TUNBRIDGE WELLS (ROYAL)** Kent *Map 5
TQ53*
**GH The Guest House** 89 Frant Rd ☎25596
18 Jan–19 Dec 10rm 5➛ 5⋔ (2fb) ✶CTV
12P ▥ S% B&bfr£10

**GH Marlborough Hotel** 57 Mount Ephraim
☎21328 Lic 25hc 7➛ ⋔ (5fb) CTV 7P ▥
B&bf£12.50–£13.50 Bdi£16.50–£17.50
Wf£85.95 D7.45pm

**TURVEY** Beds *Map 4 SP95*
**INN Three Cranes** ☎305 rs Xmas 3hc
🚗 ⅋ nc14 20P S% B&b£10.92–£12.65
Bdi£14–£20 W£69.50–£81.50 ⋈ sn L£3.50alc
D9.30pm£5.50alc

**TWO BRIDGES** Devon *Map 2 SX67*
**GH Cherrybrook Hotel** ☎Tavistock 88260
Closed Xmas & New Year Lic 8hc 1⇌ 4🛏
(1fb) 15P 🎱 S% ✳ B&b£9.25 Bdi£14.25 W£96
⅃ D7.30pm

**TYWARDREATH** Cornwall *Map 2 SX05*
⋈⅃ **GH Elmswood** Tehidy Rd,
Tywardreath Pk ☎Par 4221 Lic 7hc (3fb) CTV
P S% ✳ B&b£6 Bdi£8 D6.30pm

**TYWYN** Gwynedd *Map 6 SH50*
**GH Greenfield Private Hotel** High St
☎710354 Feb–Nov Lic 14hc (3fb) ⅋ CTV 1P
B&b£7.25–£8.25 Bdi£10.25–£11.25
W£69.50–£76 ⅃ D8.30pm

**GH Min-y-Mor** Marine Pde ☎710139 Lic
6hc 2🛏 (4fb) ⅋ CTV sea B&b£9 Bdi£12.75
W£83 ⋈ D9pm

**GH Monfa** Pier Rd ☎710858 rsNov–Feb 8hc
4🛏 (3fb) ⅋ CTV 2P 🎱 sea S% ✳ B&bfr£6.50
Bdifr£10 Wfr£67.50 ⅃ D5pm

**UPLYME** Devon *Map 3 SY39*
**INN Black Dog Hotel** Lyme Rd ☎Lyme
Regis 2634 Mar–Oct 6hc 🚗 CTV 19P S%
✳ B&b£8.50 W£52.50 ⋈ sn L£1.50alc
D9.30pm£1.50alc

**VENN OTTERY** Devon *Map 3 SY09*
**GH Venn Ottery Barton** ☎Ottery St Mary
2733 Mar–Oct Lic 13hc 4⇌ 1🛏 (4fb) CTV
14P 🎱 B&b£10–£11.50 Bdi£12–£13.50
W£77–£85 ⅃ D7pm

**VENTNOR** Isle of Wight *Map 4 SZ57*
**GH Channel View Hotel** Hambrough Rd
☎852230 Apr–Nov 14hc CTV 6P sea S%
B&b£10.35–£12 Bdi£12.50–£13.35
W£76–£87 ⅃ D6.30pm

**GH Delamere** Bellevue Rd ☎852322 Apr–
Sep 8hc (4fb) CTV 8P sea S% B&b£6–£7.50
Bdi£7.50–£9 W£48–£60 ⅃ D3pm

**GH *Macrocarpa*** Mitchell Ave ☎852428 Etr–
Oct & Xmas Lic 20hc 11⇌ 🛏 (A 3hc) (8fb) 🆑
CTV 20P sea D7.30pm

**GH Picardie Hotel** Esplanade ☎852647
Apr–Oct Lic 15hc (4fb) ⅋ CTV sea S%
B&b£7.50–£9 Bdi£9.50–£10.30
W£66.50–£70 ⅃ D6pm

**GH Richmond Private Hotel** Esplanade
☎852496 Apr–Oct Lic 12hc 4🛏 (2fb) CTV 6P
sea S% ✳ B&b£8–£10 Bdi£11.50–£14 W£70–
£72 ⅃ D6pm

**GH St Maur Hotel** Castle Rd ☎852570 Lic
16hc (8fb) ⅋ nc2 CTV 12P 🎱 sea S% B&b£7–
£8.50 Bdi£10–£11.50 W£67–£73.50 ⅃
D6.45pm

**GH Under Rock Hotel** Shore Rd, Bonchurch
(1m E) ☎852714 Mar–Sep Lic 7hc ⅋ nc10
CTV 12P 🎱 S% B&b£9 Bdi£13 W£91 ⅃
D6.30pm

**WADHURST** E Sussex *Map 5 TQ63*
**INN *Fourkeys*** Station Rd ☎2252 Lic 8hc
CTV 25P 🎱 D11pm

**WALLASEY** Merseyside *Map 7 SJ29*
**GH Divonne Private Hotel** 71 Wellington
Rd, New Brighton ☎051-639 4727 Closed
Xmas & New Year Lic 15hc 5🛏 (2fb) CTV
10P 🎱 B&b£8.05–£9.20 Bdi£12.08–£13.23
D7pm

**GH Sandpiper Private Hotel** 22 Dudley Rd,
New Brighton ☎051-639 7870 6hc (1fb) ✻
[Ch] CTV 6P ⬛ S% B&b£7–£8 Bdi£10–£12
W£63–£75.60 ⅃ D4pm

**WALL HEATH** W Midlands *Map 7 SO88*
**INN Prince Albert Hotel** High St
☎Kingswinford 287411 5hc ⬛ CTV 40P ⬛
S% ✻ B&b£7 Bar lunch £1.25&alc

**WALTON-ON-THE-NAZE** Essex *Map 5
TM22*
**GH** *Blenheim House Hotel* 39 Kirby Rd
☎Frinton-on-Sea 5548 Closed Xmas Lic 7hc
1⇨ 🛏 ✻ TV 16P

**WANSFORD** Cambs *Map 3 TL09*
**INN Cross Keys** ☎Stamford 782266 3🛏 (A
3🛏) ✻ nc7 TV in all bedrooms P ⬛ S%
✻ B&b£18 Bar lunch£1.25–£3.75
D9.30pm£3.75–£7.50

**WAREHAM** Dorset *Map 3 SY98*
**GH Kemps Country House Hotel** East
Stoke (2m W on A352) ☎Bindon Abbey
462563 Mar–Jan Lic 6hc (A2⇨) (3fb) ✻ [Ch]
CTV 15P ⬛ ✻ B&b£10.35–£12 Bdi£13.80–
£16.10 W£80.50–£103.50 ⅃ D8pm

**WARWICK** Warwicks *Map 4 SP26*
⊢⊣ **GH Avon** 7 Emscote Rd ☎491367
Closed Xmas day 7hc (4fb) ✻ CTV 6P 1⚗ ⬛
S% B&b£5.50–£6

**GH Cambridge Villa** 20A Emscote Rd
☎491169 10hc (3fb) ✻ CTV 10P ⬛ S%
B&b£6

**GH Guy's Cross Hotel** 122 Coventry Rd
☎491208 Lic 10hc (3fb) CTV 6P ⬛ S%
B&b£8 Bdi£11 D6pm

**INN Wheatsheaf Hotel** 54 West St ☎42817
6hc CTV 14P ⬛ S% B&b£14 Bdi£20 sn L£6alc
D9.30pm

**WASHFORD** Somerset *Map 3 ST04*
**GH Washford House** ☎484 6rm 5hc 1⇨
(2fb) ✻ CTV 10P ⬛ ✻ B&b£5.50–£6.50
Bdi£9–£9.50 D4pm

**WATERLOO** Isle of Skye, Highland
*Inverness-shire Map 13 NG62*
**GH Ceol-na-Mara** ☎Kyle 323 Etr–Sep 6hc
(1fb) TV 6P sea S% ✻ B&b£5.50 Bdi£10 W£70
⅃ D9pm

**WATERLOOVILLE** Hants *Map 4 SU60*
**GH Far End Private Hotel** 31 Queens Rd
☎3242 Closed Xmas wk Lic 10hc 1⇨ 1🛏
(3fb) [Ch] CTV 20P 4⚗ ⬛ S% B&b£14.95–
£17.25 Bdi£19–£22 W£105–£115 ⅃ D4pm

**WATERMILLOCK** Cumbria *Map 12 NY42*
**GH Knotts Mill Country House** ☎Pooley
Bridge 472 Apr–Oct Lic 5hc (2fb) ✻ TV 15P ⬛
lake B&b£7 D6pm

**WATERROW** Somerset *Map 3 ST02*
**INN Rock** ☎Wiveliscombe 23293 7rm 2hc
5⇨ CTV 12P ⬛ S% B&b£10.50 Bdi£15.50
W£105 ⅃ D9.15pm
**See advert on page 220**

**WATFORD** Herts *Map 4 TQ19*
**GH White House Hotel** 26–29 Upton Rd
☎37316 Lic 38hc 12⇨ 21🛏 (A 28hc 14⇨
6🛏( (7fb) CTV 32P ⬛ �givechair S% ✻ B&b£9.50–
£21.50 Bdi£14.95–£26.95 W£95.15–£167.15 ⅃
D8.30pm
**See advert on page 220**

**WEEK ST MARY** Cornwall *Map 2 SX29*
⊢✕⊣ **GH Lambley Park** ☎368 Apr–Oct Lic
6hc 1🛉 (2fb) CTV 7P sea S% B&b£4.50–£6
Bdi£9–£10.50 W£58.50–£70 ↓ Dnoon

**WELLINGTON** Somerset *Map 3 ST12*
**GH *Blue Mantle Hotel*** 2 Mantle St ☎2000
Lic 9rm 8hc (3fb) ✻ CTV ▥ D7.30pm

**WELLS** Somerset *Map 3 ST54*
**GH Bekynton House** 7 St Thomas St
☎72222 10hc 2🛉 (2fb) CTV 6P B&b£6–£7.50
Bdi£9.50–£12 Dnoon

**GH Tor** 20 Tor St ☎72322 8hc (6fb) CTV 10P
S% B&b£7.25–£7.90 Bdi£11.20–£12.50 D5pm

**WELLS-NEXT-THE-SEA** Norfolk *Map 9
TF94*
**GH Arch House** 50 Mill Rd ☎Fakenham
710696 Mar–Oct Lic 5hc (1fb) TV 5P ▥ B&b£7–

£7.50 Bdi£12–£12.50 W£79–£82.50 ↓ Dnoon

**WEST CHARLETON** Devon *Map 3 SX74*
**INN Ashburton Arms** ☎Frogmore 242
Closed 2nd & 3rd wk Oct & Xmas wk 5hc ✻
nc7 CTV 20P ▥ sea B&b£8.63–£9.20
W£56.35–£60.38 Ⅿ Bar lunch42p–£4 D9.45pm

**WESTCLIFF-ON-SEA** Essex **See
Southend-on-Sea**

**WESTGATE-ON-SEA** Kent *Map 5 TR36*
**GH Edgewater Private Hotel** 99 Sea Rd
☎Thanet 31933 Lic 9hc (4fb) ✻ CTV 6P ▥
sea S% ✱ B&b£7.50–£8.50 Bdi£10–£11
Wfr£59 ↓ D8pm

**WEST LINTON** Borders *Peebleshire Map 11
NT15*
**GH *Rutherford Coaching House*** ☎231 6hc
(2fb) CTV 12P 1🏠 ▥ D9pm

**WEST LULWORTH** Dorset **See Lulworth**

**WESTON-SUPER-MARE** Avon *Map 3 ST36*
**(See Plan)**
**GH Beachlands Hotel** 17 Uphill Rd North
☎21401 Plan:**1** Closed Xmas & Jan–Feb Lic
20hc 4⇔ 1🏠 (6fb) CTV 12P 2🅰 🎨 sea
✳B&b£9.48–£10.35 Bdi£13.51–£14.38
W£77.91–£81.93 ⅃ D7pm

⊢⊣ **GH Fourways** 2 Ashcombe Rd
☎23827 Plan:**2** Apr–Oct rsOct–Apr (Mon–
Fri only) 6hc (A 3hc) (1fb) ✶ nc9 TV 8P 🎨 S%
B&b£5–£6.50 Bdi£8–£9.50 W£49–£56 ⅃
D6.30pm

**GH Glenelg** 24 Ellenborough Pk South
☎20521 Plan:**3** Apr–Nov Lic 15hc (3fb) CTV
14P 🎨 B&b£7.50–£8.50 Bdi£9.50–£10.50
W£54–£65 ⅃ D5pm

**GH Inwood Hotel** 59 South Rd ☎29756

Plan:**4** Lic 16hc 2⇔ (A 2⇔) (7fb) CTV 14P
sea S% B&b£7.50–£8.50 Bdi£8.50–£9.75
W£59–£68 ⅃ D6.30pm

**GH Kew Dee** 6 Neva Rd ☎29041 Plan:**5**
Tem 6hc (2fb) CTV 6P 🎨 S% ✳B&b£4.50–
£5.50 Bdi£6.50–£7.50 D4pm

**GH** *Lockaine* 45 Locking Rd ☎29906 Plan:**6**
9hc (5fb) CTV 3P 🎨 D4.30pm

⊢⊣ **GH Lydia** 78 Locking Rd ☎25962
Plan:**7** Lic 6hc (3fb) CTV 6P 🎨 S% B&b£5–£7
Bdi£7.50–£9.50 W£45–£56 ⅃ D5pm

**GH Newton House** 79 Locking Rd ☎29331
Plan:**7A** Lic 7hc (4fb) ✶ CTV 9P 🎨 S%
✳B&b£5–£7 Bdi£7.50–£10 W£48–£62 ⅃ D4pm

**GH Oaklands** 26 Severn Rd ☎25253 Plan:**8**
Etr–Oct Lic 10hc (3fb) ✶ nc10 CTV 6P 🎨 S%
B&b£7–£9.50 Bdi£11–£14 W£58–£78 ⅃ D4pm

**GH Owl's Nest Hotel** Kewstoke ☎417672
Plan:**9** Mar–Nov & Xmas Lic 7hc (1fb) ✶ nc6

CTV 10P ▥ S% B&b£7.25 Bdi£10.75 W£67.50–£73 Ɫ D7pm

**GH *Russell Hotel*** 15–17 Clevedon Rd ☎20195 Plan: **10** Lic 23hc 5⇌ ⋔ (2fb) ⊁ nc5 CTV 20P ▥ D7.30pm

**GH St Annes Hotel** 35 Severn Rd ☎20487 Plan: **11** Apr–7 Oct rs21 Oct–Mar (B&b only) Lic 12hc ⊁ nc12 CTV 8P S% B&b£6.62–£7.68 Bdi£9.78–£11.50 W£57.50–£71.84 Ɫ D4.30pm

**GH Scottsdale Hotel** 3 Ellenborough Pk North ☎26489 Plan: **12** Apr–Oct 13hc ⊁ nc14 CTV 13P ▥ S% *B&b£9.50 Bdi£11 W£70–£76 Ɫ D5.15pm

**GH Shire Elms** 71 Locking Rd ☎28605 Plan: **13** Feb–Nov Lic 11hc 1⇌ (2fb) ⊁ [ch] CTV 12P ▥ S% B&bfr£6.75 Bdifr£10 Wfr£63 D5.15pm

⋈ **GH Southmead** 435 Locking Rd East ☎29351 Plan: **14** Closed Xmas 6hc (2fb) CTV 9P ▥ S% B&b£5–£6 Bdi£9–£10 W£60–£65 Ɫ

**GH Stanton Lodge Hotel** Kew Rd ☎22261 Plan: **15** Apr–Oct Lic 13hc ⊁ nc9 CTV 12P ▥ *B&b£5.75–£8.05 Bdi£9.20–£11.50 W£57.50–£69 Ɫ (W only in season)

**GH Tower House Hotel** Ellenborough Pk North ☎21393 Plan: **16** Apr–Oct rsNov & Mar (B&b only) 16rm 13hc 1⇌ 2⋔ (3fb) CTV 12P *B&b£7.75–£8.20 Bdi£10.75–£11.20 W£68–£74 Ɫ D4pm (W only 21 Jul–5 Sep)

**GH Westgate Private Hotel** 5 Ellenborough Cres ☎21952 Plan: **17** Apr–Sep Lic 8hc (4fb) ⊁ nc8 CTV S% B&b£8.50–£10.50 Bdi£11.50–£15 W£80–£108 D5pm

**GH Willow** 3 Clarence Rd East ☎413736 Plan: **18** Apr–Oct 9hc (4fb) ⊁ CTV 8P ▥ S% *B&b£5–£6.50 Bdi£6.50–£8 W£43–£50 Ɫ

**GH Wychwood Hotel** 148 Milton Rd ☎27793 Plan: **19** Lic 10hc (3fb) CTV 12P ▥ S% B&b£6.90–£9.20 Bdi£9.78–£12.08 W£58.65–£72.45 D4pm

**WEST PENNARD** Somerset *Map 3 ST53*
**INN *Red Lion*** ☎Glastonbury 32941 Lic 7hc 100P 4⌂ ▥ D9.30pm

**WESTWARD HO!** Devon *Map 2 SS42*
⋈ **GH Culverkeys** Buckleigh Rd ☎Bideford 4218 Apr–Sep Lic 6hc (3fb) ⊁ CTV 8P ▥ S% B&b£6–£7 Bdi£8.50–£9.50 W£50–£65 Ɫ D3pm (W only Jul & Aug)

**WETHERBY** W Yorks *Map 8 SE44*
**GH Prospect House** 8 Caxton St ☎62428 6hc (1fb) CTV 6P ▥ S% B&b£7.50–£8

**WEYBRIDGE** Surrey *London plan 4 E1 (page 134)*
**GH Warbeck House Hotel** 36 Queens Rd ☎48764 3 Jan–21 Dec Lic 10hc 1⋔ (1fb) ⊁ nc4 CTV 20P ▥ S% *B&b£13.80–£19.55 W£82–£123 M

**WEYMOUTH** Dorset *Map 3 SY67*
**GH Beechcroft Private Hotel** 128–129 Esplanade ☎786608 Mar–Oct Lic 34hc 1⇌ (15fb) ⊁ CTV 11P sea B&b£8.50–£10 Bdi£12.50–£14 D6pm

**GH Hotel Concorde** 131 Esplanade ☎76900 Feb–Nov Lic 17hc 5⋔ (8fb) CTV 4P sea S% B&b£8.05–£10.45 Bdi£11.75–£12.65 W£64.10–£74.20 Ɫ D6pm

**GH *Dorincourt Hotel*** 183 Dorchester Rd ☎786460 Etr–Oct rsNov–Etr Lic 11hc 2⇌ ⋔ (1fb) ⊁ nc5 TV 16P ▥ D5pm

**GH Ellendale Private Hotel** 88 Rodwell Av ☎786650 Lic 11hc (3fb) ⊁ [ch] CTV 10P 3⌂ ▥ S% B&b£7–£9 Bdi£9.25–£11.25 W£58–£70 D6.30pm

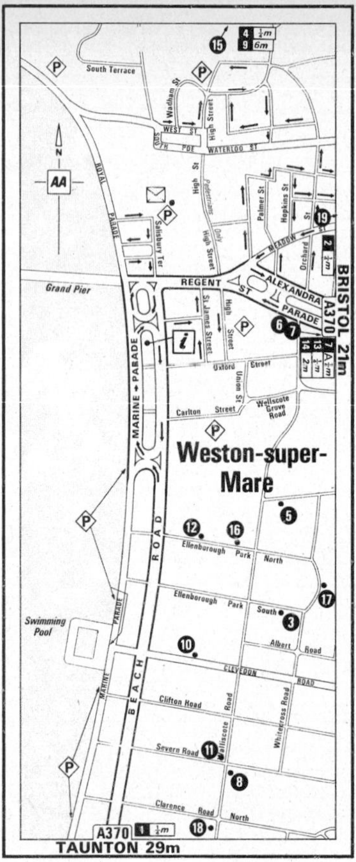
South Terrace
Grand Pier
REGENT ST
ALEXANDRA PARADE
BRISTOL 21m
A370
MARINE PARADE
ROYAL PARADE
BEACH ROAD
Swimming Pool
Weston-super-Mare
Ellenborough Park North
Ellenborough Park South
Albert Road
CLEVEDON ROAD
Clifton Road
Severn Road
Clarence Road North
A370
TAUNTON 29m

| | | | |
|---|---|---|---|
| **1** | Beachlands Hotel | **12** | Scottsdale Hotel |
| **2** | Fourways | **13** | Shire Elms |
| **3** | Glenelg | **14** | Southmead |
| **4** | Inwood Hotel | **15** | Stanton Lodge Hotel |
| **5** | Kew Dee | **16** | Tower House Hotel |
| **6** | Lockraine | **17** | Westgate Private Hotel |
| **7** | Lydia | **18** | Willow |
| **7A** | Newton House | **19** | Wychwood |
| **8** | Oaklands Hotel | | |
| **9** | Owl's Nest Hotel | | |
| **10** | Russell Hotel | | |
| **11** | St Anne's Hotel | | |

**GH Greenhill Hotel** 8 Greenhill ☎786026 Mar–Oct Lic 18hc 3⋔ (4fb) ⊁ nc3 CTV 10P sea S% B&b£8–£10 Bdi£10.50–£12.50 W£66–£75 Ɫ D6pm

⋈ **GH Hazeldene** 16 Abbotsbury Rd, Westham ☎782579 Feb–Nov Lic 7hc (4fb) ⊁ nc5 CTV 7P ▥ S% B&b£5.50–£7 Bdi£7.50–£9.50 W£49–£65 Ɫ D5pm

**GH Kenora** 5 Stavordale Rd ☎71215 Closed Xmas rs Nov–Mar Lic 18hc (7fb) ⊁ CTV 12P *B&b£7.50–£9 Bdi£10–£12 W£63–£73 Ɫ D4pm

**GH Kings Acre Hotel** 140 The Esplanade ☎782534 Feb–Nov Lic 14hc (6fb) ⊁ CTV 9P ▥ sea S% B&b£7.50–£8.50 Bdi£10–£11 W£64–£74 Ɫ D6pm

**GH Kingsley Hotel** 10 Kirtleton Av ☎785676 Mar–Oct Lic 7hc (3fb) CTV 7P ▥ D6pm

**GH Leam Hotel** 102–103 The Esplanade
☎784127 Apr–Nov Lic 22hc (8fb) nc3 CTV
sea B&b£7.77–£8.34 Bdi£11.50–£12
W£63.25–£67.28 ⚊ D6.30pm

**GH** *Marina Court Hotel* 142 The Esplanade
☎782146 Lic 14hc CTV 10P

**GH** *Redlands* 14–16 Carlton Rd South
☎786204 May–Sep Lic 14hc nc2 CTV 10P 🚿

**GH Richmoor Hotel** 146 The Esplanade
☎785087 Lic 22hc 1🍽 (12fb) ✸ CTV 9P lift
sea S% ✱B&b£8–£10 Bdi£12–£14
W£62–£80 ⚊ D4.30pm

**GH Rosedene** 1 Carlton Rd North ☎784021
May–Sep 6hc (4fb) ✸ nc3 CTV 8P 🚿 S%
B&b£6 Bdi£8.50 W£59.50 ⚊

**GH Southdene Hotel** 24 Carlton Rd South

☎784621 Lic 17hc (3fb) ✸ nc5 CTV 14P
B&b£10–£12 Bdi£12–£14 D6.15pm

**GH Sou'west Lodge Hotel** Rodwell Rd
☎783749 Lic 10hc 2🏠 (3fb) nc3 CTV 14P
🚿 S% B&b£7.02–£7.51 Bdi£8.66–£10.01
W£55–£60 ⚊ D6.15pm

**GH Sunningdale Private Hotel** 52 Preston
Rd, Overcombe ☎Preston (Dorset) 832179
Mar–15 Dec Lic 20hc 3🍽 (5fb) CTV 16P 2🚗
S% B&b£9.50–£12.25 Bdi£12.25–£15.25
W£78.50–£96 ⚊ D5.45pm

**GH Tamarisk Hotel** 12 Stavordale Rd,
Westham ☎786514 Mar–Sep Lic 18hc (7fb)
✸ CTV 19P 🚿 S% B&b£6.78–£7.60 Bdi£8–
£9.20 W£56–£64.40 ⚊ D6pm

**GH Treverbyn Court Hotel** 65 Dorchester
Rd ☎786170 Closed last 2wks Oct, Xmas &
New Year Lic 14hc 3🏠 (7fb) Ch CTV 14P S%

---

B&b£6–£13 Bdi£9.50–£17 W£52–£97
Ⓛ D9pm

**WHIMPLE** Devon *Map 3 SY09*
**GH Woodhayes** ☎822237 Feb–Dec Lic 6hc
2⇌ CTV in bedrooms 16P 2♠ ▥ S%
B&b£15–£19 Bdi£22–£25 W£140 Ⓛ D9pm

**WHITBY** N Yorks *Map 8 NZ81*
**GH Beach Cliff Hotel** North Prom, West
Cliff ☎Middlesbrough 602886 Etr–Sep
rsOct (B&b only) Lic 10hc 2🏠 ✦ nc8 CTV 5P
▥ sea S% B&b£7.50–£9 Bdi£11–£12.50
W£72–£86 Ⓛ D4.30pm

**GH Europa Private Hotel** 20 Hudson St
☎602251 Closed Xmas 7hc (3fb) ✦ nc2 CTV
S% ✳B&b£5.50–£6.50 Bdi£8–£9 W£52.50–
£58.50 Ⓛ D4pm

**GH Hudsons Hotel** 24 Hudson St ☎605277
Lic 6hc (2fb) CTV ▥ B&b£9.20–£10.35
Bdi£13.80–£15 Dnoon

**GH Prospect of Whitby** 12 Esplanade
☎603026 Mar–Sep Lic 16hc CTV ▥ S%
B&b£8.45–£8.95 W£74.50–£79.50 Ⓜ

**GH Sandbeck Hotel** Crescent Ter, West
Cliff ☎604012 Apr–10 Oct Lic 20hc 4🏠 (3fb)
CTV sea S% B&b£9.25 Bdi£12.75 W£89 Ⓛ
D6pm

**GH Seacliffe Hotel** North Prom, West Cliff
☎603139 Lic 20hc (3fb) CTV 8P sea
B&b£9.50–£10.50 Bdi£13–£14 W£84–£89 Ⓛ
D6.30pm

**WHITCHURCH** Heref & Worcs *Map 3 SO51*
**GH Portland** ☎Symonds Yat 890757 8hc
(2fb) Ⓒⓗ CTV 4P ▥ S% B&b£8–£10 Bdi£12–
£14 W£84–£91 Ⓛ D2pm

**WHITFORD** Devon *Map 3 SY29*
🏠 **GH Chantry House** ☎Colyton 52359

Etr–Sep 7hc (3fb) ✦ CTV 12P S% B&b£4.50–
£6 Bdi£7.50–£9 W£50–£60 D4pm

**WHITING BAY** Isle of Arran, Strathclyde
Bute *Map 10 NS02*
**GH Trareoch Hotel** Largie Beg ☎226 Apr–
Sep Lic 8hc (2fb) ✦ CTV 12P sea S%
✳B&b£9 Bdi£12.50 W£82.50 Ⓛ D7pm

**WHITLEY BAY** Tyne & Wear *Map 12 NZ37*
**GH Croglin Hotel** 35/41 South Pde
☎523317 Lic 40hc 7⇌ 1🏠 (10fb) CTV 16P ▥
S% ✳B&b£9.75–£17 Bdi£13.75–£21 D9pm

**WHITNEY-ON-WYE** Heref & Worcs *Map 3
SO24*
**INN Rhydspence** ☎Clifford 262 3hc 1⇌ ⇏
✦ nc10 TV in all bedrooms 60P ▥ B&b£10–
£15 Bdi£14–£19 W£98 £133 Ⓛ Bar lunch£1–
£5&alc D9pm£7.50–£8.50&alc

**WICKFORD** Essex *Map 5 TQ79*
**GH Wickford Lodge** 26 Ethelred Gdns
☎62663 6hc (2fb) ✦ CTV 6P ▥ S%
B&b£10.25–£10.75

**WICKHAM** Berks *Map 4 SU47*
**INN Five Bells** ☎Boxford 242 4hc TV in all
bedrooms P ▥ S% B&b£10.50 sn L£2.20–£5
D9.30pm£3.50–£5&alc

**WIDEGATES** Cornwall *Map 2 SX25*
**GH Coombe Farm** ☎223 Mar–Oct Lic 8hc
(5fb) ✦ CTV 12P ▥ S% B&b£6–£8
Bdi£11–£14 W£70–£90 Ⓛ D7.30pm

**WIDEMOUTH BAY** Cornwall *Map 2 SS20*
**GH Beach House Hotel** ☎256 Apr–Oct Lic
13hc 2🏠 (6fb) ✦ CTV 20P ▥ sea S%
B&bfr£7.50 Bdifr£11.75 Wfr£78 Ⓛ D7pm

**WIGAN** Gt Manchester *Map 7 SD50*
**INN Coach House Hotel** 240A Warrington Rd, Lower Ince, Ince in Makerfield ☎862281 4rm 30P ⦰ S% B&b£8.62 Wfr£60.34 Ⱨ sn L60p–£1.50&alc D10pm£1.50–£3.90&alc

**WIGHT, ISLE OF** *Map 4*
**Places with AA-listed accommodation are indicated on location map 4. Full details will be found under individual placenames within the appropriate gazetteer sections**

**WILLITON** Somerset *Map 3 ST04*
**GH Fairfield House** 51 Long St ☎32636 Lic 6hc (4fb) CTV 8P ⦰ S% B&b£7.50–£8 Bdi£11–£12 D6.30pm

**WILMINGTON** E Sussex *Map 5 TQ50*
**GH Crossways Hotel** ☎Polegate 2455 Lic 10hc 2⇌ 1♒ (2fb) nc2 CTV 20P 8🐾 ⦰ S% B&b£16–£19

**WILSHAMSTEAD (WILSTEAD)** Beds *Map 4 TL04*
**GH Old Manor House Hotel** Cotton End Rd ☎Bedford 740262 Lic 9hc CTV 10P ⦰ B&b£10.92 Bdi£14.92

**WINCHESTER** Hants *Map 4 SU42*
**GH Clownstown** Sleepers Hill ☎63990 Closed Xmas & New Year rsOct–Mar (no dinners) 6hc 1⇌ ⸸nc10 CTV 8P ⦰ S% B&bfr£8.50 Bdifr£15 D4pm

**WINCLE** Cheshire *Map 7 SJ96*
**GH Four Ways Diner Motel** (Cleulow Cross, 1m N of A54) ☎228 Lic 6hc (2fb) TV in all bedrooms 40P ⦰ ♿ S% B&b£10–£12 D7pm

**WINDERMERE** Cumbria *Map 7 SD49* **(See Plan)**
**GH Archway** College Rd ☎5613 Plan:**1** 6hc (3fb) CTV 2P ⦰ S% B&b£6.50–£7 Bdi£10.20–£10.70 W£68–£71.50 ⊬ D4pm

**GH Brooklands** Ferry View, Bowness ☎2344 Plan:**2** Lic 6hc 2♒ (2fb) ⸸ CTV 6P ⦰ lake B&b£8–£8.62 Bdi£12.50–£14.37 W£87.50–£97.75 ⊬ D6pm

**GH Clifton House** Ellerthwaite Rd ☎4896 Plan:**3** Lic 6hc nc12 CTV 5P 1🐾 ⦰

**GH Craig Foot Hotel** Lake Rd ☎3902 Plan:**4** Apr–Nov Lic 11hc 1⇌ ♒ (A 1⇌ ♒) ⸸nc CTV 16P ⦰

**GH Elim Bank Hotel** Lake Rd, Bowness on Windermere ☎4810 Plan:**5** Jan–Nov Lic 7hc (1fb) ⸸ CTV 7P ⦰ S% B&b£9.77 Bdi£15.52 W£108.64 ⊬

**GH Fairfield Country House Hotel** Brantfell Rd, Bowness on Windermere ☎3772 Plan:**6** Mar–Nov Lic 8hc 1⇌ 4♒ (5fb) CTV in bedrooms 10P ⦰ S% B&b£9.50–£12.50 Bdi£15.50–£19.50 W£98–£120 ⊬ D5pm
**See advert on page 227**

⋈ **GH Green Riggs** 8 Upper Oak St ☎2265 Plan:**7** Mar–Oct 6hc (2fb) ᴄʜ CTV 3P ⦰ S% B&b£5.50 Bdi£9 W£60 Ⱨ D5.30pm

**GH Haisthorpe** Holly Rd ☎3445 Plan:**8** Etr–Oct 7hc nc4 CTV ⦰ D2pm
**See advert on page 227**

**GH Hilton House Hotel** New Rd ☎3934 Plan:**9** Lic 7hc 3♒ (2fb) ⸸ CTV 11P ⦰ S% B&b£8.25–£9.50 Bdi£13.50–£15.95 W£87.50–£104.50 ⊬

**GH Hollythwaite** Holly Rd ☎2219 Plan:**10** 7hc (2fb) CTV S% ✳ B&b£5.75–£6.33 Bdi£9.20–£9.78 W£68.43 ⊬ D5pm

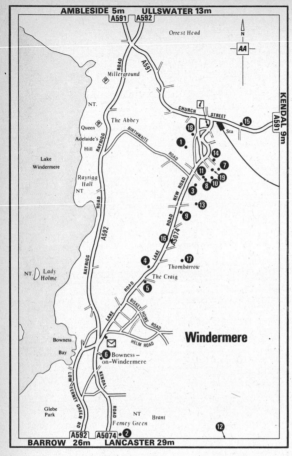

**GH Kenilworth** Holly Rd ☎ 4004 Plan:**11** Mar–Oct 7hc (1fb) ⚊ CTV ▥ S% B&bfr£6.25 Bdifr£10 Wfrf£66 ⚊ D2pm

**GH Lindeth Howe Country** Lindeth Dr ☎5759 Plan:**12** Mar–Oct Lic 7hc (3fb) ⚊ CTV 8P ▥ lake S% B&bf£11.50–£13 Bdi£17–£20 Wf£110–£135 ⚊ D4.30pm

**GH Mylne Bridge Private Hotel** Brookside, Lake Rd ☎3314 Plan:**13** Lic 13hc (2fb) ⚊ nc7 CTV 13P ▥ S% B&bf£8–£8.50 Bdi£13.25–£14.25 Wf£88–£96 ⚊ D5.30pm

**GH Oakfield** 46 Oak St ☎5692 Plan:**14** Lic 5hc (4fb) CTV ▥ S% B&bf£6–£6.50 Bdi£9–£9.50 Wf£60–£65 ⚊

**GH Orrest Head House** Kendal Rd ☎4315 Plan:**15** mid Mar–Oct Lic 7hc ⚊ nc5 CTV 10P S% B&bf£7–£8 Bdi£11.50–£13.50 Wf£80–£87.50 ⚊

**GH Rosemount** Lake Rd ☎3739 Plan:**16** Lic 8hc 2fr (2fb) CTV 6P 2☎ ▥ S% B&bf£7.50–£8.50 Bdi£12.50–£14 Wf£84–£95 ⚊ D4pm

**GH Thornleigh** Thornbarrow Rd, Bowness on Windermere ☎4203 Plan:**17** Etr–Oct Lic 6hc (4fb) ⚊ CTV 6P ▥ S% ✱ B&bf£6–£8 Bdi£9.50–£11 Wf£66.50–£77 ⚊

**GH Waverley Hotel** College Rd ☎3546 Plan:**18** Lic 11hc (4fb) ⚊ CTV 8P ▥ S% B&bf£8.05–£9.78 Bdi£12.65–£14.38

Wf£56.35–£68 ▨ D4.30pm (W only Jul & Aug)

**GH White Rose** Broad St ☎5180 Plan:**19** Feb–Nov & Xmas 5hc (3fb) ⚊ nc3 CTV 5P 2☎ ▥ S% B&bf£6–£7 Bdif£9–£11 Wf£63–£77 ⚊ D7pm

**WINTERBOURNE ABBAS** Dorset *Map 3 SY69*

**GH Church View** ☎Martinstown 296 Lic 9hc (3fb) CTV 9P 1☎ ▥ S% B&bf£6–£7 Bdif£9.50–£10.50 Wfrf£62 ⚊ D9pm

**GH *Whitefriars*** ☎Martinstown 206 Mar–Oct Lic 7hc Ch CTV 18P ▥

**WISBECH** Cambs *Map 5 TF40*

**GH Glendon** Sutton Rd ☎4812 Mar–Oct Lic 18hc 2⚌ (2fb) CTV 60P ⚊ S% B&bf£11.50

**WITHAM** Essex *Map 5 TL81*

**INN Spread Eagle** Newland St ☎512131 13rm 7hc (A 4hc)

**WITNEY** Oxon *Map 4 SP30*

**INN Red Lion** Corn St ☎3149 6hc CTV 2P 1☎ S% B&bf£9.25 Bdifr£11 sn Lf£1.50alc D8.30pmf£3alc

**WIVELISCOMBE** Somerset *Map 3 ST02*

**INN Bear** 10 North St ☎23537 5rm 4hc CTV

5P ▥ S% B&b£9–£9.50 Bdi£11.50–£12.50 W£69.50–£74 ⫞ sn L80p–£3&alc D9.30pm£2.50–£5.60&alc

**WOMENSWOLD** Kent *Map 5 TR25*
**GH Woodpeckers Country Hotel**
☎Barham 319 Closed Xmas Lic 11hc 4♒ (A 4hc 1♒) (5fb) ⌞Ch⌟ CTV 40P 2♨ ▥ & S% B&b£9–£12.50 Bdi£12.50–£16.50 W£87.50–£98 ⫞ D9pm

**WOODSTOCK** Oxon *Map 4 SP41*
**INN *Star*** 22 Market Pl ☎811209 Closed Xmas day 3hc nc14 CTV 6P D2pm

**WOODY BAY** Devon *Map 3 SS64*
**GH Red House** ☎Parracombe 255 14 Mar–Oct 6hc (2fb) nc4 CTV 8P sea S% B&b£7–£8 Bdi£11.30–£12.30 W£72–£80 ⫞ D5pm

**WOOKEY** Somerset *Map 3 ST54*
**GH Worth House Farm Hotel** Worth ☎Wells 72041 Lic 6hc (3fb) ✦nc3 CTV 12P ▥ S% B&b£7.50 Bdi£11.50 W£77 D4pm

**WOOLACOMBE** Devon *Map 2 SS44*
**GH Barton House Hotel** Barton Rd ☎870548 May–Oct Lic 12hc 6⇨ ♒ (5fb) CTV 12P D6pm

**GH *Combe Ridge Hotel*** The Esplanade ☎870321 Etr–Sep 8hc (3fb) ✦nc3 CTV 9P sea D4.30pm

**GH Holmesdale Hotel** Bay View Rd ☎870335 Lic 15hc 2♒ (10fb) ⌞Ch⌟ CTV 12P ▥ sea S% ✳B&b£7.50–£9.50 Bdi£9–£11.50 W£50–£74 ⫞ D8pm (W only Jul–Aug)

**GH Seawards** Beach Rd ☎870249 Etr–early Oct 6hc (2fb) nc2 TV 6P sea S%

B&bf£6.50–£7.50 Bdi£9.25–£10.50 W£57.50–£62.50 Ⅼ D4.30pm

**GH Wave Crest** Sunnyside Rd ☎870334 May–Sep 6hc (1fb) nc3 CTV 6P ▥ sea S% B&bf£6.50–£7.50 Bdi£8.50–£9.50 W£59.50–£65.50 Ⅼ D6pm

**GH White Rose Hotel** The Esplanade ☎870406 May–Sep Lic 16hc 10⋔ (11fb) [Ch] CTV 12P ▥ sea S% B&bf£10–£12.50 Bdi£15–£17.50 W£100–£125 Ⅼ D7.45pm (W only mid Jul–Aug)

**WOOLHOPE** Heref & Worcs *Map 3 SO63*
**INN Butchers Arms** ☎Fownhope 281 3hc ✱ nc14 80P ▥ S% B&bf£10 Bdi£12–£16.50 W£63 M Bar lunch£1.50alc D9pm£6.50alc

**WOOTTON BASSETT** Wilts *Map 4 SU08*
**GH Fairview** 52 Swindon Rd ☎Swindon 852283 8hc (2fb) CTV TV available in bedrooms P 1 ▥ S% B&bf£7.50 D7pm

**WORCESTER** Heref & Worcs *Map 3 SO85*
**GH Loch Ryan Hotel** 119 Sidbury Rd ☎351143 14hc 1⋔ (A 4hc) (2fb) ✱ CTV ▥ S% ✻B&bf£8.05

**INN Five Ways Hotel** 14 Angel Pl ☎23129 7hc ✱ TV ▥ S% B&bf£7.50 Bar lunch£1alc D9.30pm

**WORKINGTON** Cumbria *Map 11 NY02*
**GH Morven** Siddick ☎2118 Lic 6hc 2⇌ (A 2hc) (3fb) CTV 25P ▥ S% B&bf£6.50–£8 Bdi£9–£10.50 W£56–£60 Ⅼ D4pm

**WORTHING** W Sussex *Map 4 TQ10*
**GH Belmont Private Hotel** 211 Brighton Rd ☎202678 Lic 6hc (2fb) nc5 CTV 3P 5 ▥ sea S% B&bf£6–£7.50 Bdi£9–£10.50 W£40–£55 D9pm

**GH Blair House** 11 St Georges Rd ☎34071 Lic 7hc 1⇌ 1⋔ (1fb) ✱ CTV 6P ▥ B&bf£6.50–£8.50 Bdi£9–£11.50 W£63–£85.50 Ⅼ D6.30pm

**GH *Burcott*** 6 Windsor Rd ☎35163 5hc ✱ CTV 4P ▥

**GH Camelot House** 20 Gannon Rd ☎204334 Closed Xmas Lic 6hc (2fb) ✱ CTV TV in all bedrooms 3P ▥ S% B&bf£6.50–£7.80 Bdi£9.35–£10.50 W£63.25–£70.95 Ⅼ D4pm

**GH *Eleanor Lodge*** 9–11 Alexandra Rd ☎33788 Closed Xmas 11hc CTV ▥

**GH Meldrum House** 8 Windsor Rd ☎33808 Feb–Oct 5hc (2fb) ✱ nc3 CTV ▥ S% B&bf£7.50–£8.50 Bdi£10.50–£11.50 W£70–£75 Ⅼ D5pm

**GH Pleasington** 2 Wyke Av ☎201143 Closed Xmas 8hc (1fb) ✱ nc5 CTV 1P ▥ S% B&bf£7–£9 Bdi£11–£13 W£64–£74 Ⅼ D10am

**GH *St Georges Lodge Hotel*** Chesswood Rd ☎32621 Lic 9hc 2⇌ ⋔ (2fb) ✱ [Ch] CTV 10P 2 ▥ D7pm

**GH Small Hotel** 3 Salisbury Rd ☎30543 rsXmas wk (B&b only) 6hc (2fb) nc6 CTV ▥ S% ✻B&bf£8.50–£9.50 Bdi£12–£13 W£72.50–£79.50 Ⅼ D10am

**GH Southdene** 41 Warwick Gdns ☎32909 Lic 5hc (2fb) ✱ nc10 ▥ S% B&bf£8 Bdi£11 W£72 Ⅼ D6pm

**GH Wansfell Hotel** 49 Chesswood Rd ☎30612 12hc 4⋔ (1fb) ✱ nc3 CTV 8P ▥ S% B&bf£9–£11 Bdi£12.50–£14.50 W£75–£85 Ⅼ D7.30pm

**GH Williton** 10 Windsor Rd ☎37974 6hc (2fb) ✱ TV 2P S% ✻B&bf£6.50–£8 W£39–£48 M

**GH Windsor House** 16–18 Windsor Rd ☎39655 Lic 26hc 3⇌ 5⋔ (5fb) CTV 19P ▥

B&b£8.62–£11 Bdi£12.12–£15.50 W£80.50–£99.50 ⌁ D5pm

**GH** *Windsor Lodge* 3 Windsor Rd ☎200056 6hc nc5 CTV 2P 🏢 sea D1pm

**GH Wolsey Hotel** 179–181 Brighton Rd ☎36149 Lic 14hc (3fb) CTV 🏢 sea S% B&b£10.85 Bdi£15.65 W£107.50 ⌁ D5pm

**WROTHAM** Kent *Map 5 TQ65*
**INN Moat Hotel** London Rd ☎Borough Green 882263 8hc 2⇔ 300P 🏢 S% B&b£11–£12 sn Lfr£3.95&alc D10.30pmfr£5&alc

**WYE** Kent *Map 5 TR04*
**INN New Flying Horse** Upper Bridge St ☎812297 rsXmas day 5hc (A 4rm) TV in all bedrooms 50P 🏢 S% B&b£11–£17.50 Bdi£17–£24 W£102–£129 ⌁ sn Lfr£6&alc D9.30pmfr£6&alc

**YARCOMBE** Devon *Map 3 ST20*
**GH Belfry** ☎Upottery 234 mid Jan–mid Dec Lic 7⇔ ✸nc14 CTV 10P 🏢 S% B&b£11–£14 W£77 Ⓜ

**YARMOUTH, GT** Norfolk *Map 5 TG50*
**GH Frandor** 120 Lowestoft Rd, Gorleston-on-Sea (2m S A12) ☎62112 Apr–Oct Lic 8hc (4fb) CTV 7P S% B&b£6–£8.50 Bdi£8.50–£10.50 W£41.50–£54 Ⓜ D4.30pm

**GH Georgian House Private Hotel** 16 & 17 North Dr ☎2623 Closed Xmas rsWinter Lic 22hc 8⇔ (4fb) ✸nc4 CTV 10P 🏢 sea S% B&b£7–£16 W£40–£80 Ⓜ

**GH Palm Court Hotel** 10 North Dr ☎4568 Etr–20 Oct & Xmas Lic 45hc 10⇔ 19🛗 (8fb) CTV 35P 🏢 lift sea S% B&b£12–£16 Bdi£15–£22 W£77–£120 ⌁ D8pm

**GH** *Porthole* 52 Avondale Rd, Gorleston-on-Sea (2m S A12) ☎61451 Apr–Sep rsXmas 6hc (2fb) CTV 🏢

**YARNSCOMBE** Devon *Map 2 SS52*
**GH Chapple Farm** ☎High Bickington 391 Closed Xmas 7hc (3fb) CTV 10P S% B&b£6.50–£7.50 Bdi£9–£11

**YATTON** Avon *Map 3 ST46*
**INN Prince of Orange** High St ☎832193 Closed Xmas 8hc 5🛗 🖤 CTV B&b£12.97 Bdi£18.03 Bar lunch75p–£2.50 D9.30pmfr£4&alc

**YEOVIL** Somerset *Map 3 ST51*

**GH Pickett Witch House Hotel** 100 Ilchester Rd ☎4317 Closed Xmas Lic 8hc 2⇔ (A 6hc 1⇔) (3fb) CTV 14P 2🏠 🏢 B&b£12 Bdi£16.50 W£63 D8.30pm

**GH Wyndham** 142 Sherborne Rd ☎21468 Closed 23 Dec–3 Jan Lic 6hc (2fb) CTV 6P S% B&b£6 Bdi£9 W£63 ⌁ D5pm

**YORK** N Yorks *Map 8 SE65*
**GH** *Acomb Road* 128 Acomb Rd ☎792321 Jan–Nov 14hc (4fb) CTV 15P 🏢 D4pm

**GH Alhambra Court Hotel** 31 St Marys, Bootham ☎28474 Lic 21hc 12⇔ 6🛗 (4fb) CTV 20P 🏢 S% B&b£6–£10.50 Bdi£10.50–£15 W£70.50–£101.50 ⌁ Dnoon

**GH Avenue** 6 The Avenue, Clifton ☎20575 6hc (1fb) ✸ CTV 🏢 S% B&b£6.50–£8 Bdi£10–£11.50 W£65–£75 ⌁ Dnoon
**See advert on page 230**

**GH Beech** 6–7 Longfield Ter, Bootham ☎34581 Lic 7hc (2fb) ✸nc5 CTV 4P S%

B&bf£6–£7.50 Bdi£9–£11.50 W£60–£77 Ł D4pm

**GH Bootham Bar Hotel** 4 High Petergate ☎58516 Closed Xmas 10hc (2fb) nc6 CTV ⦿ lift S% B&bfr£7.48

**GH Clifton Bridge Hotel** Water End ☎53609 Lic 10hc (1fb) CTV 12P ⦿ S% B&bf£10.50–£12 D7.30pm

**GH Coach House Hotel** Marygate ☎52780 Lic 12hc CTV 10P ⦿

**GH Crescent** 77 Bootham ☎23216 Closed Nov 8hc (2fb) ⚡ CTV 4P S% B&bf£7–£8 W£49–£56 M

**GH Croft Hotel** 103 Mount Rd ☎22747 Feb–Dec 10hc (1fb) ⚡ nc2 CTV 3P ⦿ S% B&bf£7–£10 Bdi£12–£15 W£80–£100 Ł D4pm

**GH Dairy** 3 Scarcroft Rd ☎39367 Apr–Oct

5hc 1⇔ (1fb) CTV S% B&bf£6–£7.50 W£42–£52.50 M

**GH Fairmount Hotel** 230 Tadcaster Rd, Mount Vale ☎38298 Lic 7hc 2⇔ 1⋔ (3fb) ⚡ CTV 6P ⦿ S% B&bf£8–£9 Bdi£11–£12 D5pm

**GH Field House Hotel** 2 St Georges Pl ☎39572 Closed Xmas Lic 17hc 1⇔ 10⋔ ⚡ nc12 CTV 17P ⦿ S% B&bf£12.50–£16 Bdi£20.50–£24 Dnoon

**GH Grasmead House Hotel** 1 Scarcroft Hill, The Mount ☎29996 Lic 6⇔ nc5 CTV in all bedrooms 1☎ ⦿ S% B&bfr£15 Bdifr£20

**GH Hobbits Hotel** 9 St Peters Gv ☎24538 Lic 9hc ⚡ CTV 5P ⦿ ✻ B&bfr£9.48 Bdifr£16.09 Dbreakfast

**GH Inglewood** 7 Clifton Gn ☎53523 6hc (2fb) ⚡ CTV 1☎ ⦿ S% B&bf£7–£7.50

**GH Jorvik Hotel** 52 Marygate, Bootham
☎53511 Jan–Nov Lic 16hc 2⇌ 6⋔ (1fb) ✦nc
CTV 24P ▥ S% ✳B&b£8–£9.90 Bdi£12–
£13.90 D5pm

**GH Linden Lodge** Nunthorpe Av, Scarcroft
Rd ☎20107 Jan–Nov Lic 7hc (2fb) ✦nc7
CTV ▥ S% B&b£6.50–£7 Bdi£10–£11 W£70–
£77 ⱇ D1pm

**GH Mayfield Hotel** 75 Scarcroft Rd ☎54834
Lic 7hc 2⋔ (2fb) ✦CTV ▥
S% B&b£8–£12.50 Bdi£13.50–£18
W£94.50–£126 ⱇ D9pm

**GH Moat Hotel** Nunnery Ln ☎52926 Mar–
Oct rsNov–Feb 9hc 6⋔ (3fb) CTV 10P S%
B&b£7.50–£10.50

**GH Orchard Court Hotel** 4 St Peters Gv
☎53964 2 Jan–23 Dec Lic 10hc 3⋔ (5fb) ✦

CTV 10P ▥ S% B&b£8–£11.50
Bdi£10.50–£16 W£52–£74.75 Ⓜ D9pm

**GH Parkside Hotel** 98–100 Bishopthorpe
Rd, South Bank ☎33365 Closed mid Dec–
mid Jan 15hc 1⇌ 4⋔ (4fb) CTV 5P ▥ S%
B&b£7.50–£11 Bdi£12–£15.50 W£49–£75
Ⓜ D2pm

**GH Priory Hotel** 126 Fulford Rd ☎25280
Closed Xmas 18hc 3⋔ (3fb) ✦CTV 18P ▥
S% B&b£8–£9

**GH St Raphael** 44 Queen Anne's Rd,
Bootham ☎54187 Closed Xmas 7hc (2fb) ✦
CTV ▥ S% B&b£7.50–£8.50

**GH Sycamore Hotel** 19 Sycamore Pl
☎24712 Lic 6hc (3fb) ✦CTV 3P ▥ S%
B&b£7–£8 Bdi£10.50–£11.50 W£70–£80 ⱇ
D9am

---

# PRIORY HOTEL

**126 Fulford Road, York YO1 4BE**
**Tel: Reception 25280 Guests 34809**
**STD code 0904**

The Priory offers comfortable accommodation
and English breakfast and is situated on the
A19 south of the City with adjacent riverside
walk to the City centre.
Some of the 17 bedrooms have shower and
toilet facilities and all have H & C and razor
points. Large private car park.
Full central heating.

---

**For that WEEK—END STAY**
**IN THE COUNTRYSIDE**

**Phone Trevor or Wendy Johnston**
**YORK (0904) 705609 or 703888**

# The SHIP INN
**ACASTER MALBIS, YORK.**
Set in glorious countryside on the
banks of the River OUSE just
3½ miles from the centre of the
CITY of YORK.
 The SHIP INN incorporates a
delightful old-world restaurant known
as 'The Wheelhouse.'
 Truly 300 years of atmosphere
with excellent food.

**The 'INN by the RIVERSIDE'**

---

# The Sycamore Hotel

**19 Sycamore Place, Bootham, York YO3 7DW.**
**Telephone: (0904) 24712**

Proprietors: Judy & David Broadhead

This family run hotel is a member of both the English Tourist Board and the
York Hotel & Guest House Association. We are situated in a quiet cul-de-sac
only 5 minutes walk to the City and Minster. We offer bed and full English
breakfast, with evening meal available on request. The hotel is licensed for
the sale of drinks to residents. All rooms have hot and cold water, shaver
points and central heating. A guests lounge with colour TV is available.

# FARMHOUSE SECTION

The gazetteer gives details of AA-listed farmhouses in England, Wales and Scotland. Listed in alphabetical order of placenames. (*Note: there are no AA-listed farmhouses within the Channel Islands, Isle of Man, or Isles of Scilly*). Details for islands are shown under individual placenames; the gazetteer text also gives appropriate cross-references. A useful first point of reference is to consult the location maps which show where farmhouses are situated.

**ABBERTON** Essex *Map 5 TM01*
Mr S. Miller **Oxley Hill** *(TM002194)* Layer Rd
☎Colchester 66422
*Modern bungalow farmhouse with its own private nature reserve. Beautiful countryside views.*
Feb–Dec 6hc (2fb) nc5 CTV 12P 3🐾 ▥ river
55acres arable sheep S% B&bfr£10.50 Bdi fr£15

**ABBEY CWMHIR** Powys *Map 6 SO07*
Mr M. Hamer **Home** *(SO091724)* ☎Penybont 666
*Smart, stone-built house in the village. Small trout stream passes through the farm.*
3hc (1fb) TV 6P ▥ 440acres mixed S% B&b£5
Bdi£8 W£66 D9.30pm

**ABBOTS BICKINGTON** Devon *Map 2 SS31*
Mr C. Bellew **Court Barton** *(SS385133)*
☎Milton Damerel 214
*Stone-built farmhouse in an area of great natural beauty. Panoramic views from most windows. Rough shooting, fishing and riding available.*
May–Sep 4rm 3hc (1fb) ✟ nc4 TV 5P 600acres
arable beef sheep S% B&b£3.50–£4 Bdi£7–£8
D5.30pm

**ABBOTS BROMLEY** Staffs *Map 7 SK02*
Mrs M.K. Hollins **Marsh** *(SK069261)* ☎Burton-on-Trent 840323
*Large two-storey, cement rendered farmhouse set in open countryside 1 mile from village.*
2rm Ⓒⓗ TV 10P ▥ 43acres dairy S%
B&b£5.50–£6.50 Bdi£7.50–£9.50 Wfr£52.50
℔ D6pm

**ABEREDW** Powys *Map 3 SO04*
Mrs M.M. Evans **Danycoed** *(SO079476)*
☎Erwood 298
*Stone-built, two-storey farmhouse. Pleasant situation on edge of River Wye.*
Etr–Oct 3rm 2hc ✟ 6P river 235acres mixed S%
B&b£6–£6.50 Bdi£9–£10 W£58–£65 ℔ D4pm

**ABERFELDY** Tayside *Perths Map 14 NN84*
Mr A. Kennedy **Tom of Cluny** *(NN875515)*
☎20477
*Small hillside farmhouse reached by long steep tarmac/rough drive. Magnificent views southward across the River Tay and Aberfeldy.*
3rm (1fb) CTV 2P river 36acres mixed S%
B&b£5–£6 Bdi£7.50–£8.50 D8pm

**ABERGAVENNY** Gwent *Map 3 SO21*
Mrs D.V. Nicholls **Newcourt** *(SO317165)* Maerdy
☎3734
*16th-century, stone-built farmhouse with views of Sugar Loaf Mountain.*
3hc (1fb) ✟ nc4 CTV P 🐾 ▥ 85acres
dairy B&bfr£8

**ABERHOSAN** Powys *Map 6 SN89*
Mrs A. Lewis **Bacheiddon** *(SN825980)*
☎Machynlleth 2229
*From the windows there are lovely views of the surrounding mountains and countryside. Off unclassified road linking Machynlleth and Dyliffe/Staylittle (B4518).*
Apr–Nov 3rm 3🐾 (1fb) ✟ CTV P 850acres mixed
S% B&bfr£6.50 Bdi fr£11 Wfr£77 ℔ D3pm

**ABERMULE** Powys *Map 7 SO19*
Mrs J.E. Wigley **Upper Bryntalch** *(SO172961)*
☎252
*1m NE of Abermule off B4386.*
Mar–Oct 3hc (1fb) TV P 180acres mixed S%
B&b£5.50 Bdi£8.50 D3.30pm

**ABINGTON** Strathclyde *Lanarks Map 11 NS92*
Mr G. Hodge **Craighead** *(NS914236)*
☎Crawford 356
*Large farm building in courtyard design. Set amid rolling hills on the banks of the river Duneaton. Main building dates from 1780. Off unclassified Crawfordjohn road. 1m N of A74/A73 junc.*
May–Oct 3rm (1fb) Ⓒⓗ CTV 8P 4🐾 river
800acres mixed S% B&bfr£5.50 Bdi fr£8.50
D6pm

Mr D. Wilson **Crawfordjohn Mill** *(NS897242)*
Crawfordjohn ☎Crawfordjohn 248
*Two-storey, brown-brick farmhouse. Set in its own land. Off A74 1m SE of Crawfordjohn on unclassified rd.*
May–15 Oct 3rm (1fb) TV 4P ▥ 180acres arable
dairy S% B&bfr£6 Bdi fr£8 Wfr£52 ℔ D6.30pm

Mrs M.E. Hamilton **Kirkton** *(NS933210)*
(1m S A74) ☎Crawford 376
May–Sep 3rm ✟ nc7 CTV 3P river 750acres beef
sheep S% B&b£5–£5.50

Mrs J. Hyslop **Netherton** *(NS908254)*
(on unclass road joining A74 & A73) ☎Crawford 321
3hc (1fb) Ⓒⓗ CTV 4P ▥ 3000acres sheep S%
B&b£5–£5.50 Bdi£8.50–£9 D8pm

**ACHARACLE** Highland *Argyll Map 13 NM66*
Mrs M. Macaulay **Dalilea House** *(NM735693)*
☎Salen 253
*A splendid turreted house with surrounding grounds giving excellent views over farmland, hills and Loch Shiel. A blend of the ancient and modern.*
Mar–mid Oct 6hc (1fb) 8P 14,000acres beef
sheep S% B&bfr£7.50 Bdi fr£12.10 Wfr£80.50 ℔
D7pm

**ALDWARK** Derbys *Map 8 SK25*
J.N. Lomas **Lydgate** *(SK228577)* ☎Carsington 250

Stone-built traditional farmhouse, about 300
years old, in quiet rural setting.
3rm (1fb) ✹ CTV 3P 2🐴 ⊞ 300acres beef
dairy sheep S% B&b£7 Bdi£10 W£70 ⫪ D2pm

**ALFRISTON** E Sussex Map 5 TQ50
Mrs D.Y. Savage **Pleasant Rise** (TQ516027)
☎870545
Attractive farm set in typical Sussex downland.
Adjacent to B2108 Seaford road.
1hc (A 2hc) (1fb) ✹ nc5 6P ⊞ 100acres non-
working S% ✱ B&b£7–£7.50

**ALLENSMOOR** Heref & Worcs Map 3 SO43
Mrs O.I. Griffiths **Mawfield** (SO453366)
☎Belmont (Hereford) 266
Large farmhouse set in narrow lane off the
beaten track, but close enough for Hereford's
amenities.
Apr–Oct 3rm 2hc ✹ nc8 CTV 6P 176acres arable
mixed S% B&b£5–£6.50 Bdi£8–£9.50 Wfr£56 ⫪
D4.30pm

**ALVERDISCOTT** Devon Map 2 SS52
Mrs C.M. Tremeer **Garnacott** (SS516240)
☎Newton Tracey 282
Farmhouse standing in small garden surrounded
by open fields. Traditional farmhouse
furnishings. Facilities nearby include fishing, golf
and bathing.
Etr–Oct 3rm 1hc (2fb) ✹ TV 4P 85acres mixed
S% B&b£5.25–£5.75 Bdi£8–£8.50 W£52.50–
£56 ⫪

**ANNAN** Dumfries & Galloway
Dumfriesshire Map 11 NY16
K.E. Yates **Beechgrove** (NY213652) ☎2220
Attractive redstone house with pleasant garden,
surrounded by pastureland. Views of Solway

Firth.
5hc (4fb) CTV 10P ⊞ sea non-working S%
✱ B&b£7.60–£9.60 Bdi£12.60–£14.60
D7.30pm

**APPLEBY** Cumbria Map 12 NY62
Mrs M. Wood **Gale House** (NY695206) ☎51380
Comfortable, quiet farmhouse with friendly
atmosphere. Situated in delightful position 1m
from centre of Appleby.
Apr–Sep 2rm (1fb) ✹ nc5 2P 167acres dairy S%
B&b£5.50 Bdi£8 W£56 ⫪ D3.30pm

**ARDBRECKNISH** Strathclyde Argyll Map 10
NN02
Mrs H.F. Hodge **Rockhill** (NN072219)
☎Kilchrenan 218
Loch-shore farm. Trout and perch fishing (free),
and on the farm's private loch, by arrangement.
Apr–Sep 6hc (4fb) nc5 CTV 8P ⊞ lake 200acres
sheep S% B&bfr£7 Bdi fr£11 Wfr£66 ⫪
(W only mid Jul–Aug) D7pm

**ARDEN** Strathclyde Dunbartons Map 10
NS38
Mrs R. Keith **Mid Ross** (NS359859) ☎655
Farmhouse pleasantly located close to Loch
Lomond 3m N of Balloch off A82.
May–Oct 3hc (2fb) CTV P ⊞ lake 32acres mixed
S% B&b£5.50

**ARDERSIER** Highland Inverness-shire Map
14 NH75
Mrs L.E. MacBean **Milton-of-Gollanfield**
(NH809534) ☎2207
Stone farmhouse set on north side of A96 5m W
of Nairn.
Apr–Oct 3rm 2hc (1fb) ✹ Ch CTV P 365acres
mixed S% B&b£5–£10

**ARDFERN** Strathclyde *Argyll Map 10 NM80*
Mrs G. McKinlay **Corranbeg** *(NM801045)*
☎Barbreck 207
*Large rambling farmhouse in quiet spot.*
*Surrounded by beautiful scenery.*
Whit–Sep 3rm (1fb) ♔ P lake 208acres mixed
S% B&b£5 Bdi£9 W£63 D5pm

Mrs M.C. Peterson **Traighmhor** *(NM800039)*
☎Barbreck 228
*Farmhouse offering magnificent views towards*
*Loch Craignish.*
Apr–Oct 3rm (1fb) ♔ Ch CTV 8P lake 75acres
mixed S% B&b£6 Bdi£10 Wfr£70 ⚖ D5pm

**ARPINGE** Kent *Map 5 TR13*
Mrs J.A. Matthew **Lower Arpinge** *(TR187386)*
☎Folkestone 78102
*Restored farmhouse with natural beams and*
*inglenook fireplace in lounge. Spacious grounds.*
*From the London–Folkestone road (A20) follow*
*B2065 northward to Etchinghill, turn right*
*(unclass) then right at successive junctions for*
*2¼ miles.*
Apr–Oct 5hc (1fb) ♔ CTV 5P 3acres non-
working S% B&b£7 Bdi£11 W£73.50 ⚖ D9am

**ASHBURTON** Devon *Map 3 SX77*
Mrs H. Young **Bremridge** *(SX785701)* ☎52426
*Clean and brightly decorated farmhouse, parts*
*of which date back to early 16th century.*
4hc (3fb) Ch CTV 6P 18acres mixed S%
Bdi£8–£10 W£45–£50 ⚖

**ASHFORD** *(Nr Barnstaple)* Devon *Map 2*
*SS53*
Mrs G. Hannington **Fair Oak** *(SS530348)* ☎
Barnstaple 73698
*Modern farmhouse, arranged as mini-farm*
*specially catering for children, with pets corner*
*and aviaries with mixed birds. Overlooks River*
*Taw Estuary.*
May–Oct 4hc (4fb) ♔nc2 Ch CTV 6P river
89acres mixed S% B&b£6–£7.50 Bdi£9.50–
£12 W£60–£72 ⚖

**ASPATRIA** Cumbria *Map 11 NY14*
Mrs J. Mashiter **Scales Demesne** *(NY183461)*
☎20847
*Comfortably furnished accommodation. Two*
*separate staircases and front doors offer*
*independence. Within easy reach of sea and*
*Lake District.*
Jun–Aug 3rm (1fb) ♔nc3 CTV 3P 1🏠 231
acres dairy S% B&b£5 Bdi£8 W£56 ⚖ D5pm

**AUCHENCAIRN** Dumfries & Galloway
*Kirkcudbrights Map 11 NX75*
Mrs D. Cannon **Bluehill** *(NX786515)* ☎228
*Farm offers panoramic views overlooking the*
*Solway Firth and the English lakeland hills.*
May–Sep 4hc (1fb) ♔ nc12 CTV P ▦ 120acres
dairy B&b£6–£6.50 Bdi£9.50 D6pm

**AUSTWICK** N Yorks *Map 7 SD76*
Mrs M. Hird **Rawlinshaw** *(SD781673)* ☎Settle
3214
*200-year-old farmhouse with attractive views to*
*the front of the house.*
Etr–Sep 2hc (2fb) ♔ CTV 5P ▦ 206acres dairy
mixed sheep

**AVONWICK** Devon *Map 3 SX75*
Mrs C. Scott **Sopers Horsebrook** *(SX711587)*
☎South Brent 3235
*Old farmhouse situated in quiet valley*
*overlooking brook.*
Apr–Sep 2hc (2fb) ♔ CTV 2P 140acres mixed
S% B&b£5.50–£7 Bdi£8.50–£10.50 W£35–£45
Ⓜ (W only Jul & Aug) D9am

**AXBRIDGE** Somerset *Map 3 ST45*
L. Dimmock **Manor** *(ST420549)* Cross (on A38)
☎732577
*400-year-old farmhouse, formerly a coaching*
*inn. Farm offers horse riding facilities.*
9rm 3hc (3fb) CTV P 250acres mixed D5pm

**AXMINSTER** Devon *Map 3 SY39*
Mrs S. Clist **Annings** *(SY299966)* Wyke
☎33294
*Large secluded farmhouse with modern*
*furnishings. Situated in elevated position with*
*fine views. Coast nearby. S of town on*
*unclassified road between A35 & A358.*
Mar–Sep 4rm 3hc (1fb) ♔ CTV 4P 54acres dairy
S% B&b£5.50–£6.50 Bdi£8.50–£9.50

**AYLESBEARE** Devon *Map 3 SY09*
Mrs E.A. Slade **Rosamondford** *(SY027918)*
☎Woodbury 32448
*Old thatch and cob farmhouse with large front*
*garden. Conveniently placed for Exeter, the*
*airport and East Devon.*
Etr–Oct 2hc (1fb) ♔ CTV 6P 125acres dairy
Dnoon

**AYR** Strathclyde *Ayrs Map 10 NS32*
Mr & Mrs A. Stevenson **Trees** *(NS386186)*
☎Joppa 270

Comfortable accommodation in a quiet
location. 4m E on unclassified road, between
A70 and A713.
Etr–Sep 3rm (1fb) ⊁ CTV P ▥ 125acres beef
S% B&f£5.50–£6 Bdi£9–£9.50

**BABELL** Clwyd *Map 7 SJ17*
Mrs M.L. Williams **Bryn Glas** *(SJ155737)*
☎Caerwys 493
Feb–Nov 2rm (2fb) CTV 3P 2☎ ▥ 40acres mixed
S% B&bf£5.50–£6.50 Bdi£8.50–£9.50
(W only May–Sep) Dnoon

**BALA** Gwynedd *Map 6 SH93*
Mr D. Davies **Tytandderwen** *(SH944345)*
☎520273
*Two-storey manor house-style farmhouse in
open country. Stone-built and modernised in
parts. Borders on River Dee.*
Etr–Nov 3hc (2fb) CTV 10P ▥ 40acres mixed
S% B&bfr£7 Wfr£40 ℳ

**BALFRON STATION** Central *Stirlings Map
11 NS58*
**Clachanry** *(NS512888)* ☎Balfron 335
*Pleasant little hillside farmhouse with
reasonable access from the main road.*
Apr–Sep 3rm ⊁ TV 3P ▥ 135acres mixed

**BAMPTON** Devon *Map 3 SS92*
Mr & Mrs R.A. Fleming **Holwell** *(SS966233)*
☎452
*14th-century farmhouse with thatched roof,
studded oak front door and many oak beams
inside. Attractive gardens.*
3hc ⊁ nc CTV 6P 1☎ ▥ 25acres mixed S%
B&bf£6.50 Bdi£10 Wfrf£65 ℓ D4.30pm

Mrs R. Cole **Hukeley** *(SS972237)* ☎31267
*16th-century farmhouse, on edge of Exmoor.*

*Fine old beams. Rooms are comfortable and
well decorated.*
Etr–Oct 2hc (2fb) ⊁ CTV 4P 198acres mixed S%
B&b£6.50 Bdi£9 Wfr£55 ℓ

Mrs A. Campbell **Valeridge** *(SS918220)*
Oakfordbridge ☎Oakford 346
*A centuries-old farmhouse in elevated position
with superb view of the Exe Valley. 3m W of
Bampton on A361.*
3hc nc12 CTV 4P 2☎ 17½acres mixed S% B&f£
Bdi£11.50 Wf£70 ℓ Dnoon

**BAMPTON Oxon** *Map 4 SP30*
Mrs J. Rouse **Morar** *(SP312026)* Weald Street
(½m SW off A415) ☎Bampton Castle 850162
Closed 20–30 Dec 3rm ⊁ nc6 CTV 4P ▥
450acres mixed S% B&bfr£6.50 Bdi fr£10 Wfr£68
ℓ D2pm

**BANAVIE** Highland *Inverness-shire Map 14
NN17*
Mrs A.C. MacDonald **Burnside** *(NN138805)*
Muirshearlich ☎Corpach 275
*Small, stone-built farmhouse with open views
over Caledonian Canal, Loch and north face of
Ben Nevis. 3m NE off B8004.*
Apr–mid Oct 3hc CTV 3P 75acres mixed S%
B&b£5 Bdi£7.50 Wf£50 ℓ D7pm

**BARBRECK** Strathclyde *Argyll Map 10
NM80*
**Glenview** *(NM841079)* Turnalt Farm ☎277
Apr–Oct 4rm ⊁ CTV 4P 3,500acres sheep D6pm

**BARNSTAPLE** Devon *Map 2 SS53*
Mrs M. Lethaby **Home** *(SS555360)* Lower
Blakewell, Muddiford ☎2955
*Farmhouse situated in peaceful North Devon
countryside. Pony, many pets and Wendy*

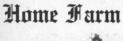

*House available for children.*
Mar–Oct 4hc (3fb) CTV 4P 40acres mixed
S% B&bf5–£8 Bdif8–£10 Wf50–£60 ⅃ D7pm

**BARRA, ISLE OF** Western Isles *Inverness-shire Map 13* **See Borve**

**BASSENTHWAITE** Cumbria *Map 11 NY23*
Mrs A.M. Trafford **Bassenthwaite Hall (East)**
*(NY231322)* ☎Bassenthwaite Lake 393
*Fully modernised 17th-century farmhouse in picturesque village close to quiet stream.*
Closed Xmas 2hc (2fb) TV 5P 200acres beef
sheep S% B&bf5–£6

Mrs D. Mattinson **Bassenthwaite Hall (West)**
*(NY228323)* ☎Bassenthwaite Lake 279
*On west side of village not to be confused with the Bassenthwaite Hall Farm on east side.*
May–Nov rsApr (B&b only) 3hc (1fb) ⅏ TV 4P
135acres mixed S% B&bf5–£5.50 Bdif9.25–£9.50
Wf63 ⅃ D5pm

**BEESWING** Dumfries & Galloway
*Kirkcudbrights Map 11 NX86*
R.H. Littlewood **Garloff** *(NX912702)* ☎Lochfoot
225
*Pleasant farmhouse set at end of farm road on south-east side of A711 6m west of Dumfries.*
6hc (2fb) Ⓒ CTV 6P ⅢⅢ 220acres dairy S%
B&bf6.32–£6.90 Bdi frf11.73 Wfrf76.95 D5pm

**BERRIEW** Powys *Map 7 SJ10*
Mrs E.G.M. Jones **Upper Pandy** *(SJ149995)*
☎338
*Isolated, black and white timbered farmhouse.
Berriew 1½ miles.*
Etr–Oct 3rm 2hc (1fb) CTV P (1fb) 140acres beef
sheep S% B&bfrf6 Bdi frf9.50 Wfrf63 ⅃

**BETHLEHEM** Dyfed *Map 3 SN62*
Mrs J. Jones **Rhuadymôn** *(SN684246)*
☎Llandeilo 823465
*An old farmhouse on the slopes of Garn Goch, an iron-age hill fort, at Bethlehem, overlooking the Towy valley and in the Brecon Beacons National Park.*
Closed Xmas & Etr 4rm 2hc 1⇼ TV 6P 2🐾 ⅢⅢ
5acres non-working S% B&bf5 Bdif9 Wf56 ⅃

**BETWS-YN-RHOS** Clwyd *Map 6 SH97*
Mrs A. Jones **Pen-y-Bryn** *(SH914732)*
☎Dolwen 223
2rm (1fb) ⅏ TV P 130acres mixed D6pm

**BICKINGTON** *(Nr Ashburton)* Devon *Map 3
SX77*
Mrs B. Heath **West Downe** *(SX794705)* ☎258
*Modernised, 16th-century farmhouse situated on edge of Dartmoor. Ponies available for riding from the farm.*
May–Oct 2hc (2fb) ⅏ CTV 2P 74acres mixed S%
B&bfrf5 Bdi frf7.50 Wfrf50 ⅃ (W only Jun, Jul &
Aug) D6pm

**BIRCHER** Heref & Worcs *Map 7 SO46*
Mr & Mrs Powell **Leys** *(SO471673)* Leys Ln
☎Yarpole 367
*17th-century farmhouse in rural setting with pleasant grounds. Close to Croft Castle and Bircher Common with its magnificent views.*
4rm 1hc (2fb) CTV P ⅢⅢ 110acres dairy S% B&bf6
Bdif8 D6.30pm

**BISSOE** Cornwall *Map 2 SW74*
**Holly Tree** *(SW763416)* Fernsplatt ☎Devoran
862126
*Isolated farmhouse in beautiful countryside.
Large garden with putting, pets' corner and pony rides.*
May–Oct 5hc CTV 10P 10acres mixed

**BLACK CROSS** Cornwall *Map 2 SW96*
Mr & Mrs J.P. Edwards **Homestake**
*(SW910606)* ☎St Austell 860423
*Pleasant house with garden on main village road. In central position for touring Cornwall.*
Etr–Oct 8hc (4fb) Ⓒ CTV 15P 82acres dairy
S% B&bf5.50–£6 Bdif7–£7.50 Wf49–£53 ⅃
(W only Whit–mid Sep) D6pm

**See advertisement on page 264.**

**BLACK DOG** Devon *Map 3 SS80*
Mr & Mrs D.J. Maunder **Lewdon** *(SS776105)*
☎Tiverton 860766
*Lewdon farm is a very old Devon farmhouse which has been in the Maunder family since 1856. Situated in a picturesque and peaceful position. Access from south side B3042 ⅓m W of Thelbridge Arms Inn (not in Black Dog Village).*
Closed Xmas 5hc 1⇼ (1fb) ⅏ Ⓒ CTV P 3🐾
220acres arable beef sheep S% B&bf6.50
Bdif9.50 Wf77 D7.30pm

**BLEADON** Avon *Map 3 ST35*
R.H. House **Purn House** *(ST334571)* ☎812324
*Pleasantly situated amid open fields with views of the Mendip and Quantock Hills and Brent Knoll.*
⅏nc3 CTV 6P ⅢⅢ river 400acres mixed D6.30pm

**BLORE** Staffs *Map 7 SK14*
M.A. Griffin **Coldwall** *(SK144494)* Okeover
☎Thorpe Cloud 249
*Stone-built farmhouse approximately 200 years old. Good views of the surrounding hills. 4 miles NW of Ashbourne.*
Mar–Oct 2hc (2fb) ⅏ TV 6P 184acres mixed S%
B&bf6–£7.50 Bdif8–£10 D6pm

**BOGHEAD** Strathclyde *Lanarks Map 11
NS74*
I. McInally **Dykehead** *(NS772417)*
☎Lesmahagow 892226
*Rough cast, two-storey farmhouse just fifty yards from Strathaven/Lesmahagow road.*
Mar–Oct 2rm (1fb) CTV 3P 1🐾 ⅢⅢ 200acres dairy
sheep S% B&bf5 Wf35 Ⓜ

**BORELAND** Dumfries & Galloway
*Dumfriesshire Map 11 NY19*
Mrs I. Maxwell **Gall** *(NY172901)* ☎229
*Situated on a hill looking towards the Moffat Hills.*
Apr–Oct 2hc ⅏ Ⓒ CTV 2P 1,066acres beef
sheep S% B&bf5.50–£6.50 Bdifrf9.50

**BORVE** Isle of Barra, Western Isles
*Inverness-shire Map 13 NF60*
Mrs M. MacNeil **Ocean View** *(NF655014)*
☎Castlebay 397
*Detached bungalow standing in natural farmland facing west over Atlantic Ocean.*
3rm (3fb) ⅏ TV P sea 3acres sheep B&bf6–£6.50
Bdif9.50–£10

**BOTALLACK** Cornwall *Map 2 SW33*
Mrs J. Cargeeg **Manor** *(SW368331)*
☎Penzance 788525
*Previously known as 'Nanparra'; home of Ross Poldark from the television series filmed here.
Area steeped in history.*
Closed Xmas 6hc (2fb) ⅏ CTV 6P ⅢⅢ 150acres
mixed S% B&bfrf6 Bdi frf10

**BOVEY TRACEY** Devon *Map 3 SX87*
A.R. Roberts **Willmead** *(SX795812)*
☎Lustleigh 214

*Farmhouse dating from 1327 situated on edge of Dartmoor National Park in a delightful valley.*
Closed Xmas & New Year 3hc ✙ nc10 CTV 10P 31acres beef ✳ B&bf£9 Bdif£15 D8pm

**BOW** Devon Map 3 SX70
Mrs V. Hill **East Hillerton House** (SX725981)
Spreyton (3m S unclass) ☎393
*Farm is located 2m NE of Spreyton village.*
Closed Xmas 2hc (1fb) ✙ CTV P ⅢⅢ 340acres mixed S% B&bfr£5 Bdifr£8

**BRADNINCH** Devon Map 3 SS90
Mr & Mrs Cole **White Heathfield** (ST012029)
☎Hele 300
*Farmhouse in typical East Devon scenery. Off southside of B3181.*
Apr–Sep 3rm (2fb) ✙ TV 4P 127acres mixed S% B&bf£4.50–£5 Bdif£7–£7.75 Wfrf£44 ⅃ D8pm

**BRADWORTHY** Devon Map 2 SS31
**Dinworthy** (SS311156) ☎297
*Farmhouse set in secluded locality. Fishing and rough shooting available.*
Apr–Sep 3hc ✙ TV 3P 105acres beef, dairy & mixed Dnoon
**Lew** (SS326140) ☎404
*Stone-built farmhouse on the outskirts of the village.*
Jun–Sep 3rm 2hc ✙ nc5 CTV 2P 60acres mixed D4pm

**BRAUNTON** Devon Map 2 SS43
Mr & Mrs Barnes **Denham Farm Holidays** (SS480404) North Buckland ☎Croyde 890297
*Large farmhouse, parts of which date from the 18th century, set in lovely countryside. 2 miles from Croyde and within easy reach of Barnstaple and Ilfracombe.*
8hc (5fb) ✙ CTV 7🐾 160acres beef S% B&bf£5.50–£6.50 Bdif£9.50–£10.50 Wf£60–£70 (W only Jul & Aug) D4pm
J.E.J. Tucker **Middle Spreacombe** (SS479421)
☎Woolacombe 870370
*Well-decorated, comfortable farmhouse 3m N of A361. Good location for country walks, fishing and bathing.*
May–Sep 3hc ✙ TV 3P 200acres mixed D6.30pm

**BREAGE** Cornwall Map 2 SW62
**Sethnow** (SW614286) ☎Helston 3603
*Long, low, 17th-century granite farmhouse with oak panelling. Fully modernised. Picturesque setting.*
Apr–Oct 3hc TV 4P 110acres mixed

**BRECHIN** Tayside Angus Map 15 NO56
Mr J. Stewart **Wood Of Auldbar** (NO554556)

Aberlemno ☎Aberlemno 218
*Fairly large farmhouse well back from road amid farmland and woods 5m SW on unclassified road, between B9134 and A932.*
3rm (1fb) CTV 3P ⅢⅢ 187acres mixed S% B&bf£4.50–£5 Bdif£7–£7.50 Wf£49

**BRENDON** Devon Map 3 SS74
Mrs A. South **Farley Water** (SS744464) ☎272
*Comfortable farmhouse adjoining the moors. Good home cooking and freedom for children.*
May–Oct 5rm 4hc (2fb) TV P 223acres mixed S% B&bf£4.60 Bdif£7.76 Wfrf£51.75 ⅃ (W only end Jul–Aug)
Mr & Mrs J.G. Phipps **Wingate** (SS780490)
☎285
*This 18th-century stone-built farmhouse is set 1,000ft up on Exmoor. The farm runs down to the edge of the Countisbury cliffs—giving marvellous views of sea. 1¼m NE off A39.*
May–Sep 7hc (3fb) ✙ CTV 9P sea 200acres beef sheep S% B&bf£7.50–£8 Wf£49 Ⓜ

**BRENT ELEIGH** Suffolk Map 5 TL94
J.P. Gage **Street** (TL945476) ☎Lavenham 247271
*A most beautiful period house, tastefully furnished to a high standard.*
Apr–Oct 2hc ✙ nc14 TV 2P ⅢⅢ 140acres arable S% B&bf£8–£8.50 Wf£56–£59.50

**BRIDESTOWE** Devon Map 2 SX58
Mrs M.A. Down **Little Bidlake** (SX494887)
☎233
*Neat, clean and efficient farmhouse adjacent to A30 between Bridestowe and Launceston.*
Whit–Oct 2hc ✙ ⒸⒽ CTV P ⅢⅢ 150acres beef dairy Dnoon
Mrs M.A. Ponsford **Stone** (SX503890) ☎253
*Large Victorian farmhouse with gardens and fishing lake at the rear.*
mid May–mid Sep 7hc (2fb) ✙ CTV ⅢⅢ 260acres beef sheep S% B&bf£7 Bdif£9.50 Wfrf£55 ⅃ D6pm
Mrs J. Northcott **Town** (SX504905) ☎226
*Tile-hung farmhouse with a pleasant, homely atmosphere.*
May–Oct 3hc (1fb) CTV 4P 150acres dairy S% B&bf£6–£7 Bdif£8–£10 D7.30pm
Mrs M. Hockridge **Week** (SX519913) ☎221
*Farm is situated east of Bridestowe and signposted from A30.*
6hc (4fb) ⒸⒽ CTV 10P 163acres mixed S% B&bf£6.50–£7.50 Bdif£8.50–£9.50 Wf£59–£65 ⅃ D6pm

**BRIDGERULE** Devon Map 2 SS20
**Buttsbeer Cross** (SS266043) ☎210
*Modernised farmhouse dating from 15th*

century. Within easy reach of Bude and
North Cornish coast.
Etr–Oct 3rm 2hc ⌇ nc11 CTV 3P 143acres
mixed D5.30pm

**BROADWINDSOR** Dorset Map 3 ST40
Mrs Poulton **Hursey** (ST433028) ☎68323
Stone-built farmhouse in very quiet rural setting
in rolling Dorset countryside.
Closed Xmas wk 2hc ⌇ TV P 2acres non-working
B&bfr£6.50 Bdi fr£10 Wfr£65 ⌇ D6.30pm

**BROMPTON REGIS** Devon Map 3 SS93
Mrs G. Payne **Lower Holworthy** (SS978308)
☎244
Small 18th-century hill farm overlooking and
bordering the Wimbleball Lake in Exmoor
National Park.
Closed Xmas 3rm 2hc ⌇ TV 4P ▥ lake 160acres
beef sheep Dnoon

**BROUGH** Cumbria Map 12 NY71
Mrs J. M. Atkinson **Augill House** (NY814148)
☎305
Stone-built Victorian farmhouse 1 mile from
village. Quiet, clean and comfortable.
Closed Xmas & New Year 3hc (1fb) CTV 6P ▥
40acres dairy S% B&b£5.50 Bdi£9 Wfr£60 ⌇
D4pm

**BRUTON** Somerset Map 3 ST63
Mrs A.M. Eastment **Gilcombe** (ST696364)
☎3378
Small, well-furnished farmhouse surrounded by
countryside, 1 mile from Bruton.
Apr–Sep 3rm 2hc nc3 CTV 6P ▥ 400acres dairy
S% B&b£6

**BRYNGWYN** Powys Map 3 SO14
Mrs H.E.A. Nicholls **Newhouse** (SO191497)
☎Painscastle 671
200-year-old, two-storey, stone-built farmhouse
set in 150acres of mixed farmland.
2hc ⌇ CTV 3P ▥ 150acres mixed B&bfr£6.50
Bdi fr£10 Wfr£70 ⌇ D5.30pm

**BUCHLYVIE** Central Stirlings Map 11 NS59
J. McArthur **Balwill** (NS548927) ☎239
White-painted farmhouse and buildings set off
main road in the upper Forth Valley.
Etr–Sep 2rm 1hc (1fb) ⌇ CTV 3P ▥ 200acres
beef S% B&b£6 Bdi£8

**BUCKIE** Grampian Banffs Map 15 NJ46
M.E.B. McLean **Mill of Rathven** (NJ446657)
☎31132
Farmhouse with attractive garden. On edge of
village of Rathven and surrounded by arable land
and several outbuildings.

Closed Xmas 3rm CTV 3P S% B&b£6.50 Bdi£8–
£10.50 D6pm

**BUCKLAND BREWER** Devon Map 2 SS42
Mrs M. Brown **Holwell** (SS424159) ☎Langtree
288
16th-century farmhouse with a friendly and
homely atmosphere.
rsOct–Apr 5hc (3fb) CTV P 310acres mixed S%
B&b£6.50 Bdi£8.50 W£50 ⌇ (W only Aug)

**BUDOCK** Cornwall Map 2 SW73
A.J. Dunstan **Menehay** (SW787322) Bilckland
Rd ☎Penryn 72550
Pleasant farmhouse with good standard of
furnishings and decoration, convenient for
beach.
Apr–Sep 3hc (1fb) CTV P 70acres mixed

**BULKWORTHY** Devon Map 2 SS31
Mrs K.P. Hockridge **Blakes** (SS395143) ☎Milton
Damerel 249
Pleasant, comfortable and well-decorated house
in peaceful setting close to the River Torridge.
May–Sep 2hc (1fb) ⌇ nc13 CTV 3P 155acres
arable beef sheep S% B&bfr£5.75

**BURNHOUSE** Strathclyde Ayrs Map 10
NS35
Mr & Mrs Robertson **Burnhouse Manor**
(NS383503) ☎Dunlop 406
Large farmhouse in own grounds. Visible and
well signposted from main Paisley/Irvine road.
Off B706.
Closed 2nd & 3rd wk Oct & New Year rsSun
(Nov–Etr) & Mon (B&b only) 6hc (1fb) ⌇ CTV 40P
▥ 111acres arable beef S% B&b£6.50–£7.50
Bdi£11–£12 D8.30pm

**BURNISTON** N Yorks Map 8 TA09
Mrs D. Muir **Beaconsfield House** (NZ014928)
South End ☎Scarborough 870439
Well-furnished and decorated farmhouse in
village.
Spring Bank Hol–Sep 3rm (1fb) ⌇ nc3 TV 4P 1☎
▥ 50acres mixed S% B&bfr£5.50 Wfr£35 Ⓜ

**BUTE, ISLE OF** Strathclyde Bute Map 10
**See Rothesay**

**BUTTERLEIGH** Devon Map 3 SS90
Mrs B.J. Hill **Sunnyside** (ST975088) ☎Bickleigh
322
The farmhouse, built about 1700, is situated in
the heart of the Devonshire countryside 3 miles
west of Cullompton.
Closed Xmas 5hc (3fb) CTV 6P 150acres mixed
✻ B&bfr£6 Bdi£8.50–£10

**CABUS** Lancs *Map 7 SD44*
T. & E. Cornthwaite **Wildings** *(SO489479)*
☎Garstang 3321
*Modernised Victorian farmhouse on A6. Clean and pleasant with plenty of home produce used in cooking.*
Etr–Oct 3hc ✸ nc12 TV 10P 60acres mixed S%
B&b£6

**CADELEIGH** Devon *Map 3 SS90*
Mrs I. Crimp **West Ridge** *(SS904093)*
☎Bickleigh 295
*Part 16th-century farmhouse set in a secluded, wooded valley. Farmhouse fare is home-produced.*
Apr–Sep 3rm 1hc (1fb) ✸ CTV 3P 93acres dairy
S% B&b£6–£7 Bdi£8–£10 Wfr£45 ⅃

**CADNAM** Hants *Map 4 SU21*
Mrs A.M. Dawe **Budds** *(SU310139)* Winsor Rd,
Winsor ☎2381
*Picturesque dairy farm adjacent to the New Forest with thatched roof and attractive gardens.*
Mar–Oct 2hc (1fb) ✸ TV 3P 140acres dairy
S% B&b£6–£7

Mrs M. Garrett **Copythorne Lodge** *(SU308148)*
☎2127
*Two-storey Victorian house set back from the main road in wooded and rural surroundings.*
3rm 1🛏 (2fb) TV 6P 30acres dairy S%
B&b£5.50

Mr & Mrs R.D.L. Dawe **Kents** Winsor Rd,
Winsor ☎3497
*Picturesque thatched farmhouse, recently renovated. Accommodation of high standard.
2m NE unclass.*
Etr–Sep 2rm 1🛏 (1fb) ✸ CTV 6P 140acres dairy S% B&b£6–£6.50 W£42 🅼

**CAIRNIE** Grampian *Aberdeens Map 15 NJ44*
Mrs P.M.F. Moir **Smallburn** *(NJ469441)*
☎Cairnie 219 (Approach road to farm is from southside of A96 mid way (approx 6m) between Huntly and Keith at signpost Wyndraw 1m of Cairnie.)
Apr–Oct 2rm (1fb) ✸ [Ch] CTV 6P 400acres mixed S% B&b£5.50–£6 Bdi£8–£8.50
W£50–£54 ⅃ D6pm

**CALDBECK** Cumbria *Map 11 NY33*
Mrs D.H. Coulthard **Friar Hall** *(NY324399)*
☎633
*Modernised two-storey stone-built farmhouse. Well-decorated and contains good quality furniture. Overlooks river and village church.*
Etr–Sep 2hc (1fb) ✸ CTV 4P river 140acres dairy sheep S% B&b£5.50–£6.50 Bdi£9–£10 D3pm

Mrs J.M. Coux **Hudscales** *(NY332375)* Hesket Newmarket (off unclass rd 1m W of Hesket Newmarket) ☎637
*A charming farmhouse dating back to the mid 1800s, with more recent extensions, set high in the Caldbeck fells which tower to the river and panoramic views over the Eden valley to the front.*
May–Oct 2rm CTV P 🏚 350acres sheep
✳B&b£6 Bdi£9.50 D7pm

**CAMELFORD** Cornwall *Map 2 SX18*
Mrs H. MacLeod **Melorne** *(SX099856)*
Camelford Station ☎3200
*Situated approximately 1m N of village near site of old railway station. Fishing and rough shooting available to guests.*
Etr–Oct 7rm 6hc (3fb) CTV 12P 95acres dairy
B&b£5.75 Bdi£9.20 W£64.40 ⅃

Mrs R.Y. Lyes **Pencarrow** Advent ☎3282
*Large stone farmhouse in a pretty hamlet, 1½ miles from Camelford.*
Etr–Oct 2hc ✸ TV 2P 2🏚 40acres dairy S%
B&b£5–£6 Bdi£7.50–£8.50 W£50–£55 ⅃

**CAPEL BANGOR** Dyfed *Map 6 SN68*
G. Humphreys **Fron** *(SN663804)* ☎221
*Elevated, stone-built farmhouse with splendid views of the Rheidol Valley.*
2rm 1hc CTV P 🏚 mixed

**CAPEL GARMON** Gwynedd *Map 6 SH85*
**Maes y Garnedd** *(SH816548)* ☎Betws-y-Coed 428
*Isolated farmhouse in elevated position.*
2rm ✸ nc TV P 150acres mixed

**CAPEL SEION** Dyfed *Map 6 SN67*
Mrs S.J. Davies **Rhoslawdden** *(SN628794)*
Moriah ☎Aberystwyth 612585
*Comfortable farmhouse overlooking fields.*
Apr–Oct 3rm 1hc CTV 3P 112acres arable dairy
S% B&b£5–£6 Bdi£8–£10 Wfr£56 ⅃

**CAPUTH** Tayside *Perths Map 11 NO04*
Mrs R. Smith **Stralochy** *(NO086413)* ☎250
*Situated in lovely spot looking down a valley, trees merging in Sidlaw hills.*
May–Oct 3rm (1fb) ✸ TV 3P 239acres arable S%
Bdi fr£7 Wfr£49 ⅃ D4pm

**CAREY** Heref & Worcs *Map 3 SO53*
Mr & Mrs Davidson **Pear Tree** *(SO561306)*
☎201
Closed Xmas 3rm 1hc ✸ nc10 CTV 6P 🏚 23acres beef S% B&b£7.50 Bdi£11.50

**CARKEEL** Cornwall *Map 2 SX46*
**Eales** *(SX414605)* ☎Saltash 2865

---

# *Friar Hall*

## *Caldbeck, Wigton, Cumbria*

### *Telephone: Caldbeck 633*

### **Mrs. D. Coulthard**

Friar Hall is a very old farmhouse with oak beams in most rooms. Situated in a peaceful position in the village of Caldbeck overlooking the river and Caldbeck Fells. Ideal situation for touring. English Lakes, Scottish Border and Roman Wall, also for fellwalks and fishing. This is a dairy and sheep farm a good place for people to stay when breaking their journey to and from Scotland.

2 double rooms and one family room.

Terms 1982: Bed & Breakfast £5.50-£6.50 Dinner from £3.50 (if ordered)

*Clean and well decorated farmhouse.*
*Saltash 2 miles.*
4rm TV 6P 11acres dairy

**CARNO** Powys *Map 6 SN99*
R.G. & P.M. Lewis **Y Grofftydd** *(SN981965)*
☎274
*Farmhouse is situated off A470 overlooking*
*typical mid-Wales scenery. Ideal centre for*
*walking. Sporting clay-pigeon shoot on*
*premises.*
4hc Ch CTV 3P 180acres mixed S% B&bf6
Bdif10

**CARRONBRIDGE** Central *Stirlings Map 11*
*NS78*
Mr A. Morton **Lochend** *(NS759856)* ☎Denny
822778
*Modernised, 18th-century hill farm. Pleasant*
*farmyard with rose garden in centre. Set in*
*quiet, isolated position. 1½m off unclass rd*
*towards Bannockburn.*
Jun–Sep 2rm 1hc ⅙ nc3 TV P ☎ ▥ 380acres
beef sheep S% B&bf5.50–£5.75 Bdif6.50–£6.75

**CARRUTHERSTOWN** Dumfries & Galloway
*Dumfriesshire Map 11 NY17*
Mrs J. Brown **Domaru** *(NY093716)* ☎260
*Modern, detached, two-storey farmhouse built*
*at side of farm road. About 300 yards from farm*
*buildings. Carrutherstown ½ mile.*
Apr–Oct 3rm 2hc TV in all bedrooms 3P ▥
140acres dairy S% B&bfrf5 Bdifrf8 Wfrf56 ⅃
D6.30pm

**CASTLE CARROCK** Cumbria *Map 12 NY55*
B.W. Robinson **Gelt Hall** *(NY542554)* ☎Hayton
260
*An old-world farmhouse built around a courtyard*

*directly off the main street of this tiny village.*
3rm (1fb) CTV 6P 2☎ 120acres beef dairy S%
B&bf6 Bdif9 Wfrf60 ⅃ D7pm

**CATLOWDY** Cumbria *Map 12 NY47*
J. & M. Sisson **Bessiestown** *(NY457768)*
☎Nicholforest 219
*Neat farmhouse, tastefully furnished and*
*comfortable. Visitors welcome to stroll around*
*farm buildings.*
5hc CTV 12P ▥ 53acres sheep S% B&bf6–£7
Bdif11–£12 D4pm

**CAWDOR** Highland *Nairns Map 14 NH85*
*Little Budgate (NH834503)* ☎267
*Small, cottage-style farmhouse set amid fields.*
*Cawdor 1 mile.*
May–Sep 2rm (A 2hc) ⅙ P 50acres arable

**CEMMAES** Powys *Map 6 SH80*
Mrs D. Evans-Breese **Rhydygwiel** *(SH826056)*
☎Cemmaes Road 541
*Remote, detached, stone-built farmhouse on*
*north side of Dovey Valley. Attractive gardens at*
*back of house.*
3rm (1fb) P river 200acres mixed S% B&bfrf5.50

**CERNE ABBAS** Dorset *Map 3 ST60*
R. & M. Paul **Giants Head** *(ST675029)* Old
Sherborne Rd ☎242
*A modernised, detached farmhouse in elevated*
*position at the head of the famous Cerne Giant.*
*Open rural views.*
Apr–Sep 5rm 3hc ⅙ nc10 CTV 10P 4acres sheep
S% B&bf6 Bdif9.50 Wf55 D2pm

**CHAGFORD** Devon *Map 3 SX78*
D.G. & S.A. Bennie **Beechlands** *(SX694877)*
☎3313

*Views of Dartmoor, Meldon and Nattadon Common. Also views of Castle Drogo and surrounding countryside.*
Mar–Nov 4rm 3hc (A 1⇦) (1fb) ✸ CTV 14P
28acres mixed S% B&b£8.50

**CHAPELTON** Strathclyde *Lanarks Map 11 NS64*
Mr R. Hamilton **East Drumloch** (NS678521)
☎236
*Large stone-built farmhouse with a modern, well-furnished interior.*
4rm (2fb) CTV P 260acres beef S% B&b£5.50–£6
W£40–£47 Ⓜ

Mrs E. Taylor **Millwell** (NS653496) ☎East Kilbride 43248
*Small, 18th-century farm set in tree-studded land.*
3rm CTV 4P 94acres dairy S% B&b£5 Bdi£6.50

**CHAPMANSLADE** Wilts *Map 3 ST84*
Mrs M. Hoskins **Spinney** (ST839480) ☎412
*Two-storey stone-built farmhouse surrounded by fields and woodland with farm buildings at rear.*
Closed Xmas 3hc (2fb) 10P 2➊ 🎇 4acres sheep
S% B&b£6–£6.50 W£35–£38 Ⓜ

**CHEDINGTON** Dorset *Map 3 ST40*
Lt Col & Mrs I. Stanford **Lower** (ST485054)
☎Corscombe 371
Closed 2nd wk Oct & Xmas 3hc nc5 TV 4P 🎇
130acres beef sheep S% ✱ B&b£6.50 Bdi£12
W£80 Ⅼ

**CHERITON FITZPAINE** Devon *Map 3 SS80*
Mrs D.M. Tricks **Brindiwell** (SS896079) ☎357
*Farmhouse situated on the side of a valley with views of Exe Valley and Dartmoor.*
3rm 1hc (1fb) ✸ CTV 4P 130acres mixed
S% B&b£5–£6 Bdi£8.50–£10 D8pm

**CHURCHILL** Avon *Map 3 ST45*
Mrs J. Sacof **Churchill Green** (ST429602)
☎852438
*Modernised 16th-century farmhouse still retaining its character, the large garden faces south overlooking the foothills of the Mendips.*
7hc (4fb) ✸ Ⓒⓗ TV 50P 🎇 25acres arable beef

*Primrose* (ST456609) ☎852358
*Attractive two-storey, stone-built farmhouse with a pretty, landscape garden.*
6rm nc5 CTV 6P 🎇 12acres non-working
D6.30pm

**CHURCHINFORD** Somerset *Map 3 ST21*
M. Palmer **Hunter Lodge** (ST212144)
☎Churchstanton 253
*Detached, two-storey farmhouse with slate roof*

*and large garden.*
4rm 3hc (1fb) CTV 6P 🎇 30acres mixed S%
B&b£6–£7 Bdi£9.50–£10.50 W£65–£70 D10am

**CHURCH STRETTON** Salop *Map 7 SO49*
Mrs J.C. Inglis **The Hall** (SO478925) Hope Bowdler (1m E B4371) ☎722041
*The Hall is an old farmhouse which has recently been completely modernised. It is set on the edge of the tiny peaceful village of Hope Bowdler, and surrounded by beautiful hills.*
Mar–Oct rsNov & Feb 3hc ✸nc10 4P 🎇 22acres sheep S% B&b£6 W£35–£38.50 Ⓜ

**CLACHAN** Isle of Skye, Highland *Inverness-shire Map 13 NG46*
Mr & Mrs C. MacDonald **Windyridge** (NG492666) ☎Staffin 222
*Small, white-painted croft with blue-tiled roof. At north end of Island in a very pleasant situation.*
mid May–mid Oct 3rm (1fb) ✱ B&b£5 Bdi£7.50 D7pm

**CLARENCEFIELD** Dumfries & Galloway *Dumfriesshire Map 11 NY06*
Mrs S.C. Hogg **Kirkbeck** (NY083705) ☎284
*Attractive farmhouse with a high standard of décor. Near to Solway coast. Fishing and golf. N on A724.*
Apr–Oct 3hc (1fb) ✸ CTV 3P 106acres arable pigs S% B&b£5 Bdi£7.50 W£50 Ⅼ D8pm

**CLAVERHAM** Avon *Map 3 ST46*
K. Dee-Shapland **Green** (ST454662) ☎Yatton 833180
*Long, low farm cottage located in a 'picture postcard' setting. Ponies & donkeys for children to ride.*
4rm 3hc (2fb) CTV P 2➊ 6acres non-working S%
B&b£8

**CLAWDDNEWYDD** Clwyd *Map 6 SJ05*
G. Williams **Maestyddyw Isa** (SJ054535) ☎289
*Old farmhouse filled with antiques. In rural setting on the outskirts of Cleanog Forest.*
Mar–Nov 3hc (1fb) ✸ CTV P 🎇 365acres mixed
S% B&b£6.50 Bdi£9.50 W£63

**CLEARWELL** Glos *Map 3 SO50*
Mr & Mrs P. Jones **Tudor** (SO569083) ☎Dean 33046
Closed Xmas 3hc 3🔥 Ⓒⓗ CTV P 🎇 14acres mixed S% B&b£5–£6 Bdi£8–£9 W£56–£63 Ⅼ D7pm

**CLOVELLY** Devon *Map 2 SS32*
Mrs E. Symons **Burnstone** (SS325233) Higher Clovelly ☎219
*Large, comfortably furnished farmhouse with open fire in spacious lounge. Good farmhouse fare.*

3hc (1fb) ✦ CTV 4P ▥ sea 400acres arable dairy S% ✳ B&bf£5.50–£6.50 Bdi£10–£10.50 W£56.50–£59.50 ⫼ D5.30pm

**CLUN** Salop *Map 7 SO38*
*Llanhedric (SO283841)* ☏203
*Large and well-furnished farmhouse with oak beams and antique furniture.*
May–Oct 2rm 1hc ✦ Ch CTV 2P 400acres dairy & mixed

**CLUNTON** Salop *Map 7 SO38*
Mrs J. Williams **Hurst Mill** *(SO318811)* ☏Clun 224
*Small stone-built farmhouse in picturesque setting, surrounded by tree-clad hills. Friendly atmosphere.*
3rm Ch CTV 6P 100acres mixed S% B&bf£5–£6 Bdi£8–£8.50 W£62

**CLYRO** Powys *Map 3 SO24*
Mrs J. Harris **Crossway** *(SO216459)* ☏Hay-on-Wye 820567
*Small farm situated in the hills. Quiet and peaceful surroundings. Clyro village 1¾ miles.*
Mar–Oct 2rm (1fb) ✦TV P 50acres mixed S% B&bf£5 Bdi£7.50 W£50 ⫼ D5pm

**CLYST ST MARY** Devon *Map 3 SX99*
Mrs B. Freemantle **Courtway** *(SS981918)* Bishops Court ☏Topsham 4506
*Modern farmhouse with views over surrounding countryside.*
Mar–Oct 2hc (1fb) CTV 4P ▥ 200acres mixed S% B&bf£6 Bdi£8.50 W£49 ⫼ Dnoon

Mrs L. Freemantle **Ivington** *(SX985912)* ☏Topsham 3290
*Large brick-built farmhouse surrounded by lawns and gardens, situated 200yds from A3052.*
Jan–Nov 3hc (2fb) CTV 4P 200acres dairy S% B&bf£5 W£35 Ⓜ

**COLEFORD** Devon *Map 3 SS70*
Mrs D.M. Hockridge **Butsford Barton** *(SS764004)* ☏Copplestone 353
*New brick-built farmhouse with fine pastoral views over Devonshire countryside.*
Etr–Sep 3rm 2hc (1fb) ✦CTV P 156acres mixed S% B&bf£5–£5.50 Bdi£8–£8.50 W£52–£56 ⫼ D3pm

**COMBE MARTIN** Devon *Map 2 SS54*
Mr & Mrs M. Stephens **Longlands** *(SS614451)* ☏3522
*Farmhouse and unspoilt woods and valleys with fine views.*
Apr–mid Oct & Xmas 6hc (2fb) TV 15P ▥ sea 27½acres mixed S% B&bf£5–£6 Bdi£8–£9 W£54–£60 ⫼ (W only Jul & Aug)

**COMRIE** Tayside *Perths Map 11 NN72*
Mrs J.H. Rimmer **West Ballindalloch** *(NN744262)* ☏282 (due to change to 70282)
*Cosy, small farmhouse with neat garden set amid hills in secluded glen. Comrie 4 miles.*
Apr–Sep 2rm (1fb) ✦CTV 3P 1,500acres sheep S% B&bf£5–£5.50

**COOKLEY** Suffolk *Map 5 TM37*
Mr & Mrs A.T. Veasy **Green** *(TM337772)* ☏Linstead 209
*17th-century farmhouse with exposed timbers in an area of rural peace and quiet. Friendly atmosphere.*
Apr–Oct 3hc ✦ nc8 TV 3P 45acres mixed S% B&bfr£7 Bdi fr£10.50 D3.30pm

**COOMBE** Cornwall *Map 2 SW95*
Mrs J. Scott **Treway** *(SW945505)* ☏St Austell 882236
*Pleasant, comfortable farmhouse in isolated rural setting about 8 miles from St Austell.*
Etr–Oct 3rm 2hc (2fb) nc3 CTV 4P ▥ 170acres dairy S% B&bf£5–£5.25 Wfr£35 Ⓜ

**COTLEIGH** Devon *Map 3 ST20*
Mrs J. Boyland **Barn Park** *(ST218050)* ☏Upottery 297
*Comfortably furnished farmhouse offering tasty country fare.*
Mar–Oct 2rm (2fb) ✦ CTV 3P 82acres dairy S% B&bfr£6 Bdi fr£9 Wfr£50 ⫼ D6pm

**COVERACK BRIDGES** *(Nr Helston)* Cornwall *Map 2 SW63*
Mr & Mrs E. Lawrance **Boscadjack** *(SW673311)* (2½m N of Helston, off B3207) ☏Helston 2086
*Modernised farmhouse set in 52 acres of dairy farmland, situated in the Cober Valley amidst delightful, unspoiled countryside 2 miles from Helston.*
Etr–Oct 4hc (2fb) ✦CTV P ▥ 52acres dairy B&bf£5.18–£6.33 Bdi£8.63–£10.06 W£57.50–£69 ⫼ (W only mid Jul–Aug)

**CRACKINGTON HAVEN** Cornwall *Map 2 SX19*
Mrs M. Knight **Manor** *(SX159962)* ☏St Gennys 304
*Attractive gardens with beautiful view in secluded position 1m from beach. Most sports in area, bathing, fishing, golf, gliding, riding, walking, bird watching, pleasure boat trips, museums.*
3rm 1👁 ✦ nc13 CTV 6P ▥ 180acres arable mixed S% B&bf£7 Bdi£11 Wfr£70 ⫼

**CREDITON** Devon *Map 3 SS80*
Mr & Mrs M. Pennington **Woolsgrove** *(SS793028)* ☏Copplestone 246

*17th-century farmhouse overlooking acres of grassland. 3m NW on unclass (Morchard) road and 1m N of A377.*
Feb–Nov 3rm 2hc (1fb) ⚹ TV 4P 160acres mixed D8pm

**CROESGOCH** Dyfed *Map 2 SM83*
Mr & Mrs A. Charles **Torbant** *(SM845307)*
☎276
*Well-kept farmhouse, tastefully furnished. Situated in pleasant spot overlooking open country.*
Etr–Oct 11hc (A 2⇨) (5fb) ⚹ CTV 40P ▥ 133acres arable beef sheep S% B&bf£5.50–£6.50 Bdif£10.50–£12 Wf£70–£79 ⥮ D6.30pm

Mrs B. Jenkins **Trearched Farm** *(SM831306)*
☎310
*Farm overlooks St George's Channel. Ideal for touring south-west Wales and Coast.*
8hc (3fb) CTV 20P ▥ sea 139acres arable S% B&bf£5.75–£7 Bdif£9.20–£10.45 D7.45pm

**CROIK** Highland *Ross & Crom Map 14 NH49*
Mrs K.M. Moffat **Forest** *(NH454914)* ☎The Craigs 322
*1870 farmhouse in beautiful location but very isolated. 10 miles off single track road from Ardgay.*
Apr–Sep 3rm ⚹ CTV 5P river 3,000acres mixed S% B&bfr£4.50 Bdi fr£8.50 D8pm

**CROMHALL** Avon *Map 3 ST69*
Mrs S. Scolding **Varley** *(ST699905)* Talbot End ☎Wickwar 292
*Spacious, two-storey, stone-built farmhouse with garden. Well-maintained and neatly decorated throughout.*
Etr–Sep 4hc (4fb) ⚹ CTV 5P ▥ 75acres dairy pigs S% B&bf£6 Bdif£9 (W only Aug) D3.30pm

**CROOK** Cumbria *Map 7 SD49*
Mrs I. Scales **Greenbank** *(SD462953)*
☎Staveley 821216
*Attractive farmhouse near village centre. Pleasant gardens. Mainly dairy plus small mushroom farm.*
Mar–Nov 5hc (2fb) CTV 6P ▥ 14½acres dairy mushroom S% B&bf£6–£6.50 Bdif£10–£11 D7pm

Mrs M. Clark **Warriner Yeat** *(SD438950)*
☎Windermere 3828
*Large, attractive house in small garden. Pleasant setting with fine views.*
Jun–Sep 3rm 2hc 1⚹ 6p 75acres mixed S% B&bf£4.50–£5

**CRUCKTON** Salop *Map 7 SJ41*
Mrs M. Birchall **Woodfield** *(SJ432108)*
☎Shrewsbury 860249
*Large, modern, detached farmhouse with neat gardens.*
3rm nc5 CTV 3P ▥ 84acres mixed S% ✳B&bfr£6

**CRYMYCH** Dyfed *Map 2 SN13*
Mr & Mrs Hazelden **Felin Tŷgwyn** *(SN162355)*
☎Crosswell 603
*Approximately 2 miles from Crymych, at the foot of the Preseli Mountains, surrounded by farmland. Within easy reach of Newport beach, Cardigan, Carmarthen and Haverfordwest.*
6rm 5hc (A 1hc) (2fb) CTV 10P ▥ 8acres mixed S% Bdi fr£9.85 Wf£62.72–£73.40 ⥮ (W only Spring Bank Hol–Aug)

**CUBERT** Cornwall *Map 2 SW75*
Mr & Mrs J. Whybrow **Treworgans** *(SW787589)* ☎Crantock 830200
*Detached bungalow, situated approximately 1m from the village of Cubert.*

---

---

Closed Xmas 5hc CTV 6P 70acres mixed S%
B&b£5.50–£6.50 Bdi£7.50–£8 W£50–£55 ⊾
D4pm

**CULLODEN MOOR** Highland *Inverness-shire* Map 14 *NH74*
Mrs E.M.C. Alexander **Culdoich** *(NH755435)*
☎268
*18th-century, two-storey farmhouse in isolated position near Culloden battlefield and Clava standing stones.*
Etr–Oct 2rm (1fb) ⊀ TV P 200acres mixed S%
B&b£5.50–£6 Bdi£8–£8.50 D6pm

**CULLOMPTON** Devon *Map 3 ST00*
Mrs A.C. Cole **Five Bridges** *(ST026095)*
☎33453
*Well-maintained, brick-built farmhouse. Clean and well decorated.*
Closed Xmas 4hc (3fb) CTV 6P 1⋒ 22acres non-working S% B&b£5 Bdi£7.75 W£51 ⊾ D4pm

**CURY** Cornwall *Map 2 SW62*
Mrs R.E.U. Benney **Nanplough** *(SW687215)*
☎Mullion 240232
*Attractive, comfortable farmhouse. Access via ½ mile gravel lane.*
Etr–Sep 5rm 4hc (1fb) ⊀ nc5 CTV 3P ▥ 50acres arable beef sheep S% B&b£5.50–£6 Bdi£9–£10 D6.30pm

**CURY CROSS LANES** Cornwall *Map 2 SW62*
Mrs M.F. Osborne **Polglase** *(SW286213)*
☎Mullion 240269
*5 miles from Helston.*
Etr–Sep 6rm 5hc (2fb) ⊀ CTV 4P 65acres mixed S% B&b£7 Bdi£10 W£70 ⊾ D6.30pm

**CUSHNIE** Grampian *Aberdeens* Map 15 *NJ51*
**Brae Smithy Croft** *(NJ520108)* ☎Muir of Fowlis 215
*Approach from A980 (3m) W or B9119 (3m) N.*
Apr–Sep 3rm CTV P ▥ 20acres arable

**CYNWYD** Clwyd *Map 6 SJ04*
Mrs B. Williams **Ceamawr** *(SJ048419)*
☎Corwen 2421
*Pleasant, two-storey, stone-built farmhouse in an elevated position.*
5hc (1fb) ⊀ CTV P ▥ river 60acres dairy

**DALWOOD** *(Nr Axminster)* Devon *Map 3 ST20*
Mrs S.W. Cobley **Elford** *(ST258004)*
☎Axminster 32415
*17th-century farmhouse in country setting. Panoramic, pastoral views.*

Mar–Oct 4hc 2⇔ (2fb) ⊀ TV 8P ▥ 37acres beef dairy sheep S% B&b£7–£9 Bdi£10–£12.50 W£66.50–£77 ⊾ D5pm

**DAVIOT** Highland *Inverness-shire* Map 14 *NH73*
Mrs E. MacPherson **Lairgandour** *(NH720376)*
☎207
*In a quiet location, near to Culloden Moor, Loch Ness and the Cairngorms. Lies E of A9 at junction with B9154.*
Apr–Sep 5rm 3hc (3fb) ⊀ CTV 5P 1,000acres mixed S% B&b£5–£5.50 Bdi fr£7.50 Wfr£48

**DEBDEN GREEN** Essex *Map 5 TL53*
Mrs K.M. Low **Wychbars** *(TL564313)* (1½m SW off Bishops Stortford road) ☎Bishop's Stortford 850362
*Moated farmhouse in 3½ acres of garden. Open views over fields.*
2⋒ ⊀ CTV TV in all bedrooms P ▥ 600acres arable S% B&b£7 Bdi£11.50 D5.30pm

**DEVIL'S BRIDGE** Dyfed *Map 6 SN77*
Mrs E.E. Lewis **Erwbarfe** *(SN749784)* (2m NE A4120) ☎Ponterwyd 251
3hc (2fb) ⊀ Ch CTV 5P ▥ 400acres mixed S% ✻ B&b£6–£7.50 Bdi£9–£10.50 W£50–£60 ⊾ D4pm

**DIDDLEBURY** Salop *Map 7 SO58*
Mrs E. Wilkes **Glebe** *(SO507856)* ☎Munslow 221
Mar–Nov 3rm 2hc ⊀ nc12 TV 6P 2⋒ 123acres beef sheep Dnoon

**DILWYN** Heref & Worcs *Map 3 SO45*
Mrs J. Anthony **Bedford House** *(SO435536)*
☎Pembridge 260
Etr–Oct 3hc (2fb) CTV 3P ▥ 17acres mixed D6.30pm

**DOCKLOW** Heref & Worcs *Map 3 SO55*
Mrs M.J. Bolward **West End** *(SO558578)*
☎Steens Bridge 256
*Large, three-storey 17th-century farmhouse. Solid oak floors and huge doors. A listed building with large garden and coarse fishing pool.*
May–Sep 4rm (2fb) ⊀ nc5 TV 6P lake 91acres beef sheep S% B&b£5 W£48 ⊾

**DOLGELLAU** Gwynedd *Map 6 SH71*
Mrs E.W. Price **Glyn** *(SH704178)* ☎422286
*Stone-built farmhouse of historical interest with oak beams, floors and doors. Well situated for coastal resorts.*
Mar–Nov 5rm 4hc (1fb) CTV 5P river 150acres mixed S% B&b£5–£6 Bdi£7–£8 W£45 ⊾ D previous day

**DORNIE** Highland *Ross & Crom Map 14
NG82*
Mrs M. Macrae **Bungalow** (NG871272) ☎231
*Farmhouse situated on main A87.*
rsEtr–Oct 3hc (1fb) ✝nc5 4P mixed S%
B&b£5.50–£6

**DOUNBY** Orkney *Map 16 HY22*
**Chinyan** (HY307200) ☎Harray 372
*Small farm cottage overlooking Loch Harray.
Free loch fishing.*
2rm ✝ Ch TV P lake 342acres arable beef
D2pm

**DRIMPTON** Dorset *Map 3 ST40*
Mr J.W.Johnson **Axe** (ST415061) ☎Crewkerne
72422
*Small brick-built farmhouse with extension at
one side, farmyard at rear and large garden at
front.*
3hc ✝nc10 TV 3P ▥ 160acres arable dairy S%
B&b£6.50–£8 W£45–£50 M

**DULFORD** Devon *Map 3 ST00*
Mrs M. Broom **Nap** (ST069065) ☎Kentisbeare
287
*Well-appointed farmhouse set in hamlet of
Dulford on main road to Cullompton.*
Closed Xmas 5hc (2fb) CTV 5P ▥ 36acres mixed
S% B&b£4.50–£5 Bdi£6–£6.50 W£37.50–£42 ⅃
Dnoon

**DULVERTON** Somerset *Map 3 SS92*
**Warmor** (SS944259) ☎23479
*Very old farmhouse with a lot of character, parts
of which are 400 years old.*
May–Sep 3hc ✝CTV 4☀ 70acres mixed D5pm

**DUNLOP** Strathclyde *Ayrs Map 10 NS44*
Mr & Mrs R.B. Wilson **Struther** (NS412496)
☎346
*Large farmhouse in its own gardens. On edge of
Dunlop village.*
6hc (2fb) CTV 10P 50acres non-working
B&b£6.50–£7.50 Bdi£13.50–£14.50 W£90 ⅃
D8.30pm

**DUNSYRE** Strathclyde *Lanarks Map 11
NT04*
Mr L. Armstrong **Dunsyre Mains** (NT074482)
☎251
*A two-storey stone farmhouse dating from 1800
in courtyard style with splendid views and small
garden.*
Mar–Oct 3rm 2hc (1fb) ✝ Ch CTV P 400acres
beef sheep S% B&bfr£5.50 Bdi fr£9.50 Wfr
£66 ⅃ D6pm

**DUNVEGAN** Isle of Skye, Highland
*Inverness-shire Map 13 NG24*
Mr A. Munro **Feorlig House** (NG297422) ☎232
*Two-storey, white-painted farmhouse dating
from 1820. Situated off main road looking onto
Loch Cavoy.*
Apr–Sep 3rm TV 10P lake 1,112acres beef
sheep S% B&b£5 Bdi£8.50–£10 W£59.50–£70
⅃ D7pm

**EAGLESFIELD** Dumfries & Galloway
*Dumfriesshire Map 11 NY27*
Mrs S. Johnstone **Newlands** (NY240741)
☎Kirtlebridge 269
*Attractive white-faced farmhouse in secluded
position at end of ⅓ mile drive.*
May–Oct 2hc (1fb) ✝CTV 2P ▥ 150acres mixed
S% B&b£5 Bdi£7.50 W£52.50 ⅃ D6pm

**EAST CALDER** Lothian *Midlothian Map 11
NT06*
Mr & Mrs D.R. Scott **Whitecroft** (NT095682)
7 Raw Holdings ☎Mid Calder 881810
*Surrounded by farmland and only ½ mile from
Almondell Country Park. Good views of
Pentlands to the south and Ochils and Forth
road bridge to the north.*
3rm (1fb) ✝ 5acres arable S%
B&b£5.50 W£38.50 M

**EAST MEON** Hants *Map 4 SU62*
Mrs P.M. Berry **Giants** (SU696207) Harvesting
Lane ☎205
*Modern farmhouse, set in ½ acre. Views from all
rooms of the surrounding countryside. Queen
Elizabeth Country Park of 1,400 acres, with
facilities for pony-trekking and grass skiing, is
nearby.*
Mar–Oct 3rm 2hc 1🛏 (1fb) ✝CTV 4P ▥ 55acres
arable S% B&b£5–£6.50 Bdi£9–£13 W£55–£65
⅃ D4pm

**EAST MEY** Highland *Caithness Map 15
ND37*
Mrs M. Morrison **Glenearn** (ND307739)
☎Barrock 608
*Small croft situated on the main coast road.
Thurso 15 miles.*
Etr–Oct 4rm 2hc (2fb) CTV 5P sea 7½acres
mixed S% B&b£5–£5.30 Bdi£8–£8.50
D2pm

**EDINBURGH** Lothian *Midlothian Map 11
NT27*
Mrs J. Jack **Tower Mains** (NT267693) Liberton
Brae ☎031-664 1765
*Farmhouse in its own grounds within residential*

*area, but backed by farmland. Overlooks golf course, city centre at Arthur's Seat.*
Apr–Oct 5hc (2fb) CTV P 🏠 200acres arable
S% B&b£5.30–£6

**EDLINGHAM** Northumb *Map 12 NU10*
Mrs M. Oates **Lumbylaw** *(NU115096)*
☎Whittingham 277
*Modernised stone-built farmhouse in rural surroundings.*
May–Oct 3hc (1fb) Ⓒ 4P 4🏠 🏠 1,000acres
mixed S% B&b£6–£7 Bdi£10–£12 W£60–£75
Ⅼ (W only Jun–Aug) D6.30pm

**EGERTON** Kent *Map 5 TQ94*
Mr & Mrs J.T. Lamb **Mundy Bois House**
*(TQ906456)* ☎Pluckley 436
*Mundy Bois is a 15th-century half-timbered farmhouse with beamed sitting room and stove fire. Views from the bedrooms are of the hills behind the house.*
2rm 1hc (1fb) TV 2P 1🏠 🏠 10acres mixed S%
B&b£8 Bdi£12 W£84 Ⅼ

**EGLINGHAM** Northumb *Map 12 NU11*
A.I. Easton *West Ditchburn* *(NU131207)*
☎Powburn 337
*Comfortable farmhouse with garden available to guests. Overlooking unspoilt countryside.*
Feb–Nov 4rm 3hc (2fb) Ⓒ CTV 10P 🏠

**EGLOSHAYLE** Cornwall *Map 2 SX07*
F.D. Acocks *Croanford* *(SX034715)* Ford ☎St Mabyn 349
*Small, compact farmhouse in pleasant countryside. Stream in side garden. Wadebridge 2½ miles.*
May–Oct 3rm ✸nc3 CTV 2P 1🏠 113acres mixed
D5pm

**ELLESMERE** Salop *Map 7 SJ33*
*Mereside* *(SJ408343)* ☎2404
*Three-storey farmhouse, 17th century in parts. Close to local beauty spot, The Mere.*
5hc TV 🏠 55acres dairy

**ELSDON** Northumb *Map 12 NY99*
Mr & Mrs T. Carruthers **Dunns** *(NY937969)*
☎Rothbury 40219
*Old farmhouse in quiet position amongst the Cheviot Hills and Coquet Valley.*
2hc (1fb) ✸CTV P 1,000acres mixed S%
✳B&bfr£6

Mrs J. Armstrong **Raylees** *(NY926915)*
☎Otterburn 20287
*Comfortable, well-furnished farmhouse.*
4rm 1hc (1fb) ✸nc5 CTV 4P 🏠 700acres beef
sheep S% B&b£6 Bdi£9 D7pm

**ETTINGTON** Warwicks *Map 4 SP24*
Mrs J. Wakeham **Whitfield** *(SP265506)*
Warwick Rd ☎Stratford-on-Avon 740260
*Pleasant house set in active farm with a wide variety of animals for interest.*
Apr–Aug 3hc ✸CTV 3P 🏠 220acres mixed S%
B&b£4.75

**ETTRICK** Borders *Selkirks Map 11 NT21*
J.R. Hall **Thirlestane Hope** *(NT285167)*
☎Ettrick Valley 229
*Quaint, white-painted farm in border hill country. Small burn flows through farmland. Good access by ¾ mile track.*
Mar–Oct 2🍴 (1fb) CTV P 900acres non-working
S% B&b£5.50–£6 Bdi£9–£10 D4pm

**EXETER** Devon *Map 3 SX99*
*Hill Barton* *(SX956932)* 133 Hill Barton Rd
☎67630
*Attractive, well-built farmhouse with small, trim garden and lawn. Situated on Exeter bypass (A30).*
Closed Xmas 7hc TV 15P 80acres mixed

**EXMOUTH** Devon *Map 3 SY08*
Mrs A.J. Skinner *Maer* *(SY018803)* Maer Ln
☎3651
*In large garden which has views of sea and Haldon Hills. Approximately 5 min walk to beach and 20 min walk to town.*
3rm 1hc (2fb) Ⓒ TV 4P 🏠 sea 300acres
arable beef dairy S% B&b£6–£8 Wfr£42 Ⓜ

Mrs J. Reddaway **Quentance** *(SY037812)*
Salterton Rd ☎Budleigh Salterton 2733
*Superior-style farmhouse. Bedrooms overlook south-east Devon coastline.*
Apr–Oct 3rm 2hc (1fb) ✸CTV 4P 260acres
mixed S% B&b£6–£6.50 Bdi£8–£9 Wfr£56 Ⅼ

**FALFIELD** Avon *Map 3 ST69*
Mrs D.S.E. Wood *Green* *(ST687943)* ☎260319
*A two-storey, colour-washed, stone-built farmhouse. Lawns, hard tennis court and swimming pool in the grounds.*
Closed Xmas 6hc (2fb) CTV 10P non-working
D3pm

**FARRINGTON GURNEY** Avon *Map 3 ST65*
Mrs D.H. Davis **Hayboro** *(ST628555)* ☎Temple
Cloud 52342
*Small farmhouse adjacent to the Farrington Inn. Garden adjoining the farm and fields.*
Mar–Nov 3rm (1fb) TV 5P 78½acres dairy
B&b£6.25–£7.50 Bdi£10.25–£11.50 W£42–
£47.25 Ⓜ Dnoon

**FELINDRE** W Glam *Map 2 SN60*
Mr F. Jones **Coynant** *(SN648070)* (3m N off
unclass rd towards Ammanford) ☎Ammanford
2064
5hc (3fb) ✸ CTV 10P ▥ 150acres sheep S%
✱ Bdi fr£8.50 W£59.50–£63 D7.30pm

**FELMINGHAM** Norfolk *Map 9 TG22*
J. Burton **Felmingham Hall** *(TG245275)*
☎Swanton Abbott 228
*Large, interesting old manor house. Remote but
near North Walsham. Big rooms comfortably
appointed.*
12hc 6⇨ 1♫ (2fb) nc10 CTV 100P ▥ 60acres
sheep B&b£13.80–£16.10 Bdi£17.25–£18.40
W£92–£115 ⅃ D7pm

**FINTRY** Central *Stirlings Map 11 NS68*
Mrs M. Mitchell **Nether Glinns** *(NS606883)*
☎207
*Well-maintained farmhouse situated among
rolling hills. Access via signposted ½ mile gravel
drive.*
15 Apr–Sep 3rm (1fb) CTV 6P river 150acres
arable dairy S% B&bfr£5.50

**FLASH** (Buxton, Derbys) Staffs *Map 7 SK06*
Mrs C.M. Povey **Far Brook** *(SK017670)*
Quarnford ☎Buxton 3085
*Old stone-built farmhouse situated in
picturesque and peaceful surroundings in upper
reaches of Dane Valley.*
Etr–Oct 3rm 2hc (1fb) nc5 P 2☎ 65acres beef

**FORDEN** Powys *Map 7 SJ20*
Mrs K. Owens **Llettygynfach** *(SJ255022)* ☎272
*Views of Shropshire Hills and Powys Valley from
farmhouse.*

2rm 1hc (1fb) ✸ CTV P ▥ 220acres dairy sheep
S% ✱ B&b£5.50–£6 Bdi£8.50–£9 W£59.50–
£63 ⅃ D7pm

**FORDOUN** Grampian *Kincardines Map 15
NO77*
Mrs M. Anderson **Ringwood** *(NO743774)*
(2m N on A966) ☎Auchenblae 313
*Small modernised villa in open setting amidst
farmland and with its own neat garden and
outhouse. Very high standard of décor and
furnishings. 1m north-west of village on B966.*
Feb–Nov 4hc (1fb) ✸ CTV 6P ▥ 17acres arable
S% B&b£6–£7 Bdi£9–£10.50 W£60–£70 ⅃
(W only Oct–Nov & Feb–May) D6pm

**FOWEY** Cornwall *Map 2 SX15*
Mrs M. Dunn **Trezare** *(SX112538)* ☎3485
*Farmhouse conveniently situated 1m from
Fowey. Pleasant atmosphere and good
farmhouse fare.*
May–Sep 3rm 2hc ✸ CTV 6P sea 230acres
mixed S% B&b£6.50–£7 W£45.50–£49 M

**FRESSINGFIELD** Suffolk *Map 5 TM27*
Mrs R. Willis **Priory House** *(TM256770)* Priory
Rd ☎254
*Attractive 400-year-old brick-built farmhouse
with beamed interior. Quality furniture.
Secluded garden. Ideal touring centre.*
3rm ✸ nc10 CTV 6P ▥ 2acres S% B&bfr£8

**FYVIE** Grampian *Aberdeens Map 15 NJ73*
Mrs A. Runcie **Macterry** *(NJ786424)* ☎555
*Two-storey farmhouse with adjoining farm
buildings in rural setting.*

May–Sep 3rm 1hc ✸ nc3 CTV 3P 105acres
arable S% B&bf6–£7 Bdif10.50–£12 Dnoon

**GARTHMYL** Powys *Map 7 SO19*
Mrs P. Jones **Trwstllewelyn** *(SO189984)*
☎Berriew 295
*Spacious 17th-century farmhouse, traditionally
furnished with some antiques and open fires in
the recently-discovered and restored inglenook
fireplace.*
Etr–Sep 5rm 4hc (1fb) ✸ Ch CTV 6P 300acres
mixed S% B&bf7  Bdif10 Wfrf67 ⅃ D4.30pm

**GATEHEAD** Strathclyde *Ayrs* Map 10 NS33
Mrs R. Elliot **Old Rome** *(NS393360)* ☎Drybridge
850265
*Situated in a completely rural setting 300 yards
off the A759 to Troon (5 miles). Farmhouse has
charm and character and dates from 17th
century.*
3hc CTV 20P 6☎ 圖 10acres non-working S%
B&bf5–£6.50 Bdif8–£10.50 D9pm

**GATE HELMSLEY** N Yorks *Map 8 SE65*
Mrs K.M. Sykes **Lime Field** *(SE693534)* Scoreby
☎York 489224
*Comfortably-furnished farmhouse with big
garden, set in the largely agricultural Yorkshire
Wolds.*
Mar–Oct 4rm 2hc (3fb) nc3 CTV 4P 125acres
arable beef S% B&bf6–£7

**GAYHURST** Bucks *Map 4 SP84*
Mrs K. Adams **Mill** *(SP852454)* (1m S off B526
unclass road to Haversham) ☎Newport Pagnell
611489
*A working farm with facilities for fishing and*

*riding on site and where children are made
especially welcome.*
3hc (1fb) TV 6P 4☎ 圖 505acres arable beef
sheep S% B&bf8 Bdif11–£11.50 Wf70 ⅃
D7.30pm

**GEDNEY HILL** Lincs *Map 8 TF31*
Mrs C. Cave **Sycamore** *(TF336108)*
☎Whaplode Drove 445
*Situated on the edge of the village overlooking
open countryside and surrounded by trees.*
Closed Xmas 3rm (2fb) CTV 6P 圖 80acres mixed
S% B&bf8 Bdif11 Wfrf77 D6pm

**GIGGLESWICK** N Yorks *Map 7 SD86*
Mrs Bessie T. Hargreaves **Close House**
*(SD801634)* ☎Settle 3540
*17th-century farmhouse with tree-lined private
drive. Well-kept gardens. River bathing and
fishing nearby.*
4hc ✸ nc 6P 230acres dairy B&bfr12 Bdifr20.50
Wf128.80–£140 ⅃ D9am

**GLAN CONWY** Gwynedd *Map 6 SH87*
Mrs C. Williams **Plas Ucha** *(SH818752)* ☎276
*Elizabethan farmhouse of historical interest with
oak beams, floors and doors. Well situated for
coastal resorts.*
Jul–Aug 3rm ✸nc 6P 250acres beef sheep

**GLAN-YR-AFON** Gwynedd *Map 6 SJ04*
Mr J.G. Jones **Llawr-Bettws** *(SJ016424)* Bala
Rd ☎Maerdy (Clwyd) 224
*Rambling, stone-built farmhouse with pleasant,
homely atmosphere. At Druid traffic lights on A5
follow A494 Bala road for 2m.*
4rm 3hc (A 2rm 1hc 1⇔ 圓) (2fb) ✸ CTV 6P 2☎ 圖
72acres mixed sheep D9.30pm

**GLASBURY** Powys *Map 3 SO13*
Mrs B. Eckley **Fforrdd Fawr** *(SO192398)* ☎332
*1m E of Glasbury-on-Wye on B4350 towards Hay-on-Wye.*
Closed Xmas 2hc ⊁ CTV 4P 280acres mixed
S% B&b£6–£7 Bdi£10–£12 Wfr£65 ⊾ D2pm

**GLASFRYN** Clwyd *Map 6 SH95*
Mrs Ellis **Growine** *(SH927502)*
*(N of A5, E of village)*
☎Cerrigydrudion 447
Apr–Oct 2rm ⊁ TV 70acres beef

**GLASTONBURY** Somerset *Map 3 ST53*
Mrs H. Tinney **Cradlebridge** *(ST477385)*
☎31827
*Large, renovated farmhouse with vegetable and fruit garden.*
Closed Xmas 4hc (1fb) CTV 6P ⠿ 165acres dairy
S% B&b£6.50–£7.50 Bdi£12–£14 W£72–£84 ⊾
Dnoon

**GLENMAVIS** Strathclyde *Lanarks Map 11 NS76*
Mrs P. Dunbar **Braidenhill** *(NS742673)*
☎Glenboig 872319
*300-year-old farmhouse on the outskirts of Coatbridge. About ½ mile from town boundary N off B803.*
3hc (1fb) CTV 4P ⠿ 50acres arable S% B&b£7

**GRAMPOUND** Cornwall *Map 2 SW94*
Mrs L.M. Wade **Tregidgeo** *(SW960473)*
☎St Austell 882450
*Tregidgeo is a comfortably-furnished farmhouse in a beautiful secluded and peaceful setting.*
mid May–Sep 4rm 3hc (2fb) ⊁ TV 4P 216acres mixed D10am

Mrs M.H. Thomas **Ventonwyn** *(SW957501)*
☎St Austell 882349
*Well-preserved, 13th-century farmhouse ¾ mile from the main St Austell to Truro road.*
Etr–Oct 5rm 2hc (2fb) ⊁ CTV 6P 177acres mixed
S% B&b£5

**GULVAL** Cornwall *Map 2 SW43*
Mrs M.E. Osborne **Kenegie Home** *(SW481327)*
☎Penzance 2515
*15th-century, 'olde-worlde' farmhouse 1 mile from Penzance. Accent on good farmhouse food.*
Apr–Sep rsOct & Mar 3hc (1fb) ⊁ CTV 4P
300acres mixed S% B&b£6–£8 Bdi£10–£12
W£70–£80 ⊾ D4pm

**GUNNISLAKE** Cornwall *Map 2 SX47*
Comdr RN & Mrs W.R. Fowler **Whimple** *(SX428708)* ☎Tavistock 832526
*Attractive 17th-century farmhouse. Oak beams and panelling in lounge. On banks of River Tamar.*
Closed Xmas 3hc ⊁ CTV 6P river 50acres beef
dairy S% B&b£8 Bdi£11 W£66 ⊾

**GWINEAR** Cornwall *Map 2 SW53*
Mrs R. Rapson **Chycoose** *(SW608367)* 33 Wall
Rd ☎Leedstown 357
*Modern farmhouse situated in old Cornish village. Small front garden. Home-produced farmhouse meals.*
Etr–Oct 3rm 2hc ⊁ nc10 TV 3P ⠿ 40acres arable
beef S% ✳ B&b£5–£6 Bdi£7–£8 Wfr£49 ⊾

**GWYDDELWERN** Clwyd *Map 6 SJ04*
Mrs E.M. Lloyd **Bryngwenalt** *(SJ067473)*
☎Corwen 2312
*Situated in a rural setting with excellent views of countryside.*
Jun–Sep 3rm ⊁ CTV 3P 110acres mixed S%
B&b£5
250

**GWYSTRE** Powys *Map 3 SO06*
Mrs C. Drew **Gwystre** *(SO070656)* ☎Penybont
316
*Typical Welsh hill farm near to Elan Valley reservoir.*
Mar–Oct 2rm (1fb) TV P 150acres mixed S%
B&bfr£5 Bdi fr£8.50

**HABBERLEY** Salop *Map 7 SJ40*
P.J. Madeley **Hall** *(SJ397036)* ☎Pontesbury 689
*Farmhouse reputed to be 16th century. Large, comfortable rooms with antique furniture.*
Jan–Nov 3rm 1hc (1fb) ⊁ 4P 138acres mixed
S% B&b£5–£6 Bdi£8–£10 W£50–£60 ⊾

**HAILSHAM** E Sussex *Map 5 TQ50*
Mrs S.A.L. Rose **Chicheley** *(TQ576103)*
Hempstead Ln ☎841253
*Large house divided in two; set in typical Sussex countryside.*
3hc (2fb) ⊁ nc3 TV 6P 5½acres poultry S% B&b£6

**HALFWAY HOUSE** Salop *Map 7 SJ31*
Mrs E. Morgan **Willows** *(SJ342115)* ☎233
*Small farm cottage well situated for those travelling to Wales. Cottage surrounded by Long Mountain and Middlebar Hills.*
Mar–Oct 3rm 1hc (1fb) nc8 10P 35acres mixed
S% B&b£4.50–£5 Bdi£9–£10 W£45–£50 ⊾
D5.30pm

**HALTWHISTLE** Northumb *Map 12 NY76*
Mrs J.W. Laidlow **White Craig** *(NY713649)*
Shield Hill ☎20565
*Stone-built Georgian-style bungalow in an elevated position, providing excellent views. Within walking distance of Hadrian's Wall.*
Closed Xmas 3hc ⊁ nc10 CTV 3P 30acres
mixed S% B&bfr£7.25 Bdi fr£11.25 Wfr£75 ⊾
D9am

**HANMER** Clwyd *Map 7 SJ44*
C. Sumner & F. Williams-Lee **Buck** *(SJ435424)*
☎339
*On the A525 Whitchurch (7m)–Wrexham (9m) road, the farmhouse is an ideal base from which to explore the area.*
4hc ⊁ CTV 12P ⠿ 7acres mixed S% B&bfr£6.50
Bdi fr£10 Wfr£70 ⊾ D9pm

**HARBERTON** Devon *Map 3 SX75*
Mrs I.P. Steer **Preston** *(SX777587)* ☎Totnes
862235
*Old farmhouse on outskirts of quaint and attractive village. Totnes about 2½ miles.*
Apr–Sep 3hc (1fb) ⊁ nc3 CTV 3P 200acres dairy
B&b£6 Bdi£8.50 W£58 ⊾ (W only Aug)

R. Rose **Tristford** *(SX780594)* ☎Totnes 862418
*Charming house with 'olde-worlde' atmosphere. Good centre for touring the coast between Plymouth and Torbay.*
3hc ⊁ nc CTV 3☎ ⠿ 150acres mixed S% B&b£6

**HARMER HILL** Salop *Map 7 SJ52*
Mrs C.P. Williams **Hill** *(SJ487232)* Newton-on-
the-Hill ☎Clive 273 (due to change to Bomere
Heath 290813)
*Two-storey, red-brick house in quiet rural position.*
Apr–Sep 2rm (1fb) ⊁ nc4 CTV 3P 76acres dairy
S% B&b£6 Bdi£7.50 W£49 ⊾

**HARRIS, ISLE OF** Western Isles *Inverness-
shire* **See Scarista**

**HARROP FOLD** Lancs *Map 7 SD74*
Mr & Mrs P. Wood **Harrop Fold** *(SD746492)*
☎Bolton-by-Bowland 600
*Lancashire longhouse built around 17th century.*

*Nestling in pleasant quiet valley. Excellent accommodation, interesting meals.*
3⇔ (A 2⇔) nc CTV 10P ▥ 280acres beef sheep S% ✳ B&b£10–£14 Bdi£14–£20 W£67.50–£80 Ⓜ D9pm

**HARTLAND** Devon *Map 2 SS22*
Mrs D.R. Walter **Edistone** *(SS249219)* ☎212
*Isolated farmhouse offering wholesome country fare.*
May–Sep 2rm ⚹ CTV 3P 84acres dairy

Mrs P.J. Wade **Holloford** *(SS289236)* ☎275
*Two-storey, stone-built Devonshire farmhouse in rather isolated countryside. Oak beams in bedrooms. Near Hartland Point.*
May–Sep 3hc (1fb) ⚹ CTV P ▥ 280acres arable dairy S% B&b£7.50–£8.50 Bdi£10–£11 W£60–£65 Ⓛ

P. Mengland **Mettaford** *(SS284245)* ☎249
*Attractive Georgian farmhouse, 2 miles from the village of Hartland. In woodland setting with panoramic views of coastline and Lundy.*
6rm (2fb) ⒸⒽ CTV 2☎ 17acres mixed S% B&b£6–£7 Bdi£9.50–£10 W£65–£70 Ⓛ
(W only Aug)

**HATHERSAGE** Derbys *Map 8 SK28*
Mr & Mrs T.C. Wain **Highlow Hall** *(SK219802)*
☎Hope Valley 50393
*16th-century house of character. Well-furnished interior containing several antiques. Isolated position south of Hathersage.*
Apr–Oct 6hc (2fb) CTV 12P 300acres sheep B&b£9.50 Bdi£15 W£95 Ⓛ D6pm

**HAUGH OF URR** Dumfries & Galloway *Kirkcudbrights Map 11 NX86*
Mrs G.J. MacFarlane **Markfast** *(NX817682)*
☎220
*Typical modernised farmhouse. Situated at the gateway to Galloway's historical and picturesque scenery with wide choice of beaches, fishing, etc.*
3rm (3fb) ⚹ TV 3P 140acres beef S% B&b£5 Bdi£7 W£49 Ⓛ D3pm

**HAVERFORDWEST** Dyfed *Map 2 SM91*
Mrs J.H. Evans **Cuckoo Grove** *(SM928162)*
☎2429
*Comfortable accommodation for non-smokers only, in recently refurbished farmhouse. Swimming pool in grounds and views of the distant Prescelly Mountains.*
Closed Xmas wk 5hc ⚹ CTV P ▥ 206acres mixed B&b£5.50–£6 Bdi£9.50–£10.50 W£37–£40 Ⓜ

**HELENSBURGH** Strathclyde *Dunbartons Map 10 NS28*
**Duirland** *(NS299872)* Glen Fruin ☎3370
*A comfortably-sized farmhouse situated away from main road.*
Jun–15 Sep 3hc ⚹ nc5 CTV 5P 2☎ 775acres mixed

**HELSTON** Cornwall *Map 2 SW62*
*Within a short radius of this town there are several AA-listed farmhouses at the following locations: (see appropriate gazetteer entry for full details)* **Coverack Bridges, Sithney, Trenear, Trevenen Bal**

**HENFIELD** W Sussex *Map 4 TQ21*
Mr & Mrs M. Wilkin **Great Wapses** *(TQ243192)*
Wineham (3m NE off B2116) ☎2544
*Part-16th-century and part-Georgian farmhouse set in rural surroundings.*
4rm 2hc 1⇔ 1🏠 (1fb) TV in bedrooms 7P 1☎ 33acres mixed S% B&b£6.50–£9

**HENSTRIDGE** Somerset *Map 3 ST71*
Mrs I. Pickford **Manor** *(ST692206)* Bowden
☎Templecombe 70213
*16th-century, stone-built farmhouse with lattice windows. Surrounded by grassland and wooded areas.*
Apr–Oct 2rm CTV P ☎ ▥ 250acres arable dairy S% B&b£7.50 W£50 Ⓜ

**HETHERSETT** Norfolk *Map 5 TG10*
Mr & Mrs P.G. Gowing **Park** *(TG148037)*
☎Norwich 810264
*Modernised Georgian farmhouse. Interestingly furnished; part modern, part antique. Well situated for excursions to Norfolk Broads.*
6hc 3⇔ 1🏠 ⚹ nc5 (Jul & Aug) ⒸⒽ CTV 30P ▥ 210acres mixed B&b£11.38 Bdi£16.44 W£100 D9pm
**See advertisement on page 252**

**HITCHAM** Suffolk *Map 5 TL95*
Mrs B.D. Elsden **Wetherden Hall** *(TL971509)*
(1m W off unclass rd to Kettlebaston)
☎Bildeston 740412
Mar–Nov 1rm (1fb) ⚹ nc11 CTV 6P ▥ 280acres mixed S% B&b£6–£7 W£40–£47.50 Ⓜ

**HOLBETON** Devon *Map 2 SX65*
Mrs J. Baskerville **Keaton** *(SX595480)* ☎255
*Large, stone-built and well-maintained farmhouse. Some walls 18in thick. Isolated rural position. Yachting at Newton Ferrers 3 miles away.*
Apr–Sep 2rm (1fb) ⚹ nc5 TV 2P sea 117acres beef S% B&b£6–£7

**HOLLYBUSH** Strathclyde *Ayrs Map 10 NS31*
A. Woodburn **Boreland** *(NS400139)* ☎Patna 228
*Two-storey farmhouse with roughcast exterior, situated on the banks of the River Doon. West off A713 south of village.*
Jun–Sep 3rm (2fb) ★ TV 10P ▥ 105acres dairy
S% B&bfr£5.50

**HOLNE** Devon *Map 3 SX76*
S. Townsend **Wellpritton** *(SX716704)* ☎Poundsgate 273
*Tastefully modernised farmhouse in Dartmoor National Park. There are panoramic views and the farm has its own swimming pool.*
Closed 25 & 26 Dec 4hc (2fb) nc7 (except for babies) ☐Ch CTV 4P ▥ 15acres mixed B&b£6–£8 Bdi£10–£12 W£55–£65

**HOLSWORTHY** Devon *Map 2 SS30*
Mr & Mrs E. Cornish **Leworthy** *(SS323012)* ☎253488
*Low, white-fronted farmhouse with attractive garden facing open country. Pleasantly situated.*
Closed Xmas 10rm 9hc 3🛏 (6fb) ★ nc4 CTV 20P 2🚗 ▥ 240acres mixed S% Bdi£12–£15 D6.30pm

**HOLT** Clwyd *Map 7 SJ35*
Mrs G.M. Evans **New** *(SJ394538)*
Commonwood ☎Farndon 270358
*Small, comfortable and cosy farm.*
Apr–Oct 2rm ★ CTV 4P 92acres dairy sheep S%
✱B&bfr£5.25 Bdi£6.75 Wfr£47 ↳ D9.30am

**HOLYWELL** Clwyd *Map 7 SJ17*
Mrs A.M. Kendrick **Garneddwen Fawr** *(SJ173707)* Lixwm ☎Halkyn 780298

*16th-century, stone-built farmhouse with oak beams.*
Etr–Oct 2hc 1⇌ ⚲ CTV 3P 66acres non-working S% B&bf5.50 W£35 Ⓜ

**HONITON** Devon *Map 3 ST10*
Mrs I.J. Underdown **Roebuck** *(ST147001)* Weston ☎2225
*Modern farm on western end of Honiton bypass. 8 miles from the coast.*
4rm 3hc (2fb) CTV 3P ⬜ river 179acres mixed S% B&bf5.25–£5.50 Bdif7.50

**HORNS CROSS** Devon *Map 2 SS32*
Mrs B. Furse **Swanton** *(SS355227)* ☎Clovelly 241
*Modern, dormer-style bungalow pleasantly situated overlooking Bristol Channel.*
Closed Xmas 3rm 2hc (2fb) ⚲ TV P sea 50acres dairy S% B&bf5.50 Bdif7.50 W£48 Ⓛ D previous day

**HOWEY** Powys *Map 3 SO05*
Mrs C. Nixon **Brynhir** *(SJ067586)* (1m E on unclass rd) ☎Llandrindod Wells 2425
*Remote 17th-century hill farm, traditionally furnished. Good walks and views. Pony for children to ride.*
4rm 3hc (1fb) 10P 150acres mixed S% B&bf5–£6 Bdif8–£9 W£55–£60 Ⓛ D5pm

Mrs R. Jones **Holly** *(SJ045593)* ☎Llandrindod Wells 2402
*18th-century building close to the A483, on the edge of the village, surrounded by open country.*
Apr–Nov 3hc (1fb) CTV ⬜ 70acres mixed S% B&bfrf5.50 Bdi frf8.50 Wfrf59.50 Ⓛ D4pm

Mr & Mrs R. Bufton **Three Wells** *(SO062586)* ☎Llandrindod Wells 2484
*Detached farmhouse built at around the turn of the century.*
Closed Xmas 7hc (2fb) Ⓒⱨ TV 20P ⬜ 50acres mixed S% B&bf5.50–£6 Bdif8.50–£9 W£59.50–£63 Ⓛ D5pm

**HUNDRED HOUSE** Powys *Map 3 SO15*
Mrs M. Kinsey **Box** *(SO129531)* ☎240
*Two-storey, 17th-century stone farmhouse. In elevated position with good views of the Edw Valley.*
Apr–Oct 3rm 1hc ⚲ nc1 TV 6P 175acres sheep S% B&bfrf6.50 Bdi frf9 Wfrf70 D5pm

**IDOLE** Dyfed *Map 2 SN41*
Mr & Mrs A. Bowen **Pantgwyn** *(SN419157)* ☎Carmarthen 5859
*Spacious rebuilt farmhouse. 3 miles south of Carmarthen.*
May–Oct 3rm (2fb) ⚲ CTV 4P 35acres dairy B&bf5.50–£6

**ILAM** Staffs *Map 7 SK15*
C. & J. Fortnam **Beechenhill** *(SK129525)* ☎Alstone Field 274
*Two-storey, stone-built farmhouse with exposed beams. Built about 1720. Unspoilt rural area with panoramic views.*
Jun–Nov 2rm (1fb) nc6 CTV 2P 92acres beef dairy S% B&bf6 W£42 Ⓜ

**INGLETON** N Yorks *Map 7 SD67*
G.W. & M. Bell **Langber** *(SD689709)* ☎41587
*A large detached property in open countryside in an elevated position situated in a quiet country lane about 1 mile south of Ingleton village.*
Feb–Oct 6hc (5fb) Ⓒⱨ CTV 6P ☂ ⬜ 7½acres sheep ponies goats S% B&bf5.50–£6 Bdif7.50–£8.25 W£52–£57 Ⓛ (W only mid Jul–Aug) D5pm

**INVERGARRY** Highland *Inverness-shire Map 14 NH30*
Mrs G. Swann **Ardgarry** *(NH286015)* ☎226
*Warm and comfortable traditional Scottish farmhouse and lodge dated 1868 in a quiet position off A87.*
Mar–Oct 1hc (A 3hc) (1fb) CTV 6P 10acres mixed S% B&bf6–£6.50 Bdif9–£9.50 W£63–£66.50 Ⓛ D4pm

Mrs L. Brown **Faichem Lodge** *(NH286014)* ☎314
*Modernised old stone house.*
3hc (1fb) CTV 4P ⬜ 7½acres mixed S% B&bf5–£6 Bdif9–£10 D7pm

**IPSTONES** Staffs *Map 7 SK04*
J.M. Brindley **Glenwood House** *(SK006488)* ☎294
*Large house about 100 years old built of dressed sandstone blocks in very picturesque and peaceful rural surroundings.*
Closed Xmas & New Year 2rm Ⓒⱨ CTV 6P ⬜ 58acres beef S% B&bf6.50–£7.50 Bdif10.50–£11.50 W£70–£77 Ⓛ D2pm

**IRTHINGTON** Cumbria *Map 12 NY46*
**Seat Hill** *(NY483634)* ☎Kirklinton 226
*Sandstone building dating from 1726. Interior fully modernised. Attractive flower garden and lawn. On A6071.*
Mar–Oct 3rm 1hc CTV P 2☂ 217acres mixed

**ISLE OF SKYE** Highland *Inverness-shire Map 13*
**See Clachan, Dunvegan, Portree, Uig**

**ISLE OF WIGHT** *Map 4*
**See Ryde**

**JACOBSTOWE** Devon *Map 2 SS50*
Mrs J. King **Higher Cadham** *(SS585026)*

☎Exborne 647
*Well-decorated and comfortably-furnished
16th-century farmhouse. Ideal base for
touring.*
Apr–Sep 4hc (1fb) ✸ nc3 CTV 12P 139acres
mixed B&b£5 Bdi£8 W£48 ⌁ D4.30pm

**KEA** Cornwall *Map 2 SW84*
E.J. Hobbs **Higher Lanner** *(SW831414)* ☎Truro
3037
*Farmhouse 3 miles west of Truro on
unclassified road. Overlooks River Fal.*
Etr–Oct 3hc CTV P river 150acres dairy S%
B&bf4.50–£5.50 Bdif7.50–£8.50 W£50–£56 ⌁
D2pm

**KEITH** Grampian *Banffs Map 15 NJ45*
Mrs J. Jackson **Haughs** *(NJ416515)* ☎2238
*Attractively decorated farmhouse. 1 mile from
Keith off A96.*
May–15 Oct 4hc (1fb) ✸ Ch CTV 8P 2☎
220acres mixed S% B&bf5–£5.50 Bdif£7.50–
£8 W£50–£54 ⌁ D9pm

Mr & Mrs J.H. Farquhar **Mains of Tarrycroys**
*(NJ404537)* Aultmore ☎2586
*Attractive stone farmhouse with large farmyard
and several outbuildings surrounded by arable
land.*
4rm 2hc (1fb) ✸ nc5 TV 6P 43acres arable S%
B&bf5.50 Bdif8.50 Wfrf56 ⌁ D7pm

Mrs E.C. Leith **Montgrew** *(NJ453517)* ☎2852
*Farmhouse with several outbuildings and
pleasant views. 2m E off A95.*
May–Sep 4rm 1hc (1fb) CTV 4P 211acres arable
beef S% B&bfrf4.25 Bdi frf6 Wfrf42 ⌁ D7pm

Mrs G. Murphy **Tarnash House** *(NJ442490)*
☎2728
*Two-storey, stone farmhouse with well-
maintained garden to the front. Surrounded by
farmland 1m S off A96.*
May–Oct 4hc (1fb) CTV 10P 1☎ ⦙⦙⦙ 100acres
arable S% B&bf5.50

**KENDAL** Cumbria *Map 7 SD59*
Mrs D. Atkinson **Bank Head** *(SD496926)*
Underbarrow Rd ☎21785
*Set back off the road, 1m from Kendal town
centre. 7m from Lake Windermere and
surrounded by pleasant countryside.*
Etr–Nov 3rm 2hc (2fb) ✸ TV 4P ⦙⦙⦙ 240acres dairy
sheep S% B&bf6.50

Mrs S. Beaty **Garnett House** *(SD500959)*
Burneside ☎24542
*A 15th-century stone-built farmhouse standing
in an elevated position overlooking Howgill Fells.
Close to both Windermere and Kendal.*
Closed Xmas & New Year 5hc (2fb) ✸ Ch CTV
6P 270acres mixed S% B&bfrf£6 Bdi frf8
D4pm

Mrs E. Gardner **Natland Mill Beck** *(SD520907)*
☎21122
*17th-century, local-stone farmhouse with
original beams, doors and cupboards. Large
well-furnished rooms.*
Mar–Oct 3rm 2hc (1fb) ✸ Ch CTV 3P ⦙⦙⦙
100acres dairy S% B&bf5.50–£6

**KENNFORD** Devon *Map 3 SX98*
Mrs R. Weeks **Holloway Barton** *(SX893855)*
☎Exeter 832302
*Well-appointed house retaining its old charm
situated 1 mile from the M5 and 1 mile from
Haldon Racecourse. Well-kept garden and large
lawn.*
4hc (1fb) CTV 4P 1☎ ⦙⦙⦙ 350acres mixed S%
B&bf5.75–£6 Bdif9.75–£10

Mrs G.J. Weeks **Lynwood** *(SX892859)* ☎Exeter
832517

254

*Well-furnished farmhouse, about 5 miles from
Exeter. Rough shooting in grounds. Views of
Haldon Forest and Exe estuary.*
3hc (1fb) CTV 4P ⦙⦙⦙ river 350acres mixed S%
B&bf6.50 Bdif10 D6.30pm

**KERRY** Powys *Map SO19*
Mrs M. Perry **Goitre** *(SO176918)* ☎248
*Modernised farmhouse with traditional
furnishings, standing in 190 acres. Conveniently
situated for touring.*
3rm 1hc ✸ CTV 4P 2☎ ⦙⦙⦙ 190acres beef sheep
B&bf6 Bdif9.50 W£63 ⌁

**KESWICK** Cumbria *Map 11 NY22*
**Low Nest** *(NY291226)* ☎72378
*Comfortable farmhouse with beamed ceiling in
dining room. Clean and tidy décor.*
May–Oct 5rm 4hc nc4 6P 120acres mixed
D4pm

**KILKHAMPTON** Cornwall *Map 2 SS21*
Mrs W. Heywood **Ley Park** *(SS271136)* ☎303
*Small farmhouse in isolated position, 2 miles
from the village.*
Spring Bank Hol wknd–Sep 2hc (1fb) ✸ TV P
143acres mixed S% B&bf4.50–£5 Bdif6.50–£7
W£45–£49 ⌁

**KILMACOLM** Strathclyde *Renfrews Map 10
NS36*
J.A. Blair **Pennytersal** *(NS338714)* ☎2349
*Well-maintained building and courtyard set in
rolling farmland. Kilmacolm 2 miles.*
Jun–Sep 3rm 2hc (1fb) ✸ TV P 125acres mixed
S% ✱B&bf5

**KIMBOLTON** Heref & Worcs *Map 3 SO56*
M.J. Lloyd **Menalls** *(SO528611)* ☎Leominster
2605
*Delightful farmhouse set in Herefordshire valley
scenery.*
Apr–Oct 2hc (2fb) ✸ CTV P 40acres mixed S%
✱B&bf5

**KING EDWARD** Grampian *Aberdeens Map
15 NJ75*
**Blackton** *(NJ726583)* ☎205
*A well-run working farm catering for family
holidays. Banff 6 miles.*
May–Oct 5hc Ch CTV 6P 113acres arable
beef D6pm

**KINGSCOTT** Devon *Map 2 SS51*
L. & H. Hookway **Flavills** *(SS538182)* St Giles
☎Torrington 3250
*Well-maintained, large Elizabethan farmhouse,
situated in the village of Kingscott, Torrington 3½
miles.*
Mar–Oct 4rm (1fb) ✸ CTV 6P 130acres mixed
B&bf5–£6 Bdif6.50–£7 W£49 D4pm

**KINGSLAND** Heref & Worcs *Map 3 SO46*
Mrs F.M. Hughes **Tremayne** *(SO447613)* ☎233
*Deceptively large, two-storey building on one of
main routes to Leominster.*
3hc (1fb) CTV 4P ⦙⦙⦙ 40acres sheep S% ✱B&bf5

**Westfield** *(SO436622)* ☎348
*Two-storey, 17th-century farmhouse with
original oak beams and brasses. Trout fishing in
River Pinsey which runs through farm.*
Etr–Oct 2rm ✸ nc CTV 2P 1☎ 60acres mixed

**KINGSTONE** Heref & Worcs *Map 3 SO43*
Mrs G.C. Andrews **Webton Court** *(SO421365)*
(off B4348) ☎Golden Valley 250220
6hc (4fb) CTV 10P 280acres mixed
✱B&bfrf6.50 Bdi frf8.50 Wfrf35 Ⓜ D9.30am

**KINGSWELLS** Grampian *Aberdeens Map 15 NJ80*
Mrs M. Mann **Bellfield** *(NJ868055)* ☎Aberdeen 740239
*Modernised and extended farm cottage on quiet road and set amid farmlands. 4m W of Aberdeen city centre off A944.*
3hc (2fb) [Ch] CTV 6P ⬛ 200acres arable dairy S% B&b£5 Bdi£8 D5pm

**KINGTON** Heref & Worcs *Map 3 SO25*
Mrs E.E. Protheroe **School** *(SO266550)* Up Hergest ☎230453
*Large farmhouse dating back to c1625 perched high on Hergest Ridge, overlooking valley of the River Arrow 2m SW of town.*
5hc 1🛏 (2fb) [Ch] CTV 7P 290acres arable beef sheep S% B&b£6 Bdi£9.50 W£66 ⥣ D7pm

**KIPPEN** Central *Stirlings Map 11 NS69*
Mrs J. Paterson **Powblack** *(NS670970)* ☎260
*Pleasant farmhouse near the River Forth on the Kippen to Doune road.*
May–Sep 2hc (1fb) CTV 4P ⬛ 300acres mixed

**KIRKCONNEL** Dumfries & Galloway *Dumfriesshire Map 11 NS71*
Mrs E.A. McGarvie **Niviston** *(NS691135)* ☎346
*Pleasant, well-maintained farm delightfully set in elevated position overlooking Nithsdale.*
May–Oct 2rm (1fb) CTV P 1🐎 345acres beef sheep S% B&b£4.50 Bdi£7.50 W£52 ⥣ D previous night

**KIRKHILL** Highland *Inverness-shire Map 14 NH54*
Mrs C. Munro **Wester Moniack** *(NH551438)* ☎Drumchardine 237
*Small, modern, two-storey house with a relaxing, tranquil atmosphere.*
Apr–Oct 2hc (1fb) [Ch] CTV 3P ⬛ 600acres mixed S% B&b£4.50–£5 Bdi£7.50–£8 W£50–£54 ⥣ D5.30pm

**KIRK IRETON** Derbys *Map 8 SK25*
J.& E. Brassington **Sitch** *(SK260515)* ☎Wirksworth 2454
*Large sandstone farmhouse with extensive outbuildings standing in a fairly remote but picturesque area.*
Closed New Year's Eve 4hc (2fb) [Ch] CTV 12P 2🐎 ⬛ 327acres mixed S% B&b£7.50 Bdi£12 W£84 ⥣ D8pm

**KIRKTON OF DURRIS** Grampian *Kincardines Map 15 NO79*
Mrs M. Leslie **Wester Durris Cottage** *(NO769962)* ☎Crathes 638
*Attractive roadside cottage with well-tended garden. Farm 200yds.*
May–mid Oct 2rm (1fb) 4P 300acres arable S% B&bfr£4.25

**KIRKWALL** Orkney *Map 16 HY41*
Mrs M. Hourie **Heathfield** *(HY413108)* St Ola ☎2378
*Two-storey, stone farmhouse on a gently sloping hill. There are distant views over Scapa Flow.*
3hc (2fb) ⚲ 4P ⬛ 500acres mixed S% ✳B&bfr£5 Bdi fr£8.50 D5.30pm

**KNAPTOFT** Leics *Map 4 SP68*
A.M. Knight **Knaptoft House** *(SP619894)* Bruntingthorpe Rd ☎Peatling Magna 388
*Modern building on site of Georgian farmhouse. Medieval fishponds restored and stocked with coarse fish. Off Shersby–Bruntingthorpe rd, 1m W from its junction with A50. Or leave M1 at*

junc 20 then via Kimcote and Watton.
Closed Xmas Day 3hc (1fb) [Ch] CTV 5P 145acres mixed S% B&b£5.75–£6.75 Bdi£8.75–£10.75 Wfr£55 ⥣ Dnoon

**KNIGHTON** Powys *Map 7 SO27*
R. Watkins **Heartsease** *(SO343725)* ☎Bucknell 220
*Large, mellow-stone residence over 300 years old. Country house atmosphere. Large garden.*
3rm 1hc 1⇆ 1🛏 (1fb) [Ch] CTV 3P 2🐎 ⬛ 600acres mixed S% B&b£6.50–£7.50 Bdi£12–£14 D8pm

**KNOWSTONE** Devon *Map 3 SS82*
Mrs J.M. Millman **Eastacott** *(SS837231)* ☎Anstey Mills 215
*Isolated farmhouse in the heart of North Devon. Large sun lounge at entrance.*
Feb–Nov 3rm (1fb) ⚲ 120acres dairy S% ✳B&b£5.50–£6 W£32–£35 Ⓜ

**LADOCK** Cornwall *Map 2 SW85*
Mrs P.M. Davies **Tregear** *(SW870506)* ☎Mitchell 214
*Attractive farmhouse set slightly back from unclassified road. Lawn at front.*
Etr–Sep 3rm (1fb) ⚲ CTV P 250acres mixed S% B&b£5.50–£6

**LAIRG** Highland *Sutherland Map 14 NC50*
Mr A. Mackay **Alt-Na-Sorag** *(NC547123)* 14 Achnairn ☎2058
*Attractive farmhouse with good views of Loch Shin. Lairg 5 miles.*
May–Sep 3rm (1fb) CTV 4P 1🐎 lake 125acres mixed S% ✳B&bfr£5

Mrs V. Mackenzie **5 Terryside** *(NC570110)* (3½m N off A838) ☎2332
*Two-storey stone farm building situated in rolling farmland with distant views of Loch Shin. Roadside location.*
May–Sep 3rm CTV P lake 50acres mixed S% B&bfr£5

Mrs M. Sinclair **Woodside** *(NC533147)* West Shinness ☎2072
*Homely house surrounded by fields and overlooking Loch Shin. Lairg about 7 miles.*
May–Sep 3rm ⚲ CTV 4P lake 360acres mixed S% B&b£5

**LANGPORT** Somerset *Map 3 ST42*
**Woodstock** *(ST442264)* Pibsbury ☎250394
*Small, well-furnished and decorated farmhouse with a pleasant garden.*
Apr–Sep 4hc nc8 CTV 8P 1🐎 river 60acres dairy D4pm

**LANLIVERY** Cornwall *Map 2 SX05*
Mr & Mrs J. Linfoot **Treganoon** *(SX065589)* ☎Bodmin 872205
*Farmhouse with small garden in fairly isolated position and beautiful countryside.*
May–mid Oct 7rm 6hc (3fb) ⚲ [Ch] CTV 8P 100acres beef S% B&b£6–£8 Bdi£8–£11 W£54–£66 ⥣ (W only Jul & Aug) D7pm

**LATHERON** Highland *Caithness Map 15 ND13*
Mrs C. Sinclair **Upper Latheron** *(ND195352)* ☎224
*Two-storey house in elevated position with fine views out across North Sea. Farm also incorporates a pony stud.*
May–Sep 4rm (1fb) ⚲ CTV 6P sea 200acres mixed S% B&bfr£5

**LAUNCELLS** Cornwall *Map 2 SS20*
Mr & Mrs A. Colwill **Moreton Mill** *(SS283085)*
☎Kilkhampton 306
*Pleasant, 15th-century, cottage-style farmhouse
with oak beams. Small, attractive garden.*
Mar–Oct 5rm 3hc (3fb) ⊁ TV 10P 2☎ 52½acres
mixed S% B&b£5–£5.50 Bdi£7.25–£8 W£50–
£55 ↓ (W only Jun–Aug) D5pm

**LAWERS** Tayside *Perths Map 11 NN63*
*Croftintygan* *(NN676389)* ☎Killin 534
*Secluded stone farmhouse standing on hillside
with dramatic views over Loch Tay. Between
A827 and Lochside.*
May–Sep 6rm 4hc TV lake 3,000acres mixed

**LEAMINGTON SPA** Warwicks *Map 4 SP36*
Mrs R. Gibbs **Hill** *(SP343637)* Lewis Rd, Radford
Semele (2½m SE off A425) ☎37571
3rm (1fb) ⊁ Ch CTV 4P ▥ 350acres mixed S%
B&bfr£6 Bdifr£10 W£53 ↓

**LEEK** Staffs *Map 7 SJ95*
Mrs D. Needham **Holly Dale** *(SK019556)*
Bradnop ☎383022
*Two-storey, stone-built farmhouse typical of the
area. 2m SE on an unclassified road off A523.*
Apr–Oct 2rm ⊁ TV 3P 72acres dairy S% B&b£5–
£5.50 Bdi£8–£9 W£55–£60 ↓ D2pm

**LEOMINSTER** Heref & Worcs *Map 3 SO45*
Mrs S.J. Davenport **Stagbatch** *(SO465584)*
☎2673
*14th-century, half-timbered farmhouse which is
a listed building. Peaceful setting 2m W off
A4112.*
rsNov–Apr (wkdys only) 3⇔ ⊁ nc10 CTV 10P ▥
40acres mixed S% B&b£6.50–£8 W£45–£55 ฬ

Mrs H.C. Davies **Wharton Bank** *(SO508556)*
☎2575
*Extensively modernised farmhouse.
Comfortable pleasant atmosphere.*
Closed Xmas 3hc 1⇔ (1fb) nc6 CTV 4P 1☎
▥ 212acres mixed S% B&b£6.50–£7.50
Bdi£10–£11 D7pm

**LEW** Oxon *Map 4 SP30*
M.J. Rouse **University** *(SP322059)* ☎Bampton
Castle 850297
*17th-century farmhouse, modernised without
losing traditional character. House set back from
road in secluded position behind farm buildings.*
Closed Xmas & New Year 6hc 2⇔ 3⋔ (2fb) ⊁
nc6 CTV 8P ▥ 216acres mixed S% B&b£8–£10
Bdi£13.50–£16 W£92–£110 ↓ D4pm

**LEWDOWN** Devon *Map 2 SX48*
Mrs M.E. Horn *Venn Mill* *(SX484885)*
☎Bridestowe 288

*Large modern bungalow set in attractive
countryside. Guests welcome to watch farm
activities.*
Etr–Sep 4rm 3hc (1fb) ⊁ CTV 4P 2☎ 160acres
dairy mixed D4pm

**LIFTON** Devon *Map 2 SX38*
*Markstone* *(SX429825)* ☎289
*Pleasant, well-decorated house with small
attractive garden.*
Etr–Sep 3rm 2hc TV 3P 48acres dairy

**LINLITHGOW** Lothian *W Lothian Map 11
NS97*
W. Erskine **Woodcockdale** *(NS973760)* ☎2088
*Modern two-storey house lying about 50 yards
from farmyard and outbuildings.*
4rm (2fb) Ch CTV 12P ▥ 300acres dairy S%
B&bfr£6 Bdifr£8 Wfr£50 ↓ D4pm

**LISKEARD** Cornwall *Map 2 SX26*
S.A. Kendall **Tencreek** *(SX265637)* ☎43379
*A clean well-decorated farmhouse set in
beautiful countryside. Liskeard 1 mile.*
2hc ⊁ 3P 250acres mixed S% ✳B&b£5.50–£6

**LITTLE EVERSDEN** Cambs *Map 5 TL35*
Mrs F. Ellis **Five Gables** *(TL371535)* Bucks Ln
☎Comberton 2236
*Historic farmhouse of 15th and 17th centuries.
Oak beams and inglenook fireplace. Listed as
being worthy of preservation.*
May–Sep 3rm 2hc (1fb) ⊁ nc12 TV 6P 240acres
arable S% B&b£7

**LITTLEHEMPSTON** Devon *Map 3 SX86*
Mrs E.P. Miller **Buckyette** *(SX812638)*
☎Staverton 638
*19th-century stone farmhouse. Set in a spacious
garden, its position provides excellent views of
surrounding Devon.*
May–Sep 7rm 6hc (4fb) ⊁ Ch TV 6P 51acres
arable S% B&b£7.60 Bdi£10.50–£11 W£68–
£73.50 D7pm

**LITTLE MILL** Gwent *Map 3 SO30*
Mrs A. Bradley **Pentwyn** *(SO325035)* (off A472
½m E of junc with A4042) ☎249
*A 16th-century farmhouse, which has been
modernised but still retains its character. The
building stands in an ½ acre of garden with its
own heated swimming pool.*
Closed Xmas 4hc (1fb) ⊁ nc18mths CTV P ▥
150acres arable beef S% B&bfr£6 Bdi fr£9 Wfr£63
D12.30pm

**LITTLE TORRINGTON** Devon *Map 2 SS41*
Mrs J. Watkins **Lower Hollam** *(SS501161)*
☎Torrington 3253

*Historic house in an unusually peaceful position. Good play facilities for children.*
May–Sep 4hc (3fb) ⚹ Ch CTV 4P 160acres
mixed S% B&bf5–£6.50 Bdi£6.50–£8.50
W£45–£56 ⅃ D5pm

**LITTON** Derbys *Map 7 SK17*
Mrs A. Barnsley **Dale House** *(SK160750)* (off
B6049 W of village) ☎Tideswell 871309
Mar–Oct 3rm (1fb) ⚹ CTV P 🎨 100acres beef
sheep S% B&bf5–£6

Mr & Mrs H. Radford **Hall** *(SK159754)*
☎Tideswell 871124
*Stone-built farmhouse about 100 years old,
situated in the village.*
Closed Xmas 3rm 1hc (2fb) ⚹ Ch TV 5P 🎨
10acres mixed ✱B&bfr£5.50 Bdi fr£8 Wfr£53
D7pm

**LLANARTH** Gwent *Map 3 SO31*
Mr & Mrs J. Morgan **Llwynderi** *(SO382130)*
☎Llantilio 226
*Secluded stone-built farmhouse with many
period features, including a classical oak
staircase. Rooms larger than average.*
Etr–Sep 5hc (2fb) ⚹CTV 6P 120acres arable
beef dairy S% B&bf7.50

**LLANARTHNEY** Dyfed *Map 2 SN52*
Mrs M.M. Bowen **Brynheulog** *(SN533195)*
☎Dryslwyn 567
*Farmhouse with large lawns, located about ½
mile from the village.*
Closed Xmas day 3hc ⚹ CTV 3P 1🐴 🎨 21acres
dairy S% B&bf5–£5.50 Bdi£7.50–£8.25 W£56 ⅃

Mrs W.M. Edwards **Glantowy** *(SN534206)*
☎Dryslwyn 275
*Spacious, well-maintained farmhouse near River
Tywi.*
Etr–Sep 2hc (1fb) ⚹ TV 5P 🎨 128acres dairy S%
✱B&bf5.50 W£35–£38.50 ⋈

**LLANBOIDY** Dyfed *Map 2 SN22*
Mrs B. Worthing **Maencochyrwyn** *(SN181243)*
Login (3½m WNW of Llanboidy on unclass rd to E
of Login/Llanglydwen rd) ☎Hebron 283
*Small isolated farmhouse in elevated position
overlooking its own farmland and hills.*
Apr–Oct 3rm (1fb) CTV P 120acres dairy S%
B&bf5 Bdi£8 W£53 ⅃ D5pm

**LLANDEGLA** Clwyd *Map 7 SJ15*
Mrs M.J. Edwards **Dol Ddu** *(SJ188503)* ☎219
*Modern, two-storey farmhouse.*
2rm (1fb) ⚹ nc10 CTV 2P 95acres mixed S%
✱B&bf4.50–£5 Bdi£7–£8 D previous day

Mr & Mrs H. Roberts **Graig** *(SJ202506)* ☎272
*Recently-built (1974) farmhouse in elevated
position. 1m S of junc A525/A5104.*
Etr–Oct 2hc (1fb) ⚹ TV 2P 🎨 mixed sheep D6pm

B.C. Lightfoot **Pentre Isa** *(SJ195498)* ☎220
*Pleasant, stone-built, two-storey farmhouse in
elevated position.*
Whit–Nov 1rm (1fb) ⚹ TV P 128acres mixed
B&bfr£6 Bdi fr£8.50 Wfr£55 ⅃ D 9am

**LLANDINAM** Powys *Map 6 SO08*
Mrs G.F. Lloyd **Llandinam Hall** *(SO028903)*
☎Caersws 234
*Two-storey, half-timbered farmhouse probably
of late 17th century, backing onto River Severn.
Fine views of the Cambrian Mountains.*
Mar–Oct 6rm 5hc (2fb) ⚹CTV P 450acres mixed

Mrs M.C. Davies **Trewythen** *(SJ003901)*
☎Caersws 444
*2m south-west of Caersws, on unclassified road
off B4569.*
Apr–Oct 3hc (1fb) CTV P 200acres mixed S%
B&bfr£6 Bdi£9–£9.50

**LLANDOVERY** Dyfed *Map 3 SN73*
***Glangwydderig*** *(SN789347)* ☎20381
*Small farmhouse on the outskirts of Llandovery
alongside the Brecon Beacons National Park.
Fishing available in farm grounds.*
May–mid Oct 2rm 3P 75acres sheep

**LLANDRINDOD WELLS** Powys *Map 3
SO06*
**See also Howey**
Mrs P. Lewis **Bailey Einon** *(SO078616)* Cefnllys
(2m E of town on unclass rd) ☎2449
Jan–Nov 3hc ⚹ CTV 3P 280acres mixed
S% ✱B&bf5.50 Bdi£8.50 Dnoon

Mrs D. Evans **Dolberthog** *(SO048602)*
Dolberthog Ln (1m SW off A483) ☎2255
Apr–Oct 2hc (2fb) ⚹ TV 3P 🎨 150acres mixed
S% B&bf5.50–£6 Bdi£8.50–£9 Wfr£60 ⅃

Mrs M.A. Davies **Highbury** *(SO044623)* Llanyre
☎2573
*Typical Welsh beef and sheep farm. Situated 2m
W of Llandrindod Wells, ½m off A4081.*
Apr–Sep rsOct & Mar 4rm 3hc (1fb) Ch CTV 4P
184acres beef sheep S% B&bf5.50 Bdi£9
Wfr£63 ⅃ D3pm

**LLANDYSSIL** Powys *Map 7 SO19*
Mrs C. Parry **Gwern Yr Uchain** *(SO193960)*
☎Montgomery 298
*Modern well-built farmhouse overlooking the
Severn Valley.*
Apr–Oct 3hc (1fb) ⚹ Ch CTV P 190acres
mixed S% B&bfr£6 Bdi fr£9 Wfr£60 ⅃

**LLANEGRYN** Gwynedd *Map 6 SH60*
E. Pughe **Argoed** *(SH604057)* ☎Tywyn 710361
*Homely, comfortable farmhouse with tasty
country food.*
Etr–Sep 3hc TV 3P 7acres

**LLANELIDAN** Clwyd *Map 6 SJ15*
M. Mosford **Trewyn** *(SJ138515)* Rhydymeudwy
☎Clawddnewydd 676
*Homely farmhouse in valley of fields and trees.
Ruthin about 5 miles. 2m E of B5429.*
Mar–Oct 3rm 1hc (2fb) TV P 🎨 80acres mixed
B&bf4–£4.50 Bdi£5.50–£6 W£38.50–£42 ⅃
D5.30pm

**LLANFACHRETH** *(Nr Dolgellau)* Gwynedd
*Map 6 SH72*
Mrs C.T. Owen **Rhedyncochion** *(SH762222)*
☎Rhydymain 600
*100-year-old, stone-built farmhouse with
extensive views of surrounding countryside and
mountains.*
Etr–Oct 2rm 1hc (1fb) ⚹ TV P 🎨 120acres mixed
S% B&bf6 Bdi£11.50 W£80 ⅃

**LLANFAIR DYFFRYN CLWYD** Clwyd *Map 6
SJ15*
Mrs E. Jones **Llanbenwch** *(SJ137533)* ☎Ruthin
2340
*Modernised farmhouse with oak beams
situated on the A525, Wrexham to Ruthin road.*
Feb–Nov 3hc (2fb) ⚹ TV P 🎨 40acres mixed S%
✱B&bfr£4.50 Bdi fr£6.50 Wfr£42 D6.30pm

**LLANFAIR TALHAIARN** Clwyd *Map 6 SH96*
**Bodrochwyn** *(SH938731)* ☎Abergele
823525
*Large, brick-built, L-shaped farmhouse of
distinction.*
Etr–Oct 3rm 1hc TV 174acres

**LLANFAIR WATERDINE** Salop *Map 7 SJ27*
Mrs J.M. Morgan **Selley Hall** *(SJ264766)*
Waterdine ☎Knighton 528429
*Old stone-built three-storey house dating back*

to 1780. Situated in rather remote but very picturesque area. Offa's Dyke runs within 200yds of farm. 5m NW of Knighton; take A488 then unclassified road on N side of River Teme.
May–Sep 3rm 1hc (2fb) ✸ 4P 500acres mixed S% B&b£6 Bdi£10 Wfr£70 ⅃ D3pm

**LLANGERNYW** Clwyd Map 6 SH86
Mr & Mrs E. Roberts **Tan-Y-Craig** (SH875669) ☎249
Large farmhouse on hillside. Situated 1 mile north of village.
Mar–Nov 3hc ✸ nc5 TV 3P 100acres mixed

**LLANGOLLEN** Clwyd Map 7 SJ24
Mrs A. Kenrick **Rhydonnen Ucha Rhewl** (SJ174429) ☎860153
Large, stone-built, three-storey farmhouse. Pleasantly situated. Shooting on farm. Trout fishing in River Dee (permit).
Mar–Oct 7rm 6hc (4fb) CTV 8P river 120acres dairy S% B&b£6–£6.50 Bdi£9–£10 W£60–£70 ⅃ D.5.30pm

**LLANRHAEADR** Clwyd Map 6 SJ06
C. Evans **Pen-Y-Waen** (SJ074615) ☎Llanynys 234
Positioned between sloping hills with views of valleys.
May–Oct 2rm (1fb) ✸ CTV P 🔲 100acres mixed

**LLANRUG** Gwynedd Map 6 SH56
Mr & Mrs D. Mackinnon **Plas Tirion** (SH524628) ☎Caernarfon 3190
Farmhouse dates back over 100 years and is set in open position with traditional farm buildings and gardens.
4hc (1fb) ✸ Ch CTV 6P 🔲 250acres mixed S% B&b£5–£6.50 Bdi fr£8.50 W£59.50 ⅃ (W only Jul & Aug)

**LLANRWST** Gwynedd Map 6 SH86
Mrs M. Owen **Bodrach** (SH852629) Gwytherin ☎640326
Farm in peaceful setting approximately 5 miles from Llanwrst
Mar–Nov 2rm (1fb) ✸ TV 6P 🔲 184acres mixed B&b£4.50–£5 Bdi£7.50–£8 D6pm

**LLANSANNAN** Clwyd Map 6 SH96
Mrs G. James **Fferwd** (SH933658) ☎230
Remote, brick-built farmhouse on the main Denbigh to Llansannan road. Denbigh about 7 miles.
May–Oct 3rm 1hc (1fb) ✸ nc8 CTV 2🌣 280acres mixed B&bfr£5 Bdi fr£6.50 Wfr£35 D6pm

**LLANSANTFFRAID-YM-MECHAIN** Powys Map 7 SJ22
D.B. & M.E. Jones **Glanvyrnwy** (SJ229202) ☎258
Two-storey, stone-built, detached farmhouse set back from road behind pleasant lawns and orchard.
Mar–Oct 3hc (2fb) ✸ nc5 CTV 6P 43acres dairy S% B&b£6.50–£7.50 Bdi£10–£11 Wfr£70 ⅃ D6pm

**LLANUWCHLLLYN** Gwynedd Map 6 SH83
D. Bugby **Bryncaled** (SH866314) ☎270
Farmhouse with beamed ceiling. Overlooking Aran Mountains, has fishing river running through grounds.
Closed Xmas day 3rm 2hc ✸ CTV 🔲 500acres sheep S% B&b£7 Bdi£10.50–£11 D8pm

**LLANVAIR-DISCOED** Gwent Map 3 ST49
Mrs Barnfather **Cribau Mill** (ST454941) Cribau Mill, The Cwm (off unclass rd joining Llanvair Discoed and Shirenewton) ☎Shirenewton 528
Closed Xmas 2hc 2🛏 ✸ CTV 2P 🔲 33acres mixed S% B&b£6 W£40 Ⓜ

**LLANWARNE** Heref & Worcs Map 3 SO52
Mrs I.E. Williams **Llanwarne Court** (SO503275) ☎Golden Valley 540385
Closed Xmas 6rm 3hc 1🛏 (1fb) ✸ Ch CTV 10P 2🌣 🔲 282acres mixed B&b£6–£6.50 Bdi£11–£11.50 D4pm

**LLANWDDYN** Powys Map 6 SJ01
H.A. Parry **Tyn-Y-Maes** (SJ048183) ☎216
Farmhouse is on edge of the nature reserve at Lake Vyrnwy.
May–Sep 3hc (1fb) CTV 4P 🔲 420acres mixed S% B&b£5.50–£6 Bdi£8.50 £9 W£60 ⅃ D5.30pm

**LLECHWEDD** Gwynedd Map 6 SH77
Mrs C. Roberts **Henllys** (SH779466) ☎Conwy 3269
Large, stone-built farmhouse, signposted from main road.
Apr–Oct 2rm (1fb) TV 4P 130acres mixed S% B&b£5–£6 Bdi£8–£9 D9pm

Mr & Mrs J.A. Jones **Lechan Ucha** (SH755757) ☎Conwy 2451
Modern farmhouse in isolated position. High on mountainside with good views of the surrounding area.
Apr–Oct 3rm (1fb) CTV 3P 🔲 river 102acres mixed S% B&b£5.75–£6.90 Bdi£8.05–£9.20 W£55.20–£59.80 ⅃ D3pm

**LLEDROD** Dyfed Map 6 SN67
P. & G. Steiner **Brynarth** (SN669698) ☎Crosswood 367
300-year-old stone and slate-built farm in pleasant countryside, in the foothills of the Cambrian Mountains.
Etr–Oct & 25 Dec–10 Jan 1rm 1🛏 (A 8rm 5➦ 2🛏) (1fb) ✸ CTV 10P 🔲 7acres non-working S% B&b£9.50 Bdi£12.60 W£88.50 ⅃ D7pm

**LOCHGOILHEAD** Strathclyde Argyll Map 10 NN10
Mr J. Jackson **Pole** (NN192044) ☎221
Pleasant well-kept farmhouse. Lochgoilhead 2 miles.
Etr–Oct 3rm (1fb) TV 3P 🔲 7,500acres sheep S% B&b£5.50–£7.50 Bdi£9–£10.50 W£60–£70 ⅃ D7pm

**LOCHWINNOCH** Strathclyde Renfrews Map 10 NS35
Mrs M. Mackie **High Belltrees** (NS377584) ☎842376
Situated 1 mile off the A737 1 mile S of Howwood. Overlooks Castle Semple Loch which has an R.S.P.B. Bird Sanctuary and yachting facilities.
5rm 3hc (2fb) ✸ CTV 10P 🔲 180acres dairy S% B&b£5.50–£6 Bdi£7.50–£8 W£50–£54 ⅃ D1pm

**LODDISWELL** Devon Map 3 SX74
E.N. Pethybridge **Reads** (SX727489) ☎317
Two-storey stone-built farmhouse in isolated position. Fine countryside views. Full working farm using own produce.
Mar–Oct 2rm 1hc (1fb) ✸ TV 3P 100acres mixed S% B&b£5–£5.50 W£34–£36

**LODDON** Norfolk Map 5 TM39
Mrs & Mrs A.E. Rackham **Stubbs House** (TM358977) ☎20231
Fine old house with excellent kitchen producing

*delicious, professional meals.*
9hc 1⇔ 1🛁 (1fb) ⫟ nc9 CTV ▥ 300acres
arable S% B&bfr£9 Bdi fr£13.50 W£70–£85
D am

**LONGDOWN** Devon *Map 3 SX89*
Mrs D.E. Booker **Steep Acres** *(SX885912)*
Bakers Hill ☎291
*Modern, bungalow-style farmhouse, situated in
an elevated position, with views of the moors.
Off B3212.*
May–Sep 4hc (1fb) 8P 10acres mixed S% B&b£5

**LONGDOWNS** Cornwall *Map 2 SW73*
Mr E.J. Lavers **Calamankey** *(SW746343)*
☎Stithians 860314
*Small farmhouse of Cornish granite; down a
short lane off A394.*
Etr–Oct 3rm (3fb) ⫟ nc6 CTV P 55acres dairy
S% B&b£4.75–£5.50 W£32 Ⓜ

**LONGLEAT** Wilts *Map 3 ST84*
J. Crossman **Stalls** *(ST806439)* ☎Maiden
Bradley 323
*Detached Bath-stone house, originally the home
farm for Longleat House. Sun terrace with trim
lawns and garden to stream. Access off A362 at
Corsley Heath.*
Apr–Oct 3hc ⫟ CTV 5P 281acres dairy S%
B&b£7.50

**LONGMORN** Grampian *Moray Map 15
NJ25*
Mrs M. Shanks **Cockmuir** *(NJ232571)* ☎Elgin
227
*Clean, pleasant farmhouse in attractive position.
Farm is set off main road down farm track.*
Jun–Aug 3rm (1fb) TV 4P 50acres mixed S%
B&bfr£4.75 Bdi fr£6.25 Wfr£43 D6pm

**LOOE** Cornwall *Map 2 SX25*
Mr & Mrs K. Hembrow **Tregoad** *(SX272560)*
☎2718
*Large, well-built, stone farmhouse on high
ground with sea view over Looe.*
Apr–Sep 6hc (4fb) CTV 12P 60acres dairy D3pm

**LOSTWITHIEL** Cornwall *Map 2 SX15*
Mr & Mrs R.C. Dunn **Pelyn Barn** *(SX091588)*
Pelyn Cross ☎872451
*Large farmhouse, formerly an old toll house,
with a well-kept lawn enclosure at rear.*
4hc (1fb) ⫟ CTV 10P 157acres mixed S%
B&b£7.50–£8 W£52.50–£56 Ⓜ

**LUSS** Strathclyde *Dunbartons Map 10 NS39*
**Duchlage** *(NS350872)*
*Pleasant, homely house. Luss 4 miles, S off
B832.*
Etr–Sep 3rm ⫟ nc12 TV 2P 1🐴 135acres mixed

**LYDBURY NORTH** Salop *Map 7 SO38*
Mr & Mrs R. Evans **Brunslow** *(SO366849)* ☎244
*Old brick-built Georgian farmhouse in rural
setting.*
Closed Xmas wk 4rm 3hc (2fb) ⫟ CTV 4P ▥
150acres dairy sheep S% ✳ B&b£5.25 Bdi£9.25
D6pm

**LYDFORD** Devon *Map 2 SX58*
Mrs J. Wild **Kirtonia** *(SX524862) Vale Down*
☎331
*Detached farmhouse adjacent to main A386.
Bedrooms enjoy scenic views of Dartmoor and
surrounding countryside.*
Apr–Oct 5hc (3fb) ⫟ Ⓒⱨ CTV 6P 6acres mixed

**LYDHAM** Salop *Map 7 SO39*
Mrs A. Williams **Pultheley** *(SO324945)* ☎Linley
214

*Pleasant farmhouse set amidst picturesque
countryside. 2¾m N A488.*
Mar–Oct 2rm (2fb) ⫟ 3P 290acres mixed S%
B&b£5.25 Bdi£7.75 W£53 Ⅼ D6pm

**LYONSHALL** Heref & Worcs *Map 3 SO35*
Mrs M.A. Eckley **Holme** *(SO339553)* ☎216
*Fully-modernised farmhouse standing on
outskirts of village.*
Etr–Oct 4rm 3hc (1fb) 8P ▥ dairy S% B&b£5–£6

J.A. Layton **Park Gate** *(SO332575)* ☎243
*Two-storey, stone-built farmhouse with land
overlooking Wales. Offa's Dyke runs through
part of the farm.*
Mar–Nov 2hc (1fb) ⫟ Ⓒⱨ CTV P ▥ 230acres
mixed S% B&b£5.50–£6.50 Bdi£10–£11
W£65 Ⅼ

**MALPAS** Cheshire *Map 7 SJ44*
Mrs N. Evans **Kidnal Grange** *(SJ473493)* ☎344
*Clean comfortable farmhouse. Attractive rural
surroundings. Duck pond. Much home produce
used in cooking.*
Apr–Oct 5rm 2⇔ (2fb) TV 12P 120acres mixed
S% B&b£7–£7.50

**MALVERN WELLS** Heref & Worcs *Map 3
SO74*
J.L. Morris **Brick Barns** *(SO783420)* Hanley Pl
☎Malvern 61775
*Imposing old farmhouse standing in its own
grounds.*
Etr–Sep 3rm (1fb) CTV 4P ▥ 200acres mixed
S% B&b£5–£6

**MANATON** Devon *Map 3 SX78*
Mr & Mrs R.V. Hugo **Langstone** *(SX747823)*
☎266
*Long, low granite farmhouse in traditional
Dartmoor style. Lawn with children's swings.
On edge of the Moor. Fine views.*
Mar–Oct 3hc ⫟ nc5 CTV 3P 130acres beef S%
B&b£6.50–£7 Bdi£9.50–£10 D7.30pm

**MARDEN** Heref & Worcs *Map 3 SO54*
Mrs M. Morris **Woodbine** *(SO520477)*
☎Sutton St Nicholas 291
*Two-storey, red-brick, Georgian-style
farmhouse. Large lawns at front. Situated on
edge of small village.*
Closed Xmas & New Year 1rm ⫟ nc TV 1P ▥
46acres mixed D5pm

**MARK CAUSEWAY** Somerset *Map 3 ST34*
Mrs E. Puddy **Croft** *(ST355475)* ☎Markmoor
206
*Comfortable and well-decorated farmhouse
with traditional furnishings throughout.*
Closed Xmas Eve ⫟ nc14 CTV 3P 130acres dairy
S% B&bfr£6 Bdi fr£7 W£38–£40 Ⅼ D6pm

**MARSHFIELD** Avon *Map 3 ST77*
Mrs E. Saville **Motcombe** *(ST784718)* ☎201
*Modernised, Cotswold-stone farmhouse in
pastureland and woodland. Views across valley
to Salisbury Plain and Mendip Hills.*
Apr–Sep 3hc ⫟ nc6 6P ▥ 40acres beef sheep
S% B&b£8.50–£9.50

**MARSHGATE** Cornwall *Map 2 SX19*
Mrs P. Bolt **Carleton** *(SX153918)* ☎Otterham
Station 252
*Farmhouse is situated adjacent to the Boscastle
road in Marshgate. Views over the surrounding
farmlands.*
Etr–Sep 3rm (1fb) ⫟ CTV 3P 120acres dairy
D8pm

**MARSHWOOD** Dorset *Map 3 SY39*
Mr & Mrs D. Edwards **Marshwood Manor**
*(SY396993)* ☎Broadwinsor 68442
*Set in the beauty and peace of Marshwood Vale
five miles from Charmouth's unspoilt beach.*
Closed Xmas day 8rm 4hc 2⇌ 🏠 (4fb) Ⓒⓗ CTV
25P ⬛ 50acres mixed D7pm

**MARYBANK** Highland *Ross & Crom Map 14
NH45*
Mr R. MacLeod **Easter Balloan** *(NH484535)*
☎Urray 211
*Roadside farmhouse standing in its own garden
on edge of village.*
Etr–Sep 5rm (2fb) ✙ CTV 10P 230acres mixed
S% ✱ B&bf£5 Bdi£8 D8pm

**MATHON** Heref & Worcs *Map 3 SO74*
Mrs Williams **Moorend Court** *(SO726454)*
☎Ridgeway Cross 205
*Beautiful 15th-century farmhouse in secluded
position with panoramic views towards
Malvern. Trout fishing on farm.*
Closed Xmas 3hc (1fb) TV in all bedrooms P ⬛
120acres mixed S% B&bf£7 Bdi£11 D10am

**MATLOCK** Derbys *Map 8 SK36*
M. Haynes **Packhorse** *(SK323617)* Matlock
Moor ☎2781
*Former inn on much-travelled Chesterfield to
Manchester packhorse route. Tastefully
furnished. Lawns and putting greens. 2m NE of
Matlock off A632 at Tansley signpost.*
Closed 20–31 Dec 4hc (2fb) ✙ nc2 CTV 6P ⬛
52acres beef dairy S% B&bf£5.50

Mrs J. Hole **Wayside** *(SK324630)* Matlock Moor
☎2967
*Pleasant, modernised, stone-built farmhouse
adjacent to A632 Matlock–Chesterfield road.*
Closed Xmas & New Year 6hc (2fb) ✙ nc3 TV 6P
⬛ 35acres dairy S% B&bfr£5.50

**MATTERDALE END** Cumbria *Map 11 NY32*
Mrs S.E. Hindson **Ivy House** *(NY396235)*
☎Glenridding 227
*Small stream runs close by farmhouse.*
Etr–Oct 3rm 2hc (2fb) 3P 19acres mixed S%
B&bf£5–£5.50 Bdi£6.50–£7 Wfr£45.50 ⅃ D4.30pm

**MATTISHALL** Norfolk *Map 9 TG01*
Mrs M. Faircloth **Moat** *(TG049111)* ☎Dereham
850288
*Period farmhouse standing back from road.
Good friendly atmosphere.*
Jun Oct 2rm (1fb) ✙ nc4 TV 2P 50acres mixed
D5.30pm

**MAWNAN SMITH** Cornwall *Map 2 SW72*
Mrs H. Mann **Penwarne Barton** *(SW773301)*
☎250331
*Interesting, well-equipped farm with many
animals. In very good position within sight of the
sea.*
May–Sep 3rm (1fb) ✙ TV 3P 118acres mixed
S% B&bf£7–£7.50

**MENDHAM** Suffolk *Map 5 TM28*
Mrs J.E. Holden **Weston House** *(TM292828)*
☎St Cross 206
*Fine old house about 300 years old. Fishing
nearby.*
Apr–Oct 4hc (1fb) nc6 CTV 6P ⬛ 300acres
arable dairy S% B&bf£6 W£30 Ⓜ

**MENHENIOT** Cornwall *Map 2 SX26*
Mrs S. Rowe **Tregondale** *(SX294643)*
☎Liskeard 42407
*Farm situated 1½ miles north of A38 east of Liskeard.*
3rm (1fb) Ch CTV 3P 400acres mixed S%
B&b£5–£6 Bdi£7.50–£8 D8pm

**MERRYMEET** Cornwall *Map 2 SX26*
B. Cole **Merrymeet** *(SX279660)* ☎Liskeard 43231
*Small two-storey, tile-hung farmhouse with small front garden. Yard and buildings at rear.*
May–mid Sep 2rm ⚹ TV 1P 1🐎 40acres mixed S% ✱ B&b£5 Bdi£7 W£45 ⓛ

**MIDDLETON ON THE HILL** Heref & Worcs *Map 3 SO56*
Mrs C.E. Moseley **Moor Abbey** *(SO545633)*
☎Leysters 226
*Former monastery about 400 years old. Original oak staircase and upper floors. Dining room in refectory with open log fire. Access to farm is from A4112 1m SW of Leysters.*
Apr–Oct 4hc (2fb) ⚹ nc6 8P 246acres mixed S%
B&b£5–£6 Bdi£6–£7 D5pm

**MIDDLETOWN** Powys *Map 7 SJ21*
Mrs E.J. Bebb **Bank** *(SJ325137)* ☎Trewern 260
*Traditional farmhouse with rear garden and attractive outlook.*
Mar–Oct 2hc (1fb) ⚹ CTV P 🎱 30acres sheep S% B&bfr£5 Bdifr£8

**MILBORNE PORT** Somerset *Map 3 ST61*
Mrs M.J. Tizzard **Venn** *(ST684183)* ☎250208
*Modern purpose-built farmhouse in mellow stone. Situation amid rural scenery on outskirts of village.*
Mar–Nov 3rm 2hc (2fb) ⚹ CTV 6P 🎱 300acres dairy S% B&b£6 W£40 Ⓜ

**MILNGAVIE** Strathclyde *Dunbartons Map 11 NS57*
Mrs L. Fisken **High Craigton** *(NS525766)*
☎041-956 1384
*Two-storey, stone-built farmhouse with numerous outbuildings. Good access road.*
2hc (2fb) CTV 10P 🎱 1,100acres sheep S% B&b£5 W£35 Ⓜ

**MINSTER LOVELL** Oxon *Map 4 SP31*
Mr & Mrs C. Brown **Hill Grove** *(SP334110)* (off B4047 1½m E of village towards Crawley village)
☎Witney 3120
Closed Xmas 2rm ⚹ 2P 🎱 80 acres beef S% ✱ B&B£7–£9

**MOLLAND** Devon *Map 3 SS82*
Mrs P. England **Yeo** *(SS785266)* ☎Bishops Nympton 312
*Well-maintained farmhouse with good furnishings and décor. Set in large garden.*
Apr–Oct 4hc (1fb) ⚹ CTV 4P 🎱 200acres mixed S% B&b£5.50–£6.50 Bdi£9–£10 W£58–£65 ⓛ

**MONEYDIE** Tayside *Perths Map 11 NO02*
Mrs S. Walker **Moneydie Roger** *NO054290)*
☎Almondbank 239
*A substantial, two-storey farmhouse standing amid good arable land. Perth 7 miles.*
Apr–Sep ⚹ 1P 143acres mixed S% B&b£5–£5.25

**MONKSILVER** Somerset *Map 3 ST03*
Mrs L.R. Watts **Manor House at Rowdon Farm** *(ST082381)* ☎Stogumber 614
*Farmhouse overlooking Quantock Hills.*
Closed Xmas 6hc 1🛏 🏠 (2fb) CTV P 🎱 300acres mixed D4pm

Mrs S.J. Watts **Rowdon** *(ST082381)*
☎Stogumber 280
*Solidly built stone farmhouse overlooking Quantock Hills.*
4hc (2fb) CTV 6P 🎱 150acres mixed

**MONKTON** Devon *Map 3 ST10*
Mr & Mrs Bowra **Pugh's** *(ST186029)* ☎Honiton 2860
*Well-situated farmhouse on the A30 at Monkton. Honiton about 1½ miles.*
Mar–Oct 3rm 2hc (1fb) nc12 CTV 4P 🎱 7½acres mixed S% B&b£6–£6.50 Bdi£9–£9.50 W£52–£54 Ⓜ D5pm

**MONTGOMERY** Powys *Map 7 SO29*
Mrs S.M. Davies **East Penyllan** *(SO244941)*
☎246
*Farmhouse is in England, 2m SE of Montgomery on B4385.*
Apr–Nov 3rm (1fb) Ch CTV 5P 200acres mixed S% B&b£4.50–£5 Bdi£6.50–£7 D6.30pm

**MONTROSE** Tayside *Angus Map 15 NO75*
Mrs A. Ruxton **Muirside of Gallery** *(NO671634)*
☎Northwater Bridge 209
*Situated in beautiful countryside facing the Grampian Mountain range, and only 5 miles from the seaside.*
2rm 1hc (1fb) TV 3P 110acres arable S% ✱ B&b£4.50–£5 Bdi£8–£8.50 W£56 ⓛ D7pm

**MORNINGTHORPE** Norfolk *Map 5 TM29*
Mrs O.K. Gowing **Hollies** *(TM212939)* ☎Long Stratton 30540

---

*Large Georgian property standing in own
grounds, in quiet rural area. ¾m E of A140.
Good atmosphere, plenty of amenities.*
Apr–Oct 9hc 2⇋ (4fb) ⋇ CTV 8P ⦰ 350acres
arable B&b£8 Bdi£10 W£75 ⱡ (W only Jul &
Aug) D6.30pm

**MORVAH** Cornwall *Map 2 SW33*
Mrs J. Mann **Merthyr** *(SW403355)* ☎Penzance
788464
*Well-appointed farmhouse on B3306 north-west
of Penzance.*
Jun–Oct 6hc (3fb) ⋇ CTV P sea 100acres beef
S% B&bfr£6 Bdifr£8.50 Wfr£48.50 ⱡ (W only high
season)

**MOUNT** Cornwall *Map 2 SX16*
E.J. Beglan **Mount Pleasant** *(SX152680)*
☎Cardinham 342
*Farm 6 miles east of Bodmin in open country on
the edge of Bodmin Moor. Own transport
essential.*
Etr–Oct 8hc (2fb) CTV 8P ⦰ 50acres arable
sheep S% B&b£5.50–£6.50 Bdi£8.25–£9.50
W£54–£60 D4pm

**MOYLGROVE** Dyfed *Map 2 SN14*
Mrs A.D. Fletcher **Penrallt Ceibwr** *(SN116454)*
☎217
*A very pleasant farm off A487. ½m from Ceibwr
beach.*
6hc (3fb) Ⓒⱨ CTV 20P ⦰ 250acres mixed
B&b£7–£8 Bdi£11.50–£12.50 W£75–£85 ⱡ

**MUSBURY** Devon *Map 3 SY29*
Mrs S.L. Cligg **Higher Bruckland** *(SY284933)*
☎Colyton 52371
*Farmhouse completely surrounded by farmland.
Seaton 4 miles.*
Etr–Oct 3hc (1fb) ⋇ CTV P 236acres mixed
D4.30pm

**NANTGAREDIG** Dyfed *Map 2 SN42*
Mrs J. Willmott **Cwmtwrch** *(SN497220)* ☎238
*Early 19th-century Welsh-stone farmhouse,
carefully modernised and furnished.*
3hc 1fⱨ (1fb) ⋇ TV 10P 30acres mixed S%
B&b£6–£7 Bdi£10–£12 W£70–£84 ⱡ D8.30pm

**NETHER COMPTON** Dorset *Map 3 ST51*
Mrs C.D. Allard **Halfway House** *(ST603163)*
☎Sherborne (Dorset) 2781
*Mellow stone-built house in elevated position.
Well-kept gardens. Interesting display of
horseriding awards. On A30.*
Mar–Oct 3hc (1fb) CTV 12P ⦰ 119acres beef
S% B&b£7

**NEWBOLD ON STOUR** Warwicks *Map 4
SP24*
Mrs J. Kerby **Berryfield** *(SP216483)* ☎Ilmington
248
*A deceptively-large farmhouse in secluded
position. Situated off the Armscote–Ilmington rd.*
Etr–Oct 3hc (1fb) ⋇ P ⌂ 100acres mixed S%
B&b£5.50–£6 W£35 Ⱨ

**NEWBRIDGE** Lothian *Midlothian Map 11
NT17*
Mr & Mrs W. Pollock **Easter Norton**
*(NT157721)* ☎031-333 1279
*Small attractive farmhouse. Excellent position
for motorway and Edinburgh Airport.*
Apr–Sep 3rm (2fb) CTV P ⦰ 7acres poultry S%
B&bfr£5

**NEWBURGH** Fife *Map 11 NO21*
**Glen Duckie** *(NO283188)* ☎352
*A large farm set amid rolling hills with main
farmhouse dating from 16th century.*
May–Sep 2rm ⋇ TV 4P 358acres mixed

**NEWCASTLE** Salop *Map 7 SO28*
Mrs P.M. Reynolds **Newcastle Hall** *(SO246824)*
☎Clun 350
*Large stone-built Georgian farmhouse in
peaceful setting. Surrounded by tree-clad hills.*
Etr–Oct 4rm 3hc (1fb) P 278acres beef sheep
S% B&b£6.50–£7 Bdi£9.50–£10 D4.30pm

**NEW CUMNOCK** Strathclyde *Ayrs Map 11
NS61*
Mr & Mrs A. Howat **Polshill** *(NS652132)* ☎301
*Pleasant, well-kept old mill house, parts of
which date back 300 years.*
Jun–Sep 2rm (2fb) ⋇ nc5 CTV 4P 230acres beef
S% B&b£4.50–£5

**NEWQUAY** Cornwall *Map 2 SW86*
**Legonna** *(SW834594)* ☎2272
*Granite farmhouse in beautiful wooded valley.
Swimming pool, tennis court, private fishing
lake, children's play area and pony riding. 2¼m
SE of Newquay.*
May–Sep 10hc TV 10P 140acres mixed

Mr & Mrs A.R.E. Wilson **Manuels** *(SW839601)*
Lane ☎3577
*17th-century farmhouse in sheltered, wooded
valley 2 miles from Newquay on A392.*
Closed Xmas 4rm (2fb) Ⓒⱨ CTV 4P 35acres
mixed

**NEWTON** *(Nr Vowchurch)* Heref & Worcs
*Map 3 SO33*
Mrs J. Powell **Little Green** *(SO335337)*
☎Michaelchurch 205
*Modernised farmhouse which used to be an inn.*

*Friendly atmosphere.*
Closed Xmas 3hc (2fb) 🄲ⓗ CTV 4P 50acres
beef sheep S% B&b£5–£6 Bdi£7.50–£9
W£50–£60 ⅃

**NEWTOWN** Powys *Map 6 SO19*
L. Whitticase **Highgate** *(SO111953)* ☎25981
*15th-century half-timbered farmhouse with
wonderful views over valley and hills.*
3hc 2🔥 (1fb) 🟊 🄲ⓗ CTV P 🛏 300acres mixed
S% B&b£6.50 Bdi£10 D5pm

Mrs I. Jarman **Lower Gwestydd** *(SO126934)*
Llanllwchaiarn (2m E off B4568) ☎26718
3hc (2fb) 🟊 🄲ⓗ TV 3P 1🐾 200acres mixed
S% B&b£5.50 Bdi£8.50 Wfr£59.50 ⅃ D6pm

**NORMANBY** N Yorks *Map 8 NZ90*
D.I. Smith **Heather View** *(NZ928062)* ☎Whitby
880451
*Attractive modern farmhouse. Well-appointed
and comfortable. Conveniently situated for
coastal visits.*
Mar–Sep 5hc (3fb) 🟊 nc5 CTV 5P 🛏 40acres
mixed S% B&b£5.50–£6.50 Bdi£8–£9 D5.30pm

**NORTH CADBURY** Somerset *Map 3 ST62*
Mrs A.G. Robson **Ferngrove** *(ST637274)*
Woolston ☎329
*In a pleasant secluded locality. Lawn and
produce garden adjoining house.*
4rm (1fb) 🟊 🟊 TV P 🛏 90acres mixed S%
B&b£6.25 Bdi£9.75 W£62 ⅃ D5.30pm

E.J. Keen **Hill** *(ST634279)* ☎40257
*Two-storey, red-brick, double-fronted
farmhouse with front garden and extensive
outbuildings.*
Etr–Oct 3rm 1hc (1fb) 🟊 TV P 🛏 100acres dairy
S% B&bfr£5.50 Bdifr£9

**NORTH DUFFIELD** N Yorks *Map 8 SE63*
Mr F.B. Arrand **Hall** *(SE692374)* (½m NE of
village) ☎Bubwith 301
*In low-lying territory the farmhouse is
surrounded by rich farming land overlooking the
River Derwent in a secluded area away from the
village.*
May–Sep 3rm 2hc (2fb) 🟊 CTV P river 170acres
mixed S% B&b£5.50

**NORTH WOOTTON** Somerset *Map 3 ST54*
Mrs M. White **Barrow** *(ST553416)* ☎Pilton 245
*Stone-built farmhouse fronted by tidy gardens at
edge of village.*
Mar–Nov 3hc (1fb) 🟊 CTV 4P 150acres dairy S%
B&b£6.50 Bdi£8.50 Wfr£56 ⅃

**NORTON** Notts *Map 8 SK57*
Mrs J. Palmer **Norton Grange** *(SK572733)*
☎Mansfield 842666
*A 200-year-old stone-built farmhouse fronted by
tidy gardens at edge of village.*
Etr–Sep 3rm 2hc (1fb) CTV 4P 172acres mixed
S% B&b£7.50–£8

**NOTTER** Cornwall *Map 2 SX36*
Mrs E.A. Tamblyn **Notter** *(SX390609)* ☎Saltash
3593
*Quietly situated farmhouse a few yards off the
A38 overlooking the valley.*
3hc (1fb) TV 5P 207acres mixed S% B&b£5–£6

**ODDINGLEY** Heref & Worcs *Map 3 SO95*
Mrs P. Wardle **Pear Tree's** *(SO909589)*
☎Droitwich 778489
*Large modern farmhouse in quiet country lane
close to M5 motorway.*
Etr–Sep 4rm 2hc 🟊 nc5 CTV P 🛏 17acres mixed
S% B&b£7 Bdi£9 W£49–£52.50 ⅃ D24hrs notice

**OKEHAMPTON** Devon *Map 2 SX59*
Mrs E. Maile **Agiestment** *(SX603979)* ☎2359
*Well-appointed farmhouse with extensive moor
and forest views.*
Mar–Sep 2rm (2fb) 🟊 nc12 CTV 3P 🛏 260acres
mixed S% B&b£6–£7 W£70–£72

Mrs M. Pennington **Hill Barton** *(SX594984)*
☎2454
*Good working farm in peaceful setting in the
heart of beautiful, well-wooded countryside.*
Mar–Nov 3rm 2hc 🟊 nc8 TV 6P 280acres beef
sheep S% B&b£7–£7.50 Bdi£11–£11.50

Mrs K.C. Heard **Hughslade** *(SX561932)* ☎2883
*Pleasant farmhouse on the edge of town. Ideal
base for exploring Dartmoor and north and south
Devon coasts.*
Closed Xmas 4hc (1fb) CTV 6P 500acres mixed
S% B&b£6.50–£9 Bdi£9–£10.50 Wfr£60 ⅃
D5.30pm

**OKEOVER** Staffs *Map 7 SK14*
E.J. Harrison **Little Park** *(SK160490)* ☎Thorpe
Cloud 341
*Red-brick and stone farmhouse, interior
abounds with oak beams.*
May–Sep 3rm 2hc (2fb) 🟊 nc3 CTV 3P 123acres
dairy S% B&b£6 Bdi£8 D3.30pm

---

## Hughslade Farm Okehampton, Devon

The farm is ideally situated for touring Devon,
Cornwall, Dartmoor and Exmoor. Hughslade is a
large working farm with plenty of animals around.
The farmhouse is comfortably furnished. Lounge
with colour TV and central heating on the ground
floor. Meals served in the dining room, are mainly
made from home-produced vegetables and meat.
Bed, breakfast and evening meal or bed and
breakfast daily. Okehampton is just 2 miles from
the farm and has a superb golf-course, tennis courts
and covered swimming pool. Horse riding available
at the farm. Happy holiday assured.

SAE please for terms to Mrs K C Heard,
Hughslade Farm, Okehampton, Devon.
Tel: Okehampton 2883.

**OLD DALBY** Leics *Map 8 SK62*
Mrs V. Anderson **Home** *(SK673236)* Church Lane ☎Melton Mowbray 822622
*19th-century farmhouse, parts from 1730, in the Vale of Belvoir. Former bailiff's house when property was part of estate.*
Closed Dec 3hc (A 2rm) (1fb) TV 6P ▥ non-working S% B&b£6.75–£7.50 Bdi£10.25–£11 D24hrs notice

**ONICH** Highland *Inverness-shire Map 14 NN06*
Mr & Mrs A. Dewar **Cuilcheanna House** *(NN019617)* ☎226
*Large Victorian house with gardens set in sloping fields leading to Loch Linnhe. Excellent views over lochs and mountains.*
Etr–Sep 9rm 8hc (2fb) Ch 8P ▥ lake 120acres beef S% B&b£5.50–£6.50 Bdi£10.25–£11.25 W£69–£75 L D7pm

**ORKNEY** *Map 16*
**See Kirkwall, Rendall**

**OTTERBURN** Northumb *Map 12 NY89*
Mr & Mrs G.F. Stephenson **Monkridge** *(NY913917)* ☎20639
*Well-cared-for, comfortable farmhouse in the attractive environment of the Northumberland Moors.*
Closed Dec 2rm (1fb) ✱ CTV 3P 1🚗 ▥ 1,400acres mixed S% B&b£7 Bdi£11 Dnoon

**OXENHOPE** W Yorks *Map 7 SE03*
Mrs A. Scholes **Lily Hall** *(SE023362)* Uppermarsh Ln ☎Haworth 43999
*Pleasant farmhouse in 9-acre smallholding rearing turkeys and hens. Overlooking pleasant valley in Brontë country. Horse riding, golf, tennis and bathing 4 miles.*
Closed Xmas 3hc ✱ CTV 12P ▥ 9acres mixed S% B&b£6 Bdi£9 W£56 L D6pm

**OXWICH** W Glam *Map 2 SS58*
Mrs D.M. Tucker **Norton** *(SS492866)* ☎Gower 241
*Modernised farmhouse conveniently located for beaches, clifftop walks, and many local beauty spots.*
2rm ✱ CTV 🚗 ▥ 45acres mixed S% B&bfr£5 Bdifr£7.50 Wfr£50

**PADOG** Gwynedd *Map 6 SH85*
Mrs L. Davis **Dylasau Isa** *(SH832157)* ☎Betws-y-Coed 265
*Stone-built farmhouse ½ mile from A5, east of town.*
Apr–Oct 3hc (1fb) ✱ CTV 4P 300acres mixed S% B&b£5 W£35 M

Mrs E.A. Jones **Pant Glas** *(SH846513)* Pentre Foelas Rd (½m W of A5/B4407 junction) ☎Pentrefoelas 248
late Apr–Oct 3rm 1⚲ (1fb) ✱ CTV 6P 179acres S% ✱B&b£4.60–£5.17 Bdi£8.05–£9.20 D5.30pm

Mrs D.O. Jones **Ty-Uchaf** *(SH830503)* ☎Pentrefoelas 280
*Stone-built farmhouse on hill farm.*
Closed Xmas day 3hc (2fb) Ch CTV 20P 300acres beef sheep S% B&b£5.50–£6.50 Bdi£8.50–£10 W£56–£65 D5pm

**PANCRASWEEK** Devon *Map 2 SS20*
M.A. Brown **Higher Kingford** *(SS285061)* ☎Briderule 281
*Small working farm 6 miles from Bude.*
Apr–Nov 5rm 2hc (1fb) ✱ CTV 5P 84acres mixed S% B&b£5.75 Bdi£8.05 W£48.30 L

**PANDY TUDUR** Clwyd *Map 6 SH86*
Mrs G. Roberts **Llwyn du Uchaf** *(SH854640)* (¼m SW of B5384 towards A548) ☎Llangernyw 622
*17th-century stone farmhouse at the end of its own drive with good views over surrounding countryside.*
May–Oct 2🛁 (1fb) CTV 3P 53acres mixed S% B&b£6 Bdi£8 D8pm

***Llywn Llydan*** *(SH851647)* ☎Llangernyw 243
*Modernised farmhouse in an elevated situation. Magnificent views.*
2rm 1hc ✱ nc8 4P river 85acres mixed

**PANTYGELLI** *(Nr Abergavenny)* Gwent *Map 3 SO31*
Mrs M.E. Smith **Lower House** *(SO314159)* Old Hereford Rd ☎Abergavenny 3432
*Isolated stone-built farmhouse. Well situated 3 miles from Abergavenny.*
Etr–Oct 3hc (1fb) CTV 6P 200acres arable beef sheep S% B&b£5.50–£6

**PEASEDOWN ST JOHN** Avon *Map 3 ST75*
Mr & Mrs R. Birk **Carlingcott Mill** *(ST695584)* Carlingcott (1m NW) ☎Radstock 32197
*Alongside the river in a secluded valley, this trout farm is adjacent to a mill.*
Closed Xmas 3rm 2hc 1🛁 ✱ nc10 TV 6P ▥ river 16acres trout S% ✱B&b£9 Bdi£13.75 W£84 L D6pm

**PEBWORTH** Heref & Worcs *Map 4 SP14*
Mrs M.J. Jordan **Pebworth Fields** *(SP134459)* ☎Stratford-on-Avon 720318
*Unusual, colonial-style farmhouse. Trim grounds fairly remote and ideal for local tourist areas.*

May–Aug 3rm 1hc (1fb) ⚹ TV P 100acres mixed S% B&b£6.50–£6.75

**PELYNT** Cornwall *Map 2 SX25*
Mrs E. Tuckett **Trenderway** *(SX214533)*
☎Polperro 72214
*Comfortable and well-maintained farmhouse about 3 miles from Looe.*
May–Sep 3hc (1fb) ⚹ CTV 4P 360acres mixed S% B&b£5–£6.50

**PENMACHNO** Gwynedd *Map 6 SH75*
**Tyddyn Gethin** *(SH799514)* ☎392
*Farm situated high on mountainside with panoramic views of surrounding country.*
3hc ⚹ TV P 60acres beef, mixed and sheep

**PENRUDDOCK** Cumbria *Map 12 NY42*
Mrs S.M. Smith **Highgate** *(NY444275)*
☎Greystoke 339
*250-year-old stone-built farmhouse with beamed ceilings; tastefully modernised. Good base for towing and recreational facilities. Children's playground. 2m E on A66.*
Feb–Oct 4hc ⚹ nc10 CTV 4P 2☎ 400acres beef sheep S% B&b£6 Bdi£9 W£60 ⌊ D5pm

**PENTREFOELAS** Clwyd *Map 6 SH85*
M. Thomas **Tai Hirion** *(SH839525)* ☎202
*Two-storey, stone-built house. Adjacent to A5 Corwen to Betws-y-Coed road.*
2hc (1fb) ⚹ TV P 204acres mixed S% B&b£5–£6 Bdi£7–£8

**PENYBONT** Powys *Map 3 SO16*
Mrs D. Hughes **Bwlch y Cefn** *(SO121612)* (3m S of Penybont village on unclass road) ☎657
May–Sep 3rm (2fb) CTV 10P 356acres mixed S% B&b£5 Bdi£7.50 W£52.50 ⌊ D6.30pm

Mrs S.F. Cox **Neuadd** *(SO092618)* Cefnllys
☎Llandrindod Wells 2571
*Two-storey, isolated farmhouse situated in elevated position. Fine views.*
Apr–Sep 4rm 3hc (2fb) Ⓒʰ CTV 6P ⫛ river 329½acres mixed S% B&b£6.50 Bdi£9.50 W£65 ⌊ D5pm

**PILSDON** Dorset *Map 3 SY49*
K.B. Brooks **Monkwood** *(SY429986)*
☎Broadwindsor 68723
*With pleasant views the farmhouse is in a peaceful rural area.*
2rm (1fb) P 130acres mixed S% ✳ B&b£6–£6.50 Bdi£7.50–£8.50 W£50–£55 ⌊

**PITLOCHRY** Tayside *Perths Map 14 NN95*
Mrs M.M. Hay **Faskally Home** *(NN918601)*
☎2007
*Pleasant 'U'-shaped farm with popular caravan site attached. Set on west side of A9 on northern outskirts of Pitlochry. Sheltered from Loch Faskally by trees.*
Apr–mid Oct 8rm 6hc (2fb) P 100acres non-working S% B&bfr£5.50

**PLAYING PLACE** Cornwall *Map 2 SW84*
**Halvarras** *(SW814415)* ☎Devoran 862305
*Typical stone-built farmhouse about 1½ miles from A39.*
Apr–Sep 6hc ⚹ 6P 115acres arable & beef

**PONSWORTHY** Devon *Map 3 SX77*
Mr & Mrs. Fursdon **Old Walls** *(SX697745)*
☎Poundsgate 222
*Farmhouse standing in its own small estate. Isolated, near Dartmoor. Pleasant atmosphere.*
Apr–Oct 3rm Ⓒʰ 4P ⫛ river 36acres beef S% B&b£6.93

**PONTARDULAIS** W Glam *Map 2 SN50*
Mr & Mrs G. Davies **The Croft** *(SN612015)*
Heol-y-Barna ☎883654
*Farmhouse has open aspect to the Gower Peninsula and the Loughor Estuary.*
Closed Xmas & New Year 3rm 2hc 1⋒ (1fb) nc5 TV 4P 1⌂ ▥ sea 5acres beef S% B&b£6–£9 Bdi£8.50–£12 W£55–£75 Ⱡ D5pm

**PONTSHAEN** Dyfed *Map 2 SN44*
Mr & Mrs R. Morris **Glan Dwr** *(SN445491)* (2m N off B4459 onto unclass rd) ☎255
*Stone-built traditional Welsh longhouse, approximately 300 years old, set in 12 acres on a hillside, some 800 feet above sea level, overlooking Clettwr Fach Valley.*
5hc 1⋒ (3fb) TV 20P 1⌂ ▥ 12acres mixed S% B&b£5.50–£6 Bdi£11–£12 W£65–£70 Ⱡ D5.30pm

**POOLEY BRIDGE** Cumbria *Map 12 NY42*
Mrs A. Strong **Barton Hall** *(NY478251)* ☎275
*Attractive farmhouse, well-furnished and decorated. Large garden with lawn and summer house. Boating, fishing and golf nearby.*
Mar–Oct 3rm 2hc (1fb) ★ nc8 P 65acres dairy S% B&b£6

**PORT OF MENTEITH** Central *Perths Map 11 NN50*
Mrs J. Fotheringham **Collymoon** *(NN593966)*
☎Buchlyvie 268
*Attractive white-painted farmhouse near lane. Situated just off B8034.*
Apr–Oct 3rm 1hc (3fb) ★ CTV 3P ▥ river 350acres mixed S% B&b£5.50 Bdi£8

**PORTREE** Isle of Skye, Highland *Inverness-shire Map 13 NG44*
Mrs M. Bruce **Cruachanlea** *(NG513373)* Braes
☎Sligachan 233
*Situated 6 miles SE of Portree on B883, overlooking sea to the Isle of Raasay. Hill views everywhere.*
4hc (2fb) CTV 8P ▥ sea 10acres arable sheep S% B&b£5–£5.50 Bdi£8–£8.50 W£56–£59.50 Ⱡ D7pm

***No 1 Uigishadder*** *(NG430463)* ☎Skeabost Bridge 279
*Small crofting farm situated high on moor in isolated position facing north-west. Portree about 4 miles.*
Apr–Sep 3rm ★ 6P 6acres arable

Mrs S. MacDonald **Upper Ollach** *(NG518362)*
Braes ☎Sligachan 225
*Grey, stone crofting farm in 7 acres of hilly farmland with gardens and trees screening the house. Close to coastline 6½m SE of Portree on B883.*
Mar–Oct 3rm (1fb) ★ TV 4P sea 7acres mixed S% B&bfr£5.50 Bdifr£8.75 D6pm

**POUNDSGATE** Devon *Map 3 SX77*
Mrs G. Fursdon **Lowertown** *(SX712729)* ☎282
*Pleasantly-situated farmhouse with wooden beams in entrance hall.*
Mar–Nov 3rm (1fb) TV 3P 120acres beef S% B&b£6

**PWLLHELI** Gwynedd *Map 6 SH33*
Mrs M. Hughes **Bryn Crin** *(SH379358)* ☎2494
*Large, stone-built farmhouse in an elevated position overlooking Cardigan Bay and Snowdonia. Within easy reach of sandy beaches.*
May–Oct 3rm 2hc (2fb) ★ 3P sea 70acres mixed S% B&b£5–£5.50

Mrs J.E. Ellis **Gwynfryn** *(SH364357)* (1m NW)
☎2536
Closed Xmas & New Year 2hc (1fb) ★ nc5 CTV P ▥ 350acres mixed B&b£5.50–£7 Bdi£9–£12 W£38–£40 M̸ D10am

**REDMILE** Leics *Map 8 SK73*
Mrs A. Barton **Olde Mill House** *(SK789358)*
☎Bottesford 42460
*A beautiful house approximately 250 years old, which has been considerably modernised; set in peaceful Belvoir valley.*
4hc nc10 CTV 4P ▥ 5½acres non-working S% B&b£8–£8.50 Bdi£12.50–£13 W£84–£87.50 Ⱡ D am

Mr & Mrs P. Need **Peacock** *(SK791359)*
☎Bottesford 42475
*Modernised 250-year-old farmhouse. Hunter stud farm with paddocks. Horse riding available. In rural Vale of Belvoir close to Castle.*
Closed Xmas 4rm 1hc (2fb) [ch] CTV 10P ▥ 5acres mixed S% B&b£7 Bdi£11 W£77 Ⱡ D8.30pm

**RENDALL** Orkney *Map 16 HY32*
Mrs H.R. Harcus **Lower Ellibister** *(HY386213)*
☎Evie 224
*Farmhouse set amid beautiful countryside with extensive views across the bay to Kirkwall.*
3rm (1fb) CTV 4P 344acres mixed S% B&bfr£5 Bdifr£8.50 Wfr£77 D6pm

**RHANDIRMWYN** Dyfed *Map 3 SN74*
Mrs G.A. Williams **Galltybere** *(SN772460)*
☎218
*Isolated farmhouse 9 miles north of Llandovery amid splendid scenery. Ideal for bird watching and hikers.*
1rm (A 2hc) (1fb) ★ nc5 CTV 4P 325acres mixed S% ✱B&b£6 Bdi£10 Wfr£70 Ⱡ

**RIEVAULX** N Yorks *Map 8 SE58*
Mrs M.E. Skilbeck **Middle Heads** *(SE584869)*
(1m E of B1257 & 3m NW of Helmsley)
☎Bilsdale 251
Apr–Nov 3rm (1fb) ★ TV 6P ▥ 170acres mixed S% ✱B&b£6 D6pm

**ROBOROUGH** Devon *Map 2 SS51*
***Rapson Court*** *(SS573179)* ☎High Bickington 246
*Typical small Devonshire farmhouse dating from 17th century. Thatched roof, oak beams, horse brasses. Good views of surrounding countryside.*
Etr–mid Sep 2hc ★ nc5 TV 2P 125acres mixed

**ROCHESTER** Northumb *Map 12 NY89*
Mrs G.E. Wilson **Woodlaw** *(NY821985)*
☎Otterburn 20686
*The farmhouse was built about 1800 and overlooks the valley. It's about 100 yards from A68.*
Apr–Oct 3rm (1fb) nc2 CTV 3P 800acres mixed S% B&b£5.50 Bdi£8.50

**ROGART** Highland *Sutherland Map 14 NC70*
Mrs C.F. Moodie **Rovie** *(NC716023)* ☎209
*Farmhouse situated in the Strathfleet valley 4 miles from sea. Rabbit shooting on farm and fishing locally in River Fleet. S off A839.*
Apr–Oct 7hc (1fb) CTV 6P 120acres mixed S% B&b£6–£6.50 Bdi£10–£10.50 W£70–£75 D6.30pm

**ROSEDALE ABBEY** N Yorks *Map 8 SE79*
Mrs D.J. Rawlings **High House** *(SE698974)*
☎Lastingham 471
*18th-century modernised farmhouse, stone-built and oak-beamed. Log fires. Panoramic*

*views over dale.*
3hc (1fb) 4P 🎢 100acres beef sheep S%
B&b£6.50–£8.50 Bdi£11–£13.50 W£77–£94 ⓛ
D7pm

**ROSTON** Derbys *Map 7 SK14*
Mrs E.K. Prince **Roston Hall** *(SK133409)*
☎Ellastone 287
*Former Manor House, part Elizabethan and part Georgian, in centre of quiet village. Ideal centre for touring Peak District.*
May–Sep 2rm 1hc (1fb) 🛠nc14 TV 4P 100acres arable beef S% B&b£6–£7 Bdi£7.50–£10 D10am

**ROTHESAY** Isle of Bute, Strathclyde *Bute Map 10 NS06*
**Birgidale Crieff** *(NS073591)* ☎Kilchattan Bay 236
*Well cared for, attractively furnished farmhouse on south end of island. Well-maintained garden. 3m S off A845.*
Apr–Oct 2rm nc4 TV 3P 🎢 sea 300acres arable dairy

**RUSHTON SPENCER** Staffs *Map 7 SJ96*
Mrs J. Brown **Barnswood** *(SJ945606)* ☎261
*Large stone-built farmhouse. Grounds stretch to edge of Rudyard Lane. Splendid views across lake to distant hills.*
Apr–Dec 3rm 2hc (2fb) 🛠CTV 4P lake 100acres dairy S% B&bfr£6.50 Bdi fr£10.50 Dnoon

**RUSKIE** Central *Perths Map 11 NN60*
Mrs J. H. Bain **Lower Tarr** *(NN624008)*
☎Thornhill (Stirling) 202
*Large, well-maintained farm over 200 years old, with partly-modernised interior. Good views over rolling hill land.*
Etr–Oct 2rm 1hc (1fb) 🛠TV P 161acres mixed S% B&b£4.50–£5 Bdi£7.50 D4pm

**RUTHIN** Clwyd *Map 6 SJ15*
M.E. Jones **Pen-y-Coed** *(SJ107538)* Pwllglas
☎Clawdd Newydd 251
*Isolated farmhouse on high ground with extensive views. Stone-built with timbered ceilings.*
Closed Xmas 3hc (3fb) TV P 🎢 160acres mixed S% ✷B&bfr£5 Bdi fr£7 Wfr£45 ⓛ

Mrs T. Francis **Plas-y-Ward** *(SJ118604)* Rhewl
☎3822
*Period farmhouse, dating back to 14th century. 2m N A525.*
Jun–Sep 2rm 1hc (1fb) 🛠nc5 TV 6P 216acres arable dairy sheep S% B&b£7

**RUYTON-XI-TOWNS** Salop *Map 7 SJ32*
Mrs V. Mason **Lower** *(SJ362261)* Shotatton
☎Knockin 461
*Smallholding with well-furnished accommodation. Well placed for touring. Two acres of private ground. Fishing and golf 3 miles.*
4hc 1♒(1fb) CTV 6P 🎢 2acres arable S% B&b£7.50 Bdi£10.50–£11 W£60 D7pm

**RYDE** Isle of Wight *Map 4 SZ59*
Mrs C. Morey **Aldermoor** *(SZ582906)* Upton Rd
☎64743
*Two Victorian cottages situated in rural surroundings. 1½m from Ryde.*
Etr–Oct 3hc (2fb) CTV 3🐾 60acres dairy S%

**ST AGNES** Cornwall *Map 2 SW75*
W.R. & K.B. Blewett **Mount Pleasant** *(SW722508)* Rosemundy ☎2387
*Spacious bungalow set in the farm meadows. Stands in its own large garden with beautiful views.*
May–Oct 11hc (6fb) CTV 20P 40acres dairy S%

B&b£5–£6 Bdi£7.50–£8.75 W£51.75–£60 ⓛ
(W only last wk Jul–1st wk Sep)

**ST BURYAN** Cornwall *Map 2 SW42*
Mr & Mrs W. Hosking **Boskenna Home** *(SW423237)* ☎250
*Farmhouse situated in a convenient position. Beaches a few miles away. Pleasant spacious rooms with traditional furniture.*
Etr–Sep 3rm 2hc 🛠 ⓒⓗ CTV P 75acres arable dairy S% B&b£5 Bdi£7 W£49 ⓛ

Mrs M.R. Pengelly **Burnew Hall** *(SW407236)*
☎200
*Former 'gentleman's residence' with spacious rooms. Farm has its own coastline with safe bathing.*
mid May–mid Oct rsWed 3hc (1fb) 🛠CTV 3P sea 150acres dairy S% B&b£5–£5.50 Bdi£9–£9.50 W£55–£60 ⓛ D4pm

**ST DOGMAELS** Dyfed *Map 2 SN14*
Mrs M. Cave **Granant Isaf** *(SN126473)* Cipyn
☎Moylegrove 241
*The Pembrokeshire Coastal Path runs along the boundary of this farm which enjoys spectacular views of the sea and cliffs.*
May–Oct rsApr 2rm (1fb) CTV 2P 🎢 sea 400acres dairy S% B&b£5–£5.50 Bdi£8–£9 W£52.50–£59 ⓛ D5pm

**ST ERME** Cornwall *Map 2 SW85*
F. Hicks **Pengelly** *(SW856513)* Trispen
☎Mitchell 245
*Attractive, well-built farmhouse. Good central base for touring Cornwall.*
Mar–Oct 4hc (1fb) 🛠nc10 CTV 4P 240acres mixed S% B&b£5–£5.50 W£31.50–£35 Ⓜ

Mrs B. Dymond **Trevispian Vean** *(SW850502)*
Trispen ☎Truro 79514
*Extensively modernised farmhouse. Clean and well maintained. Large sun lounge at the front.*
Mar–Oct 7rm 6hc (3fb) 🛠CTV P 200acres arable beef sheep S% B&b£5–£6 Bdi£7–£8 W£48–£49 ⓛ D6pm

**ST EWE** Cornwall *Map 2 SW94*
Mrs J.G. Kent **Lanewa** *(SW983457)*
☎Mevagissey 843283
*Comfortable farmhouse situated in the small village of St Ewe. St Austell about 6 miles.*
mid May–mid Oct 3hc (1fb) ⓒⓗ CTV 3P 60acres mixed S% B&bfr£5 Bdi fr£7.50 Wfr£50 ⓛ

**ST JOHN'S IN THE VALE** Cumbria *Map 11 NY32*
Mrs H. Harrison **Shundraw** *(NY308236)*
☎Threlkeld 227
*Large, well-maintained, stone-built farmhouse; parts dating from 1712. In elevated position with views across valley.*
Etr–Oct 3rm (1fb) 🛠TV 3P 52acres sheep S% B&b£4.75–£5

**ST JUST-IN-ROSELAND** Cornwall *Map 3 SW83*
Mrs W. Symons **Commerrans** *(SW842375)*
☎Portscatho 270
*Pleasant modernised farmhouse, attractively decorated throughout. Large garden. Wonderful scenery in the area.*
Mar–Oct 4rm 3hc (2fb) 🛠CTV 6P river beef sheep B&b£7–£7.50 Bdi£9–£9.50 W£60–£65 ⓛ D am

**ST KEW HIGHWAY** Cornwall *Map 2 SX07*
Mrs N. Harris **Kelly Green** *(SX047758)*
☎Bodmin 850275

*Old, two-storey farmhouse with lawn at the front.*
5hc (4fb) ⚹ CTV 5P 300acres mixed

**ST KEYNE** Cornwall *Map 2 SX26*
Mr V.R. Arthur **Killigorrick** *(SX228614)*
☎Dobwalls 20559
*Farmhouse lies 3½ miles from Liskeard 1m W off Dulce–Dobwalls road.*
4hc (1fb) ⚹ nc5 TV 4P 1🅿 21acres mixed S%
✱ B&b£5 Bdif£7.50

**ST MARGARET, SOUTH ELMHAM** Suffolk
*Map 5 TM38*
Mrs H.B. Custerson **Elms House** *(TM310840)*
☎St Cross 228
*Delightful period farmhouse in extremely quiet location; friendly atmosphere.*
Apr–Oct rsMar & Nov 3hc (1fb) ⚹ nc10 CTV 4P ⫿
200acres arable sheep S% B&bfr£8.50 Bdi fr£15
Wfr£80 ⅃ D5pm

**ST MARGARET'S AT CLIFFE** Kent *Map 5
TR34*
C. & L. Oakley **Walletts Court** *(TR347446)* West Cliff (1m W B2058) ☎Dover 852424
Apr–Oct 4hc (2fb) ⚹ Ch CTV 8P sea 3acres beef S% B&b£7 Wfrf£45.50 Ⓜ

**ST OWEN'S CROSS** Heref & Worcs *Map 3
SO52*
F. Davies **Aberhall** *(SO529242)* (on B4521 1½m W) ☎Harewood End 256
*200-year-old farmhouse situated 4½ miles from Ross-on-Wye on the B4521. Hard tennis court for guests' use.*
Mar–Oct 3hc (2fb) ⚹ nc3 CTV 3P ⫿ 132acres arable dairy S% B&b£6–£7 Bdi£9–£10 W£60–£70 D5pm

**SAMPFORD PEVERELL** Devon *Map 3 ST01*
Mrs M.H. Parkhouse **Higher Shutehanger** *(ST030133)* ☎820569
*Secluded farmhouse adjacent to the Grand Western Canal. Well situated for touring Devon and the Dartmoor and Exmoor National Parks.*
Mar–Oct 3hc (1fb) ⚹ CTV 3P 3🅿 ⫿ 15acres mixed S% B&b£5.50 W£37 Ⓜ

**SAXELBY** Leics *Map 8 SK62*
Mrs M.A. Morris **Manor House** *(SK701208)*
☎Melton Mowbray 812269
*Part 12th-, part 15th-century farmhouse in high Leicestershire village. Feature is 15th-century staircase.*
Etr–Oct 2hc (2fb) ⚹ TV 4P ⫿ 125acres dairy sheep S% B&bfr£7 Bdi fr£11.50 Wfr£72 ⅃ D5pm

**SCANIPORT** Highland *Inverness-shire Map
14 NH63*
Mr D.A. Mackintosh **Antfield** *(NH616371)*
☎219
*Large, two-storey building, ½ mile off B852.*
May–Sep 2rm (2fb) ⚹ nc4 CTV 10P 354acres mixed

**SCARISTA** Isle of Harris, Western Isles
*Inverness-shire Map 13 NG09*
Mrs M. Macdonald **Croft** *NG002926)* 1 Scarista Vore ☎201
*Small, well-maintained croft which doubles as local Post Office. Good position facing west overlooking golden sands and ocean.*
Apr–Oct 2rm nc10 2P sea 19acres mixed S%
B&b£6–£7 Bdi£10.50–£12

**SEABOROUGH** Dorset *Map 3 ST40*
Mrs C.R. Creed **West Swilletts** *(ST428056)*
☎Broadwindsor 68264

*Modernised early 17th-century farmhouse with oak beams and low ceilings, situated in remote part of West Dorset.*
Mar–Sep 4hc ⚹ TV 4P 200acres arable beef S% B&b£6.50 W£45.50 Ⓜ

**SEBERGHAM** Cumbria *Map 11 NY34*
Mrs E.M. Johnston **Bustabeck** *(NY373419)*
☎Raughton Head 339
*Stone-built farmhouse dating from 1684. Extensively modernised.*
Spring Bank Hol–Oct 3rm TV 5P 72acres mixed S% B&bfr£4.50 Bdi fr£8 Wfr£50 Ⓜ

**SHAP** Cumbria *Map 12 NY51*
E. & S. Hodgson **Green** *(NY551121)* ☎619
*Large farmhouse dating from 1705. Countryside suitable for walking holidays.*
Etr–Sep 2hc (2fb) ⚹ TV 4P 167acres mixed S% B&bfr£6

S.J. Thompson **Southfield** *(NY561184)* ☎282
*Farmhouse set in pleasant area with good views. Guests are welcome to interest themselves in farm work.*
Etr–Oct 2rm 1hc (2fb) ⚹ nc10 CTV 3P 110acres mixed S% B&b£4.50–£5

**SHAWBURY** Salop *Map 7 SJ52*
Mr & Mrs J.C. Gollins **Braggs Country Suppers** *(SJ602228)* Longley Farm, Stanton Heath ☎Shawbury 250289
*Originally dating back to 1710, this attractive brick and tile cottage was named after Paul C. Bragg, the world authority on Natural Farming.*
2½m NE off A53.
1rm (A 3rm 2hc 1⇔) (2fb) Ch TV 15P ⫿
15acres mixed S% B&b£6.50–£8.50
Bdi£10.50–£18 Wfr£90 D9pm

**SHAWHEAD** Dumfries & Galloway
*Dumfriesshire Map 11 NX87*
Mrs M.D. Riddet **Henderland** *(NX872746)*
☎Lochfoot 270
*Small farmhouse about 5 miles from Dumfries. Golf, fishing and tennis are available.*
May–Oct 3rm (2fb) ⚹ CTV 3P 207acres dairy S% B&b£5–£6 W£35–£40 Ⓜ

**SHELFANGER** Norfolk *Map 5 TM18*
Mr B. Butler **Shelfanger Hall** *(TM102832)* (S of village off B1077) ☎Diss 2094
*16th-century moated farmhouse, in peaceful setting of 2 acres of wooded grounds, set back 1 mile from the road.*
Apr–Sep 2hc ⚹ nc3 CTV 10P ⫿ 400acres dairy S% B&b£7 Bdi£10 W£65 ⅃ D6pm

**SHILLINGFORD** Devon *Map 3 SS92*
J.R. Holloway **Zeal** *(SS998226)* ☎Clayhanger 231
*Old farmhouse with low ceilings and oak-beamed rooms.*
Etr–Nov 3rm 1hc (1fb) ⚹ 4P 253acres mixed S%
✱ B&b£5–£8 Bdi£8–£12 W£49–£56 ⅃ D5pm

**SHIPMEADOW** Suffolk *Map 5 TM38*
Mrs M. Steward **Manor Farm** *(TM379903)*
☎Beccles 715380
*Delightful old farmhouse, improved and modernised.*
Etr–Oct 2hc ⚹ nc12 CTV 4P 2🅿 ⫿ 144acres arable S% B&bfr£8.70 Bdi fr£13.70 W£80 ⅃ Dnoon

**SHIRWELL** Devon *Map 2 SS53*
Mrs G. Huxtable **Higher Upcott** *(SS585384)*
☎216
*Situated in a quiet picturesque area on the foothills of Exmoor. The bedrooms overlook the unspoilt Devon countryside.*

Etr–Nov 3rm (1fb) ⒸⒽ CTV 2P 104acres beef sheep S% B&b£4.50 Bdi£7

**SIMONSBATH** Somerset *Map 3 SS73*
*Gallon House (SS810394)* ☏Exford 283
*Small, detached farmhouse, formerly an inn. Surrounded by grassland. Horse riding facilities are available.*
Apr–Oct 4rm 2hc nc13 CTV 4P 圖 50acres beef

**SKELSMERGH** Cumbria *Map 7 SD59*
E. Johnston **Hollin Root** *(SD526976)* Garth Row ☏Selside 638
*Clean and comfortable farmhouse situated in attractive valley.*
Etr–Oct 4hc (1fb) ⅀nc10 TV 4P 60acres mixed S% B&b£5.50–£6 Wfr£38.50 Ⓜ

**SKYE, ISLE OF** Highland *Inverness-shire Map 13*
**See Clachan, Dunvegan, Portree, Uig**

**SLAGGYFORD** Northumb *Map 12 NY65*
Mrs D.M. Staley **Crainlarich** *(NY680523)* ☏Alston 329
*Attractive, modern farmhouse built of local stone. Situated in rolling hill land.*
May–Oct 6rm 5hc 2⇌ (1fb) ⅀nc10 CTV 4P 1♨ river 1,500acres beef sheep S% B&bfr£5 Bdifr£7.50 D5.30pm

**SLAIDBURN** Lancs *Map 7 SD75*
Mrs P.M. Holt **Parrock Head** *(SD697527)* Woodhouse Ln ☏614
*Modernised farmhouse dating back to 1677, set in the Bowland Fells.*
Closed Xmas 3⇌ (A 4⇌) (2fb) CTV 8P 圖 250acres mixed S% B&b£11 D8pm

**SMEATON, GREAT** N Yorks *Map 8 NZ30*
Mrs N. Hall **East** *(NZ349044)* ☏336
*A 17th-century working farm on the edge of the village. Spacious rooms of period character; clean, well-furnished and comfortable. Situated in rural surroundings.*
May–Oct 3hc ⅀nc3 CTV 4P 圖 120acres mixed S% B&b£6.50–£8 Bdi£7.25–£10.75 W£42–£50 Ⓜ (W only May–Sep) D8pm

**SOUTH BRENT** Devon *Map 3 SX66*
M.E. Slade **Great Aish** *(SX689603)* ☏2238
*Situated near Dartmoor National Park. Extensive views of countryside from farmhouse.*
Closed Dec 5rm (3fb) ⅀CTV 6P 60acres mixed S% B&b£5–£5.50 Bdi£7–£7.50 D4pm

**SOUTHLEIGH** Devon *Map 3 SY29*
A. Espanton **Lower Wadden** *(SY215939)* (1m E of village off unclass Colyton rd) ☏Colyton 52236
Etr–Oct 4hc (2fb) CTV 10P 圖 35acres mixed S% B&bfr£5 Bdi fr£7.50 Wfr£47.50 Ⓛ

**SOUTHMOOR** Oxon *Map 4 SU39*
Mrs A.Y. Crowther **Fallowfields** *(SU393979)* Fallow Field (on W side of village S of A420) ☏Oxford 820416
May–Sep 4rm 3hc 1⇌ (1fb) nc10 CTV 15P 圖 12acres beef sheep horses B&b£9–£10 Bdi£15–£16 W£59.75–£66.50 Ⓜ D6.30pm

**SPARROWPIT** Derbys *Map 7 SK08*
Mrs E. Vernon **Whitelee** *(SK099814)* ☏Chapel-en-le-Frith 2928
*Modernised farmhouse, parts built in 1600. In pleasant hillside setting. Good centre for hill walking or touring.*
Etr–Oct 3rm 1hc TV 6P 圖 42acres dairy S% B&b£6 Bdif£9.50 Wfrf£66.50 Ⓛ D4.30pm

**STALBRIDGE** Dorset *Map 3 ST71*
Mrs M. Selway **Thornhill** *(ST741149)* ☏62751
*Mellow stone, modernised farmhouse with gabled outbuildings in elevated position offering open views across Dorset.*
Apr–Oct 1rm (1fb) ⅀nc8 P 320acres mixed S% B&b£5.50–£6 W£35–£38 Ⓜ

**STANDLAKE** Oxon *Map 4 SP30*
Mrs C. Ross **Church Mill** *(SP396038)* ☏524
*A grade II listed 17th-century Mill House with adjoining watermill working various livestock in 20 acres. Private fishing is available on the River Windrush.*
Apr–Oct 2hc 4P 25acres mixed S% B&b£6.50–£7.50 W£42–£49 Ⓜ

Mrs S.R. Pickering **Hawthorn** *(SP373048)* (2m NW off A415 towards Yelford) ☏211
*A working farm primarily cultivating soft fruit but with a few livestock. A renovated old Cotswold stone building. Facilities nearby for various watersports.*
Apr–Sep 2rm 3P 圖 25acres mixed S% B&b£6.50–£7.50 Wfr£42 Ⓜ

**STAPLE FITZPAINE** Somerset *Map 3 ST21*
Mrs D.M. Jee **Rutters Leigh** *(ST261164)* ☏Buckland St Mary 392
*Small, very pleasant farmhouse off A303.*
3rm (1fb) ⅀CTV 3P 70acres dairy

**STAUNTON** Glos *Map 3 SO51*
Miss S.J. Fairhead **Upper Beaulieu** *(SO530118)* (off A4136 SW of village) ☏Monmouth 5025
*Situated on the Gloucester/Gwent border, near the Forest of Dean. Riding facilities can be arranged.*
3rm (2fb) ⅀CTV 8P 1♨ 圖 25acres mixed S% ✳B&b£5–£6 Bdi£9.50–£10 W£94.50–£108 D7pm

**STIRLING** Central *Stirlings Map 11 NS79*
Mrs R. Johnston **Kings Park** *(NS787936)* ☏4142
*Large, modernised farmhouse situated on the outskirts of the town and offering splendid views of Stirling Castle.*
Etr–Sep 3rm (2fb) ⅀CTV 4P 圖 230acres mixed S% B&b£6

*Powis Mains (NS819959)* Causewayhead ☏3820
*Well-sited, stone farmhouse dating from 1840. Stands in Forth Valley overlooked by Wallace Monument and Ochill Hills. 3m NE A91.*
Jun–Sep 2rm ⅀CTV 6P 250acres mixed

**STOKE HOLY CROSS** Norfolk *Map 5 TG20*
Mr & Mrs Harrold **Salamanca** *(TG235022)* ☏Framingham Earl 2322
*Old house with large garden on city outskirts. Simple but comfortable.*
Mar–Sep 3hc (A 1⇌ 🏠) (1fb) ⅀nc6 CTV 6P 168acres arable dairy D9am

**STOKEINTEIGNHEAD** Devon *Map 3 SX97*
W.J. & E.A. Cluett **Rocombe House Hotel** *(SX910701)* ☏Shaldon 3367
*Large farmhouse situated in secluded valley.*
12hc (10fb) ⅀CTV 15P 8acres beef S% B&b£8.50 Bdi£13.25 W£63–£86.25 Ⓛ D5.30pm

**STOKE PRIOR** Heref & Worcs *Map 3 SO55*
Mrs G.M. Pugh **Norman's** *(SX524555)* ☏Steensbridge 221
*Secluded hilltop farm approached by rough track, entrance of which is near the village Post Office.*
Etr–Sep 3rm 1hc (1fb) ⅀TV 3P 50acres mixed

S% B&b£5–£5.25 Bdi£7–£7.50 W£49–
£52.50 ⊬ D5pm

**_Wheelbarrow Castle_** *(SO516573)*
☎Leominster 2219
*Large, imposing, brick-built manor house
overlooking River Luss. Four-poster bed
available. Numerous antiques.*
3rm ✻ Ch TV 6P 2☎ ▥

**STON EASTON** Somerset *Map 3 ST65*
J. Doman **Manor** *(ST626533)* ☎Chewton
Mendip 266
*Well-kept and attractively-furnished farmhouse.
Lawn at the front, and fruit and vegetable
garden. Situated in quiet minor road.*
Closed Xmas 2hc (1fb) ✻ CTV P ▥ 250acres
mixed

**STONE (in Oxney)** Kent *Map 5 TQ92*
Mrs E.I. Hodson **Tighe** *(TQ937268)* Tighe
☎Appledore 251
May–Oct 3hc ✻ nc8 CTV 4P ▥ 100acres sheep
S% B&b£7–£8 W£49 ▯

**STOWFORD** Devon *Map 2 SX48*
Mr & Mrs C.T. Brown **Stowford Barton**
*(SX434870)* ☎Lewdown 272
*Signposted from main road, north of the A30.*
Apr–Oct 3rm (1fb) ✻ Ch CTV 4P 53acres dairy
S% B&b£5–£5.50 Bdi£7–£8 W£50–£55 ⊬
(W only Jun–Oct) D4pm

**STRAITON** Lothian *Midlothian Map 11 NT26*
Mrs A.M. Milne **Straiton** *(NJ273667)* Straiton
Rd ☎031-440 0298
*Georgian farmhouse with garden, situated on
southern outskirts of Edinburgh. Swing,
climbing frame and lots of pets for the
children.*
Apr–Oct 4hc (3fb) Ch CTV 10P 200acres
mixed S% B&b£6.50

**STRATFORD-UPON-AVON** Warwicks *Map
4 SP25*
Mrs M.K. Meadows **Monk's Barn** *(SP206516)*
Shipston Rd ☎293714
*Well-appointed farm offering clean and tidy
accommodation. Adjacent to A34 Stratford–
Oxford rd.*
Closed 25 & 26 Dec 4hc (1fb) ✻ CTV 5P ▥
75acres mixed S% B&b£4.75–£5

**STRATHAVEN** Strathclyde *Lanarks Map 11
NS74*
Mrs E. Warnock **Laigh Bent** *(NS701413)*
☎20103
*Attractive, stone-built farmhouse with
outbuildings surrounding the courtyard. 1½m SW
of Strathaven on the A71.*

Jun–Sep 2⇔ ✻ nc8 TV 4P 1☎ ▥ 100acres beef
S% B&b£5 W£35 ▯

**STREET** Somerset *Map 3 ST43*
N.J. Tucker **Marshalls Elm** *(ST485348)* ☎42878
*Old well-preserved farmhouse with back and
front gardens, set in country surroundings.
Street 1½ miles.*
May–Oct 3rm nc10 TV 2P 200acres mixed S%
B&bfr£5 Bdi fr£8 Wfr£30 ▯

**STURTON BY STOW** Lincs *Map 8 SK88*
Mrs S. Bradshaw **Village Farm** *(SK889807)* (W
off B1241) ☎Gainsborough 788309
Mar–Oct 3hc ✻ CTV 6P ▥ 350acres mixed S%
✱B&b£7.50

**SUMMERCOURT** Cornwall *Map 2 SW85*
Mrs W.E. Lutey **Trenithon** *(SW895553)* ☎St
Austell 860253
*Modern farmhouse situated in quiet location in
open country a few miles from the coast.*
Jan–Nov 4hc (2fb) CTV 6P ▥ 148acres mixed
S% B&b£4.50–£4.60 Bdi£6.40–£6.50 W£40–
£44 ⊬ D3pm

**SWINSCOE** Staffs *Map 7 SK14*
Mrs D.S. Salt **Calton Moor House** *(SK115487)*
☎Waterhouses 221
*Large, Georgian-style farmhouse.*
Etr–Oct 2hc (2fb) ✻ nc5 CTV 12P ▥ 200acres
dairy S% ✱B&b£5

**TACOLNESTON** Norfolk *Map 5 TM19*
Mrs R.F. Easton **White House** *(TM142940)* 24
Bentley Rd ☎Bunwell 220
*Small, well-kept property fairly close to Norwich.
Large rooms, comfortably appointed.*
Etr–Oct 4hc nc3 4P ▥ 1,200acres mixed S%
B&b£7.55–£8.95 Bdi£10.40–£12.70

**TALATON** Devon *Map 3 SY09*
J. Buxton **Harris** *(SY068997)* ☎Whimple
822327
*17th-century thatched cob farmhouse set in
quiet village. Large concrete yard. Lawns and
gardens.*
2rm 1hc (2fb) ✻ CTV 10P 1☎ 130acres dairy S%
B&bfr£6

**TAUNTON** Somerset *Map 3 ST22*
Mrs B. Cozens **Musgrave** *(ST269236)* Henlade
(3m E off A358) ☎Henlade 442346
*Oak-beamed farmhouse, comfortably furnished.
Side garden and orchard. 400yds from main
road.*
Closed Xmas 2rm (1fb) ✻ nc7 CTV 3P 107acres
dairy S% B&bfr£5 Bdi fr£7.50 Wfr£45 ⊬
D previous day

**TAVISTOCK** Devon *Map 2 SX47*
Mrs E.G. Blatchford **Bungalow** *(SX464731)*
Parswell ☎2789
*Well-situated building on the Callington road,
commanding good views of surrounding
countryside.*
Etr–Nov 2rm (2fb) ✚ TV 2P 106acres mixed S%
B&b£5–£6 Wfr£35 ₥

**TEMPLE CLOUD** Avon *Map 3 ST65*
Mr J. Harris **Cameley Lodge** *(ST609575)*
Cameley (1m W unclass) ☎52423
*Newly-converted barn attractively designed in
keeping with the area, overlooking 13th-century
church and trout lakes.*
5hc 1⋔ (2fb) ✚ TV in all bedrooms 30P 2☎ ⋙ lake
220acres fish S% B&b£10–£16 Bdi£16–£24.50
W£95–£185 ⅃ D9.30pm

**TEMPLE SOWERBY** Cumbria *Map 12 NY62*
**Skygarth** *(NY612262)* ☎Kirkby Thore 300
*Attractive farmhouse with high standard of
facilities and furnishings. Large airy rooms.
Overlooks River Eden.*
May–Oct 3rm ✚ CTV 6P river 220acres
mixed ₥

**THORNCOMBE** Dorset *Map 3 ST30*
Mr P.J. Atyeo **Higher** *(ST376034)* ☎Winsham
340
*Detached, two-storey, brick and stone
farmhouse. Milking parlour and farmland
adjacent. Large lawn.*
3hc (2fb) CTV 6P ⋙ 50acres dairy S% B&b£5
W£30 ₥

**THORNHILL** Dumfries & Galloway
Dumfriesshire *Map 11 NX89*
Mr J. Mackie **Waterside Mains** *(NS870971)*
☎30405
*Farmhouse set on banks of River Nith. Fishing
parties catered for.*
Etr–Oct 3hc (1fb) ✚ nc CTV 3P ⋙ river 160acres
arable dairy S% B&b£5–£5.50 Bdi£8–£8.50
D4pm

**THROWLEIGH** Devon *Map 3 SX69*
Mr & Mrs C. Mosse **East Ash Manor**
*(SX680911)* ☎Whiddon Down 244
*17th-century thatched, oak-beamed farmhouse
situated in beautiful countryside. 1m E on
Whiddon Down road.*
3hc (1fb) ✚ Ch TV 4P ⋙ 160acres mixed S%
B&b£7

**TIDEFORD** Cornwall *Map 2 SX35*
Mrs B.A. Turner **Kilna House** *(SX353600)*
☎Landrake 236

*Stone-built house set in a large pleasant garden
on main A38, ¼ mile outside village.*
Closed Xmas 6hc (4fb) CTV 6P 12½acres beef
S% B&b£6.50–£7.50 Bdi£11–£12

**TILLINGTON** Heref & Worcs *Map 3 SO44*
Mrs J. Seaborn **Stone House** *(SO443465)*
☎Hereford 760631
*Views of Herefordshire countryside.*
3rm 2hc CTV 6P ⋙ 60acres mixed D7pm

**TIVERTON** Devon *Map 3 SS91*
Mr L. Heywood **Lodge Hill Farm** *(ST945112)*
Ashley (1m S of town off A396) ☎252907
6rm 5hc (2fb) CTV 8P 35acres mixed S%
B&b£6.75 Bdi£10 W£65 ⅃ D am

R. Olive **Lower Collipriest** *(SS953117)*
☎252321
*Modernised, scheduled building on the banks of
the River Exe.*
Apr–Oct 4hc 2⇌ 2⋔ ✚ nc10 CTV 6P 3☎ ⋙
221acres beef dairy S% ✱ Bdi£10–£12 W£65–
£67 ⅃ Dnoon

**TODMORDEN** W Yorks *Map 7 SD92*
Mrs R. Bayley **Todmorden Edge South**
*(SD924246)* Parkin Lane, Sourhall ☎3459
*Converted 17th-century farmhouse on rural
hillside. Clean, comfortable rooms. Cosy
residents' lounge. Ample entertainments
nearby.*
3hc (1fb) ✚ nc8 CTV 10P ⋙ 1acre non-working
S% B&b£6.50 Bdifr£11 Wfr£43 ₥ D7.30pm

**TOMDOUN** Highland *Inverness-shire Map
14 NH10*
Mrs H. Fraser **No 3 Greenfield** *(NH201006)*
☎221
*Small modern bungalow set in isolated position
in rugged, hilly countryside. 3m E, on S side of
Loch Garry.*
20 May–Sep 3rm (1fb) TV 6P 172acres mixed
S% B&b£5–£5.50 Bdi£8.50 W£55 ⅃ D7pm

**TOTNES** Devon *Map 3 SX86*
Mrs G.J. Veale **Broomborough House**
*(SX793601)* ☎863134
*Spacious, country-manor-style house in hilly
parkland. Games room. Views of Dartmoor and
surrounding countryside. Local game fishing.*
Mar–Nov 3hc (1fb) ✚ Ch CTV P ⋙ 600acres
mixed S% B&b£7.50 Bdi£12 W£50 ₥ D10am

**TREFEGLWYS** Powys *Map 6 SN99*
Mrs J. Williams **Cefn-Gwyn** *(SO993923)* ☎648
*Clean and homely farmhouse.*
3rm 1hc (1fb) ✚ Ch CTV 12P 2☎ ⋙ 55acres
mixed S% B&b£5–£5.50 Bdi£7–£8 W£49–
£56 ⅃ D8pm

**TREFRIW** Gwynedd *Map 6 SH76*
Mr & Mrs D.E. Roberts **Cae-Coch** *(SH779646)*
☎Llanrwst 640380
*Pleasant farmhouse in elevated position on side of Conwy Valley.*
Etr–Oct 3rm (1fb) ⚡ nc3 TV 4P 1☎ 50acres mixed S% B&b£6.50 W£42 Ⓜ

**TRENEAR** *(Nr Helston)* Cornwall *Map 2 SW63*
Mrs G. Lawrance **Longstone** *(SW662319)*
☎Helston 2483
*Well-appointed farmhouse set in beautiful countryside. Facilities include a playroom and sun lounge. From the Helston–Redruth rd (B3297) take unclass rd SW–(Helston 1½m); (Trenear 1m)–thence via Coverack Bridges.*
Mar–Oct 5hc (3fb) CTV 5P 62acres dairy S% B&b£6.30–£7 Bdi£8.75–£9.20 W£60.40–£64.40 Ⓛ D6.30pm

**TREVALGA** Cornwall *Map 2 SX08*
**Reddivallen** *(SX099887)* ☎Boscastle 361
*Comfortable house with garden in isolated position off the B3266.*
Jun–Sep 2rm ⚡ CTV 2P 320acres arable, dairy & sheep

**TREVEIGHAN** Cornwall *Map 2 SX07*
Mrs M. Jory **Treveighan** *(SX075795)* ☎Bodmin 850286
*Two-storey, stone-built farmhouse with farm buildings attached. Situated in isolated village. Views over valley.*
Etr–Oct 3rm (1fb) ⚡ [Ch] TV 3P 140acres dairy S% B&b£5 Bdi£9–£9.50 W£63 Ⓛ D6.30pm

**TREVENEN BAL** *(Nr Helston)* Cornwall *Map 2 SW62*
Mrs W.M. Dallas **Roselidden House** *(SW676297)* ☎Helston 2118
*Approach from unclass rd off A394, ½m N of Helston or from B3297 near Wendron.*
Etr–Sep 4hc ⚡ nc5 CTV 4P sea 17½acres beef ✽ Bdi£9.77–£10.35 W£62.10–£66.70 Ⓛ (W only mid Jun–mid Sep)

**TROON** Cornwall *Map 2 SW63*
Mrs H. Tyack **Sea View** *(SW671370)* ☎Praze 831260
*Farmhouse has been modernised, yet still retains atmosphere of family-run farm. Tastefully furnished with extensive pinewood décor.*
10hc (3fb) [Ch] CTV 10P 3☎ 🎜 sea 10acres mixed S% ✽ B&b£4.40 Bdi£6.90 W£47.50 Ⓛ D5pm

**TROUTBECK** *(Nr Penrith)* Cumbria *Map 11 NY32*
R.G. Bird **Askew Rigg** *(NY371280)* ☎Threlkeld 638
*17th-century stone-built farmhouse. Attractively modernised to retain original character. Entrance to drive is situated only a few yards from the A66.*
4rm 1hc (2fb) CTV P 🎜 200acres mixed S% B&b£5.50 Bdi£8–£8.50

Mrs M. Dobson **Riverside** *(NY382253)*
☎Greystoke 220
*Stone-built house and buildings in quiet rural setting. Fine views of surrounding hills.*
Etr–Sep 3rm (2fb) ⚡ nc4 CTV 4P 87acres mixed S% B&b£4.50 Bdi£7 W£49 Ⓛ D3pm

**TYWARDREATH** Cornwall *Map 2 SX05*
**Great Pelean** *(SX085563)* ☎Par 2106
*Situated near Pempillick with walled garden to front entrance. Par beach 2 miles. ½m N towards*

*A390.*
May–8 Sep 6rm 5hc ⚡ TV P 140acres mixed

**TYWYN** Gwynedd *Map 6 SH50*
Mrs A.E. Jones **Dolgoch** *(SH648049)*
☎Abergynolwyn 229
*Two-storey, brick farmhouse with stream running by. Five Minutes' walk from the Dolgoch Waterfalls.*
May–Mid Sep 3hc (1fb) ⚡ 4P 356acres mixed S% B&b£5–£6 Bdi£8–£9 W£55–£62 Ⓛ

Mrs Davies **Dyffryngwyn** *(SH632984)* Happy Valley ☎710305
*Modern clean bungalow. Follow A493 south for 1¾m, then unclassified road east (signposted Happy Valley) for 2½m. The farmhouse is on the right.*
May–Oct 3rm (1fb) 3P 600acres beef sheep D5.45pm

**UFFCULME** Devon *Map 3 ST01*
Mrs M.D. Farley **Houndaller** *(ST058138)*
☎Craddock 40246
*Very old attractive farmhouse standing in beautiful garden.*
Mar–Oct rsNov–Feb (B&b only) 3hc (2fb) ⚡ CTV 4P 1☎ 176acres mixed S% B&b£8–£10 Bdi£10–£12 W£69–£79 Ⓛ D4.30pm

Mrs C.M. Baker **Woodrow** *(ST054107)*
☎Craddock 40362
*Farmhouse set in pleasant lawns and gardens with meadowland stretching to River Culm. Trout fishing available.*
Closed Xmas 4rm 3hc (A 3rm) (2fb) ⚡ CTV 7P 200acres mixed S% ✽ B&b£6 Bdi£9.50–£10 D8pm

**UFFINGTON** Salop *Map 7 SJ51*
Mr & Mrs D. Timmis **Preston** *(SJ530118)*
Preston-on-Severn ☎Upton Magna 240
*1½m S on unclass road joining B5062 and A5.*
2rm 1hc (2fb) TV 6P 2☎ 🎜 150acres mixed S% B&b£6–£7.50 W£42 Ⓜ

**UIG** Isle of Skye, Highland *Inverness-shire Map 13 NG36*
Mrs J. Macleod **No 11 Earlish** *(NG388614)* (2m S of Uig off A856) ☎319
*House and smallholding sheltered by conifers and lying approximately 300yds from main road.*
early May–mid Oct 3rm (1fb) TV 6P 36acres sheep S% B&b£5–£5.50 W£33–£35

**ULEY** Glos *Map 3 ST79*
Mrs N. Hill **Newbrook** *(ST775980)* ☎Dursley 860251
*Stone-built farmhouse with lawn, garden and orchard. In attractive village below western escarpment of Cotswolds.*
Closed Xmas 3rm 2hc (1fb) ⚡ nc5 CTV 4P 🎜 120acres mixed S% ✽ B&b£6 Bdi£9 W£56 D1pm

**ULLINGSWICK** Heref & Worcs *Map 3 SO54*
Mrs P.A. Howland **The Steppes** *(SO586490)*
☎Burley Gate 424
*17th-century listed building, being noted for its many points of historical and architectural interest, and although it retains its original features, including a wealth of exposed beams throughout, it has been sympathetically modernised.*
3🎜 nc12 CTV & TV in bedrooms 6P 🎜 1½acres non-working S% B&b£7.50–£9 Bdi£15–£18 W£90–£105 Ⓛ D7pm
**See advertisement on page 274.**

**UPOTTERY** Devon *Map 3 ST20*
Mr J. Gregory **Hoemoor** *(ST218104)*
☎Churchstanton 265

*Well-kept, small, modern farmhouse. Rather isolated but with beautiful views.*
Apr–Oct 4rm 1hc (1fb) nc12 2P 2🐎 50acres mixed S% B&b£7 Bdi£9 W£60

Mrs M.M. Reed **Yarde** *(ST193045)* ☎318
*17th-century farmhouse with interesting oak panelling and beams. Overlooks the Otter Valley. Near Monkton on the A30.*
Mar–Nov 3rm 2hc (1fb) ⚭ CTV 3P 1🐎 river 80acres beef dairy S% B&b£5–£6 Bdi£8–£9 W£50 ⟂

**UPPER ELKSTONE** Staffs *Map 7 SK05*
Mrs C.R. Faulkner **Mount Pleasant** *(SK056588)* ☎Blackshaw 380
*Stone building, parts of which date back 250 years. Situated on hillside with excellent views across Elstone Valley. Off B5053. Donkeys for children to ride.*
Etr–Oct 3hc nc6 CTV 4P 〰 2acres non-working S% ✱B&b£6.75 Bdi£10.75

**UPPER HULME** Staffs *Map 7 SK06*
Mrs J. Lomas **Keekorok Lodge** *(SK005616)* (1m NW of village towards The Roaches landmark) ☎Blackshaw 218
*Modernised stone-built house with views over Tittesworth reservoir, well known locally for fishing.*
Etr–Oct 3rm 2hc (1fb) ⚭nc2 CTV 6P 〰 12acres mixed S% B&b£8 Bdi£13.50 D10am

**UPTON PYNE** Devon *Map 3 SX99*
Mrs Y.M. Taverner **Pierce's** *(SX910977)* ☎Stoke Canon 252
*Large farmhouse about 1 mile north of A377 Exeter to Barnstaple road.*
Etr–Sep 1hc (1fb) ⚭ CTV 6P 〰 310acres mixed S% B&b£6.50 W£42 Ⓜ

**USK** Gwent *Map 3 SO30*
J. Arnett **Ty Gwyn** *(SO391045)* ☎2878
*Large modernised farmhouse situated between Raglan and Usk at Gwehelog 3m NE off Raglan road unclass.*
Closed Xmas day 3rm (1fb) ⚭ nc3 TV 3P 〰 25acres mixed S% B&b£5.50–£6.50 Bdi£9–£9.50 W£65 ⟂ Dnoon

**UTTOXETER** Staffs *Map 7 SK03*
Mrs P.J. Tunnicliffe **Moor House** *(SK102327)* Wood Ln ☎2384
*Stone-rendered farmhouse, about 200 years old, extensively modernised and renovated and containing antiques. Rural setting overlooking racecourse and fields.*
3hc (1fb) Ⓒʰ CTV P 〰 180acres dairy ✱B&bfr£7 Bdi fr£11 Wfr£72

**WALL** Cornwall *Map 2 SW63*
Mrs A. Rowe **Reawla** *(SW605363)* ☎Leedstown 320
*Pleasant well-situated farmhouse close to beaches, with small, well-kept garden.*
Etr–Sep 3hc (1fb) CTV P 40acres beef

**WARCOP** Cumbria *Map 12 NY71*
Mrs E. Collinson **Highwood Holme** *(NY760150)* Flitholme ☎Brough 304
*Modern bungalow of local stone adjacent to original farmhouse. Well decorated and comfortable.*
Apr–Sep 2rm (2fb) CTV 2P 〰 S% B&b£4.25

**WAREHAM** Dorset *Map 3 ST98*
Mrs J. Barnes **Redcliffe** *(SY932866)* ☎2225
*Modern farmhouse in quiet, rural surroundings. Pleasant location adjacent to River Frome and overlooking hills and fields. ½ mile from Wareham.*
5rm 3hc (1fb) ⚭ CTV 2P 2🐎 〰 250acres beef

**WATERPERRY** Oxon *Map 4 SP60*
S. Fonge **Manor** *(SP628064)* ☎Ickford 263
*Stone farmhouse standing in large garden.*
3rm 2hc (1fb) Ⓒʰ TV 4P 250acres mixed S% B&b£5–£8 Bdi£9–£12 W£62–£65

**WATERROW** Somerset *Map 3 ST02*
Mr J. Bone **Hurstone** *(ST056252)* ☎Wiveliscombe 23441
*Set on the edge of Brendon Hills overlooking the valley of the River Tone. Comfortably furnished with log fires during winter months and on chilly evenings.*
5hc CTV 10P 65acres mixed S% B&b£7.50–£8.50 Bdi£11.50–£12.50 W£65–£75 ⟂ (W only Jul & Aug)

**WEEDON LOIS** Northants *Map 4 SP64*
Mrs B. Raven **Croft** *(SP600465)* Milthorpe ☎Blakesley 475
*New detached house in rural surroundings.*
Feb–Nov 2rm CTV P 〰 25acres pigs & turkeys S% B&b£7.50 Bdi£10.50 W£69 ⟂ D7pm

**WEETON** Lancs *Map 7 SD33*
Mrs T. Colligan **High Moor** *(SD388365)* ☎273
*Compact, homely farmhouse. Clean and tidy. Much farm produce used in cooking.*
Closed Xmas 2rm (1fb) ⚭ CTV 20P 〰 7acres mixed S% B&b£5 W£35 Ⓜ

**WELSHPOOL** Powys *Map 7 SJ20*
Mrs E. Jones **Gungrog House** *(SJ235089)* Rhallt ☎3381
*300-year-old farmhouse in quiet situation high*

*on hillside. Commanding superb views of
the Severn Valley. 1m NE off A458.*
Apr–Oct 2hc 🖌 Ch CTV 6P 📖 15acres beef
S% B&bf6.50 Bdif10 Wf68 D7pm

Mr & Mrs W. Jones **Moat** *(SJ214042)* ☎3179
*Situated in Severn Valley. Games room in house
and tennis court in garden.*
Apr–Sep 3hc (1fb) 🖌 CTV 3P 📖 255acres
dairy S% ✱ B&bf6 Bdif9 Wf60 ⅃ D2pm

Mr & Mrs J. Emberton **Tynllwyn** *(SJ215085)*
☎3175
*Large, brick-built farmhouse, dating from 1861,
in peaceful surroundings with lovely views. One
mile from Welshpool.*
6hc (3fb) CTV P 150acres mixed S% B&bfrf6
Bdifrf10 Wfrf68 ⅃

**WESTBOURNE** W Sussex *Map 4 SU70*
Mr & Mrs E.D. Edgell **Tibbalds Mead**
*(SU750873)* White Chimney Row ☎Emsworth
4786
*Elizabethan farmhouse with recent addition,
some beamed ceilings. Situated on the south
side of village.*
Feb–Nov 2rm 🖌4P 📖 70acres mixed S%
B&bf7–£10

**WEST CHILTINGTON** W Sussex *Map 4
TQ01*
A.M. Steele **New House** *(TQ091186)* ☎2215
*This is a listed 15th-century farmhouse with oak-
beamed rooms and Inglenook fireplace. Situated
in the heart of the picturesque village of West
Chiltington.*
Jan–Nov 3hc (2fb) 🖌 nc10 CTV 4P 1🐎 150acres
mixed S% B&bfrf8.50

**WEST TAPHOUSE** Cornwall *Map 2 SX16*
Mrs K.V. Bolitho **Penadlake** *(SX144636)*
☎Bodmin 872271
*Old-world farmhouse with large garden set in the picturesque Glynn Valley.*
Mar–Oct 2rm (1fb) TV 3P 250acres mixed S%
✱B&bf5–£6

**WETTON** Staffs *Map 7 SK15*
J.G. Stubbs **Yew Tree** *(SK111553)*
☎Alstonefield 202
*Natural stone house with pleasant lawns and rose gardens. In village in renowned Manifold Valley, part of Peak District National Park.*
4rm 2hc (1fb) TV 4P 178acres dairy & sheep

**WHATSTANDWELL** Derbys *Map 8 SK35*
A.J. Clarke **Watergate** *(SK328545)*
☎Wirksworth 2135
*Stone house built in 1779. Set in quiet surroundings.*
Closed Dec–Feb 2rm 1hc 1⇌ ⋔ (1fb) TV 6P ▥
120acres non-working

**WHEDDON CROSS** Somerset *Map 3 SS93*
**Triscombe** *(SS921377)* ☎Winsford 227
*Large, modernised, 17th-century farmhouse on elevated site. Secluded from main road. 1 mile from village.*
Etr–Oct 5hc CTV 16P ▥ 30acres mixed ⬤ D7pm

**WHIDDON DOWN** Devon *Map 3 SX69*
Mrs J.S. Robinson **South Nethercott**
*(SX688947)* ☎276
*Most attractive cob and brick farmhouse in large gardens in quiet backwater on Devon Dartmoor National Park.*
3rm 2hc 1⇌ ✱nc12 CTV 5P 170acres arable dairy B&bf8.50–£10 Bdif13–£15

**WHIMPLE** Devon *Map 3 SY09*
Mrs H.I. Pinn **Down House** *(SY056968)*
☎822475
*Spacious farmhouse with large garden of lawns, attractive flower beds and shrubs. Pleasant and homely atmosphere.*
6hc nc5 TV 8P 5acres mixed S% B&bfr£6
Bdi fr£8.50 Wfr£56 ⬤ D4pm

**WHITE CROSS** Cornwall *Map 2 SW97*
**Torview** *(SW966722)* ☎Wadebridge 2261
*Modern farmhouse on main A39. Wadebridge 1½ miles.*
4hc CTV 6P 22acres mixed ⬤ D6pm

**WHITE MILL** Dyfed *Map 2 SN42*
Mr & Mrs J.F. Grant **Pencnwc** *(SN464232)*
☎Nantgaredig 325
*Two-storey, stone-built Victorian residence. Large lawned and wooded garden adjacent. 1 mile from village.*
Etr–Oct 4rm 3hc (2fb) ✱CTV 6P 82acres mixed
S% B&bf5.50 Bdif8.50 D 4.30pm

**WHITESTONE** Devon *Map 3 SX89*
Mrs S.K. Lee **Rowhorne House** *(SX880948)*
☎Exeter 74675
*Farmhouse set in attractive gardens and lawns. Exeter 6 miles.*
3hc (2fb) ✱CTV 6P 90acres dairy S% ✱B&bf5
Bdif7.50 Wf52.50 ⬤

**WHITLAND** Dyfed *Map 2 SN21*
C.M. & I.A. Lewis **Cilpost** *(SN191184)* ☎280
(due to change during the currency of this guide)
*Two-storey, 300-year-old farmhouse in an elevated position. 1½ miles north of the village amid extensive gardens.*
Apr–Sep 7hc 3⇌ 3⋔ (3fb) 20P ▥ 160acres dairy

B&bf10–£10.50 Bdif14–£15.50 Wf90–£100 ⬤
(W only Jul & Aug) D6pm

Mr & Mrs Daniels **Waungron Farm Hotel**
*(SN191157)* Waungron Isaf (1m SW off B4328)
☎682 (due to change during the currency of this guide)
13hc 7⇌ 6⋔ (4fb) ✱ Ⓒⓗ CTV in all bedrooms
30P ▥ 110acres beef S% B&bf8.50 Bdif12
Wf83 ⬤

**WIDDINGTON** Essex *Map 5 TL53*
Mrs L. Vernon **Thistley Hall** *(TL556311)*
☎Saffron Walden 40388
*This historic farmhouse is pleasantly surrounded by gardens and pastureland with beautiful views of the countryside.*
Jan–Nov 3rm 2hc (1fb) nc5 TV 6P ▥ 30acres mixed S% B&bf6.75–£7.50

**WIDECOMBE IN THE MOOR** Devon *Map 3 SX77*
Captain & Mrs R.E. Curnock **Scobitor** *(SX725750)*
☎254
*Well-appointed, moorland farmhouse set in the heart of Dartmoor National Park.*
Closed Xmas 5hc 3⇌ Ⓒⓗ CTV 10P 2🏠 ▥
50acres beef S% Bdif18–£26

**WIGHT, ISLE OF** *Map 4*
**See Ryde**

**WILBERFOSS** Humberside *Map 8 SE75*
Mrs J.M. Liversidge **Cuckoo Nest** *(SE717510)*
(1m W of village on S of A1079) ☎365
Mar–Oct 2hc (1fb) ✱nc2 TV 3P 80acres mixed
S% ✱B&bf5

**WILLAND** Devon *Map 3 ST01*
Mrs J.M. Granger **Doctors** *(ST015117)*
Halberton Rd ☎Tiverton 820525
*Farmhouse situated in garden and farmland. Tiverton and Cullompton 4 miles.*
Mar–Oct 3rm (1fb) ✱CTV 6P 90acres mixed S%
B&bf5.50 Bdif7.50 Wf48 ⬤ D3pm

**WIMPSTONE** Warwicks *Map 4 SP24*
Mrs J.E. James **Whitchurch** *(SP222485)*
☎Alderminster 275
*Lovely Georgian farmhouse built 1750. Listed buildings set in park-like surroundings on edge of Cotswolds. 4½ miles from Stratford-upon-Avon.*
3hc (2fb) ✱ TV 3P ▥ 500acres mixed S%
B&bf4.50–£5.50

**WINFRITH** Dorset *Map 3 SY88*
Mrs H. Cox **Wynards** *(SY802846)* (½m W off unclass rd) ☎Warmwell 852817
*Small farm on the outskirts of the village, has pleasant views over surrounding countryside.*
Mar–Oct 6rm 2hc (1fb) Ⓒⓗ CTV 8P ▥ 11acres mixed B&bf9–£11 Bdif12–£14 Wf75–£80
⬤ D4pm

**WITHIEL** Cornwall *Map 2 SW96*
Mr & Mrs P.U.G. Sharp **Tregawne** *(SX002662)*
☎Lanivet 303
*Charming, carefully modernised farmhouse furnished with antiques. Stands in Ruthern valley away from the farm. Heated outdoor swimming pool.*
Closed Xmas 4rm 2hc 1⇌ ⋔ (1fb) 6P ▥
160acres dairy

**WITHLEIGH** Devon *Map 3 SS91*
**Jurishayes** *(SS913121)* ☎Tiverton 2984
*Warm and comfortable farmhouse with pleasant atmosphere. Well positioned for touring North and mid Devon.*
5rm 2hc ✱ TV 100P 134acres mixed D6pm

**WIVELISCOMBE** Somerset Map 3 ST02
**Deepleigh** (ST079294) Langley Marsh ☎23379
16th-century farmhouse, converted into small
hotel. Comfortable lounge with original beams,
panelling and log fire. 1m N unclass rd.
6hc 1⇌ ⋔ Ch CTV 6P ∭ 15acres mixed ⅃
(W only Jul & Aug) D5.30pm

E.M. Wyatt **Hillacre** (ST104275) Croford
☎23355
Traditional farmhouse set back about 200yds to
the north of A361.
2hc ⊁ CTV 4P 850acres mixed S% B&b£5.50
Bdi£8 W£52 ⅃

**WOODBURY SALTERTON** Devon Map 3
SY08
Mrs M. Hamilton **Stallcombe House**
(SY039891) Sanctuary Ln ☎32373
Old comfortable farmhouse with large attractive
garden in peaceful position.
Etr–Nov 3rm 2hc (1fb) ⊁ CTV 3P 55acres dairy
S% B&bfr£6

**WOOKEY** Somerset Map 3 ST54
Mr & Mrs L.J. Law **Honeycroft** (ST509453)
Worth ☎Wells (Somerset) 78971
Large whitewashed cottage with lawns and
orchard, on B3139.
Feb–Nov 3rm 1hc (2fb) ⊁ nc4 CTV P ∭ 37acres
beef poultry & pigs S% B&b£5.25

Mrs A. Barnard **Manor** (ST508454) Worth
☎Wells (Somerset) 72838
Modernised old farmhouse.
Closed Xmas 4hc (3fb) nc3 TV P ∭ 40acres dairy
poultry S% B&bfr£5 Bdi fr£7.50 Wfr£49 ⅃ D4pm

**WOOLFARDISWORTHY** Devon Map 2 SS32
Mr & Mrs R. Hancock **South View** (SS335213)
☎Clovelly 397
Farmhouse set in very quiet and peaceful
surroundings.
Etr–Oct 2rm 1hc (1fb) ⊁ CTV 2P 40acres arable
dairy S% B&b£5.50

R.C. & C.M. Beck **Stroxworthy** (SS341198)
☎Clovelly 333
Tastefully decorated and set in beautiful
countryside offering a variety of farm produce
on menu. Herd of Guernsey cows.
10rm 9hc (4fb) ⊁ CTV 20P 90acres dairy B&b£6–
£6.50 Bdi£9.50–£10 W£66.50–£70 (W only Jul &
Aug)

Mrs P. Westaway **Westvilla** (SS329215)
☎Clovelly 309
Well-decorated accommodation. Good
farmhouse meals served.
Mar–Sep 3hc (1fb) ⊁ CTV P 22acres beef sheep
S% B&b£6–£7 Bdi£7.50–£8.50 W£48–£50
(W only Jul & Aug)

**WOOLLEY** Cornwall Map 2 SS21
G. Colwill **East Woolley** (SS254167)
☎Morwenstow 274
Farm set in undulating pastureland, close to
A39. Homely atmosphere. Play area with
swings, see-saw and pony for children.
Apr–Oct 3rm (1fb) CTV 6P 190acres arable beef
S% B&b£5–£5.50 Bdi£8.50–£9 W£50 ⅃ D6pm

**WOOTTON COURTENAY** Somerset Map 3
SS94
**Ford** (SS929426) ☎Timberscombe 211
A genuine working farm.
5rm 4hc ⊁ TV 5P 150acres dairy D6.30pm

C.T. Gooding **Ranscombe** (SS947433)
☎Timberscombe 237
Dark redstone house with gardens at front and a
duck pond to the side. Easy access via M5.
Etr–Oct 3hc (2fb) 6P 100acres mixed ✲ Wfr£60
⅃

**WORMBRIDGE** Heref & Worcs Map 3 SO43
Mrs P.M. Thomas **Wormbridge Court**
(SO429309) ☎239
A 400-year-old manor house standing adjacent
to A465 Hereford–Abergavenny road. Horse
riding, with lessons available from qualified
instructor.
Mar–Oct 5rm 4hc (3fb) Ch CTV 6P 250acres
arable beef S% B&bfr£8.50 Bdi fr£12.50
Wfr£82 ⅃

**WORMELOW** Heref & Worcs Map 3 SO43
Mrs E.P. Jones **Lyston Smithy** (SO495292)
☎Golden Valley 540368
Old stone farmhouse, formerly blacksmith's
cottage, extensively renovated to a high
standard. South facing with views towards
Gloucester, Forest of Dean and Wye Valley.
Guests have use of lawns and recreation area.
Closed Xmas & New Year 3hc 1⇌ 2⋔ (2fb) nc6
CTV P ∭ 14acres fruit B&b£7–£9 W£49–
£63 M

**YARCOMBE** Devon Map 3 ST20
Mrs V. Rich **Broadley** (ST239069) ☎Upottery
274
Traditional-style farmhouse in remote, East
Devon countryside. Good home cooking.
May–Sep 2rm ⊁ nc5 TV P 136acres dairy sheep

Mrs N.S. Dyer **Crawley** (ST259079) ☎Chard
2259
Attractive stone building with a thatched roof.
Etr–Nov 3rm 2hc ⊁ CTV 3P 250acres mixed

**YEALMPTON** Devon Map 2 SX55
Mrs A. German **Broadmoor** (SX574498)
☎Plymouth 880407
Stone-built farmhouse and outbuildings,
situated in open countryside enjoying distant
views of Dartmoor.
3hc ⊁ nc7 CTV P 207acres mixed S% B&bfr£6

**YEAVELEY** Derbys Map 8 SK14
Mrs J. Potter **Eddishes** (SK179396) ☎Great
Cubley 486
Etr–Oct 2rm ⊁ nc3 CTV 4P 62acres dairy S%
B&b£6 Bdi£9.50 D7.30pm

**YEOVIL** Somerset Map 3 ST51
Mrs M. Tucker **Carents** (ST546188) Yeovil
Marsh ☎6622
Clean, pleasant traditional-style farmhouse on
the outskirts of Yeovil 2m N of A37.
Feb–Nov 3rm 1hc (1fb) ⊁ CTV P 350acres arable
beef S% B&bfr£6 Bdi fr£9.50 D2pm

**YSBYTY IFAN** Gwynedd Map 6 SH84
Mrs F.G. Roberts **Ochr Cefn Isa** (SH845495)
☎Pentrefoelas 602
Farm set in elevated position with good views
high above A5.
Etr–Dec 3rm 2hc (2fb) ⊁ nc3 TV 3P 123acres
mixed S% B&b£5–£5.50

**ZELAH** Cornwall Map 2 SW85
**Honeycombe** (SW827527) ☎411
Detached house on smallholding. Lawned
garden at front. Fine views over unspoilt
countryside. ½m S of A30, 300yds E of junction
A30/B3285.
May–mid Sep 3hc ⊁ nc12 TV 4P 13½acres beef

**ZENNOR** Cornwall Map 2 SW43
Mrs M.C. Osborne **Osborne's** (SW455385)
Boswednack ☎Penzance 796944
Farmhouse offering own dairy produce and
vegetables. Wholesome country food. Lands
End about 10 miles. Bathing in nearby coves.
2hc (2fb) ⊁ CTV 4🏾 sea 70acres beef S%
B&b£5–£5.65 Bdi£7.50–£8.65

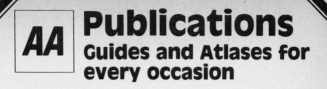

# **AA** Publications
## Guides and Atlases for every occasion

## SUPERGUIDES

### Hotels and Restaurants in Britain
Impartially inspected and updated annually, this guide lists 5,000 AA approved places to stay or wine and dine in comfort.

### Camping and Caravanning in Britain
1,000 sites around Britain, checked for quality and maintenance of facilities and graded accordingly. A special colour feature gives details of sites in particularly attractive surroundings.

### Guesthouses Farmhouses and Inns in Britain
Thousands of inexpensive places to stay, selected for comfortable accommodation, good food and friendly atmosphere. Special feature on the search for "Guesthouse of the Year".

### Self Catering in Britain
A vast selection for the independent holiday-maker — thatched cottages, holiday flats, log cabins and many more, all vetted by AA inspectors.

### Stately Homes, Museums, Castles & Gardens in Britain
An unlimited choice for all the family, including zoos, wildlife parks, miniature and steam railways, all listed with opening times, admission prices, restaurant facilities etc.

### Travellers' Guide to Europe
### Camping and Caravanning in Europe
### Guesthouses, Farmhouses and Inns in Europe

## ATLASES

### Complete Atlas of Britain
Superb value for the modern motorist. Full colour maps at 4 miles to 1 inch scale. 25,000 place name index, town plans, 10-page Central London guide, distance chart and more.

### Motorists' Atlas of Western Europe
AA atlas covering Europe at 16 miles to 1 inch scale. 10,000 place name index, route planning section, town plans of capital cities.

*All these publications and many more are available from AA shops and major booksellers.*

# The National Grid

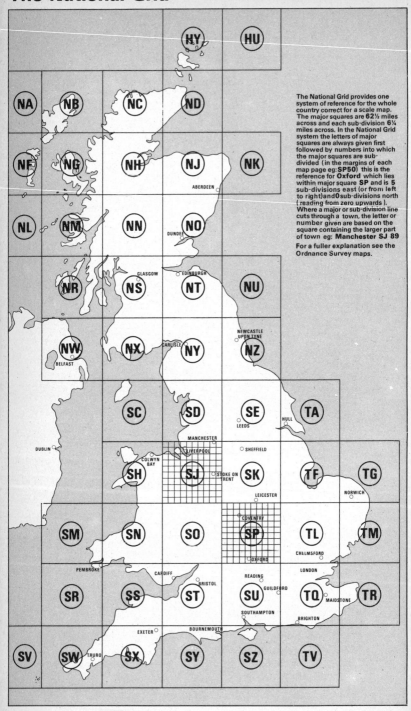

The National Grid provides one system of reference for the whole country correct for a scale map. The major squares are 62½ miles across and each sub-division 6¼ miles across. In the National Grid system the letters of major squares are always given first followed by numbers into which the major squares are sub-divided (in the margins of each map page eg: **SP50**) this is the reference for **Oxford** which lies within major square **SP** and is **5** sub-divisions east (or from left to right) and **0** sub-divisions north (reading from zero upwards). Where a major or sub-division line cuts through a town, the letter or number given are based on the square containing the larger part of town eg: **Manchester SJ 89**

For a fuller explanation see the Ordnance Survey maps.

# Key to Atlas

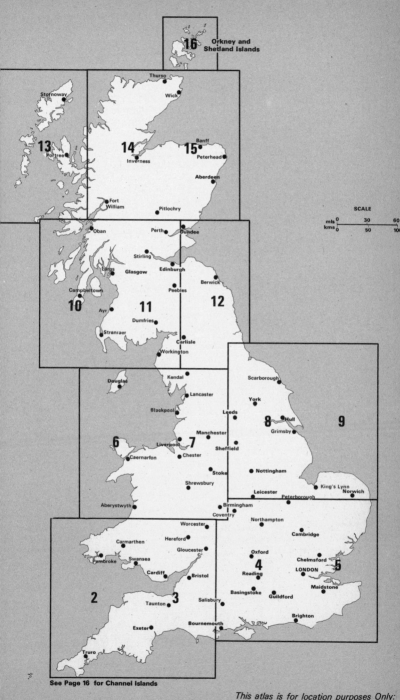

SCALE

mls 0 — 30 — 60
kms 0 — 50 — 100

See Page 16 for Channel Islands

*This atlas is for location purposes Only:
see Member's Handbook for current road
and AA road services information*

*Maps produced by
The AA Cartographic Department
(Publications Division), Fanum House,
Basingstoke, Hampshire RG21 2EA*

*Based on the Ordnance Survey Map with
the Sanction of the Controller H.M.S.O.*

For continuation pages refer to numbered arrows

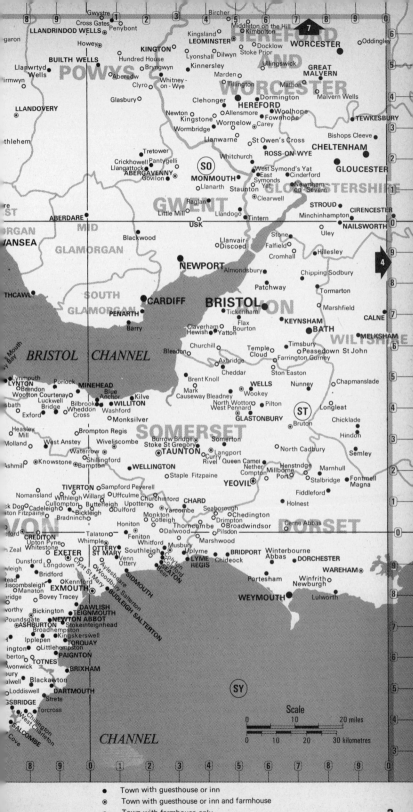

Scale

0        10        20 miles

0    10    20    30 kilometres

- ● Town with guesthouse or inn
- ◉ Town with guesthouse or inn and farmhouse
- ○ Town with farmhouse only

3

For continuation pages refer to numbered arrows

4

Scale

| 0 | 10 | 20 miles |
| 0 | 10 | 20 | 30 kilometres |

● Town with guesthouse or inn
◉ Town with guesthouse or inn and farmhouse
○ Town with farmhouse only

5

Holmrook

**DOUGLAS**

Port Erin
Port St Mary

SC

*IRISH    SEA*

PENMAENMAWR  LLANDUDNO  **COLWYN**  **PRESTATYN**
                **CONWY**   **BAY**
Trearddur  Bodedern            **BEAUMARIS**        Glan      **RHYL**
Bay                  **LLANFAIRFECHAN**      Conway    **ABERGELE**
        Gaerwen            Llechwedd          Llanfair
                    **BANGOR**        Betws - yn - o    Talhaiam   Rhu
                Tal-y-Bont        Rhos
                        Llangernyw      **DENBIG**
        Llanrug        Trefriw  Pandy
**CAERNARFON**          Dinorwic    Tuduro  Llansannan
        Bontnewydd          **LLANRWST**              Llanrha
                Llanberis                    **RUTH**
    Betws  Garmon              Capel Garmon   CLEV
    Pontllyfni          **BETWS-Y-COED**          Pentrefoelas
                    Dolwyddelan  Padog        Clawddnewydd
                SH              Glasfryn   Gwyddelwern
                    Penmachno  Ysbyty            Cc
                    Beddgelert      Ifan      Glan-yr-Afon
                **BLAENAU FFESTINIOG**                Cyr
    Morfa Nefyn  Nefyn        **FFESTINIOG**
            **CRICCIETH**          GWYNEDD      Llandderfel
    Llanystumdwy            **PORTHMADOG**              **BALA**
        **PWLLHELI**              Llanuwchllyn
    Llanbedrog      Harlech
    Abersoch                        Llanwd
                        Llanfachreth
                Bontddu            **DOLGELLAU**
**CARDIGAN BAY**      **BARMOUTH**        Dinas Mawddwy
            Fairbourne
            Llwyngwril    Tal-y-Llyn  Cemmaes
                    Llanegryn
                **TYWYN**
                        POWYS
        Aberdovey      Aberhosan          Carno
                    Trefeglwys  **NEWTOW**
                        Llandinan
    **ABERYSTWYTH**    Capel
                Bangor
                DYFE
            Capel    Devil's
            Seion    Bridge
        SN
            Lledrod            Abbe
                        Cwml

For continuation pages refer to numbered arrows

Scale
0        10        20 miles
0    10    20    30 kilometres

6

Town with guesthouse or inn
Town with guesthouse or inn and farmhouse
Town with farmhouse only

**7**

For continuation pages refer to numbered arrows

8

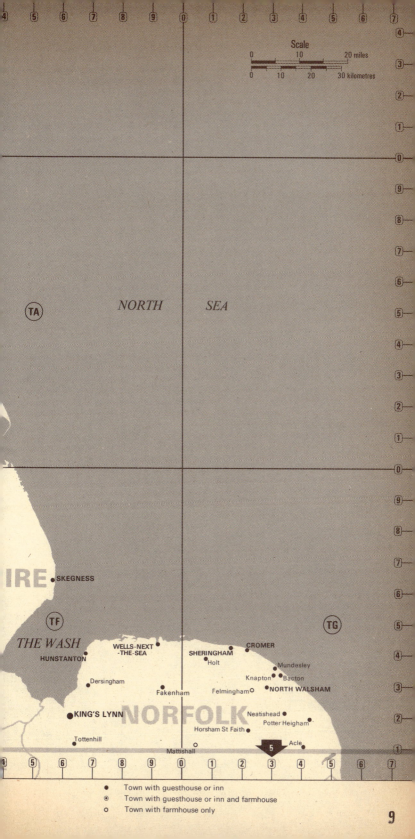

## Scale

| 0 | 10 | | 20 miles |
| 0 | 10 | 20 | 30 kilometres |

**TA**

*NORTH SEA*

IRE ● SKEGNESS

**TF**

*THE WASH*

**TG**

WELLS-NEXT-THE-SEA    CROMER

● HUNSTANTON    ● SHERINGHAM    Mundesley

● Holt    Knapton ● Bacton

● Dersingham    Felmingham○ ● NORTH WALSHAM

● Fakenham

**NORFOLK**

● KING'S LYNN    Neatishead ●

Horsham St Faith ●    Potter Heigham

● Tottenhill

Mattishall ○    **5**    Acle ●

- ●    Town with guesthouse or inn
- ◉    Town with guesthouse or inn and farmhouse
- ○    Town with farmhouse only

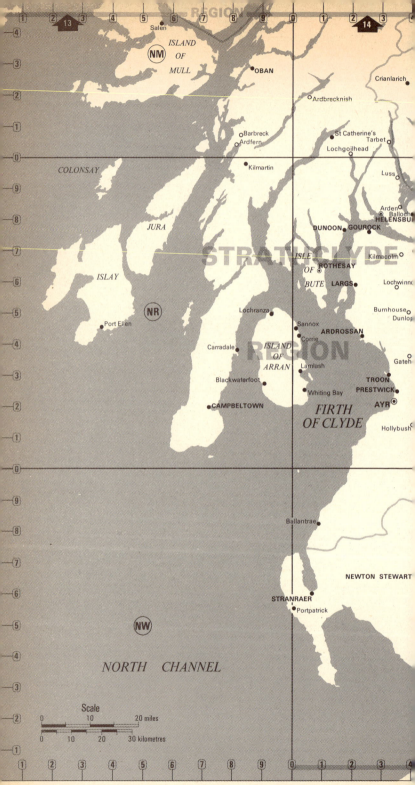

**13** **14**

Salen

ISLAND
NM OF
MULL

OBAN

Crianlarich

Ardbrecknish

COLONSAY

Barbreck
Ardfern

St Catherine's
Tarbet
Lochgoilhead

Kilmartin

Luss

Arden
Balloch
HELENSBU

JURA

DUNOON GOUROCK

STRATHCLYDE

ISLE Kilmacolm
OF ROTHESAY
BUTE LARGS

ISLAY

Lochwinn

NR

Lochranza

Burnhouse
Dunlo

Port Ellen

Sannox
Corrie

ARDROSSAN

Carradale

ISLAND
OF
ARRAN

Lamlash

REGION

Gateh

Blackwaterfoot

Whiting Bay

TROON
PRESTWICK
AYR

CAMPBELTOWN

FIRTH
OF CLYDE

Hollybush

Ballantrae

NEWTON STEWART

NW

STRANRAER
Portpatrick

NORTH  CHANNEL

Scale

0          10          20 miles

0      10      20          30 kilometres

● Town with guesthouse or inn
◉ Town with guesthouse or inn and farmhouse
○ Town with farmhouse only

11

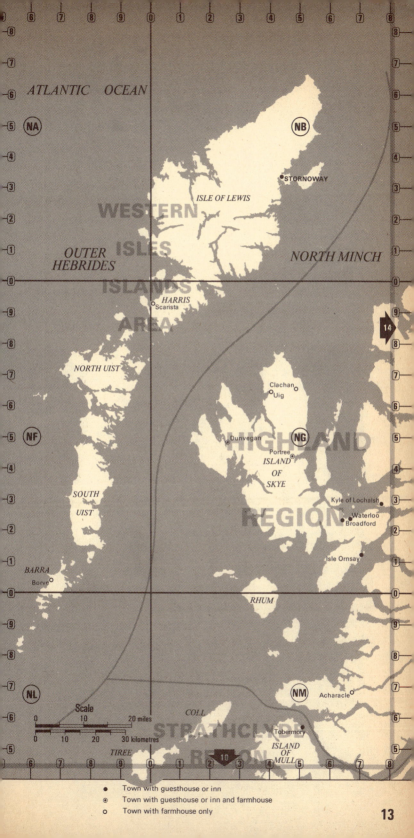

ATLANTIC OCEAN

**NA**

**NB**

●STORNOWAY

*ISLE OF LEWIS*

WESTERN

OUTER
HEBRIDES

ISLES

*NORTH MINCH*

ISLANDS

*HARRIS*
○Scarista

AREA

NORTH UIST

○Clachan
○Uig

**NF**

●Dunvegan

**NG**

HIGHLAND

Portree◉
*ISLAND
OF
SKYE*

Kyle of Lochalsh●
●Waterloo
●Broadford

REGION

SOUTH
UIST

*BARRA*
Borve○

●Isle Ornsay

*RHUM*

**NL**

**NM**

●Acharacle

### Scale

|     |     |     |          |
|-----|-----|-----|----------|
| 0   | 10  |     | 20 miles |
| 0   | 10  | 20  | 30 kilometres |

*COLL*

STRATHCLYDE

●Tobermory

*TIREE*

**10**

*ISLAND
OF
MULL*

●    Town with guesthouse or inn

◉    Town with guesthouse or inn and farmhouse

○    Town with farmhouse only

**13**

**14**

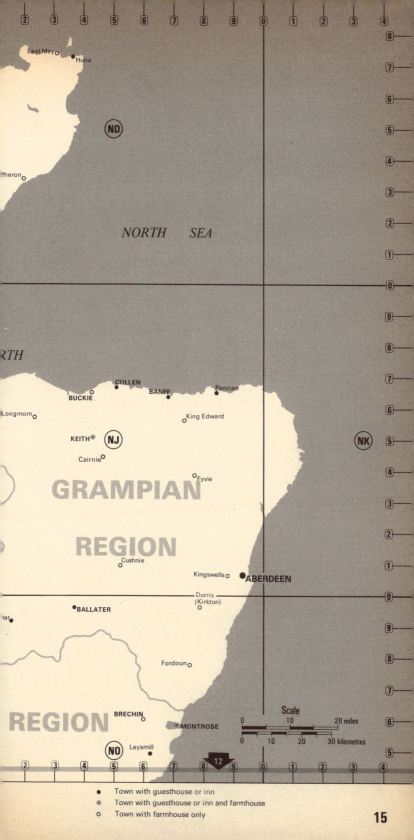

NORTH SEA

GRAMPIAN

REGION

REGION

ND

NJ

NK

NO

East Mey
Huna

theron

Longmorn

CULLEN
BUCKIE
BANFF
Pennan

King Edward

KEITH

Cairnie

Fyvie

Cushnie

Kingswells
ABERDEEN

Durris
(Kirkton)

BALLATER

Fordoun

BRECHIN

MONTROSE

Leysmill

Scale
0          10          20 miles
0     10     20     30 kilometres

12

- Town with guesthouse or inn
⊙ Town with guesthouse or inn and farmhouse
○ Town with farmhouse only

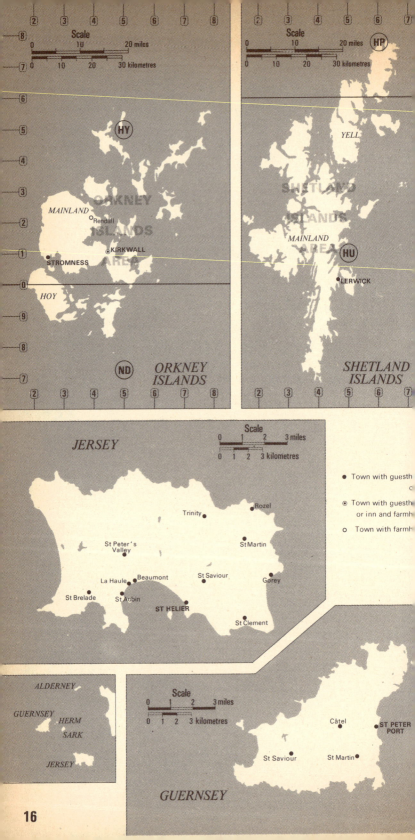

## ORKNEY ISLANDS

⑧
⑦
⑥
⑤
④
③
②
①
⓪
⑨
⑧
⑦

### Scale
0    10    20 miles
0   10   20   30 kilometres

(HY)

ORKNEY
ISLANDS
AREA

MAINLAND

○ Rendall
◉ KIRKWALL

● STROMNESS

HOY

(ND)

## SHETLAND ISLANDS

### Scale
0    10    20 miles
0   10   20   30 kilometres

(HP)

YELL

SHETLAND
ISLANDS
AREA

MAINLAND

(HU)

● LERWICK

## JERSEY

### Scale
0   1   2   3 miles
0   1   2   3 kilometres

Trinity
● Rozel

St Peter's
Valley

StMartin

La Haule ● Beaumont    St Saviour
St Brelade    Gorey
St Aubin   **ST HELIER**

St Clement

● Town with guesth...
    o...
◉ Town with guesth...
    or inn and farmh...
○ Town with farmh...

ALDERNEY

GUERNSEY

HERM

SARK

JERSEY

## GUERNSEY

### Scale
0   1   2   3 miles
0   1   2   3 kilometres

Câtel
● ST PETER
PORT

St Saviour    St Martin

# REPORT FORM

To:
The Automobile Association,
Hotel and Information Services Department,
9th Floor,
Fanum House,
Basingstoke,
Hampshire
RG21 2EA

Name of establishment

| Town | County |
|---|---|

Date of visit

**Did you find:**

|  | above expectation | satisfactory | below expectation |
|---|---|---|---|
| Service | | | |
| Accommodation | | | |
| Meals | | | |

| | | |
|---|---|---|
| **Do you agree with the listing of this establishment** | YES | NO |
| **May we quote your name when taking up any complaint with the guesthouse/farmhouse/inn?** | YES | NO |
| **Did you take up your complaint with the manager at the time of your visit?** | YES | NO |

Name

Address

| Date | Membership No. |
|---|---|

Signature

*Further copies of this form can be obtained from any AA office*

**Additional remarks:**

---

For office use:

| Head office action | Regional office action |
|---|---|
| Acknowledged | Inspected by |
| Recorded | Date |
| Action | |
| File | |
| Inspect | |